CE

TEACHING

COMPOSITION

AND LITERATURE

in Junior and Senior High School

LUCIA B. MIRRIELEES, PH.D.

Revised Edition

GREENWOOD PRESS, PUBLISHERS
NEW YORK

Contents

Appendices

Indices

Introduction

Ye know ek that in forme of speche is change. . . .

MANY changes in educational theory, some changes in educational practice, and much new educational terminology mark the years since 1931, when the first edition of this text was printed. The major changes in these twelve years seem to have arisen from five conditions—conditions which had long existed, but which finally reached public consciousness and aroused rather general discontent. These were: narrow departmentalism, rigid courses of study, undemocratic classroom procedures, submergence of the individual pupil, and separation of school and community. Little by little departmental lines were blurred in numerous communities by timid introduction of materials from science or social science—readings and discussions foreign to the conventional work in literature. Then in many of the more progressive communities appeared those courses termed "fused" or misnamed "integrated." Later the "core" curriculum and the "experience" curriculum banished content courses based solely upon academic attainment. In these schools half of the school day was devoted to the exploration of the pupils' needs, abilities, ambitions, home environment and responsibilities. Here pupil-teacher planning was substituted for authoritative instruction. In many schools this exploratory course approximated and extended the orientation and self-examination formerly to be found in the most successful "home rooms." Or these courses might concern themselves with man's development and advancing state of culture; but such study was for the primary purpose of acquainting the pupil, indirectly rather than directly, with himself and his own environment. In these courses the pupil was no longer submerged, but was an active participant, consciously and voluntarily co-operating with the members of his group. In many

v

towns and cities the ideal of the school as a community center has already been attained, largely through various war activities, so that an increased interrelation of school and community now exists.

Yet, in spite of these changes and this educational ferment, much school life has remained static. There are hundreds upon hundreds of schools in our forty-eight states where, with community approval, strict discipline is imposed upon pupils, and where traditional-minded teachers offer traditional courses in literature and the history of literature, regardless of the community level of culture or the needs and interests of the students. In such schools the "progressive" teacher is still regarded as an unsafe faddist, a troublemaker, usually weak in discipline.

But in the English departments of less conventional schools, and, to some degree, in practically all departments of English, eight changes are now obvious. These are:

1. *Disappearance of many of the older classics.* Those works which held their place through tradition and eminent respectability rather than through their intrinsic interest and value to twentieth-century youth are gradually disappearing.

2. *Increase of wide reading rather than intensive study of single books.* Intensive study of one text, even to the point of dislike on the part of the student, so that he might learn how to enjoy other books has little by little given way to wider and more varied reading.

3. *Appearance of much modern material dealing with present-day problems.* The day when no pupil might read fiction in study hall is long since past, and today magazines, newspapers, plays, biography, semiscientific and historical books and articles, modern drama and verse, and translations from many foreign writers all find a place in our English classrooms.

4. *Recognition of the teachers' duty to create a democratic atmosphere and to awaken students to the privileges and responsibilities of citizenship in a democracy.* Discussion of the rights of minority groups, the dangers of race or religious prejudice, the problems confronting the world today, find their way into the interpretation of both classics and modern books.

5. *Organization of all material around centers of interest.* In more and more schools several interests (such as English arts, social studies, music, drawing) combined into a core curriculum built upon the general idea of understanding man's social, political, spiritual, and artistic life have replaced the traditional courses in history, English, art, and so on.

6. *Instruction in library use to further individual research.* Individual research, particularly in the thirty experimental schools, has played an important part in decreasing the lock step in classroom teaching. The reading ability and interest of each individual pupil determine the material which he reads. Anthologies and simplified books have also increased in number and in use.

7. *Introduction of language study not primarily to secure correct usage, but to picture its history, its method of development, its numerous pitfalls for the uninitiated.* This study of semantics and propaganda, practically unknown in the majority of high schools twelve years ago, reflects significantly our recognition of the need for national and international understanding.

8. *Instruction in the science of reading, in the last dozen years, perhaps the most universal change.* Those schools and those teachers not offering skilled instruction in remedial reading are at least aware of their omission, and are now apologetic for its absence.

Various forces, in part responsible for these changes, have been brought to bear upon high-school English departments. For example, the Progressive Education Association has awakened teachers to the necessity of considering the pupil as an integral part in planning and carrying out any program. It has stressed the idea that educational development of the individual pupil does not rest solely upon his acquirement of facts and skills. But, above all, the National Council of Teachers of English, founded in 1913, has provided a constant stimulus through books, pamphlets, the *English Journal,* and the *Elementary Review.* It has kept teachers aware of the possibilities for service and for accomplishment. To illustrate this new freedom and the development of each pupil according to his own ability and interest, the National Council has provided such studies as *Pupils Are People,* such guidance as *Basic Aims in English Teaching* and the *English Journal*, filled with experiments and theories by classroom teachers.

The present text, addressed to those students in normal schools and colleges who intend to teach English, presents the problems which later they will face in their classrooms. Since they must be both *informed* concerning literature and composition (both written and oral) and *awakened* to the problems in the teaching of English, the text is so planned that:

1. It states the problem in composition or literature as a challenge demanding original thinking.

2. It tests the prospective teachers' knowledge and ability in oral and written expression.

3. It requires them to make and to present orally exercises and assignments planned for and discussed by the class and then solved and presented before the class by the individual. By means of these class presentations—given in class hours or in special meetings termed "laboratory" periods—prospective teachers are led to test their ability of awakening interest in a subject, organizing it, and lucidly explaining and presenting the idea in such a way as to solicit co-operative activity.

These three steps should awaken prospective teachers from the passivity of the usual college "learner" and stimulate the creative attitude necessary for the teacher-pupil participation of the modern schoolroom. In order to make the work as realistic and practical as possible, all material is illustrated by actual class situations. In order, however, to avoid repetition of the work in college courses termed Educational Theory and Methods, no discussions of the general theory of education and of different curriculums have been included.[1] In the "Foreword," however, in

[1] For those readers unfamiliar with the curriculum of a modern experimental high school, the following books would serve for a quick summary: Spears, Harold: *The Emerging High School Curriculum and Its Direction*, American Book Company, 1940; Joint Committee in Curriculum: *The Changing Curriculum*, Appleton-Century, 1937; Educational Policies Commission: *Learning the Ways of Democracy*, National Educational Association, 1210 Sixteenth Street N.W., Washington, D.C., 1940.

spite of the possibility of repetition, there are a few illustrations of progressive practices and theories drawn from various experimental high schools. They may be the means of arousing question of, and perhaps discontent with, the all-too-familiar regimentation of pupils and of subject-centered teaching still found in many of our public schools. These illustrations may also serve to suggest to the young teachers placed in a departmentalized high school how, little by little, they may bootleg into their own classrooms many of the attitudes and practices found in more progressive schools. By this method it is hoped that prospective teachers may avoid the disillusionment which overwhelms many enthusiastic beginners when, unwarned, they are confronted by small-town conservatism and hostility toward change. Hence the whole text is carefully balanced between what is desirable and wholly possible in some schools and what may be done in a small, conventional high school.

With this text go my appreciative thanks to those who have from the results of their research or teaching experience added to the theories and practices that I should like to call my own. Grateful acknowledgment is due my many students in both Montana State University and the Bread Loaf School of English, Vermont, and the many librarians and teachers and high-school pupils who have given me aid and suggestions. Elsewhere many of their names appear in connection with their various contributions. Throughout years of enthusiastic co-operation, Miss Winnifred Feighner, Assistant Librarian, Montana State University, and the library staff have been of invaluable service. To Dr. H. G. Merriam, Montana State University, and to Miss Edith R. Mirrielees, Stanford University, who have aided me in the writing of the original text and the two revisions, I am most deeply indebted.

L. B. M.

Missoula, Montana, 1943

Some Experiments in Present-Day Teaching

I. EARLY EXPERIMENTS IN TEACHING JUNIOR-SENIOR HIGH-SCHOOL ENGLISH

EVER since the appearance in 1917 of the bulletin *Reorganization of English in Secondary Schools* [1]—a challenge to college domination, fixed curriculum, and pupil regimentation—the creative teacher of English has suffered from an uneasy conscience. In the 1920's some programs encouraged pupil activity. By 1930, chosen "experimental schools," released from college and school-board restrictions, attempted pupil-centered programs. In these carefully planned courses, the individual pupil's ability, need, and interest determined the type of material given him. He was treated as an individual, but also as a class member. Today (1952) this concept is an accepted ideal, though perhaps "more honor'd in the breach than the observance." Yet with the publication of *The English Language Arts*,[2] Volume I, a new understanding of this ideal and of practical schoolroom procedures should do much to widen the scope of indivdualized instruction. The teaching of English, like all teaching, is still experimental. Does this statement discourage you? As you recall the thousands who have taught, it may seem to you that some few should have discovered a *best way*. If so, they might, perhaps, have patented it and proclaimed it to the world. Such procedure would seem sensible, economical, humane—but, also, impossible.

When conservative folk scoff at the constant experimentation

---

[1] Department of the Interior: Bureau of Education. Bulletin No. 2, 1917.
[2] Appleton-Century-Crofts, Inc., April, 1952. This book from the N.C.T.E. Commission on the English Curriculum is the outcome of a six-year study, and the work of more than 176 experienced teachers, directed by Dora V. Smith and others.
In text see page 572.

3

in modern teaching of English and complain of the "fads and frills" (why a "fad" has necessarily a "frill" attached has always interested me) they forget one important fact. How can the resultant output remain unchanged when one combines three constantly changing ingredients? In school there are changing groups of children from changing groups of parents with varying backgrounds. These changing groups of children, as years pass, are brought up under changing religious, social, political, and economic conditions. In this educational experiment the most slowly changing entity is the teacher, but even she, particularly if she began her own high-school study since rather than before 1914, is not an unchanging factor.

Creative teachers of English have always experimented. I remind you of their experimentation for two reasons: (1) to emphasize that though you can provide yourselves with a few principles and much information, you cannot find a ready-made pattern for your own teaching; and (2) to bespeak a sympathetic attitude toward the new-type courses in English. These courses are not perfected. The teachers in the experimental schools are themselves the first to point out defects. But the principle upon which experimental courses are built appears a sound one. It is this: *A teacher of English must aid each pupil to develop himself at his own rate and must assist him to integrate what he learns at school, at home, and in his community.* Many teachers add a second principle. *Teachers of English must attempt directly and indirectly so to form the minds of their pupils that these potential citizens will uphold rather than menace those democratic ideals we assert but as yet have failed to achieve.* Various educators in discussing the experimental school have said that the ideal teacher for them would be one who holds the archeologist's point of view. Ideally at least, when an archeologist studies prehistoric man, it is not grammatical man, literary man, historical man whom he seeks to know, but man with all his learning and ability integrated into one rounded personality, a member of a social group. Of course analogy is often misleading. If you embalmed your pupils, you, too, in the restful quiet of your classroom could regard each "rounded personality" undisturbed. But they would be dead. Your question is a more difficult one: "How can I help my all too active twentieth-century boys and girls to fuse the various materials acquired at school, so that school, home life, community life, and later their lives as citizens may be saner, happier, and perhaps more altruistic?"

How have some teachers of English, in co-operation with teachers of other departments, attempted to answer this question? You are accustomed, in both college and high school, to speak of the Department of History, the Department of English, the Art Department, or the Music Department. Have you familiarized yourself with the experiment now being made at the University of Chicago or with the work carried on in any one of those numerous universities utilizing the Chicago plan? If you have, you will recall that freshmen in these institutions no longer take Freshman English or Freshman History, but that they all enroll in a course given some such title as "Humanities." There they are asked to consider certain aspects of man's history: events which have occurred; ideas that have dominated men's minds; and literature, sculpture, painting, music which throw light upon man's spiritual and intellectual life. In some of the universities where such a course is offered, the students are free to attend lectures or to remain away. They may read as widely or as narrowly as they choose. When ready, they attempt a comprehensive examination upon this panorama of man's artistic, social, and political ideals and accomplishments.

Contrast such a course with your own freshman work. The difference is probably striking. In this newer-type curriculum, students are responsible for their own learning. The slow and the brilliant are not shackled together by hours and credits, but each may progress at his own rate. And most significant of the changed attitude is the fusion of material. Departmental lines

are broken. Students are not registering for four hours of literature, unrelated perhaps to the life and thought of the time; or
for three hours of history, minus the literature, philosophy, and
art of the period. Material from four departments is so correlated
that not four courses with similar objectives, but one course with
four phases, each motivated by the same objectives, is offered the
entering freshmen. The attempt—as yet often unsuccessful, often
confusing—is to assist the freshman to integrate the history, literature, philosophy, art, and music of certain periods of the past.
If the whole is intelligently fused, it should present to the entering student a balanced picture of certain epoch-making periods
in the life of our race.

Look at the other end of the educational ladder. In kindergarten and in the first two grades fusion such as that just described has long existed. The teachers in these early years center
their attention upon the child, not upon the specific departmentalized information that each child must obtain. The pupil tells
stories (English) about his number work (mathematics) and
illustrates with a picture or cutting that he has made (art).
Part of his tale he acts or pantomimes (dramatics). Or he brings
a polliwog to class and displays it (biology) as a prologue to the
"Polliwog Song" (music) in which the class joins. Whether or not
these kindergarten teachers have an archeologist's attitude of
mind is open to question, but you will note that their pupils
work with thoroughly fused material which both teacher and
pupil use quite innocent of departmental boundaries.

In this new tendency in college and the old in kindergarten
you will recognize a certain likeness. What is it?

1. The pupil must be seen as a person, as a mind reaching out in
all directions, regardless of departmental boundaries, not as a sponge
which merely absorbs, more or less permanently, specific information poured into it.[1]

[1] Featherstone, W. B.: "The Place of Subjects in an Integrated Curriculum,
California Quarterly of Secondary Education, Vol. 9 (1933-34), p. 235.

2. The individual must be an active and creative participant. He must assume responsibility for himself, and, in so far as he is able, direct his own activities.

3. The teacher must see not only her own subject but that subject in relation to the pupil and in relation to present-day society. She must seek material to enrich her course or must discard it according to the needs of the student, regardless of departmental boundaries or of past conventions.

Having glimpsed college and kindergarten, you might now consider your own years in junior-high-school work; then, if you are interested, read *Western Youth Meets Eastern Culture*.[1] It is not only delightful reading, but it will give you a glimpse of what knowledge and skill, plus resources, can do to revitalize the often dry husks of junior-high-school English, history, geography, and art. Perhaps in this course, as in a course called "The American epic," offered by certain Los Angeles schools in the seventh and eighth grades, the outstanding qualities are the teacher's dramatic presentation of a large quantity of related material and her imaginative approach to that material as shown in part by the creative activities of the pupils. Below are given the general objectives of the course in which English (consisting of literature, mechanics, oral and written work), social studies, geography, art, and music are fused.

A. "The American Epic," an Integrated Course

GENERAL OBJECTIVES

1. The acquiring in socially helpful ways of a partial appreciation of what our forefathers did for us.

2. The beginning of an understanding of how the life about us has evolved out of the life of the past.

3. A recognition of the more important present-day American trends and problems.

4. The cultivation of a taste for reading worth-while literature and the development of skills in oral and written expression. (You

[1] By E. F. Barry, F. G. Sweeney, and A. E. Schoelkopf.

will note the pageant-like quality, the dramatic element, in the topics listed for the first unit of work.)

UNIT I [1]

THE CURTAIN RISES

Introduction (Aims)
A. Prologue
B. In Search of Gold
C. Trappers and Traders
D. Looking for the Northwest Passage
E. For Queen and Country
F. Terminal Group Activities

This unit of work may well occupy two periods a day for the first ten weeks of the B7 semester. The time should be carefully allotted to Approach, Individual Activities, and Terminal Group Activities. The period of Approach should be one of general reading and discussion for the purpose of creating or broadening the pupils' interest. (Aims: (1) to learn why America was rediscovered; (2) to become somewhat familiar with the kind of people who came to America; (3) to understand why these people came to America.) Several days should be allowed for the Approach to each of the subtopics and two to three weeks may not be too much to give to the Terminal Group Activities.

(To illustrate more fully the work done here, note the readings and the activities that accompany one of the five subdivisions of this unit of work. The history and geography and literature, the oral and the written work, are all motivated by one topic of interest. Do not be misled by the fact that no grammar and no drill upon sentences appear on the chart. It is taken for granted that the teacher in charge will stop whenever it seems wise to give the necessary spelling drill on those words that pupils need to know in order to do the work suggested, or will spend time on

---

[1] Prepared by the Secondary Course of Study Committee from materials furnished by Helen Lucille Berg, Emily Rice Huntsman, Evelune Naomi Warder, and Mary Bernice Young, of the John Burroughs Junior High School; quoted from the February, 1934, pamphlet by permission of Mr. Arthur Gould, Deputy Superintendent of Los Angeles City School District.

sentence structure when the sentences used show that drill is needed. Of course spelling, sentence structure, correct usage, punctuation receive time—when and where they are necessary for the pupil to do the work he elects to do.)

PROLOGUE

After the fall of Rome, Europe was engaged for several centuries in assimilating the civilization of the invading barbarians. Such famous figures as Clovis, Mohammed, Charlemagne, and Alfred the Great successively occupied the stage of history. Feudalism and the Church came to dominate all Europe. The Normans invaded and conquered England. Europe experienced contact and intercourse with a different and in many respects a more advanced civilization through the Crusades. Feudalism was undermined by the Crusades and the invention of gunpowder. The Humanists arose and the control of the Church was weakened. Men began to think for themselves. Science was revived and an impetus given to invention. Marco Polo's visit to the East increased the trade with the Orient. The printing press, which was to revolutionize learning, came into existence. Constantinople fell to the Turks and the trade routes with the East were closed.

1. **Approach.** Read excerpts from books dealing with Our Homes in the Old World, bringing in such information as Where Americans Came From, Why Europeans Came to America, How They Lived before They Came to America, and What Americans Brought from the Old World. Encourage as much reading as possible in order to create or broaden the interests of the children. Medieval castle life is especially interesting to pupils of this age.

2. **Text References** [1]
> Beard and Bagley: *The History of the American People,* Chaps. I and III
> Smith: *Human Geography,* Book I, pp. 219-275, 305-342; Book II, pp. 203-301, 304-349

3. **Reading List** (Junior High)
> Beard and Bagley: *Our Old World Background*
> Brooks: *Story of Marco Polo*
> Casner and Gabriel: *Exploring American History*

[1] These references provide an extensive reading list.

Church: *The Crusades*
Coulomb, McKinley, and White: *What Europe Gave to America*
Forman: *Stories of Useful Invention.*
Finnemore: *The Story of Robin Hood and His Merry Men*
Gordy: *Beginnings in Europe*
Gray: *The Children's Crusade*
Hall: *Boy's Book of Chivalry*
   Our Ancestors in Europe
Harding: *Stories of the Middle Ages*
    Old World Background to American History
Hewes: *Boy of the Lost Crusades*
Lamprey: *In the Days of the Guild*
    Masters of the Guild
Mace and Tanner: *The Story of Old Europe and Young America*
Nida: *Dawn of American History in Europe.*
  Early Men of Science.
Pyle: *Robin Hood*
  Otto of the Silver Hand
Quennell: *History of Everyday Things in England*
Rugg: *History of American Civilization*
Stein: *Our Little Crusader Cousin of Long Ago*
  Our Little Norman Cousin of Long Ago
  Troubadour Tales
Stevens: *Story of Children's Crusade*
Tappan: *Heroes of the Middle Ages*
   When Knights Were Bold
Terry: *Lord and Vassal*
Wilmot: *Stories of the Crusades*

4. Reading List (Elementary) [1]

Barker, Dodd, and Webb: *The Growth of a Nation*
Beard and Bagley: *The History of the American People*
Chapman and Whitney: *The History of Our Nation*
Foote: *The Story of Our Republic*
Kelty: *Beginnings of the American People*
Rugg: *History of American Civilization*

[1] See materials of the Visual Education Section of the Los Angeles City Schools.

Tryon, Lingley, and Morehouse: *The American Nation Yesterday and Today*

5. Activities

1. Wandering minstrels often came to the banquet hall of the castle. Since the people had few books and no magazines, a welcome was given to the minstrels who sang of great deeds of heroes in other lands and times. Dramatize such a scene.

2. Suppose you were to go to sleep and awake one thousand years ago in a castle in Southern France. Give an account of the things which a person of your age would do in the regular life of the castle.

3. Imagine you are the lord of an English manor, and a group of stranded people ask to remain overnight. Invite them in, show them over the grounds, and tell them all about the life lived there.

4. Write and present a dialogue between yourself and a master workman of a medieval guild. In the conversation, bring out the steps which you must take to become a master workman. Also, have the master workman persuade you that his guild is the best one for you to join.

5. Collect pictures or make drawings to show the nature of the Gutenberg printing press. Explain how it worked and compare with a modern press.

6. Write and present a series of dramatic episodes which might be given over the radio, depicting King John and the signing of the Magna Charta.

7. Imagine yourself a guest at a banquet in an old English castle. Tell about the people there, the arrangement of the table, what they had to eat, what they wore, and what they talked about.

8. Make an outfit of armor with shield, weapons, and trappings for both knight and horse. Use paper and paste and cut the knight and horse from cardboard if you do not have some toy forms to use.

9. Make a map showing the routes of the Crusades and give accounts of the experiences and hardships endured by the Crusaders.

10. Read an interesting book dealing with life in Europe before 1492; make an original jacket for the book and on the inside flap write a brief review with the idea of interesting others in the book.

11. Draw a map showing the route of Leif Ericson and give the

class an account of his trip. Also explain why his expedition was not followed by colonization.

12. Write a newspaper article on one of the following:

> The Angles and Saxons Make War on Britain
> The Danes Make War on Britain
> The Fair in the Middle Ages
> Printing Is Invented
> The Spanish Armada Is Defeated
> Constantinople Taken by the Turks
> The Hundred Years' War Is Ended

If the whole unit of work were before you, you would see that prose and poetry, oratory and drama, are all a part of the course, as are also brief, superficial explorations into the science of agriculture, mining, transportation, and domestic science. Perhaps you would also note a dearth of real literature. Here, more than in the first course mentioned, *Western Youth Meets Eastern Culture,* whimsical or imaginative verse and prose, although it would be possible to introduce them, apparently play but small part. Factual material predominates.

The attempt to correlate material and to present this material largely through pupil activities is clear to you, is it not? Consider the detailed description of the course given in *Western Youth Meets Eastern Culture,* or even the briefly sketched Los Angeles course, and then contrast them with the work offered in many states in the last two years of the grade school. There in many systems the literature studied is bound in three or four grade-school readers, and those books comprise practically all the reading required or expected. Or again compare these newer courses with the travesty existing in certain states where schools are dominated by a state eighth-grade examination. There you may find one year given over largely to grammar drill, practically unmotivated by oral or written use. This drill is termed "English." (Is it any wonder that high-school pupils fight shy of later courses so designated?) Reading belongs in another class, and is termed "Literature." Yet it is wise to remember one thing. Even under so unpropitious an organization, good teachers have in the past taught interestingly and well. Remarkable as it may seem when one considers all the restrictions of subject and of examinations imposed upon them, they have succeeded in giving broadly humane courses and have by their teaching increased their pupils' understanding of literature and therefore of life. It is important to remember that character, knowledge, skill, pleasing personality, and enthusiasm are still and have always been the dominant factors in successful teaching.

B. "Social Living," an Integrated Course

A third practice found in many of these fused courses is this: not only do teachers of English in co-operation with teachers of other departments attempt through geography, history, music, art, and literature to re-create the life of past times with its problems and beliefs; and not only do they try to aid their pupils to integrate this material in their own brains, but they also begin with modern problems and work from the present to the past. By this reversal of the chronological order they believe that interest is aroused, and the ultimate purpose of the course—a clearer understanding of the social and political life of the present—is more readily kept in mind by both teacher and pupils.

A glimpse of several such courses may prove useful, and will indicate to you the outstanding experiments being carried on in those schools where English is fused with material drawn from other subjects. These classes sketched, remember, are not found in conventional but in experimental schools.

A course more or less typical of the work carried on in experimental schools is one for freshmen and sophomores called "Social Living" which includes fusion of English, Social Studies, Art, and Music. The course opens with discussion of the pupils' own problems—economic, social, moral. It then broadens to the community problems and to the problems confronting the pupils' parents. Finally a study is made of national and international problems. On the part of the teachers, preparation for this course covered a period of two years, during which time faculty committees laid a foundation for their work by the reading of psychology, and social and economic theory. The school is provided with a "Social Living Room" in which celebrated pictures are placed and discussed, and where pupils can play phonograph records of recognized masters and hear discussions of the men and their work. Teachers of various training are working toward a common goal and are co-operating in order to provide for each pupil for two years an approximation of a cultured home in which art, music, literature, personal and national problems, are studied and discussed.[1]

Assume that this two-year experimental course is well conceived and well presented; then ask yourself three questions.

1. Would you have enjoyed and profited by it as a high-school underclassman?

2. Would it have given you as a college freshman a basis more or less satisfactory than the one you had upon which to found your knowledge of the world about you and to meet cultured people in intelligent discussion?

3. As the teacher of such a course, how would you have to supplement your present mental equipment? Do you note the greater necessity for training in history, sociology, economics, and art for these teachers in experimental schools?

C. *"Along the Forty-first Parallel," an Integrated Course*

A fourth experiment is one that attempts correlation in the tenth year between English and social studies by presenting a cross-section of present-day America, the forty-first parallel of latitude being chosen as the line for cross-sectioning. Such a study seems, at first sight, too ambitious for high-school sophomores, but, naturally, the work is both elementary and superficial. The attempt, however, to correlate material, to awaken intelligent interest, and to give boys and girls of high-school age

[1] Quoted by permission of Principal A. C. Argo, Sequoia Union High School, Redwood City, California, from the records of the English Section Meeting, Curriculum Conference, Stanford University, California, June, 1934.

some definite knowledge of their own land in both its physical and social aspects shows again the earnest attempt to aid pupils in integrating that material which heretofore has been unrelated and presented in separate departments. This survey, given two hours a day throughout the sophomore year, the first hour taught by the social-science teacher, the second by the teacher of English, consisted of six units of work. Throughout the six units the objectives held by both teachers were the same, and when feasible, both teachers remained in the room for the two hours. To correlate the work as closely as possible, the two teachers (1) used the same room, (2) accepted the same oral and written reports, reading lists, and topics. Such correlation or fusion of materials did not, of course, preclude drill upon oral and written composition, spelling, and the mechanics of writing. It insured emphasis upon correct speech and writing during at least two hours of the pupils' school day. The units of work in the order presented were as follows: a study from east to west along the forty-first parallel of (1) geologic formations, (2) racial problems, (3) economic problems, (4) social problems, (5) political problems, (6) institutions and problems of the individual (home, church, school, literature, arts, amusements). The advantage of having two teachers present this work rather than having it presented by either a teacher trained in social studies or one trained in English is at once apparent. Unlike certain of the experimental courses, in this one neither teacher is attempting to present material with which she is only superficially acquainted. Hence misinformation or unsound theory is avoided, and neither the pupil's factual information nor his imaginative growth is neglected. Furthermore two personalities and two approaches to the same problem offer stimulus to the pupils, particularly in a two-hour period. But such a course also offers serious difficulties. The most serious, probably, is that of securing two differently trained teachers, each accustomed to a strictly departmentalized system, who can and will work together with complete harmony and one-ness of objective.

D. *"An Analysis of an American's Rights," an Integrated Course*

In stimulating fashion, Principal Frank L. Cummings presents an experiment carried on in the high school in Chico, California, which, if you find it interesting, you can investigate for your-selves.[1] The course, a fusion of English and social studies, con-sists of six units, each unit motivated by one of the six rights of American citizens set forth in the preamble of the Constitution: (1) to form a more perfect union; (2) to establish justice; (3) to insure domestic tranquillity; (4) to provide for the common defense; (5) to promote the general welfare; and (6) to secure the blessings of liberty. In this course each topic begins with a consideration of present-day conditions. After this investigation, the class traces each topic back to Colonial days, thus seeking an explanation and better understanding of present life. The benefits from such fusion are well summarized in the following statement:

Such a course might enable pupils to realize for the first time that American literature is an outgrowth of the American experi-ment in democracy and to realize that their expanding acquaintance with history should challenge them to accurate and adequate writing and speaking. Too often history has valuable content but atrocious English; too often English has correctness but no content. Education might flourish best if one course had both points of emphasis. Teach-ers capable of teaching combined courses certainly can be found to-day, and many more can be trained. In short, the difficulty of amal-gamated courses is not in the theory of amalgamation; the difficulty lies in reactionary, visionless teachers, wedded to extreme depart-mentalism on the one hand and on the other to the fetish of school credits. Happily, a few schools are catching the vision of new possibilities.[2]

---

[1] Cummings, Frank L.: "Practices in Fusion of Subject Matter in Various Courses," *California Quarterly of Secondary Education*, Vol. 10 (1934), pp. 13-18.

[2] Lyman, R. L.: *The Enrichment of the English Curriculum,* Supplementary

II. LATER EXPERIMENTS IN JUNIOR-SENIOR HIGH-SCHOOL ENGLISH

You will find the general pattern of the earlier experimental work in English repeated more or less in the various curricula (1952) listed below. As yet, the majority of schools in this country teach English or language arts as a separate subject. Among English teachers there is, however, a strong movement, begun in the thirties, "to see that the normal relationships are carefully maintained between expression of ideas and the skills needed; between reading, and talking and writing about what one reads; and between writing and speaking and the necessary search for ideas in print, by interview, or over the radio." [1] If, years ago, English teachers had practiced these "normal relationships," is it possible that English would not appear in "subject-combined" courses today?

From the many present-day curricula I have listed only eight: I a, For Slow Readers; b, Work-Experience; c, Life Adjustment; d, Nonacademic. II a, Fused Courses; b, Common Learnings; c, Core Curriculum; d, Correlated Subjects. [2] The titles grouped under I are self-explanatory. But surprise awaits you in the life adjustment program. Look for literature. There *Consumers' Guide* ranks high. The work-experience curriculum is, apparently, often an unsolved tangle of hours, jobs, and credit for work, but the purpose has merit. The "fused" and "correlated" programs combine two or perhaps three subjects, but "core" or "common learnings," practically the same, may serve as a total program "—designed to look after the socially misfit . . . and . . . those below

Educational Monograph No. 39, January, 1932, pp. 210-11. University of Chicago Press.

[1] Smith, Dora V.: *English Journal*, Vol. 37 (March, 1948), p. 121. See also Monograph of the *National Survey of Secondary Schools*, No. 20, *Instructions in English*, Bul. 17 (1932).

[2] Reading references for these eight curricula are on page 29.

average in scholastic power." [1] In 1950-51 adoptions of the core curriculum increased rapidly. But, as the "Suggested Readings," page 29, show, many administrators tend to have a radically different point of view from that of teachers of English. Why? Apparently because administrators view English as a helpful aid to one or more factual subjects. As teachers consider our factual minded, keenly competitive society, marked by lessening moral restraints, many are concerned over the gradual elimination of literature reading and discussion—those stimuli to mental, emotional, and imaginative growth. They question whether factual material should replace the type of thinking and writing that develops an understanding of oneself and others. Today in public life, unsubstantiated charges and sweeping generalizations confuse readers and listeners. Teachers realize the need of slowly developing in pupils an understanding of language, its dangerous misrepresentations, and bombast as well as its honesty, clarity, and accuracy.

Read Chapter I in *The English Language Arts*,[2] a book referred to as the "English Teachers' Bible." There you will find "The Purpose of Teaching the Language Arts." Only after you understand what English courses can mean in the development of pupils, are you prepared to consider English in a fused, combined, or correlated curriculum. Consider, too, the pupils of average, lesser, and greater ability. All students need the same types of stimulation. But growth occurs only if the ideas, materials, and methods are carefully fitted to the student's ability and environmental conditioning.

[1] Yardumian, Leona: " 'Correlated Studies': A Custom-Built Curriculum," *California Journal of Secondary Education,* Vol. 25 (1950), p. 271.

[2] N.C.T.E. Curriculum Series, Vol. I, by the Commission on the English Curriculum, Dora V. Smith, Director, Appleton-Century-Crofts, April, 1952, $3.75. See also Appendix B, p. 572.

If as yet you have not this volume, read Dr. Smith's article in the *English Journal*, Vol. 37, March, 1948, "Basic Consideration in Curriculum Making in the Language Arts."

III. GENERAL TENDENCIES APPARENT IN THESE COURSES

It is too soon to draw more than tentative conclusions concern-ing the various innovations introduced into experimental schools. What their faculties ask, with almost pathetic eagerness, is the right to work quietly, undisturbed by criticism or by praise, until they have themselves had time to reach some satisfactory deci-sions concerning their experiments. Such being the case, it is un-fair for a casual visitor to attempt evaluation. Since, however, you may wish to utilize in your own teaching some practices based upon these courses, tentative observations may be allow-able. Obviously the courses are as yet experiments. But, so far, what straws in the wind may one observe? Apparently two tendencies are discernible.

1. In the ninth and tenth grades much of that material termed cultural which was formerly found in high-school courses has dis-appeared.

2. In the last two years, the work, although it approximates more closely the high-school classes of the past, covers a wider field, and the pupils are encouraged to adventure more independently.

You will observe that in teaching in an experimental school one serious difficulty confronts the teacher. In those classes where widely different material is fused, or where each pupil is encouraged to follow his own interests more or less regardless of the unit material planned, teachers must at times find themselves conducting classes and presenting material about which they have but scanty information. The secondary school, it is true, demands neither research workers nor eminent scholars, but when the blind lead the blind—in this case, perhaps their most serious injury is not physical. At present, respect for sound learning, good craftsmanship, and definite information is men-aced. Yet good may come from this very danger. If in the future departmental lines are to be far less clearly drawn than today—and I believe that they are—it is evident that a more generous education in history and sociology must be demanded of those who are to teach English in secondary schools. Greater breadth of vision, deeper insight into the possibilities of literature teaching—sadly needed in the past and needed today—will be even more necessary. Fused material from social studies and art may, if wisely used, immeasurably enrich the pupils' study of literature; if unwisely used, they may readily usurp the place of real literature, thus eliminating the spiritual and aesthetic growth now possible—even though often not attained. This substitution in English classes of factual for imaginative content, a substitution of which doubtless you have been aware and which is particularly obvious in the last course of study mentioned, is given challenging form by an administrator in one of the large city systems:

If the classics stand in the way of vital education, so much the worse for the classics. They will have to pass over into the other area of the social studies curriculum organized for the benefit of bright pupils going to college or pupils whose parents wish them to have a conventional education.[1]

Such a comment shows well the present-day attitude toward literature teaching held by many administrators. It implies that for pupils unfitted for college, literature of the past has nothing to offer. Back of the comment just quoted, however, lies a serious misapprehension. Many classics, it is true, are ill suited for high-school study; many classics demand careful preparation on the part of the teacher, and an imaginative treatment. Much bad teaching is done. But the classics, carefully selected and wisely taught, had in the past and still have permanent value, not for the brilliant only, but for the butcher, the baker, and the maker of Mazda lamps—people who need even more than their more gifted companions the strength and beauty to be drawn from Homer or Shakespeare, the pathos and humor of Dickens, the

[1] Featherstone, W. B.: "The Place of Subjects in an Integrated Curriculum," *California Quarterly of Secondary Education*, Vol. 9 (1933-34), p. 242.

courage of Kipling's verses, and the philosophy of an Emerson or a Wordsworth or a Thoreau. Because English—once admitted to be of supreme importance and required for all twelve of the school years—has been taught badly, you find it today in temporary disgrace. And it has been taught badly because many ill-prepared teachers, teachers who themselves lacked intellectual, imaginative, emotional, or aesthetic appreciation for it, have attempted to teach literature in hundreds of classrooms throughout the United States. And too often even potentially good teachers have taught literature as divorced from life and present living. They did not see, or at least did not make their pupils see, *Coriolanus* as the age-old and present-day struggle of the idealistic aristocrat against the vulgar stupidities of those who would pull all down to their own level; they did not see Ulysses as Byrd or Scott or Peary "forever roaming with a hungry heart," nor yet as the age-old symbol of courage and unwavering persistence. Teach modern literature, of course, but be careful not to eliminate from your pupils' reading menu everything except the modern. Do not impute to the classics the teacher's stupidities and lack of vision.

For you the chief interest in these experimental courses probably lies in the vista of related material which they open to you and in the constant emphasis upon aiding each pupil to develop himself. They should make clear, too, the necessity for keeping your classes alive and interesting, and seeing your teaching as a means of liberating each pupil and training him to use all his faculties. But most important of all, they should show you the necessity for a truly "liberal" education on your own part, so that you can offer to your pupils not only literature, but literature richly set with its accompaniment of history, sociology, art, and music. Obviously no young teacher has this wealth of background, but the realization that such a background is desirable for the teacher of literature is the first necessary step in acquiring it.

IV. WHAT ARE SOME PROGRESSIVE IDEALS THAT YOU CAN REALIZE IN A DEPARTMENTALIZED HIGH SCHOOL?

Suppose that you are not a free agent in curriculum building, but that you are confronted by closely drawn departmental lines and a more or less fixed course of study. What progressive work can you do? Your own progressive or nonprogressive attitude will determine that question. If you are one type of person, you will continue to teach selection after selection as if your sole purpose were to see that every sophomore in your class knew the plot, setting, characters, and style of each book studied; that your seniors knew the main names, personalities, titles of works, and one selection from each outstanding author from Chaucer to Matthew Arnold. (You would hardly have time to introduce twentieth-century authors.) Or you may feel genuinely advanced if you divide your work and for one semester drill upon grammar and mechanics and for the second teach selected classics instead of the three-day literature, two-day composition schedule used perhaps by your predecessor.

But suppose that you are not that type. What can you do?

1. **A laboratory workshop.** You can transform your classroom into a laboratory where each pupil is working at his own rate. If you make a laboratory or workshop the ideal for your classroom, it is no longer a place where pupils come to answer questions in order to convince the teacher that reading has been done. Instead, it may become a place where ideas are paramount, where teacher and pupils come bringing material bearing upon some problem (the unit of work), material which may be read, or acted, or written, or merely discussed, but which is closely related to the lives of the pupils and to the fundamental problems of the present—whether the literature itself comes from ancient Athens or contemporary Chicago.

2. **Wide reading.** You can so arrange your material—given a reasonable number of books—that each pupil begins to read at

his own level; hence, for you a course of study may become merely a suggested line of progress for some few pupils in your class, while many pupils are reading either simpler or more difficult material. In certain schools where pupils buy their own texts, this experiment has been tried. The classroom is provided with empty shelves. When the pupils arrive, each is led to consider his past reading and to list the books which he has read, marking those he has particularly enjoyed. Also he is led to discuss his hobbies and interests. Together he and the teacher decide upon two books, not to exceed a dollar each in price, which he believes he might enjoy reading. The books are purchased, placed upon the waiting shelves after they have passed through the hands of the appointed or elected class librarian; and under the eye of the teacher reading is done. The English classroom has become a library reading room. Four classes of thirty would line the classroom with two hundred and forty books, attractive books in fresh covers. At the end of the year each pupil takes his own books home, battered to be sure, but each reader has also had an opportunity to enjoy his neighbors' volumes.

The plan is by no means perfect. Books are lost; some pupils continue reading upon too low a level; the unity which can grow out of a common reading background and the stimulus of class discussion of a recently read play or story (when that discussion is stimulating) is largely forfeited. Poetry, plays, and essays fill but a small space on the classroom shelves. But in the eighth, ninth, and tenth grades when our great ambition is to make readers of our pupils, how successful do you think this plan would prove? Each pupil begins his reading where he can read with enjoyment.

A system used by Miss Adela Klumb in a public high school in Wisconsin is as follows: The teacher surveys her full shelves and estimates the quality of each book, assigning an A, B, C, or D for each. But length of book is also considered; hence *The Count of Monte Cristo* would count A6 because of its length, but

Shadows on the Rock only A1, and *Riders of the Purple Sage* only C2. In this manner each pupil, although he reads at his own level, understands what that level is—at least in the eyes of his teacher—and also he is encouraged to read either a long or a short book as he chooses. No tests are given, but the reading is done to a great extent in the schoolroom. And although there are no formal tests, there are discussions with the teacher and with others in the classroom.

The plan is an interesting one. Probably one text and one book for wide reading for each pupil might be a possible stepping-stone to greater freedom. There was a time, you may remember, when in grade school supplementary readers were unknown. If Mary had a book, she was amply supplied. In your book ordering, remember this plan or a modification of it as a possibility.

Another change that is altering literature teaching in class-rooms all over the United States is the introduction of an anthology to replace separate texts. There, inside two covers, is a little library for each pupil. Where texts are owned by the state, the ease of checking out to the student and collecting again from him one book instead of four or five might readily recommend the anthology to the teacher because of the saving in time, effort, and nervous energy. Perhaps the saving is even greater in those schools where pupils must be led to buy their texts or, if unable to buy them, must secure money from the board of education. But there are other benefits to be gained. One pupil can finish *Silas Marner* in two evenings; another plods on slowly, taking two weeks to complete the tale. The first student has in his hands ample material to read while student number two is laboriously digesting his novel. What an anthology means to both teacher and pupils can hardly be realized by those of you who have yet to see a school "library" which consists of a locked hall closet containing some twenty books.

To be sure there is one serious objection to most anthologies.

As a rule they are unwieldy. One cannot put a volume of *Literature and Life* in his pocket and forget it while viewing a basketball game; *Hidden Treasures in Literature* had better be read by the junior-high-school girl before she begins her long walk home. And yet perhaps the strong incentive to get one's literature read during study periods to avoid carrying so bulky a book home is in itself good training.

How familiar are you with modern anthologies planned for junior- or senior-high-school pupils? The better ones are carefully organized, one unit of reading leading on to the next. It behooves a prospective teacher to analyze an anthology carefully, securing if possible a teacher's manual prepared by the editors. I think that you will admit that these carefully considered, thoughtfully graded units in an anthology may—at least during your first two years of teaching—provide a better course than you, unaided, can build from single texts. Why? Because experienced teachers have selected material suitable for junior- or senior-high-school pupils. I recall a young teacher who recommended Eugene O'Neill's *Ah! Wilderness* for sophomore readin; and possible class production, another who suggested that freshmen act *Dead End* because they could do the children's parts successfully, and a third who, enthusiastic over *Tom Jones,* suggested that robust book for sophomore class reading. Use your initiative; of course draw on your college training and modern reading; but also be guided by the suggestions of experienced teachers. Remember that in junior and senior high school there is often a great difference between intellectual grasp and emotional development. It may be entirely possible for a pupil to read an adult novel or play, but at the same time it may be either impossible or undesirable for him to grasp it emotionally. Since this is the condition, but one difficult for the young teacher to realize, the anthology, with its wealth of material adjusted to the needs of the pupils, safeguards you against your own inexperience.[1] A second advantage is this: modern anthologies list after each unit suitable material from all types of literature. These, adapted to different reading abilities, stimulate class reading. These titles may serve as guides for the wide reading of your better pupils, but they may also serve as a guide for you in ordering library books.

In many classrooms the change in world conditions has altered literature teaching. American students need to know the literatures of other nations. In some schools such material is given as an elective course in the senior year; in other schools "World Literature" becomes a part of the regular senior work. But whatever arrangement is made for offering the course, the purpose for offering it is this: We as a nation are too provincial. Our pupils forget that the foreign day laborer would probably be a day laborer in his own country. They tend to believe that *all* Chinese, Italians, French, and Germans are like the vegetable vender, the bootblack, the laundryman, or the restaurant keeper whom they know. As a nation we need to know more of the art, music, and literature of other nations. But it has taken two World Wars, the United Nations, foreign travel, and radio and television to convince us of that fact. Today courses in world literature are fairly new, but where they are offered the object is, of course, to increase the students' appreciation of other nations. Many teachers question the wisdom of attempting to portray twelve or fifteen different civilizations through the medium of brief poems or excerpts from longer works. Others believe the need for some comprehension of other countries and of their literary products is so great that an anthology of world literature, although frankly superficial, should be used as a means of interesting students in the peoples of foreign lands. One thing becomes immediately apparent. Any teacher who attempts such a course must not only know much more than the anthology offers, but must organize her material so that there will be carefully directed wide reading, well-motivated class re-

---

[1] In later chapters you will be asked to examine various anthologies.

ports, and intelligent discussion of important national tendencies.[1] Probably you as a young teacher would not attempt such
a course in your first year of teaching, but you should be informed
as to its existence in many schools. And the fact that such a
course does exist may give you courage to attempt to widen the
intellectual horizons of the pupils in your classroom.

3. **Teaching by units.** Unit work demands free reading and
individual exploration. But small schools with meager library
books may await you. Esther Niebel, Bozeman, Montana, states
that the best material for the least cost is found in five or ten
single copies of anthologies. Why? You have approximately 60
or 100 short stories, 20 or 50 plays, articles, essays, biographies,
and 5 or 10 novels. Consult your principal, then your pupils, then
the P.T.A. Make earning the money and reading new books an
exciting adventure.

4. **Teaching by testing.** Create a workshop atmosphere, co-
operative, free from criticism or competition. Explain that some
run and some read faster than others; then give diagnostic reading
tests and drills on *how* to read, stressing comprehension more than
speed. Constant interest in and encouragement of slow readers,
plus simple reading material, and analysis of their difficulties are
all essential.

5. **Book-discussion days.** You can stimulate much free reading
both by eliminating time spent in fruitless class discussion of material already comprehended and by awakening interest in many
books rather than centering interest upon a few. More probably
than you now realize, you can increase reading by the elimination
of the old-style book report and by substituting book-discussion
days.

[1] The volume *Adventures in World Literature* by Rewey Belle Inglis and
William K. Stewart provides ample reading lists, so that in this particular
text the teacher's problem is somewhat simplified. Books on art and music as
well as books concerned with the literature of the various countries are also
listed, so that the volume becomes a selective but interesting guide to the intellectual and artistic life of some sixteen nationalities.

6. **Enriched teaching.** Through pictures, magazines, newspapers, occasional assembly programs, and the utilization of all related material available, you can present literature units that are truly cultural, rich in their picture of the past, and significant because of the emphasis which you place upon the interpretation of life, past and present.

One thing becomes more and more apparent, does it not? It is the teacher's own zest for reading, her taste and abundant vitality, plus her tact and good humor, which determine her success in literature teaching. Careful planning is necessary, accumulation of material is necessary, but nothing can take the place of the teacher's own enjoyment of both a good detective tale and a delicate lyric, a profoundly moving drama and an excellently clear, cool analysis of some idea or situation. Read. Read wisely. Know the literature that will appeal to youth, but be aware of the necessity of feeding your own brain with the finest in literature in order to retain both your mental vigor and your literary taste.

Although the modern schoolroom is equipped with an address system, a radio, and phonograph records, and although the modern assembly is equipped with a motion-picture machine, I have purposely omitted all references to these most useful aids, since I discuss them later.

In contrast to these "experimental" courses described earlier, here is a quotation from a live and certainly "progressive" unit from a state course of study of 1941 vintage. I quote it from *General English,* a course of study for the State of Missouri.[1]

---

[1] *Missouri at Work on the Public School Curriculum, Bulletin* 3A, 1941. Secondary School Series. *Language Arts: General English.* Lloyd W. King, State Superintendent of Public Instruction.

IDEAS FOR YOUR CONSIDERATION

These quotations are taken from one of the many articles published by Dr. Dora V. Smith in which are foreshadowed the programs found in *The English Language Arts,* Volume I, discussed earlier.

1. "We hope, above all, to develop in them [pupils] a personal habit of reading for sheer fun as well as for information and enlightenment, which will bring them deeply personal satisfaction so long as reading days last."

2. "In the realms of social and civic life, we believe that through literature and discussion our pupils should develop a sensitivity to human relationships. *Reading Ladders for Human Relationships* . . . reveals the power of literature to present human experiences in the concrete with all the warmth of personal emotion."

3. "The power of literature to promote understanding and to engender loyalties lies in its appeal to the emotions, for in emotions are the wellsprings of action."

4. "The first problem in interrelationships in English . . . is . . . to see that the normal relationships are carefully maintained between expression of ideas and the skills needed; between reading, and talking and writing about what one reads; and between writing and speaking and the necessary search for ideas in print, by interview or over the radio."

5. "Our students must leave school understanding that newspapers, radio programs, and many magazines exist for the purpose of setting forth particular points of view. It is imperative that each reader and listener understand what mode of thought is being presented; that he demand evidence; and that he compare both the evidence and the point of view with that of other programs and other periodicals."

SUGGESTED READINGS

The English Language Arts, Vol. I, N.C.T.E. Curriculum Series, Dora V. Smith, Director

Read Part III, Chapter 9, "Relationship of the English Curriculum to the Total School Program" and then consider Part IV, Chapter 18, "Methods of Evaluating Instruction." This last chapter will aid you in all your teaching.

Consult: Educational Index; *The High School Curriculum,* H. R. Douglass, ed., Ronald Press, 1947; G. S. Wright: "The Core in Secondary

Schools" (Biblio.), *School Review,* Vol. 60 (1952), pp. 46-54; U. S. Office of Education, 1950 Circular, No. 323 (Free)

1. Sheean, M. H.: *Slow Learners,* "What Currriculum for the Slow Learners?" *Nat. Assoc., Secondary-School Principals,* Bul. 34, Vol. 167-74 (1950), pp. 4-16

2. Ivens, Wilson H., and Runge, B.: *Work Experience in High School,* Ronald Press, 1951

3. *Life Adjustment Education for Every Youth,* Office of Education, Bul. No. 22, 1951, Washington 25, D. C. (30 cents)

Martens, E. H.: "Toward Life Adjustment through Life Adjustment," *School Life,* Vol. 33 (1951), pp. 52-4.

4. "Vitalizing the High-School English Curriculum with Special Reference to Non-Academic Students," *Education,* Vol. 69 (1948), pp. 250-53

5. La Brant, Lou, ed.: *English in Common Learnings,* N.C.T.E., 1951 (50 cents)

Cramer, R. V.: "Common Learnings Program in Junior High School," *Nat. Assoc. of Secondary-School Principals,* Bul. No. 35, 1950, pp. 158-66

6. Alberly, Harold: "A Proposal for Reorganization on the Basis of a Core Program," *Progressive Education,* Vol. 28 (Nov., 1950), pp. 57-61

Burnett, Lewis W.: "Core Program in Washington State Junior High School," *School Review,* Vol. 59 (1951), pp. 97-100

Drederich, P. B.: [1] "How Fare the Core Courses?" *School Review,* Vol. 57 (1949), pp. 13-14

7. Yardumian, Leona: " 'Correlated Studies': A Custom-Built Curriculum," *California Journal of Secondary Education,* Vol. 25 (1950), pp. 271-83

* Jordan, S. Stewart: "Literature in Correlated Programs," *English Journal,* Vol. 39 (1950), pp. 313-17 (What is it?)

* Burge, A. M.: "English Class Uses Social Studies Readings," *Clearing House,* Vol. 22 (1947), pp. 105-7 (An improvement?)

8. Cox, W. M.: "Life Adjustment for Youth," *High Points,* Vol. 320 (Oct., 1950), pp. 19-24 (For vocational schools)

9. Lindsay, F. B.: "Life Adjustment Education and the Framework," *California Journal of Secondary Education,* Vol. 25 (1950), pp. 406-10

---

[1] What factor in English is ignored? See the report on programs in 71 junior high schools, "Junior High Schools of Today," Lauchner, A. H., *Calif. Jour. of Secondary Education,* Vol. 26 (1951), pp. 470-74.

10. Rogers, H. J.: "Emerging Curriculum of the Modern Junior High School," *National Association of Secondary-School Principals*, Bul. No. 34 (April, 1950), pp. 128-38

11. Hyer, L. D.: "Life Adjustment through Literature," *English Journal*, Vol. 40 (1951), pp. 28-33

12. Leonore, Sister Gertrude: "Life Adjustment in an English Class," *Catholic Educational Review*, Vol. 48 (1950), pp. 163-70

13. Trabue, M. R.: "Personal Development and the English Curriculum," *Elementary English*, Vol. 28 (1951), pp. 215-20

14. Holton, S. M.: "Flexibility in Secondary Schools through the One Subject Plan," *High School Journal*, Vol. 32 (1949), pp. 113-22. (Condensed in *Education Digest*, Vol. 15 (1949), pp. 28-31.)

15. Pooley, R. C.: "English in the Coming High School," *English Journal*, Vol. 37 (1948), pp. 284-91

PART ONE
Written and Oral English

CHAPTER I

The Teacher's Attitude toward Composition: Theme Prevision, Correction, Evaluation

I. WHAT OUGHT YOUR THEME PILE REPRESENT?

WHEN you consider the changing sheaf of themes on your desk, that ever growing, never decreasing pile, just how do you regard them? That they are not impersonal bits of fact, similar to the popular true-false tests whose value (if you have the key) is immediately recognizable, you may be sure. Nor do they, except at rare intervals, contain bits of fancy, pure and undefiled. What are they?

Far more than you now realize, the answer to that question depends upon you, the teacher. Within reasonable limits you will get what you prepare for, what you encourage and foster, what you expect and reward. Do not misunderstand me. Presumably you will not find a young Macaulay endowed with unusual vocabulary; you will not find a young Shelley; nor will you discover one of the Brontë sisters. But there is always the gold-miner's lure—you may. If you have not any of these celebrities, however, you do have some twenty or two hundred and twenty personalities that in sports, on the street, at home, in clubs, at the movies, have strong likes and dislikes, have keen hopes and fears and disappointments, have admirations that move them far more than you now are ever moved. And yet some teachers of composition complain that their classes have nothing about which to write, have no ideas to express, and have no vocabularies in which to wrap the puny little shoots of thought they do possess.

Just who are these godlike beings? Who are these teachers, on another plane, going to faculty meetings and to English Associations where they "sit like gods together, careless of mankind"? Do not be condescending. You are not dealing with children. Neither are you dealing with mere brains. If you are really teaching your pupils and meeting them on the common footing of workshop interest in composition, you are meeting whole, more or less rounded personalities. You are concerned with their hopes, their ideals, their prejudices, their emotions, their manners; in fact you are concerned with them as people, younger than you but on the whole like you. They are like you, but more easily hurt, more easily discouraged, and, remember, more easily fired with enthusiasm if you can once gain their liking and their respect.

After all these generalities, let us return to the pile of themes on your desk. What ought they represent? First of all, they should be the visible sign of that careful prevision which you practiced before the themes were written. Perhaps they represent:

1. A question flung out to the class two weeks ago, just to set them thinking

2. A dictation where some few technical points and a word or two in spelling were stressed, both of which they would probably need in the later theme

3. A class discussion where some material was read to touch off imaginations, or to provide a point of view, or to open possible ways of developing an idea

4. A laboratory writing period with teacher supervision, suggestion, brief conferences when necessary

5. A time for writing, either in study hall or at home, and for rereading, revising, and, at last, preparing a final draft

6. A class period spent in reading aloud in groups, and in preparing a few penciled notes for the teacher concerning the best papers submitted

Does your sheaf of papers, or do some of the papers in your sheaf, represent that much thoughtful prevision on your part, and that much careful work on the part of your class? Might the

pile represent something else? Does it represent your own vigorous, enthusiastic, but half-questioning presentation of the general
idea or pattern for this type of work? Does it show the development of the idea by the class so that, in their own minds, the
thought seems to have been largely their own? More and more
you will realize that both your initiation of ideas in the classroom
and your enthusiastic reception of pupils' ideas have a definite
effect upon the compositions which you receive. And yet there
is a certain temptation here. A principal recently remarked in
discussing two teachers: "Both are good. Miss X gets excellent
work from her classes, but she always gets what *she* wants; the
work is really hers. Miss Z simply opens the gates for the pupils
and their ideas troop out. Her classwork is often on an inferior
plane compared to that of the other class, but it is spontaneous,
original, and really their own." Since English should be a tool,
a usable tool, the latter teacher apparently is doing more than
the former to liberate the ideas of her pupils and to provide a
usable medium for them.

You may agree with this open-gate theory and condemn
guidance. Many teachers fresh from college would agree with
you. And I admit, of course, the danger of overguidance, of
cramping the ideas of pupils, those ideas that come purling forth
like crystal springs, bubbling up spontaneously. A pretty thought.
But look at the facts. You will find that your pupils as a rule
are not filled with ideas that they urge upon you. Many classes
have, apparently, nothing about which to write. You set pen and
paper before them; you say in effect: "A theme will be due next
Tuesday. Write something interesting that we shall all enjoy."
Have you had a somewhat similar experience? Have you ever
been presented by a tactless hostess to some stranger with the
comment "I know you two will get on well together. You are
both so clever." What is the effect? The springs of conversation
are dried at the source. There is literally nothing to say.

In the same way an assignment and a class when brought

together by a tactless teacher confront each other with hostility. The introduction has been made, but what of it? The teacher has provided no lead, has aroused no interest, has suggested no common ground for beginning. The desire to talk or to write is killed, or at least is not kindled. Does this comparison seem fantastic? I do not believe that it is. I am not suggesting that no labor accompany writing, that pupils be cajoled into theme work. I am, however, urging that the work, the hard work, that they do be clearly motivated, be made interesting, be prepared for carefully by both teacher and pupils, and that the final product be something of which the pupils may be reasonably proud. Perhaps you agree with me now, but later you will realize even more keenly the close connection between that final product and the teacher's preparation, introduction, and intelligent supervision while the discussion and the writing are in progress.

There is also another point to consider. After you have taught for a time and have had an opportunity to realize how crowded your schedule is, you will come to the conclusion that the amount of prevision suggested is impossible unless the amount of original writing is lessened. One finished theme in two weeks would be possible; one finished theme a week or a daily theme would be impossible both for you and for the pupils. By finished themes I do not mean those daily exercises suggested later. Remember that you as teacher must analyze each theme, weigh it, comment upon it, grade it. The pupils must get an idea, let it grow, jot it down, prune it, and prepare it for class inspection and for your grading. Obviously there are two points of view here to be considered. First, why should you, a busy teacher, who must be vigorous and humorous, sympathetic and stimulating, waste time and energy upon papers which do not represent the best or even the second-best effort of your pupils? Why read, mark, and, unconsciously, learn and inwardly digest perfunctory writing?

Consider also the pupil's predicament. How can he develop

any instinct for good workmanship—if such a thing exist—if he must always work at top speed? How can he develop any genuine interest in writing if he never improves upon his first draft? Many a conscientious teacher has overworked herself and killed interest in her classes by increasing the number of papers. Pride in any one paper is rendered impossible because of the hasty preparation of the many. You will hear teachers say: "But my pupils never will begin a paper until the night before it is due. It's just human nature. Hence all this prevision does not work in my classes." Of course it does not. No prevision "works" unaided. The teacher, through prevision—that is, through foreseeing the problems awaiting her class—prepares them to meet those problems. If she piles up too many problems, she has no time for proper preparation; if she gives assignments by chance, luck, accident, she can foresee no problems. If she does not make the specific paper seem important or an interesting challenge to the members of the class, they do not undertake the work sooner than necessary.

II. HOW CAN YOU SECURE THOUGHTFUL PREPARATION?

Have you thought about the question of early preparation, of dilatory preparation, of late papers? Let us consider the teacher's personal problem. If she has five classes, she has five sets of themes to keep properly separated, to consider, to comment upon, to grade. Naturally she has a different standard for her freshmen and for her juniors. She has, also, a different problem in each class. It is obviously much more difficult for her to grade themes fairly if she draws a theme from each of her four years and grades one of each. Her senior work seems much better than the freshman theme just read. She tends to grade the freshman theme too severely, forgetting that by her list of minimum essentials she has tacitly promised the freshman not to see certain faults; and her senior theme she grades too leniently. Life will be simpler for her, grades will be fairer, if she grades all of the

papers from one class at one time and if she can view them in
the light of the problem presented in that particular class, the
prevision they represent, and the minimum essentials for that
particular group. Is it unidealistic to consider the teacher's labor
before considering the convenience of the pupils? Not at all.
Teachers have too long, I believe, neglected themselves. For that
reason they are often less amiably vigorous, less interesting, less
stimulating, than they should be for the good of the pupils whom
they teach.

Let us now consider themes and theme assignments from the
standpoint of the pupils. Most pupils carry four or five subjects,
and in addition have music, or athletics, or tasks at home, or a
job. Pupils are busy people, and the fact that at home they are
not considered adults and are often not consulted as to guests,
radio concerts, interruptions of all kinds, makes the task of
studying harder than it would otherwise be. Then too there is
often no place, even in the homes of rather fair grade, where
paper, ink, and reasonable quiet can be obtained. All writing
must, therefore, be done during study hours at school. But English teachers seem often strangely unaware of these facts. Were
they keenly conscious of them, assignments would be made far
enough in advance to allow a little for chance interruptions. A
week is none too much for the growth and writing of an idea that
is to be read by some of one's peers, judged by the teacher, and
perhaps given even wider publicity. Some teachers, to encourage
early preparation, suggest at the time of assignment that there
will be a laboratory period when first drafts may be brought to
class for suggestions and help. This period should come some
two or three days before the theme is due. The plan works with
many, for this lure of free aid and class time spent upon homework seems a bargain not to be overlooked. With other pupils,
however, more than suggestion is needed.

Although it is most unwise to make an unbreakable rule, many teachers—with exceptions and loopholes for themselves—state that all late themes will be dropped a certain number of points in grade. Other teachers find it more effective to give the original grade that would have been received had the theme been on time, but circle it, thus indicating a deduction in grade. Some teachers find comment without grade more effective. But here the beginner needs warning. Since a grade, either in numerals or in letters, must be given every four weeks, six weeks, or semester, it is dangerous to have no accumulated grades in your class book. Beware of giving grades based upon your general impressions of pupils' work. You cannot show a general impression to a pupil, a parent, or a principal; and there is often the questioning football coach who adds himself to the trio.

III. HOW CAN YOU PROTECT YOUR PUPILS FROM FAILURE?

Before we discuss the question of grade further let us consider the question of correction. When that topic is first mentioned, it presents no difficulties. All one does, apparently, is to read the theme, mark all of the mistakes, and tell the pupil in a brief note how good or how poor his theme is. It is, of course, timetaking, but not difficult.[1] That may all be true, but let me ask you how good or how poor *is* his theme? Then, too, what are mistakes? Are mistakes in a senior theme the same as mistakes in a freshman paper? What of the theme brimming with fresh observation, genuine experience, interest, but at the same time fairly sizzling with bad grammar and original spelling? Is that a good or a poor theme? There is one more question. What of the properly written, perfectly innocuous theme that says nothing? Perhaps an illustration will make these points clearer. Will you read these two brief freshman themes, themes written apparently without any prevision but assigned with the certainty that "One Day" must bring forth something?

[1] See Appendix D, "Suggestions on Correcting and Grading Papers."

I. ONE DAY

My father took me to see the smealter in Anaconda. We live there now. It is a smaller town quite different than I had expected. We lived in Chicago before. At first it seemed funny to live in a small place.

We went to see the smealter at night. Lots of people seemed to be working around. There cloths were black with dirt and their faces were dirty. My! I shall never forget when we walked in the door. There before us was a bowl shaped thing full of fire. It was hot in the room and my father kept wipping his face. The bowl full of fire was tiped over and the gold fire ran out into a mould. Some of it splashed out in the dirt. Men ran around and got excited. Something was the matter with the mould, it had a crack or something and it had to be emptied out. It was some job to do it and do it quick so as not to let the hot metal get cold so as it wouldn't flow out like it flowed in. Some job for those men! They just ran about swearing and sweating until a big man come and then everything was alright. He knew what to do and told all of them what to do quick.

I guess I enjoyed that night as much as any thing I've ever done. I felt funny inside all the way home thinking how I'd like to work like the men I saw and father said he enjoyed it to.

II. ONE DAY

My father took me to visit a mine on a certain day last fall. All was lovely and peaceful as we walked along. We were very happy and thankful that we lived in the pure air above ground. It must be hard for humans to live in the dark.

When we reached the mine we put on suitable clothes. We descended with some others. We were in the mine about an hour, but it seemed longer than that to me. We came up just at noon, and many people came out of the buildings with us. Some got on the street cars. We thought the cars were too crowded so we waited a little while. Then a man in a car asked us to ride with him.

The day was pleasant. I was glad I had gone to see a mine.

What do you know of these two writers? Obviously the writer of the first theme has not acquired sentence sense, cannot spell and is vague about correct grammatical forms. He does not distinguish between the essential and the nonessential, as is shown in paragraph one. But what good touches that first theme has! Look at "a bowl shaped thing full of fire," "gold fire," "Some of it splashed out in the dirt." And how interestingly he makes authority step into the scene where men "ran about swearing and sweating" until the big man "told all of them what to do quick." If you too know anything of the tense excitement, the flicker of light on bare muscle, the dull glow of molten metal, you too will feel "funny inside" when you read this boy's paper, for you realize how his whole nature responded to that scene, and how faithfully he attempted to record the epic labor that he witnessed.

Do you see now more clearly what I mean by prevision? This boy's theme full of genuine enjoyment and real vigor cannot and should not go back to him a mass of red ink. Why? Because you must not kill his desire to write. Because his theme has ten times the possibilities of theme two, written by a smug little girl who sees nothing, feels nothing, but who can both spell and punctuate. Am I unfair? Yes, certainly. Again in her theme we see the need of prevision. Had she grasped the idea that her paper must make her readers see and feel and experience what she saw and felt and experienced, the topic would, doubtless, be different. She is here uninteresting, perfunctory. But the fault is the teacher's.

Suppose you had in mind some such theme assignment as the one that obviously brought forth the two papers we have just examined. You know, for example, that your pupils have had interesting experiences. The general-science group has visited the shredded-wheat factory; three other pupils have visited a canning factory; a third group has seen dairy farming on a large scale; some of the girls have not had any of these experiences, but with encouragement they remember with interest the operations of a wrecking machine at work eating away the foundations of some old building. One girl seems never to have seen anything, but upon a suggestion from the teacher recalls how her mother pickled green tomatoes and how the whole house smelt of spices and cooking vinegar. Then the mine and the smelter are mentioned by the writers of themes one and two. Perhaps this discussion grew out of some class reading, some theme, some incident in the morning's paper that you or the class mentioned. It might have been the outcome of "Caliban in the Coal Mines," a favorite with high-school pupils.

Before there is any talking of a theme it would be wise to make sure that all of the class realize what makes a description real and vivid. It would, for example, be wise to forestall the usual endless introduction by the suggestion, "Don't feel that you must tell us how you got there (wherever it is) or all that you saw on the way. Just pick some three or five minutes that you enjoyed or found exciting or interesting. Make us see and feel what you felt and saw." Naturally this injunction is not the only one of its kind. Work on visualization has gone on since the first day. Conrad's injunction in the introduction to *The Nigger of the Narcissus*, "by the power of the written word to make you hear, to make you feel . . . it is, before all, to make you *see*," has perhaps become a well-known slogan in the class.

Before writing begins, other things are necessary. So far each member of the class is thinking about his five minutes. With one, it may be a description of the moment before and the one after his motorcycle skidded into a passing car; with another the moment when, coming from twenty below into a warm room, he found that his ears and nose were frozen; with a third it will be the moment on a Jersey dairy farm when all the cows' heads, pinioned between perpendicular poles, turned toward the door, and the smell of cows, fresh milk, and alfalfa greeted the stranger. While the class is thinking, there will be some dictation stressing sentence completion. There will be board work and a reminder of minimum essentials. Perhaps a spelling rule for verbs (*stopped, dropped,* etc.,) will be driven home with numerous examples upon the board and reference to the pupils' individual lists of words. Illustrations of some of the five minutes experienced by real writers will be read: Arnold Bennett, James Oppenheim, Frank Norris—all are fish for the classroom net if they have pictured, and pictured vividly. Then comes a day for beginning work. The teacher is available for conference and keeps an eye upon these beginnings, advising elimination here, a different word there, or occasionally, if a fault seems to occur often, interrupting long enough to make the correct form plain before individual work is continued.

But for writing, as for pears and persimmons, there is a ripening stage that should go on in the dark. Therefore these compositions are laid aside for a day; then in rough draft they are again brought to the light. Other pupils, perhaps, look them over to make suggestions; perhaps the teacher can be consulted upon some knotty point; last, the theme is checked over in the light of the list of minimum essentials for that grade, and then a final draft is made. In groups the themes are read, and the best—that is, the most vivid and interesting—are selected. When all are handed in, these better ones are passed to the teacher with penciled comment from the group leader. Later all the class will hear these few. A genuinely good theme, a really vivid picture, is thus given general recognition and reward.

Do you realize that nothing begets good writing so much as discriminating praise? Perhaps in some themes but one sentence or one word is outstandingly good. To encourage future good writing you must be sure that that one good feature has recognition. I recall a boy who in a hopeless theme spoke of the "patchwork quilt" flung over the hills. The different trees and shrubs, the plowed ground, the fields of grain, the tawny stretches of brown grass, were all there in his two words, and the class and I held high holiday over his success. With what result? It seemed worth while to pick words that made pictures; all the class realized that fact.

IV. HOW SHALL YOU GRADE THEMES?

But these themes must be corrected, evaluated, graded. You know and I know, of course, the absurdity of marking one bit of human experience 85 and another 87. What is 85 per cent success in bringing pictures before our eyes, or making us experience an incident, or leading us to comprehend an explanation?[1] Letters are simpler to bestow, perhaps, because each one represents a wider spread. But how do you or I know that one theme deserves A and another C? Why should it not be B and D? And there is always the disconcerting possibility that beneath the pencil of another teacher the grades might be reversed. There is also the matter of mechanics. If it is bad, should a theme fail? How bad must it be? Is "bad" a fixed or a relative term?[2]

A device used by many teachers in an attempt to deal justly with themes is the following one. You are in good company if you accept the idea; you are in good company if you reject it

[1] Many private schools have eliminated grades and give comments only to pupils and to parents. This practice (in spite of the example set by the University of Chicago) will not, in all probability, be adopted by public schools during your teaching career; hence you must consider the problems of grade giving.

[2] One account of variation in theme grading well worth your investigation is found in the *Twenty-second Yearbook* of the National Society for the Study of Education, Part I, Chap. III. There are numerous scales for measuring theme value, and it would be well if you had some knowledge of them, but the chief difficulty of these scales is that of applying them. One pupil differs so greatly from another in vocabulary, style of writing, personality, that it is difficult to compare a pupil's paper with a printed model and reach a conclusion. Teachers can train themselves to use composition scales, but the average teacher with a full schedule will find that while scales dealing with mechanics are invaluable (see Appendix C for tests), scales dealing with composition content are exceedingly difficult and timetaking. Three of the well-known composition scales are these: *Hudelson's English Composition Scale; Nassau County Supplement to the Hillegas Scale for Composition;* and the letter scales called *Scales for Measuring Special Types of Compositions*. All three are published by the World Book Company, Yonkers, N. Y.

indignantly. Personally I like it because I find it has an admirable disciplinary effect upon the teacher. It forces her to consider a pupil's theme from two standpoints, from that of content and from that of form. I believe also that it clarifies composition for the pupil, but it is because of the discipline for me, the teacher, that I practice it. Here is the plan: On every theme two grades are given $\left(\dfrac{C \quad B \quad A \quad D}{c \quad c \quad 81 \quad 85} \right)$ and as a rule two comments. One grade, that on the top line, is the teacher's estimate of the value of the theme's content. The grade below the line is the teacher's estimate of the form or mechanics of the theme. The two comments accompany the two grades. One, put in the most conspicuous place, deals with content, the subject matter of the theme, the way that subject matter has been selected, realized, organized, presented. Commendation for whatever is good in a theme should appear here, and suggestions for future writing. The second comment is primarily, I am afraid, concerned with the technical errors made, but a nicely varied use of sentences, a neat apposition, or even a feeble attempt to put into practice some of the devices taught in drill work should be here commended. In the first grade and first comment you try to appraise the somewhat intangible quality in composition; in the second you give a more accurate evaluation of the pupil's use of mechanics.

And what effect has this double appraisal had upon you, the teacher? It has compelled you to look at the theme in two lights. No matter how bad the mechanics, how erratic the sentence construction and spelling, you have been forced, not as teacher to pupil, but as one human being to another, to look at this bit of human experience and to see where it is real, where it is wanting or untrue, or where it obscures truth. For example, it makes the writer of the smelter experience feel "funny on the inside all the way home" to have witnessed one of man's greatest industrial achievements. And you, another human being who have also felt "funny on the inside" and who have also experienced that excited interest, tension, and envy, cannot score such a theme merely upon its errors and damn it for its ignorances. You must give due recognition in this paper to the sense of the picturesque, to the crude re-creation of the scene. Too often, as I have said before, we teachers of English discourage the good brains of our schools by our absurd evaluations. Life *is* greater than a comma; vigor and interest *are* far greater and far more important than incorrect verbs or misspelled words. "What," pupils must say among themselves in disgust, "what does *she* know of life anyway, just sticking red marks on theme papers?" But pupils are really marvelously patient. If they feel that you are doing as well as you can, and that you like them, they will overlook many of your English-teacher idiosyncrasies. They can, for example, be led to see the necessity for decent English, the justice of minimum essentials, and the fair play in failing papers where incorrect forms persist—forms that have been adequately presented and drilled upon in class. They are patient, but do not try their patience too far. Recognize and, in some way, reward life and vitality.

You should not accept this double marking system blindly. Many teachers object strongly to it. Their main objection is this: One cannot divorce thought from form. Bad form, they feel, so distracts the reader from the content of the paper that the content is weakened. Perhaps this is true. Perhaps thought and expression are one. There are of course certain errors in sentence order and construction that so obscure the thought that the reader loses the content. But I find that though I regret *wipping* or *tiped* and would prefer a transfer of p's, yet the thought, the content, is not obscured. I do not minimize the error; I merely divorce those errors, those rambling "and" sentences and the bad grammar, from the thing that the pupil attempted to do. I shall give him a failure on the form of his theme, this theme that I should never have let him submit in its present state, but I shall give him a B on the observation, the sensing of the situation, the spirit underlying the theme. He must, however, revise and rewrite, for he must provide good material with decent form. What will happen to him eventually? Eventually he must improve his form or fail. I have minimum essentials to support him; I have spelling drills; and he keeps an individual list of all misspelled words. I have sentence-manipulation drills, grammar drills, a consultation board which will remind him of certain dangers. According to my minimum requirements the existence of certain errors, such as a comma between whole sentences, automatically fails a paper. And my experience leads me to believe that pupils will, as a rule, learn what has to be learned, particularly if it is presented clearly, logically, interestingly, and with sufficient emphasis and repetition.

There is another point in regard to grading that must be discussed. When you pick up one of the papers on your desk, what do you expect? Is it for you potentially a 100-per-cent paper, and does it remain so until the theme itself convinces you that it is not? Or, as you unfold it, do you regard it as potentially a paper of 75 per cent, and do you continue to think of it in that light until its added virtues or its diminishing virtues change your estimate? After all, what difference does it make? If you read Mr. Ward's stimulating chapter on "What Is Theme Value?" in *What Is English?* you will find him clinging optimistically to the miner's certitude that a gold nugget lies just ahead. With what result? Read and discover. But for my own part, much as I appreciate Mr. Ward's position, and much as I recognize the common sense that underlies his discussion, I prefer, both for myself and for my pupils, a double grade: a 90-per-cent theory for form, but a 75-per-cent theory for content.

Before I begin upon a pile of themes, I know, both from study of the normal distribution curve and from my own common sense, that about half of those papers will, in the very nature of things, be mediocre in content (I use the term in its original sense of *medius*). Some will be poor; some will be fair or good;

a few may be excellent. I am, you remember, speaking now of the content grade only. If a mediocre pupil writes a theme that is mediocre, you do him an injustice if you grade that theme as excellent in content, no matter how much effort he has put into the writing of it. With care and patience he can make his paper excellent in mechanics. Let his reward come to him in his grade on form. But to give him a grade on his theme content that his content does not deserve is injurious both to him and to the class as a whole. In teaching composition your greatest effort should be expended in developing your pupils' ability to think clearly. You try to make them realize what qualities in writing make writing excellent. You stress clarity, logical sequence, emphasis. You point out for praise vivid wording, appeal to the senses, keen observation, interesting imaginative expressions, well-expressed humor. You submit papers for class judgment. What happens if you mark as excellent in content a paper that shows none of these qualities, a paper that is not excellent? You confuse your class. You break down what you are attempting to build up. You assure the writer by your grade that he possesses qualities or abilities that he does not possess, or at least that are not present in his paper.

Be sympathetic with your pupils; deal kindly with their efforts in writing; but do not be intellectually dishonest in judging the content of their themes. A poor theme might grade 60 (or F), not passing; a fair theme 75-80 (C); a good theme 80-90 (B); an excellent theme 90-100 (B+ or A). Under normal circumstances you may find in every pile of high-school themes a 95-per-cent paper; you will probably find two or three 60-per-cent papers; almost certainly you should find that more than half fall between 75 per cent and 85 per cent. I state these figures dogmatically because the usual tendency of young teachers is at first to grade too leniently. It seems to them remarkable that "children" write as well as their pupils do. Then, slowly, the teacher discovers that her standards are too low. She finds, suddenly, that she is considered "easy"—a word that you will learn to fear. But if her grades run too high at first, what great harm is done? In answer to that question consider the case of one Tom Mansard, sophomore, who finds that his first four months' rating in English runs: 95, 80, 80, 75. Apparently he is doing more and more poorly. The more he tries, the worse his grade. Why try? In reality his new teacher of English may be just waking up to his shortcomings. But if his first rating had been 60, 70, or 80, he would have had some incentive to work. When you begin, of course, you must be careful to differentiate between papers that are poor, fair, good, or excellent. But in your first month of teaching it would be wise to mark nothing (short of a work of genius) higher than 90 per cent.

In grading the mechanics of a theme, I use a different system. I make 90 the mark for mechanics given every paper in which occur none of the errors listed in the minimum-essentials requirements for that group. If such errors occur, I deduct a certain percentage from 90, the exact amount for each error having been determined earlier by the class. Thus a tiresome writer who avoids all taboo errors will have 90. A clever writer who uses his words effectively and who avoids taboo errors will also have 90. But I have a bonus of 10 which I may give for positive merits in expression, for words and phrases that give life to the theme. Such a bonus seems to me only fair. For it is often true that a dull, conscientious pupil will gain his 90 by timid avoidance of any complicated expression, while his neighbor invites disaster by his imaginative daring. If you too employ this system, you will find that it has one great virtue. Pupils understand what a grade on form means. They know that 70 is a danger signal. They know that 90 means that they are doing what they have contracted to do. They know that 95 means that their themes possess some positive merit other than correctness. Of the content grade they are less certain, and, I confess, so am I. But they know that a paper marked $\frac{F}{90}$ demands another paper in its place, for though no listed errors occur, the thought value is zero. They learn, too, that a paper graded $\frac{A}{60}$ has to be rewritten, for, admirable as the content is, decent form also is demanded.

Let me summarize very briefly. When that sheaf of themes confronts you, there are certain problems which you must face. What are they? First, you must recall the prevision, the assignment, the problem it included; then, with these facts in mind, you must examine your papers. Mr. Hitchcock has used the admirable figure of "cargo" and "ship" in discussing themes. "What," you ask yourself, "is the thought cargo in each theme?" After you have considered the content, the way it is organized and presented, you are ready for your first grade and first comment. But as you read you are also checking the papers for certain specific faults—not for all errors but merely for the few fundamental ones listed for each grade. Much you overlook. If a certain number of those tabooed errors occur, the paper fails. Later you and the class will increase the penalty. Perhaps then one comma fault may fail a paper. If all minimum-essentials faults are avoided, and the pupil has made an honest workmanlike use of the teaching you have given (variety of sentence beginnings, varied sentences, etc.) that pupil has done well. Whether his paper does or does not show charm (I quote Mr. Ward) is a matter of relatively little importance.

In every walk of life extra ability is rewarded. Why should it not be so in English classes? You will find, perhaps, three in the sophomore class who write better than the majority of your seniors; ten in your senior class that do heavy, honest work that ranks below your junior average of writing. If, however, these seniors keep their agreement to conquer the minimum essentials for the grade and if their themes contain a reasonable amount of orderly thinking, they deserve a passing mark. It is, of course, wise to seek out for praise any tiny gleam of originality they may show, or any logical statement, or even any neat listing of facts. That much they deserve. On the other hand, to convince them that they possess qualities that they do not possess is neither wise nor kind. Grades are honest payment for work done. A pupil's intentions, his need for encouragement, the amount of effort he has expended, have nothing to do with the final mark received. If you grade upon anything but the paper itself, how can you justify your mark to the members of your class? Nor should a class be misled in its judgments as to what is and what is not good work.

Clever as well as dull pupils suffer, however, from unwise grading. It would, perhaps, do high-school teachers good to listen to the college freshmen when they discuss their high-school preparation. Often there is the puzzled dismay of the "bright" student who finds himself in a subfreshman group, condemned to spend college time upon the mechanics of writing not learned in high school. His record at the registrar's office (for no student statement is regarded as authentic) shows, perhaps, an 85 or a 90 in composition. Yet he can neither recognize whole sentences, spell, nor punctuate. When he talks, he uses words well; he has done some reading; he has, perhaps, managed the high-school paper; and he is pleasantly at home in adult society. Dozens of such baffled freshmen, some more, some less attractive, have in my office puzzled over their high-school training. Apparently their high-school teachers graded upon potential ability or upon content only. At any rate, the freshmen were led to believe themselves well equipped for college when in reality they were badly prepared. As a consequence of this teacher deception they were humiliated in their own eyes, and were forced to deduct time from college work and college sports in order to make up for their high-school teachers' sympathetic encouragement, or their aesthetic pleasure in "cargo" and their unseamanlike disregard of the "ship." With poor minds, however, with students ranked low by their teachers of high-school composition, no college should find fault. With them the high-school teacher has, doubtless, labored and labored ineffectually through no fault of her own. Many a freshman admits ruefully that in high school he "didn't know enough to get down to work" and adds the thoughtful tribute that the teacher "kept after" him for all four years.

V. HOW SHALL YOU SECURE INTELLIGENT REVISION?

There is one phase of theme work that is all too little considered. After you have graded a composition, after you have evaluated its contents and noted its mechanics—what then? When his corrected paper is returned to the pupil, what does he do? You have expended energy and effort in pointing out to him the beauties and deficiencies of his theme. How does he profit by your labor? In many schools it is no exaggeration to say that teachers spend hours putting little marks upon papers, papers that pupils glance at and then throw away. Such a method, you will agree, is absurdly inefficient.

When you have corrected and graded a theme, you have, in reality, reached the second important stage in composition teaching. (The first and most important step is, without question, creating in pupils a desire to write.) You and I know the importance of revision, the profit received from correcting mistakes and laboring over passages until they say just what the writer intended them to say. But it is hard to make pupils see the advantage of such work. They write—often with enjoyment. But when a theme is once handed in, though they are curious to see what the teacher will say or what grade she will give, their interest in the theme itself is dead.

How are you to secure intelligent revision? Some teachers have their pupils file their returned themes in a notebook, number the errors checked, and, on the back of the preceding page, under the correct number write the proper form. Sometimes, of course, it is simpler to rewrite the theme. Sometimes, perhaps, no corrections need be made. In the *English Journal* for January, 1917, you will find a plan by Dr. Stith Thompson entitled "The Notebook System of Theme Correction." He suggests a classification of errors, divisions in the pupil's notebook, one for each type of error, and a classification *by the student* of all the mistakes marked in each of his themes. In Appendix E I am quoting, with the permission of the authors, an extract from "A Summary of Methods in Composition Work" printed in the *English Journal* for October, 1930. Here you will find forty-eight suggested procedures, all of which have been used by experienced teachers. You will not, of course, wish to use all of them nor to use any one of them invariably, but the list, compiled by Dr. S. C. Crawford of the University of Southern California and Miss Marie C. Phelan, John Burroughs Junior High School, Burbank, California, should prove interestingly suggestive.

VI. WHAT POLICY SHALL YOU ADOPT?

On your desk a sheaf of themes will await you. What your policy toward them will be, you must decide for yourself. But *decide*. Few things are more wearing, more disquieting, than to approach each set of themes with hesitating uncertainty. If you have no fixed policy, what is the result? One set finds you buoyantly flinging out good grades; another finds you unhappily failing all but three in the class. From experience I suggest these four precautions:

1. Have a clear-cut policy.
2. Have this policy clearly understood by the class.
3. Have proof for all grades given—proof that the pupils feel free to seek and that they can understand.
4. Have enough marks in your grade book before the report cards are sent home so that you may base your grades upon concrete evidence.

SUGGESTED EXERCISES

At the end of this chapter you will find a number of references. Read as many as you can before you attempt these exercises.

1. Refer to the two themes in this chapter entitled "One Day." Select from literature two or three examples that would illustrate quickly and vividly to the second writer what is meant by "concrete detail," "making the reader share the writer's experience," "painting word pictures." Copy these two illustrations. It would be wise to file them for future use in your own classroom.

2. Select from literature two brief examples that will illustrate the statement, "Any experience, no matter how trivial, can be made interesting if the writer is sufficiently interested in it and shares this interest with his reader." (Are you familiar with Conrad's description of landing a horse for the native in *A Personal Record?*)

3. Make a ten-minute dictation that: (a) illustrates vivid picturing of an active scene; (b) illustrates a rapid, interesting beginning; (c) uses a number of words in which the consonant is doubled before *-ed* or *-ing;* (d) is interesting to high-school age.

4. Write the two grades and the two comments that seem suitable for the two themes quoted in this chapter. Since these themes have been submitted to experienced teachers and have received widely different treatment, it might be interesting later to compare your comments with others.

5. Write, as your contribution to your future high-school class discussion of themes, a paper that would fulfill the requirement of the assignment sketched in this chapter.

a. At the end list several of the vivid words or phrases used.

b. List three or four examples of varied sentence beginnings used.

c. Indicate in a sentence or two how the paper is made interesting by both elimination of and concentration upon certain details. The object of this tabulation is to indicate what points you might perhaps discuss to advantage in connection with the mechanics of getting an idea down upon paper.

SUGGESTED READINGS

The English Language Arts, Vol. I, N.C.T.E. Curriculum Series, Dora V. Smith, Director
Read Part III, Chapter 11, "The Challenge of Individual Differences."
Do you plan to use *one* standard for grading class papers?

From the English Journal

1. Reedy, Sidney J.: "What Composition Is Functional?" Vol. 27 (1938), pp. 127-32
If at first you feel lost, this list of most and least important items should prove helpful.

2. Piper, Francis K.: "Condensing Magazine Articles for Tape Recording," Vol. 40 (1951), pp. 222-24

3. Minton, Arthur: "Design for Composition," Vol. 30 (1941), pp. 136-46

4. Cauley, Thomas: "Evaluating Topic Sentences," Vol. 39 (1950), p. 394

5. Merriam, H. G.: "Who Can Teach Creative Writing?" Vol. 36 (1947), pp. 464-69
Read. "The student has not learned that he's a developing mind and spirit that should be constantly trotting out into new pastures." Teachers must "encourage experiments."

6. Kitchen, Aileen Traver: "The Language Belongs to Them," Vol. 39 (1950), pp. 373-79
A good summary of purposes. In language teaching "we have sufficient information to give a new shape and a new direction."

7. Fatout, P.: "Sit Down and Write," Vol. 37 (1948), p. 536

From Elementary English

1. Jensen, A. C.: "Composition Can Be Interesting," Vol. 25 (1948), pp. 312-19

2. Mercille, Margaret G.: "Creating on the Air," Vol. 27 (1950), pp. 507-10
Equally desirable for junior high school age either "on the air" or in the classroom.

3. Cooper, Jane Wilcox: "Creative Writing As an Emotional Outlet," Vol. 28 (1951), pp. 21-23
True at any age.

CHAPTER II

Developing a Semantic Approach Toward Language

M ANY teachers have spoken of semantics as if the subject were either unimportant or so difficult that it was "beyond the ken of ordinary man." For that reason—and I hope that I do not insult your intelligence—the ideas here are expressed with the greatest simplicity. Also they are loaded, perhaps overloaded, with illustrations and with suggested class work for different grade levels. Possibly the two attitudes expressed by different teachers have been fostered unconsciously in some English departments where work in semantics is nonexistent. Even yet some linguists regard semantics as an intruder, an upstart in established linguistic study. On the other hand, the National Council of Teachers of English (N.C.T.E.) strongly endorses such instruction in junior-senior high school—though tactfully omitting the term *semantics*. The N.C.T.E. resolution committee states the urgent need for such language training, in ". . . a world where the word of men and of nations has become suspect, where using language to promote confusion and false values is a wide-scale undertaking." [1] But without some basic philosophy concerning language itself, teachers may easily lack conviction as to the permanent value of vocabulary study. Explaining a word here and a word there arouses no continuity of interest in language. Discouraged, some teachers make the dictionary an unsatisfactory substitute for live classroom discussion. [2]

So much for generalizations. When Breal, in 1897, introduced

[1] "The Milwaukee Meeting" (resolutions), *English Journal*, Vol. 40 (February, 1951), p. 111.
[2] See "Dictionary Study," pp. 158-60.

the term *semantique,* he explained it as "the meaning of words." Today "the nature and meaning of words" seems a more adequate definition. Thus, after essential preparation, you would attempt to teach junior-senior high-school pupils to understand the:

1. Nature of words themselves
2. Ways in which words may fail to express an idea accurately
3. Personal responsibility of listener or reader to analyze and to test the accuracy of generalizations
4. Recognition of the power over and danger to thinking inherent in words
5. Need on the part of each individual for a sense of responsibility as to the accuracy and honesty in his own wording

Do not let this list overwhelm you. After you grasp the basic idea of a semantic or analytic approach to language and then make it your own (if you do not have it already), you will realize one fact. Pupils from the sixth grade on are capable of understanding the five steps listed. But, remember, their ability to understand and to learn depends entirely upon your appropriately simple language at each grade level, and your use of illustrations within the pupils' span of interest. Obviously this work cannot be taught as a course or unit. It is an attitude toward language to be fostered whenever students question, use certain types of words, or lack a term to express their ideas. Such opportunities allow you to illustrate with *their* familiar terminology various principles in *your* planned semantic program. The difficulty in this teaching does not lie in the subject matter, but in the method. The teacher must be Argus-eyed, alert through all her teaching to attempt to detect and utilize those words which will illustrate the nature of language.

By the time you have read thus far, probably four questions have occurred to you.

1. To the multiplicity of topics now termed English, why add semantics?

2. If I have had no college preparation in semantics, how shall I acquire enough understanding and information to lead pupils intelligently?

3. For teaching in junior-senior high school, what material should I select?

4. How shall I interest boys and girls in so intangible a subject?

The rest of this chapter will attempt to answer these questions. Do not accept the answers blindly. Remember that no two people think alike or teach alike. Your kind of teaching—even if you and I agree in theory—must be determined by your personality, knowledge, and training.

ANSWERS TO THE FOUR QUESTIONS JUST LISTED

Question 1. "To the multiplicity of topics now termed English, why add semantics?"

Training in semantics provides a basis for understanding the nature of words, and, finally, the nature of language. It can also provide pupils with a means of testing the accuracy or truth of what they hear or read or think. Gradually over a period of years such training should develop a new way of thinking and of expressing those thoughts. Yet pupils in the past had no such training. Why add it now? One might answer this question by a second query: has past training in language met our need for truth, clarity, and moderation? Recall the words of the N.C.T.E. resolution committee. Consider the environment in which pupils now live. Then consider, too, the minds of your pupils, uninformed, uncertain, confused. At home and abroad, words from radio, television, and motion picture assail their ears. Words from comic books, newspapers, and magazines allure their eyes. At home, at work, at school, at play, they find words forced upon their attention. In this hubbub of language, when do they think? And in this welter of words, what means have they for distinguishing truth from falsehood? Recall the accusations, apparently minus proof or accurate statistics, in the era of McCarthyism. Recall the credulous listeners who, unquestioning, applauded these outbursts. And, last and most important, recall the illogical confusions evidently existent in the minds of many adults. These are the adults, who, ignoring individual differences, spread prejudices against *all* people of a certain race, or creed, or color. If a semantic approach to language could improve the pupils' ability to think straight, to listen critically, to demand proof, to test unsound generalizations glibly uttered, would not such training be of the utmost importance to future citizens? [1]

Question 2. "If I have had no college preparation in semantics, how shall I acquire enough understanding and information to lead pupils intelligently?"

Acquiring the needed information is not too difficult: "Read, mark, learn, and inwardly digest" the following brief, annotated list, arranged in chronological order.

USEFUL BOOKS

Three Scholarly Works

Ogden, C. K., and Richards, I. A.: *The Meaning of Meaning,* 5th ed., rev., Harcourt, Brace, 1938 (First edition, English, 1930)
A lasting source book and reference for later writers.

Korzybski, Alfred: *Science and Sanity,* Science Press, Lancaster, Pennsylvania, 1933
An authority for all later books listed here.

Zahner, Louis C., and others: *Language in General Education,* Appleton-Century, 1940

Two Popular Books

Chase, Stuart: *The Tyranny of Words,* Harcourt, Brace, 1938
A highly readable, journalistic presentation of semantics, based upon *Science and Sanity,* one that immediately aroused general interest.

Hayakawa, S. I.: *Language in Action,* Harcourt, Brace, 1939; revised as *Language in Thought and Action,* 1949
An amusing, clever Book-of-the-Month in 1939.

[1] For a longer discussion of this whole question, read Lou La Brant's *We Teach English,* Part 1, Harcourt, Brace, 1950.

Three Books on Teaching Semantics in High Schools

Progressive Education Association: *Semantics in Secondary Schools,*
Appleton-Century, 1940

A simply written, practical discussion, the last fifty pages devoted to
"Suggested Application and Methods."

La Brant, Lou: *We Teach English,* Harcourt, Brace, 1951

A challenging book. Part One, "We Face a Class," defines the background in linguistics which the author deems necessary.

DeBoer, John J., Kaulfers, Walter V., and Miller, Helen Rand: *Teaching Secondary English,* McGraw-Hill, 1951

Chapter V, "Semantics as a Common Learning" gives an over-all view
of this work as taught in high-school English.

In addition to the books listed, *Elementary English,* beginning with the
January, 1951, issue, has published a series of articles dealing with "the
nature of language and of linguistic pitfalls." This material in pamphlet
form can be obtained from the National Council of Teachers of English.[1]

Although here chronologically aranged, the books are probably
best read in another order. The least difficult are those concerned
with teaching semantics in junior-senior high school. If these are
consulted first, then one of S. I. Hayakawa's books, *The Meaning
of Meaning* should not prove difficult, though probably less immediately helpful than *Language in General Education.* This list
gives a bare minimum. When you have time, much more awaits
you.

Question 3. "For teaching in junior-senior high school, what
topics should I select?"

Five topics or nine topics may meet your needs, but the seven
listed below include material that seems to me essential.

TOPICS SELECTED FOR JUNIOR-SENIOR HIGH-SCHOOL TEACHING

I. Meaning of the word *symbol* gained from pupils' experiences
and discoveries (traffic lights, soldiers' insignia, railroad crossing
signs)

II. Words as mere symbols for (a) concrete objects (*key, cup,*

[1] 211 West 68th Street, Chicago 21.

knife—sensory referents) ; (b) abstractions (*happiness, embarrasment, poverty, technocracy*—nonsensory referents)

III. Word usage—factual and metaphorical (a) factual (*key* to the garage) ; (b) metaphorical (*key* to the situation)

IV. Connotation of words—a study of implication

V. Context—guide to word meaning: (a) Words in the sentence or passage surrounding the word in question; (b) Situation or condition under which words are used; (c) Background or former experiences of speaker or writer

VI. Types of language destructive to straight thinking: (a) Abstract nouns (generalizations) minus referents or used with vague, confused, or overexaggerated referents; (b) Emotive words minus adequate thought content; (c) Words (mere symbols) to which people attribute qualities of the referent; (d) Devices common to propaganda (slanting, card stacking, implications, etc.)

VII. One method of detecting unsound statements

These seven listed topics, necessary at each level of teaching, should be taught consistently and repetitiously. But the illustrative words and illustrative topics must, in each instance, be adjusted to the students' level of understanding and interest.

The order in which you present this material after topic one and two (first steps toward an understanding of words as symbols) can not be predetermined. Since the discussions must arise from the students' needs, these needs and your own common sense will determine the order. Metaphor, connotation, and context would, of course, be discussed in connection with literature, listening, and the students' own speech and writing. After students understand words as symbols, you will probably guide the discussion into topics VI and VII ("Language destructive to straight thinking" and "One method of detecting unsound reasoning"). Over and over again, grade after grade, you teach the same concepts but at different levels of maturity. Finally, one hopes, these concepts will become a guide to the students' thinking.

Question 4. "How shall I interest boys and girls in so intangible a subject?"

After you have finished the suggested readings and have considered the seven topics listed, you will find the material far more "tangible" than you expected and more interesting. To awaken interest in language, some first steps are suggested on pages 152-57. This material, appropriate at any level, must alter in length of discussion and terminology according to the maturity of the students. More than in earlier periods, students can be interested in foreign lands, languages, and language relationships. Foster this interest; and when possible, attempt to destroy your students' intellectual isolation.

After some such beginning, why not discuss with your pupils *levels of speech*, an excellent means of sensitizing them to word usage? It will lead to a discussion of what level of English is appropriate in different situations. Teachers have long used the term "correct English." Today, many have substituted the term "appropriate for the occasion," as more courteous, honest, and educationally provocative. Through socio-drama you could introduce imaginary situations requiring "standard English," speech used by educated people. In this way you offer pupils a practical reason for learning to avoid "I seen" or "ain't" or "would have went." And, too, you are doubtless providing much oral practice on accepted forms.[1]

When you have aroused interest in words by these or other devices, introduce the word *symbol*. Give pupils much experience with that word through symbol hunts.[2] Do not hurry this work; make certain that each pupil experiences and recognizes the empty form called a symbol and the thing for which it stands. One fact

[1] See pages 93-94 and 256 on ear training.
[2] Encourage students to collect symbols: soldiers' insignia, red and green traffic lights, nods, flexed finger, raised eyebrows. Older students may find symbols in Chaucer's Tabard Inn sign, or in pink tissue paper floating over Mexican pulque shops.

often overlooked is this: *no word contains meaning unless some past experience, real or vicarious, provides it.* Without experience with the referent, students can verbalize but cannot fully comprehend. Obviously teachers must, as with the word *symbol,* provide classroom experience. An unpublished study made in 1940 indicates the predominance of verbalization.[1] Two tests, one using the textbook terminology, the second using identical questions in non-textbook language, were given in seventeen Class B Iowa high schools to all students in social studies. A majority passed the first test but failed the second. Evidently, like Hamlet, these students had been reading "Words, words, words." Aware of the possibility of verbalism, vary your own terminology in order to discover how clearly students comprehend the ideas under discussion, and the full meaning of words used. For you, how rich in meaning are the following terms? "All I want is one more example of zeugma." "Most of the inhabitants are xanthochroid." Words that you use in class may be just as empty of meaning, perhaps, for your students as these are, mayhap, for you.

When your students understand symbols in the world about them, then, and only then, introduce words as symbols. S. I. Hayakawa amusingly points out that words, mere noises, differ in different languages. If you have students of foreign-born parents, here is an opportunity for them to inform the class, gain self-confidence, and realize the importance of their parents' native language—an importance teachers should not fail to recognize and foster. Symbols understood, students are ready to accept words as symbols, symbols for tangible things or for feelings or conditions that exist in people's minds or in the world about them. Begin with symbols for concrete objects; for example, use the words *cup, knife, key.* In the seventh grade I would ask, "Could you drink from the word *cup?*" "Were you cut by the word *knife?*" Absurd? Of course. Yet such questions can accomplish

[1] *High School Students' Understanding of Modern Society,* by W. J. Maucker, President of Iowa State Teachers' College, Cedar Falls.

two things: the class realizes that the words are symbols; they laugh, perhaps suggest similar absurdities, thus underlining in their memories the fact taught. They may discuss the incident, perhaps, outside of class, a sign of interest. In order to drive home a fact or principle, attempt to illustrate, when apt and appropriate, with amusing or surprising statements. For, as Chaucer remarks, "Swiche thinges kan they wel reporte and holde." Much is yet to be done with symbols such as *cup, knife, key*. Challenge pupils to discover for such words as many different meanings *in context* as possible. Illustrate first, making sure that the term "context" is understood in its simplest form. Illustrate with such examples as "I lost the door *key*." "This is the *key* to the situation."

After students recognize the symbolic character of *cup* and *knife*, much repetition of other concrete terms is still necessary before introducing nonsensory words. Some teachers bridge this shift from concrete to abstract by illustrations from the talk of children. Others turn to primitive languages such as the Bantu.[1] Use of both is probably wise, one familiar to the class, the other unknown and amusing. Both illustrations show that as speakers grow less childlike in the use of language, words often cease to point out just *one* object (referent); then, as we well know, confusion may arrive.

When you teach abstractions in the seventh grade, make your teaching and illustrations simple. But from seventh grade through senior high school use abstract words to foster more mature thinking. Many students report and report well on what they see or hear, but they draw no conclusions. They are mirrors, reflectors in one sense of the word but decidedly not in the other. If you consider this mirrorlike condition of some students' minds, you

---

[1] Otto Jespersen in discussing the Bantu speech (see page 617) states that the natives had a different word for each animal's tail. When White men used the same word for the tail of a fish and a horse, the natives laughed scornfully. This same growth from specific words to generalizations is, of course, characteristic of children.

will realize that teaching students to draw sound generalizations is essential to their development. Little by little in the seventh grade you have to urge abstract words upon them and encourage them to draw conclusions. In senior high school, on the other hand, it is not the use of abstract terms or conclusions, but the elimination of abstract terms minus needed modification and referents, and of unthought-out conclusions that await you. If your teaching is to hasten intelligent thought and speech, you must struggle with these two grave errors. But it calls for tact and sympathetic understanding thus to hasten intelligent thought without discouraging the students' desire to share their ideas with you.

One error in thinking is obvious in children, adolescents, and adults: the use of words that have no referent or one that the symbol grossly exaggerates. For seventh-grade use I have termed this "Allness," a name easily remembered and recognized. Such an expression as *"All* our parents want school to close early," will gradually disappear as a result of questioning. *"All* of the parents? You asked each one?"[1] Soon it will be the students themselves who recognize and eagerly question such statements. To make them realize most quickly the falsity of generalizations that ignore individual differences, apply the generalization (termed stereotype) to the members of the class. For example, "All seventh-grade boys deliver papers" will bring immediate protest, as will "All junior students prefer Walt Whitman to Carl Sandburg." In this way the students themselves discover that the truth or untruth of a symbol can be ascertained by comparing the symbol with the referent. As you realize, this is a far more effective method of learning than would be a similar statement from the teacher. In the long, long process of stereotype elimination, such stress upon individual differences is just a beginning, just a first step. Simple

[1] For more detailed discussion, see Lou La Brant's *We Teach English,* Part I, or Engelbert J. Neumayer's "Teaching Certain Understandings about Language," *English Journal,* Vol. 39 (November, 1950), pp. 505-15.

and limited as this "Allness" method is, students begin to learn two processes essential to straight thinking. First, they learn to question the symbol, and, therefore, abandon passive acceptance. Second, they learn to seek proof from the world about them by which to measure the symbol used. Do not, however, be too optimistic. A change in process of thinking is not accomplished in one lesson or one month or one year. It is a slow growth that must be fostered throughout the whole English program. But you can, even in one year, break certain habits and begin the formation of others.

Another difficulty with symbols and referents should be considered. Any child knows that the words *cup* and *knife* are neither the thing symbolized nor are they possessed of those qualities belonging to the referent. But abstract terms are more confusing. Many an adult fails to dissociate the word from the emotions that surround the referent. This type of self-hypnosis with words is not uncommon.[1] Such a situation was illustrated by the decision of a certain judge. A drunken mother appeared before him seeking a divorce and possession of the children. The judge, himself a devoted son, granted her requests on the basis of "the sacred rights of motherhood." The word *mother,* that is, was charged with the emotion which for him surrounded the referent. A different situation is that of a speaker who, seeking from a hostile audience approval of higher appropriations for education, wrapped about this issue, repeating the words over and over, three charged abstractions—Christianity, democracy, and parental love. When his speech ended, the audience rose, shouting approval, completely convinced—through their emotions. Listen for similar examples of confused thinking. You will have little difficulty in finding them. Do you remember in *The Hunting of the Snark* that bit

---

[1] In *Teaching Secondary English* John J. DeBoer illustrates this fact with the Coué daily repetition of "Day by day in every way I grow better and better."

of semantic truth concerning the power of words over thought? "The proof is complete if only I've stated it thrice." Thus adults who repeatedly condemn *all* Russians, plumbers, capitalists, or union members limit their capacity for unprejudiced thinking by each repetition of the stereotype.

"Language," as J. C. Seegers has said, "is not simply a subject to be taught. It is a way of thinking, of responding, of participating. . . . It is a manifestation of growth." [1] But growth is gradual. Do not expect your happy-go-lucky boys and girls to be suddenly metamorphosed into able semanticists. But do see that you provide them with a method for testing important abstractions. Thus you offer them protection against exaggerated wording and emotional confusion of word and referent, both of them protections against the floods of propaganda in our highly verbal nation.

In no sense, however, is this training applicable to the future only. Particularly in the senior high-school classrooms and auditorium such training is badly needed. Classroom discussions and auditorium debates have often seemed hotbeds of misused generalizations. Certain types of high-school students, uniformed but interested in adult problems, are prone to toss about assertions as unqualified as they are unfounded. They maintain, for example, that *"Loyalty* is a virtue." (Loyalty to whom? To thieves? kidnapers? arsonists?) "Everyone should have liberty." (Liberty to "shoot up the town"?) As in the seventh grade, such questioning as to the referent will show immediately that unmodified abstractions are meaningless. [2]

In senior high school, and, in simplified form, in junior high

[1] "Interpreting Language—An Essential of Understanding," *Elementary English*, Vol. 28 (January, 1951), pp. 35-38.

[2] Read "Teaching Thinking and Teaching English" by Arthur Minton, *Hi Points,* Vol. 31 (October, 1949), pp. 5-20. Here is an analysis of correct and incorrect statements, judged by the criterions of (1) completeness, (2) exactness, (3) relevance.

school also, a study of propaganda offers still further useful work on abstractions and emotive wording. To the thoughtless or credulous student this work provides an awakening experience. Here he is asked to analyze straight, slanted, or frankly biased reports from newspapers or radio commentators. In junior high school, pupils will, probably, seek similar material in signs and advertisements that utilize the seven steps in propaganda.[1]

Connotation, often an ally in propaganda, should play an important part in all teaching of English.[2] It is, of course, essential to the pupil's growth in understanding what he hears and what he reads. But it is also most important as a protection to the naïve high-school graduate. In business, college, or social meetings he is handicapped if he blunders, unaware of the implied meaning of his words. One man, admiring his hostess's dress, assured her, "I always like loud clothes." And a prospective minister, a college freshman, discussing in class a passage from *Paradise Lost*, was impressed by the angels "all yelling around the throne of God." It is a part of your responsibility, through class activities and incidental comments, to protect students from tactless errors. The more fortunately trained student, recognizing with enjoyment the use of implication in literature, may also gain interest through attempting to express his ideas and comments less obviously and with more skill in wording.

But since this ability to test ideas is limited by the pupils' understanding of words, be sure that you *provide much training on*

[1] This topic and the seven steps mentioned, plus suggested class exercises, are discussed on pages 169-71. The best library reference is *Propaganda Analysis,* Vol. II, published by the Institute for Propaganda Analysis, now nonexistent.

[2] See Porter Perrin's discussion of connotation in *Writer's Guide and Index to English,* rev. ed., Scott, Foresman, 1950, pp. 322-28. You would profit from having this book in your own professional library.

See pages 167-71 for suggested exercises on the different connotations of a word at different social or financial levels or from those of different political beliefs.

the essential qualities of words in action. That a word's meaning depends, in very considerable part, upon context is one of the first principles to inculcate. You will find that pupils, stopped by an unfamiliar word, avoid using their own brains to puzzle out its meaning. They tend to skip it, ask what it means, or—if so trained—brave the complications of a dictionary.[1] Using the context, actually reading the whole sentence to glean the word's meaning, is a habit slow to develop. As stated earlier, the term *context* should vary according to the age of the pupil and the simplicity of the topic. For the first two years of junior high school, words in the sentence and in neighboring sentences are probably sufficient. For the later grades, according to the students' abilities, the term should also mean (1) the purpose, (2) the situation or condition under which the words are used, and (3) the background of the speaker or writer.

But the first duty of the teacher is to see that students consult the sentence, paragraph, or whole passage. This practice must be repeated over and over again until the habit is acquired. Why?

First, only the context can indicate whether, for example, the word *key* is used factually or metaphorically.

Second, as *Time* magazine states,[2] 570 words commonly used in English have approximately 7,000 different uses. The word *run,* with its compounds, has 800 different meanings, illustrated by such uses as "run on the bank" and "run in a stocking." How, except from the context, can one select from the 800 possibilities?[3]

Third, the irresponsible or dishonest omission of words or sentences from quoted material (particularly common in political campaign literature, in radio speeches, and in newspaper reports on controversial issues) should be illustrated and discussed. If

---

[1] See "Dictionary Study," p. 158, and protect pupils from the confusing erudition of the dictionary.

[2] "Education," *Time,* Vol. 55 (January 9, 1950), p. 42. You will also find this statement quoted in *Teaching Secondary English,* p. 133.

[3] Why not use the word *run* in class to emphasize through students' volunteered sentences the necessity of consulting the context?

competitive debates abound in your own and neighboring schools, you may find that these debates also offer numerous examples. This latter source, and the students' papers in which deceitful omissions appear, provide more effective teaching material than do the materials suggested earlier. This study should so train students that they condemn such omissions. The obvious purpose, however, is to develop in them an unwillingness to accept unquestioned even what seems to be exact quotation. An intelligent procedure.[1]

Fourth, in order to develop intelligent understanding of what is heard or read, it is necessary to consider three things: the condition under which statements are made; the purpose for those statements; and the background of the speaker or writer. Here are two brief incidents illustrative of the influence background has had upon comprehension and conclusion reached. In a girls' school in China, Browning's "My Last Duchess" evoked from the class complete agreement with the Duke who killed his wife. She had not (as a Chinese wife would have) properly valued his "gift of a nine-hundred-year-old name"; hence she deserved death. A second example is that of a tenth-grade boy who, reading a poem about a witch, was puzzled by the line, "She laid on the water a spell," and asked, "Why did she want to lay down for a spell in water?" No one of us is educated, only less ignorant.

Aside from difficulties in connotation, still other pitfalls exist for the factual-minded student. Metaphor, long taught as though it belonged exclusively in poetry, or poetry and slang, plays an important part in prose writing and in speech. From the seventh grade on through high school, this fact should be stressed and illustrated. Particularly for practical-minded students, language possesses a new fascination when they are awakened to the fact

---

[1] You will discover much illustrative material if you investigate *past* election speeches (the farther back the better), in which the speaker quoted his opponent. There you could glean illustrations of honorable uses and dishonorable omissions of context. Be wary, however; leave to your students the discovery of current errors.

of their own unconscious use of metaphor.[1] More important, however, is their awakening to this strange use of language, a use nonfactual, suggestive. When metaphor is at last understood as a shorthand version of analogy, showing some one characteristic *shared in common,* the class is ready to consider metaphor in prose readings. Discussion should, of course, center upon the way in which a particular metaphor illuminates and enriches meaning. Without much discussion of this type, students unaccustomed to stretching their imaginations may, secretly, consider metaphor as unnecessary words that "get you off the track."[2] Such discussion will soon reveal the difference between metaphors that illuminate the idea and those that tend to obscure it. So far the work has concerned with prose. Might this type of discussion contribute later to the student's enjoyment of poetry? In Chapter XIII I have stressed the impatience of those students who ask "If he [the poet] wanted to say it, why didn't he say it so people could understand?" If metaphor has been recognized by the students in their own speech and in "sensible" prose, one great barrier to the enjoyment of poetry has been removed.

One warning is, perhaps, appropriate. Throughout this chapter and this book, I have repeatedly urged classroom discussion. Its use? To develop students' ability for straight thinking, effective wording, and courtesy toward others. Make sure that both the students and their parents (the latter probably educated through "book learning") understand these purposes.[3]

[1] For further discussion, see p. 184, reading 9.

[2] Are *stretching* and *track* metaphors? Why not scatter appropriate metaphors plentifully through your own classroom speech—a type of game in which the students may soon outdo you? Slang should also be estimated in terms of its contribution to the idea.

[3] Read "The Public School Crisis," *Saturday Review of Literature,* Vol. 34, No. 36 (September 8, 1951), pp. 6-12 ff., giving the school situations in six large cities. The article will convince you of the necessity for keeping in touch with the parents and for teaching language without introducing strange "learned" terms. Develop a semantic approach toward language, but do not ride forth on a white charger proclaiming the fact.

You, on the other hand, will recognize that semantic study offers other rich by-products; one is the encouragement of analysis and speculation which may lead some students to objective thinking—a consummation devoutly to be wished.

SUGGESTED EXERCISES [1]

1. Prepare a three- to five-minute talk for, or write a letter to, parents in the P.T.A. in which you explain tactfully the importance of "word study and discussion" (semantics). Several parents have complained, "All this talking in class about words is a waste of time."

2. In a ninth- or twelfth-year class introduce *levels of speech*. Make your illustrations both instructive and amusing but also essential for the assignment that you dictate.

3. Socio-drama. Before attempting this exercise, read Henry M. Buckell's article in the *English Journal*, Vol. 39 (1950), pp. 256-61.

4. Original work. Work out for some one class level a class period in which you introduce, discuss with the high-school class, and illustrate how you would teach one of the following topics: (a) *words, factual* and *metaphorical;* (b) *connotation;* (c) *context;* (d) *abstract nouns,* (1) minus referents, (2) emotive, (3) confused with referents.

SUGGESTED READINGS [2]

References for Your Own Guidance

The English Language Arts, Vol. I, N.C.T.E. Curriculum Series, Dora V. Smith, Director

Read Part III, Chapter 17, "Reading Semantics" and Chapter 14, "The Program in Listening."

1. Reconsider "Useful Books" listed in this chapter.

---

[1] These exercises may take the form of papers, class talks, or group talks in student-arranged "laboratory periods" (see page viii). Some might be used in cadet teaching. For each written or spoken exercise, *adjust your wording and illustrative material to the vocabulary and interests of the grade selected.* If written, ask yourself, "Am I clear, definite, interesting?" If spoken, ask yourself, "Am I easily heard? Do I talk to all class members? Am I unhampered by notes, erect, clear, pleasant in tone, interesting?"

[2] See Appendix B, pages 572-75, for references on listening, audio-visual aids, and other language uses.

2. Seegers, J. Conrad: "Interpreting Language—An Essential of Understandings," *Elementary English,* Vol. 28 (1951), pp. 35-8

This article introduces a series of articles, sponsored by the National Conference Research in English, which you will find listed in Appendix B, page 573.

From the English Journal

1. Adams, Harlen M.: "Learning to Be Discriminating Listeners," Vol. 36 (1947), pp. 11-15

2. Larson, P. Merville: "Discussion—a Basic Procedure in Teaching English," Vol. 20 (1951), pp. 379-82

3. Heaton, Margaret M.: "Stereotypes and Real People," Vol. 35 (1946), 327-32

4. Gregory, Margaret, and McLaughlin, W. J.: "Teaching the Newspaper in Junior High School," Vol. 40 (1951), pp. 23-28

5. Bennett, E. C.: "How to Teach a Magazine that Transcends Mass Appeal," Vol. 38 (1949), pp. 82-6

From Different Sources

1. Minton, Arthur: "Teaching Thinking and Teaching English," *Hi Points,* Vol. 3 (October, 1949), pp. 5-20

2. Siepmann, Charles A.: *Radio, Television, and Society,* Oxford University Press, New York, 1950

A survey of the whole field, one necessary for any teacher who wishes to be as well educated in radio background and present use as are some students.

3. Moreno, J. L.: *Psychodrama,* Vol. I, Beacon House, Beacon, N. Y., 1946

See "Socio-drama," Section viii, pp. 315-78.

4. Deighton, Lee: "A Plea for Co-operative Effort in the Study of Language," *English Journal,* Vol. 38 (1949), pp. 218-25

". . . we choose . . . the most appropriate [language] for a particular occasion."

CHAPTER III

Teaching Functional Grammar

I. TO SECURE SENTENCE SENSE

A. *The Meaning of the Term Functional Grammar*

ARE YOU familiar with the term "teaching functional grammar"? It means, as the name implies, the teaching of those forms in grammar that are essential to the pupil who would express his thoughts correctly. But it means something more definite than that. It means the teaching of *only* those grammatical forms without a knowledge of which the pupil is unable to know whether a sentence is or is not correct. If you subscribe to the idea that you will teach functional grammar only, and if you follow that belief and practice consistently, you pledge yourself to three things:

1. You will eliminate much formal grammar that has cluttered and confused the brains of past generations of pupils.
2. You will, if you are intelligent, change grammar drill from a process of memory to a process of thinking.
3. You will show your pupils at the end of each drill period how the grammar work for that day can and should function in their own speech and writing.

B. *Economy and Skill in Grammar Teaching*

If you are to teach functional grammar, how economically and skillfully are you to do it? In high-school teaching today there is often little economy because the material to be taught has not been efficiently pared down to the essentials. For example, it is absurd to stress gender except for foreigners accustomed in their own tongue to an arbitrary use. The classification of nouns into concrete and abstract serves no useful purpose, but since pupils must learn to use capitals, the distinction between common and proper nouns deserves careful teaching. Then again, is not the differentiation between the uses of *shall* and *will* an absurd technicality for those pupils who are still misusing *seen, done, good?* Think of the effort expended in the average grade school upon *may* and *can* with little foreigners who still say, "I t'ink dat ain't no gut." If you are dealing with children of intellectual aristocrats, teach the niceties; if you are not, spend time and effort where time and effort are needed. And, by the way, how about *may* and *can* in your own speech? Much of the time wasted in school comes from the teacher's attempt to follow a textbook too closely, a textbook that emphasizes niceties which perhaps even you, an expert in English, use only occasionally.

In the crowded curriculum which the English teacher carries today, it is no longer possible to teach one thing at a time. In either grade or high school you will have to fit in mechanics economically so that you fill each class period to the maximum. "Oblique teaching" is the term that I apply to this method. Ostensibly you are teaching one point in mechanics; incidentally, however, you are stressing some three others. Each board illustration, for example, presents the point under consideration, but it also illustrates other points. It has been estimated that about two-thirds of the pupils' errors made are errors in the use of either verbs or pronouns. Surely it is a wasted opportunity not to slip pronouns into all illustrative sentences so that the proper case of the pronoun after a transitive verb or after a preposition may be often seen and heard. Also a wise teacher will select certain "demon" verbs (*ring, come, raise, lie, set, went*) and use them repeatedly in her illustration for subject-verb sentence training. Again, there is an opportunity here in illustrative sentences to teach certain uses of the comma. These uses should be taught incidentally, gleaned from those board sentences that, primarily, are written to illustrate some other principle. For example, one might teach such uses as (1) the comma to set off a series, direct address, appositives; or (2) to separate co-ordinate clauses joined by *and, but, for ;* or sentence elements that might be improperly joined in reading were there no comma.

In addition to economical presentation of material, there is need of skill in presentation. In grammar lessons or in sentence corrections, I have often witnessed greater stupidity, it seemed to me, on the part of the teacher than on the part of the class. As a rule one of three reasons seemed to account for the teacher's lack of skill. Either she knew her grammar imperfectly, and hence was bookish and unable to discuss her material readily; or she was so bent upon making her point that she was unobservant of class difficulties; or she was provided with too little illustrative material. Handicapped by one or more of these difficulties, she would try to force one illustration, not realizing that often a mind blocks upon one combination of words when it could grasp the same thing with another word grouping. As an illustration of the difficulties inherent in a certain word group, consider this sentence in subject-verb agreement: "The length of the fields vary with the width." I have seen the members of a class stalled upon that sentence, confused for the moment because, while they recognized that subject and verb must agree, they felt that *s* indicated the plural: hence for them *varies* would at the moment seem plural, and they knew that the sentence demanded a singular predicate. The teacher should have comprehended that a quick reference to other sentences, "The size changes," "The sizes change," "The man goes," "The men go," would have straightened out the pupils' thinking.

As I have said, the presentation of material ought to be economical and skillful. A fruit-packer prides herself upon the skill and rapidity with which she can sort and pack apples. Any intelligent factory makes economy, speed, efficiency, its watchwords. If English teaching were one half as intelligent as industry, English teachers would pride themselves upon their specific skill. You would hear one say: "I spend one forty-minute period on participles and gerunds. After that the class knows the difference between them," or "Miss Jones can teach the principles of adjective and adverb clauses in thirty minutes so that they are as clear to a class as one-word modifiers and as immediately recognized." Why do we not hear such comments? Because we clutter our own minds and our pupils' minds with unnecessary material. Because we are not content to teach functional grammar. Because we are not yet able to recognize it as the best way of implanting the habit of writing decent sentences. Because we have a lazy man's attitude toward inventing what, for us, is the best and easiest inclined plane upon which to slide information, unobstructed, into the minds of average pupils.

C. Where to Begin

After these generalities concerning the whole field of grammar teaching, let us consider two questions that you will ask yourself when you meet your first high-school classes. First, where shall I begin? Secondly, how can I present this material efficiently, economically, skillfully, with a logical growth through the four years?

When you receive the first set of themes from your high-school classes, the first question will probably be answered for you. Some papers will contain complete sentences. Many (if your class is a typical one) will contain such errors as these: "While my friend and I waited on the shady side of the street," or "He walked toward me with a fish on his hook, it was bigger than any I had caught." Obviously the writer who composed those two groups of words did not understand the essential unit, the sentence, upon which all writing is based. Your immediate duty, then, is to inculcate the idea that *every group of words punctuated as a sentence must contain one principal subject and predicate.* It is all very well to teach that a sentence expresses a complete idea if you believe in that statement. Labor for a time with that definition if you like it, but eventually you will find that there are pupils to whose ears that formula means nothing. To them "Hearing a noise" sounds correct. For the difficulty of the complete-idea formula is this: The measure is purely subjective. If, to a pupil, a group of words sounds "complete," it does. That is all there is to it. I have seen teachers struggle until the accommodating pupil lied valiantly, and the weary teacher was fain to believe—until the next incomplete group of words revealed the pupil's polite deception.

No, the complete-idea formula, reasonable and logical as it is, will not do. You have to go deeper. You have to take a sentence to pieces and say dogmatically: "You cannot have a complete idea, a sentence, without a main predicate and for it a main subject, expressed or understood. What is the predicate? What is the subject?" In other words, you cannot teach *all* pupils to write whole sentences without teaching functional grammar. There are, it is true, some pupils with logical minds who invariably write complete sentences. You may have been one of them. But if your purpose is, as it must be, to teach *all* your pupils to write reputable English, you will have to teach them to recognize subjects and predicates in ready-made sentences, to put subjects and predicates into their homemade sentences, and to read their own and their neighbors' themes critically with subjects and predicates in mind.

Are you surprised to learn that the writing of whole sentences properly terminated is often more correctly done in the seventh and eighth grades than in the second year of high school? Does that statement discourage you? Remember that expression and thought are indivisible. The first two years that a pupil spends in high school should be and often are a time of very rapid mental and emotional growth. Blunderingly, boys and girls are attempting to find words for their more complicated thinking. They dimly recognize that their thought is more complicated, and attempt, often awkwardly, to show thought relationships by placing all related material in the same sentence or in a following sentence fragment.

Your business is to train yourself to grasp the tenuous thought connection that they have in their own minds; then you must show them how that relationship may be made clear to the reader. Too often the busy teacher feels satisfied if at the board she has turned some pupil's awkward or incomplete sentence into a reputable one. But if the finished product does not exactly express the idea the pupil had in mind, her work is practically useless, or perhaps worse than useless, so far as the author of the sentence is concerned. Over and over again the question "Does that sentence say just what you mean?" should be on the lips of the teacher. After a while, pride in good workmanship can be awakened in some few pupils—pride in searching for the word or construction that exactly expresses the thought. A Sentimental Tommy will rarely brighten your classroom; but in many pupils a desire for sincere expression can be awakened by a teacher who herself strives for sincerity.

In other words, you have to remind yourself constantly that you are not teaching sentence structure for its own sake. You are attempting to liberate thought and to clarify thinking by providing a flexible, responsive medium for its expression. Remember this purpose. Otherwise you are satisfied with parrotlike reproduction of textbook models, with form instead of thought, with glibness instead of sincerity. You may, perhaps, have taught your pupils to write with fair correctness, but you have not assisted them to develop so that written English may become for them a usable tool.

D. How to Begin

Let us now consider the first step in the mechanics of composition writing, the complete sentence. I have already suggested that it is well to discard the logically correct test, "Does the sentence sound complete?" in favor of "Has it a subject and a predicate?"

To work from sentences on the board is a wise beginning. If you ask the class for the shortest possible sentence, they will probably arrive at the answer "Go." I should take that one and build from it on the board in some such manner as this, the class assisting.

1. Go.
2. (The man) (goes).
3. (The tall man) (goes quickly).
4. (The tall man in the blue coat) (goes quickly toward the red barn).
5. (The tall man in the blue coat who, I believe, is a policeman,) (goes quickly toward the red barn, from which tiny puffs of white smoke are issuing).

Here the class witnesses the growth of a sentence, but sees the unchanging quality of its two parts, its predicate and its subject. In just the same fashion pupils can unwind a sentence and convince themselves that, no matter how many words a sentence may contain, it has but two parts, the subject and all that belongs to it, and the predicate with all that belongs to it. Since grammar is difficult, this apparent simplification is comforting to pupils. But this division of a sentence into but two parts, the whole subject and the whole predicate, has also another advantage. It encourages a class to read by units, by groups of words, rather than to pick and choose a noun and a verb regardless of context.

How are you going to teach your pupils to find the predicate and the subject? And why place the verb first and give it particular stress? Before discussing any rule or definition of a subject or a predicate, one general principle, true in all teaching, must be recalled: No definition should be given until after many illustrations have been placed upon the board and thoroughly discussed. Then and then only is it wise to crystallize the information thus gained into a definition. But even then it is wiser to allow variation and personal expression of the idea in the words of the pupil than to demand a set formula. Why? Because grammar must be kept a process of thinking, not a function of memory. It is surprising how many youngsters can define all parts of speech and yet fail to recognize any—except, perhaps, adjectives and nouns. A definition given first, before the principle it stands for is perfectly clear, becomes a group of words that jingles in the memory; becomes a group of words to be learned exactly and to be reproduced, often, without awakening thought. An unvarying rule, therefore, is this one: Always illustrate a principle fully before crystallizing the idea into the form of a definition.

For a beginning class it is sufficient to know that a subject is the principal person or thing one is talking about; a predicate is the assertion made about the subject. It is wise also in order to keep your pupils thinking, not guessing, to give them various types of subjects. To teach a group that a subject must be a noun is to mislead them. Even more important to remember is this fact: To teach pupils that an isolated word has the power of being some specific part of speech is to undo all the emphasis that you are putting upon grammar as a thought process and to substitute memory work instead. *Run* looks like a verb to us, but "The run is short" makes it serve as subject. *Mother* seems to us a noun, but "See the hen mother the little turkeys" makes the word a verb. This insistence upon the fact that no word is anything in itself, that we cannot tell what part of speech a word is until we see it function in a sentence, has done much to insure common-sense methods in the teaching of grammar.

Remember these two principles: No word is in itself a part of speech, and no definitions are to be given until numerous examples of the idea have provided a definite concept for the terms used. Then I repeat the question: How are you going to teach subjects and predicates? And why place particular stress upon the predicate?

E. *The Importance of the Verb*

To consider the second question first, look at the would-be sentence "Hearing a noise." The pupil recalls that *hear* is a verb. At the present stage I, too, would admit *hearing* as a kind of verb, but I should rule out all *-ing* endings as possible for predicates, that is, for verbs that can make an assertion about a subject. If the class recognizes early that *-ing* disqualifies a verb for the office of predicate, much trouble and time is saved. But to talk of gerunds and of participles while predicates are still little-known entities is confusing. Hence a "so-called verb" or a "kind of verb" will do for the present. A second reason for stressing the predicate, aside from the elimination of *-ing* forms, is this: The use of vigorous verbs obviously and rapidly improves a pupil's writing, while his hunt for exactly the right verb greatly increases his interest in composition. It is, therefore, an encouraging bit of technique to confide early to the writer of themes. You are the skilled workman; the pupil is the apprentice. Teach him those tricks of the trade that give a beginner some appreciation of later skill and some feeling for the art that lies far ahead.

For example, pupils have seen on the board and have in class found and discussed the subject and the predicate in such sentences as the following:

1. John made a home run.
2. Hockey is a good sport.
3. Swimming is a favorite sport of mine.
4. "Gobble" is an ugly word.
5. To swim is excellent exercise.
6. That he is shortstop is lucky for the team.
7. Going out in a boat frightens me.
8. Out in the garden are radishes.
9. _____ Run to the drugstore.

Next it is wise to elicit sentences from the class, writing them on the board and underlining the two parts of the sentence, subject and predicate. But if the class seems not to remember any of its grammar-school training, it is probably wiser to begin not with the stripped subject and predicate but with the subject plus all of its modifiers (the whole subject) and the predicate plus all of its modifiers (the whole predicate).[1]

As a rule, however, in the first year of high school the teacher can begin with the simple subject and predicate.[2] It is also wise in these early stages of subject-predicate drill to stress the reading of complete and incomplete word groups, indicating expectancy by the voice in such a group as "Out on the wet slippery deck of the great steamer as it pulled away from the wharf . . ." to make evident that the idea is incomplete in contrast to "We squatted on the slippery decks of the little steamer," with its satisfactory drop of voice at the end. I mention this method of reading because many pupils have a persistently inquiring lift of the voice at the end of sentences. The habit is apparently a peculiarly difficult one to break.

As you consider those sample sentences given above, you may say that it must be confusing to the class to have the teacher use so-called nouns, verbs, gerunds, infinitives, noun clauses, for the subjects of these sentences. Of course it is—to those pupils who are looking for the word, not for the idea. And, naturally, you will provide the class with many simple noun subjects first until they comprehend their uses. But you should early divorce your pupils from the idea that a subject must be one word, that it must be a noun, or that there exist any words or word which may

[1] Occasionally even high-school teachers of some experience forget professional etiquette so far as to wonder aloud why their students have been taught nothing in their previous training. Needless to say, pupils are able to forget more than they are taught; hence your successor may have to exercise quite as much patience as you. Also remember that you do not know the number of outside activities carried on by your predecessor.

[2] It is convenient to accustom pupils to the term "substantive" for nouns, pronouns, or nounlike groups of words.

not serve as a subject. Challenge your class to find something that you cannot turn into a subject for them. You are quite safe. Challenge them to think of unusual words that they can make into predicates. By changing grammar from memory drill to thinking process, you are making it a brightening, not a dulling, influence. You will find that "grammar-drill day" becomes one of the liveliest skirmishes of the week. Occasionally these skirmishes prove too rapid for the slower pupils, but a daily five-minute test will show you what pupils are lagging.

At first in your teaching, appalled at the number of different things you are supposed to do, you will feel that a daily five-minute sentence drill is too timetaking. Just remember that nothing is too timetaking if you can implant sentence sense thoroughly and completely in your first year so that it will function in all later themes. Then, too, you must economize by oblique teaching and by utilizing small bits of time. Five minutes may be spent on sentence drill at the first of the hour: drill based upon sentences that you have previously placed upon the board, sentences written on the board by some four or five pupils between classes, after school, before school in the morning. These five-minute drills are of more value (as you already know from your study of the "laws of learning") than is one whole period set aside for drill work.

F. A Combined Vocabulary and Grammar Drill

One of the numerous subjects that you must teach is vocabulary building. And though part of another chapter is devoted to that topic, I want to illustrate here how it may be introduced with oblique emphasis upon subject-predicate training. In pupils' themes perhaps the most monotonous predicates used are those two useful but colorless verbs *said* and *go*. A device such as the following—one capable of much variation—not only interests and excites a class while it stresses the subject-predicate relationship, but it is, perhaps, one of the most useful devices for awakening

Interest and pride in writing. The teacher places some such list as the following upon the board:

1.	sparrow	6.	schoolboy
2.	elephant	7.	tramp
3.	cow	8.	athlete
4.	mouse	9.	large housewife
5.	small lady	10.	old man

The class is then asked to jot down in a line the numbers from one to ten and to write after each number the best possible descriptive predicate for each subject, telling how it moves. After two minutes' consideration and writing, the class will volunteer its information. It will discuss suggestions, and finally adopt the most suitable predicates. On the board will appear some such list as this:

1. sparrow—hopped—swooped—skimmed
2. elephant—lumbered—padded
3. cow—meandered—trotted—loped
4. mouse—crept—scuttled—scampered
5. little lady—minced—tripped
6. schoolboy—scuffed—sauntered
7. tramp—slouched—slumped
8. athlete—strode
9. large housewife—bustled—heaved—trod
10. old man—tottered—shuffled

In the final selection of each word or words, a discussion of what each word means and how different words change the character of the subject awakens interest in words themselves and in words as honest tools of thought. I have long used a sentence to illustrate the fact that a predicate can alter the entire idea of a subject, and have asked the class to record what mental image each gets of the actor as I substitute verb after verb in the blank below. "He —— between Henry and me down the long avenue into the sunlight." (And may I remark in passing that "between Henry and me" is another bit of oblique teaching?) On the pupil's mental screen *toddled* produces the image of a baby; *tot-tered,* an old man or an intoxicated man; *skipped,* a youngster; *slouched,* either a "down-and-out" or a disgruntled schoolboy. By changing *he* to *she* one can run through a new catalogue, finding new traits for the child or woman who *strides, minces, skips, races,* or *elbows* her way along. Does all this work seem too much like play?

In the same way, the monotonous overuse of such a word as *said* can be banished from pupils' themes, to be replaced by verbs perhaps less desirable, but words showing forethought, interest, a desire for more accurate expression. Another old favorite of mine is the statement " 'It's a lie,' he ——." (You will note that both quotations and the apostrophe of contraction are being taught obliquely here.) The average class is delighted with the changes in tone, character, circumstances, it can produce by the succession of verbs inserted. " 'It's a lie,' he whined," gives a Uriah Heep in pleasant contrast to Mr. Murdstone's " 'It's a lie,' he thundered," or to the malicious, sly " 'It's a lie,' he chuckled," of a Quilp. *Snuffled, snorted, murmured, protested,* and many others, in turn alter the character of the speaker.[1]

For a moment may I digress here on the subject matter of the sentence used? Teachers used to assume that boys and girls, innocent and childish, were occupied with beautiful thoughts about birds and bees and butterflies; hence all board illustrations must be sweet or at least innocuous. The fact of the matter is that while those of us who have passed forty may be fond of the alliterative and innocent trio given above, high-school boys and girls like competitive sports, tragedies, and the sophistication of the moving pictures. It is, therefore, often necessary to violate our own creed of sweetness and light and to attune ourselves to the age in which our high-school pupils live. You, perhaps, will find this violation less painful than I, but you, too, are behind

---

[1] After a brief drill on this sentence, one pupil at the next class meeting brought in a list of 114 possible verbs.

the procession if you think of your pupils, even the freshmen, as "children." They are adults, remember, learning a trade, the trade of writing. For many it will never rise to an art, but for all it is a tool to be used in the real world, not in the highly selective atmosphere created only in a class in English.

G. *The Assignment*

Let us next consider what type of outside work pupils might do as an outcome of the class discussions on subject-predicate sentences. It is wise to remember that in addition to the class period about forty minutes belong, as a rule, to the study of English. If from the very first you do not assign work for that forty-minute period, you will soon find that science, mathematics, Latin, or athletics has usurped it, and that you cannot regain that time for outside study. From the first, then, assignments— sensible, important, constructive assignments, not "busywork" —should be given. I have heard the following work dictated: "Tomorrow bring in twenty-five sentences of your own. Underscore the subject once, the predicate twice." Can you find a poorer assignment for an intelligent or even a semi-intelligent group? What would be the result? Twenty-five brief statements something like this: He saw it. She saw it. They came here. Mary is ill. Baseball is over. If twenty-five such sentences are written, some physical exercise is required, but the mental effort equals, perhaps, that demanded in the second grade. And why should a class do more? They have complied with the request. On the other hand suppose we take the same assignment and make it an intelligent one.

Bring in twenty-five sentences of your own in which you underscore the subject once, the predicate twice. Of these:

1. Make five in which the verb exactly describes or pictures the subject. (Example: The quartz glittered in the sunlight. The blind man tapped his way along the pavement.)

2. Make five in which the predicate suggests the motion or speech of the subject. Try to use other words than those suggested in class.

3. Make five in which several words come before the subject and the predicate. See if you can catch the class on these.

4. Make five in which one or more words separate the subject from its predicate. (Example: The boy whom I know ran down the steps.)

Don't be stingy with ideas, but don't waste words.

H. Summary

What is the object of this discussion? It has, as I see it, five purposes:

1. To make clear the mooted term "functional grammar"

2. To drive home the principle that much illustration must precede definition

3. To promulgate the doctrine that a word's function in a sentence determines its part of speech

4. To indicate how subject-predicate recognition and drill may be interestingly combined with word selection

5. To contrast live, practical work closely associated with theme writing and oral composition with dead, mechanical, busywork assignments

II. TO SECURE SENTENCE VARIETY

A. Be Practical

Once more, why are you teaching grammar? A wise check on yourself, as has been suggested earlier, is a five-minute summary at the end of every class recitation. At that time you and your pupils sum up the actual use of the day's work as it applies to composition writing. High-school pupils are not interested in storing their minds for some remote future. Of course they are not. But they *are* interested in learning when they can see a definite, practical reason for the effort. Your business, then, is to eliminate the impractical and, daily, to correlate the grammar work studied with the themes written and the revisions made.

Grammar taught as an isolated phenomenon is about as useful to your pupils as were Shakespeare and the musical glasses to certain ladies of doubtful fame. If, in your teaching, grammar is to be more than a classroom ornament adorning the speech of your pupils with new words and odd phrases, *see that the theory they learn is applied to the sentences they write.* If you do not make the grammar learned function in the sentences written, you are about as consistent as the imaginary teacher of piano who demands dutiful attention to finger exercises throughout the week but on Saturday encourages her pupils to pound at will. Be practical. See that you teach only that which is useful; then demand that use be made of it.

Each of you will eventually work out your own method, but until you have done so these suggestions may help you to correlate grammar teaching with theme writing. In the preceding paragraphs methods were given for teaching sentence sense. We shall now consider the next step after the recognition and use of subjects and predicates have become habitual, and end punctuation no longer gives way to commas. When this millennium is reached, what comes next?

B. *Attack Monotony*

If you look at the average high-school freshman composition, the next step will present itself. You will find that in the case of the well-prepared pupil compound and simple sentences strew the page. (If the pupil is poorly prepared, you will find that incomplete sentences litter the paper. In that case, no "next step" is possible until he can habitually write complete sentences.) Too often these incorrect or dull sentences are marked, and the pupil is advised to alter them, but he is given no clear-cut advice by his teacher of English as to *how* such alteration may be made. Of course we know that the successful manual-training teacher shows a boy how to use a T square, how to use an adz; that the penmanship teacher concerns himself with arm movement, position, and formation of letters before he expects good writing. But we, the teachers of English composition, too often forget the necessity of concrete aid, and expect sentence manipulation to come as a natural gift. Therefore, we condemn poor constructions but do nothing toward teaching the principles underlying their improvement.

What can you do? First, after you have secured whole sentences, *you can attack simple sentences that are tiresomely alike.* Take, for example, this passage: "He had his breakfast and went to the office. He found no one there. He rang the bell with one hand and he tried to work the telephone with the other. The telephone was out of order, he found. He rang the bell furiously. He rang and rang and the office boy did not answer." Obviously, if this were put on the board, a class would object to the repetition. But what constructive suggestions would you as teacher offer?

The first step is, is it not, to alter the subject-verb beginnings? While you teach parts of speech, phrases, and clauses, teach, step by step, that monotony can be avoided by placing at the beginning of the sentence:

1. A phrase—prepositional or one having an *-ing* verb form
2. A single adverb
3. A transposed word
4. A transposed clause

On the board would appear something like this:

After breakfast (1. prepositional phrase) he went to the office. There (2. adverb) he found no one. Ringing the bell furiously (1. *-ing* verb form) with one hand, he tried to work the telephone with the other. The telephone (3. transposed word) he discovered was out of order, and no office boy answered the bell (4. transposed clause) in spite of all his ringing.

Both passages are immature, but the second shows the pupil that there are simple mechanical means of ridding his composition of repetitious constructions. Here you provide prac-

tical devices that any pupil can grasp. Of course you will introduce them gradually: first, perhaps you will consider the prepositional phrase or simple adverb that can be switched to the beginning of the sentence. "He saw him again, later," is a commonplace. "Later he saw him again" may be a bright spot in a pupil's
flock of subject-verb sentences. Remember, however, that only
through much board work can pupils be brought to an appreciation of the value of word placement. And only through grammar
drill can they be made familiar enough with prepositional
phrases, adverbs, dependent clauses, to understand the component parts of the sentences they write, and to grasp the teacher's
suggestions as to change.

C. Develop Self-criticism

It is necessary to consider one other point here. How well do
you write? Are your own sentences above reproach? Perhaps one
reason for the pathetic constructions used by college students is
that many of their high-school teachers—obviously unskilled
architects as judged by their own written work—were not sensitive to their pupils' clumsy sentences. Teachers of English do
not, on the whole, write so well as the average newspaperman.
We are likely to be stiff, self-conscious, labored. Do you read
your own papers aloud softly to see how they "listen"? Ear training for your pupils is valuable, more valuable by far than all the
grammar training you can give them. But who ever heard of a
course in listening in either high school or college? What you
should attempt to get is *both* the auditory sense of a strong or
weak sentence and the grammatical knowledge. As you well
know, many a sentence while grammatically correct is still hopelessly awkward. Do you yourself listen intelligently? With your
own manuscripts do you read aloud, very softly, noting the sound
of the words, of the sentences, of the paragraphs? Do you listen
for the transitions between sentences, between paragraphs, and
for unfortunate similarities of sound? Try yourself; then in the

classroom test your pupils. Put their sentences on the board so that they can have both a visual and an auditory impression. Then show them how you discover weaknesses, why you suggest changes, and how those changes should be made.

D. Teach Variety in Sentence Beginnings

Aside from board work chosen from student themes, how are pupils to get enough practice so that they will begin to be critical of their own sentences? You will have to work out many exercises. Unfortunately ideas penetrate slowly, and the Biblical admonition "Line upon line, and precept upon precept: here a little and there a little" applies nowhere more appropriately than to the teaching of composition. A pupil sees that "He saw him then" is perhaps bettered by the change "Then he saw him." He grasps the idea so clearly that when called on for another sentence, he can make this one, "John saw her then," and change it triumphantly to "Then John saw her." But in his own themes he will continue to write one after another subject-verb sentence—"I went there later"; "He confessed it all to me afterwards"—with no realization of the fact that monotony of form could be avoided by transposition.

What are you to do? You may give out twenty sentences to be changed so that each begins with either an adverb or a prepositional phrase. You may praise highly a revised sentence set amid a flock of subject-verb sentences. You may read a theme composed of monotonous subject-verb sentences with malign emphasis, such emphasis that the class will squirm in anticipation of conclusively damning it. And, by the way, you will find that your pupils are much more censorious than you would ever dare to be. Often you will be forced to moderate their criticism, to plead that though of course the form *is* bad, yet the idea is a good one; that though repetition weakens the thought, yet some verb is well used. As soon as possible it is well to rouse your class so that they condemn and you willingly admit the evils of con-

struction. Why? For two reasons: (1) the offender who perpe-
trates a bad theme heeds the criticism of his peers much more
than he will ever take to heart your own comments; (2) he will
be grateful for your championship and your sympathy. You
admit that the dress of his thought is outlandish, but you approve his thought. He and his companions, however, must be
reminded of one thing. A simple subject-verb sentence is often
the best type to use; it is only monotonous repetition of the same
kind of sentence that is tedious. A monotonous series of sentences
beginning with adverbs or prepositional phrases would be even
more undesirable, because less natural. Monotony, then, is the
crime that your pupils must realize and, having realized, must
attempt to eradicate from their themes. And how are they to
realize it? Through reading themes aloud softly, listening to each
sentence.

So far, only sentence variation gained through the placement
of adverbs and prepositional phrases has been discussed. The use
of a participle or an infinitive at the beginning of a sentence will
be taught later. Many college students seem to feel that some
magical rite is necessary before they can comprehend the use of
a participle or a gerund. If a participle (*swimming* fish: *flying*
birds: *running* quickly, the boy . . .) is taught as an adjective
with the queries "What is swimming? What is flying? Who is
running?" it is not difficult for pupils to see that an *-ing* verbal
which describes or limits a noun or nounlike word is a participle.
A recognition of its usefulness to them in sentence building, however, may come much more slowly. What is its use? A pupil
might write, "John was running downhill *and* his foot caught on
a snag *and* he fell headlong." The use of that last word would
make one grateful to the pupil, but even gratitude may not restrain a teacher. In lumbering country "cutting waste timber"
becomes a recognized phrase. Here the waste timber is apparent.
A class will suggest various versions—*snagging his foot; running
downhill*—and will be quick to see the undesirable repetition of
and.

E. Teach That the Idea Should Determine the Sentence Form

Since thinking and sentence making are related even in the writing of the poorest pupils, much board work is necessary to illustrate the fact that the emphasis placed upon an idea depends upon the form in which that idea is expressed. Here the participle, the dependent clause, the prepositional phrase, should be shown as desirable for expression of the minor statements, the main clause for expression of statements of importance. Keep that fact in mind in order to make idea rather than mere form of dominant importance. But how are you to do it?

"Alice dusted the piano and broke Father's statue of Psyche." That sentence will pass the average class unchallenged unless you suggest that the daily dusting is scarcely so important as the unusual happening. What will the class then do with the sentence? It may suggest: "When Alice was dusting . . ." or "Dusting the piano, Alice . . ." or "Alice broke Father's statue of Psyche as she was dusting the piano," or "Father's statue of Psyche was broken by Alice while she was dusting the piano." If the idea of cutting waste timber is kept to the fore, that last monstrosity will soon disappear from the board, though not before it has served its purpose as a warning against ungainly construction and awkward use of the passive.

It is difficult to stress this particular point, the teaching of sentence construction, strongly enough. Young teachers, enamored of names and titles, seem convinced that there is some intrinsic virtue contained in the words *simple, complex,* and *compound.* Consider your own introduction to those terms. In school presumably you went through a period of spying upon ready-made sentences, intent upon pinning one of these names upon them. Why did you? Unless you were better taught than are the majority of pupils, you did it apparently for the sole purpose of naming them. But what's in a name? Unless this study of sentences is attacked from the standpoint of the idea to be expressed, and unless the influence of that idea upon the form is kept to the fore, sentence classification becomes a piece of pure theory. And beware pure theory for the practical brains of thirteen and fourteen.

Your business is to show that a simple sentence, long or short, is used to make one statement. It may be "John ran well." It may be "While standing in the downpour of rain, looking hopelessly for our defeat at the hands of Lakeport High, suddenly I saw John's long, lean body forge ahead, inch by inch, past Lakeport's famous two-miler." In a simple sentence, the writer has one thing to say. That one thing he must say, undimmed by coordinate or subordinate clause. Its dominance must be made clear by the kind of sentence used. But suppose the writer has two ideas of equal importance. We may not know of the race and its outcome. The writer tells us, "John ran well, but Lakeport's runner outdistanced him." Both ideas are true; both ideas are balanced in the mind of the writer. He wishes to do justice to both athletes; hence he must use a compound sentence. But if the case were different, a compound sentence would misrepresent the actual happening, as it takes shape in the teller's mind. His enthusiastic interest centers on the Lakeport man. All else is subordinate; therefore the form must indicate that fact as it does in the complex sentence, "Lakeport's two-miler easily outdistanced John, although our man ran well."

I have prolonged this discussion because on that special Judgment Day for Teachers when their sins of omission are to be blazoned to the world, among the first crimes to be reckoned with will be this practice of teaching sentence classification as an end and aim in itself, divorced from actual writing, unrelated to the thought expressed, a mere busywork for restless minds.

F. Teach the Meaning of Common Connectives

As soon as you approach complex sentences, another responsibility is yours. Are you well trained in the use of connectives?

From freshman to senior in high school and again in college from freshman to senior, thought relationships and the appropriate connectives expressing these relations must be consistently emphasized. Perhaps no better test of a person's accurate or inaccurate expression can be had than that provided by his discriminating use of connectives. You should, of course, begin with the simplest, the co-ordinate. What does *and* imply concerning the ideas it connects? What does *but* tacitly promise the reader? What does *for,* the conjunction, mean? (And here it is a simple matter to fix for all time the idea, "*For* preceded by a comma is a conjunction meaning *because; for* without a comma is a preposition"; and to illustrate that idea by the statements "He went for the doctor" and "He went, for the doctor called him.") In the pressure of schoolwork many composition teachers overlook the necessity of *teaching* the various shades of meaning contained in connectives. It is as if they believed that the very urgency of thought would necessitate the right choice of word—as it does eventually with those interested in writing, but as it never does with the less interested group. Would it not be sensible to list for your own guidance the main co-ordinate connectives, those that express addition, contrast, consequence, alternative ideas, repetition; and those used with subordinate adverbial clauses that express concession, condition, time, place, manner, degree, or comparison, result, purpose, cause? Then you would be ready to make intelligent illustrations of the different ways an idea may be expressed.

Naturally you would not pour out all of these different types at once upon the defenseless heads of your pupils. But through the four years you should build up their knowledge of the relation existing between the meaning desired and that implied by certain connectives. For example, *because, unless, since, although, admitting that, meanwhile, yet, consequently, for example, on the other hand, moreover,* have each a definite use, and each implies a somewhat definite thought relationship between the two clauses. What is it? How are you to make the difference clear?

G. Cut Waste Timber

One more effective device for cutting waste timber is the use of apposition. "Mr. Jackson, who is a plumber, came to our house" becomes "Mr. Jackson, the plumber, came to our house." It is also a simple matter to teach the proper punctuation while emphasizing the use of apposition as an economy in sentence making. At first it is necessary to have board exercises in reduc-tion of wandering clauses; soon, however, these changes should be demanded in theme revision before the theme is handed in. To drive home the construction upon which you are working, ask for the number of appositive constructions used in certain com-positions, just as earlier in the work you will ask for the number of non-subject-verb sentences that the pupil has used. Too often in the past, boys and girls have been censured for short themes; hence there has been little incentive to make themes compact, and sentences brief, or to strive for a concise wording of an idea. Frequent emphasis upon the idea "Here are one hundred and fifty words to spend. Who can get the most for his one hundred and fifty?" or "You may have six sentences and no more in which to give your picture," will tend to strengthen sentences by compressing much material into little space. At least it will neces-sitate the use of apostrophe, participial phrase, prepositional phrase, in place of the longer clauses. It will also necessitate some thinking about the medium used.

III. TO SECURE SENTENCE UNITY, COHERENCE, EMPHASIS

A. A Warning

So far we have discussed sentence sense and the simpler forms of manipulation used to secure variety in sentence beginnings. The work suggested might readily be presented in junior high

school. It is in no sense difficult; it in no sense depends upon maturity of the students' minds. But whether it is taught to seventh-grade pupils, to juniors in high school, or to freshmen in college, it must be presented, amply illustrated, grasped by the students, and habitually practiced by them in their own writing *before* it is desirable to pass on to more mature problems. Up to this point we have been dealing with foundation work. Obviously such work should precede any superstructure even if one has to wait until the senior year in high school before considering more advanced problems. Be warned by the following statement: Much of the difficulty experienced by advanced students arises directly from the mass of half-understood material over which they have been hurried. Some conscientious teachers have felt that, willy-nilly, they must "cover" the prescribed course; hence the pupils have suffered.

B. Lack of Agreement

A form of error that continues throughout grade school, high school, college, and even lingers upon the lips of adult educated men and women is that of agreement. It is a problem with which you must cope from the beginning of your sentence work until the night of graduation when you hear your honor student ask: "Has everyone their diploma?" Under the general heading "Lack of Agreement" you will find listed in any textbook a series of statements concerning agreement of (1) subjects and verbs; (2) antecedents and pronouns; (3) antecedents, relatives, and following verbs and pronouns. These three types provide a problem in instruction that you must face and solve.

Why stress antecedents? Because you will probably find in the papers of your juniors and seniors that their most flagrant error is the use of a floating *which, this,* or *it* minus a clear antecedent. Hence any training that makes the pupil antecedent conscious assists him indirectly to avoid both the floating-*which* error and errors in agreement. Is that term "floating *which*" familiar to you? For example, a pupil writes: "He ran into a truck which cost him twenty dollars." Obviously the first clause is the only possible antecedent for *which*. Just as obviously, the sentence does not mean what it says. But if you tell your pupils, "Tack down your floating relatives or pronouns with a definite antecedent," you have done three things for them:

1. You have given them a definite slogan to remember, and they like slogans.
2. You have pointed out and thus aided them to detect and correct a particularly insidious type of error.
3. You may have improved their thinking by making that thinking more specific.

You must glean examples of the floating *which* from class papers. You must illustrate on the board, by inserting an antecedent or by recasting the sentence, how by an intelligent use of antecedents a statement may be made clear and definite. Eventually this work ought to result in such improved sentences as these—improved before the final paper is handed in: "He ran into a truck, an accident which cost him twenty dollars," or a complete revision such as: "He had to pay twenty dollars' damages because he ran into a truck and scattered its contents."

Many teachers, utilizing the pupils' enjoyment of cartoons, use original ones to impress upon their students' minds the relationships existing between the various parts of a sentence or the various uses of verbs, pronouns, and other difficult forms. Why? Because they find that humor combined with visual appeal is an effective way of driving home those facts which, expressed in the sedate language of the textbook, make all too little impression upon the pupils' minds. If you are doubtful as to how cartoons can be used successfully, consult the *Using English* series by Lucy H. Chapman and Luella B. Cook, and illustrated with cartoons by Fred G. Cooper. For example, the cartoon of an agonized pup *rising* in air, *raised* by a mounting airplane, differentiates dramatically the difference between *raise* and *rise*. Some teachers use stick drawings when teaching sentence structure: Father Stick for a simple sentence, Mother and Father Stick for a compound sentence, and Mother Stick holding the baby for a complex one. These devices are mere devices, but do not scorn them if they accomplish their purpose. It is an unimaginative teacher who overlooks such opportunities to make her material visual. At present you think of such drawings as useful for the grades, but do not overlook their use with older pupils if those pupils are still struggling with junior high-school problems.

C. Shifts in Construction

Another type of error, termed shift in construction, arises from poor thinking. The pupil begins his sentence with one form in mind; he loses sight of his beginning and strays off into some other form. For example a pupil may make:

1. A shift in person:

One must enjoy new sights and sounds and even smells to overlook the discomforts *you* have to suffer in Oriental countries.

2. A shift in subject:

Just put your flag up and soon a *person* will see flags on every house in the block.

3. A shift in voice:

One *can go* in an airplane one hundred miles an hour and at the same time little motion *is felt*.

4. A shift in tense:

When he *got* the news, he *runs* home excitedly, shouting to all the people he met.

Remember that any dogmatic assertion in class concerning shift in tense within a sentence would be unwise, since often the thought demands such change.

How shall you meet these four types of errors? Some minds that think clearly will practically never run into such constructions as those illustrated above in 1, 2, or 4. Other pupils who think confusedly, and pupils who write carelessly, must have board work drawn from their own themes, questions that force them to think out the relationship between sentence parts, and models discussed in which authors have written clearly and consistently.

Perhaps further suggestion is futile, but this one fact is certain: If pupils can once be convinced that shift in person, subject, or tense *is not* "just another mistake in English," but *is* a sign of confused, weak thinking, improvement is possible. Just so long, however, as pupils regard these errors as places "where it doesn't sound good" or places where it "maybe could be said better," there is little hope of securing clear thought or of making any permanent improvement in the pupils' written work.

Nothing so far has been said of shift in voice. Probably the best method of combating this error is to present many concrete examples in which you show a weak sentence containing a passive, then the same sentence recast in active voice. The constant query: "Who hears? Who sees? Who is sad?" will soon rid themes of such expressions as: "I climbed a hill. A beautiful landscape was seen"; "I opened the door. A noise was heard"; "We looked at the poisoned dog. Sorrow was felt." Pupils may not care particularly whether they write smoothly and beautifully, but as a rule they do want to say a thing sensibly and vigorously. Some few pupils probably can be awakened to an appreciation of and pleasure in good workmanship for itself, but if the majority learn to write clearly and with some attempt at vigor, what more can you reasonably desire?

D. Parallel Construction

We have now reached what I term a more advanced problem in sentence composition, a problem that should wait until the foundation of complete sentences is firmly established. It is the question of parallel and nonparallel construction, and is perhaps one of the most difficult problems in sentence building because it is so closely connected with both logical thinking and grammatical knowledge. Normally this form belongs to rather more mature thought and rather more complicated sentence forms than you will find in freshman or sophomore writing. Certainly it is well to ignore errors in parallel construction until after the less difficult errors have been conquered. But when your class is ready to consider it, how are you to explain it?

Since pupils are familiar with the term "parallel" from their study of mathematics, I have found the easiest approach a visual one. Take such a sentence as: "When the boat left Honolulu, the natives commenced (1) to shout good-by, (2) to throw flowers, and (3) waving their arms above their heads." If you place on the board

$$\ldots \text{ natives commenced} \begin{cases} (1) \text{ ———} \\ (2) \text{ ———} \\ (3) \text{ ———} \end{cases}$$

with the question, "What is the relation between *commenced* and the three following statements?" the grammatical connection is at once clear. Then follows the logical conclusion that parts of a sentence serving the same grammatical function must have the same grammatical form. Again take such a pupil-made specimen as this: "My father told us how as a boy he had come to this country, when it was winter he had suffered from cold and hunger, and that at times homesickness had made him completely wretched." Obviously the writer wishes a summary statement and feels, correctly enough, that these three facts belong in one sentence. What are you to do? Surely you have not used this sentence to its maximum capacity if you are content to let it pass with the quick revision of: "My father told us how as a boy he had come to this country, how in winter he had suffered from cold and hunger, and how at times he had been so homesick that he had been completely wretched." That revision will do, but the pupil should see that there is not just *one* way but several ways of expressing this idea. Too often pupils feel that the teacher's way, for mysterious reasons, is the right one. It would be wise to make sure that the principle of parallel construction is clear by again using some such device as this:

My father told us
    1. how . . . 1. that . . . 1. in his boyhood . . .
    2. how . . . 2. that . . . 2. in the winter . . .
    3. how . . . 3. that . . . 3. during the first year . . .

This last device may seem a little absurd to you, but until pupils grasp the idea of parallel form, it is wise to call for all possible construction. Classes then see how flexible sentence building may be and begin to realize that not *one form* but *any form used consistently* will give the desired parallel relationships.

While teaching parallel construction you should also consider connectives, so that the pupils may see the promise of parallel construction contained in the correlatives *either . . . or, neither . . . nor, not only . . . but also, both . . . and.* If, however, the pupils are to use these forms with habitual correctness, their ears must also be trained so that they can "listen" intelligently to their own sentences. Over and over again it is the sound of the sentence that determines whether the use of correlatives is or is not desirable. With training, pupils can learn to detect by sound the ragged effect of nonparallel wording even before they are conscious of the shift in grammatical construction.[1]

But the intelligent use of parallel construction, like intelligent use of the balanced or periodic sentence, calls for a certain maturity of mind, since all three are closely concerned with the

---

[1] Seniors in high school ought to be sufficiently "ear-minded" to recognize a balanced sentence or—perhaps with a suggestion from the teacher—to reorganize their own sentences in the following manner:

First version: "The ninth-year boys liked Tom Sawyer best of any fiction character, which was different from the girls who voted Jo Marsh the best character."

Changed version: "The ninth-year boys liked Tom Sawyer best of any fictional character; the girls preferred Jo Marsh."

logic of thinking. When pupils' thinking becomes less childish, then provide them with a more mature form to match their more mature thoughts. But it is wise to remember one thing: If you place your emphasis upon form, you tend to shackle your pupils' thoughts. If you place your emphasis upon the logic of the idea and show repeatedly how thought relationship may be indicated by form, you are aiding pupils to develop the power to think more clearly. In other words, you are assisting them to make intelligent use of English as a tool.

Another type of nonparallel error in high-school composition is known as "nonparallelism through omission." An example of this form is: "She is a woman who has no love nor interest in her children." Since the preposition *in* cannot serve for *love* as it does for *interest,* it is necessary to insert the preposition *for* after the word *love.* But remember that the same statement is not true in such a sentence as: "He played baseball, but he took no interest nor pleasure in golf." Here the one preposition *in* is suitable for both *interest* and *pleasure;* hence its omission following *interest* is desirable. A second type of omission that leads a pupil into difficulty is illustrated by this sentence: "John knew what was customary, but his friend did not." The substitution of "knew what was customary" after "His friend did not" is, of course, ungrammatical, but it is the only substitution logically possible. The sentence, therefore, must be altered to read: "John knew what was customary, but his friend did not know." A third type of careless omission is that of leaving out the second *the* when that word determines whether the writer is talking of one or of two separate things or persons. This type of error is illustrated by the sentence, "I went to the stove and icebox." Here a second *the* is essential. Again it is seen in the omission of the second *to* in such a sentence as "He wrote to his father as well as me."

E. Develop Your Pupils, Not Your Theories

In working with sentence manipulation, it is obvious that punctuation must be discussed. Although a later chapter will deal with the general topic of punctuation, it enters here, for you must realize that the pupil's writing cannot be developed systematically, one topic at a time. Spelling cannot occupy one year, grammar a second, punctuation a third, sentence manipulation a fourth, and theme writing a fifth. The use of the comma belongs to your grammar lesson when you are teaching the use of long introductory dependent clauses; it belongs when you teach reduction of clauses to participial phrases; it belongs when you teach apposition and its uses. You should show the necessity of a comma with certain introductory adverbs or prepositions where the sense of the sentence depends upon its use. For example, "Ever since we have protected him" means nothing; but "Ever since, we have protected him" is a clear statement.

What advantages do you see in interpreting "Functional Grammar," the title of this chapter, in so broad a fashion that rhetoric, punctuation, and devices for limiting themes may be discussed under that heading? The disadvantages are, of course, obvious at once. It is certainly much easier to teach one thing at a time. You can make neat, clear-cut plans; you can progress logically—if no one asks an anticipatory question—from point to point in orderly fashion; you can cover ground rapidly. Probably the lecture method would be most effective. But, fortunately, pupils in high school are not given to passive listening. In high school a subject must be made alive, and material must be taught when needed. If theme writing is being done, many problems arise at once. Of course it is wise to emphasize one thing at a time—grammar at first, perhaps—but while teaching that one topic, you should give incidental instruction in allied topics that belong with it and enrich it. You will find a discussion of "oblique" teaching in the first paragraph of this chapter, but remember here that functional grammar, taught for the purpose of making sentences correct, clear, and forceful, must also be stretched to include: (1) sentence formation; (2) sentence variety; (3) rhetorical effect of sentences; (4) word choice; (5) punctuation. In other words (although functional grammar is your subject), you are not actually teaching functional grammar. You are teaching growing boys and girls who have immediate need of the material which you can give. Your business is—as expertly as possible—to help them to grasp some of the recognized devices for expressing thought clearly and forcefully.

If you are an inexperienced teacher you are in danger of losing your perspective. You may think of the bulk of information to be imparted as of primary importance. Just as long as you are "subject-minded," you are looking at your problem from an uneconomical point of view. Boys and girls are not empty bowls to be filled as you see fit. Rather they are swimmers who should be acquiring the necessary technique to keep them afloat. You are the swimming teacher. You may (many teachers of English do) throw them out into the troubled waters to sink or swim. You may be a theorist and keep them long on dry land teaching them breathing exercises and arm and leg movements. But it is to be hoped that you sense their pleasure in actuality and put them into the water with just enough knowledge to float them. When they can float, you give clearly, one by one, the needed instructions. The teacher of English who attacks grammar without correlating it with actual sentence improvement in written themes is like the swimming teacher who instructs one month in leg movements, the next in arm movements, but who concerns herself not at all with actual swimming.

How are you to begin?

1. You should look at your pupils and their needs.

2. You should think out the clearest method of imparting what you know.

3. You should correlate the material that can most easily be learned in related form.

4. You should study your group and your individuals to see what processes block their minds, what prove easy for them, and how you, the expert, can most efficiently clarify difficulties.

This plea for clarification is not a plea for "learning made easy." It is a plea for teaching made intelligent. Much teaching has been stupid, clumsy, dull, in spite of the fact that any mechanic knows that there are right and wrong ways of working.

Below are exercises to test both your own knowledge and your skill in presenting that knowledge to a class. Remember that it is necessary for a teacher to have endless illustration of the *same* principle under *different* guises, so that a class may learn to recognize the principle without becoming distracted by its dress; hence each principle below calls for varied illustrations. You will find it wise, presumably, to refresh your memory on certain technical points before you attempt to give expert advice on the best way of teaching them. The reading references will give you suggestions, but it would also be wise to consult your grammar and *Practice Leaves*—if you possess them.

SUGGESTED EXERCISES

Read a number of the references listed at the end of this chapter before you attempt these exercises. In these exercises you test both your knowledge and your ability to impart that knowledge with interest and dexterity. You should file under the general head of Sentence Manipulation any work that you do here. It should be useful to you later in your high-school classes. See Appendix A, "Your Filing System."

1. **Variety.** Make a series of related simple subject-verb sentences upon some topic of interest to high-school pupils. Alter these sentences by the devices suggested so that the passage has greater force, brevity, interest gained through variety. List the exact grammatical constructions that you have used in your changes. In parentheses after each change in your second set of related sentences indicate what grammatical construction you have used.

2. Adverbs. Make ten original sentences, containing adverbial elements that would serve for a high-school dictation exercise. Indicate what use in the sentence is served by the position of the adverbial element. Emphasis and sound should, of course, determine the position.

3. Revision. Plan a ten-minute lesson to be carried out on the board in which you—with the aid of your imaginary high-school class—build, revise, "listen to," and finally obtain a paragraph of some eighty words upon some topic of interest to high-school pupils.

4. Participles. Work out a simple twenty-minute exercise with participles in which you have a wealth of illustration. Write a brief paragraph explaining how you would teach participles, as distinct from gerunds. Remember that the subject matter need not be dull.

5. Models. Garner from your reading some dozen sentences that show vitality and excellent economy. In each instance indicate the grammatical device used to obtain the desirable result.

6. Transposition. Work out eight sentences each of which will permit from two to four changes in emphasis by shifting the subordinate elements. Again take care to make the changes striking, perhaps amusing.

7. Connectives. Work out four ten-minute board lessons on connectives. Teach the implied relationship in some of the more usual words or phrases, progressing from the simple *and* and *or* to the more difficult *but* and then to the more subtle implications. Do not try to cover too much ground.

8. Conjunctive adverbs. Make a twenty-minute board lesson on conjunctive adverbs with proper semicolon punctuation. Make clear by many illustrations why they are conjunctions, why adverbs, and how they differ from those identical words used in such a sentence as "He is, nevertheless, a very good player." This last point is confusing. This type of work would be unsuitable for freshmen or perhaps for sophomores; their ideas are not semicolon ideas.

9. Reduction. Plan a lesson in sentence reduction in which you place long grammatically correct sentences upon the board, and then slash out various parts. Reduce those sentences to about half their former length without reducing their thought. Make this a dramatic example of intelligent cutting. Label with the grammatical name the part cut and the part substituted. (Recall Stevenson's "Any story can be made a good story by judicious use of the blue pencil.")

Before you attempt to write any of these suggested exercises, turn to Chapter IX and note what use is made of varied sentences in actual theme writing.

SUGGESTED READINGS
References for Your Own Guidance

The English Language Arts, Vol. I, N.C.T.E. Curriculum Series, Dora V. Smith, Director

Read Part III, Chapter 12, "The Modern View of Grammar and Linguistics." Observe that "usage" or "functional" grammar is "grammar" taught intelligently.

1. Perrin, Porter: *Writer's Guide and Index to English,* rev. ed., Scott, Foresman, 1950

An excellent teacher's guide—particularly for the first years of teaching. Consult chapter headings.

2. Pooley, Robert C.: *Teaching English Usage,* Appleton-Century, 1946

Read entire. Common sense and knowledge are here combined as in *Writer's Guide* listed above.

3. Hodges, John C.: *Harbrace College Handbook,* Harcourt, Brace, 1946

Convenient for quick reference.

4. Richards, I. A.: *The Meaning of Meaning,* Harcourt, Brace, 1938

Appendix A. Read paragraph one. Does it shock you? Many modern teachers agree in large part.

5. Fries, Charles Carpenter: *American English Grammar* (N.C.T.E.), Appleton-Century, 1940

Read Chapter 11, "Some Inferences from This Study for a Workable Program in English Language for the Schools"; then examine former chapters.

6. Kaulfers, Walter V.: "Grammar for the Millions," *Elementary English,* Vol. 26 (1949), January and February issues

From the English Journal

1. Minton, Arthur: "Grammar Makes Sense," Vol. 36 (1947), pp. 26-29

Teaching sentence building: a combination of functional grammar and ideas expressed.

2. Moir, William: "Glamour in Grammar," Vol. 40 (1951), pp. 388-491

Grammar required, the teacher makes it "much less painful" than "the usual approach."

3. Tichenor, T.: "Sentence: Basis for Grammar and Composition," Vol. 37 (1948), pp. 361-64

4. Leer, Margrete: "Building Sentence Patterns by Ear," Vol. 38 (1949), pp. 197-200
Try it.

5. Frogner, Ellen: "Grammar Approach and Thought Approach in Teaching Sentence Structure," Vol. 28 (1939), pp. 518-26
Students show greater ability in writing if they work on combining their own choppy sentences instead of studying grammar or diagraming.

6. Davison, Ethel B.: "Power from Sentence Patterns," Vol. 39 (1950), pp. 379-84
"Discriminate between the false and the true . . . ideas expressed." Place ideas above grammatical terms. Ironic that such advice is needed, but it is.

7. Loban, Walter: "Studies in English Which Assist the Teacher," Vol. 36 (1947), pp. 518-23
Read; then attempt to banish nonessentials. "Teaching systematic grammar is no substitute for teaching English usage."

8. Depew, Ollie, and Bork, Edith: "Grammarians' Gobbledygook" (Round Table), Vol. 39 (1950), pp. 393-94

9. Clark, Bobbie Godlove: "Maybe Exercises Aren't So Bad After All," Vol. 39 (1950), pp. 455-56
Sentence drill, dictation, blending of drill and imagination, "good fun" for the teacher and class. "An English class must be interesting."

10. Cook, Luella B.: "Teaching Grammar and Usage in Relation to Speech and Writing," Vol. 35 (1946), pp. 188-94
"The 'place of grammar' . . . is largely *inside the teacher's head* to be drawn out and used at need rather than taught outright . . . this side of college." *Read.*

11. Andrews, Joe W.: "Audio-Visual Aids for Teaching Grammar," Vol. 40 (1951), pp. 165-66

12. Robinson, Mary Margaret: "Using the Opaque Projector in Teaching Composition," Vol. 35 (1946), pp. 442-45
This plan for teaching allows all the class to center its attention on the blackboard copy and to see how sentences can be improved in wording, punctuation, spelling.
A great timesaver.

CHAPTER IV

Four Years' Growth: Spelling, Punctuation, and Interdepartmental Co-operation

W HEN you look back over the last two chapters, do you realize that four principles have been stressed? They might be summarized as follows:

1. The simpler forms of sentence construction and the most necessary mechanics of writing (*integrated with and motivated by theme work*) must be adequately illustrated and taught.

2. These few forms must be comprehended and consistently practiced by the pupils before they are allowed to pass to a higher grade.

3. Each year these few fundamentals should be augmented.

4. Throughout the four years any failure to use these fundamentals correctly must be consistently penalized with ever growing severity.

In those four statements you have the entire teaching philosophy of the chapters just completed. If you accept that philosophy, what does it imply concerning you, the teacher? Of necessity you must view your teaching not week by week nor term by term, but as an articulated whole extending through the three or four years required of high-school pupils. You must establish minima; you must penalize if the comparatively few fundamentals taught are violated; you must overlook much. Above all, you must, under various guises, repeat and repeat and repeat, for nothing less than habitual correctness within the prescribed narrow field of the minima should satisfy you or your pupils.

But mere correctness is not enough. You are not a drill master;

you are a teacher of live written thought. Beware of so emphasizing mere correctness of form that it overshadows the importance of content. Beware of shackling thought instead of liberating it. For unless mechanics and original writing are integrated, unless the need for clarity, vitality, and interest motivates your teaching, you are making the knowledge of mechanics an end in itself —truly a dull procedure. Why should a high-school pupil know compound sentences to know compound sentences, or know the correct uses of quotation marks to know the correct uses of quotation marks? You, of course, agree now that all this unmotivated learning is absurd, but wait until you get into the schoolroom. There, it is all too easy to separate subjects into various compartments and teach each one as if it were an end in itself.

Perhaps the best advice that you can follow is this: *Take a four-year view of your high-school course in English.* Otherwise you will unconsciously lose perspective; you will attempt to hurry your classes; you will attempt to teach too much at a time. Often it is difficult to realize that a word correctly spelled on Thursday or a construction understood and rightly used on Friday may both, by Monday, have disappeared into the limbo of forgotten things. For your own guidance you need some constant reminder that forms do escape. A helpful one is a year calendar, one for each class, with the minima for each class stated, and with special marks at ever increasing intervals reminding you of the necessity of minima reviews and tests. These year plans or calendars have many uses. What are they? They tend to increase the regularity of repetitious drill under different forms, to remind you of dictation *before* a certain procedure is begun. They make certain the repetition of that identical dictation later. They recall the necessity of watching a certain pupil's progress chart, of speaking a word of appreciation at the end of some particularly hard struggle, of arranging for personal conference days in advance of some special problem, of utilizing some community event, holiday, or season in timely fashion.

So far there are three important phases of high-school work that we have touched upon but incidentally. These are the teaching of punctuation, spelling, and the work in vocabulary building. Each requires slow growth throughout the four years. Each is peculiarly dependent for existence upon the teacher's own knowledge and interest, and upon her comprehension of her responsibility to the pupils and to the community. Each can, as a rule, be omitted or slighted without causing any very general discontent among the authorities of the school. In fact here are three phases of work in high-school English teaching that, important as they are, owe their existence very largely to those teachers who are endowed with a "teaching conscience" and a keen realization of the present and future needs of their pupils.

As might be expected perhaps, each phase is, unfortunately, often disregarded. Punctuation is merely a matter of clear thinking. Spelling, some high-school teachers feel, should be taught in the grades; after that, it becomes a personal problem for each pupil—and, at any rate, a crowded curriculum has no room for it.

Vocabulary building, on the other hand, is essential, they would say, in high school; but acquiring words is more or less like acquiring a knowledge of Amos 'n' Andy over the radio or like recognizing a popular tune. Neither of these things is taught; pupils merely acquire them. Of course a particularly bad ear will not retain words, just as it has no flair for a tune; or a poor eye cannot visualize, just as some eyes cannot recognize color. For these unfortunates there is little hope.

It is a pleasant philosophy for a busy teacher, and it is evidently more widely practiced than widely admitted. But it is a philosophy that works hardship upon the future teachers, stenographers, businessmen of small means, writers of friendly letters, and college freshmen. Except in rare instances they need to be *taught* how to spell, how to punctuate, and how to use new words intelligently.

I. SPELLING

Let us consider first the question of spelling. What theories do you cherish about it? How well and how easily do you spell? Have rules helped you? Have you ever consulted the dictionary for the same word more than twice? When you were in grade and high school, were you *taught* spelling or were you merely required to spell words? When all is said and done, is spelling a thing that can be taught? Or is it simply a thing that can be learned? Do you think of spelling and the teaching of spelling as dull or interesting?

After all those queries, let us begin with the last. Like almost any other thing in high school (I except carnivals, athletics, and dramatics) spelling is interesting or dull according to the way that you, the teacher, regard it. Perhaps in no other one phase of English teaching has more concentrated research been carried on than in that of spelling. It is not sufficient, therefore, that you recall how *you* were taught and follow in the footsteps of your former instructors. You must find out what modern thinkers believe concerning its teaching; you must discover what methods are advised, advised after scientific investigation; and you must attempt to build your teaching of spelling upon a scientific basis.

One note of warning is necessary. As you read, you will gradually become aware of the fact that most of the research is based upon grade-school groups; hence many of the words are presented with emphasis upon their meaning. Your problem is somewhat different. High-school pupils tend to misspell words like *too, disappear, separate, dropping*. The meanings of the words are clear; they have appeared in the pupils' writing, correctly and incorrectly spelled, for many years. Not less but more difficult, then, is the problem that awaits you in high school, for you must:

1. Awaken your pupils to discontent with their former careless spelling.

2. Arouse in them a sense of their own responsibility for spelling all the words in their themes correctly (a sense of responsibility often termed "spelling conscience").

3. Show them the necessity for keeping a personal list of all their misspelled words upon which, from time to time, you will test them.

4. Teach them *how* to study a word intelligently.

5. Provide them, through tests *before* they have studied their lists, with a knowledge of what words they do and do not know.

6. And supply tests of spelling—spelling words in interesting sentences and paragraphs—frequently enough and with sufficient repetition of the same words so that the correct forms may become fixed.

There is, doubtless, nothing new to you in these six statements. But back of these statements must lie carefully planned and conscientiously, vigorously prosecuted campaigns if they are to be more than an amiable declaration of theory decorating your course of study. Probably the most helpful book that you can buy (fortunately an inexpensive one) is Lippincott's *Horn-Ashbaugh Spelling-Book*, for grades one to eight, compiled after long scientific investigation by Drs. Horn and Ashbaugh. When you consider that even in the sixth-grade lists such words occur as *hoping, dropped, surprise, ninth, until, occurred, forty,* you will, if you have viewed high-school themes, realize that there is much here to interest you. Although I shall summarize them, I shall not give in detail the directions for learning words—directions given in four pages of instruction—for you should consult the book and, if possible, possess it. The steps advised are as follows: The pupil should: (1) look at the word, pronounce it, try to visualize it syllable by syllable; (2) say or whisper it; (3) compare the mental vision with the printed page while saying the letters; (4) again attempt to visualize it; (5) again compare the image with the original; (6) write the word; (7) compare it with the original; (8) write it again three times. If any of the three copies contain an error, the pupil is told to begin with the first direction and to repeat the process.

The proper procedure for the teacher is also definitely stated. (At the end of this chapter see the reference to the investigation by Dr. Horn recorded in the *Eighteenth Yearbook*.) Unless further research contradicts the method given here, you would do well to conform to it, although there is at present some slight disagreement with Dr. Horn's suggested procedure. In the various spelling books [1] widely used today you will find, for example, some lack of uniformity upon the following two points: (1) whether the teacher should test pupils *before* they have studied their spelling lesson; (2) whether the teacher should dictate spelling words or should dictate paragraphs in which these words appear. The compilers of popular spelling books, however, if they mention the following questions at all, are agreed that:

1. Each pupil should keep a list of his individual errors, and this list should form the basis for much of his spelling work.
2. Reviews should be given at specified times and at varying intervals.
3. Individual progress charts should be kept.
4. If spelling lessons are given in the form of dictated paragraphs, these paragraphs should contain interesting material. They also agree that pupils must be awakened to a pride in correct spelling before spelling can be taught effectively.

A. *Changing Fashions in Spelling Instruction*

In the past, emphasis has been laid upon spelling words in lists. As you know, this method has very generally given place to paragraph dictation, paragraphs which employ the words to be tested. Also in the past much emphasis has been placed upon trouble spots in words, those letters that pupils find most difficult to remember correctly. Probably the word *separate,* with its troublesome *a* often written *e* in the second syllable, is one of the best-known examples. The practice of pointing out this trouble

[1] Bohne, Emmitt: "Methods of Teaching Spelling. Analysis of Spelling Books" (1928), an unpublished investigation made under the direction of Dr. Almack, Stanford University.

spot [1] and in some fanciful way centering pupils' attention upon it is now under debate. Recent scientific investigators seem to discourage this device. They substitute careful pronunciation, syllable division, attempted visualization—attempted until successfully accomplished. All the teacher-pupil activity of the past expended upon 'devising ingenious and amusing methods by which to remember the correct letter placement is today frowned upon as a bit of waste energy. "Why not," the investigator would say, "teach the word itself? Why invent machinery, spending time and effort to do it, when all that you need to do is to get your group to visualize the word as it is?" At times that scientific admonition will remind you of the statement "To catch a bird, put salt on its tail." *When* you get a pupil near enough to a word to visualize it, correct spelling is practically assured.

In the past, perhaps "sugar coating" played a rather important part in the use of elaborate devices. In my own case—and I used it lavishly—I suspect that ignorance of a better method, amusement at my own inventiveness, and an honest desire to obtain correct spelling (motives not equally worthy) all goaded me on in my spelling activities. I had not analyzed my own procedure until a foreign child, regarding me stolidly, made the analysis for me: "I like to spell. You bees so funny in it." The injunction "Be funny" would be bad advice. Each one of you must, to a certain extent, invent your own method, and scientific investigation should keep you from certain of my aberrations; and yet—I am not a complete convert to any *one* way of presenting *all* words. Logical as the suggested methods doubtless are, you, as a classroom teacher, must recognize that live boys and girls may at times demand an unscientific procedure—or rather a procedure which becomes scientifically correct if it produces the desired emotional and intellectual responses that you must have for successful work. High-school pupils thrive upon a procedure which

[1] Ward, C. H.: *What Is English?* pp. 45-53.

is scientifically methodical, but it must be enlivened by the dramatic, the unexpected, the humorous. It is true that pupils learn correct spelling by correct visualization, but how does that bit of pedagogical information profit you if you cannot make your pupils desire to visualize? Remember this generalization: Any device that distracts a pupil from the issue at hand is harmful; any device that centers attention more firmly upon the problem (if more concentration is needed) is desirable. You must be the judge. But even in these days of change you will find the following three statements true:

1. The correct spelling of a word must be made to seem of importance. The more common the word and the more commonly misspelled, the more effort will be required. Thus *its, too, their,* require herculean effort to give them significance, while *the moon's shinning through the trees* can by its absurdity impress itself.

2. Self-correction of these common words *before* papers are accepted becomes a dramatic necessity—dramatic if the teacher but make it so. If you treat a word as sufficiently important so that conquering it seems worth while, you may eventually find it impossible to pass a paper in which this demon is misspelled.

3. A genuine concern as to whether words are correctly spelled must be aroused if the poor speller is ever to conquer his weakness.

Once more, let us consider trouble spots in words. What is your own experience with them? You have Dr. Tidyman's authority for the practice of underlining those letters that allow themselves to become confused. You have Dr. Horn's statement that the practice is probably a waste of time. Is there a middle ground?

A rather enlightening experiment was carried on by Mr. Harry V. Masters [1] in which he submitted a certain list of words to three groups of two hundred each. These groups were drawn from eighth-grade pupils, seniors in high school, and college seniors. The statistics obtained for two of the words, *pneumonia*

[1] Masters, Harry V.: "An Investigation to Determine the Type and Causes of Spelling Errors," *Elementary School Review,* Vol. 4 (1927), pp. 113-116.

and *divine,* show an interesting difference. The two charts below
will illustrate it.

Spelling record for the word *pneumonia:*

> 200 eighth-grade pupils spelled it in 75 different ways.
> 200 high-school seniors spelled it in 39 different ways.
> 200 college seniors spelled it in 21 different ways.

Spelling record for the word *divine:*

200 eighth-grade pupils	90 correct	97 "devine"	8 other spellings
200 high-school seniors	130 correct	61 "devine"	no other spellings
200 college seniors	155 correct	43 "devine"	2 other spellings

Obviously the word *pneumonia* possesses no fixed trouble spot—
or it might be called a very Job of a word, and covered with them.
The word *divine,* on the other hand, has a fixed trouble spot.

Years from now, after you have corrected several miles of
pupil writing, you will discover that there are other words which,
like *divine,* lend themselves to but one type of error. There are,
for example, *seperate, grammer, supprise, goverment, discription,
finaly, Febuary, droped, fourty, truely, mathamatics.* These are
a few of the best known. After you have met them often, you
will realize that it is possible for you to foresee the *one* error
pupils will make if they make any; to arouse pupils to the danger; and, eventually, to make each pupil conscious of that misspelling in his own papers. Might it not be a wise middle course
to avoid pointing out any particular trouble spot in Job-like
words, but to stress and stress hard the recalcitrant letters in
those words possessing but *one* form of misspelling?

And how shall spelling words be tested? Since the death of
the social spelling bee, oral spelling has fallen into disrepute. Its
only business or social use today is the telephonic "Z as in zebra.
P as in Peter," which demands little training, each speaker selecting his own examples; hence written spelling (usually words in
paragraphs) is advocated.

B. *Spelling Rules*

Since the early thirties the question as to whether one should or should not teach spelling rules has been hotly argued. Through these years there has also been a growing recognition of pupils' individual differences and need for individualized instruction. In spite of such formidable names as those of Messrs. Horn, Ashbaugh, O'Shea, and Stormzand, all opposed to rule teaching (and by "rule teaching" I mean inductive teaching),[1] some voices have protested their elimination of all rules. Of three things you can be certain: A rule half-taught is a menace to correct spelling; a rule rich in exceptions is a source of confusion; only four of the many spelling rules have remained popular in schoolrooms.[2] In Harry V. Masters "Possible Value of Four Spelling Rules in Debate," [3] you will find an early protest, one worth reading. Mary S. Robinson, educated in schools that omitted rules and phonetics, writes: "When I began teaching, the fear that I should misspell a word on the blackboard . . . was a veritable nightmare. . . . I shall never forget my exultation when I found the rule about doubling final consonants. I felt as Christian must have felt when the burden slipped from his shoulders." [4] Another writes, "Much of the confusion in spelling is caused by the breakdown in phonetics, by double letters, and by variation of vowel combinations. . . . Certain rules, even though they have exceptions, provide directive value." [5]

[1] The inductive method: class or individual consideration of a word; search for other words similar in one particular respect; discussion of similarities, practice in spelling, formulation of a rule based upon many examples, learning of rule, class-made or teacher's version.

[2] Doubling the final consonant, dropping the final *e, ie* and *ei,* and changing *y* to *i* in certain plurals.

[3] *Elementary English Review,* Vol. 5 (1928), pp. 212-19.

[4] "A Plan for Remedial Spelling," *English Journal,* Vol. 37 (1948), pp. 35-38. Dictate no word lists, but words in sentences. Why?

[5] Ellenjarden Nolde, psychologist and English teacher, German Friends School, Philadelphia, *English Journal,* Vol. 38 (1949), p. 280. See also Chapter 12 in J. N. Hook's *The Teaching of High School English,* Ronald Press, 1950.

Conscious as we are of individual differences, is it odd that we attempt to banish rules for the Miss Robinsons in our classrooms or to force rules upon those students for whom spelling is no problem?

C. Possessives

Teaching the correct form of the possessive, an apparently easy process, calls, you will find, for much skill and patience. Unless you approach this work by first excluding all mention of plural possessives, and by fixing attention upon singular possessives only, pupils become hopelessly confused. The one rule: "Write your word; add an apostrophe; then add an *s*," deduced by the pupils from a study of many expressions such as *the chair's legs, Mr. Wells's novels, our school's reputation, Burns's poems*, seems simple. Personally, though I do not mention the fact in class, I always write *Wells' novels, Burns' poems*. For years I tried to teach that form in defiance of *chair's legs* and to the detriment of our *school's reputation*. Finally, realizing how often I received such agonized forms as "I saw Agne's mother," I determined that one rule must function for all singulars, common and proper. When a pupil did succeed in writing *Mr. Wells' novels*, I said nothing, but I did not teach that form. Why? I believe that a teacher should attempt to make the use of accepted forms automatic; then pupils can concentrate upon ideas.

After the singular possessives have been grasped and practiced, it is time to consider plural possessives. A class confronted by *horses' hoofs, chairs' legs, ladies' tailor*, and also by *men's clothing, women's hats, oxen's horns*, will finally formulate the rule: "Write the plural form. If the plural ends in *s*, add an apostrophe. If the plural does not end in *s* add an apostrophe and an *s*." It sounds easy, does it not? Just wait. After your town paper announces the coming of a *Ladys' Tailor*, and your pupils have written *Ladie's* and *Ladies's*, you will better understand how difficult the form is, and will agree with Mr. Ward that it is ". . . a mental feat to write men's and boys' clothing." [1]

D. Summary

How, then, shall you teach spelling?

1. Arouse in your classes a feeling that spelling is important.

2. Explain intelligibly to your pupils how words are to be studied.

3. See to it that the approved method of study is practiced by every pupil.

4. Secure evidence from each pupil that he has, and is working upon, his personal spelling list made from his own errors.

5. Drill upon selected weekly lists, tested, studied, and again tested in dictation.

6. Construct dictations that will contain systematic review of words formerly tested. (Remember oblique teaching.)

7. Encourage pupils to improve upon their previous records through frequent inspections of their individual progress charts and by occasional individual aid.

8. Last, hammer patiently upon those few errors which occur over and over again in the average high-school theme, and which must, a few at a time, be included in your minimum essentials.

If you do get results, it will mean that you are honestly meeting responsibilities that all high-school teachers tacitly agree to assume.

SUGGESTED EXERCISES

Read the references listed at the end of this chapter before beginning these exercises. Each exercise here suggested should be brief, should include some oblique teaching, should conform to the principles of teaching spelling just discussed, should be as arresting, interesting, amusing, as you can make it. A sensible plan to follow would be to establish a place in the college library where these plans can be examined. It would be wise to pool your ideas, to copy any device from a class member's paper that seems to you useful, and to keep these ideas in your permanent files. Try to develop a workman's pride in skillful and original devices. See "Your Filing System," Appendix A.

[1] Ward, C. H.: *What Is English?* p. 96.

1. Select three words that are difficult for you, if possible three that you have occasionally misspelled. Practice on them the instructions laid down in the Horn-Ashbaugh spelling book and summarized in your text. Observe your own reactions carefully. At what point do you tend to depart from instructions? Does the process require patience? What difficulties will presumably confront your pupils? Can you here apply any of your work in psychology?

2. If possible find a child (or an adult who has never conquered spelling) and persuade him to let you teach him how to spell. Many a freshman—and freshman instructor—would be honestly appreciative of your work, *but your approach must be tactful.* If the patient will follow directions, you will be entirely repaid for the time and effort expended.

3. Dissect some four words comparable to *tele graph, phono graph,* but containing other word elements, and for each of the four collect as many commonly used words obviously containing the same element as you can find. Think of some pictorial device to illustrate on the board each word group. Write a five-minute discussion of these words. Include here origin, original meaning, history of adoption—whatever seems to you valuable.

4. Make a separate dictation exercise not more than 150 words in length illustrating the two spelling rules (doubling the final consonant and dropping silent *e*). Each exercise: (a) should be a complete episode; (b) should be amusing or interesting; (c) should use at least twenty words to be spelled according to the rule illustrated; (d) should include three punctuation rules other than those of end punctuation; (e) should contain the test words underlined. If possible give this dictation to class members.

5. Make an interesting dictation containing all forms of the possessive. Combine with these forms some five spelling demons and two uses of quotation marks. At the end, list the demons and the rules in punctuation illustrated. Be brief.

6. Select from the following list five words. For the benefit of the other members of the class write a statement as to how you could teach them effectively so that: (a) interest is awakened in them; (b) the trouble spot (if one exists) is apparent; (c) each type of appeal is used.

It would be sensible to so distribute the words that all are illustrated.

across	guard
athlete	immediately
benefit	library
business	occasionally
calendar	occurred
chose—choose	probably
description	proceed—procedure
embarrass	restaurant
exaggerate	seize
February	sophomore
finally	vegetable
four—forty—fourteen	wondering—wandering
grammar	whose—who's
government	your—you're

II. PUNCTUATION

What is to be your attitude toward punctuation and toward the teaching of punctuation in high school? It might also be a pertinent question to inquire: How do you punctuate—by instinct, by rule, by the general sense of the passage, by all three?

Perhaps in no other phase of English teaching is there less clear thinking than in the field of punctuation. Normally the teacher who comments upon an oral report differentiates between such spoken errors as *would have went* and the far less noxious *everyone . . . they*. Normally also the corrector of a written theme deducts more for the misspelling of *disappear* than for the misspelling of *Diarbekr*. But too often that same corrector recognizes no hierarchy among the marks of punctuation. In an excess of democracy the omission of a period, a forgotten comma between co-ordinate clauses connected by *and,* or an apostrophe omitted between *8* and its accompanying *s* in such a sentence as "The 8's have it," are all marked with equal severity. And why not, the corrector might ask, since each is an error in punctuation?

Before we go further, it may be wise to recall that punctuation usage is a matter of custom, changing less rapidly, it is true, than fashions in dress or in manners, but changing certainly. That its purpose is to separate sentence elements becomes obvious by a glance at Caxton's slanting lines:

As a Cok ones sought his pasture in the donghylle/ he found a precious stone/ to whome the Cok sayd/ Ha a fayre stone and precious thow arte here in the fylth And yf he that desyreth the had found the/ as I have he wold have taken the up/ and sette the ageyne in thy fyrst estate/ but in vayne I have found the/ . . .

Or we might turn to the eighteenth century. The laced and boned lady in Amy Lowell's "Patterns" is not unlike the eighteenth-century sentence with its elaborate commas, its colons, its inset parenthetical expressions. Today the devotee of thickset punctuation, if he scanned our novels or periodicals of the twentieth century, would sigh in vain for the complicated constructions and punctuation of yesteryear. Glance at these two passages, one from Fanny Burney's *Evelina* (1778), the other from Edith Wharton's *The Children* (1928).

I made no answer, but quickening my pace, I walked on silently and sullenly; till this most impetuous of men, snatching my hand, which he grasped with violence, besought me to forgive him, with such earnestness of supplication, that, merely to escape his importunities, I was forced to speak, and, in some manner, to grant the pardon he requested: though it was accorded with a very ill grace; but, indeed, I knew not how to resist the humility of his entreaties; yet never shall I recollect the occasion he gave me of displeasure, without feeling it renewed.

But perhaps it added to the mystery and enchantment that to see her he had to climb from the dull promiscuity of his hotel into a clear green solitude alive with the tremor of water under meadow-grasses, and guarded by the great wings of the mountains.

Emancipate yourself from the idea, if you ever held it, that punctuation is a dead, unchanging thing. It is as alive as language itself. It is a convention of manners, as binding and as arbitrary as those courtesies of each age that mark the civilized from the savage. But just as we have discarded the Elizabethan ruffs or labored conclusions—"Believe me, dear Sir, your humble and obedient servant"—that marked our correspondence of a certain period, so we have discarded the long, elaborate, subdivided sentence. On the whole, dress, manners, expressions, have each become simplified. Instead of the cumbersome though magnificent sentences of Milton, we have briefer statements, shorter thought units. Similarly punctuation has been modified.

Before you begin teaching, you should discover what conventions are now accepted. To make your pupils punctuate like Scott is absurd. To draw your punctuation illustrations from Dickens is only a little less unreasonable than to pattern your dress after Dora Copperfield's or, if age require, Betsy Trotwood's. Where do you gather ideas as to how you should dress? From shopwindows, from other people, but principally from fashion magazines—conservative ones, I hope. For the current usage of punctuation marks, recent books published by reputable firms, and particularly magazines of good standing, are your safest guides. Mr. Ward in his entertaining and illuminating chapter on punctuation in *What Is English?* urges the editorial pages of good magazines as the safest guides, and particularly stresses the consistency and clarity of the *Saturday Evening Post* in its use of punctuation. In both of these statements I agree.

But if you admit to your pupils this state of flux in punctuation, will they feel that each may place his period or comma as he chooses? Not at all. You as teacher must find what uses are prevalent today; then, one after the other, teach those uses. And where should you begin? First, teach your pupils the fixed and unvarying use of the period or question mark at the end of a complete statement. Be dramatic about it. Make your class consider an omitted period or a comma supplanting a period at the end of a complete statement as ignorant as a *would have went* in an oral theme, as uncountenanced as the eating of peas with a knife, as shameful as confusing a track meet with steam engines and railroads. Obviously your drill upon subjects and predicates in grammar, your stress upon complete sentences, and your dogmatic insistence upon a period, not a comma, between unconnected, grammatically complete statements must be carried on at the same time. It is really all the same work. But later you must be careful not to overemphasize the importance of quotation marks, or of commas in series, or of any other mark in punctuation. If you do, you obscure the fact that the period omitted or wrongly placed is the supreme crime. Just recall what little effect capital punishment had upon crime when minor offenses were punishable by death. Remember the cry "Might as well hang for a sheep as a lamb." A boy may, perhaps with discomfort but certainly not with public disapprobation, come to school minus a handkerchief; but he is seized by an officer if he comes minus his trousers. It is unfortunate if through mishap a pupil loses his commas around a parenthetical expression, but it is iniquitous if he jams two separate sentences together with a comma. Is it more serious to telescope two sentences than to punctuate as complete an incomplete group of words?[1] If a pupil asked me that question, I think I should inquire, "Is it more serious to kill one man or two?" For, after all, language is not dead. Sentences if made of wingèd words live. And I should want my pupils to cultivate a feeling for each sentence. It is for this reason that I later advocate short themes, in which each statement may be considered.

[1] No longer can an incomplete statement be invariably termed incorrect. And it certainly is illogical to admit that what a writer like Sinclair Lewis does habitually is forbidden the beginner. To obviate this difficulty, I urge pupils to do as they please, but, since they are beginners and should know what liberties they are taking when they take them, I ask them to mark with a star every incomplete group of words punctuated as if complete. This idea, I believe, I derived from Professor Seward of Stanford University.

A. *What Punctuation Marks Must You Teach?*

Before you begin teaching it would be sensible to survey the whole field of punctuation and to determine if possible upon three things: (1) the uses of each mark; (2) the relative importance of each mark to the pupil; and (3) the order in which they should be taught together. It would be well, also, to decide what your attitude is on this question: Should pupils punctuate according to a given rule, or according to the thought of the passage, or sometimes in one way, sometimes in the other? When you have made up your mind concerning these questions, one more awaits you: What devices are best for inculcating the various uses of punctuation marks? Suppose we begin this investigation with a survey of what punctuation marks exist and how each is used. I shall number them according to the general order in which I should probably teach them, but since no two people would agree, the order is not, perhaps, significant.

1. Period:
    a. After a complete declarative or imperative sentence
    b. After abbreviations
1. Question mark:
    a. After a direct question
    b. Within parentheses to express uncertainty as to the correctness of the assertion (not taught before the third year)
2. Comma:
    a. To separate members of a series.
    b. To set off parenthetical elements
    c. To separate quotations from such expressions as *he said*
    d. To separate clauses
    e. To separate parts of a sentence that might wrongly be read together
3. Quotation marks:
    a. To inclose quotations
    b. To inclose titles of chapters, single poems, etc. (not book titles)

3. Apostrophe:
   a. To mark possession
   a. To mark contraction
   b. To form certain plurals (*D's, 9's, and's*)
4. Italics:
   a. For book titles, periodicals (taught as soon as books are discussed in written themes)
   b. For steamships
   c. For foreign words and words taken out of their context (*français; Its* is a pronoun)
5. Colon:
   a. To set off the greeting which begins a letter
   b. To introduce formally a word, list, statement, question, or long quotation
6. Exclamation point:
   After words, expressions, or sentences to show strong emotion
7. Dash:
   a. To mark an abrupt break in thought
   b. To set off a summary statement from a statement or statements preceding it
8. Semicolon:
   a. Between co-ordinate clauses where the conjunction is omitted.
   b. Before conjunctive adverbs
   c. Between long clauses one or more of which contains commas
9. Dots:
   To mark omissions
10. Parenthesis marks:
    a. To inclose matters foreign to the main idea of the sentence or paragraph
    b. To inclose a confirmative symbol after a word (*two (2) dollars*)
11. Brackets:
    To inclose explanatory material

B. In What Order Shall You Teach Punctuation Marks?

If you admit the device of underlining to indicate italics as a part of punctuation, you have, all told, thirteen symbols. Some of these symbols your freshmen should know and use, not all of them. Probably the average freshman concerned with whole sentences and with gaining some variety in his sentence beginnings will have no use for a semicolon. As yet his thoughts are not semicolon thoughts. Probably he is better off without parenthesis marks and without dashes except to mark a broken thought. Brackets and dots of omission as yet are of little use to him. What is left?

1. The period, the most important mark of all, should concern him first and with it the question mark.

2. After the period, he needs to know the use of the comma (a) in series, (b) with quotation marks, (c) to set off parenthetical elements, (d) to separate long introductory adverbial clauses from the main clause, (e) to separate co-ordinate clauses joined by a conjunction, particularly with *but* and *for*.

Let us go back for a moment to see just what we mean by the words "to set off parenthetical elements." Certainly not all parenthetical uses should be considered, but in the freshman year these might well be taught: (a) appositives; (b) geographical names that explain other names, and dates that explain other dates; (c) mild interjections; (d) and explanations like *as you know, it seems to me,* etc.

If in the first year or year and a half or two years your pupils really learn to use the marks suggested and use them invariably when on their best behavior, you have done well. You have not bothered their heads about absolute phrases. You have never mentioned restrictive or nonrestrictive clauses. You have not mentioned semicolons unless you have perhaps suggested some day the substitution of one in lieu of an *and* that was weakening an otherwise good sentence. But you have given them tools for the kind of sentences they presumably write. If they need more tools, give them more. Three in the class may. Show these three, but others in the class are not ready and should realize that they are not.

C. How Shall You Teach Punctuation?

When you approach punctuation with a high-school class, you may be surprised to find that they consider each mark of punctuation and each use of each mark as a distinct law unto itself. For example, commas must surround words in direct address or in parenthetical expressions; they must also surround words in apposition; likewise they must surround names that explain other names and dates that explain other dates. But the average class will be slow to see that underlying those four uses is the general principle: Separate parenthetical material from the element that it explains or interrupts. Take the sentences:

> Will you, John, open the door?
> It is, I believe, too warm in here.
> Bob, the short stop, has a strained tendon.
> Chicago, Illinois, passed the law March 23, 1929.

When pointed out, not before, a class realizes the truth stated earlier: Punctuation from the days of Caxton down has existed for the purpose of separation. You are supplying reason that supplements and explains the rules. Am I urging you to tell your pupils, "Reason out all punctuation"? No indeed. The reason should be obvious to them just as the reason for saying "Good morning" should be obvious. In the latter case we wish to be polite, or are afraid of being rude. In the former case we wish, in order to be easily understood, to separate parenthetical material from that which it explains or interrupts. In both cases we have no particular choice; established usage largely determines what we do, though more dogmatically, of course, in the case of punctuation than in that of our morning salutation. Over and over again the question should arise: "Look at this comma. What are you separating?"

Perhaps you disagree with this self-conscious method of punctuation. You are, perhaps, convinced that punctuation should be almost automatic. If we write "March 23" our pen should instinctively add ", 1929." Very good. I agree, too. But what about automatic shifting of gears when you drive? Now, you may shift automatically, but just recall how long you found it necessary to go through a formula beginning: "What must I do? I should shift gears. First I must . . ." In teaching punctuation I should suggest the following order: First, write upon the board a sentence correctly punctuated. Present custom dictates the form. Second, discuss the reason underlying the custom and then show many examples before a definite rule is given. Third, present many examples for the pupils to punctuate, at first identical, later similar, and at last, similar but with the likeness well obscured.

Punctuation can be learned only through many repetitions. Where can you get examples? Mr. Ward in his *M.O.S. Book* series provides much material. *Trail Fires,* by the Misses Walker, Bartels, and Marye, is original and interesting. Other sentence booklets abound and may be had for little money. These printed pages which can be torn out are a saving to both teacher and pupil: to the teacher, for print is easier to read than manuscript; to the pupil because the elimination of all work connected with the sentence except that of placing punctuation marks, emphasizes punctuation unobscured by all the labor of writing, copying the correct spelling, keeping the margin straight. Here one factor, punctuation, has been isolated, and the pupil may center his full attention upon it. After he has punctuated, under guidance, one page or four pages or seven pages, if necessary, each one of which illustrates the setting off of parenthetical expressions and explanatory names or dates, he probably will not use the commas with invariable correctness in his own writing, but he is dull indeed if he does not comprehend the underlying principle. And if he comprehends it, what better foundation could you give him upon which to build correct form in his original themes?

It may seem more practical and logical to you to have a pupil work almost entirely from his own writing and properly punctuate that. But there is one flaw in such practice. Probably two-thirds of his sentences demand more or less complicated punctuation because they are awkward, badly made, rambling affairs. First, you need to show the pupil how to transpose, simplify, chop up his statements. By the time revision in material has been accomplished, he is in no state to fix free, unhampered attention upon the subject of punctuation.

But one difficulty may arise of a very practical nature. Suppose your principal disapproves of having pupils buy practice books. What can you do? You can buy several different ones yourself, have material placed on the board, dictate some of it, lend your books to the dullest. There are many ways of overcoming difficulties. There are also many textbooks that will clear or obscure the issue. An excellent guide which you would do well to follow is Porter G. Perrin's *An Index to English*. Open and closed punctuation, disputed questions as to the comma use, and the latest approved uses of that much-disputed mark, the hyphen, are there discussed and well illustrated. An older book but one that attempts some synthesis is the Greever and Jones *Century Handbook of Writing*. There, very clearly and sensibly, similarity of uses is pointed out. For example, the fourteen or fifteen uses of the comma are first stated as five; then subdivisions of these five uses follow.[1]

By this simplification, punctuation is made to appear easier and more reasonable. I used to go farther. It seemed to me reasonable to teach the semicolon and the comma together, since their functions are on the whole similar though of different magnitude. Now I know that I was in error. Beginners do not and

---

[1] Some texts still differentiate between single words in series and phrases or clauses in series, as if there were really an essential difference between the following sentences:

1. He heard the dull, heavy, blurred sound beneath his feet.

2. He listened to the purring sound, felt the jarring shudder of machinery, sensed the mastered power of the great machine.

3. If you look to the right, if you look to the east, if you look to the south, the same sight will confront you.

should not think in terms of semicolons. But when the time comes for instruction in semicolon uses, then, surely, the similarity in use should be pointed out. For example, the following sentences are alike and call for the same treatment.

1. The Boy Scouts started, each with his bacon, dried fruit, bread, and roll of bedding.

2. The sheep came in bunches of twenty, in straggling herds of a hundred, in great flocks of more than a thousand.

3. The girls decided upon the following division of labor: Marian was to secure music for dancing; Alice was to tell fortunes; and Mrs. Hellweg was to provide refreshments.

Probably the most difficult bit of punctuation to employ correctly, and therefore the most difficult usage to teach, is that of the comma in nonrestrictive expressions. Here very skillful teaching is necessary. Your business is (1) to fix in the minds of your pupils a clear idea of what constitutes a restrictive and a nonrestrictive expression, (2) to manufacture many examples, and (3) to withhold the name "restrictive" until the class comprehends clearly the logic underlying the construction.

Any textbook will tell you that a restrictive clause is one that "points out" or "limits" or "restricts" the word it modifies so that the thought of the main clause would be changed by its omission. Conversely, a nonrestrictive clause is one that can be omitted without affecting the thought of the main clause. As you realize, such a construction calls for far more intelligent thought than is demanded by the use of apposition, series, or even quotations. Here you are requiring adult thinking. Be reasonable. Postpone this work until the simpler uses of the comma and semicolon have become fixed habits. Then attack it after careful preparation. Unless the teacher is particularly skillful in her first discussion of this construction, pupils emerge with the idea that a sentence from which a restrictive clause is omitted will not "make sense." Why they get this idea is not clear. But since they do get it, of course all clauses look to them nonrestrictive. Then, apparently without reason, the teacher calls some one thing, some another. Since the sentences, with parts deleted, continue to "make sense," the pupils' minds block completely. Punctuation is not for them.

How shall you begin this dangerous subject? Often the use of a diagram clarifies the beginning. "Here for example," you explain as you put a square on the board, "is a yard. Here is the gate. Here," as you locate the gate by a mark and add some five crosses, each with a name, "are five fruit trees: two peach, two pear, and one apple. The apple tree stands by the gate." Then on the board you write, "The apple tree, which stood by the gate, blew down last night." The class sees that there is but one apple tree; it sees that the statement of its position is nothing but additional information; and it realizes that commas cut out the nonessential additions (nonrestrictive clauses) from the essential fact of the main clause. The real gist of the sentence is, "The apple tree blew down last night."

It is wise to choose your first illustration carefully so that the class does not at once discover how dependent the punctuation is upon the writer's interpretation. If that discovery comes too early, while the idea of restrictive clauses is only half-grasped, many pupils throw up their hands in despair. They believe that no one really knows about the construction, and that unless one is a teacher it is no use trying to grasp it. To make clear the meaning of "restrictive" some such sentence as this is useful: "Mary Smith who lives on Chestnut Street is not the Mary Smith whom you met yesterday." Obviously the sentence cannot read "Mary Smith is not the Mary Smith." After this idea of a restrictive clause has been made clear, it is time to return to the drawing on the board, to label all of the trees "apple" and then to reconsider the sentence. Again obviously, the clause "which stood by the gate" this time is essential to make clear which of the five apple trees blew down.

Perhaps all this seems to you rather childish. It really is not. If by diagram, by altering the context of sentences, by placing the emphasis upon the idea, not upon the commas, you can quickly and definitely fix in the pupils' minds the principle of restrictive and nonrestrictive clauses, you have done an admirably adult, admirably expert bit of classroom teaching. Of this you can be certain: By a wandering, confused discussion of restrictives and nonrestrictives you can block the minds of your pupils so successfully that many of the group will never understand the subject.

In your classroom as you present the various problems in punctuation, you will, if you are wise, garner a large quantity of illustrative material and file it for future use, with comments jotted on the margin indicating the kind of misunderstandings that arose. After a time you will have what for you and for your classes proves to be the soundest, most economical, most skillful approach to various knotty points. Before I mention a few of my favorite devices, I must call attention to that serpent lurking to corrupt your little Adams and Eves. These are the serpent's words "Place a comma wherever there is a pause." Satan must have cogitated long upon that sentence, for nothing else could so successfully undo your work in punctuation. Thomas hearkens to the voice. Thomas has adenoids and gasps for breath as he reads. Lucy across the aisle stammers with long pauses before all W's when she reads. Robert takes no chances and scans each individual letter; hence he dishes out his words like an ice-cream vender, one word spooned out at a time. And so following. Put your heel on the head of the serpent quickly if that head is ever reared in your own classroom.

D. What Devices May Prove Useful?

And now I shall end the discussion of punctuation with a list of a few devices that I have found practical.

1. **Cartoons.** Have you ever considered the desirability of using cartoons to drive home certain uses in punctuation? Just

as in teaching sentence forms you will find "stick" drawings useful (Father Stick for a simple sentence; Mother and Father Stick
for a compound sentence; Mother, Father, and Baby Stick for a
compound-complex sentence), so in punctuation, an absurd cartoon showing the use of the period, the comma, the semicolon
will serve to fix in the pupil's mind the use of that mark. Some
years ago no textbooks included cartoons; now they are widely
used. It may be that the popularity of the Sunday "funny paper"
first suggested their use to textbook makers. If the use of cartoons
in the schoolroom is new to you, you would do well to examine
the series called *Using English* by Lucy Chapman and Luella B.
Cook; the junior-high-school series called *English Activities* by
W. W. Hatfield, E. E. Lewis, and others; or *The Arch of Experience* by M. E. Clemo, and E. A. and L. V. Everett. At once you
will see how cleverly the well-made cartoon attracts attention,
drives home the idea, and renders that idea memorable. Punctuation teaching can be amusing and interesting or merely dull routine; all depends upon the skill and resourcefulness of the teacher.

2. **Reminders on the blackboard.** If you can do so, it is wise
to set aside a strip of blackboard in your classroom and upon
it keep more or less permanent reminders of the right forms to
be used. Thus you can train your pupils to consult it and to correct their own themes for these particular errors *before* the paper
comes in to you. One of the reminders that I should use on such
a consultation board would be this:

His Her Its Our Their	These are pos-sessive pronouns.	Don't Can't It's Shouldn't	These are con-tracted forms. The apostrophe indicates that a letter is omit-ted.

The forms *its* and *it's* are easily confused. If each is taught with
similar words and if the two forms are not first associated, less
confusion occurs.

3. **Repeated practice.** Because freshmen need to write about books, they should learn early how to write book titles. On the consultation board it is wise to place the title of some book with which they are familiar and in the same sentence write also the title of one of the chapters in order that they may have the correct forms before their eyes. For example: Do you remember in *Ivanhoe* the chapter called "The Black Champion"? In *Poems of Today* you will like "The Highwayman" by Alfred Noyes.

4. **A consultation board.** When pupils advance to semicolons, they are often disturbed over what is and what is not a conjunctive adverb. It is a simple matter to list the more usual ones on the consultation board in some such fashion as this:

The following words when used as conjunctive adverbs are pre-ceded by a semicolon:

; hence	; therefore	; besides
; thus	; accordingly	; still
; then	; consequently	; nevertheless

But you have not ended the probable confusion, for you will have some dull but conscientious pupil writing, "He is; nevertheless often late to school." It is wise, therefore, to supplement the statement and the list with some such illustration as this:

He is, nevertheless, a parasite. (*Nevertheless*—parenthetical.)
He is a parasite; nevertheless he has his uses. (*Nevertheless*—conjunctive adverb.)

5. **Homely comparisons.** Each person must of course work out his own way of teaching quotation marks. But it is well to remember that pupils take pleasure in discovering the ingenuity by which the marks wigwag information as to the speaker and distinguish between his own words and words that he quotes. San Francisco children are familiar with the Chinese wooden or ivory egg that as it is taken apart reveals an ever smaller egg inside. Double and single quotation marks in a sentence such as

the following recall this toy. After a time pupils enjoy attempting to catch others by their ingenious inventions.

"Do you," Harold chuckled, "remember when we studied 'The Ancient Mariner,' and Miss Jackson said, 'John, please begin "Alone, alone, all, all alone," ' the day after your accident when you had to guard the wrecked machine all night?" Of course you would not begin with this complicated form. You would begin with a simple, "Come at once!" Harry shouted. Then you would probably say: "If Harry were speaking now, just what words would you hear?" You would show that quotation marks box in just what one would actually hear, and exclude all else. But there are other niceties. "Won't you come," Mary said, "to the dentist's with me?" takes careful explanation as to why the *t* in *to* is not a capital, why the question mark comes where it does, and why two commas are needed. "Won't you come?" Mary asked. "You'd enjoy it," takes much discussion before the reason for the period after *asked* becomes clear. Go slowly when you begin with quotation marks; don't be tempted by the Chinese egg too early, for capitals, commas, quotation marks, and end punctuation all seem difficult at first to the beginner.

6. **Verbal similarities.** Even in my college classes I find repetition of the term "absolute" rather helpful in order to fix the idea that an absolute phrase or, as it is often called, the "absolute nominative" stands "absolutely" alone, is not grammatically connected with the rest of the sentence, and must, therefore, be set off with a comma.

7. **Inconsistencies.** And what is your private belief and practice in regard to the comma before *and* in an a, b, and c series? Personally I like it. Personally I think that it indicates good thinking. But professionally I have to recognize that its use is passing. The writing upon the wall, particularly if I choose the wall called the *Saturday Evening Post*, contains no comma before the third of a series connected by *and*. If I am logical, I must let my pupils discard it. But with human weakness I write on the

board, "The Boy Scouts enjoyed their beefsteak, fried onions and ice cream." And even the most radical in my classes feel the sentence bettered by a comma.

8. **Changing standards.** In the same way you cannot afford to be overparticular about commas after introductory adverbial clauses if the meaning is clear, for periodicals are not. Watch the magazines and have your upperclass pupils watching. It is the height of the ridiculous to follow a manual that is not in step with the best usage of today.

9. **A local style book.** I have one suggestion for those of you who find yourselves burdened with an outdated manual of punctuation. Discuss with your classes this woeful condition. Wake them to a feeling bordering upon indignation that the school should have to use an old book. Why? Because you can stir them into the suggestion that you and they should make a style book for the school. There is no better way of teaching mechanics. Each usage must be canvassed thoroughly; numerous illustrations for each usage must be brought in; careful exercises must be made. Of course it is wise to arm yourself first with style books recently published, and with the best and most recent authorities; but even so your own reading, if wisely done, ought to prove your most valuable source of information.

III. CO-OPERATION IN TEACHING MECHANICS

There is one other practical device for securing decent form in mechanics, but I admit that it is full of difficulties. Let us take a purely imaginary case. Suppose that you require from your classes clean, orderly, fairly well-organized papers in which only whole sentences will be accepted. Suppose that in the papers and examinations in chemistry, history, and Latin the same standard is not demanded, and that the paper is graded upon content only. How much longer will it take you to gain the kind of paper that you wish? How much will the acceptance of careless writing in other courses undo the teaching in your own classes? Is it not like expecting good table manners from children but demanding them at only one meal out of four? The case is purely an imaginary one when certain schools are considered. Many a teacher of Latin or science is as demanding as or more demanding than you will be in his or her requirements concerning written work. But schools exist where just this type of illogical training continues. Would it not be wise for you to attempt to find out, quietly, courteously, the state of your pupils' writing in courses other than your own? No teacher *desires* poorly expressed papers. But in the pressure of teaching history or mathematics or science a teacher may readily feel that there is no time for giving instruction in the elements of English composition. After all, if a boy solves a problem rightly, why should he be censured for misspellings or for misused grammar? If he knows the facts concerning William the Conqueror, he knows his history whether he expresses it in half-sentences or in whole sentences. What do you think about this situation?

A device tried in some twenty or thirty schools—prosecuted vigorously or half-heartedly according to the principals' interest and the tact, enthusiasm, and energy of the teacher of English— was this: All teachers promise to do four things:

1. To agree upon one form for all papers and reject all other forms

2. To mark all misspelled words, and assume the responsibility for teaching the spelling of those often-used words peculiar to that particular subject. (Latin: *Caesar, tribune, forum,* etc. Mathematics: *geometry, triangle, parallel,* etc. Science: *oxygen, hydrogen, symmetrical,* etc.)

3. To require, except in outline work, whole sentences properly capitalized at the beginning and properly terminated

4. To report to the teacher of English on lists furnished by her, and on certain dates before the issuing of report cards, the standing in English usage of each pupil on the list. (These grades were in most instances merely plus or minus. They indicated whether the

teacher did or did not find the pupil able or, perhaps, willing to write neat papers, express ideas in whole sentences, and spell with reasonable correctness. If a minus was reported, the pupil receiving it was given a lowered grade in English composition, no matter how good the work was that he handed in to his teacher of English. The theory underlying this seeming injustice was that if he knew as much as he apparently knew in English, it would function in his other work.)

You may easily object to the system as I have sketched it. It was and is an experiment. It does, of course, work certain injustices. One teacher reports strictly; another is lax. A pupil who has done admirable work in composition is dismayed to find a lowered grade because of slovenly papers in history. You may argue that poorly expressed history is poor history; hence a lowered grade should be given. I agree, perhaps, but if in your school you want to get co-operation in the teaching of the mechanics of writing, as a practical measure it is wise to assume as much of the extra work as possible and to shoulder the unpleasant reduction of grade yourself. Some teachers of composition feel that it is unfair to ask them to assume this extra work. Perhaps it is. But there is a question as to whether, in the long run, it is extra work. Suppose a teacher of English felt that her pupils gained more from being checked on (1) form, (2) whole sentences, (3) spelling, in every paper they wrote, even if that checking were a little erratic and sometimes unfair, than they gained from one set of papers a month? To be quite honest, the teacher would gain some hours' time, for checking, deducting, recording even two hundred grades (and few teachers have that many pupils) would take less time than correcting, commenting upon, recording, two hundred themes. As I look at it, it seems to me that *from the standpoint of the teacher of English, this co-operation, if she can get it, is pure gain.*

But a word of warning is needed. If you have never taught, you may not realize just how difficult and how delicate a situation can arise in a school over this problem of co-operative teaching. You, the teacher of English, cannot, as a rule, broach the subject to the faculty. Why? Because you would seem to be criticizing them for receiving poor papers. You can, however, working through your principal, succeed perhaps in having some of the faculty look into the state of writing in your school. Almost without doubt they will find it to be bad. Your principal will feel that something should be done, and you and the committee may stumble upon some such plan as that just outlined. Someone will suggest that only the unsatisfactory pupils be reported. That idea sounds the death knell to the scheme, for teachers are both busy and human; hence be ready to meet such a suggestion. In one high school, Flathead County High School, Kalispell, Montana, the principal, Mr. Payne Templeton, instituted in addition to some such scheme a series of minimum-essentials tests given throughout the entire school. All of his teachers recognized the fact that decent form in writing was essential, and co-operated in an effort to obtain it. But even this system of co-operation under a principal who fully appreciates the importance of co-operative work was not established in a month or a year.[1] Do not rush into any co-operative scheme. Think it over, for it has many dangers ahead.

When you consider the first four chapters of this book, what do you find stressed? The teaching of a very few essentials through repetition, through the introduction of the game spirit and self-competition, through the blending of mechanics with the artistry of expression. And what are these few essentials, and how are they presented? I might summarize them as follows:

1. **Functional grammar** based upon the making of whole, properly terminated sentences and given life and vitality through its immediate use and through its constant association with vocabulary work and sentence manipulation.

[1] Templeton, Payne: "Putting the English Department in Its Place," *High School Teacher*, Vol. V (1929), pp. 214-215.

2. **Vocabulary work** scattered throughout all phases of class discussion, but motivated by the constant inquiry "Is this the best word to make your reader *see*, to make him *feel*, to make him *realize* your thought connection?"

3. **Spelling** first tested, then studied, each pupil the maker of his own spelling list—a list studied and retested in all the ways that an ingenious teacher can devise, a teacher who places full emphasis upon visual recall.

4. **Punctuation** taught slowly and in orderly sequence, not as a subject in itself but as a part of all written expression, with much information withheld until the writing of whole sentences is established.

5. **A minimum-essentials program** established through the co-operation of pupils and supported by the principal, a program unambitious in its scope, but inflexible in its demands within its narrow range of essentials.

6. **Co-operative teaching of the mechanics of written English** practiced by every teacher in the high school and vigorously promoted by the principal, so that decent manuscripts and the use of correct grammar, reputable wording, spelling, and punctuation are demanded in every high-school paper.

SUGGESTED EXERCISES

Before attempting these exercises read a number of the references listed at the end of this chapter. All material that you use should be suitable for pupils of high-school age and high-school interest.

1. Plan a board talk illustrating the fact that parenthetical elements are separated from the main idea of a sentence. Make a brief original dictation illustrating this principle. Write the steps of the introductory discussion and the dictation. State what oblique teaching you have attempted.

2. Plan three lessons, the last to follow some month or months after the other two, in which you teach quotation marks. Try to be clear, original, and interesting. Write out, with board illustra-

tions, the steps in each discussion. State with illustrations what oblique teaching you have attempted.

3. Make a set of twelve sentences in which commas are required. These commas are to illustrate only this one rule: "A comma is used to separate parts of a sentence which might erroneously be read together."

4. a. Write a dictation exercise consisting of twelve sentences illustrating restrictive and nonrestrictive clauses. Punctuate properly. With two of the sentences indicate how you would explain to the class that one of the sentences was and one was not restrictive.

b. Write why you consider the following sentence restrictive or nonrestrictive: "An old sailor who had been growing more and more angry jumped to his feet and stamped out of the meeting."

5. Construct a twenty-minute lesson on the semicolon with conjunctive adverbs. Write a clear explanation of why the words are termed "conjunctive adverbs," and give illustrative material to make your point clear and easily remembered.

6. Give a lesson upon the colon. Hand in an outline of the steps of your talk and eight illustrative sentences. State what oblique teaching you attempt.

7. As dramatically as you can, illustrate how the dash may be used to give life and vigor to a sentence. Make eight sentences without dashes; then in each sentence show the improvement brought about by the insertion of a dash, and probably by some slight rearrangement of words.

8. Teach one very brief lesson on the difference between parentheses and brackets.

9. Make a dictation exercise for a senior class that covers all uses of the comma, semicolon, apostrophe, period, and question mark. Number each mark. At the end of the paper repeat each number and state the use. Make this work as brief as possible.

SUGGESTED READINGS

I. WORK IN SPELLING

A. References for Your Own Guidance

The English Language Arts, Vol. I, N.C.T.E. Curriculum Series, Dora V. Smith, Director

Read Part III, Chapter 8, "Planning Minimum Essentials, and Relative

Emphasis on Aspects of the Program." Does this chapter surprise you?
If so, why?

1. Horn, Ernest: "Principles of Method in Teaching Spelling as Derived from Scientific Investigation," National Society for the Study of
Education, *Eighteenth Yearbook,* Part II, Chap. III, pp. 52-77

2. ———, and Ashbaugh, Ernest J.: Lippincott's *Horn-Ashbaugh Spelling Book,* Lippincott, 1927, the Preface
The instructions to the teacher should be studied carefully and filed for
later use.

3. Perrin, Porter: *Writer's Guide and Index to English,* rev. ed., Scott,
Foresman, 1950
See page 766, groups of words that have traits in common. *Do not teach
lists of words,* but be ready to explain likenesses and, where useful, see
the separate article in the Index. Read the chapter "Spelling," pages 155-
68. The four rules listed have proved valuable.

The discussion of hyphens, pages 595-98, will prove useful, for fashions change.

4. Masters, Harry V.: "Possible Value of Four Spelling Rules in Debate," *Elementary English Review,* Vol. 5 (1928), pp. 212-19
In 1952 they are still accepted. See *Writer's Guide.*

5. ———: "An Investigation to Determine the Type and Causes of
Spelling Errors," *Elementary School Review,* Vol. 4 (1927), pp. 113-16

6. Cody, Sherwin: "A New Way to Teach Spelling," *Elementary English Review,* Vol. 5 (1928), p. 186

7. Archer, Clifford: "Transfer of Training in Spelling," *Elementary
English Review,* Vol. 5 (1928), pp. 55-61

8. Jenkins, William A.: "The Educational Scene," *Elementary English,*
Vol. 28 (1951), pp. 301-04
Much information on topics aside from spelling is also given here.

9. Chapman, Lucy, and Cauley, Thomas: *Language Skills,* Grade 10,
Harcourt, Brace, 1948
Read "Improving Your Spelling," pp. 452-79. How the rate of learning
can be increased through board work, illustration, division into types of
words, and dictation.

B. References Concerned with the Teaching of Spelling

1. *An Experience Curriculum in English: A Report of a Commission
of the National Council of Teachers of English,* W. W. Hatfield, Chairman, Chapter XIX, "Spelling," pp. 257-61
How closely does this chapter agree with your text?

From the English Journal

2. Brown, Corinne B.: "Teaching Spelling with a Tachistoscope," Vol. 40 (1951), pp. 104-05

". . . a 43 per cent increase in retention of each spelling lesson as tested weekly." Do you approve of lists of words or of words selected from individual errors?

3. Broehl, Francis: "Spelling in Senior High School," Vol. 37 (1948), pp. 200-02

". . . basic lists . . . continued through junior-senior high school should be individual lists of errors." Ideas for spelling emphasis.

4. Nolde, Ellenjarden: "Remedial Spelling," Vol. 38 (1949), pp. 279-81

5. Robinson, Mary S.: "A Plan for Remedial Spelling," Vol. 37 (1948), pp. 35-38

A time-taking but efficient program for correcting misspellings. Causes of misspelling analyzed.

II. WORK IN PUNCTUATION

A. References for Your Own Guidance

1. *A Manual of Style*, 11th ed., University of Chicago Press, 1949

You will find here a recent authoritative statement on punctuation usage. But remember that punctuation varies; there are few ironclad rules.

2. Perrin, Porter: *Writer's Guide and Index to English*, rev. ed., Scott, Foresman, 1950

Read Chapter V, pp. 131-54. ". . . a realistic view of punctuation instead of an approach from fixed rules . . ." Also consult page 716.

3. Hodges, John C.: *Harbrace College Handbook*, Harcourt, Brace, 1946

Excellent for quick consultation and exercises, pages 105-62.

B. References Concerned with the Teaching of Punctuation

1. Brown, Rollo: *The Writer's Art*, Harvard University Press, 1921, pp. 133-35

This paragraph on the subject of punctuation, quoted from Poe, raises the plebeian comma, semicolon, and dash into the realm of art. Consider it. Pupils can see the dramatic use of the dash; they can even see the neatness of the semicolon, but you will have difficulty in making the use of the commo appear to them aught but commonplace.

2. Olsen, Helen F.: "Teaching Basic Language Skills," *English Journal*, Vol. 39 (1950), pp. 249-53

What methods here are approved for teaching punctuation? What four classifications for teaching commas? Many useful suggestions.

3. Kinney, Lucien, and Dresden, Katharine: *Better Learning Through Current Materials,* Stanford University Press, 1949

Read "Current Materials in Teaching Fundamental Skills," pp. 19-23.

To awaken interest in punctuation and its relation to thought, pupils select passages from magazines or newspapers to read aloud. "Because the material is meaningful and important, the pupils are concerned that the complete idea be communicated." The reader asks the class "to judge from context and inflection" how the sentence should be punctuated. Punctuation, sentence construction, listening, and vocabulary are here combined.

4. Chapman, Lucy, and Cauley, Thomas: *Language Skills,* Harcourt, Brace, 1949

See pp. 380-451. Clear, logical progress shown here.

5. Lyman, R. L.: "Fluency, Accuracy, and General Excellence in English Composition," *School Review,* Vol. 26 (1918), pp. 85-100

BRIEF LIST OF STANDARDIZED TESTS
Mechanics and Effectiveness of Expression

1. *Cooperative English Test A: Mechanics of Expression,* Cooperative Test Service. For grades 7 through 12

Measures various phases of correct English and recognition of acceptable usage, grammatical usage, punctuation, capitalization, and spelling. Four forms: Q, R, S, and T. (Cost: 10-99 copies, 6 cents. For 100 or more, 5½ cents. Specimen set, 25 cents.)

2. *Cooperative English Test B-1: Effectiveness of Expression (Lower Level).* For grades 7 through 12

Measures elements influencing the effective use of English, including sentence structure and style, active vocabulary and organization. Three forms: R, S, and T. Prices are the same as for the preceding test.

Address: Cooperative Testing Service, 15 Amsterdam Avenue, New York 23, New York. It is economical to get the *Cooperative English Test, Single Booklet Edition (Lower Level).* Available in forms R, S, and T, it contains three complete tests, both 1 and 2 above plus *Reading Comprehension.* Price 13 cents a copy. Range is 7 through 12. Scales scores are provided.

3. *Ohio Scholarship Tests, English Usage,* Grades 10, 11, 12, *Every Pupil Test,* State Department of Education, Columbus, Ohio

CHAPTER V

Vocabulary Study

IT IS a brave person who dares discuss vocabulary building in the light of actual classroom procedures. No other subject in high school, not even spelling, is so entirely dependent upon the common sense, interest, and intelligence of the teacher. Usage, however, demands a comprehension of shades of implications more difficult by far than the mere arrangement of letters in a word. But the very fact that it is difficult and must of necessity grow with the growth of ideas makes it essential that vocabulary work should permeate every discussion, every piece of literature read, every composition assignment planned with the class, every talk by the teacher, every spelling lesson, every oral report.[1] It is almost as absurd to study words one day out of every week as it is to eat one's week's supply of salt every Wednesday at twelve. For both word study and salt must be scattered lightly over much of our food for brain or body.

The first stumbling block that appears when a teacher surveys the subject of vocabulary building is the size of the undertaking; the second is the difficulty of beginning. You visit one school. Every third verb used orally is wrongly used, but every pupil's book is open to an exercise based upon the accepted use of *may* and *can*. You go elsewhere. The seventh-graders are struggling with *shall* and *will*. The eighth-graders are lost in the mazes of *who* and *whom*. But these same youngsters *would have went* joyfully forth if they *seen* a circus parade approaching. You listen to a high-school report. The pupil has not the faintest conception that *and* may not be used in lieu of *but*. All, however, are concerned as to whether the speaker looked at his audience and stood

[1] For Vocabulary tests, see Chapter XII.

151

straight, hands out of pockets. Farther up in high school you find semicolons under discussion, but there is no discussion in progress as to the meaning of words such as *hence, consequently, therefore*—words that in themselves contain a distinct implication concerning the thought relationship existing between the two parts of the statement. The exact meanings of words—words important to thought, not mere niceties of the language—must be discussed and taught both directly and indirectly. Only by continuous oblique teaching of words and word combinations can pupils be provided with a language which is for them a usable tool.

How shall we make vocabulary study interesting? A colorless ninth-grader, after listening to a glowing talk by the principal, sought her out to say: "I liked your talk a lot. It had so many nice words in it." There it is. Those "nice" words that we want pupils to know must be beautiful in our mouths before we as teachers can interest others in using them. Would it, I wonder, improve our pupils' speech if we, as teachers, occasionally let ourselves build up in the classroom a story, a scene, an incident, an argument, so clearly, so dramatically, so vividly, that we were models of clarity and interest to our pupils?

I have profited by the late Dr. Krapp's scornful term "schoolma'rm English," correct, anemic, colorless English, that—afraid of mistakes and cowed by authority—has not vitality enough to make an impression upon pupils' minds.

I. HOW DO YOU MEAN TO BEGIN TEACHING VOCABULARY BUILDING?

There are three different approaches:

1. A study of the history of our tongue and of individual words
2. A study of "applied semantics"
3. A survey, with remedial work, of the pupils' knowledge and use of language

All three types of study are desirable in a well-organized curriculum. But remember, this type of work is not to be crowded into a day, a week, a "unit," nor confined to any one semester or year. The classics, written composition, magazine and newspaper reading, oral work—all offer rich opportunities for discussion of language, of words, of the influence of certain kinds of words upon thought. The grammatical and rhetorical approach we have always with us, taught either interestingly or dully. It is an important but often unrecognized part of grammar drill; discussion in spelling of roots, prefixes, and suffixes; sentence manipulation; reorganization of talks or written papers. (This type of work I have treated elsewhere.) Interest in words and in expression must be kept alive. Doubtless the first and most appealing approach is the historical, but before you picture dramatically the evolution of the different Indo-European tongues, it is well to awaken interest in words themselves. Then you are ready. Even junior-high-school pupils can grasp with genuine interest and enjoyment your picture of Parent Latin in Rome sending out his Sons to France and Spain. Later their great grandchildren return to Rome to find themselves embarrassed because of their "country" speech, their dialect, later to be termed "Italian" or "French" or "Spanish." [1]

Remember, it is the concrete picture that makes the abstract statement of interest. My own device is to picture an isolated farm where the father and mother, unable to say the letter *p*, rear their children in utter isolation. Would the children learn to say this unpronounced letter? The class agrees that they would not. Then, as you foresee, I turn to Grimm's law and suggest the Latin *pater* which became the English *father;* the Latin

[1] Quite small children can be disabused of the conviction that English is the "right" language, that "foreigners" are a bit ignorant when they choose to speak Russian or German or Chinese. In an Italian pension a woman at a table asked the Italian word for spoon. When told *cucchiaio*, she remarked, "Fancy all that just for *spoon*." Even adults may suffer from an arrogant attitude concerning the "rightness" of English.

piscis or *pes* which became the English *fish* and *foot*. Here, just as when you display the famous circle of Indo-European tongues—what are you teaching? Information? Not entirely. You are breaking down the unfortunate feeling of superiority common to young (and sometimes to adult) Americans, and increasing the self-respect of the foreign-born pupil. In college you learned this material as information; in high school you teach it, perhaps primarily, to engender attitudes of mind. The importance of this work? Who knows? Perhaps if all junior-high-school pupils recognized the relationships of tongues, this sense of kinship might destroy at least *one* barrier between nations.[1] Reference books can provide you with lists of German, or Dutch, or Scandinavian words. It would be wise to select according to the type of foreign pupils you have; then they can "bring words from home" and shine in the glory of knowing something that "Teacher" considers important. What are you doing? Trying to give your pupils a feeling for language, trying to inculcate in these voters-to-be some sense of international unity.

A. Devices for Arousing Interest

From your memory or from college texts you might chart a river named "The English Language." What would you have? Probably a spring of Celtic into which seeps a little Latin and a trickle of Danish; a broad stream of Norman French swelling the spring to a river of some importance; and then the intricate network of rivulets, streams, springs, pouring into this river—learned Latin, Parisian French, Greek, Spanish, Italian, Dutch,

---

[1] Try listing words, the German, then the English.

German	English	German	English
Vater	father	*Gelt*	gold
Mutter	mother	*See*	sea
Schwester	sister	*Schiff*	ship
Bruder	knave (boy or child)	*Blume*	bloom
Knabe	brother	*Geist*	ghost
Kinder	children (kindergarten)		

Russian, Hindu, Chinese, African, American Indian. You see what I mean by the necessity of not only *knowing* but also visually and imaginatively *realizing* the relationships and the resources of the English language. If your training did not include a study of our tongue, consult the books suggested at the end of the chapter; then, later, at summer school you can supplement your self-instruction. But don't deprive your pupils of this work.

Informally and simply you must establish in the minds of your pupils:

1. An interested attitude toward language
2. A curiosity as to *why* words are what they are
3. An amused interest in their peculiarities and human qualities

Be certain that you have captured interest; be certain that you have stirred the imagination of your group *before* you demand such individual labor. Group work at first—discussion, wonder, a volunteered investigation, much give-and-take talk where you provide the incentive—must lay a basis for further study. Later, you will deal: (1) with semantics (or semasiology, as it is also termed), the study of word growth and changes in meaning; and (2) with "applied semantics." These topics could prove as interesting and profitable to your pupils as any phase of their schoolwork, but each topic must be skillfully introduced and pursued.

To arouse interest I have long used the simile of the F.B.I. man or the sleuth whom he employs. I explain that we are too untrained to join the F.B.I. (in language study, the learned philologists), but that we can be humble sleuths. And our business? From the movies pupils are all too ready to explain that a sleuth employs himself shadowing the unwary, unmasking those in disguise, or confronting some apparently innocent person with the crimes of his earlier years or with those of his disreputable ancestors. But before a pupil can be a recognized sleuth, I explain, he must prove himself. *First,* he must show that he is observant.

Second, he must manifest some ability in looking below the obvious surface. *Third,* he must indicate his ability to draw conclusions from what he finds. To illustrate: If the pupils are garden-minded, I propose an imaginary expedition to a garden where we sprinkle the *sweet william,* the *forget-me-nots,* the *bleeding hearts.* Then I wait. At last I see someone has a glimmer. I encourage him to see the hoop-skirted maidens and the bewhiskered beaux saturated in sentiment who exchanged these flowers. Next we look at the *hen-and-chickens, Dutchman's-breeches,* or *nasturtiums,* and together enjoy the absurd comparisons, stressing that *nasus* means nose, and *tortum,* twisted. Then we turn to the world of people. Pupils agree, a bit unwillingly, that people have probably been pretty much the same always. And I, still stressing that a good sleuth is one who can see resemblances, suggest that we try to find out by modernizing a sentence full of "adopted" words from Greek and Latin. On the board I place "The supercilious Roman fool, who had accumulated his wealth, insulted his neighbors and uttered diatribes against them because of their poverty." After some explanation of meanings I list my words and their translations.

ADOPTED WORDS   CLASS WORDS

supercilious (L. *super*—over; *cilium*—eyelid)......highbrow
fool (L. *follis*—bellows)................blowhard, windbag
accumulated (L. *cumulus*—to heap up)........made his pile
insulted (L. *salire*—to leap)..jumped on them (with both feet)
diatribes (G. *dia-tribein*—to rub)................rubbed in

Their modern version reads: "The highbrow Roman windbag, who had made his pile, jumped on his neighbors and rubbed in their poverty."

Why spend time, you might ask, on such nonliterary writing? Because here time is eliminated; behind both dignified terms and slang the same pictures formed in the minds of the Latin citizen and the American pupils. In fact, words often remind one, perhaps

you add, of family albums. In spite of the hoops, curls, and de-
mure expression, Great-grandmother Mehitable McGregor and
young Gladys Mae in shorts have the same features. (Such passing comparisons are like fishhooks. Important facts separate
readily from pupils' minds; these illustrations remain.)

B. Levels of Speech

The two sentences just discussed, dignified and undignified, introduce another topic: levels of speech. Early I should admit, if
I were you, that "good" English is appropriate English, English
appropriate for the particular occasion for which it is used.
Clothes being an outward and visible sign that even the stupid-
est can comprehend, I like to speak of the various levels of speech
in terms of appropriate clothing. No one would, for example,
wear his baseball suit and catcher's mask to a funeral, nor would
he wear the black suit and white gloves of a pallbearer when
playing third base. To accost a mechanic with vague reference to
"little white things" when talking of spark plugs would earn his
pitying contempt, but for a tiny child "little white things" becomes good English. Be honest with your class. If there is "A
time to weep, and a time to laugh; a time to mourn, and a time
to dance," be sure there is a time for every level of speech, where
the level is appropriate and that English "good" English. It is
important, though, to see that the level of the classroom is somewhat higher than the level of the street or the football field, just
as the writing level should again be a little higher, though not
stilted in its correctness.

Long ago when discussing language I gave up the idea of
"right" and "wrong" except in generally admitted questions of
grammatical constructions, those constructions which are important to high-school pupils. I adopted those more flexible standards
of good usage and appropriate levels of speech. With what effect?
The right and the wrong stood out sharply, unblurred by questions of taste. *Shall* and *will* are not in the same class with *ain't*

got no ; a misused *may* or *can* is not so wrong as *he done it.* By adopting these two standards, the significant and the comparatively insignificant were made evident. Debatable points were omitted unless a pupil brought them up for discussion. And— even more important to the whole topic of vocabulary building— by this device language that belonged to the boy or girl on the street and on the athletic field still belonged to him or to her in the classroom. Each could have ideas about it ; each could find the illustrations of different levels and of better ways of meeting a speech situation ; each might be waked up imaginatively to some interest in words. Few pupils are interested unless they can contribute something to discussion.

C. Dictionary Study

It is only *after* your pupils are sensitive to levels of speech, and alive to the intrinsic interest in words, that the dictionary becomes to them an important, even an indispensable, companion. *But approach dictionary study warily and slowly, a little at a time.* In many schools, consulting the dictionary is accepted by the pupils as a form of punishment to be avoided when possible. This attitude is of course unfortunate, but it seems to me a natural one in schools where dictionary drill is thrust upon a class as an end in itself, or in too great quantity at any one time. You and I know how to use a dictionary, but suppose a freshman comes across the sentence "He was weighed down by a sense of his own inferiority." He does not know the last word ; hence the sentence means nothing to him. Conscientiously he looks it up. He finds on his first trial: "Inferiority. Inferior quality or state" —and bangs the dictionary shut. But he soon realizes that the wording has told him nothing. Again he secures the *infer* page and goes back to *inferior*. Here he finds the following information:

a. (L., compar. of *inferus* that is, below, underneath.) 1. Situated lower down; lower; nether. 2. Specif.: a. *Astron.* Nearer the sun than the earth is; as the *inferior* or interior plants. b. *Print.* Standing at the bottom of the line, as small figures or letters; as A_2B_c. 2 and c are *inferior*. **c.** *Bot.* (1) Situated below some other organ. (2) On the side of a flower which is next the bract: opposite or farthest from the axis; anterior. 3. Of low degree or rank. 4. Of less importance, value, or merit; of poorer quality; as, the *inferior* poets. 5. Of poor quality; mediocre; second-rate; as *inferior* goods.—*n.* One who, or that which, is inferior to another.

Can you blame the freshman if he hesitates before he again looses upon himself such a flood of unusable information? [1]

Teachers are prone to think too highly of a dictionary, not realizing the difficulties that beset the pupils' dictionary route to knowledge. A pupil learns a word by hearing it, seeing it, reading it in connection with other words. Even the dictionary synonyms are not to be trusted, as a certain Dutch artist learned when he spoke at tea of the delicious stink of the roses. Synonyms are only approximations. But since pupils must learn to glean facts from the dictionary, how shall they begin? What should you teach them?

1. Alphabetical arrangement of words
2. Intelligent use of guide words at the top of the page
3. Intelligent use of key words at the bottom. (To ask any class to learn diacritical marks is a waste of time, for the key word can be quickly consulted.)
4. The mark for long and for short vowels (breve and macron)
5. The way accent is marked, both primary and secondary
6. The way syllables are divided in contrast to the way compound words are joined
7. The way parts of speech are indicated
8. The way in which a capital for the word indicates that it is a capitalized word (except in certain pernicious pocket dictionaries where all words are capitalized and where no sources for words are given)
9. The abbreviations used

[1] An intelligent approach to dictionary teaching is given in *Gaining Language Skills*, Book III, by Lucy H. Chapman, pp. 120 ff.

10. The existence and location of the special lists that may be consulted, such as the Pronouncing Gazetteer, the Biographical Dictionary, Foreign Words and Phrases, Christian Names.

But again, you as teacher must go slowly. You have four years. For a while look up words in the dictionary yourself. Illustrate the use and interest of the volume. Talk of word histories. Give occasional one-word speed tests to your freshmen. Above all, I should advise you not to make the dictionary a penance, a bore, a book associated with disappointments and drudgery. In its place the dictionary is a valuable book. Admit to your class its many virtues and its frequent faults.

Your pupils as they shadow words, following them through various disguises, can be led to discover an important fact. Although reputable dictionaries may be trusted as to ancient word histories and meanings, with contemporary meanings or pronunciations they lag from five to fifteen years behind accepted usage. Why shake the pupils' faith in the dictionary? Because you can thus show for a fact that language is an alive, growing, changing entity; that a dictionary merely records what at various times educated people have made correct by their usage.[1] Perhaps the more imaginative of your pupils will one day have a sudden vision of language as a whole. This vast body of words, hoary with age, full of the "do's" and "don't's" of teachers and textbooks, he realizes is not a fixed thing, handed down like Moses' tablets of stone or Brigham Young's tablets of gold, but is a living organism. He may realize that words are being born, degenerating, dying, or being regenerated.[2]

---

[1] Do you know the story Hardy tells? His wife, objecting that no such word as the one in his manuscript existed, made Hardy look in the dictionary. There he found it. She, still suspicious, asked, "On whose authority?" Hardy's classic response was "On mine."

[2] Words once of importance:

Carpetbagger, Hooverize, spinning jenny, horsecar

Degeneration of words

villain...farm laborer	*wench*...girl or child
boor...farm laborer	*vile*...cheap

If pupils are familiar with the sea, they are quick to realize that the urge to communicate ideas is like a heaving ocean. Bits called words, are swept up into prominence, or subside, or are lost beneath the waves. Some, though dead, are caught in fixed form and are kept afloat for generations. These fossils interest pupils. All that you need do is to start them on the quest by suggesting *fro* caught by *to* and floated along in the phrase "to and fro" (though no one *"fros"* alone); *hue* inseparable from *cry;* *rack* floating along in *rack* and *ruin.*

Most classes are surprised to see that single words convey a history of man's fears or suspicions. The patient sleuth will find, however, that we as a race are a suspicious lot, convinced that the people about us are no better than they should be. The epitome of man's cynicism appears in the word *gossip* (*God-sib,* a "sponsor in baptism" or "relation in God"). This *God-sib* talked too much of what he knew; the present *gossip* resulted.[1]

This dour disposition of our ancestors was not, you convince your class, confined to their judgments of people. Of future events they expected evil rather than good. Such conviction appears in today's unpleasant connotation of the word *accident*

knave...boy	*beldame* (*belle dame*)...beautiful woman
insane...not healthy	
crisscross...Christ's cross	*brat*...child

Regeneration of words

steward...sty-ward	*lady*...loaf-kneader (Bread was the staff of life.)
sergeant...servant	
pluck (*courage*)...pluck (viscera)	*lord*...loaf guardian
guts (*courage*)...guts (viscera)	*butler*...bottle-server
marshal...horse servant	

[1] Other terms which display still further our ancestors' suspicious nature are:

sanctimonious...saintly (Sometimes we question if the virtue is genuine.)

to persecute...to follow (What more undesirable than to be followed by the uninteresting?)

smug...trim or neat (When ill dressed, how we dislike meeting the well dressed.)

outlandish...foreign (Our ancestors were as provincial as we.)

officious...serviceable (But who wants help thrust upon one?)

(originally *to happen*); or in that more sinister word *casualty* (originally *chance happening*); or in *doom* (A.S. *dōm*) (originally any legal judgment).

D. Idioms, Metaphor, Simile

Idioms offer another field for adventuring. Your pupils will realize that even if they have never seen a ship, they lightly use such tragic terms as "to keep one's head above water," "to break the ice," "to cut and run." And even the man who has never owned, ridden, or raced a horse may still say "in at the finish," "a dark horse," "a walkover," "to pull it off," or even "a horse-laugh"—whatever that means.

After you have awakened interest, after you and your pupils have wondered, guessed, investigated, found amusement, philosophized, and developed a genuine curiosity about words, you will doubtless stress even more than in your casual beginnings the use *of metaphor and simile in language development*. For example, in junior high school you can catch pupils' interest by asking them to flex their arms, feel the movement under the skin, and describe the sensation. As they feel the ripple of muscle under their fingers, it interests them that "muscle" comes from the Latin word *mūs*—little "mouse." This looking behind words for the faded metaphor is probably one of the most attractive methods of arousing interest. Your class is off on an adventure if you ask "Why do we use the following words?"

Arm: Armchair, arm of the sea, long arm of the law, we arm our navy; an armory

Head: Head of a pin, head of a bed, head of an army, the headland, headlight, headliner

Leg: He flew the first leg of his journey.

Then there are such terms as:

1. hoisting *crane* (why crane?)
2. gymnasium *horse*
3. *key* to the situation
4. *key* to the city
5. *fired* with ambition
6. suffered *gnawing* fear

7. a *mannish* woman
8. a *manly* little fellow

9. touched to the *bottom* of his heart
10. feeling *deeply* hurt

Encourage the use of original similes. Soon the pupils will themselves debar trite, stale expressions from class speech and writing. Try this exercise: "How would you finish?"

1. eyes like ———
2. white as a ——— or a ———
3. dry as ———
4. hard as ———
5. tit for ———
6. rough and ———
7. blind as a ———
8. spick and ———
9. sly as a ———
10. busy as a ———
11. hungry as a ———
12. drink like a ———
13. stubborn as a ———

Naturally, you would do nothing to soften the disgust aroused for those faded, secondhand expressions still appearing in some of our less-distinguished conversation. But, just as naturally, you and the class are led to discover, perhaps to invent, fresh wordings. Encourage originality. (Is it unfair to suggest that the dullness found in much high-school speech and writing arises in part from the teacher's failure to develop an adventurous attitude toward the use of words?)

With interest in fresh metaphor and simile you can combine— you and the class—disapproval of clichés, those stale word combinations that through long use have become the bane of editor and listener alike. (Girls and woman are "the fair sex." Western men are "he-men," or "red-blooded.")

Those of us who have lived long in the West and the Northwest have seen much picturesque terminology in the making. Cowboys "ride the rimrock," "earmark" their stock, or "get a drop" on thieves who "rustle" cattle. Placer miners "rock their cradles," "strike it rich," or "pull up stakes" if the mine does not "pan out." These terms, and hundreds like them, are fresh, striking, original. If you reward fresh wordings, and if you and the class discourage the cliché and the colorless, you might be able to bring into your classroom originality, vigor, picturesqueness, marks of American speech—the speech of the football field and street. That our speech is picturesque and vigorous Mr. Mencken will convince you in his stimulating book *The American Language*. Of course slang (and poetry) spring from this desire for fresh, vigorous expression. Insist that if slang is used it is fresh; you might even rid your pupils' speech of such well-worn terms as *lousy, foul, fierce, neat*. H. L. Mencken terms slang "a kind of linguistic exuberance, an excess of word-making energy." (Such energy we see running riot in the magazine *Time*.) It would be well to admit at once that there are two kinds of slang, *good* (appropriate and expressive) and *poor* (far-fetched, artificial, or unneeded).

II. APPLIED SEMANTICS

The work so far discussed lays a foundation for the last and most adult approach, "applied semantics." [1] You can, by prompting, see that your pupils ask "Why do even educated people use language so blunderingly, misunderstanding what is said and distorting what they hear?" Probably your best answer—if you wish to take the whole topic out of what I term the " 'tis and 'taint" talk that confuses many a class—lies in reading that famous quotation on conversation from *The Autocrat of the Breakfast Table:*

. . . there are at least six personalities distinctly to be recognized as taking part in that dialogue between John and Thomas.

Three Johns.
1. The real John; known only to his Maker.
2. John's ideal John; never the real one, and often very unlike him.
3. Thomas's ideal John; never the real John, nor John's John, but often very unlike either.

[1] "Applied semantics," the study of words not as solitary entities, not as subjects for phonetics and semantics—not even as factors in the stream of speech, but as factors in the stream of meaning."—Isaac Goldberg, *The Wonder of Words*, p. 296.

Three Thomases.
$\begin{cases} \text{1. The real Thomas.} \\ \text{2. Thomas's ideal Thomas.} \\ \text{3. John's ideal Thomas.} \end{cases}$

Today, blinded by conflicting war reports and battling ideologies, your pupils will not hesitate to admit how slow they (and we) are to use words with careful discrimination.

A. Taboo

A simple approach to "applied semantics," used in several senior high schools, is a consideration of taboo words, beginning perhaps with some of the customs of primitive people. (Have you, by the way, an acquaintance with Sir James George Frazer's *Golden Bough,* perhaps in the concise one-volume edition?) Illustrations from the taboo words of early peoples lead naturally to a consideration—with much amused condescension on the part of your pupils—of the euphemisms of their grandparents and great-grandparents, such as *limbs—*never *legs;* hose—never *stockings; flannels* or *linens—*never *underwear.*

Your class is less amused, in fact a little shocked, to note in present-day speech and newspapers the prevalence of this same primitive tendency. For moral delinquency we politely avoid the specific by using such terms as *in trouble, a misdemeanor, misconduct, a transgression, a slip, a lapse, misguided;* and rather recently the two terms *wanted* and *sent up* have taken on specific connotation from their association with the law courts. The class recognizes this tendency in the avoidance of the word *death.* War also provides gruesome facts veiled by the terms *cleaning up, mopping up,* and *taking proper precautions.*

The excerpt given below comments, with admirable economy of words, upon this same tendency.

A NOTE ON VERBAL TABOO

The affective connotations of some words create peculiar situations. In some circles of society, for example, it is "impolite" to speak of eating. A maid answering the telephone has to say, "Mr. Jones is at dinner," and not, "Mr. Jones is eating dinner." The extensional meaning is the same in both cases, but the latter form is regarded as having undesirable connotations. The same hesitation about referring too baldly to eating is shown in the economical use made of the French and Japanese words meaning "to eat," *manger* and *taberu;* a similar delicacy exists in many other languages. Again, when creditors send bills, they practically never mention "money," although that is what they are writing about. There are all sorts of circumlocutions: "We would appreciate your early attention to this matter." "May we look forward to an immediate remittance?" "There is a balance in our favor which we are sure you would like to clear up."[1]

B. Propaganda

The consideration of the taboo and of the euphemistic statements are, however, merely a mild introduction to the more rigorous thinking that you will demand of your pupils. You would do well to familiarize yourself with Mr. Hayakawa's recent book, *Language in Action,* from which I have just quoted. Here you will find straightforward wording, full of apt, often amusing comment, and illustrations useful to you in classroom discussions. It is perhaps as usable a guide as you will find, with the exception of the material sent out by the Institute of Propaganda Analysis. There is one word of warning, however, which you should heed. Discovery of the unsuspected affectation, prejudice, snobbishness, unfair dealing, or actual deceit in the words of their elders is heady wine for the high-school junior or senior. Your business is to attempt to see that while your pupils discover the muddled thinking, the confusions, and the emotional reactions in the thought about them, and in their own thinking, they also keep a sane outlook upon life. What you want to avoid while teaching your pupils to read warily is the blighting cynicism which arro-

[1] S. I. Hayakawa: *Language in Action,* copyright, 1941, by Harcourt, Brace and Company. Used by permission of the publisher.

gantly suspects and belittles all virtue, and thus makes normal growth for both mind and emotions impossible.[1]

How would you avoid the dangers cited? Probably you would begin your discussion of propaganda with a consideration of *how* the wise advertiser succeeds in attracting our attention and in arousing our interest in his product. From some such innocuous study you might emerge to the realm of conjecture. By class discussion you and the group would agree that everyone is influenced by environment and heredity, by personal interest or prejudice, to feel in some particular way about the problems that concern them. Note that word *feel*. Although they "feel," they are unaware that their opinions and beliefs may be determined by their emotion, not by their brains. Many illustrations are necessary before pupils realize the fact that lack of clear thinking, not possession of evil intentions, often leads to wrong though completely sincere conclusions.

Here are a few suggested class exercises for illustration. They may or may not prove appropriate for your classes or for your community.

EXERCISE I

1. There is a movement on foot for a new high-school gymnasium and swimming pool. In one sentence each give a public statement concerning this movement by: (a) a miser, owner of much taxable property; (b) a seller of real estate; (c) the high-school principal. Have each speaker slant his speech so that it may influence community voters.

2. It is urged, beginning June first, that the high-school tennis

---

[1] "With critics who say that propaganda-analysis work with young people brings unhealthy cynicism, we cannot agree—not if such classroom work is conceived and carried out *for* the child and *with* the child. Not if we do not confront children and young people with questions, with concepts, with social and economic or political problems about which they can do nothing—the difference is 'the difference between the teacher who imposes her own in. ests upon her pupils, who "propels" them through a unit of study on propaganda,' and the teacher who as a guide to maturity helps her students to think critically and to act intelligently on the everyday problems they are meeting."—*Propaganda Analysis*, Vol. II, pp. 108-09,. published by the Institute for Propaganda Analysis, 211 Fourth Avenue, New York City. Reprinted with permission.

courts be used by members of the senior high school only. In one sentence express the point of view of: (a) the senior-high-school principal; (b) the junior-high-school principal; (c) the mother of the eighth-grade champion in tennis.

EXERCISE II

Suggest in one sentence for each point of view represented by the character that would be ascribed to the following:

1. William the Conqueror
    a. As seen by a Norman follower
    b. As seen by Harold, "last of the Saxon kings"
2. Mr. Wendell Willkie
    a. As viewed by Democrats before the 1940 election
    b. As viewed by Democrats after his return from England in 1941
3. The Ford plant
    a. As viewed by Messrs. William Green (A. F. of L.) and John Lewis (C.I.O.) after the agreement establishing a closed shop
    b. As viewed by Messrs. Green and Lewis three years earlier

Such exercises may convince you that, as Mr. Hayakawa stresses, there is strong human predilection for conceiving all questions as right or wrong, as good or bad. He suggests that "in our expression, 'We must listen to both sides of the question,' there is an assumption, frequently unexamined, that every question has, fundamentally, only two sides." Perhaps to lessen this type of thinking you can present questions and exercises demanding three or four, not two, attitudes of mind or possibilities of action.[1]

This type of discussion, a matching of wits against wits in the classroom, breaks down the pupils' conviction that in all questions only two sides exist.

Not only do people view ideas from different angles, but their emotions become involved. For example, the word "person" seems

[1] You might remind your pupils that many a well-prepared debate has been lost because the losing team did not foresee a third possible solution.

colorless. But once hear the contemptuous "My daughter never associates with such *persons*." What happens? Wolf, tiger, and snake appear, by contrast, almost desirable. The first and Second World Wars give much evidence; labor-capital disputes also provide ample illustrations. We have the unfortunate habit, your pupils will find, of naming or classifying a person or a thing (Democrat, Jew, Catholic, Methodist, German, Englishman, jitney, movie), then endowing that person or that thing with the qualities which we attribute to the name.[1]

Probably you are familiar and will familiarize your pupils with the seven ways of influencing the public for or against any movement or thing or person. If not, consult *Using Periodicals,* the N.C.T.E. pamphlet [2] by Ruth Mary Weeks, for a discussion of these methods [3] of influencing opinion. Get them to accept this definition: "Propaganda is the expression of opinion or action by individuals or groups deliberately designed to influence opinion or actions of other individuals or groups with reference to predetermined ends." [4]

In this work your business is to build upon pupil interests. Turn to advertisements, school programs, sports or drama, historical situations encountered in other classes, attitudes of book characters, town or city questions. During the last two years in high school, you should consciously try to broaden your pupils' interests to include those questions which as voters should concern them keenly. (Before that time, though you try to broaden their interests, remember that their normal interests may not be your own.) Consult the history teachers; supplement, but do not repeat, the work in social science. There is, remember, the news-

[1] Do you recall *Alice in Wonderland?* " 'When I use a word,' Humpty Dumpty said, in rather a scornful tone, 'it means just what I choose it to mean—neither more nor less.' "

[2] Order from 211 West 68th St., Chicago 21. 60 cents.

[3] Methods are name-calling, glittering generalities, transfer, testimonials, plain folks, card-stacking, and band wagon.

[4] From Institute for Propaganda Analysis, Vol. I, p. 51.

paper and periodical field. You will find interest aroused by contrasting editorials. Take for example the same event or topic as treated by the *Saturday Evening Post* and the *Nation,* the *New Republic, Business Week,* or other publications with contrasting policy. It will become obvious that "The truth is this to me and that to thee," but it will also become apparent that the different tone is secured by words, words colored by emotion.

Your community and state problems, the maturity or immaturity of your group, your own information, interests, and wisdom, will determine the scope and success of this work. Remember *clear thought, not heedless and impassioned argument, is your objective.* The following suggestions for class discussion might or might not be suitable; you alone can determine that question.

EXERCISE

What connotation exists in the use of the following terms:

1. Non-Aryan
    a. Used in the dictionary
    b. Used by Hitler
2. Labor organizer
    a. Used by a California fruit-grower
    b. Used by A. F. of L. members
3. Used by three different types of speakers
    a. "Okie"
    b. "Migratory worker"
    c. "Itinerant laborer"
    d. The Pearl Harbor incident
    e. Line to Moscow
    f. Closed shop and open shop
4. Conservative and reactionary
    a. Used by a Republican banker in Maine
    b. Used by a Communist in Los Angeles

Perhaps you feel a certain uneasiness about introducing controversial topics or terms. Perhaps you wish to wander pleasantly in the past, occupied with Tennyson, Arnold, Emerson, or Shakespeare. Controversy—that is, an honest differing of minds, not of emotions—is a necessary adjunct to intellectual growth. Of course keep to a *rational,* not an *emotional,* discussion, for the very purpose of this work is to lay bare the unfortunate effect upon thinking of emotion and prejudice. (Do you recall the phrase "a person who can discuss without arguing"? He should be your ideal.) Your purpose is also to lay bare the unsuspected power of the word (that mere assortment of letters) over human thought.

What value, you may ask, lies in all this work? Do pupils spell better? Can they hold a job better? What does it "get them"? It is sometimes hard to make pupils (or even you, the prospective teacher) realize fully the value of intangibles. Yet if you can get your pupils to think of words, to look behind their surface, to be curious about new words, you have provided them with a lasting interest. It is an interest that overwork, poverty, illness, sorrow, cannot completely abolish. You are also bestowing upon them a protection against being duped. You have laid a foundation for clear, logical thinking. But an awareness of words can do still more. A sense of the flavor and shades of meaning in words heightens the beauty, deepens the tragedy, of speech and literature. Thus it enriches emotionally those hard, factual, sometimes cynical youngsters who fear emotion, sentiment, reverence, as saints of old feared the Devil. If you can help it, do not let your pupils "live by bread alone."

III. SURVEYING THE PUPILS' KNOWLEDGE AND USE OF LANGUAGE

But, you may say, all this work—interesting, stimulating as it may be—is not teaching the pupils correct use of such everyday words as *accept—except, most—almost, already—all ready.* True, from babyhood until final interment all of us, consciously or unconsciously, are at work on our vocabularies. The steps that we follow and that you must follow in teaching include:

1. Disentangling like forms that have become more or less jumbled

2. Sharpening and defining the uses and meanings of those words already known

3. Growing accustomed to the usual idiomatic combinations of certain words

4. Gaining power from a knowledge of prefixes, roots, and suffixes so that the meaning of new words may be inferred

5. Learning new words which are useful in talking, writing, and reading.

When you glance back over these five processes, the learning of new terms, you note, is given a subordinate position. Remember that high-school boys and girls have already a stock of words on hand. Many of these terms they know; many they half-know. Some belong only in their reading vocabularies. These they understand in a general way but do not use. Some they might write, aided perhaps by the dictionary, but would feel self-conscious about using orally. And some they might like to use occasionally were they certain of prefixes or positive as to accent. But for the most part, words bother them little. They supplement their limited vocabulary with stock phrases and words (*pep, nice, definitely, neat, awful, swell, lovely, fine*) which serve to express all action, being, or state of being. New words they must of course learn, but at first is it not wiser to attempt to clarify for them the words that they already possess than to introduce strangers into the existing confusion?

A. *Vocabulary Teaching—a By-product*

If you grant that these five processes should be carried on, how is one to do it? Scattered throughout this book you will find answers to that question, for vocabulary training, I feel sure, must be subordinated to some other purpose if it is to be really effective. For example, in Chapter IX you will find a discussion of transition words and their teaching. In this chapter, as well as elsewhere throughout the book, the necessity of teaching the implications expressed in connectives has been stressed. But this work, of course, demands a four-year growth; it cannot be hurried, for it requires both analysis of the thought of the sentence and the breaking down of careless *and* and *then* habits already established.

In practically every school, much good vocabulary work goes on, I feel certain, hardly recognized as vocabulary work because it is so closely associated with grammar, theme correction, or sentence manipulation. For example, you will be doing admirable vocabulary work, simple as it seems, if you teach the meaning and correct use of *but* in contrast to *and,* or again if you eliminate the floating *which, it, that,* of pupils' themes. As I have already suggested in Chapter III, the easiest way of arousing interest in words is to inquire for vivid, characteristic *go* and *said* substitutes. You may be teaching sentence sense, but obliquely you are training your pupils in vocabulary selection. In the same way, as mentioned later in Chapter IX, when you insist upon clear, vivid words that appeal to one of the five senses and discuss these words, discarding those that are least successful, you are again working on vocabulary; you are sensitizing your pupils to word meanings and to word power. Or if you consider Chapter VII, you will find that excellent vocabulary drill underlies the analysis of every business letter in the light of its courtesy, its friendliness, its appropriateness. And so it is, probably, with the best work that we do in vocabulary building. We use words merely as tools. Our interest is centered elsewhere, but to accomplish what we need to accomplish, we must consider words.

Perhaps, though, it is in the realm of literature studied or in the world of radio that we find the most fruitful sources. Not all words here need to be known; but key words, essential words, or words that in themselves are interesting and usable for pupils should be made clear.

And just what are you to do? Each of you will, of course, work out methods of your own for these five phases of vocabulary study, but here are a few suggestions upon which, doubtless, you will elaborate.

1. **Disentangling like forms that have become more or less jumbled.** First to consider (and last to use correctly) are such common words, confused primarily as to spelling, not meaning, as *to, too, two; piece, peace; principal, principle; council, counsel; alter, altar; accept, except; course, coarse.* Then there are these terms which illustrate slightly different types of confusion: *affect—effect; wonder—wander; compliment—complement; formerly—formally; eminent—imminent; lose—loose; practical—practicable; chose—choose; party—person; quite—quit—quiet; respectfully—respectively; reputation—character; suspicion—suspect.*

Why do you not jot down misused words, misused in either pupils' speech or writing, and then compile a list applicable to *your* particular group? Your better pupils would rather enjoy making from these lists a series of word tests. These you can dictate, place on the board, or better yet, pass out on mimeographed sheets. Here is one type.[1]

EXERCISE

compliment—complement

Marian and Helen are so completely opposite in appearance and disposition that they ——————— each other delightfully.

At least that ——————— is often paid them.

2. **Sharpening and defining the uses and meanings of words already known.** Work on synonyms not only fixes the meaning and shades of meaning but is an excellent device for increasing a pupil's usable vocabulary. Why not list and ask your pupils to list synonyms for words?

[1] It is well to remember that often *one isolated word carries little meaning;* hence *place words in sentences,* or better yet, *paragraphs,* and ask your pupils to *illustrate new or confusing words in sentences.*

EXERCISE

1. Place, 2. Posture, 3. Position, 4. Pose, 5. Attitude, 6. Bearing, 7. Inarticulate, 8. Speechless, 9. Mute, 10. Silent, 11. Dumb

a. "Did you find a ——————— on the top floor and a ——————— for the desk which pleased you?" Marian asked.

b. "Shall we do something to improve your ———————?" the gymnasium instructor suggested, sorry for the shy, ——————— youngster before him.[1]

In discussion of synonyms you have again an opportunity to stress that most useful topic, *levels of speech*. Good taste in speech is not inherent. Levels of speech must be explained in schools, and practice in distinguishing levels must be a part of classwork. Many present-day texts include slang, colloquial, informal, and formal terms, such as *chew the rag, chin, palaver, chat, chatter, talk, converse,* to make sure that in composition work, both oral and written, there is class discussion of appropriate terms, and that such discussion plays an important part.

3. Growing accustomed to the usual idiomatic combinations of certain words. You will find that prepositions cause much trouble. I should admit at once, if I were you, that there is neither rhyme nor reason in our idiomatic expressions. *Usage,* not *reason,* has determined what is correct speech. Here is a typical exercise on one kind of idiom.

EXERCISE

(If you yourself are unsure, consult Fowler's *Modern English Usage,* Oxford University Press, 1946, for the correct preposition-verbal idiom.)

1. The new dish consists ——————— fish, potatoes, onion, spices, and milk

2. Courtesy consists ——————— unfailing consideration for others

3. All his ambitions failed ——————— realization because each day a new ambition seized him

---

[1] You will note (an example of oblique teaching) that not only are you working on synonyms, but you are also giving practice in proper use of quotation marks and in variety in sentence patterns.

4. The meeting was deferred ——————— Saturday
5. Of course I shall defer ——————— your wishes
6. Their fears were confirmed ——————— the F.B.I. bulletin
7. The Governor announced, "I am more confirmed ———————
my opinions."

This work is important, but be sure that you are not wasting
time on nonessentials. One safe guide is this: *Never insist upon
teaching your pupils niceties of language which you and the
majority of your educated friends violate in speech and writing.*

**4. Gaining power from a knowledge of prefixes, roots, and
suffixes so that the meaning of new words may be inferred.**
The dissection of words so that their parts may be clearly recognized should take an important place, five minutes one day, two
another, three a third, in all classwork. This dissection should be
so employed that it helps pupils to recognize the meanings of
other words more or less similarly constructed. For example,
there would appear on the board *anti* (against) and *ante* (before); *pre* (before); *mono, bi, di, tri,* and so on, with the ever
growing list of *monologue, monotone, monogram, monoplane;
bicycle, biped, bicuspid; dialogue, diameter, dimeter; tricycle,
triangular, trident, triumvirate,* and so on. A board list such as
the following would also sensitize pupils to the meanings of
terms that they employ unthinkingly, and should make them the
readier to comprehend a new word employing any one of these
elements. (I use the word *should* advisedly.)

geo	(earth)			geo	(earth)	
phono	(sound)	—graph (y)		physio	(nature)	—logy
auto	(self)	(writing)		theo	(God)	(word)
photo	(light)			psycho	(soul, mind)	

tele (at a distance)—
- graph (writing)
- phone (sound)
- scope (sight)

micro (small)—
- scope (sight)
- phone (sound)
- photograph (picture)

It is a temptation to linger here. You as teacher are doing a valuable thing if you arouse your pupils to speculation, and if you break down a long-established evil habit, often encouraged unconsciously by teachers of language. In the past, pupils have been penalized for guessing at the meaning of words. But you want your pupils to guess—intelligently. Or, to put it more accurately, you want them to use all of the intelligence that they have when a new word confronts them. Before they look it up or give it up, they should attempt to force out a meaning from the word itself and from its context. If, by way of illustration, a boy knows that *geo* means *earth* in the word *geography,* he ought to be able to "guess" *geophysics* or *geocentric* or even *geometry* with a little help, although that last word may seem to him so very far removed from "earth measure" that without your encouragement he will scarcely credit his own wisdom.

If you are logical in your building through the four years, do you realize what an excellent foundation you can lay for your pupils' knowledge of words?

5. **Learning new words which will be of actual use to pupils in talking, writing, and reading.** As to the type of words which you teach, you yourself will have to be the judge, but the words should be immediately useful. The activity in the classroom and the reading carried on will largely determine what is needed. If your ninth grade is occupied with myths, stress such words as *panic* and *tantalize.* Or you might list, as suggested earlier, words gathered from radio programs, talks, literature, assemblies—words of value to the group. The wisdom of foreseeing that poor readers have already met key words before they face them in assigned reading has also been stressed in Chapter VI. The pupils' interest in these new words rests in part upon the type of test you give. You can, of course, buy vocabulary tests which are useful, but in the lower grades the class-made variety is more satisfactory. Remember: *Pupils strive to excel in*

those phases of work that the teacher regards as important. Be sure that vocabulary building falls in this category.

TWO SAMPLE TESTS

A. Can you fit the right word into the right place and spell it correctly? Use the first letter and the suggested words in parentheses to help you find the *one* needed word. Do not use one of the words in parentheses. Write the correct word on the right-hand blank.

1. Mr. Johnson is now engaged in the hardware b————— (occupation).   1. —————————

2. Your lawyer is noted for his sound j————— (decisions, advice, conclusions) on problems of finance.   2. —————————

B. An easier type, of course, is multiple choice, the desired word being used in either a sentence or a phrase.

A *circuitous* approach

a. hesitating manner. 1. pleasing, 2. stupid, 3. deliberate, 4. dull

b. unusual sight. 1. everyday, 2. painful, 3. unsightly, 4. uncommon

c. mortifying experience. 1. embarrassing, 2. flattering, 3. noted, 4. deadly

d. terse expression. 1. vulgar, 2. eloquent, 3. short, 4. unfair

Basic English is a topic with which you should familiarize yourself, and should present to your high-school pupils. Read C. K. Ogden's *The System of Basic*.[1] Make your pupils aware that with more than 500,000,000 people now familiar with either Basic or English as their natural or governmental tongue, it is probable that Basic English will before long become the recognized international language. The 850 words included in its vocabulary are sufficiently simple to be mastered in a few weeks and sufficiently usable to provide a medium of expression. Of this language Mr. Ogden writes that its purpose is "To serve as an international auxiliary language; that is to say, a second language for use throughout the world in general communication, commerce, and science." He adds that since Basic is simple, it

---

[1] Ogden, C. K.: *The System of Basic,* Harcourt, Brace, 1934. See Appendix I for further discussion.

can serve as an introduction to those foreigners who may wish to learn English, but who use Basic as a preliminary step. Simple, clear, scientific statements can be made in Basic, and though it lacks the beauty and the variety of the English language that we speak, it does provide a simple, adequate medium. The dream of a world language is not new. In medieval times the wandering scholar was at home among his kind, for Latin provided a medium, flexible and beautiful. In 1887 Esperanto was created and has served many people as an international tongue. (If your pupils are interested in Latin or French or Spanish, they would find a report on Esperanto interesting.) Today it is finding a new function. Certain universities use it as a means of testing the entering students' native ability in language by offering them a passage in Esperanto and a dictionary, and then giving them time to cope with this unknown medium. Latin is now a dead tongue; Esperanto is less used today than some years ago; Basic English, its roots firmly established in a living language, offers once more the possibility of a world tongue, displacing no language, but providing a second tongue for all peoples.[1]

As your pupils (1) explore new words, (2) think over the exact meanings and implications of those long used, (3) look behind words for history, metaphor, simile, hidden meanings or connotations, they will, with your aid, reach certain generalizations.

1. They will realize that words (except mere "mortar" words like *the, of, shall*) are divided into concrete terms which conjure up a picture, and abstract terms which appeal only to the intellect. This distinction could be taught in five minutes. But you will desire pupils

[1] A strange tongue that a few of your pupils might find fascinating is the Bantu language, one so difficult that after discovering it, your pupils will consider English or English grammar mere child's play. You will find it discussed in Jespersen's *Language, Its Nature, Development, and Origin,* p. 353, and in Appendix I you will find a sample. It may remind your pupils of the "pig Latin" which they talked at ten or earlier. You will also find in the appendix a sample of that other strange jumble known as beach-la-mar, or sandalwood English, used as a trading language. In it most of the words are English, but the rules for using them seem to be determined by the natives of the West Pacific region.

to realize the difference so keenly that they know *when* to seek for the picture words to evoke images in the minds of their hearers or readers, and *when* to clear their readers' or listeners' minds from pictures so that the abstract idea comes to them uncluttered.

2. They will also realize that certain words like *mother* and *home* tend to evoke an emotional response. (How well the moving-picture industry knows this fact!) On the other hand, they will recognize that words like *lever, acid,* or *geometry* tend to awaken purely intellectual response—except, of course, in certain individual situations.

3. They will recognize the hosts of words that take on special coloration in connection with specific situations or attitudes of mind. *Politics, judge, Teachers' Union, honor,* may or may not carry a special weight or emotion.

4. You can bring them to see that language used at different levels gives very different results, and that in a sentence the skillful dip or rise from one level to another—if appropriate to the subject—adds flavor and distinction.

5. You can show them the pleasure caused by unexpected wording. It would be wise to collect examples. Try these two, both from *Harper's Magazine.* Mr. E. B. White writes, "We got out the jack, a pitiful little hydraulic affair painted a bright yellow to make it seem alert." Note the pinprick in that last word? Or in this sentence where the reader, plunged from one level of speech to another, experiences an interesting mental vibration. Speaking of "Road Signs," Mr. De Voto remarks, "Sometimes the history is *inaccurate* or even, as at Dodge City, Kansas, *faked;* and entering my native State, I ran *square* into a *thumping lie,* one which is the more *injudicious* since nearly anyone can *spot* it." [Italics mine]

Keep your eyes open for sentences or paragraphs that illustrate good modern English; better yet, have your pupils range far and wide in search of admirable models. This encouragement of casual reading is just one of the many ways in which you can meet the protest—not an unusual protest—well put in a letter from Dorothy Marie Johnson, assistant editor of the *Business Education World.*

You know, I worry about English teachers. I had two good ones in high school, but they had to teach us such dull stuff. I got the impression that there were two kinds of literature—what was bad (that was what we enjoyed), and what was good (that was what we had in school and didn't like). I also got the impression that all the good authors were dead ones. If English teachers could be taught to bridge the gap between George Eliot and Zane Grey, everybody would have more fun, and English teachers wouldn't have any trouble defending the teaching of English against the attacks of vocational teachers. I see something of these attacks, in my work, and I boil over promptly. But that doesn't stop them.

Perhaps, also, your pupils during this study of words will unlearn much which they once learned. Many a youngster's mind in its progress through school remains cluttered with don'ts: "Don't end a sentence with a preposition," "Don't use contractions," "Don't begin a sentence with a conjunction," "Don't write incomplete sentences," "Don't use slang." You and I use contractions, don't we? And when we choose, we start sentences with conjunctions. And incomplete sentences? Why not? To gain the desired effect we bootleg them into even our formal writing. Why don't you say to your pupils:

"Know your subject; know what effect you want to convey; then make words your servants to carry out your desires."

SUGGESTED EXERCISES

Read as many as you can of the references listed before you attempt these exercises. After class discussion it would be wise to file all exercises so that class members can copy for their permanent records any word histories or suggestions that seem to them useful.

1. After you have consulted at least one of the books listed, plan an introductory three-minute talk on the resources of the dictionary. Your attempt here should be to arouse interest rather than to give information. Illustrate with words *all* the different types of information to be gained from a dictionary comparable to *Webster's Collegiate Dictionary.* Such a list is not, of course, to be given to a high-school class at any one time.

2. Select three words that have histories of interest to high-school pupils. Discuss. Your main purpose is *to awaken interest* in words.

3. Select such a word as *hand* or *eye*. Show how it has broadened in meaning. Trace and seek an explanation for the various uses. (See Logan Pearsall Smith's *Words and Idioms*, Houghton Mifflin, 1935.)

4. Select three words similar to *liquor* or *ghost*. Indicate how their meaning has become narrower. (See Greenough and Kittredge, *Words and Their Ways in English Speech*.)

5. Select three words that have degenerated in meaning. Trace their history interestingly. The word *victuals* might suggest others to you.

6. Explain clearly and interestingly the terms "root," "stem," "prefix," "suffix," illustrating your statements with some twenty familiar words. Greenough and Kittredge, *Words and Their Ways*, Chap. XIII, will help you.

7. Find interesting origins for the following words. Some of the books listed you will find are indexed both by matter and by words used in illustration; hence the following words can be readily found. It would be wise to collect many examples for future use.

dunce (Trench)	surloin or sirloin (Greenough)
jitney (McKnight)	rhyme or rime (Greenough)
cowcatcher (Mencken)	touchy (Greenough)
Welsh rabbit or rarebit	Jerusalem artichoke (Greenough)
(Greenough)	sandwich (Greenough)

8. Explain the term "fossil" when applied to words. Discuss three that would be interesting to high-school pupils. Explain possible reasons why these words have lasted.

9. Make clear-cut, interesting, memorable explanations as to the difference in use of:

a. affect—effect	f. like—as (or as if)
b. accept—except	g. most—almost
c. already—all ready	h. liable—likely
d. beside—besides	i. healthy—healthful
e. due to—owing to	j. associates—companions

Provide illustrations that could appear on a consultation board for class guidance.

10. Prepare a class assignment in which you introduce and assign words borrowed from several foreign sources. Point out that often

certain types of words are borrowed from particular nations. For example, from the Dutch we have many sea terms. Why? Make your assignment specific and stimulating.

11. Are you interested in junior-high-school work? If you are, look up *Gaining Language Skills* by Lucy H. Chapman (Book III, of the Growth in Using English series). In Chap. VI note Miss Chapman's method of introducing her group to the dictionary. Note her use of cartoons. After you have studied her procedure, frankly imitate her method, but use original material in planning five lessons in language-building. (In Part V of Book IV of the same series, note the method of coping with spelling demons.)

12. Define *propaganda*. Produce for a three-minute class talk three or four of the seven ways of influencing public opinion as illustrated in newspapers or current magazines.

13. Eastman, Max: *The Enjoyment of Poetry*, Scribner, 1921. In three chapters—"Names Practical and Poetic," "The Technique of Names," "The Technique of Poetic Names"—you will find a fresh, imaginative outlook on words. Review for the class briefly.

14. Quiller-Couch, Sir Arthur: *On the Art of Writing*, Putnam, 1916. Study the chapter "On Jargon"; it will provide you with admirable ammunition with which to discourage roundabout expressions and trite phrases.

15. Frame five problems for discussion that are capable of three or more possible solutions. Present to the class.

SUGGESTED READINGS

Much material is crowded into this chapter. For that reason a list of topics as they are treated in the chapter is here given with specific references. Individual high-school pupils might well investigate some of these for class reports, since the references are clear and specific. The bibliography at the end of the chapter will supply the book titles.

1. *The Indo-European families:* Any unabridged dictionary; McKnight, Haber, Hatfield, pp. 3-35; Baugh, Chap. 2

2. *Levels of speech:* Krapp, Chap. 6; Hayakawa, pp. 154-56

3. *Dictionary study:* G. and C. Merriam pamphlets; Kennedy, pp 469-660

4. *Attitude toward language:* Krapp, Chaps. 24, 33; Kennedy, pp. 96-121, 629; Mencken, Chaps. 5 and 6

5. *Degeneration and regeneration of words:* Greenough and Kittredge, Chap. 20; Kennedy, Chap. 13

6. *Proper names:* McKnight, pp. 385-92; Kennedy, pp. 272, 337, 572; Greenough and Kittredge, p. 209

7. *Fossils:* Greenough and Kittredge, Chap. 15; McKnight, pp. 84-89

8. *Idioms:* Smith (English idioms), pp. 2-50; Kennedy, pp. 646, 577-80

9. *Figurative language:* Greenough and Kittredge, pp. 9-18; 272-83; Hayakawa, pp. 147-50; 146-47; Kennedy, pp. 549-59

10. *Slang:* Hixon and Colodny, pp. 135-55; Mencken, pp. 555-90; McKnight, pp. 37-69

11. *Applied semantics:* Goldberg, pp. 296-318; Hayakawa, pp. III-v

12. *Taboo words and euphemisms:* Jespersen, p. 239; McKnight (English words), pp. 266-79; Hayakawa, pp. 103-13; Mencken, pp. 284-311

13. *Propaganda and analysis:* Hayakawa, pp. 35-38; 69-75; 146-49; 152-53; Institute for Propaganda Analysis (bulletins and *Year Book*)

14. *Word formation:* Kennedy, (prefixes) pp. 342, 253, 386; (suffixes and roots) pp. 335-47; Hixon and Colodny, pp. 165-299

15. *Questions of correct usage:* Fowler, according to reference; Kennedy, pp. 657-60

16. *Strange tongues:* Ogden, see index; Jespersen, pp. 356-58; (Bantu and beach-la-mar), Kennedy, pp. 647-48

From the *English Journal*

1. Burnham, Josephine M.: "The Matrix of English," Vol. 38 (1949), pp. 265-71

2. Norris, Ruth E.: "Adventures in Vocabulary Building," Vol. 20 (1931), pp. 575-79

3. Greene, J. C.: "Modernizing the Teaching of Vocabulary," Vol. 34 (1945), pp. 343-44

4. Miller, Ward S.: "A Plan for Teaching Vocabulary," Vol. 27 (1938), pp. 566-73

5. Armstrong, David T.: "Dictionary Work," Vol. 34 (1945), p. 490

6. Strang, Ruth: "Levels of English," Vol. 24 (1935), pp. 577-79

To save students later embarrassment, stress this topic.

7. Young, Helen H.: "Reading a Sentence: An Exercise in the Study of Meaning," Vol. 30 (1941), pp. 450-57
This is an interesting example of close analysis of a small unit.

8. Conrad, Lawrence H.: "Advanced Reading: Senior High School," Vol. 27 (1938), pp. 19-27

9. Edelman, L.: "The Single-Word Fallacy," Vol. 29 (1940), pp. 477-82
Here are good illustrations of propaganda.

10. Zahner, Louis C.: "English, a Language," Vol. 29 (1940), pp. 470-77

11. Glicksberg, Charles I.: "The Dynamics of Vocabulary Building," Vol. 29 (1940), pp. 197-206

BIBLIOGRAPHY

Fowler, H. W.: *A Dictionary of Modern Usage,* Clarenden Press, Oxford, 1926

Goldberg, Isaac: *The Wonder of Words,* Appleton-Century, 1939

Greenough, J. B., and Kittredge, G. L.: *Words and Their Ways in English Speech,* Macmillan, 1901

Hayakawa, S. I.: *Language in Action,* Harcourt, Brace, 1941

Hixon, Jerome C., and Colodny, I.: *Word Ways,* American Book Company, 1941

Institute for Propaganda Analysis, 24 Fourth Avenue, New York City, *Year Book* and bulletins

Jespersen, Otto: *Language, Its Nature, Development and Origin,* Holt, 1922

Kennedy, Arthur G.: *Current English,* Ginn, 1935

Krapp, George Philip: *The Knowledge of English,* Holt, 1927

Merriam, G. & C.: *An Outline for Dictionary Study Designed for Use with Webster's Collegiate Dictionary,* 5th ed., Merriam Company, Springfield, Mass., 1940

Miller, Clyde R.: *How to Detect and Analyze Propaganda; A Town Hall Pamphlet,* The Town Hall, Inc., 123 West 43 Street, New York City

Ogden, C. K.: *The System of Basic English,* Harcourt, Brace, 1934

Robinson, Stuart: *The Development of Modern English,* Prentice-Hall, 1934

Smith, Logan Pearsall: *English Idioms,* Clarenden Press, Oxford, 1923 (S. P. E. Tract, No. XII)

Weekly, Ernest: *The Romance of Words,* Dutton, 1912

Other books that you might find helpful, either for information or for amusement are:

Ernst, Margaret S.: *In a Word*, Knopf, 1935

Nonsense with each word amusingly illustrated by James Thurber.

Roget's International Thesaurus of English Words and Phrases, ed. by C. O. S. Mawson (abridged), Crowell, 1930

A necessary part of anyone's library.

Picturesque Word Origins, G. & C. Merriam Co., Springfield, Mass.

A history of original meanings illustrated, one word and one picture to a page.

Word Study, ed. by Max J. Herzberg, G. & C. Merriam Co., Springfield, Mass. (Free)

McKnight, George H.: *English Words and Their Backgrounds,* Appleton-Century, 1932

Mencken, H. L.: *The American Language,* 4th ed., Knopf, 1936

CHAPTER VI

Teaching Organization of Thought

WE TEACH spelling and punctuation; we *teach* grammar and the fundamentals of sentence structure. On Monday a class does not understand the use of quotation marks; by Friday a glimmer of light is apparent; and by the following Wednesday a dictated conversation can be taken down with more than fair correctness. But when we turn to that still less tangible topic, organization of thought, even though we work as diligently to inculcate principles, we must wait longer for results. By comparing simple expository talks as given by the freshmen and the juniors we can, perhaps, see the results of our training. Or by a comparison of freshmen and sophomore themes we may see in the second year greater orderliness of thinking. The development is, however, slow, often discouragingly slow.

A few high-school pupils may write well, one or two, perhaps, better than you do. But to the average high-school pupil each theme tends to remain a thing apart, a Herculean task that he must perform alone and unaided. He cannot see that the same general principles underlie his themes whether their subject is the business of beaver-catching, the making of a municipal skating pond, or the manufacture of artificial ice. For each separate theme you will find him dragging out his material by main force and hurriedly scrawling it down as it comes out of his mind. As the confusion grows greater, as a rule he grows more and more disgusted with composition making, for he sees, if he is intelligent, how far his jumbled facts misrepresent the clear, orderly process he witnessed with interest.

What can you do for him? How can anything so intangible, so individual, as his thinking become a subject for profitable classroom discussion? And how shall you proceed if you do undertake teaching organization of thought? Because the topic is a fundamental one, teachers generally admit its importance; but because the topic is intangible, difficult, and easily obscured in specific themes by subject matter, illustrations, and odd quirks of style, a pupil's organization of thought is often neglected. Often the theme or talk is criticized adversely for its external blemishes, while no mention is made of its fundamental deformity in thought or faulty articulation of parts. When you get into the schoolroom, you will realize the reason for this neglect. You will be busy. There will be many obvious things to teach. A badly deformed sentence, a misspelled word, incorrect punctuation, misuse of a verb, are all immediately recognizable, can be quickly marked, should be corrected by the pupil. There will be times when it may seem to you that your eye, your hand, your pencil, check these errors while your mind is fixed upon a restless study hall or is busy deciding whether you should or should not report Manuel's transgressions to the principal. I admit that themes should *not* be so corrected. I am merely stating that at times they are. At other times, however, when you put your whole attention upon theme organizations, what shall you do?

I. TEACH LOGICAL SEQUENCE: B.M.E.

From the sixth grade on through the twelfth, one essential to drive home is this: Every paper that a pupil writes, every oral report that he makes, is written or spoken for an audience. This audience has a right to demand logical organization and clarity. In brief narrative where chronology predetermines the order of events, an outline is probably not necessary. Most children know that they must

1. tell of mounting a bicycle or pony before they
2. tell of the neighbor's dog that caused the accident or
3. tell of the black eye that resulted from the fall.

In this incident the audience demands of the teller:

1. a **Beginning** that is immediate and interesting;
2. a **Middle** that is clear and in which all the material given is necessary; and
3. a brief **End** which concludes with a "clincher" sentence.

From the sixth grade on, classes will profit by this stress upon the B.M.E., so called in my own classes. On the consultation board I have found it convenient to leave, until all are familiar with it, this formula:

Look at Your B.M.E.

1. Is the **Beginning** immediate and interesting?
2. Is the **Middle** clear? Are all statements necessary for the reader's complete understanding or realization?
3. Is the **End** brief? Has it a clincher sentence?

You might ask why I avoid the more elegant and sightly terms "introduction, body, conclusion." I like the homemade quality of B.M.E. Also the idea of "introduction" is exactly what I wish to eliminate. Pupils consider an introduction an excuse for some dull, irrelevant, usually self-conscious bow to the audience. By B.M.E. I eliminate the bow. In the same way the term "conclusion" suggests to the average high-school mind a postscript, an addition after he is logically through. By E, I stress the need for stopping. But E also implies the need for a clincher sentence, a sentence that conveys a satisfying sense of conclusion.

Pupils must be made to realize that every sentence has to *win* its place in composition, either by making the facts of the theme more understandable to the reader, or by making the reader enter more fully into the sensations under consideration. I offer this B.M.E. only as a patently homemade device by which pupils may (1) arrange their ideas before they write, (2) revise their own themes before making the final copy, and (3) judge their neighbors' themes or talks given in class.

More and more I realize that one of the most valuable things to cultivate is a recognition of completion. Pupils must be made to feel satisfaction in a completed sentence, a completed paragraph, a completed theme. If possible they should be led to find satisfaction in a well-rounded talk. This much you can do, whether you can get more from your class or not: You can educate them to feel dissatisfied with a theme that has no clincher sentence at the end. Their comments "It isn't finished" or "He just stopped" will, time after time, indicate that you have cultivated in them an expectancy which the writer or speaker has not satisfied. Comments of this kind, if deserved, should encourage you. They show that your pupils have grasped one essential principle of thought-organization.

You must show pupils the need for order in speaking or writing. Some teachers present scrambled lists or paragraphs where the material does not follow the B.M.E. pattern but E.B.M. or M.E.B., thus giving a painful sense of disorder. Naturally, unscrambling these facts and setting them in proper array becomes the second step.

Other teachers present numerous paragraphs for analysis, a necessary and profitable prelude to writing and to intelligent reading. No matter what method you use, this work in paragraphs and longer selections must occupy much time, and should become a part of reading, writing, and speech. From the sixth grade on, you will probably present brief interesting paragraphs. These, at first under teacher guidance, the class considers, learning how to select (1) the topic sentence, (2) the key word or words in that sentence, (3) the arrangement of details in the paragraph, and (4) the method of ending or "clinching" the idea.[1]

---

[1] Before you consider teaching paragraphing, consult the revised *Writer's Guide and Index to English* by Porter G. Perrin, Scott, Foresman, 1950. Read and digest chapters seven and eight. Build your teaching upon this concept: *The idea must determine the kind, length, and construction of a paragraph, and the paragraph's function in and relation to the whole paper.* Then aware of the purpose and goal, consult some reliable junior-senior high school series of texts. Two useful series are D. C. Heath's "English in Action," and Harcourt, Brace's "Language Skills." Note from grade to grade the shifts in

Remember that teaching pupils to grasp the topic sentence of a paragraph and teaching them to write topic sentences large enough in scope to include the necessary details is a timetaking process. Also it is a process never completed, for, year after year, the pupil is confronted by material of increasing difficulty. Be patient; build slowly. Over and over you will ask: "What does the paragraph *say?*" "Of what is the author talking?" "Is that the main idea or is that just an illustration?" You will find that in this work, as in the consideration of examination questions and in general reading, it is wise to drill upon the *key word* of a sentence. First, of course, teach the meaning of the term "key word" in a sentence. In "Discuss the chief differences that you find in the characters of Hector and Achilles," obviously the key word is *differences*. But probably several of your freshmen will tell you that both warriors are brave, both swift-footed, and so on. Why do they? Because reading is an art. Because they have not been taught to extract the meaning from a group of words. By such questions, and by frequent board exercises both as to what a question means and what type of answer will be considered successful, you may teach pupils to read more intelligently and to organize their information in more orderly fashion. Perhaps you might expect a pupil to list under the headings "Hector" and "Achilles" the chief characteristics of each, to cross out those that were similar, to rearrange those remaining, and then, when those two lists were completed and arranged, to attempt to write upon the chief difference in the characters of the two heroes. But unless you suggest this very simple device for organizing their ideas few if any of your class will employ it. The device should be taught them in frequent brief class exercises based upon ques-

emphasis, but the constant repetition, enlivened by new approaches. From these texts you can learn methods; but paragraphs, even well built ones, are useless unless they support the whole structure of the paper. Through board work, and through oral development of familiar topics, you can train students to see the *whole idea,* and then to divide it into its component parts or paragraphs.

tions demanding a contrast or a comparison of books, characters, situations.

Some teachers believe in what they call practice tests, tests given, explained, written, and corrected in one class period, a rehearsal for the more serious, graded examinations. To the pupils these tests seem a remarkable and kindly aid; but to the teacher they are just one more device for teaching organization and for securing practice in strongly motivated expository writing. The finding of the key word in the question and the ways of organizing answers are discussed. In the same fashion every graded examination upon its return should also become a subject for class discussion. There should be an analysis of each question to discover its scope, and the reading of well-organized and poorly organized answers to indicate by contrast what is and what is not satisfactory organization. In this way an examination becomes not only a testing, but an effective teaching device.

One useful method for clarifying thought, but one that pupils avoid, is that of numbering the steps. This device, I explain, is particularly useful to them in an examination. Frankly I admit to them my own effective method in examinations of appearing to know more than I do by writing "There were ———————— causes for the widespread discontent," numbering the causes as I think of them *one, two, three,* and so on, and then at the conclusion returning to my original statement and filling the blank. If you can lure your classes into writing such an introductory sentence, what have you done? Forced them to organize their material into a certain number of (one hopes) parallel statements. If you can lead a class into such clear thinking that it sees topics as wholes, subdivides them, and does not forget that a *third* demands a *first* and a *second,* you have done well. You have laid a ground plan for clear, sensible organization of your pupil's thought. By board work, by twenty minutes of class writing, by suggesting a question one day and returning to it later, you can give your class stimulating work in methods of organization. Try in the classroom a matching of wits by quick analysis of some such questions as these:

1. There were at least —————————— causes for Jessica's unhappiness in Shylock's house.

2. There are at least —————————— causes for our admiration for Winston Churchill.

3. There are at least —————————— reasons why we should have student government.

4. There were at least —————————— traits in Silas Marner that lay dormant during his long solitude.

Of course there is a danger here. You do not want to breed superficial thinkers, future citizens who mistake snap judgments for sound thought. I think, however, if you give the class sufficient time, you need not worry upon this score. If a class invariably analyzed a topic, a question, a situation, and divided it into a few essential phases, I should know that the millennium had come. What do most pupils do? Look at a question, rush headlong upon it, and write whatever comes first into their minds. Why? For years they have suffered from long examinations. Their precipitancy is an interesting comment upon our educational methods.

So far I have stressed expository material, but while you are stressing the B.M.E. (or whatever you choose to call it) of the theme as a whole—narrative, descriptive, expository—you must also, of course, concern yourself with the relation of parts within the whole. Here again the audience idea is useful. As suggested in Chapter IX, you need to teach pupils how to express time sequence by showing them how time words may be used as guides. By pointing out these guide words to your class, by asking them to find examples of a writer's use of such time words to aid readers, and by suggesting that they use similar devices, you are teaching them two things: first, to organize their thoughts into chronological series; and, second, to recognize and to use technical means of keeping their readers informed clearly as to the passage of time. When you read the assignments given in Chapter IX, will you realize, I wonder, that you are in reality concerned with teaching the organization of thought? Or will you think of those assignments as mere vocabulary instructions and attempts to get smooth sentence structure?

I ask that question, for I believe much classwork that might become effective training in organization of thought falls short of its full usefulness because it is not generalized. Teachers should show, with many examples, how author after author has used a time sequence successfully, how easy it is to follow, how essentially easy it is to write, how useful it is as an aid for organization of material. And teachers should discuss pupils' themes in the light of this general principle of organization. Often the time sequence seems so inevitable to the teacher that she does not realize one fact: The pupil may have utilized it without consciously realizing what he was doing. He merely remembered the incident; he told it as he remembered it. His composition, then, apparently so well organized, may be merely an accident, and no guide to help him when he attempts a second narration of events which he remembers, but not in chronological order.

The teaching of space sequence again presents a somewhat similar problem. Fiction will provide you with many a description or simple exposition of houses, lawns, athletic fields, main streets, decks of ships, and farms where you, the reader, are skillfully led from place to place by definite guide words. Does it seem childish to explain to high-school pupils the necessity for such guide words? Back of the words lies a fundamental process, the *process of establishing a point of view,* and of seeing the subject to be described as a whole subdivided into logical parts which, one after the other, the writer displays to the reader.

Often, of course, a mere listing of details may be desirable, as in the paragraph from *A Tale of Two Cities* quoted in Chapter IX. Here, as used by a skilled writer, the order of details is comparatively unimportant. But in high-school themes, as a rule, some definite arrangement is more satisfactory than a mere haphazard listing. Pupils should be taught, for example, to observe the order commonly illustrated in newspaper accounts. There one finds a statement of the general idea, the principal happening, followed by specific details. The morning paper announces that two American missionaries have been seized by bandits. *The first paragraph reports the bare facts,* plus the names and a statement of time, place, and possible cause. Not until the next paragraph do we learn the exact details. In a magazine article, however, just the opposite plan may be carried out. The particular detail is told first, and from this detail, our interest awakened, we are carried on to the general idea dominating the article as a whole.

Another arrangement of material with which your high-school pupils should be familiar is that of a climax sequence. If, for example, your board contains the following jumble under the heading "Loyalties," any class will protest. *Loyalties: family, nation, League of Nations, friends, state, city.* They will feel that, like the circles made by a stone dropped into water, the ever wider interest must follow, not precede, the narrower one. Just what are you doing with this list? Asking a class to arrange ideas in the order of magnitude. When planning a composition, a pupil should of course look at his topic as a whole, determine the relative value of its parts, and place those parts advantageously.

Why is all this work important? Because you are giving your junior-high-school pupils (or, alas, your high-school seniors or college freshmen) an introduction to some necessary general principles, principles that will aid them both (1) to understand the thought patterns of the material they read, and (2) to organize their own ideas for talks or papers. One word of warning is necessary: Easy as the work seems to you, it is difficult for many of your pupils, since analyzing an article—that is, viewing material objectively as to its organization—is always more difficult than merely swallowing it whole. Watch your group. Do not tire them with this unwonted mental activity, for you must not build up in the minds of your poorer pupils a dislike based upon their inability to follow the work presented.

What have you accomplished? With some such simple beginning as I have suggested here, you have shown your pupils:

1. The need for order in expressing ideas
2. The simplest form of outline
3. Several patterns of thought organization
4. Recognition of these patterns in the material that they read

This you have certainly done, but if your teaching has been successful, you have done much more. You have laid a foundation for intelligent reading and logical thinking.

II. TEACH OUTLINING

But the simple B.M.E. is only the first step in logical thinking. The outline in proper form is step two. Would you be surprised to learn that in many classrooms the whole process of outlining is treated in a perfunctory manner, and often left untaught until just before the final "long" paper in the last semester of the junior or senior year? Yet, as you realize, all six years of the high-school course in English are given over to teaching pupils to speak, write, and read organized units of thought. What is your own explanation? Is it possible that prospective teachers of English are more thoroughly trained in appreciation of literature than in logical thinking? Whatever training you have had, one thing becomes obvious. From the sixth grade on you must *teach* the principles which underlie outlining, and teach them consistently, until your pupils view their talk-to-be or their unwritten paper as an entity with *one* dominant idea which has several subdivisions. Is that statement too idealistic? Let's go further. You must teach the principles which underlie outlining until your pupils recognize that the articles or formal essays that they read have *one* dominant idea which has several subdivisions. If you approximate this ideal, you are teaching your pupils to read intelligently; you are teaching them to think more logically than was their earlier habit. Don't look on outlining as a formal, dull, but necessary drill. Think of it as one of the most useful things that you can do for each individual pupil, who will, presumably, become a talking, reading, voting citizen of the United States. Do you realize its possibilities?

So much for generalization. What are you to do?

You must show your pupils how to outline.

You recognize, do you not, that human beings are mentally lazy? (Recall the evasion of mental effort shown by our "flipping a coin.") Even though it might, in the long run, be easier to think out and to outline an expository paper or talk, pupils shirk the task—just as you and I did—hoping through luck or chance to hit upon an acceptable order of facts. Outlining is only a convenient way of signifying logical thought divisions. The outline itself, that is, is an unimportant detail. When finished, it is merely "the outward and visible sign" of that "inward and spiritual grace" called logical thinking. *Teach* the principles of thought division and arrangement of material. Then, just as convenience, *use* a simple outline to express what you and the class have decided is a logical arrangement.[1]

Are you familiar with the two types of outline: the procedure outline and the content outline? They are used for distinctly dif-

---

[1] Outline Form

   I. ....
      A. ....
        1. ....
          a. ....
            (1) ....
              (a) ....
      B. ....
        1. ....
        2. ....
  II. ....

ferent purposes. Be certain that your pupils realize the difference. The procedure outline corresponds to the plans made before one climbs a neighboring mountain or starts for Hong Kong. The traveler decides:

1. When he will start
2. How he will go
3. What he will make the chief objective of his trip

But later when he tells of his journey, it is not the procedure plan which interests his hearers; it is the substance of his trip— what he saw, felt, experienced.

For example, you are working at the seventh-grade level. You and your class are planning a talk before the P.T.A. (Parent-Teacher Association) on why your school needs a new room for the cafeteria. Together you would make a procedure outline— that is, a chart as to what you must do for such a discussion. You might write some such simple procedure outline as this:

A NEW CAFETERIA LUNCHROOM

(*Topical Procedure Outline*)

I. Why we need a new lunch-room
II. How we could pay for it
III. How we should profit from having such a room

A NEW CAFETERIA LUNCHROOM

(*Sentence Procedure Outline*)

I. We need a new lunchroom
II. We could pay for it
III. We would profit from having such a room

Only after you and the class have surveyed the topic as a whole are you ready to collect material. Later, when you know the necessary facts, you are ready to make a content outline— one giving material, not mere directions for procedure.

For many high-school pupils one of the most stimulating fresh-man courses is general science. Here are two outlines on that sub-ject: (1) a procedure outline which can be made without specific information, but charts a method for collecting facts; (2) a con-tent outline in sentence form.[1]

[1] Until you have taught parallel construction and taught it thoroughly, it may be unwise to accept topical outlines.

OUR COURSE IN GENERAL SCIENCE
(*Procedure Outline*)

I. Give a description of the course, telling its purposes and the subject matter included.
II. Show why the course is beneficial to freshmen.
III. Tell how it could be improved.

(Note the simplicity of the language. What you are striving for is clean-cut divisions of a topic.)

OUR COURSE IN GENERAL SCIENCE
(*A Sentence Content Outline*)

I. To understand the course a brief description of it is necessary.
    A. The purpose of the course is twofold.
        1. It is to awaken our interest in the world of science.
        2. It is to give us a superficial understanding of certain scientific fields.
    B. The content of the course is interestingly varied.
        1. It presents a little botany, enough to open our eyes.
        2. It introduces a little zoology.
        3. It offers a few experiments in chemistry.
II. We derive different types of benefit from the course.
    A. The work in class and in laboratory is enjoyable.
        1. The lectures are full of fresh, surprising material.
        2. The experimental work in laboratory is interestingly different from other schoolwork.
    B. The work makes us understand many scientific facts which formerly puzzled us or went unnoticed.
    C. The work makes us more interested in the world about us.
III. There are certain changes, however, that would make the work more interesting and beneficial.
    A. The lectures should cover less material and should give more explanation about the topics treated.
    B. The course should provide more laboratory equipment so that each pupil could have a desk and material of his own.
    C. The instructor should have fewer tests and more discussion periods during which pupils could ask questions.

Here is a seventh-grade attempt.

A GREEK LEGEND

(A Sentence Content Outline)

I. The sky at night has fascinated mankind.
   A. Our scientists study the stars.
   B. Our poets write of their beauty.
   C. The Greeks invented interesting stories about them.

II. One legend invented by the Greeks is of the Pleiades.
   A. The Pleiades were seven beautiful maidens who excited Orion's love.
      1. They were pursued by him.
      2. They prayed to be saved from him.
      3. The goddess changed them into pigeons.
      4. Later they were changed into a constellation made up of seven stars.
      5. Today we see only six, for at the fall of Troy one maiden hid her face.

III. Through the ages man's treatment of the stars differs.
   A. Great books are written on astronomy by scientists.
   B. Poems like "My Star" are written by modern poets.
   C. But only the Greeks have given us stories that still live and still make the night sky interesting to those who know the legends.

In the senior high school the only difference in teaching outlining lies in the type of material and the amount of detail used. To make this work concrete, I give a typical "setting-up exercise" used with a retarded junior class. The pupils were to read later the selection by Stuart Chase from his book *Rich Land, Poor Land* on the importance of grass. Some were familiar with Dust Bowl conditions; one or two had seen the movie version of *Grapes of Wrath;* two had heard of that admirable film, *The Plow That Broke the Plain*. All seemed certain that writing an article was practically impossible, and that reading one was distasteful. So

much for the background. The teacher, who was to act as class
secretary at the board, had decided upon the following steps:

First, to write down all thoughts concerning Dust Bowl conditions
as they were contributed.
Second, to discard, at class suggestion, all obviously nonessential
material, and from the pertinent suggestions to make a procedure
outline.
Third, to select one dominant idea from the several volunteered
that would unify the imaginary article.
Fourth, to list the usable suggestions in logical order.
Fifth, to develop a content outline in sentence form from this
material.
Sixth, to select a title appropriate for the dominant idea.

Fortified by these resolutions, the teacher began a discussion
of Dust Bowl conditions; then she suggested that since later the
class would write articles upon various topics, they could together
organize this topic—a sort of setting-up exercise—just to see how
it might be done. Dividing the board in half, she explained that
on the left side she would list the class suggestions; then on the
right side they would together organize those suggestions into an
orderly outline for the imaginary article. The whole procedure, a
method used by many well-known magazine writers, allows the
writer to see what he knows on a topic, and to decide what facts
or illustrations he should look up.

FIRST STEP	SECOND STEP
Class Suggestions	*Procedure Outline*
1. Nebraska companies planted grass. (III)	I. Present grass conditions contrasted to past conditions (Topics 2 and 11)
2. People are moving out of the Dust Bowl lands. Soil blows away. Bad for babies. (I)	II. Steps in destruction of grass (Topics 9, and illustration 3, 6, and 10)
3. Feuds between cattlemen and sheepmen. Sheep bad for grass. (II)	III. Steps taken to hold soil solid Topics 1 and 5)
	IV. Possible solution: govern-

4. These Dust Bowl problems are serious. (IV)

5. Russia had Dust Bowl problems. They planted kandym plants. Read about it in the *Reader's Digest*. These plants held down the soil. (III)

6. Sheep kill grass. Eat it too close. (II)

7. Trees hold water in the soil. (omit)

8. Roosevelt began planting a shelter belt. (omit)

9. Cows overgrazed the land. Too many for amount of grass. (II)

10. Dry-land farmers came in. Plowed land. Used horses, then tractors. (II)

11. Used to be lots of grass all over the plains. Had no Dust Bowl problems till recently. (I)

12. People are poor in Dust Bowls. Government will have to help them and have to help the states, too. (IV)

13. It takes about 25 years to get grass back on Dust Bowl soil. (IV)

ment aid and control (Topics 4, 12, and 13)

Sentence Content Outline

I. Dramatic contrast exists between the past and the present condition of our land in our so-called Dust Bowl areas.

  A. In the past the land was productive.

    1. Native grasses, often knee-high, covered the area and waved in the wind.

    2. These grasses sprouted, grew, seeded themselves, and withered to the roots.

  B. At present the land is a virtual desert.

    1. Swirls of dust, not waving grasses, now move in the wind.

    2. This semidesert area is ever increasing in size.

    3. Farmers are forced to abandon the land, for it is unfit for cultivation.

II. Blind or thoughtless as the inhabitants were, it is now clear, step by step, how this destruction of native grasses took place.

A. At first wild buffalo
and then a few head
of cattle grazed this
vast area.

B. Then more and more
cattle were driven up
from Texas or neigh-
boring states by in-
coming settlers.

C. Later the sheepmen
brought in new prob-
lems.

 1. Sheep in great
numbers kill the
grasses by graz-
ing too close to
the roots.

 2. Cows refuse to
graze where
sheep have been.

 3. Soon came a
cattle-sheep feud,
indicating that
the land was
overstocked and
overgrazed.

D. Following the cattle-
men and the sheep-
men came the farmers.

 1. At first they
turned over the
soil with horse-
drawn plows.

 2. With the coming
of the First
World War and
the consequent
demand for
wheat, machin-

ery was intro-
duced, and vast
areas of native
grass were plowed
under.

E. Under hot sun and
high wind year after
year the topsoil blew
away.

    1. At first there
were occasional
swirls of dust.

    2. Next there were
dust storms in
certain areas.

    3. Finally ever in-
creasing areas
loosed their top-
soil and joined
the semidesert
area.

III. This unfortunate desolation
is not peculiar to the United
States, nor is the condition
without remedy.

A. Russia suffered from
a similar condition,
brought on by a sim-
ilar cycle of events.

B. There the government
planted the kandym
plant, a weed that
takes root easily and
holds the soil solid.

C. A somewhat similar
attempt, on a small
scale, was tried in Ne-
braska, and the soil

there was anchored
successfully.

IV. It is evident that steps must
be taken to reclaim this
semidesert land.

    A. This Dust Bowl area
is needed for grazing
purposes.

    B. Unless this land is re-
claimed, it will infect
neighboring land.

    C. This reclamation
should be carried on
by the Federal Gov-
ernment.

        1. People owning
this land are now
poor.

        2. Since it takes
about twenty-five
years to reclaim
the land, few in-
dividual owners
can afford to let
their land lie idle
that long.

        3. The Federal Gov-
ernment can, by
utilizing the land
of other states,
transfer families
from Dust Bowl
lands, and can
reclaim the Great
American Desert.

Although this class-teacher product is faulty, it illustrates group work in thinking through a familiar problem and gaining some sort of orderly sequence. It is obvious that the class would have to investigate certain points were this outline developed.[1] For example:

1. The exact location of the Dust Bowl area
2. The part of Russia that was planted with kandym (kandym familiar to them under another name evidently is not here recognized)
3. Dates and facts concerning cattle-sheep-farming periods
4. Facts as to the amount and kind of government aid already given Dust Bowl sufferers

The work illustrated (1) a simple approach to teaching organization of thought; (2) one way of encouraging pupils to examine their own minds for composition material; and (3) the practical use of outlining to gain orderly organization.

Such setting-up exercises in class, used frequently, have yet another value. They encourage pupils to ask (and to be asked) five questions:

1. Exactly what is your topic?
2. How much do you know about it?
3. Into what two, three, or four big divisions does it fall?
4. What *one* impression or dominant idea do you mean to give us?
5. How are you going to support or illustrate what you have to say?

All teachers know the discouraging moment when after a really good paper has been read to an uninstructed class, the class sits silent or says, "I didn't think it was interesting," "I liked it," "I thought it was all right." By class building of themes never to be written, the class gains some idea of what can be expected and should be expected from a paper. In other words, the pupils become more intelligent and more critical concerning their own and their classmates' work. The teacher has provided a basis for class discussion.[2]

[1] It is also obvious that an imaginative pupil contributed "swirls," "vast areas," "loosed their topsoil," contrasting oddly with the teacher's "semiarid," "infect," "consequent demand."

[2] The teaching of parallel construction is always a difficult problem. If an outline is in topical, not sentence, form, you have an excellent opportunity to

There are times, however, when an outline shrinks to a mere pretense of logical thinking. Beware of that noninformational type foisted upon you in lieu of a content outline. My own favorite in high-school days, equally serviceable for exposition and for argument, for advocacy of a new municipal swimming pool, county jail, dance pavilion, or orphans' home, was this:

THE CITY OF ——————— SHOULD BUILD A NEW ———————

I. Introduction:
   A. History of the present ———————

II. The present conditions of ——————— are detrimental to the community:
   A. Financially
   B. Physically
   C. Morally

III. The proposed changes would improve conditions:
   A. Financially
   B. Physically
   C. Morally

IV. The proposed plan is practicable:
   A. Financially—Money is obtainable
   B. Physically—Ground and materials are available
   C. Morally—The community is awakened to its responsibilities

stress once more this peculiarly difficult construction. Recall the discussion in Chapter III, and practice changing the forms so that the class is aware that no *one form* is "correct," but that a word, a phrase, a clause, a sentence, may be used *if used consistently for those parts that are of equal importance.*

Example

II. Steps in grass destruction   or   II. Steps in destruction
   A. Overgrazing by cattle   A. What cattle contributed
   B. Overgrazing by sheep   B. What sheep contributed
   C. Breaking soil with plow   C. What the plow contributed

or

II. Destruction of the grass was   or   II. Native grasses were destroyed
      accomplished through   A. By cattle
   A. Herds of cattle   B. By sheep
   B. Bands of sheep   C. By farmers equipped with ma-
   C. Farmers with machinery   chinery

V. Conclusion: The City should build a new —————
   A. Because a change is necessary
   B. Because the proposed change is desirable
   C. Because the proposed change is practicable

This type of ready-made outline, a hodgepodge of procedure and content outline, runs ideas into a mold, gives a semblance of order, and allows the pretense of thought to replace thinking. The other type of outline or brief, however, one in which the actual material appears in related sequence, has a definite place, particularly in the longer expository or argumentative writings of the last two years of high school.[1]

Remember this fact: English more than other high-school subjects suffers from sporadic teaching. The habit of logical organization is not learned in one class exercise, nor in a three-week unit. Outlining is a tool, and worse than useless unless its use is understood. In planning your year's work in each class, see that simple outlining—the mere breaking up of a subject into its logical divisions—is utilized (when appropriate) both for reading and for composition, oral and written.

III. TEACH PRÉCIS WRITING

As with the work in outlining, I feel that here again a warning is necessary. Your teaching of English must not descend to mere drill for drill's sake, nor to dull repetition. You are *not* teaching outlining for any intrinsic value that lies in the outline form. You *are* attempting to show your pupils how to organize their own ideas or how to seize an author's *main* idea, freeing it from a mass of illustration and detail. The foundation for this type of work should be laid in junior high school, but if your senior-high-school pupils have had no training in organization of thought and recognition of important and subordinate ideas in the work of

[1] A question that you must decide is whether or not you intend to teach argument and debate and whether you intend to give instruction in brief-making. The condition of your class must, of course, be the determining factor. See suggested texts and reading references on debate, Appendix H.

others, what must you do? *Begin on whatever level is adapted to your pupils' needs.* Précis writing—a brief statement of the main idea of sentence, paragraph, or whole article given briefly in the pupil's own words—is another method of compelling pupils to analyze for the essential idea.[1]

If you think over your work in literature, you realize that précis, of a sort, have been a necessary but informal part of all reading. "What does it mean?" you ask about a sentence, a paragraph, an article. And, orally, the pupil may—or may not—give you an approximation of a précis. There are certain steps which you will follow, beginning in the junior high school, that will aid him in this process of understanding a passage: (1) locating the key word, (2) locating the topic sentence in a paragraph, (3) scrutinizing a paragraph to discover what pattern of development is used by the writer, (4) looking for the main statement and its supporting statements in a discussion. All these devices (discussed earlier) are preliminary steps in analysis that should precede précis writing. From précis work itself pupils learn how to read, how to condense an idea, how, shearing off illustration and repetition, to extract and set down briefly the essential thought in a passage. In those parts of the United States where the shadow of the College Board examinations darkens the last two years of high-school literature study, précis may play too important a part. I make that statement tentatively. But in the West, analysis of passages is an all too infrequent exercise. Précis writing must not, of course, crowd out original work; neither must it be injudiciously used to spoil the study of literature, as it certainly is when pupils are forced to reduce as fragile and lovely a thing as poetry to a poor prose paragraph. In the early years it serves a purpose somewhat similar to that of mental-arithmetic drills. It forces pupils to focus attention, to read accurately or

[1] For a careful analysis of the process, see *Language Arts for the Junior and Senior High Schools of Texas,* State Department of Education, Austin, Texas, *Bulletin* No. 396, Vol. XV, No. 3 (March, 1939), p. 110.

listen attentively. For the senior-high-school pupils it has added uses. Note-taking becomes important; hence précis writing—that is, brief, accurate statements of the main ideas read—becomes of increasing importance. Work in note-taking (class reports, lectures, and text assignments), with drill upon various kinds of material, ought to play some part in your classwork. How large a part depends upon the preparation and ability of your pupils.

But dangers beset the path of a new teacher who attempts précis writing before a foundation has been laid. The work itself is difficult both for the teacher and for the pupils. For the teachers it is hard because they must find desirable and relevant paragraphs, suitable in subject matter, vocabulary, length. Then, too, they must write them on the board, or mimeograph them, or read them aloud. The work is timetaking, and worse than useless if hurried. It is essential to its success, particularly at first, that it receive the stimulus of class effort, of teacher encouragement and suggestion, and of immediate discussion of the written analysis. In the last two years brief, frequent class exercises in précis writing have definite value.[1] Perhaps the work belongs more logically in history or science, but the teacher of composition must also assume responsibility for this training.

If you glance back over this chapter, you will note that the foregoing discussion is merely a series of suggestions for awakening in your pupils a recognition of the dominating idea in writing or speech and the supporting statements. By précis writing, by analysis of questions for the key word, by listing and numbering the various phrases to be discussed, by class training with such topics as "There are at least ——————— reasons why we

[1] The best précis work is drawn from material students are studying in history, science, or English, not from printed tests. Realizing that the work is sensible and useful, they undertake it willingly, many collecting examples. They are also learning an important fact: different types of material require different types of reading. Learn to center and relate your work. For aid see *Harbrace College Handbook,* pp. 371-374, Harcourt, Brace, 1946.

should have student government," you are assisting pupils to recognize the main proposition and its logical subdivisions.

IV. TEACH PUPILS TO WRITE RESEARCH PAPERS

A. *Use of the library*

If your pupils are fortunate, since grade-school days they have had access to a well-stocked library. But if they have not, if the high-school library consists of one hall closet open half an hour after school plus the usual dog-eared dictionary and encyclopedia set, you can still manage a research paper, though not under ideal conditions. It is to be hoped that a town or county library and a co-operative librarian exist somewhere in your vicinity. If a visit to that library is carefully prepared for and intelligently carried out, your pupils accomplish two things: They get some material for a paper; they acquire at least a speaking acquaintance with a library. Would the class enjoy such an outing? Would your principal approve such initiative on your part? Would the librarian, if carefully forewarned, make proper provision for the invasion? The answer is, of course, obvious. Try such an expedition, but don't rush a class into the visit *before* you have given them careful training with the free material (and perhaps some of the less expensive material) listed below. Whether or not your school library is well equipped it would be wise to equip yourself with the following free pamphlets, enough for each class member:

From G. & C. Merriam Company, Springfield, Massachusetts:
Guide to Webster's New International Dictionary
Outline for Dictionary Study for Webster's New Collegiate Dictionary
Vocabulary Building, Interesting Origins of English Words
From H. W. Wilson Co., 950-72 University Ave., New York:
Sample Pages of the Reader's Guide (Up to 50 in number for class use are sent on request. Try them in quick class drill after sufficient explanation, particularly in poorly equipped schools.)

Nine cents for stamps and enough energy to write three letters, since three of the five pamphlets listed come from the same publisher, will bring you this admirable material for classroom drill. Class drill preceded by careful explanation will teach your pupils how to find the wealth of material carefully concealed from them in dictionary, encyclopedia, *Readers' Guide,* and card catalogue. After such classroom training, after each pupil is supplied with specific and varied questions on a work sheet that is to be filled in at the library, you are almost ready for the library visit. One thing remains: You must make it clear to the librarian that once she has pointed out the location of the card catalogue, the *Readers' Guide,* and other necessary reference works, your pupils are to spend the two hours working, not listening.

But suppose you are neither on a desert island nor in a school minus an adequate library. Training in the use of the library and in organizing one or more research papers is no less important, but is a simpler and more satisfactory procedure. Most schools, although they both encourage and demand library acquaintance and use from grade-school days on, leave the formal research paper until the end of the eleventh or the twelfth year. Many reports, however, based upon intelligent use of library resources are expected from pupils in both junior and senior high school.[1] Such reports must be preceded by training in use of the library, training given by both teacher and librarian. Illustrative of the close co-operation which should exist between high-school teacher and librarian is Jessie Boyd's account, "The University High School Library Keeps Pace with Curriculum Needs."[2] Here is explained the visit of a tenth-grade pupil to the library where (1) the Dewey decimal classification is reviewed; (2) a diagram of the library is given each pupil; and (3) work sheets are passed

---

[1] See *The Secondary School Curriculum and Syllabi of Subjects,* State of Minnesota Department of Education, St. Paul, Minn., *Bulletin* No. A1, *English, for Junior High School Period,* August, 1933, p. 111.

[2] *University High School Journal,* Vol. 19, No. 1 (November, 1940), University of California, Berkeley, Calif.

out which require pupils to investigate the library materials for answers to definite questions. After these work sheets have been checked, errors discussed, and the sheets returned to the pupils' notebooks, the teacher introduces the pupils to the *Readers' Guide*; then brief research papers on hobbies or vocations are written. In the eleventh year, emphasis is placed on various periodical indexes and handbooks, editorial policies, propaganda. During this study a term paper, a research paper with bibliography, is required. Classes or individuals having difficulty with library work receive special instruction from the librarians. In the twelfth year a library test reveals those students who need more library instruction. For them (a step not taken, apparently, in many schools) "the librarian explains the University of California library, its arrangement and services offered, and thus helps to minimize the adjustment necessary for those who go to the University."

What can you do for your prospective college students that approximates this aid? In many schools an even more important question is this: How can you train your pupils who are not bound for the university so that they can get the maximum amount of aid and pleasure from the library reference and reading rooms? Brains just as good, just as curious, are outside college walls as are within them, and often they are hungrier and more eager than those inside. Your business is to make it possible for these brains to find themselves at home in that democratic university of the people—the public library.

One of the most detailed and explicit accounts of library training, given from the seventh grade through the twelfth, is included (pp. 232-85) in the *Syllabus in English* for the State of New York.[1] Consult it, or if it is not available, invest thirty-five cents and have this guide as a permanent part of your professional library. One of the virtues found in this course, outlined from the seventh-grade pupil's first visit to the library until the senior's last one, is its patient repetition. At each level, work sheets are given the pupils. Each sheet calls for laboratory work in the

[1] See footnote on next page for additional texts on library instruction.

library, and since waste of time and an invitation to idle would result from turning a whole class upon identical books or years of the *Readers' Guide,* questions are identical as to the type of material demanded, but dissimilar as to the year or the person to be investigated. *Remember to be this foresighted.*

To your pupils, the card catalogue is either an indispensable guide or an enigma. Your business is to make it the former. At first you may question as to what you would "teach" about a card catalogue except its alphabetical arrangement. Why not have made or make sample cards showing the numerous and baffling variations? These you would display and discuss. They should include:

1. Author card
2. Title card
3. Subject card (referring to the whole book)
4. Subject card (referring to part of the book)
5. Reference card ("See" reference)
6. Reference card ("See also" reference)
7. Cross reference (card for pseudonym)
8. Card giving table of contents

After this discussion, is it necessary to point out that the teacher must know, and know thoroughly, the resources of the school library? If that library is inadequate, she must also know the city or county library and co-operate with the librarians. Librarians are patient people; be certain that the "co-operation" is not one-sided.

Library training should be spread over as wide a span of years as possible.[1] But even if it is of necessity crowded into the last two years, it should be taught thoroughly and with much repetition. Just what are you to teach?

[1] Texts on library instruction: Brown, Zaidee: *The Library Key,* 7th ed., rev., 1943, 90 cents. For 25 or more, 60 cents. H. W. Wilson Co.; Toser, Marie A.: *Library Manual,* a Study-Work Manual on the Use of Books and Libraries, rev., 1949, 70 cents. For 25 or more, 45 cents, H. W. Wilson Co.

1. Parts of a book and their uses
2. Uses of the dictionary
3. Uses of an encyclopedia
4. A survey of the library, its general content and arrangement
5. A survey of the periodicals and newspapers
6. Use of the card catalogue
7. Use of the *Readers' Guide*
8. Use of the *New York Times Index* and other indexes
9. Use of familiar and needed reference books
10. Way to follow a topic through various references and cross-references, and to extract only the pertinent material

B. Method of collecting and organizing library materials for a research paper

There are teachers who omit all research papers of any length because they feel that their seniors should spend their time attempting to secure correctness. You will have to decide the matter for yourselves. But under certain conditions I question that decision. If from seven until seventeen a youth has *not* learned the generally accepted decencies of spelling, punctuation, sentence structure, and paragraphing, why do I expect that he will learn them between seventeen and eighteen? If he goes to college and survives subfreshman composition, he will, doubtless, be exposed to source-theme making. If he does not go to college, it is highly probable that he will receive no later training helpful in the collection and logical arrangement of research material for talks or discussions in club, lodge, union, or private conversation. Nor will he know how to find the facts that underlie those questions about which he is asked to vote. I am inclined to believe that the not-too-long research paper, *written on a topic of interest to the pupil,* may prove to be a stimulus to better work—even to the weak pupil. But you must use tact, patience, and good judgment. The careless, overgrown, happy-go-lucky boys emerging into manhood need a man-sized job. For them the "weekly theme" or the "class exercise" (though they can't cope with it) may not prove a sufficient challenge. If a research paper does awaken their interest, then and then only will they make an effort to improve their mechanics—about which, perhaps, we concern ourselves more than we do about their thinking.

A slow and carefully planned beginning is necessary. The high-school-senior mind seems to take perverse pleasure in confusing "bibliographical cards" and "reading cards." It also shows a pre-dilection that approaches devotion for collecting notes on large, mussy sheets of paper, scribbled on both sides. Three-by-five cards it abhors; and elastic bands about those cards are an ex-travagance rarely tolerated. Be prepared for slow, painfully slow, discussion of *how* a pupil can save himself time and effort. A few periods spent in "setting-up exercises" on procedure outlines, out-lines that are to guide future reading and note-taking, may seem to you in the rush of the senior year an uncalled-for expenditure of time. But it is not. I should advise you to begin by urging your students to look into their own minds in order to discover something about which they have long felt some curiosity. Then as they look within, I should casually suggest topics, explaining that radio, television, recorders, films, our national parks, John Buchan's novels and life (with a chapter of *Pilgrim's Way* in-cluded), Katherine Mansfield's eye for detail or the influence of her life on her stories, the invention of the submarine and its sub-sequent improvements—one and all offer excellent possibilities.

Here is a piece of work, remember, before which strong men quail—unless you give slow, careful instruction. Each step should be explained to the class deliberately (unless your group is un-usually well prepared), and work sheets should be provided for preliminary exercises. You may question why students should not immediately expend their energy upon the topic selected for their individual research paper. Perhaps they should, but a week spent increasing acquaintance with library resources, and learning how to record accurately and fully on individual cards each library reference, gives them both excellent training and time to consider just what topic is of sufficient interest for them to spend from four to six or eight weeks investigating.

Work sheets, prepared well in advance, make this preliminary drill definite, and demand library investigation that later will save time and discouragement. The seven sheets would probably cover the following material:

Work Sheet I. Some five topics for which procedure outlines are to be made.

Work Sheet II. A specimen card for bibliography and some five references (with incomplete data) that demand visits to the card catalogue, encyclopedias, *Poole's Index, Readers' Guide, International Index to Periodicals,* or other sources, depending upon your library equipment. (Since you will in class examine these cards, it would be wise to select material based upon the five topics listed on Work Sheet I. Even a teacher of English cannot "take *all* knowledge for his province.")

Work Sheet III. A specimen reading card (note-taking card) and some five assignments demanding brief and simple précis of specific articles or paragraphs from articles.

Work Sheet IV. A request that the student select one topic from those listed on Work Sheet I. For that topic a content outline is to be made. (Naturally the topic must be simple and require little reading. The purpose is to give again the difference between the procedure outline—to guide research; and the content outline—to guide the writer in making an interesting paper.)

Work Sheet V. A. A paragraph developing any part of the content outline.

B. *At least* three footnotes for the paragraph, two from the same source.

After this period of preparation, after frequent inquiry as to possible topics chosen for each pupil's research paper, and after consultation in private with those who have *no* interest and *no* desire, you and your class are ready to advance upon the article to be written. (I like to use "article." The students should feel that this is a new type of writing, a climax to their high-school work.) Each student in possession of his now filled, corrected,

and revised work sheets knows just what steps he must take in
the preparation of his own paper. And again you will check each
step. A class discussion of various excellent content outlines may
awaken the duller pupils. Then, too, the co-operative effort to
suggest added material or illustration is excellent training for the
whole class. Since the articles are being written to be read, I like
to explain the difference between the "logical" and the "psychologically correct" order of events. It is logical to tell that Washington was born, lived, died. But to arouse interest, it is doubtless better to rearrange that terse outline, attempting to interest
us by an anecdote or some reference. (For example, Chiang Kai-
shek is referred to as "the Chinese Washington.")

When your pupils have produced the first draft of both their
introduction and their first few pages, consultation again is desirable. This preview of a long paper saves you work and the
pupils discouragement. Few private interviews with pupils net
them more, I believe, than this one, for they are launched upon
a long paper, and they can immediately profit from suggestion.
Revise, cut, change, switch words and phrases, even whole paragraphs, and write in transitional words and sentences. Replace
dull words with better and slow "ands" with semicolons, but
praise passable words and strike out the dead timber that follows or precedes them. In other words, here again is an opportunity to teach vocabulary and sentence structure. It is possible
to so revise the beginning of a long paper that you inject life into
the style, courteously consulting the writer as to substance. Even
dull and careless pupils respond to this treatment and attempt
to diminish the difference in style between the later pages and
that comparatively scintillating beginning which they believe they
have practically written themselves. Am I too optimistic? Not,
I think, if you build logically, slowly, and with enthusiasm for
the various topics undertaken.

And when this article is completed, give it publicity, as much
publicity as you can invent. Some five or six articles can be

placed in the library for all the class to read. (It is judicious to give a brief quiz on them later.) One or two can be read in class. A particularly good one might be bound and placed in the library.

Interest in English classwork must compete with interest in football, dramatic performances, thrilling explosions or successful results in chemistry laboratory and—hardest of all—with those increasing pressures from outside: work, possible army conscription, aviation, dances, love affairs, and the ever present radio and motion picture. When you fully realize the condition, you see why you must dramatize your material and must make success mean far more than a mere A, B, or C. This research paper has taken many hours out of a busy senior's life; see that those hours, if well spent, bring him full returns.

When you glance back over this chapter, you will realize two things:

1. That every statement in the chapter is as applicable to oral as to written composition
2. That the chapter itself contains these four injunctions:
   a. Strive to make your pupils realize the necessity for clear thinking.
   b. Devise exercises that demand clear thought.
   c. Make these exercises challenging, interesting, but repetitious.

And last, more difficult but far more important than the other three:

   d. *Keep your perspective. Do not lose it in the clutter of daily classroom teaching.*

SUGGESTED EXERCISES

At the end of this chapter you will find a number of references. Read as many as you can before attempting these exercises. The work suggested in the first two exercises should be carried out completely or should be omitted. But the desirability of examining minutely the structure used by skilled writers before attempting to teach structure to others is obvious.

1. Read "On a Piece of Chalk" by Thomas Huxley, contained in his volume entitled *Lay Sermons*.

   a. Divide the essay into its five principal divisions.

   b. Subdivide these into their main divisions.

   c. Outline the essay, but not in detail.

   d. Select some five examples of topic sentences well used.

   e. Select some five examples of successful transition.

   f. Select some five examples of adaptation of the material to the audience, an audience demanding a simple, logical presentation.

2. Select any well-written short story in which the time sequence is marked; analyze this sequence. Plan a three-minute talk in which you explain time sequence and give definite information to your high-school class which may guide them in their writing. Use story analysis for illustration.

3. Select a description in which there is obvious space sequence. Note those words which convey this sequence to the reader. Plan a brief talk similar to the one for the story, but this time attempt to guide your pupils in their writing of systematic description.

4. Select from a newspaper a suitable incident. For contrast, select a suitable magazine article in which the interest of the reader is aroused, the main idea being developed later. Plan a brief talk with board illustrations in which you show the advantages and disadvantages of the two types.

5. Explain with interesting illustrations what is meant by "climaxed sequence" and "chronological sequence." Show when the two might be identical, when each might be desirable or undesirable.

6. Select from your reading two well-made paragraphs with easily recognized topic sentences, both on subjects of interest to high-school pupils. Bring for class discussion and for possible exchange. Give sources accurately. In each mark the topic sentence, transition words, and the clincher sentence, and indicate by Roman numerals the propositions that support the main idea or topic sentence. After each, write a one- or two-sentence précis. Perhaps you might have the more desirable mimeographed for the class members.

7. Write ten questions, suitable for high-school examination questions, that call for organization of material. In each place a definite key word.

SUGGESTED READINGS

The English Language Arts, Vol. I, N.C.T.E. Curriculum Series, Dora V. Smith, Director

Read Part I, Chapter 2, "The Language Arts and the Growth of Young People," and Part I, Chapter 3, "Goals and Experiences in the Language Arts Program."

1. Thomas, C. S.: *The Teaching of English in Secondary Schools,* rev. ed., Houghton Mifflin, 1927, pp. 44-47 and 111-12

One member might summarize the ideas given here of the use of the outline in its relation to the paragraph.

2. Minton, Arthur: "Teaching Thinking and Teaching English," *Hi Points,* Vol. 31 (October, 1949), pp. 5-20. (The pages for each month are numbered from 1 in the bound volumes.)

An admirable article, clear, logical, specific. Read or reread.

3. Hitchcock, Alfred: *High School English Book,* Holt, 1923, pp. 281-335

In this book, practically thirty years old, you will find many ways suggested of interesting pupils in orderly thinking.

From the English Journal

1. Minton, Arthur: "Structure," Vol. 37 (1948), pp. 529-33

"Relate paragraph and sentence structure and transitional devices to the structure of the whole composition." Literature is used as a helpful example.

2. ———: "Thinking Composition," Vol. 40 (1951), pp. 8-11

Suggests topics which the teacher may "stockpile" for use before topics have been developed from the class. Emphasizes the value of topics requiring moral judgments within the students' scope of interest.

3. Halperin, Irving: "Combining Art Appreciation and Imaginative Writing," Vol. 40 (1951), pp. 396-97

Students' papers are judged by: (1) originality, maturity, consistency of idea; (2) organization of the idea.

4. Cauley, Thomas: "Evaluating Topic Sentences," Vol. 39 (1950), p. 394

A two-paragraph description of a device for teaching "consideration of topic sentences." Try it.

5. Leer, M.: "Building a Sentence Pattern by Ear," Vol. 38 (1949), pp. 197-200

CHAPTER VII

The Psychology of Letter Writing

WHEN you think of composition work in high school, you realize, of course, that instruction in letter writing must occupy some place in your curriculum. What preparation shall you make? Probably you will reassure yourself concerning the various conventional wordings, spacing, punctuation, in business and friendly letters. You will, perhaps, think out explanations as to why capitals are used as they are in salutation and in complimentary close. But what else should you do? This matter of form is only a small part of your problem after all, a small part that looms mountain-size if you do not focus it rightly. You may want your pupils to know when to write *Yours truly* and when to write *Lovingly yours;* you may want them to replace the quaint *Friend John* salutation, invariably adopted by beginners, with *Dear John.* And there are other externals connected with letter writing that custom demands. But how many letters do you suppose your pupils write or should write as they conduct their lives at present? I seriously doubt if in the first two years any one of them needs to write a business letter. Also I question whether the majority of your juniors and seniors are called upon to write more than two or three business letters a year. A questionnaire might reveal an interesting discrepancy between the amount of time spent upon letter forms in the schoolroom and the actual use made of letters in school or in later life. On the other hand, there is no question but that the average citizen uses letter forms more often than he uses any other form of composition.

Under these circumstances might it be possible that letter training in high schools could be carried on merely as a phase of theme work, with some strong objective other than that of imparting correct form? Could correct form, however necessary, become incidental? Might you discuss it with your pupils and together agree that form of letters was merely a detail, though a detail that must be scrupulously correct? Little boys play baseball with a stick, and boast no masks; larger boys afford a bat and balls; the high-school team has bats, balls, masks, suits, and an umpire. Yet this paraphernalia does not make the game. It does, however, make the game better, more interesting, more spectacular.

I. USING ONE'S ENGLISH

While you are considering letters and baseball, I mean to digress for a few paragraphs to discuss the report of a committee appointed by the National Council of Teachers of English that appeared in the *English Journal* for February, 1926. This report, entitled "The Place and Function of English in American Life," was a significant piece of work, one that, I feel, deserved even more prominence than it has since been given. The committee through questionnaires attempted to discover what uses the average American found for his written and spoken English, and how well or how poorly he felt himself trained. The replies, numbering approximately twenty-six hundred, give a more or less adequate cross section of our nation. All who responded were over twenty-one years of age and had received training in our colleges, or in our high schools, or in our grade schools. The significant fact—for our purpose—brought out by this investigation is given in the following quotation from the report:

But the great majority of those who filled out the questionnaire ignored points of form and stressed points of adjustment. Two facts stand out: first, they felt themselves to be clumsy at adjustment in these various language situations (conversation, reading, public speaking, writing, interviews); second, their English instruction had done little, seemingly, to help them with the problem of making adjustment.

An astonishing revelation of many of the questionnaires, more often perhaps from persons who have attended college than from those whose formal schooling ended earlier, is the lack of realization of any correlation between the rules of usage, or the principles and devices of rhetorical art, and the conditions and exigencies of human intercourse. Often they say in substance: "I have this or that trouble in such a relationship, but I do not see what that has to do with your inquiry as to English, language, etc., for the trouble is due to defect of intellect, temperament, habit, environment, etc., and these are not related to language." That is to say, such persons have no clear conception of language as a tool.

In other words, these replies show no comprehension of the fact that school training should attempt to increase the "adequacy . . . enabling men and women of the future to meet better the language demands laid upon them." Over and over again the difficulty stressed was not owing to the individual's lack of correct form but to his inability to adjust his mind to others or to adjust to situations. The demand, expressed or implied, was not for more training in better form of expression in speech or in writing, but for greater mental and emotional adaptability. Many teachers of composition have the attitude toward English expressed by those answering the questionnaire. They feel that if a pupil speaks and writes with fair accuracy, they as teachers have succeeded. Subtlety of thought, quick adjustment to social requirements, ability to get another's thought or point of view, do not concern them.

Let us look at the situation from another standpoint. Upon what does adjustment depend? First, of course, social adjustment rests upon the individual's ability to project himself imaginatively, to set aside that preoccupation with self which limits so many people, and to see the incident or the situation through another's eyes. If you have read the often-quoted chapter in James Harvey Robinson's *The Mind in the Making* entitled "Four Kinds of Thinking," you will recall his description of the brain. He pictures it filled with reverie, too filled with dreams of self to admit willingly any other subject, and, when interrupted, returning to self as rapidly as external conditions will admit. To awaken such a brain to another's need and to arouse it to another's point of view is not easy, particularly with an unimaginative mind. But it is just such an awakening, just such an awareness of others, that we find both private and business life demand, and it is the lack of just such a quality that private and business people regret in the questionnaires mentioned. Second, quick social adjustment rests upon rapid association. All of us are unfortunately familiar with the brilliant reply concocted alone in the still watches of the night. Also we are familiar with the openings in conversation not recognized as openings until later, or the letter unfortunately mailed before the real import of the event or the action of which it tells was fully grasped.

II. TEACHING LETTER WRITING

But what has this report and what have these later paragraphs to do with the subject of teaching letter writing in high school? Unfortunately very little, I should say—in the average high school. Too often letter writing is one of the most uninteresting, most artificial phases of composition. Letters from Jane Carlyle and R. L. S. are viewed. Letters from Smith, Jones and Company and from the headquarters of the Camp Fire Girls are posted on the bulletin board. Pupils write three or thirty business letters in correct form, two or twenty friendly letters, a few formal and informal invitations and responses; then the teacher and class with free consciences return to the mutton of regular compositions.

But realizing the artificiality of letter writing in schools, teachers have tried various devices. A few years ago there was an epidemic of mailing letters written by grade-school children to various business houses. The teachers, anxious to make letter writing practical, decided that all letters should have not only an audience, but also a stamped envelope and an adult reader. The child of a friend of mine in Oakland, California, wrote to a San Francisco music house inquiring about a piano. In response the firm sent a representative across the bay to interview the possible purchaser. His time—an hour and fifty minutes—the fifty-cent boat and carfare, the human energy wasted, as well as the waste of some clerk's time who opened, read, and answered the child's letter, all combined to form an impressive illustration of the thoughtless dishonesty of some well-intentioned teacher. And yet, basically, the teacher was right; a letter should have an audience. It was merely her lack of perspective that led her into misguided activity.

After these intervening paragraphs let us return to the questions that confronted you at the beginning of the chapter. How can letter writing be made practical, useful, interesting? How can it be so taught that it may, perhaps, increase your pupils' awareness of others, their imaginative responsiveness, their sensitivity to implied meanings and to situations? I have nothing new to offer. But in order to avoid mere generalizations, I shall mention various devices and assignments, work planned and executed in the light of the principles suggested earlier.

III. SURVEYING FASHIONS IN LETTERS

When the time for instruction in letter writing arrives, I like, as in the teaching of punctuation, to stress the importance of changing fashions. I speak of changing styles in haircut, ties, shoes. Every girl in the room can appreciate the feeling of the unfortunate girl in a knee-length skirt surrounded by dresses that sweep the floor. A mention of laces that gave place to "boiled" collars that in turn were largely supplanted by "soft" ones; or of doublet and hose, followed by satin or velvet breeches, that disappeared before our present stovepipe trousers or plus fours, starts a discussion in which all can participate. And it is wise to remember that if you want to launch a subject with interest, you should lead pupils to contribute. Even grown people think an open forum is good if they have contributed to the discussion.

After the changing dictates of fashion have been discussed, the changes in that most intimate of writing, letters, follows naturally. To address a parent as *Honored Parent* is a far cry from *Mother dear, Dear Mumsy,* or *Darling Daddy.* Dr. Johnson's letter endings set a tone decidedly unlike the tone of the twentieth century. But these bits of eighteenth-century custom are far less useful as contrasts than such nineteenth-century atrocities as "Yours of the 14th inst. at hand. Will say as per schedule," or "Hoping to hear from you soon, Yours," and other clipped and mangled phrases. Oddly enough, in the high-school mind not brevity and wit but brevity and business are closely associated; hence it is well to have omissions and abbreviations dubbed old-fashioned and quaintly reminiscent of bustles and sideburns *before* any business letters are written by the class. By this device condescending remarks concerning timeworn phrases are relieved of any personal application.

Of course the next question is this: What is the fashion in letters today? Here I like to be particularly helpless. Apparently I get no business letters; hence the pupils must glean from parents, from neighbors, from corner stores, all the advertising letters they can lay hands upon. After a time you will find that there are certain firms upon which you can count to provide you with admirable models. Some fire- and life-insurance companies, some magazines, a dictionary company or two, send out letters that will prove useful bulletin-board material. Very soon your consultation board should show, inclosed within parallel and horizontal lines to indicate the paper's edge, correctly written letter heading, address, greeting, and close—all properly centered, spaced, and punctuated. On the board is the admitted fashionable, up-to-date form from which only the naïve and unsophisticated vary.

IV. TEACHING ETIQUETTE OBLIQUELY

And at this point may I interpolate one observation that may not have occurred to you? You are not only teaching English composition, but you are also teaching boys and girls with widely different kinds and different degrees of home training. For the most part, if they are to succeed in the world, they need to cultivate manners that will give as little offense as possible to their future employers and associates. In this matter of letter writing you have an opportunity to help some of them. In some Eastern schools regular class discussion centers about points of etiquette, and at least one textbook on school etiquette exists, a book, teachers report, that is read assiduously. In the West this work is largely left to chance, but in both sections, pupils are leaving high school to become cooks or clerks or office assistants, mechanics or college freshmen. Often they could happily and profitably associate with people from far better homes than their own if they knew how. When you are discussing letter forms, forms dictated by custom, why do you not draw your comparisons from other forms so dictated? For example, a certain error in a letter —an error by our present standard—is like leaving the spoon in one's coffee cup, is as bad as noisy eating, is as objectionable as public manicuring. Some letter is so good that it gives you the same pleased feeling that you have when a stranger holds the door open instead of letting it bang in your face. (It is with forethought that I use "one" in the undesirable situations, and "you" in the desirable. To use "you" in both would be objectionable, for the class and I know that none of us would commit any of the practices first listed.)

Does all this sound silly? Of course it all depends upon your group. And yet at a book counter in a five-and-ten-cent store I recently saw a cue of some twenty-five girls all obviously scanting their lunch hour to read from a certain pile of red books. When at the end of their lunch hour they replaced the books, I read the title, *Good Manners*. Today good manners are, of course, as they always have been, a social and business asset, but they are also an especially necessary lubricant in the intricate machinery of our city living. Increase awareness of others, and you do something to sensitize your pupils. Here in letter writing you will find one of many possible places where, by casual illustration, you can obliquely impart the information that should have been given in the nursery.

V. DEVISING BUSINESS-LETTER ASSIGNMENTS

When your consultation board shows what you and the class agree upon as the absolutely correct business form used in letters of today, it is time to begin writing. I like to ask, if I am working with underclassmen, that each choose a business for himself, a business that he will not tire of, for he will be asked to keep it for some time. Also I ask him to choose one in which he employs people and in which he sells goods of some sort. Then I ask him to make a letterhead for his business and display it. The letterhead, I admit to myself but not to my class, is purely for amusement and to give a sense of reality to the business chosen. After each has displayed his business letterhead, shown probably in groups of five and then, if good, to the class, real letter writing begins. Some teachers use the group method, pooling the letters in groups and drawing them out and answering them. This method has the advantage that while each day each letter is read, no one person's letter is read too frequently by the same pupil, and hence chance personal antagonisms may be avoided. Other teachers whose classes are seated in rows prefer the exchange across the aisle so that A-1 exchanges rather regularly with B-1 for some weeks, and they watch each other's correspondence and write each other letters.

As soon as the business of each pupil is established, a series of letters capable of almost endless variation is begun. Before each assignment, there must, of course, be careful prevision so that the situation, the accepted conventions in letters of the type demanded, and the reasons for those conventions will have been discussed and, perhaps, sample letters read. To make this plan definite, I have listed below some possible assignments. Each letter must, of course, be answered and the answer acknowledged, so that each person in turn is an applicant, an employer, a high-school principal.

1. Write a letter of application to the business firm across the aisle. Just what facts does the firm need to know about you? Give some person, probably your high-school principal, for reference. After your letter is written but before you copy it, reread. Try to decide if the person that you picture is like you. Consider both what you say, what you omit, and how your words sound. *The form in this and in all later letters must be correct or the letter will be discarded.*

2. Write a letter to your principal (or other person) asking him for a letter of recommendation. Remember two things: first, that he will be glad to help you to a better position; second, that he is a busy person. Reread your letter. Have you been both polite and brief?

3. Write a letter thanking the principal (or other person) for the letter of recommendation. Good manners and good policy usually go together. Do they here?

4. As employer, write to appoint a time for your applicant to appear in person. Be polite and specific. Remember that businessmen are always eager to get the very best person possible in any position of trust.

5. As a purchaser, order some goods from the business house with which you have been corresponding. Be sure you are specific. Don't make your problem too simple.

6. Unfortunately the goods sent you were not what you had ordered. Remember that the fault might have been yours, or at least that the business house also regrets the error.

And these letters can, of course, continue just as long as training is needed and pupils are interested. The reading of the letters in groups adds much to class interest. If your school has classes in shorthand and typing, by all means consult with the teacher of those classes.

VI. DEVISING FRIENDLY-LETTER ASSIGNMENTS

A transition from business to friendly letters is easily made. I rather like to explain that little by little the person directly over the former applicant has become interested in him and finally invites him to spend a week end at his country house, where his wife proves to be a very simple, pleasant, informal hostess. Naturally when the guest returns to work, he must write the wife a "bread and butter" note. Then I explain that this note is not, of course, in business form, but that it certainly is a "business" letter, and that many of our semisocial letters, letters saying thank you for the return of a lost pocketbook, for a letter of recommendation, for a message that was important, etc., may easily be both good social manners and admirable business acumen. (Is all this comment too practical, too shrewd? Perhaps as a nation we follow our patron saint, Franklin, too literally, but certainly we could to advantage be more thoughtfully polite.) The type of assignment just mentioned opens discussion of when notes are necessary and when they may be omitted.

Then in the field of friendly letters there is much to be done. There are formal and informal invitations and acceptances. To teach these in certain classes would be absurd, but in others is essential. Some teachers give them practical and immediate value by having notes written to parents inviting them to assemblies, class programs, evening performances, or even sending out invitations for certain social meetings of the Parent-Teacher Association. Of course in friendly rather more than in business letters a little sensitivity as to words, implications, tone, can be developed. I recall a hilarious senior group who, after having been presented with many varied social problems, labored most intelligently with this:

Assignment. Your brother or sister has just married. You have never met this new member of your family. Write a courteous, cordial note welcoming him or her. Be simple and sincere. Make him or her feel neither (1) that you regret having this new member in the family but think that the new member is lucky to be there, nor (2) that you are humbly grateful for the opportunity that makes the note possible. Reread your note and decide (1) how the reader would feel toward you; (2) how you wish him or her to feel. When the two agree, copy your note and be ready to have it read in class.

There is one more comment upon letter writing that is necessary because many teachers, perhaps through lack of time, through inertia, or through lack of imagination, seem not to think of it themselves. Letters written upon regular theme paper used for composition do not seem like real letters. It is hard for a pupil to be interested in proper centering, spacing, placing of heading, if the paper is lined or if three holes for some future notebook confront his eye. In the same way a brief note or an invitation that in itself demands a correspondence card looks like nothing resembling a real social communication when written on theme paper. Remember that it is an easy matter, even if you have to do it at your own expense, to get from any newspaper office paper cut the desired sizes.

VII. SECURING AN AUDIENCE

I have made no comment so far upon the custom, more or less prevalent today, of providing a real audience for class letters. I list some suggestions below. Their success depends not only upon class interest awakened by a skillful teacher, but also upon the co-operation secured elsewhere and the prompt response made to all letters sent.

1. Exchange of letters between the members of one class and members of another class (a) in the same school, (b) in other schools of the same system, (c) in schools in different parts of the

country or in foreign countries. (In the last case the interest aroused is greatest, and very good work, often illustrative of the kind of school and country the pupils know, can be secured. The difficulty is usually one of time. Teachers in this country occasionally so plan their teaching of letter writing that some such exchange may be carried out in two schools. Thus Butte, Montana, may learn of Staunton, Virginia; and two teachers in different states arouse interest in actual letters sent through the mail.)

2. Letters to "shut-ins," often absent members of the class.

3. Letters for certain organizations like the music club, for special assemblies to which outsiders are invited, for the librarian who needs much free material in the way of announcements of books, catalogues, pamphlets, etc.

4. Letters written to amuse hospital children at Christmas time, or for other holidays.

5. Actual letters, the names omitted, to be mailed later. Usually these are thank-you letters for Christmas, birthdays, etc. (In letters of this type some teachers err upon the side of correctness, forgetting that if a pupil wishes to write a friend and address him perhaps as "you old Chump" or revile him in "Listen, you old Mutton Head," he has a perfect right to do so. I have known teachers who rigorously excluded all slang and even all abbreviations from these so-called "real" letters. Naturally the class learned merely to echo what the teacher desired, and these attempts to simulate actual letters became disliked, purely perfunctory writing.)

VIII. RECOGNIZING UNDERLYING PRINCIPLES

Earlier in this discussion I spoke of some general principles which might be concretely illustrated by the suggestions made.

1. Keeping up-to-date.

Of course the first is that of creating a need for writing and a recognition of the importance of writing well since—in letters even more truly than in other written work—"Your English is you," as Mr. Hitchcock has happily expressed it. It is my experience that pupils do not mind being ignorant, nor do they very much object to being rude or incorrect—but they do dislike being thought old-fashioned; hence it seems effective to stress fashion, change, and up-to-date knowledge of purely mechanical matters. Up-to-date clothes, songs, letters, slang, appeal to modern youth.

2. **The audience.** The audience, the person who is to read the letter and who is to be affected favorably or unfavorably by it, is important. This stress upon the audience calls, of course, for some attempt on the pupil's part to imagine him, his probable attitude of mind, and the situation under which he receives the letter. These situations must be very simple at first, but should grow progressively more difficult. There must be, however, sufficient repetition of the original situation under slight disguise to make success possible. If, for example, widely different situations were proposed in rapid succession, a slow pupil might continue unable to enter into the work imaginatively. Under those circumstances, although he would learn correct letter-form, he would benefit little from the work. For example, it calls for little stretch of imagination to recognize the required attitude of mind of an applicant for a position, or of a pupil thanking someone who has written a letter of recommendation for him. Apparently it requires more to complain courteously about missent goods. Here it is necessary not only to feel the inconvenience to oneself, but to recognize that one may have ordered badly or that the firm may have been negligent and will regret the fact. The note of thanks to the hostess is again more difficult, for the writer is neither a close friend nor a mere business acquaintance. Pupils struggle here between a jocular overfamiliarity that is in strikingly bad taste or a coldly businesslike tone suggesting the probability of an inclosed check for board and room.

3. **The right tone.** The change in tone made possible by the alteration of a word or phrase, or by the inclusion of a cordial sentence in ending, awakens pupils to some realization of what is meant by "implication." Often, for the first time in their writing they realize that one word determines whether a letter is slightly hostile or entirely friendly, informal, or overfamiliar. Much good, interesting work is possible here. The following series of questions [1] put out by a large business house for the guidance of its clerks, who through their letters represent the firm, impresses the pupils with the importance of tone much more successfully, as a rule, than any teacher-made queries could do. These questions, copied in notebooks and consulted before a business letter is written in final form, help much in awakening pupils to the total effect of their letters.

[1] Found in W. H. Leffingwell's *Office Management* and copied by him, as he states, from "the correspondence manual of one large, well-conducted company."

When reading your dictated correspondence, just measure letters according to the following table:

Courteous	Discourteous
Sincere	Curt
Pleasant	Sarcastic
Friendly	Sharp
Cheerful	Impatient
Warm	Cold
Helpful	Peevish
	Overbearing
	Harsh

If to each of the words in the first column, you can answer "Yes," then your letters are all right as far as the tone is concerned. Should you have to answer "Guilty" to any of the points given in the other column, then revise the letter or letters before they leave your hands, even if it is necessary to hold them until the next day. An unfriendly letter is nothing more than the dropping of a wrench into the gears which drive the business machine. Whether the whole letter, or only a sentence, violates this principle, makes no difference. A sentence, or even a word, can undo months and years of effort.

When compared to other composition units taught, why is the work on the unit of letter writing often found to be a poor, perfunctory business? Largely, I believe, because of lack of faith. Faith is an attribute that every teacher of composition must cultivate. Unless she believes in the value of what she is doing, successful work is almost impossible. Disbelief and perfunctoriness, faith and enthusiasm, are usual companions. The letter-writing units are, perhaps, poorly taught because any intelligent teacher sees how little use the average pupil will make of his instruction. But if letter writing is dignified so that it becomes a psychological problem, a study of the reader's mind and mood, a sensitizing of the pupil's mind to moods, situations, words, it becomes well worth the doing, a unit which any teacher can plan and execute with enthusiasm.

SUGGESTED EXERCISES

At the end of this chapter a number of references are listed. Read as many as you can before you attempt these exercises.

1. Write a model letter (perfectly centered, spaced, punctuated, etc.) for each of the following situations:

a. A letter to a superintendent of schools applying for a position in his school system. Remember here that your letter is judged as an index of your character. Decide what impression of your personality you give in the letter.

b. A business letter in which you order some half-dozen different articles.

c. A friendly, courteous letter to a Mrs. Roscoe whom you do not know, explaining why her son or her daughter in your class is failing. Analyze each word as to its "tone" and its possible effect upon the reader.

d. A formal acceptance written in answer to an invitation to a banquet.

e. A letter of recommendation for a high-school boy who is applying for a position as messenger for the General Electric Company. Upon what qualities would they desire to have information? What impression of the boy do you give? What impression do you give of yourself?

Devise some way of mounting these letters, either separately or in a booklet, so that they may serve as bulletin-board models in high school. Your paper, cards, envelopes, ink, must of course be entirely appropriate. It would be wise to file this work, after class discussion and comparison, in your permanent files. (Have you manila envelopes for filing?)

2. Devise an interesting high-school assignment that will call for three imaginative situations and three friendly letters. These should be sufficiently unlike to excite interest, but sufficiently alike so that one prepares for the others. In introducing this assignment, attempt to awaken an appreciation of letter writing as a psychological problem and to arouse interest in the problem itself.

3. Devise three letter situations that call for: (a) an analysis of some high-school problem; (b) a decision by the writer; (c) an attempt to persuade the reader to the writer's point of view.

Here you should bear in mind three things: a. The assignment should suggest several possible problems and suggest them interestingly. b. It should suggest and stress the necessary difference in appeals made to different kinds of pupils. c. It should make possible a class discussion as to ways of organizing material.

4. Find and bring to your college class two letters that are in some way notable. Write out a brief introduction suitable for high school that will awaken interest and lead pupils to listen intelligently to these two. (For your own benefit and for the benefit of the class, copy the letters, or if you own them, give such accurate reference that others can find them. These, too, should be filed.)

5. Select three or four letters from the past that will illustrate changing styles of letter writing. Cutting these as you like, make copies that you can file for high-school reading.

6. If the opportunity is given you, be ready in class to discuss the best ways of filing and of displaying letter material, of collecting interesting sample letters from firms, and of securing for little money paper of the right kind and size for class use.

SUGGESTED READINGS

References Concerned with the Teaching of Letter Writing

1. Perrin, Porter: *Writer's Guide and Index to English,* rev. ed., Scott, Foresman, 1950

See "Letters," pp. 623-27; "Business English," pp. 455-56; "Social Correspondence," pp. 762-64.

2. *An Experience Curriculum in English: A Report of a Commission of the National Council of Teachers of English,* W. W. Hatfield, Chairman, Appleton-Century, 1935, Chap. XVI, "Writing Experiences, Grades 7-12," pp. 208-16

3. Write The International Friendship League, 40 Mt. Vernon Street, Boston, Massachusetts, if you wish your pupils in the junior high school to write letters to one of the "150,000 children all over the world who know English [and] are looking for American teen-agers as pen pals." Usually, the Red Cross local office will also aid letter-writing projects.

4. Wagner, Ruby: "An Effective 'Thank You' Letter," *Elementary English,* Vol. 25 (1948), pp. 114-21

A heartfelt "thank you" note for a gift from the junior-high-chool class inspired them to write the kind of letter "that makes people feel warm and happy inside."

From the English Journal

1. McCrea, Mary: "A Unit on the Letter of Application," Vol. 30 (1941), pp. 497-99

2. Irwin, Claire C., and Irwin, James R.: "A 'New Look' at Letter Writing," Vol. 38 (1949), pp. 97-99
Consider this article. Letter writing can be dull or most profitable. All depends upon the teacher's realization that in letters students can grow in their ability to understand others.

3. Palmer, Dora E.: "Out of the Rut—Into the Groove," Vol. 34 (1945), pp. 423-28
An excellent example of holding pupils' interest and of increasing their thinking power by a fresh, modern approach to traditional subjects.

4. Storm, Eugene M.: "Genuine Eighth-Grade Letters: An Idea that Clicked," Vol. 34 (1945), pp. 449-50
A letter that served several purposes.

5. Treanor, John H.: "The Significance of the Address in Letter Writing," Vol. 38 (1949), pp. 285-86
Interesting if used as part of a post office project for junior high school.

6. Moore, Doris: "Handclasps Around the World," Vol. 29 (1940), pp. 590-93
What were the six benefits received from this letter project?

7. Gossett, Bernice Tracy: "Creative Letter Writing," Vol. 26 (1937), pp. 817-19

8. Frailey, L. E.: "Writing Letters Today," Vol. 28 (1939), pp. 64-66
There is a bit of verse here containing many of the formal, taboo phrases of bad business letters.

9. *Conducting Experiences in English,* Monograph 8, National Council of Teachers of English, Angela M. Broening, Chairman, Appleton-Century, 1939, pp. 133-39
Note: Why not write for travel material for schools? It can be obtained from the Association of American Railroads, Transportation Building, Washington, D. C. Ask for *Railway Literature for Young People: Bibliography for Grades and High School.* (See Appendix G.)

CHAPTER VIII

Speech: A Basis for All English Work

IT is possible, though not probable, that you will find yourself in a school where certain English periods are given over to a speech teacher, one whose business it is to meet and know the speech problems and difficulties of every pupil in the school. Or you may find that certain courses in speech, required or elective, are offered during each year of the junior-senior high-school program. But if you are in a small school, what you are more likely to find is that you, as teacher of English, are solely responsible for the amount and quality of speech training given your sixty or one hundred and sixty students. Regardless, however, of whether there is or is not a speech specialist in the school, you, as teacher of English, are not only responsible for the speech that your pupils use, but are also responsible for inventing opportunities for speech work. In other words you should make oral work a basis for composition, an important phase of all literature study, and an outstanding factor in its own right during each semester's course.

In oral work (as in all teaching) there are many problems confronting you. It is hardly feasible in the limits of one chapter to go into the subject of oral work in detail, but it is possible: (1) to make clear a point of view; (2) to point out various possibilities for vitalizing oral work in the classroom, so that practice in speech is given; and (3) to suggest certain books, studies, and articles which can be of use to you, the teacher.

I. WHAT QUALITIES SHOULD MARK YOUR OWN SPEECH?

Before you can demand good speech from your pupils, you must, of course, set your classes a good example. Clear-cut, easily audible speech, low-pitched and pleasant in tone quality, ought to be made a requirement for all teachers. Yet, on the whole, teachers' voices are not noted for their excellence. When you are teaching, you may realize one reason for what is sometimes termed "the schoolroom voice." There is strong temptation, particularly if you teach above the roar of traffic or the reverberation from steel riveting, to center your attention, regardless of tone or quality, upon audibility alone. And yet the effect of a high-pitched voice issuing from a strained throat is more annoying than you perhaps realize. Try it at table or in some group of your friends. See how, merely by your tone of voice, you can, little by little, change the mood from a carefree, pleasant one to one that is constrained or restive. In many schoolrooms it is the teacher who, by the sense of tension and anxiety conveyed in her tone, breeds in her pupils nervousness and impatience, if not slight rudeness or open revolt. Keep yourself aware of your own voice. When it rises in pitch, make a conscious effort to pull it down. When your throat tightens, breathe deeply and make a conscious effort to relax it. And if you realized the pupils' relief when a teacher's voice slides from pitch to pitch instead of stalking along in solid monotone, you would also try so to vary what you say that pupils' ears are pleased, not assaulted.

School administrators fully realize the importance of a teacher's voice. In the questionnaires which they send out concerning possible candidates they ask specifically as to that candidate's mode of speech. And yet, odd though it is, college students frequently seem to consider voices and modes of speech as matters irrevocably fixed. A prospective teacher may alter her dress, hair, lips, eyebrows, and complexion, and yet say that she "feels it's an affectation" to alter her voice production, her enunciation, or even her pronunciation—unless the latter is flagrantly incorrect. Such an inhibition on her part is obviously unfortunate both for herself and for her pupils. If she possesses a delicate and lovely instrument (and no violin nor piano is so lovely as a beautiful speaking voice) she is under at least a tacit obligation to draw from that instrument beautiful rather than unpleasant tones. Listen to yourself. Perhaps your voice does give pleasure; if so, guard it. If it is flat or nasal or harsh, consult the speech specialist and then follow his suggestions. If it is monotonous, vary it.

But aside from a pleasant quality of voice, you must also cultivate audibility. Speech is produced to be heard; when it is only half heard, nerves are frayed and time is wasted. If you visited many grade or high-school classrooms, you would soon become conscious of three things:

1. Many teachers are oddly unconcerned as to whether pupils do or do not hear every word spoken in the classroom, or hear only by conscious straining.[1]

2. Many teachers with immobile upper lips mumble, particularly when they read aloud, and many others read aloud so rapidly that, though words are well pronounced, the effect is hurried and unpleasant.

3. Almost without exception those teachers who have a pleasant, friendly, natural atmosphere in their rooms speak and read clearly and pleasantly; they impress one as being well-bred hostesses, occupied in seeing that all of their pupil-guests hear easily and that no time is unprofitably spent.

Your own speech, audible, pleasing in quality, and correct, of course, should be as well phrased and as picturesque as you can make it. Colorless correctness (Dr. Krapp's "schoolma'rm English") should give place to vigorous, racy, natural English suitable to the subject under discussion. So far, merely your extem-

---

[1] College professors err, doubtless, in this direction more than do either high-school teachers or teachers in the grades. In this one particular, the growing courtesy of the student seems to exist in inverse ratio to that of the instructor.

poraneous speaking in the classroom has been mentioned. You should, however, do some carefully prepared work. Do not overlook the importance of preparation before giving assignments to your class and before giving a dictation; but you should also read aloud at times in order that your classes may realize in poem or drama the full beauty of the spoken word. Remember that careful cutting and practice in reading aloud are necessary before you can present to your classes effectively a dramatic scene, a poem, or a bit from some novel. Such preparation is timetaking, but for many of your pupils these readings may well be the outstanding imaginative experience of their school day, and the only real beauty that day to enter their lives. Therefore, take these readings seriously. Prepare as carefully as you would for an assembly program, and attempt to make reading aloud— your own reading and the reading of pupils—a class procedure to which you and your students look forward expectantly.

II. HOW IMPORTANT TO YOUR PUPILS IS SPEECH TRAINING?

The student's performance in the classroom and certainly his personal feeling of failure or success depend to a large degree upon his ability to present ideas quickly, succinctly, and with fair correctness—either his own ideas or ideas that he has gleaned elsewhere. At home, on the street, on the playground or athletic field, in club meetings, and especially at dances and social gatherings it is again his speech that largely determines both his own sense of success or failure and his position as follower or leader of his group. During his years of schooling, speech is to him of major importance. What of his later years? Consider your own life in college, in vacations, in whatever positions you have filled. You, of course, are hardly a fair representative of the great numbers of high-school pupils who flow through our secondary schools and from there into various homes or industries; but in your own case, how important a factor is speech? You realize almost daily, do you not, in every college class, social group, or business meeting, that those people who can easily summon and pleasantly and convincingly express their ideas have an enormous advantage over their less-articulate fellows? It is true that many speak well who have never received formal training. It is true also that many pianists play well by ear, but their special ability hardly forms a legitimate reason for rejecting formal instruction and hours of practice. In your schoolroom, recognize the importance of oral work, give as much direct and "oblique" teaching as possible wherein speech, clear-cut and vigorous, plays an important and respected part.

III. WHAT RELATION EXISTS BETWEEN WRITTEN AND ORAL COMPOSITION?

If you recall the questionnaire quoted in the last chapter, you will remember how large a number of the people replying to it expressed the opinion that they, as adults, had small use for the training in writing received in school, but that they felt themselves to be sadly lacking in speech facility. They failed, of course, to recognize that the more formal aspects of oral work rest upon written summaries and carefully organized written outlines; but, according to their own estimate of their needs, the more formal aspects of oral work seemed to them the least useful. What was your own experience? If you recall your junior-senior high-school work, you will in all probability find that an apparently disproportionate amount of time was given to composition and literature, compared to the time spent upon speech training. If you recall the grading scheme in your own school, there, too, you will recognize the phases of work in English upon which emphasis was placed. Probably you received either one grade, a grade covering all aspects of work in English, or you received a grade in literature and one in composition. This latter grade *may* in the mind of the teacher have included oral work, but I venture that in your own mind, at least, it stood for written themes and was closely connected with condemnatory marks concerning punctuation, grammar, spelling, and sentence formation. In the great majority of schools, speech and a constructive program for its improvement have in the past been subordinated both to written composition and to the study of literature.

This subordination is understandable and, in some ways, not without excuse. Obviously, training for correctness is equally applicable to speech and to writing. Just as obviously, training for effectively phrased sentences can be as profitable to the speaker as to the writer—it can, that is, if both teacher and pupil recognize the importance of ear training. And all training in organization of thought [1] applies equally to either form of expression.

But teachers have been slow to recognize the aid that each form of composition offers readily to the other. Emphasis has been placed upon written work, sometimes almost to the exclusion of all oral training, often to the detriment of written composition itself. And yet writing that is not built upon the quick interplay of ideas in class discussion, nor yet motivated by ultimate public use in class talk, club speech, or assembly program, may easily degenerate into a dreary exercise executed without motive. Important as it is, speech training has been neglected in grade school, high school, and college. Partly this neglect has come about because of the pressure of work, the number of students in each class, and the recognition by the teacher of the fact that life itself provides many possibilities for practice in speech, while practice in written work may terminate with graduation. There is, though, a second reason. If you should listen to the speech of your college professors—professors who, perhaps, write admirably —and then note the speech of some of your classmates who are about to embark upon the profession of teaching a high-school subject, this second reason might suggest itself to you. And yet the training in the two forms of composition can be related if you make a conscious effort toward such relation and do not allow

[1] See Chapter VI.

written composition, the easier of the two to deal with in large classes, to absorb an undue amount of time.

This tiny composition from a seventh-grade pupil illustrates the close relation that *can* exist between written and oral compositions. The procedure was as follows: First the children discussed possible topics and each decided upon his own. Then there was well-directed discussion as to how a speaker might by brevity, illustrations, and unity interest his audience. Each pupil then planned his talk, "tried it out" at home or before a schoolmate, wrote it as a theme, and finally, as a climax, gave it extemporaneously (that is, prepared but not memorized) before the class.

MUSIC

by Mary Lou Mason, Seventh Grade, Paxton School,
Missoula, Montana

There are many kinds of music. Every day I hear several in just my name, Mary Lou, beginning in the morning, when Daddy calls up the stairs, "Mary Lou, time to get up." That's a dirge.

When the girls call, "Mary Lou, hurry!" that is a march. And when Baby Danny calls, "Ma'y 'Ou, c'mon," that is sentimental music. But the most satisfying music of all is when Mother calls, "Mary Lou, supper's ready."

When we begin to argue, and the Mary Lou's fly thick and fast, that is not music at all; that is jazz.

IV. WHAT SHOULD BE THE CLASS ATTITUDE TOWARD ORAL WORK?

Although pupils studying literature or writing compositions profit greatly from a co-operative class, one providing opportunity for kindly, spontaneous discussions and suggestions, yet a pupil *can* in solitude read a book with enjoyment; he *can*, also, write his compositions alone. But oral work demands a speaker and an audience; hence the attitude of that audience in the schoolroom becomes an all-important factor. *Oral work must, by its very nature, be a co-operative enterprise.* The speaker talks to an audience; the audience, each member at some time to become the speaker, should listen (1) with interest in the substance of that talk, (2) with admiration for speech difficulties overcome, or (3) with frank disapproval for lazy or indifferent work. You must secure this friendly, co-operative attitude if your oral work is to be successful. Doubtless you have seen, as I have, a whole class taking pride in the progress made by some shy or some foreign pupil or a whole class politely ignoring some pupil's speech difficulty. But there are other types of schoolrooms—rooms where pupils sit tense and unhappy or even perhaps feign illness, more willing to risk an unexcused absence than three minutes before the class.

You will readily admit that such an unhappy atmosphere makes oral work, successful oral work, impossible. How can you secure a desirable class attitude? You must solve that problem for yourselves, since every group provides you with a different problem. The following suggestions, however, may perhaps prove useful.

1. When you begin in the fall, get acquainted with your class through written composition, reading, or class vocabulary discussion before making assignments for individual oral work. The unwisdom of risking a pupil's flat refusal to participate must be immediately obvious to you. It not only throws a gloom over your entire class, but it offers a most tempting example to others, particularly if the pupils recognize you as a novice. Try various ways of making speech work unembarrassing. Discussion might begin from the seats. (One is braver seated.) Then, so that all hear more easily (an old subterfuge), pupils are from time to time asked to rise. Later, to explain a point, a pupil may be asked to place on the blackboard what he understands to be the intelligent punctuation of a sentence, or chart on the board the directions which were not clear when read to the class. Be aware of the fact that for many pupils—pupils who without the slightest embarrassment can march as "twirlers" before a high-school band—the "front of the room" is terrifying. Make the approach so gradual and so natural that they feel no ordeal, merely

a rather pleasurable excitement, when they are to stand before the class.

2. The most effective way of securing a co-operative group is, of course, to introduce topics and to glean topics from your class that are of genuine interest to them. Each pupil is, remember, profoundly interested in himself, his adjustment to his own problems, the way others have met similar problems. Let that knowledge guide you to vital topics and away from those dull repetitions of strange facts taken verbatim from the *Readers' Guide* or the *Scientific American*.

3. Where you place your emphasis (upon the topic or upon the way that topic is delivered) is again important. Remember that *what* is said is always more important than *how* it is said, *even in a speech class*. Be certain that you dignify your work by stressing the idea while at the same time you stress ways and means of making that idea more interesting, more persuasive, more logical, more adult.

4. The old adage concerning the horse and his drinking habits, true of all learning, is particularly true of oral work. Unless a pupil cares to improve, he will, in all probability, improve little. Hence it is important to seize upon every opportunity for your pupils to speak in public. The school assembly offers rich possibilities, even if the pupil merely advertises a candy sale, or urges attendance at the junior play or dance. Other classes offer some possibilities. If a student is to report in history, give him the opportunity to rehearse that report before the speech class. Possibly your principal, if you discuss your project with him, can assist you by dropping in occasionally, having first been invited by some member of the class, and will thus provide an audience. An exchange of speakers between sections or between grades is also a spur to your pupils. If you are at work on parliamentary training, or class dramatization, invite pupils from study hall (if you may), or another teacher, or the head of your department. (Always warn adults that your chairman will ask them for comment; they do not care to speak badly in a speech class.)

5. Intelligent criticism, honest but encouraging, is an important factor in securing the desired attitude in class and in spurring pupils to careful preparation for class activities. Each pupil when he has given prepared work should know *how* you and the class think he has performed. In other words, the state to avoid in your classroom is perfunctory talking to talk because talk is required, not talking to inform, entertain, move to action, persuade, or picture. Be certain

that you *have a definite purpose in your assignment, a definite procedure, and a definite criticism for all prepared class presentations.* Some teachers in the senior high school have a mimeographed form which they fill while the pupil is speaking. This they hand the pupil at the end of the hour. It is either filed by the pupil or, later, by the teacher as a permanent record which both may consult, an interesting history of improvement or stagnation. May I repeat: Your first consideration must be the material and the organization of that material; then, important but secondary, you must consider the speaker's relation to the audience, his voice and diction, his vocabulary and his bodily control. Many teachers have one other general comment which might be called "total impression."

ORAL-WORK CHART FOR TEACHER COMMENT [1]

Year: Name of Pupil: Topic: Remarks:		Content	Organization	Relation with audience	Voice and diction	Vocabulary	Control of body	Total Impression
	A							
	B							
	C							
	D							
	E							
	F							

6. Since speech must be a co-operative undertaking, what are the demands that you will lead your pupils to make of themselves? Of course speech must be easily audible and, since it is for the benefit of the class, it must be given to them simply and pleasantly, as if the speaker were glad to have the opportunity to tell what he has to say. Perhaps at first those apparently simple demands are sufficient—and how long it takes to get easy speech from pupils.

7. But to secure a desirable classroom attitude the pupils must

For the idea of this chart I am indebted to Mr. Ralph Y. McGinnis, Assistant Professor of Speech at Montana State University, Missoula, Montana.

feel that they are progressing, not repeating year after year the same type of performances at the same level. It would be an error to lay before your pupils the various requirements which I shall list below, but you, the teacher, must bear them in mind and must strive to make your pupils, *little by little*, aware of them.[1] Teach pupils:

a. To walk to the front of the room naturally and stand in the center (not clinging to the wall like an ivy).

b. To act as if they were glad to have the chance to talk. Never to act bored or sigh (through embarrassment), for it discourages the audience before the talk begins.

c. To take a deep breath and, if nervous, to take an instant to shift a book on the desk, place notes on the desk, in order to delay until that long breath has fortified them.

d. To look at the audience, all of it, before speaking to the central division with an occasional glance at the left and right.

e. To have notes, if notes are necessary, on 3″ x 5″ cards, written on *one side only,* and arranged in order. These should be openly consulted, not glanced at secretly as if notes were shameful, but the less they must be consulted, the better. If reading from a book is part of the talk, the book should be fastened with clips at the place selected, or better yet, strapped open with elastic bands.

f. To move about a little, shifting weight and moving to mark a shift in topic, but neither pacing like a caged lion nor attempting to dramatize a talk. Easy bodily control is the ideal.

g. To speak distinctly and just a little louder and a little more slowly than if talking to one person. (A trained speaker watches his audience to see that all hear.) But the manner of speech should be that of natural conversation.

h. To choose language appropriate to the subject, not "elegant" or artificial. (One has spoken well if the class forgets *how* he speaks and is concerned with *what* he says.)

i. To plan carefully both the first and the last sentence; the first to catch the listeners' interest, the last to leave a clear-cut impression.[2] (An apology at the beginning is taboo, but a ragged unfinished

---

[1] At a banquet given by my first class in oral English (I had been *most* conscientious with them), I and my little speech were introduced by the words: "And will you note her enunciation, pronunciation, posture, voice variation, relation with the audience, and manner of beginning and ending her talk?" Needless to say, I learned much about speech teachers from that supposedly humorous introduction.

[2] Remember to utilize in speech the teaching you have expended upon these principles in written composition training.

close is equally undesirable. Some speakers begin with a joke. If a speaker wishes to be funny, good, but he must be sure that his jokes *further his topic*. Don't waste time on unrelated jests.)

j. To prepare carefully. Such preparation may include: a topical outline, two rehearsals carefully timed, notes on 3″ x 5″ cards written on *one side only*, readings (with the book clipped or strapped open at the correct place by rubber bands), and all equipment such as pictures, slides, or charts *arranged in the order in which they are to be presented.*[1]

Perhaps you, the teacher of speech, may think that these ten points are inelegantly expressed. They are, intentionally so. *Avoid* pompous or technical language. By simplicity in your own terminology you stress the practicality of oral work. Your pupils are training for actual use: home, business, school, social gatherings, club or lodge or union talks. Just so soon as pupils feel the work is not practical, for them all oral work ceases to have value.

Reading aloud is another phase of oral work that should play some part in your classroom. At first you will be thankful if all pupils read so that they can be heard and understood; little by little they should improve upon this scant minimum requirement, and read so that they seem to be telling the experience of the printed page, and telling it with recognition of the listeners. "Raise the eyes from the printed page" is an injunction which should follow "Hold the book so that your speech is not cut off by it."

From the seventh grade on, reading aloud should be a part of every semester's work. Pupils read to share discovered material, to show a meaning rather different from the passage as read by another, or to re-enjoy a poem or story or article with the other members of the class. Since the radio has become a necessity in practically every home, pupils are becoming speech-conscious— for others. Let an announcer slur his words, or become, through

---

[1] When in school assembly some adult breaks all ten of the injunctions above, I consider it no discourtesy for the speech class to be aware (charitably aware) of his errors. Let's be intellectually honest.

his own fault, unintelligible (pupils are charitable to "technical difficulties over which we have no control"), and even your most slovenly speaker will condemn him. Do not discount the value of the radio as a device (either with a box or a genuine "mike") for motivating readings, talks of all kinds, book reviews, even class plays. Know radio programs.

V. WHAT SHOULD DETERMINE THE TYPE OF ORAL WORK GIVEN?

In schools where the oral work is merely a part of the English classwork, and where it must be handled by teachers untrained in speech, one great difficulty is the lack of a well-organized course of study. Pupils talk from the seventh grade until they graduate, and talk, perhaps, little better in the twelfth than in the seventh year. They may even, from boredom, talk less well. Your business is *to organize your four-year or three-year course with simple, varied exercises in speech that build gradually enough and are differentiated enough so that pupils not only can succeed at each level, but also can recognize their own increasing ability.* When you survey the possibilities for oral work in a five-hour week program—a program that must include written composition, mechanics, functional grammar, vocabulary training, library training, and much literature reading—what can you do with oral English? That is the problem which next September may face you.

First, you might chart the various speech situations which your pupils must meet. Second, you might make a rough estimate of the work to be done in the other phases of English. Third, you might decide how much oral work you can combine with the other types of work in English—*to the detriment of neither.* Fourth, you might schedule separately as many of those types of oral work needed by the pupil as time will permit (types that cannot be combined with written composition or literature). Do you begin to recognize the vast importance of intelligent oblique teaching?

Your pupils, no matter what their grade, are individuals who have, as has been said, speech situations at home, at parties and socials, at class meetings or clubs or unions or lodges, in business relations, and in school. I once attempted to list all the possible speech situations in these five relationships; it made an interesting and enlightening catalogue, but proved too space-taking to include in detail. It did, however, throw some light upon the absurdity of confining oral work to "reports before the class." I could find comparatively few occasions outside of school when, either as young people or as adults, these students would rise and present at length their views on any topic. But the speech needs of these boys and girls and the speech needs they would still have as adults are represented in part by the list below.

Pupils need to know:

1. Voice and bodily control in order to be at ease with others
2. The common courtesies of greeting people, and making a few remarks easily and pleasantly in various home, social, and business relationships
3. The common courtesies of telephone conversation
4. The importance of ears and minds trained to receive, retain, and impart accurately specific information
5. The conventions upon which courteous conversation rests
6. The acceptable standard of manners for their community (with some concept of better manners if the community standard is low)
7. The simpler parliamentary procedures followed in public meetings
8. The importance of quick mental adjustment to new situations, sensitivity to the unexpressed desires and moods of others, and ability to remain silent or to speak tactfully
9. The method of collecting and organizing material for talks, reports, investigations (largely necessary for success in school or college)

As you glance back over this rather formidable array, you will, perhaps, be impressed by the fact that in your own high-school training, school needs alone were considered. Today in all up-to-date schools, teachers of English are agreed that oral work *is not of value* unless it contributes directly to the efficiency of the pupil in his out-of-school contacts. Be practical. Build your oral program on the speech needs of your pupils. *Always show your pupils the practical reason for the oral exercises before the exercise is prepared.* A program devised as a series of problems to be solved, a series made by teacher and pupils together, has in many schools proved desirable. But these problems must never become mere routine exercises or appear trivial. They must not lend themselves to either flippant or bored reception. Interest and a desire to improve are essential, and can be obtained *if* the class sees at each step the importance to them in the various out-of-school and in-school situations which *at that time* or *in the near future* confront or may confront them.

VI. WHAT PHASES OF ORAL WORK CAN BE COMBINED WITH ENGLISH ACTIVITIES?

A. Speech Work Correlated with Literature Study

Oral work in connection with literature presents a fairly simple problem. The opportunities, briefly summarized, include:

1. Prepared reading from the text. (Before a group, before the class, as "guest reader" before another section, over the radio—real or imaginary.)

2. Readings from books or magazines discovered in "free reading." (These should in some way illustrate, either by contrast or by similarity, the theme under discussion in class. A series of unrelated readings is, so far as literature study is concerned, probably a waste of class time.)

3. Choric speech.

4. Group drama reading before groups, the class, as an "activity-period" program, or over the radio. (Many teachers, realizing the charm of oral drama reading, organize a drama-reading group for one of the numerous "last-period" activities.)

5. Dramatization of ballads, stories, scenes from books.

6. Interpretation of individual speeches. (Lady Macbeth's "We fail" serves as an excellent example.)

7. Talks about books, tendencies, authors, qualities. (Such work must be clearly motivated.)

8. Oral reports on authors, settings, or summaries of world conditions. (The Crusades for *Ivanhoe*, the First World War for *Greenmantle*, a legend for *Prester John*, the author's life for *Native Son*, the actors for *Green Pastures*. Again the radio presents opportunities.)

9. Oral reports, or brief précis, in connection with the bulletin-board display. (In some schools current events on modern authors or new discoveries about older authors make an admirable three- to five-minute prelude to classwork.)

10. Discussion of book reviews and reviewers. (For this work and the one above I advise the *Books* section of the *New York Times* and the *New York Herald Tribune*, the *Saturday Review of Literature*, and for older students reviews in the *Yale Review*, the *Virginia Quarterly*, the *Nation*, the *New Republic*. For younger pupils who need direction and brevity, *Time* and special articles such as Pearl Buck, "Literature and Life" in the *Saturday Review of Literature*, August 13, 1938; Joseph Wood Krutch, "What Is a Good Review? ' in the *Nation*, April 17, 1937; the editor's "Anonymous Reviewing" in the *Saturday Review of Literature*, January 21, 1939, offers possible references.

11. Conversations on literature at imaginary (a) dining tables; (b) evening parties; (c) hostess-guest afternoons. (Pupils are quick to see the advantages of trying courteously to enter and to direct conversations.) Conversations on topics relative to the life of the author (a) with the author—represented by another pupil; (b) with an imaginary friend (à la Ben Jonson and a man from Stratford). All depends upon the seriousness with which this type of imaginary work can be carried on. In many schools, particularly where students come from homes stocked with books, this type of work is highly successful. (Notice in these exercises that your purpose is primarily to indicate impersonally what is and what is not acceptable conduct in discussion. The work should be begun at the seventh-grade level and, with increasing maturity of material, be carried on in some form throughout the high-school course. Recall the questionnaire in Chap. VII.)

12. Introductions connected with literature. Pupils at some time have to introduce strangers to each other. Introductions—both gra-

cious and awkward—can perhaps be found in literature, but the introduction of literary people (Sir Roger de Coverley, Robinson Crusoe, Becky Sharp, Dr. Samuel Johnson, Elmer Davis, Vincent Sheean, Edna St. Vincent Millay) with an appropriate introductory comment to begin easy conversation is a game that calls for tact and understanding of the characters, and is excellent training in speech.

You will find, also, excellent opportunities for pointing out the expert and the bungler in conversation in the various books and short stories which a class reads. In "Xingu" (*Xingu and Other Stories* by Edith Wharton) you can point out that the sound basis for good talk, and the only sound basis, is simple, unpretentious discussion of material known to the speaker. It is a delightful corrective for pupils who think that excellent conversation grows out of "ten easy lessons."

You might consult the *Commonweal* for June 10, 1938, which contains "Road Rules for Talkers" by Amanda B. Hall: or Milton Wright's *The Art of Conversation*.[1] Many students kill intelligent discussion by their hummingbird habit of sudden approach and equally sudden retreat from an idea. Continuity of idea in discussion develops slowly; encourage it.

Of course, good discussion demands both courtesy and ease, qualities desired by students, whether or not they admit the fact. To satisfy this desire, through literature you can lead the class discussion from past to present. How do the customs, manners, situations as shown in fiction or biography differ from those of our own day? Such an approach can lead to a thoroughly impersonal discussion that may answer for the ill-at-ease many of their unasked questions.[2]

B. Speech Work Correlated with Work in Written Composition

1. When reading compositions aloud, I like to use "article" or "incident" or "story" or "discussion" instead of "theme" or "composition." It brings the written effort into comparison with other writing in the world outside the schoolroom, where many models await the amateur.

2. Group discussions and selections of the better written papers.

[1] McGraw-Hill, publishers.
[2] a. *Boy Dates Girl,* Pocket Ed., by Gay Head, Scholastic Publishing Co.
   b. *Etiquette in Business,* by M. L. Carney, McGraw-Hill.
   c. *Behave Yourselves,* by B. Allen and M. P. Briggs, Lippincott.

(Here a chairman and businesslike methods of discussion—I advise a time limit—are essential.)

3. Oral criticism of papers read. (Time should be given for the careful formulation of opinions. Stress should be placed upon favorable comment first and constructive comment always.)

4. Class discussion of topics that may be used, or may never be used for future writing. (Note the "setting-up exercises" suggested in Chapter VI.)

C. Speech Work Correlated with Mechanics: Grammar, Spelling, Vocabulary Drill

Grammar: Particularly with younger pupils, oral drill upon correct forms is essential. By oral work only can the tongue be trained and the ear become accustomed to the correct forms of such words as *lie—lay, rise—raise, come—came,* etc. Invent such exercises as:

1. Rapid teacher-question pupil-answer dialogues, providing drill on difficult forms.

2. Rapid dialogue prepared by pupils (imaginary telephone, visitor, application for a job, errand, introduction, dinner-table conversation, nomination speech, etc.), where these difficult word-forms are frequently used.

3. Oral reading of sentences to discover the placing of misplaced modifiers. Oral illustrations of similar modifiers properly placed. The training of the pupils' ears—the only training that will give them style and enjoyment of style in others—*must* be oral.

D. Speech Work Correlated with the Study of Punctuation

1. If teachers *would* teach punctuation as merely one means of making meaning clear, then much reading of sentences to observe the changes in thought wrought by various punctuation marks would play an important part in class discussion. (See Chapter IV.)

2. Pupils should also interpret by change of voice the mood or the drama implied by punctuation. "We live as in a dream—alone." (Conrad in "Youth.") "All that night, all the next day, and all the next night he meditated." (Katherine Mansfield in "Life of Ma Parker.")

3. A brief dictation exercise made by a pupil and read by him to

the class offers again an opportunity for a "before-the-class" appearance.[1]

E. Speech Work Correlated with Spelling and Vocabulary Drill

1. Spelling again offers pupil-made dictation exercises.

2. Talks can be given on variations in spelling, on English versus American spelling, on roots, suffixes, prefixes, and meanings and legends or myths behind words.

3. For vocabulary work a series of reports, group discussions, and panel discussions is both possible and desirable.[2]

[1] Here is such a dictation made by one of my students, Shirley Knight:

DICTATION EXERCISE FOR PUNCTUATION

Are you lonely? Do others shun you? Do you wake up at two A.M. with a punctuation complex? Don't let your friends say of you, "Let's not bother with him; he's a punctuation moron." Don't be handicapped any longer by old-fashioned punctuation. Start now, without further delay, to learn punctuation in the approved style, and watch your popularity grow.

Don't be misled by long, formal rules of punctuation; consequently let simplicity and efficiency be your guiding stars toward perfection of punctuation. Punctuation is probably the most important (?) factor in your life, or your friends' lives. Commas, periods, and semicolons—these are your very destiny.

"What," you may ask, "is the price I must pay for all this?" If you so choose, only fifteen minutes of your time each day is required. Only co-operation, clear thinking, and honest effort are asked of you; patience and persistence, both necessary for good punctuation, will do the rest.

[2] The following cutting from a newspaper indicates one possibility of interesting correlation of vocabulary and speech.

ENGLISH CLASS TO BROADCAST FORUM

"The King's English," a radio forum, will be broadcast by Miss Irene Berg's senior English class at 9:15 A.M. Tuesday . . . from Flathead County high-school's Little Theater with the co-operation of T. R. Richardson's speech department. [Then follows a list of students' names.] Allan Crumbaker organized the ideas of the class into a script which will show development of the English language through the ages, from the period of Anglo-Saxon speech to the present. The discussion will show that language is the result of the author's adaptation of words to his needs. Poetry will be used as a medium of contrast between classic usage and the American vernacular.

(The topic might appall you and me, but not youth if the teacher is wise enough to guide but not curb activities.)

VII. WHAT SPEECH TRAINING MUST BE GIVEN UNCOMBINED WITH OTHER PHASES OF ENGLISH WORK? [1]

In the earliest training for bodily control, pantomime may well play an important part, just so long as you can make it a serious and enjoyable procedure. (Pantomime of characters in novels is sometimes successful, but beware attempts to represent tragic characters, for you must never make the classwork ridiculous.) Then there are numberless situations: for example: (1) telephone conversations; (2) introductions; (3) greetings and farewells to guests; (4) entering and leaving, with guests, a room, hotel, bus, streetcar; (5) the courtesy of rising for older people and greeting them properly. In fact, all this social courtesy must be a part of your oral work, a necessary and valuable part, fitting your pupils to take their places easily in the world of people. (Naturally you would modify your work according to the type of pupils you have.) [2]

From the seventh grade on pupils should act as pupil chairmen, conducting meetings according to the simpler forms of par-

[1] For those speech situations which must be handled independently, those oral compositions in which the pupils draw upon their own information or their own experiences or their own interests other than those found in the English class, consult Appendix J and the books listed at the end of this chapter.

[2] Although all teaching requires ingenuity and variety of material, oral work depends upon those qualities even more than other types of work, since the audience must be kept interested. Why not profit from the radio technique? This is a quiz-crazed world. You could have brief true-false tests on manners with instructions as to the way to score for all the etiquette problems which your class must discuss. For example, why not a telephone-manners (T.M.) quiz, a "Who goes first?" quiz, a "When stand, when sit?" quiz, an "Introduction, please" quiz, an "At table, what?" quiz? All depends upon the interest of your class; but you are safe so long as the "manners" remain those that present actual problems to boys and girls. Most of your pupils will recognize the value of knowing how, even if their manners are kept for special occasions. Be helpful. These pupils are going to need to meet people, to act in conformity with accepted standards. You are teaching pupils, not subjects. One book which, because of its detailed exercises and general tone, seems to me particularly useful is Craig, Alice Evelyn: *The Speech Arts; A Textbook of Oral English*, rev. ed., Macmillan, 1937. Consult it.

liamentary procedure. In later grades they should learn how to amend motions, what motions are in order; they should understand the necessary parliamentary procedure as used in school clubs and debating societies, so that they feel no embarrassment or uncertainty when they desire to speak or to make a motion. This work, depending upon the time you have, can be made a thoroughly enjoyable class activity in which all participate.

VIII. WHAT PART MIGHT THE PUBLIC ADDRESS SYSTEM, RECORDER, PHONOGRAPH, AND RADIO PLAY IN YOUR SPEECH WORK?

Whether you do or do not have these mechanical aids for oral work in your first school, you should know something of their use. Many teachers consider the public-address system a not unmitigated blessing. If principals are thoughtless, they may too often interrupt classes with announcements that could be delayed until the end of the hour. But for your speech class the public-address system has many uses. All sections meeting at the same period can hear a particular program or a particular talk originating in the school. It gives the broadcaster much the same thrill that one receives from talking over the radio; and it certainly stimulates careful preparation. It is of considerable advantage, too, to have a recorder. Unfortunately many of our finest radio programs are given at hours inconvenient for class use; hence pupils may miss the best speeches, acting, and readings that the United States can produce. But if you keep alive to the opportunities provided by radio, and are supplied with a recorder, you can record those programs and play them on the phonograph when you desire illustrations of the varied problems facing your class. These recordings can be repeated over and over again; thus you and the class can analyze the various methods of appeal and those elements which make speech effective. No matter how isolated your school, you are provided with admirable illustrative material.

An even more important function is the recording of your pupils' voices. Many voices can be recorded on one record, thus cutting the expense, for two sentences will show a pupil whether his voice is pleasantly or unpleasantly pitched, and whether he does or does not articulate clearly. For many schools, however, the radio is the only mechanical aid available. As suggested elsewhere, it is well to appoint a committee to keep you informed of excellent programs.

REFERENCES ON RADIO AND SPEECH

1. Abbot, Waldo: *Handbook of Broadcasting,* McGraw-Hill, 1937
Radio Speaking; Specialized Radio-speech Programs; Oral Interpretation and Dramatic Reading; Radio Pronunciation; Articulation and Dialects; Radio Dramatics.

2. *R.F.E.C. Service Bulletin,* U.S. Office of Education, Federal Security Agency, Washington, D.C.
Teachers may receive free upon request issues as they are published. They contain reviews and articles on radio education. This material will prove interesting to your radio-interested pupils.

Many teachers confess their inability to find or to help students find topics of interest for their oral compositions. Would it be wise to treat your pupils as adults and to ask their aid in collecting and distributing information on these new mechanical aids to education? It will appeal to them as a thoroughly worth-while project. Below are sources to which you could direct them.

1. *Educational Research Bulletin,* College of Education, Ohio State University, Section 2, pp. 38-59 (May 14, 1941)
Student broadcasting; types, speeches, etc. Drama, music.

2. *Sound Recording Equipment for Schools,* Committee on Scientific Aids to Learning, National Research Council, 41 East 42 Street, New York City, 1940
Single copies available to teachers without charge.

3. *Broadcast Receivers and Phonographs for Classroom Use,* same publisher as 2, 1939-40
This is a completely scientific discussion of kinds, types, uses, and performances of various types of receivers and phonographs. Thoroughly in-

teresting to your scientific pupils, and indispensable before buying equipment.

4. *How to Use Radio in the Classroom,* Educational Department, National Association of Broadcasters, 1626 K St. N.W., Washington, D.C.

By a Committee of Teachers and Radio Educators in Association with Evaluation of School Broadcasts, Norman Woelfel, Ohio State University, in charge. Here are nine brief essays on how to use radio in the classroom.

5. Bragdon, Clifford: "The Movies in High School," *English Journal* (High School Edition), Vol. 26 (1937), pp. 374-81

Why not try noon movies? Note the list given here. (In some schools five-cent noon movies are used to raise money for records and books.)

6. Films to rent, Progressive Education Association. Commission on Human Relations, Room 3867, 45 Rockefeller Plaza, New York City.

Apply for application blanks and booklets describing more than sixty films (1940) that can be secured, such films, for example, as *The Good Earth, The Life of Emil Zola, Louis Pasteur, Dodsworth.* Booklets with study material and suggestions for discussion are provided.

7. Nicoll, Allardyce: "Literature and the Film," *English Journal* (High School Edition), Vol. 26 (1937), pp. 1-9

How does the author answer the often-heard question "Why does the movie change events in the novel filmed?"

8. A complete catalogue (price 50 cents) of silent films for schools, special programs, etc. Division of Visual Instruction, Harmon Foundation, 140 Nassau Street, New York City. (Films may be rented.)

9. Teller, Irene E.: "Reading—with Sound," *English Journal,* Vol. 27 (1938), pp. 33-38

Here is an amusing article on interesting the mechanical-minded pupil in producing appropriate sound for class readings (after rehearsal) of either prose or poetry. How to get these various sound effects—whether you use them or not—would provide a pupil with an interesting topic.

IX. WHAT INDIVIDUAL AND WHAT CLASS INSTRUCTION IN SPEECH SHOULD YOU GIVE?

So far, opportunities for speech have been discussed, not the actual instruction in speech itself. The problem of instruction divides itself at once into two parts—instruction for normal pupils and instruction for those with obvious speech defects. Given normal pupils, you can find many profitable ways for teaching them to speak. What can you do with those pupils who have a serious speech defect? Unless you are trained, it is probably unwise for you to attempt correction. When they speak, you can provide a sympathetic but serenely unconscious attitude on your own part; you can secure a sympathetic courtesy from your class; and in all ways possible you should shield the pupils from embarrassment or self-consciousness. If there is a speech specialist able to cope with stammering or other speech difficulties, by all means arrange a conference for the pupil, and do all in your power to help him carry out any instructions given. But beware of attempting instruction that you are not well prepared to give. The harm you may do if, unskillfully, you try to aid a pupil who stammers or stutters is so serious that it is undoubtedly wiser to attempt no corrective work. There are, however, certain minor faults with which you might deal successfully. With the less serious cases, such as omitted final consonants, slovenly speech, monotone, clipped words, or too little flexibility of the upper lip, you might be able to give profitable instruction. But when you have forty in a class, you will find that you can do little individual work. Yet this much is possible: You can select the difficulty that appears most frequently in your group, call attention to it as a class, not as an individual, fault, and give some corrective work and oral exercises spoken in unison. But with your pupils' enunciation, voice quality, and pitch you can do little unless you are well trained; and in large classes you can do little even then, although with certain types of students you can speak a few words in private, make an occasional inquiry concerning their progress, and encourage them to work on their particular difficulties.

For the members of your class whose speech habits are normal you may be able to secure definite improvement. One thing you must do. Set certain goals for your class. The first, of course, is that all speech, whether one-word answer or prepared talk, must be audible to all members of the class. Unless you wander about your classroom you may never know how little of front-seat comment penetrates to the back row, or how many comments, understandable when the speaker faces you, you lose when you regard the back of the speaker's head. The second goal should be clarity—clarity of idea, clarity of phrasing, and clarity of enunciation. If you stress clarity of thought rather than clarity of expression, you are beginning at the root and will presumably have more effect upon your pupils' work than if you overlook the foundation and attempt to deal with the form. Confused speaking, you will find, usually has its source in confused thinking, or in lack of any definite idea to be expressed. Many teachers are satisfied if these two goals are reached, but there are other goals. You wish your pupils to stand upright, to look at their audience, to hold their bodies not too awkwardly. But remember this: The one thing that you must not do is to make classroom speaking an ordeal, and an appearance before the class a cause for commiseration. Your pupils are adolescents. They change with bewildering rapidity back and forth from sensitive adults to mischievous children. At any moment they may be unbelievably sensitive about a changing voice, a disfigurement, too much or too little weight or height. For these reasons make oral work as casual as you can. In the English classroom, speech (indulged in often during some ten of the sixteen waking hours) should be for pupils a usual, simple, un-self-conscious activity. First, of course, they must see its usefulness. You will not find it hard to show them the need for training, for most of them have at some time suffered from their own inability to cope with a social situation. Then if you can convince them of the practicality of the work that you propose (or lead them to propose), the popularity of the work ought to be assured.

It is unfortunate if your own training in oral work has been scanty, but if it has been, and if you now have no time to remedy the situation, you might consult some of the texts listed below.[1] Then you might begin to plot out for your junior or senior high school the objectives for each year. Decide upon the types of activities suitable for your group that might in each year provide stimulating speech situations. Remember that poise and good speech habits cannot be acquired quickly. You must provide many opportunities in which, under different guises, you can cultivate the same qualities—clear thought and clear, pleasing expression—with sufficient variety of purpose so that pupil interest does not wane. As the importance of speech becomes more widely recognized (the radio has done much to call attention to speech and its profitable uses) the place of oral work in the schoolroom will undoubtedly become increasingly important. Provide yourselves, therefore, with as much speech training as you can. Recognize the many distractions and the difficulties that arise from the numbers in a classroom; then work out a few very simple aims that will guide you in your teaching. Not until after those aims are clearly defined are you ready to bring to bear all your ingenuity and tact in inventing dozens of situations which will provide your pupils with an opportunity to realize at least in part the aims which you and they have established.

SUGGESTED EXERCISES

Before you attempt these exercises, read as many of the references listed at the end of the chapter as time will permit.

1. a. Consider your own voice, its quality, flexibility, and pitch. Then note the voices of those about you. Select one person whose voice thoroughly pleases you; attempt to analyze what qualities you thoroughly enjoy. Bring your observations to class in the form of a well-organized *one-minute* talk. Your topic might be some variation on the theme: "The Qualities of a Pleasing Voice."

b. Consider the voices about you. Attempt to analyze why cer-

---

[1] Later in some of the summer sessions that you will attend, secure some training in speech, in reading aloud, and in acting. Few studies will stand you in better stead in the high-school classroom.

tain voices displease. Are lips rigid? Is the tone nasal? What could the owners do to render their voices more pleasing? Prepare a *one-minute* talk on the results of your investigation. If possible, it would be wise to have a few of these talks given in class.

2. Select a *two-minute* reading to give before the class, if time allows, or before some of your class members. You might try a Shakespeare song perhaps, a brief Housman poem, or a poem by Humbert Wolfe. Your purpose here is to interpret intelligently and pleasingly for your audience and to test your own reading.

3. Plan six related eight-minute exercises in conversation (decide upon the junior- or senior-high-school year in which they might be used) and outline briefly. Show purpose, way of arousing interest, sources from which pupils are to gain material, and probable motivation for each talk. Work for slightly increased difficulty in each talk, as was suggested in teaching the letter.

4. If time allows, present in your class a panel discussion of oral English—each speaker given a definite phase, the class taking part when possible. Your readings in *English Journal* articles will provide you with much material, but you should also advance your own opinions.

5. Select one junior- or senior-high-school text and be ready to present, in brief written form, all of the oral work that might profitably be used in its study. Get variety and keep interest.

6. Select some well-written, exciting book that would appeal to junior-high-school boys and girls. From it make a brief cutting to be read aloud. Your purpose should be to awaken interest in the book. If you can, give this reading before the class or before a number of your classmates. If you would practice together, you would find that you could gain much from your own reading and from the faults and excellences of the others.

7. Prepare an assignment suitable for a senior class. It should call for careful, logical explanation on your part. Prepare it; then, if time permits, give it to your college class. Set yourself a difficult problem; then attempt to solve it logically, clearly, quickly, and in pleasant fashion.

8. Work out a related series of telephone problems suitable for a group of seventh-grade or eighth-grade children. Remember that each situation must seem interesting, probable, and important. Then work

out a second more difficult series appropriate for the ninth or the tenth year. You may feel that you do not know much concerning children of grade-school age. Look about you. Would it be wise to go visiting schools?

SUGGESTED READINGS

A. References for Your Own Guidance

The English Language Arts, Vol. I, N.C.T.E. Curriculum Series, Dora V. Smith, Director

Read Part III, Chapter 13, "The Program in Speech and Writing." Why are the two combined in one chapter?

Books That Are Texts

1. Borchers, Gladys Louise: *Living Speech,* rev. ed., Harcourt, Brace, 1949

For junior-high-school work, Grades 7-9.

2. Hedde, Wilhelmina G., and Brigance, William N.: *American Speech,* rev. ed., Lippincott, 1951

For both junior and senior high school.

3. Painter, Margaret: *Ease in Speech,* rev. ed., D. C. Heath, 1943; 2nd rev. ed., 1953

For senior high school. English teachers' various activities employing speech are included.

4. Weaver, Andrew Thomas, and Borchers, Gladys Louise: *Speech,* Harcourt, Brace, 1946

5. Robinson, Karl Frederic: *Teaching Speech in Secondary Schools,* Longmans, Green, 1951

6. Sarett, Lew, Foster, William Trufant, and McBurney, James H.: *Speech,* Houghton Mifflin, 1943

A Teaching Aid

7. Bernstein, Julius C.: "Recording and Playback Machines: Their Function in the Classroom," *English Journal,* Vol. 38 (1949), pp. 330-41

This article (written in answer to the request of Max J. Herzberg, Director of Production of Audio-Visual Materials) answers the needs of anyone wishing to select, buy, or use the recorder or playback. Here the advantages and disadvantages of disk, tape, and wire recorders are discussed; machines are listed, and a nontechnical bibliography is supplied.

*B. References Concerned with the Teaching of and the Listening to
Oral English*

1. Mercer, Jessie: "Listening in the Speech Class," *Bulletin of the
National Association of Secondary-School Principals,* Vol. 32 (1948), pp.
102-107

2. Kinney, Lucien, and Dresden, Katharine, eds.: *Better Learning
Through Current Materials,* Stanford University Press, 1949
(a) "Current Materials as a Basic Resource," pp. 51-69. Consider
"The Organization of a Teaching Unit," pp. 53-66, and "The Evaluation."
(b) "Having Effective Classroom Discussion," pp. 69-90. Observe
Madge McRae's careful preparation and class oral work based on a
school situation.

3. Grams, Jean, and Kinney, Lucien: "Sociodrama in High School
Classes," *Social Education,* Vol. 12 (1948), pp. 341-44

4. Walthew, Margaret: "What's Right with America?" *Clearing House,*
Vol. 15 (December, 1940), pp. 205-07

5. Herzberg, Max J.: *Radio and English Teaching* (N.C.T.E. Monograph, No. 14), Appleton-Century, 1941

From *Elementary English*

1. Wright, M. B.: "Let's Do: Let's Tell," Vol. 26 (1949), p. 604

2. Fry, Dorothea: "Experiences in Speaking," Vol. 28 (1951), pp. 126-
29; 171

3. Morkovin, B. V.: "Growth Through Speaking and Listening," Vol.
26 (1949), pp. 129-31

From the *English Journal*

1. Painter, Margaret: "The Dilemma of the Four-Leaf Clover," Vol.
38 (1949), pp. 254-59
Many practical suggestions are made here by the writer, chairman of
the N.C.T.E. Committee on Speech.

2. Finch, Hortense: "Wake Up and Live," Vol. 27 (1938), pp. 136-37

3. Brickell, Henry M.: "What Can You Do with Sociograms?" Vol. 39
(1950), pp. 256-61

4. Appy, Nellie: "Western Timber: The Panel in Action," Vol. 26
(1937), pp. 801-05
Read this article. Note that present-day social problems are here discussed—with good temper.

5. Cook, Margaret: "The Why Is Plain," Vol. 29 (1940), pp. 577-81
The simple beginning of a high school's use of film and radio.

6. Davison, Helen G.: "Vox Pop in the Classroom," Vol. 26 (1937), pp. 574-75
Note here how Monday morning is anything but "blue."

7. Moore, Paul: "Recording Pupils' Speech," Vol. 30 (1941), pp. 500-01

8. Waggoner, Louise: "Conversation and Courtesy," Vol. 26 (1937), pp. 569-72

9. Kirk, Marguerite: "Newark Goes to School," Vol. 35 (1946), pp. 260-64

10. Greene, Jay E.: "Teachers of English, Social Studies, and Speech Co-ordinate Efforts," Vol. 39 (1950), pp. 451-52

11. Handlan, Bertha: "Group Discussion of Individual Reading," Vol. 32 (1943), pp. 67-73

12. Stoops, Emery: "Oral English in Life Situations," Vol. 24 (1935), pp. 555-61
Seven steps in preparation and delivery of oral material. Well worth reading for teachers untrained in speech work.

13. McCarroll, Jessie M., and Poley, Irvin C.: "All the News and No Print: An Adaptation of the Living Newspaper," Vol. 29 (1940), pp. 572-76
An amusing program that you could adapt for an assembly.

14. Heaton, Margaret: "The Foreground of the American Scene," Vol. 27 (1938), pp. 335-40
An up-to-the-minute study of American types from radio, theater, books. A thoroughly interesting method of viewing the modern world.

15. Reid, Seerley: "Hollywood Hokum—the English Teacher's Responsibility," Vol. 29 (1940), pp. 211-18

16. Crocker, Lionel: "On Teaching Public Speaking," Vol. 29 (1940), pp. 219-24

17. Roberts, Holland D., and Fox, Helen: "Streamlining the Forum and Debate," Vol. 26 (1937), pp. 275-82

18. Stratton, Ollie: "Technique for Literate Listening," Vol. 37 (1948), pp. 542-44

19. Cox, Olivia M.: "A Project on Democracy in Motion Pictures," Vol. 40 (1951), pp. 169-70
A class selection prompted by an article in *SRL*.

CHAPTER IX

Motivating Composition in Relation to Pupils' Experience

I. WHY IS COMPOSITION WORK UNPOPULAR?

WHEN you consider the question of composition and com‑ position assignments, several difficulties arise. You want to arouse interest in writing; you want to present some problem that the class must solve; you want to give just enough help to stimulate your pupils to work, but not enough to do the work for them; and you want to have variety. Every teacher, I sup‑ pose, goes that far in the analysis of her problem. If, however, her analysis goes no farther than I have just suggested, she may easily decide upon some such series of assignments as the follow‑ ing:

1. A summer day that I enjoyed.
2. Which is the greater hero, Hector or Achilles?
3. An outdoor scene that filled me with —— (supply an appro‑ priate word).
4. Write a vivid description of an interesting character.
5. (a) Keep a diary for three days; see how much you can find of interest to us Or (b) report the Assembly speech given on Wednesday. Be accurate.

What do you think of these five consecutive assignments? Read them over and consider just what is demanded of the unskilled writer. You will find that in the course of five assignments he is asked for: (1) a narration of a whole day's happenings; (2) an exposition calling for critical judgment; (3) a description of some natural scenery where mood should largely determine the selection and presentation of all details; (4) a description of a person in which, presumably, external appearance is given, but in which, also, an attempt is made to interpret character; (5) a selected list of happenings, or a digest of what may easily have been a wandering and feeble talk.

It is hardly an exaggeration to say that schools still exist in which teachers, conscientious ones too, fling out assignments not unsimilar to those cited above. They want variety; they want to keep compositions interesting; they are busy about many things. Very probably, too, they feel that if pupils just write enough, they may, by the trial-and-error method, stumble upon some correct and fairly interesting way of expressing such ideas as they may happen to have on hand. Is it not probable that a close relation exists between the teacher's attitude just stated and the pupils' dislike of composition?[1]

Before examining more desirable theme assignments than those listed, we might consider why composition is often presented in undigested blocks of vaguely determined size and kind, or in a strangely jumbled sequence of assignments. Other subjects have order and sequence. Why should composition so frequently lack them? Why should it not consist of carefully graded units?

1. Many teachers fail to view their composition work as a four-year course; hence they try to teach all things at once instead of building patiently, a little at a time.

2. The teacher's failure to recognize the difficulties inherent in different types of writing and in different types of composition subjects results in ill-considered and ill-arranged assignments. This topic has been so well analyzed, however, by Mr. Hitchcock in his *Bread Loaf Talks on Teaching Composition* (pp. 8-21) that I see no need for further discussion.

3. Some teachers, apparently, look upon the physical act of writing a theme as the one important step in composition work. For that reason they slight or omit those essential preliminary steps such as arousing a desire to write, finding something worth saying,

[1] In a study made of some seventeen hundred high-school pupils in Oakland, California, I asked each pupil to rank in order of liking the four, five, or six high-school subjects he was then carrying. The result of this questionnaire showed that composition was the most unanimously disliked subject; literature ranked high.

discussing possible ways of organizing the material, determining upon a desirable form.

4. Teachers forget at times that practically all assignments should provide the pupil with (a) a clear-cut, definite problem, (b) certain specific requirements that he must meet, and (c) a definite concept as to what would be considered a successful theme. (Does all this sound dogmatic? Does it suggest fettered spirits? Just wait.)

5. As was suggested in Chapter III, many teachers in their correction of themes fail to make clear to the pupils by what changes their weak or awkward sentences may be improved. They mark a combination of words as "good" or "awkward" without giving then, or later, any analysis as to what is good or what makes a sentence weak. Perhaps the construction under consideration needs a participle or demands a dash or requires repetition to strengthen it; but unless the teacher, as skilled workman, points out just what is wrong and why, the poor apprentice stumbles on and, if he perseveres, discovers only by the costly trial-and-error method what might have been explained to him in five minutes.

6. Teachers are at times prone to forget the necessity for much repetition. A pupil learns by doing a thing until he knows how to do it. No one learning to drive a motor would willingly spend one lesson on a Ford, the next on a Buick, a third on a yacht, and a fourth on an airplane, though the general principle in all four is more or less the same. He takes a lesson on the Ford and continues to practice on that Ford until he learns or gives up. Far-fetched as it may seem, there is some slight analogy between this learning to drive and learning to write. Common sense dictates that a pupil should be confronted by much the *same* type of problem under *various* disguises until he has had enough practice to improve upon his first efforts. If, however, you return to the five topics suggested at the beginning of this chapter, you will note that "Which Is the Greater Hero, Hector or Achilles?" will be aided but little by practice upon the theme "A Summer Day That I Enjoyed." Nor will either contribute much to the pupils' ability to interpret through outward appearance the personality of that interesting character who is to be "vividly" described.

7. It has been proved that teachers grade compositions erratically. (See Chapter I.) It will suffice to say here that a grade should be a more or less accurate payment given by the teacher for tangible

products received from the pupil. If you conceive a grade to be a mark given to encourage or to reward conscientious effort, or to discipline bright but unruly pupils—well, you may still find some experienced teachers who will agree with you, but think it over.

II. HOW CAN YOU ORGANIZE AND MOTIVATE COMPOSITION?

Now let us consider what we mean by organization in composition; what some sample work might be in various grades; and what advantages seem to arise from an organized series of assignments that are lacking in the older, more haphazard method. Many teachers used to have some such sketchy arrangement for the distribution of their work as the one given below:

Monday: Drill day. (Grammar, sentence construction, etc.) Compositions handed in.
Tuesday: *Ivanhoe*.
Wednesday: Oral day. Current events.
Thursday: *Ivanhoe*.
Friday: Dictation, spelling, discussion of Monday's compositions.

Such a program had, it is true, certain advantages. Oral days were not crowded out; literature did not absorb so large an amount of time that drill was forgotten; spelling and dictation found a place in the high-school program. But the disadvantages of this mechanical division of subject matter far outweighed its advantages. Under this system it was almost impossible to elimi‑ nate the old conception of the recitation period (a time for telling the teacher what the pupil had learned) and to make each class merely a continuation of the learning process.

Today many schools teach literature one semester (literature requiring much written work), and composition another (com‑ position supplemented by much outside reading). One advantage of this division in those schools where free textbooks are supplied is that by alternating the classes—for example, three sophomore composition sections and two sophomore literature sections the first semester—fewer sets of books are required, and therefore a greater variety of texts may be purchased. This division of composition and literature into different semesters, however, is adopted because it is convenient for teachers and economical of books rather, perhaps, than because it is in itself ideal. A six- or a four-week period spent upon literature alternating with a six- or a four-week period of composition is, probably, the more popular arrangement where funds will permit or where pupils buy their own texts. The advantages of shorter units are these: They allow concentration upon one problem in composition or completion of a piece of literature plus the necessary preparation and collateral reading; they also avoid the quite possible monotony of a whole semester devoted to writing, while they provide sufficiently frequent practice to keep pupils in the writing habit.

What would be a specimen-organized, carefully motivated composition series? I shall give several in illustration, but remember, these series are merely illustrative and are in no sense ideal, for they are not made with some specific class in mind, a class that is working upon some definite problem. If you attempt to use one of them and find that it does not fit your class, just recall how seldom you are able to step into a store and walk out in a perfectly fitting suit. Usually some alterations are necessary, and these alterations make all the difference between a successful and an unsuccessful purchase. An assignment should be even more delicately fitted to the class—an abbreviation here, an enlargement there, an added series to give a broadening effect somewhere else.

A. Motivation for Freshman Work in Sense Impression

Miss Ida Wintsch, head of the high-school English Department in White Plains, New York, conducted an interesting experiment with her freshman class that will, I hope, eventually be recorded in the *English Journal* or elsewhere. Convinced that sentence sense had not been inculcated through the old-form theme assignment, and interested in the device, sketched in Chapter III, for developing discrimination in the choice of words, she worked out a logical and interesting series of assignments. These were so sequenced that a pupil tried practically the same problem, disguised slightly, three times; hence by the third time he had some possibilities of success. The following assignments are not identical with those presented by Miss Wintsch, but are made in the spirit of her experiment and are modeled upon her work.

FIVE-SENTENCE THEMES (SENSE IMPRESSIONS) FOR FRESHMEN

First Day

1. **Procedure.** Each pupil upon arrival in class was given a mimeographed sheet to be inserted in his notebook. This sheet provided a basis for class discussion and an assignment for the next day's work. (In an introductory paragraph the problem to be considered each day—some aspect of vivid telling—was discussed.) The introductory paragraph on the mimeographed sheet contained questions as to the way we receive impressions; pointed out that most of our information concerning the world about us comes through one of our five senses; and suggested that certain words like *crisp, salty, glittering, undulating, velvety, thundering, pungent,* since they appeal to some *one* sense, make a description more vivid and real to the audience than that description could be if the ideas were given without an appeal to eye, ear, taste, touch, smell. Then followed a brief list of words under each of the senses:

   a. Sight—*glittering, sparkling,* etc.
   b. Hearing—*snarling, muttering, whispering,* etc.
   c. Touch—*smooth, velvety, prickly,* etc.
   d. Taste—*salty, sour, acid,* etc.
   e. Smell—*stale, pungent, spicy,* etc.

After this list were three or four sentences indicating just what concrete advantages arise from specific terms. (For example, "the lighted match" is perfectly understandable, but "the blue spurt of a lighted match" gives the same fact more picturesquely.) After pupils considered these terms and added many more words to the list given, pupils read through the first assignment in the unit.[1]

---

[1] Naturally, you would find the following assignments dull or interesting, were you the pupil, depending upon the way they were presented. Teaching depends so largely upon the personality of the teacher that it takes courage

2. Assignment. Write five sentences, making each one an appeal to one of the senses, and arranging them in the order listed above: sight, hearing, touch, taste, smell. You have succeeded if (a) each sentence makes us see clearly or feel keenly the scene or the experience that you describe, and (b) if each group of words is a complete sentence, properly terminated. Look for your subjects and predicates. (This injunction would be repeated daily.) For example, to what sense would you appeal most strongly in each of the following situations: passing a sawmill, a popcorn stand, a flower shop; crossing a city street in heavy fog; wading in a muddy brook; getting breakfast in camp? Choose what you know and can picture. The five sentences need not be connected in thought.

Second Day

1. Procedure. Sheets were passed out again stressing sense appeal. Adjectives and -*ing* forms of the verb (probably gerunds and participles are unfamiliar terms) were particularly stressed. Then an example of the kind of theme desired was suggested. If you go nutting in the early morning you (a) see the russet leaves, (b) hear the faint twittering of birds, (c) touch the prickly burrs, (d) taste the oily meat of the nuts, (e) smell the crushed mint under foot. After these suggestions, the class built these ideas into sentences. Here a new problem arose. Connectives became necessary, and a list was made including such as *before dawn, as the sun rose, then, next, soon, but, for, later, after*. These are, of course, time-sequence connectives. Pupils were asked to volunteer other situations that might be fruitful for sense appeal, and were encouraged to choose original topics. As a suggestion for the less original, however, the following topics were mentioned as possible: sugaring off, a beach supper, football in the mud, rowing in a strong wind.

2. Assignment. Write five sentences, each appealing to one of the senses and in the order listed. These five are to be on a connected topic. When you have written them, read them aloud. Notice (a) if the appeal to the senses is vivid; (b) if each word adds to

to generalize any plan and suggest it as desirable procedure. Imagine this plan in the hands of Miss Murdstone. Each suggestion would fall of its own weight. Imagine it in the hands of Sir James Barrie. We would soar with him. Imagine it with G. B. S. We would tremble at our own stupidities, but what an unexpected yet exhilarating experience it might be! After this apology for presenting a plan that falls dead without the lift of an imaginative teacher, I shall give the assignments that might possibly follow such a beginning.

the impression; (c) if your connectives are smooth and well used; (d) if each statement is a well-made sentence.

Third Day

1. **Procedure.** Again sheets were passed. The introductory paragraph stressed the fact that the kind of person who sees a sight largely determines what is seen. Then the question was asked: What one sentence can you make for each person listed below that will illustrate the fact just stated? A puddle in the middle of Park Street might be (a) an annoyance to the high-school girl in her new slippers; (b) a pleasure to the little boy in his new rubber boots; (c) a danger to the football player on crutches; (d) an interesting bird bath to the naturalist. Before sentences were made in class, under the headings Girl, Little Boy, Football Boy, Naturalist, words were listed that might appropriately describe that puddle as it was viewed by different eyes.

2. **Assignment.** Write ten sentences, five for each, in which the same event was experienced by two different people with different points of view. Make each of the five sentences appeal to the senses. Follow the order given before.[1]

After these three assignments, the next three mimeographed sheets passed to the pupils dealt with description of *one* object familiar to all the class—a near-by lake, a park, a range of mountains, an expanse of ocean, a prairie—that in itself was large enough to have varied moods and varied aspects under different climatic conditions. These various possible aspects were suggested, and words listed as they were volunteered by the class that would suggest, through appeal to the senses, this scene under different conditions (*gleaming, angrily rumbling, rippling, laplapping, fishy,* or *tawny, rugged, rough, barren, wind-tossed*).

Since the five sentences were to be connected description, the necessary connectives were discussed and listed, and the difference pointed out between the kind used in narration and the

[1] Miss Wintsch limited her pupils to five-sentence themes for the entire term. With a very slow class I should follow her example, but with an average group I should use the assignment as given. You will note that for three successive days the class has attempted the *same* problem under slightly *different* form.

kind used here in description. The list would include such space-sequence words as *farther on, directly below me, nearer, above, turning to the right, to the east.* All of these words were drawn from the pupils in answer to the question: How can you help your reader to follow you? Then the class were assigned a five-sentence theme describing the scene now familiar to all. The pupils were asked to select some one condition (storm, calm, moonlight, severe cold) and to make their descriptions as vivid as possible, each of the five sentences appealing to one of the five senses in the order given before. After all had presented the *same* scene under *different* conditions, the pupils were confronted with the new problem of describing a scene strange to some of the class in terms that the readers could understand. To lead the class to making similes and metaphors—or, rather, to lead the class to use their imaginations and to project themselves into the mind of someone else—a series of problems was proposed: How would you describe an orange to an Eskimo who had never seen one? How would you describe a snowball to a boy from Louisiana who did not know snow? The class saw the possibilities of "a ball like snow but the color of the sun," "a ball like cotton but cold as ice," and were determined to go on concocting strange, Donne-like figures. But perhaps it is wiser to restrain them later than to curb this first enjoyment in released imagination.

Each one was then asked to find a scene familiar to him but unfamiliar to some of the class. By appealing to the five senses, the writer was to translate this scene so that it might be keenly realized by all. An orange orchard, Portland Street after rain, early morning in the Green Mountains, were suggested. As a conclusion to these exercises in description, the following assignment was made: In ten sentences, five each, show us two contrasting scenes, contrasting because of the different conditions under which you see them. As before, be sure that each sentence appeals to one of the five senses, and in the order given. Choose what you like but make it something that you have really wit nessed. Possibilities for this scene might be: the woods in autumn, in winter; State Street in July, in December; a maple grove in spring, in summer; a toboggan slide before and after the thaw; the school grounds at noon, at ten in the morning.

Perhaps these six examples indicate sufficiently the organization and motivation used in one type of series assignment. The teacher is bent upon (1) securing interested writing with a specific problem in each assignment, (2) encouraging well-selected words and the imaginative use of a pupil's vocabulary, and (3) demanding the invariable use of whole sentences. You may protest that five sentences are too brief and too arbitrary a limit. Of course pupils should not be limited to five-sentence themes indefinitely, but if they write badly, it is certainly better practice to write five sentences with care and forethought than twenty-five hurriedly. The amount of care and forethought that pupils put into their five sentences, however, is in direct ratio, remember, to your own interest and belief in the work and to your preparation, board illustration, and critical discussion of each assignment. This type of work attracts the lazy because at first it seems easy, can be thought about while other things are being done, and can be written quickly when it is once thought out. Brief as it is, however, it compels careful choice of words because the class knows just what type of appeal is expected in each sentence; hence they are quick to condemn or praise judiciously. And, last, it gives repetitious practice that can be quickly graded by the teacher. In some six brief papers it is possible to see and to show the pupil just what he has gained in power and where he is still weak. May I add without being accused of weakly truckling to the lazy, or of joining those misguided souls who would remove work and discipline from education, that this form of assignment is good because pupils enjoy it, and because they are led to use words—concrete words that produce pictures—in clear, whole sentences? What more can one ask from high-school pupils?

B. *Motivation for Exposition* (*Sophomore Year*)

A possible exposition series to be used in the last semester of the sophomore year might be built up in some such way as I give below. The previous training and the character of the class would, as I have said before, largely determine how the work should be planned and presented. Since, however, some model is necessary to give the theory concrete form, the following unit may serve, although any assignment *in vacuo* is of necessity poor.

First Day

1. **Procedure.** The teacher opens the recitation by asking for an original definition of some common object; for example, "What is a clock?" She repeats the query until the class is able to volunteer some statement that is sufficiently inclusive to admit all clocks, but sufficiently exclusive to eliminate watches, sundials, hourglasses. Next, "What is a chair?" might follow, to be succeeded by an abstract term such as *accident* or *climax*. (Here is an excellent place to attempt to eliminate the high-school formula: "A climax is when . . .") After the unit has been introduced in general class discussion, the assignment might be as follows:

2. **Assignment.** Think of three well-known words for tomorrow, two concrete (like *clock* or *chair*) and one abstract (like *happiness* or *thought*). Bring to class a definition for each one, written in complete sentences. Be so clear and definite that the class cannot criticize them unfavorably. Also bring in three other terms for class definition. As soon as you reach the room, write upon the board one definition from your three and also your list for class consideration. Sign your name after your work.

Second Day

1. **Procedure.** At the beginning of the hour, the teacher writes on the board an incorrect definition, such as, "Ink is a black fluid used for writing." The average class will accept this teacher-made definition until they realize that the existence of drawing ink and purple ink renders this statement too limited. The group is then ready to deal more critically with the board definitions placed there by members of the class, and to make more careful definitions for those words placed on the board by the pupils. Of course the assign-

ment depends upon class reading habits and library facilities, but a possible one under usual circumstances might be as follows:

2. **Assignment.** From your magazine reading (or elsewhere if necessary) bring in three brief definitions (not more than four or five sentences at most) that seem to you interesting and clear. For example, you might find a well-worded statement defining a *dirigible*, a *biplane*, an *amateur athlete*. You might find a definition of a *romantic novel*, of a *sketch*, of a *lyric*. You might find a statement of what *tariff* means, of what *personal property* consists according to state or national definition, or what distinguishing features *crullers* possess in contrast to *doughnuts*. Choose what you will.

Third Day

1. **Procedure.** After class discussion of the topics discovered and after some practice in redefining terms a brief dictation is given. It consists of clear-cut directions to a pedestrian as to how he should get from Avenue A to M Street, two well-known places. After this extract has been read, dictated, reread, corrected, and discussed, its brevity, clarity, and courtesy stressed, it is preserved in the notebook. Following the dictation, a discussion of the possible difficulties and confusions that might arise if certain words had been added or omitted leads to one conclusion: It is necessary to get the stranger's point of view before it is possible to direct him intelligently. Then or at a later period the class is asked to write, and is given this problem: "A strange pupil is taken by automobile to the gymnasium. He asks you to direct him to the principal's office." A brief time is given for writing; then when some of the papers are read, the class is asked to chart the stranger's progress. It might be well to call upon some of the less accurate pupils, so that their inexact statements may arouse discussion and increase the realization that it is essential to get another's point of view. Words like *quite, a little farther, the math room,* should be pointed out as vague or confusing to the pupil who does not know the school.

2. **Assignment.** You may take your own assignment, but make the problem fairly hard. Put a stranger somewhere in town. Tell him clearly, quickly, politely, how to reach some other rather distant destination in town. It is not fair to take him by automobile, or to show him the way. By the rules of the game he has to go unaided except by your advice and directions. He ought to go as immediately as possible. Bring in your directions written out in

whole sentences and with a map to show what you did for him.
In class these will be read in groups of five; the best will be read
to the class.[1]

Of course the ability of the class, their former training, and the
degree of success attained in these first three assignments would
determine whether the teacher should undertake a more complicated problem or should continue longer to vary the simple giving
of directions. If, however, the class has succeeded in the third
exercise, it would be well to begin in class with a discussion of
some simple process familiar to the pupils.

   1. Procedure. The class and teacher working together might
place on the board directions that they could give to a visiting child
whom they wished to entertain: How to play the ancient and divert-
ing game of tit-tat-to, for the directions there are simple. How to
play run sheep run, blindman's buff, still-water, charades. Here it
would be well to draw from the class what they used to play, and
then, if possible, to pose as ignorant, misunderstanding their directions until the board record is perfectly clear. Again, the connectives
should be stressed: *next, later, after, when one of the players, while
one group* (time sequence).

   2. Assignment. For tomorrow, choose some game that is not
too complicated, think it through, write out your directions, read
them to someone to see if he can follow each step; then look at
your sentences and use of connectives. When the directions are
clear and as brief as you can courteously make them, copy them to
hand in. Five of you will be asked to put your directions on the
board, or as much of them as time permits. In groups, all of you
will read one another's papers and give student criticism. The best
will be chosen and put on the hall bulletin board. Remember to
look at the board in the afternoon.

   After this type of assignment concerned with games and with
directions, a more difficult problem, but one easily within the
average sophomore's grasp, such as the following, might be given.

---

[1] Since, because of cost, many schools cannot afford mimeographed sheets,
I am using in this unit and in the next board work and dictation. The mimeographed sheets, though a convenience, are in no sense a necessity.

Assignment. Come to class with a clear, complete statement (150-word limit) concerning one of the following topics or a similar topic of your own choosing. Play fair. Don't select too easy a one for yourself.

1. What is a dictionary? What are its uses?
2. What is the *Readers' Guide?* What are its uses?
3. What are the functions of our student-body officers?

Bring to class also a problem about which we could write, and be ready to volunteer information concerning it. To save time, put your problem on the front board (sign your name) as you enter the class.

When these brief, simple assignments have been successfully carried out, such a spectacular problem as the following one might be given to conclude the six weeks' unit of work:

Assignment. Decide upon something that you can make and make it; be ready to tell us clearly, if the class is interested to know, how you made it. These objects may be placed upon the shelves and tables about the room. In order that your explanation may be as clear and as brief as possible, write it out. This paper will be handed in. (Of course such an assignment must be given far enough in advance so that sufficient time shall elapse between the first mention of the problem and the day for the display of the finished object.) When you come into class, look over the objects and determine what ones interest you most. By vote we shall decide what ones are to be explained.[1]

In a later composition unit more difficult problems should be presented, such, for example, as clear explanations of the Boy

---

[1] One teacher reported that when such an assignment was given, three of her class contrived an almost perfect airport with electric searchlight, tiny airplanes, hangars, etc. The interest in the class, the clarity of the explanations, and the genuine enjoyment of the group, convinced her that the time was well spent.

An Oakland High School boy, Oakland, California, found his first success, and consequently his first interest in English, when he was encouraged to perform a chemical experiment before the class and to explain it. Of course mere busywork should be avoided, but teachers of English would do well to tie their work to the live interests of their pupils.

Scouts organization or the organization of the Camp Fire Girls, the Junior Red Cross, the local Rainbow Club. As a rule pupils insist that they dislike exposition. After a time you will probably discover that much of the difficulty in and the dislike for exposition has arisen because, in the past, there has been too little oral preparation carried on by the teacher and class together. It is no easy thing to organize material, even familiar material, and much time should be spent in showing a class (1) how to collect ideas, (2) what to do with them, (3) how to make a working skeleton from which to write, and (4) how to articulate the different parts of an exposition. (See Mr. Hitchcock's *Bread Loaf Talks on Teaching Composition* and M. Bezard's *My Class in Composition*.) Many a theme that will never be written might to advantage be worked out in skeleton. You, as chief mechanic, must show your apprentices how clarity and order can be obtained. Together, you working at the board as secretary, you and the class should build up a topic. One that I have often used merely as a class exercise is based upon this introductory sentence: "Fire-fighting in cities has undergone most drastic changes since the days of my great-great-grandfather." The pupils, probably accustomed to a modern city fire department, can, through their imaginations, their reading, their occasional visits to small towns or camps, build with the teacher's aid a first rough scaffold upon the board. It might resemble this one:

SKELETON FOR A THEME ON FIRE-FIGHTING IN CITIES

1. Neighbors with pots, pans, buckets run to the fire.
2. Neighbors, supplied with buckets, run to the fire.
3. Some of the townspeople, organized into a bucket brigade, run to the fire and pass buckets of water to the burning building.
4. An organized volunteer group with hose and handcart run to the fire. (A shed is necessary for the cart and hose. City water has replaced the old well or pump system.)
5. Paid firemen with horse-drawn fire engine drive to the fire. (Firehouse necessary. Chemicals used.)

6. Paid firemen with automobile equipment go to the fire. (Fire department is now housed in a more elaborately equipped building.)[1]

After these topics have been jotted on the board, and the steps have been discussed to determine whether or not they are logical, another question arises. If one were writing upon this topic, of what length should the theme be? Could the material be given in a paragraph, a five-hundred-word theme, a book? The reason, of course, for such a discussion is in part to show the pupil that length is a variable matter depending entirely upon treatment. But also it is necessary to illustrate that in justice to the subject, the importance of any phase of an idea must determine the amount of space given it. Often in pupils' themes, not the importance of the phase but the inclination of the writer determines the relative length of the different parts. Three-fourths of a paper is spent in beginning while the rest of the material is compressed into a mere summary.

It would be wise to sketch for the class how this topic, fire-fighting, might be treated in one sentence, in one paragraph, or even, if one knew enough about it, in a book. Then another problem arises. If the various topics sketched on the board are to be treated in one theme, how are these different topics, each following the other chronologically, to be smoothly connected so that the theme does not sound like a mere listing of inventions? Of course the two words *then* and *next* present themselves. What else? On the board, volunteered by the class and the teacher, would be listed such expressions of time sequence as the following:

The next step . . .	A few years later . . .
Following the . . .	Then . . .
Shortly after . . .	Improving upon . . .
	Developing from . . .

[1] The reasons for choosing a fairly unfamiliar topic are two: first, one is not using material some pupil in the room may want to use later on; and, second, one is showing a class how much more information the average person

The teacher might or might not use parts of the outline for class writing, depending entirely upon the interest and knowledge of the class. In either case she *should* see that for the following assignments work is demanded requiring preparation similar to that illustrated in this skeleton. Why spend a day upon the topic of fire-fighting if the theme is never to be written? Because if they have built one skeleton under supervision, the pupils are better prepared to build one of their own and are also better prepared to appreciate and to criticize their own and their neighbors' themes intelligently.

But the topics so far suggested leave untouched what is today undoubtedly your most fruitful field for expository speech or writing. In this age, dominated by scientific interest, you would do well (1) to discover the scientific knowledge of your group; (2) to profess keen interest in what they know; (3) to attempt to stimulate them so that they will supplement their knowledge by simple readings, questions and observation; (4) to increase the scope of their interest by suggesting or by professing your ignorant curiosity about some related topic. For example, if you are near an airport, the radio beam provides a fascinating topic that calls for clear oral exposition, board illustration, reading, and, finally, offers material for an excellent, clear-cut scientific paper that, if well done, can be used in pamphlet form in your library to inform the ignorant. In the same way you can lead pupils to consider mankind's war on insects: the termite, the potato bug, the mosquito, the beetle in our forests.[1] Outside your classroom windows the world is teeming with admirable expository topics—if you have but the wisdom to use them. The electric light, the radio, the mysteries of the garage, the general science

has in his mind and half knows than he himself supposes. It is always difficult to get pupils to use what they know or to look into their own minds to find what is there.

[1] Probably Hans Zinsser's *Rats, Lice, and History* is much too sophisticated for your sophomores, but an article in the *National Geographic Magazine* might form an admirable basis upon which some boy or girl whose own basement is attacked by termites or whose garden is overrun by insects could learn how to observe and recount what that observation seemed to reveal.

laboratory, or kitchen (if regarded as the domain of a dietitian rather than of a mere cook), the stars at night and the lenses through which we regard them, the hospital laboratories with their blood tests and serums—all these topics and many more offer a field for oral and written exposition. And, too, these topics may serve to correlate the English class with the pupil's outside activities and interests. Any of these topics will lead the pupil into nonfiction reading. He will skim magazines, hunt out a fact in a textbook, consult the encyclopedia, ask adults about his topic. What are you doing for him? Teaching him in speech and in reading to interest himself in ideas, to speak and read like an intelligent adult.

If you feel yourself inadequately equipped, some such simple text as Frederick Houk Laws's *Science in Literature* will provide you with information, suggestions, and bibliography. Perhaps you resent such excursions outside your chosen field of English. Remember, you are not teaching English composition. You are teaching live, twentieth-century boys and girls. Find their interests; lead them to magazines and simply written books; cultivate their powers of thinking and their ability for organizing material in which they and their age can be interested. As a young teacher you will at first tend to teach your pet theories *about* composition. But remember that the most important principle in composition teaching is this: You must see to it that your students have adequate "cargo" for both their oral and written themes. If the "cargo" is adequate, you have a foundation upon which to build. Without adequate "cargo," composition becomes a farce, an empty formality, receiving and meriting the weary contempt accorded it by many of our intelligent pupils in many of our present-day high schools.

C. Preparation for Short-Story Writing

Even at the risk of being monotonously repetitious, I mean to suggest one last series assignment in composition for junior or senior work. Whether or not we approve of attempting in high school anything so technically difficult as the writing of short stories, the demand for them is insistent. We have school magazines, yearbooks, and short-story contests such as those sponsored by the *Scholastic Magazine*. High-school pupils are interested in this, their favorite form of reading, and desire to print better original stories than those appearing in the magazine of some rival school. Whether or not you think the form too difficult, in high school short stories are both read and written.

In connection with wide reading and discussion of short stories, I have with amazement heard inexperienced teachers, blandly unconscious of the difficulty of the assignment, ask pupils to produce an entire, finished story in three days, or a week, or for the next class meeting. Such an assignment, if it is not based upon ignorance alone, is certainly based upon the conviction that there is no teachable technique connected with the short story. But if you yourself do not hold that conviction, and wish to give definite aid, how might you go about it?

Of course here writing must be preceded by wide reading and discussion, wide reading definitely motivated, and discussion which concerns itself with more discriminating comment than the unpleasantly familiar "I didn't admire the man, but I'd like to be just like the girl in the story"; "I didn't mind it; it was easy to read."

You want, of course, to lead your class to some appreciation of what makes a story good or poor. How? First, in the stories read, you must begin slowly and with much repetition to stress one point in technique, then another. It is, of course, necessary to keep the story interest paramount, but the average high-school pupil, surprised to discover how much underlies story reading and story writing, follows the work with genuine interest.

Perhaps the first thing that you must decide, if it is not decided for you, is the type of textbook that you need—a historical one, devoted largely to Poe, Hawthorne, and Stevenson, or one representing the work of modern authors. I should advise the latter if your purpose is to lead your outgoing pupils into the habit of reading good magazines, for names such as Wilbur Daniel Steele, Charles Caldwell Dobie, Dorothy Canfield Fisher, Lord Dunsany, and Ben Ames Williams, found both in the text and in the magazines, will form a helpful bridge between class and the outside world.

After the textbook has been read understandingly, with discussion [1] of mood, time, methods of character presentation, point of view, underlying idea, method of repetition to drive home the main idea, the time has come for writing. Naturally it is unwise to introduce more than one principle at a time, for pupils, having slid over the surface of stories in all their previous reading, find, perhaps, that they are learning how to read fiction for the first time; hence the number of items stressed must be increased slowly. One reward, however, for this deliberate study—always interesting work because of the class absorption in the stories themselves—is the pupils' growing respect for the art of writing and their increasing sensitiveness to implication and suggestion in literature.

A short-story series of assignments in composition might be planned as follows. Their order should, of course, be determined largely by the interest of the class and by the type of stories read.[2]

D. Motivation for Junior-Senior Work in the Short Story

1. **Assignment.** Choose a setting with which you are familiar, one that suggests in itself gaiety, mystery, elegance, crudity, whole-

[1] For the sake of brevity and clarity this discussion is made dangerously dogmatic in tone, but of course in reality no two teachers would present material in the same way even though they agreed as to the procedure necessary and the objectives desired.

[2] You will find in *Developing Language Power* by Luella B. Cook a chapter entitled "Planning and Writing a Story." In it are stimulating suggestions for awakening interest in stories and story technique. The sections on "Selecting a Story Idea" and "Developing a Plot into a Story" are particularly useful.

some out-of-doors, solemnity, or solid comfort. In not more than two-thirds of a page present it to us so that we feel from the description the mood that you wish us to realize. Avoid *telling* us what we should feel, but so picture the scene that of necessity we grasp your mood.

Procedure. 1. Read to the class some contrasting settings. Then suggest how important are the choice of details and the elimination of other details that, even though true, do not contribute to the impression desired. With one of the descriptions it might be well to question as to what undoubtedly existed in the actual scene that is not mentioned by the author. Next suggest the importance of the type of word, showing on the board and building up with class aid some such distressing list as this:

SCENE TO EXPRESS	WRONG TONE	RIGHT TONE
Solemnity	frizzled	reverberations
Crudity	diaphanous	greasy
Mystery	plumped	glided

2. At the next meeting have these papers (assigned before) exchanged and read aloud in groups of five. Those pronounced best would then be read to the whole class and discussed for their virtues and for their possible improvements. To help the poorer pupils it might be well to have some member of each group analyze the kind of failure found in the less successful papers and then have the class and the teacher discuss why certain words or details omitted or added changed the atmosphere, and weakened or strengthened the impression desired. (It is, of course, necessary to work carefully here, for pupils are sensitive.)

After sufficient work has been done with these attempted backgrounds so that the majority of the class have been reasonably successful, it is time to attack the second group of assignments.

2. Assignment. Record three characteristic actions of three different people whom you see before the next meeting of the class. Decide why you term these actions characteristic rather than just accidental or chance motions. Go over the stories read and select from them some five examples for class discussion, showing how writers identify characters by some movement, action, or expression much as Homer identified them by a descriptive epithet.

Procedure. In class have these papers discussed in groups; then have those characteristics chosen by each group as the most significant and interesting reported to the class for general discussion. Attempt to emphasize the superiority of *showing* over *telling* a trait in character.[1]

3. Assignment. Take the setting just finished, or another if you prefer, and put a suitable character into it in characteristic pose. This will be a photograph, not a moving picture.

Procedure. 1. Discuss again the term "characteristic gesture" or "pose," indicating how necessary are those bits of observation which show us a character's use of hands, eyebrows, shoulders. Read from several authors to illustrate this point. It might be well to sketch on the board with suggestions from the class how some well-known figure could be given (the shady courthouse steps in summer and the figure of the sheriff; the basement steps of the schoolhouse and the janitor resting there after school; the windy street corner and the newsboy who stands there at five o'clock).

2. Have the class observe in some of the stories read the way in which not only the ideas expressed but the very words are carefully adjusted to each character so that they are subtly permeated with his own personality. To illustrate this fact read brief selections from familiar stories, perhaps from Mr. John Russell's "Jetsam" in the talk of the beachcomber and the reduced gentleman, or again in his story "The Fourth Man," for here each character stands out distinct in every gesture and word.[2] After such a discussion, the class will realize what is confronting them in the following assignment.

4. Assignment. Take two contrasting characters (for example, a small boy and his aunt, a football player and the principal, a high-school girl and the dean of girls, an inexperienced clerk and a well-to-do shopper) whom you think you can understand and see clearly. It would probably be wise to base your work upon some two people whom you know. Build up a brief dialogue between the

---

[1] An occasional quotation from a poor author—such, for example, as the quotation from Harold Bell Wright used by Mr. Leonard in his *Essential Principles of Teaching Reading and Literature*, p. 22—will, if analyzed, show clearly the emptiness and vagueness resulting from lack of concrete image or action. On the other hand, the tiny incident of the dog's slinking out of sight when Dunstan entered the breakfast room (*Silas Marner*) seems to be securely fastened in the minds of all upperclass students.

[2] "Jetsam," in Gerould, G. H., and Bayly, C.: *Representative Short Stories.* "The Fourth Man," in Mirrielees, E. R.: *Significant Contemporary Stories.*

two, interspersed with tiny bits of physical description so that we not only see and know a great deal about them but realize the contrast sharply and see the charatcer of each.

Upon the class success or failure in this work depends the amount of invention the teacher must display here in contriving various exercises of the type already suggested before allowing the class to begin work upon the final product. A short story is a kind of writing in which a pupil can take great pride; but that pride and enjoyment are somewhat dissipated, if not altogether destroyed, when the unskilled writer attempts original work without preliminary practice and suggestion. What he is doing here in this preliminary work serves as a series of warming-up exercises quite comparable to the trackman's exercise before a race. How long this trial writing should continue must be determined by the teacher's time and interest, by the interest of the class, and by the class impatience to begin in earnest upon "the" story. But not until sufficient training has been given so that the pupils can succeed to some degree is it wise to concentrate upon the final product, the climax of the unit's work.[1]

Some teachers use situation pictures such as one finds on the cover of the *Saturday Evening Post*, and suggest that their pupils draw stories from them. To this practice, however, there are two objections.

1. The people pictured are almost always slightly caricatured, so that a story based upon them would tend to picture types rather than individuals, the kind of generalized writing that the teacher is trying to avoid.

2. The situations often suggest love stories, and while high-school pupils might possibly cope with this type of tale in a Penrod spirit,

[1] Miss Mabel I. Rich (whose *A Study of the Types of Literature* you will find to be an invaluable mine of information to draw upon during your first years of teaching) has been successful in obtaining excellent plots for short stories and for one-act plays from newspaper clippings. Each pupil secures a usable clipping; the germ of the story contained in it is discussed, and the pupil develops this embryo into a finished play or tale.

their attempts are, more frequently, a combination of inanity and moving-picture emotion that no one could call good, judged by any known standard.

Probably a word of warning as to the very real difficulty of writing a story based primarily upon a love motive in contrast to the comparative simplicity of telling a story based upon plot or upon an analysis of some less complicated emotion (a boy's fear of his father, a girl's struggle because she feels herself unwanted in her home, a child's jealousy of the new baby) will guide the class away from failure.

THE STORY

First Assignment. After each pupil has decided upon the main incident of his story, it is wise—in order to insure a coherent plot, some visualization of the characters, and a definite knowledge of the setting—to make some such assignment as the following:

1. Hand in a thumbnail sketch (150 to 200 words) of the whole plot. [You as teacher should save the pupil from discouragement by discovering structural weaknesses before he has labored long over a plot which it is impossible for him to develop successfully.]

2. Hand in a two-sentence summary giving the character and the most striking physical attribute of each of your main figures. [You should try to make the characters "come alive" in the pupil's mind.]

3. In not more than five sentences make the setting of your story clear to us. [You can often save a rather good plot from seeming improbability by a change of setting.]

These preliminary sketches are, presumably, not to be used in the final draft, but are merely further warming-up exercises.

Procedure. While each pupil is working upon these problems, it is well to stress once more the art of omission, compression, and rapid beginning. It has become a byword in my own classes, "Don't begin with Adam," for the average student, whether in high school or college, tends to "begin with Adam" and trace the relationship down to Herbert Hoover before he can discuss the latter with a clear conscience. If, again, a number of well-done stories are considered in the light of what has been left unsaid, the pupil will probably grasp the idea of *implying* situations and relationships. He will also find out the advantages of arousing interest at once. The time scheme of a story, the summary telling, the use of retardation, should again be recalled. This type of work is especially valuable, for the knowledge of how and where to compress, where to omit, and how and where to expand story material will improve student writing more obviously than any other one device.

Final Assignment. When the teacher and class have together reconsidered these topics, and, through conferences, the teacher has discovered that the pupil has a plot and a set of characters offering him some chance of success, the individual work begins. Laboratory periods for individual conferences, laboratory periods for group reading and comparison of parts in the first rough draft, and laboratory periods for quiet revision should follow.

At last when the final product is handed in, it is not a short story conceived, born, matured, written, between class periods, but is the fruit of some six weeks' work spent in reading, studying, and discussing short stories, and in writing preliminary sketches. The actual amount of writing is not very great but, as in the earlier units of composition sketched, each part of the work is thoroughly understood before any writing is attempted, for all of it is based upon class discussion. This method centers the interest upon one problem at a time and repeats each problem often enough so that success is made possible, or at least so that entire failure may be avoided. A reasonably good pattern is provided, but individual invention is counted upon to supply original material.

III. WHAT IS GAINED THROUGH THIS TYPE OF ORGANIZATION AND CAREFUL MOTIVATION?

As I see it, the advantages in this unit plan are twofold: first, it defines clearly what is to be done, thus eliminating discouragement and waste effort; second, it permits intelligent class criticism and recognition by the class of those efforts that are successful. When the sense impressions, the expositions, or the stories are completed, the group method of reading them and of presenting the best for general class discussion provides each story or sketch with an interested audience, gives some student criticism to each writer, lays a foundation for critical judgment, and makes easy a selection for general class discussion.[1]

In these three dissimilar series, given as illustrations of carefully organized and adequately motivated work, you will note the importance of:

1. Oral discussion
2. Board work
3. Pattern assignments worked out in class
4. Discussion of transition with specific words suggested
5. Definite requirements
6. Original material encouraged, but suggestions provided for the unimaginative

The usual pedagogical term for this work is, I believe, prevision. It is the act of foreseeing what difficulties may confront the writer, and of inventing preliminary exercises to insure the pupil against unnecessary and discouraging errors. Such prevision seems intelligent, does it not?

Does the work seem too prescribed, too cabined, caged, confined? Do you feel that boys and girls should be given greater freedom?

At present in high school much excellent writing is done. But when one considers the great bulk of composition teaching carried on in our high schools today, it is not the excellence of the writing nor yet the zealous prevision by the teacher that impresses one. Perfunctory writing by the pupils, hasty, ill-planned assignments by the teachers, preoccupation of both teachers and pupils with matters of form rather than with worth-while contents, are not the exception but—with outstanding exceptions—the rule. And these undesirable conditions exist in schools where the same teachers who present composition poorly, often illogically, are

[1] The group method is widely used and popular but frequent regrouping is desirable. Only the best papers are read to the whole class. For other methods that teachers have used to increase the students' responsibility for the papers written such as "Pupil Self-Correction and Criticism," see Appendix E, pp. 587-88.

giving skillfully planned, intelligently presented courses in literature. Literature can, to a certain extent, be counted upon to teach
itself; composition, as you will learn later, must be taught. These
various suggestions as to organization and motivation are made
in the hope of bringing order out of what in some schools might
almost be termed chaos repetitiously presented for four years.

SUGGESTED EXERCISES

If it is possible, try presenting your plans to a group of students
or to other members of your college class. By so doing you will
realize some of the problems confronting the high-school teacher,
and will discover a little concerning your own strength and weakness. Before attempting these exercises, read a number of the references listed at the end of this chapter.

1. Plan a twenty-minute introductory discussion in which you
teach the principles underlying description, description written from
a stationary point of view. Take one scene. Choose it carefully for
its familiarity and for its richness in detail. Above all, be interesting, logical, and terse. Write out your plan, and at the end of your
paper enumerate just what you have tried to do. Recall the principles of oblique teaching. What mechanics have you stressed? What
drill have you given upon choice of words?

2. Write three assignments plus the introductory discussion in the
classroom for a high-school class (specify the year). Make them
follow logically the introduction discussed in 1. At the end of the
paper, list the principles taught directly or stressed obliquely.

3. Plan an introductory classroom discussion in which you illustrate various ways in which the reader can be informed of moving
or changed point of view. This time, see if both incorrect and correct
examples cannot be included, so that the class may discover for itself
the principles that you wish to illustrate. Write out briefly your
discussion and give the examples used. At the end of the discussion,
list the steps by which you conveyed your information. Be interesting—even amusing, if possible. State what oblique teaching was
attempted.

4. Make three assignments that have for their purpose the arousing of interest in accurate observation. Remember that most pupils

have forty minutes which they should devote to English in addition to the class recitation period; hence it is always wise that actual work of some kind should accompany any assignment. Mere looking will probably lead to no preparation at all. Indicate in each case what the classroom procedure shall be for each day.

5. Plan an introductory discussion and three assignments that have for their purpose a brief narrative in which (a) elimination of all but the most essential facts and (b) the reaching of a definite conclusion in the last sentence are demanded. Anecdotes, fables, jokes, might be useful to you. Remember that training the good taste of pupils is one of the English teacher's numerous responsibilities.

6. Plan three assignments which could occur in the process of teaching dialogue that will (a) review form; (b) call for varied *said* verbs; (c) stress the necessity of interpolated brief description of the characters; and (d) remind the pupils that conversation (to have any significance) must reveal the character of the speaker.

7. In undertaking informal discussion or debate, sketch a plan for nine meetings. This material need not be presented in detail but each step should be a logical advance over the preceding one. Remember that this is informal debate. Content concerns you more than the etiquette of formal debating.

After preparing one or more of these suggested exercises, ask yourself these questions concerning them: (a) Have I been clear? (b) Have I been interesting? (c) Have I built logically? (d) Would the majority of the students want to undertake what I have suggested?

SUGGESTED READINGS

References for Your Own Guidance

The English Language Arts, Vol. I, N.C.T.E. Curriculum Series, Dora V. Smith, Director

Read Part III, Chapter 6, "The Junior and Senior High School." Why ask pupils to record their own experiences?

1. Conrad, Joseph: *The Nigger of the Narcissus,* pp. xi-xvi

This preface gives perfect expression to its writer's creed, and deserves many readings. "My task . . . is, by the power of the written word to make you hear, to make you feel—it is, before all, to make you *see*." Make reading it a student assignment.

2. Brown, Rollo: *The Writer's Art,* Harvard University Press, 1921, pp. 193-209 and 34-76

The first selection gives De Maupassant's theories concerning the novel, theories that in their simplest aspects you may desire to pass on to high-school pupils. The second, by George Henry Lewes, contains guiding principles lucidly given. It should help to vivify your teaching of composition.

3. Mirrielees, Edith R.: *Story Writing,* The Writer, Inc., Boston, 1947

Before you attempt to teach advanced students the importance of (1) the time element in their stories, (2) character details, (3) implication, or (4) verbal revision, it might be wise to review these pages: (1) pp. 47-87; (2) pp. 135-70; (3) pp. 122-32; (4) 192-222.

4. Mearns, Hugh: *Creative Youth,* Doubleday, Doran, 1925

The experiment outlined here has become widely known. Investigate it. The quality of the verse produced by high-school pupils will surprise you.

5. *An Experience Curriculum in English: A Report of a Commission of the National Council of Teachers of English,* W. W. Hatfield, Chairman, Appleton-Century, 1935

Chapter IX, "The Nature and management of Creative Expression." *Read this assignment;* then study it carefully. It contains much wisdom.

6. Studer, Norman: "Local History: A Neglected Source," Progressive Education, Vol. 19 (1942), pp. 8-11

Here is a worth-while project for the ambitious student.

7. Perrin, Porter: *Writer's Guide and Index to English,* rev. ed., Scott, Foresman, 1950

Review Chapters 7-9 inclusive, pp. 168-236 for teaching structure of paragraphs in exposition.

8. Minton, Arthur: "Structure," *English Journal,* Vol. 37 (1948), pp. 529-33

Teaching organization of expository papers.

From the English Journal

1. Cook, Luella B.: "A Technique for Training in Thinking," Vol. 16 (1927), pp. 588-98

Is the writer's interest centered in the *process* or in the *result*? Why is it important to distinguish between the two? How does this article dignify the composition process as it is, or should be, carried on in high school?

2. Mallery, David: "Release: A Human Relations Approach to Writing," Vol. 39 (1950), pp. 429-35
Read. Admirable teaching founded upon mutual trust and thoughtful planning to obtain continuity of interest and growth in self-understanding.

3. Carlsen, George Robert: "On Understanding One's Self," Vol. 36 (1947), pp. 229-35
A method of securing satisfactory papers by giving satisfactory measuring sticks.

4. La Brant, Lou: "The Individual and His Writing," Vol. 39 (1950), pp. 185-89

5. Orton, Wanda: "Released Writing," Vol. 18 (1929), pp. 465-73
Read this article. Is your own writing "released"?

6. Lawler, Marcella R.: "Developing Personality Through Communication," Vol. 36 (1947), pp. 82-84
". . . The classroom is a place for such living." Examples of the effect of success upon pupils' development.

7. Ruhlen, Helen D.: "Free Writing in Junior High School," Vol. 19 (1930), pp. 547-51

8. Littwin, Maxwell F.: "Three Methods of Developing Imagination in Pupils' Writing," Vol. 24 (1935), pp. 654-61
Read this. It is full of concrete suggestions.

9. Ramsey, Lucille: "Original Activities in Seventh-Grade Language Arts," Vol. 37 (1948), pp. 352-58

10. Carpenter, R. H.: "We All Know Stories; Let's Write Them," Vol. 38 (1949), pp. 139-43

11. Miller, Ward S.: "We Write Our Life-Stories," Vol. 29 (1940), pp. 490-93
A pleasantly simple way of arousing interest in writing autobiography.

12. McKitrick, May: "Creative Writing in the New Era," Vol. 23 (1934), pp. 298-302
Here is recognition of English as a place for creative thinking concerning social problems.

13. Moses, Katherine: "In Behalf of Contest Writing in High Schools," Vol. 32 (1943), pp. 203-05
Here is a fresh idea; many teachers complain about the contests that interrupt classwork.

14. Willson, C. E., and Frazier, Alexander: "Learning Through Listening—to Each Other," Vol. 39 (1950), pp. 367-73

An interesting series of ninth-grade pupils' comments upon the papers written by classmates.

15. La Brant, Lou L.: "New Programs in Arkansas," Vol. 24 (1935), pp. 649-54

An interesting view of many different procedures. *Read.*

16. Robinson, Mary Margaret: "Using the Opaque Projector in Teaching Composition," Vol. 35 (1946), pp. 442-45

"Careless errors soon disappeared. Students were conscious of their audience." Few methods are more effective in the classroom; also an excellent way of encouraging nonreaders to read.

17. Clark, Helen McDonald: "Suggestions for Themes," Vol. 40 (1951), pp. 332-36

". . . Build from the practical viewpoint that the pupils are potential authors. Explain that never before . . . has there been such demand for material concerning personal adventure and experience."

18. Sheridan, Marion C.: "Can We Teach Our Students to Write?" Vol. 40 (1951), pp. 332-36

From *Elementary English*

1. Cooper, Jane Wilcox: "Creative Writing as an Emotional Outlet," Vol. 28 (1951), pp. 21-23; 34

The pupil projects his feelings into imaginary situations. "Excellent for retarded readers many of whom are emotional problems." Applicable to both high-school levels.

2. Rideout, I.: "Writing is Fun for Seventh Graders," Vol. 27 (1950), 386-88

Be sure you make it "fun."

3. Putman, R. H.: "Dynamic Approach to Behavior Through Creative Writing," Vol. 27 (1950), pp. 375-79

4. Robinson, Thomas E.: "Putting Flesh on Story Skeletons," Vol. 25 (1948), pp. 212-16

A helpful junior-high-school device that could arouse interest.

CHAPTER X

Motivating Composition in Relation to Pupils' Reading

I. DO TEACHERS AGREE ON THIS TOPIC?

WHAT relation should exist between the literature that a class reads and the compositions that it writes? Your answer to that question will probably be determined in part by your geographical location. If west of the Mississippi, you will recall that there was little connection between literature and composition in your own training, and will probably agree that such a connection is unnecessary; if east of the Mississippi, you will remember letters that you wrote impersonating Rowena, Nancy Lammeter, Gareth, or Mr. Lorry, and will agree that utilization of literary material for original theme work is desirable.

Divorcing yourself as far as possible from the memory of the way that you were taught, will you consider both sides of the question and attempt to arrive at some decision? Is it wise or unwise to link literature and self-expression? Does it depend upon circumstances, so that generalization is impossible? Or is there some underlying principle concerning the connection that determines when literary material may be used to advantage and when it may not?

First of all, it would be well to consider what attitudes of mind exist today in regard to this subject. In a few schools, literature courses are taught as literature courses only, composition being no more closely connected with them than are courses in grammar or in chemistry. But since teachers of English are usually employed to teach both literature and composition, and since time and energy are not unlimited, many teachers find it convenient and economical to utilize interest in a whole book, or a character, or a situation, and use it as a basis for written work.

Four statements, perhaps, sum up the unexpressed attitude of many teachers.

1. Compositions are required.
2. Every theme must have some subject matter.
3. A book supplies such subject matter, so that the pupil is not left wondering what subject to choose.
4. With supplied subject material, the pupil can concentrate all of his energies upon spelling, grammar, punctuation, sentence construction. Poorly trained as he is, he needs to concentrate upon mechanics, undisturbed by a hunt for ideas.

And if you reread these four statements you may agree that they seem logical.

There are teachers, however, who refuse to accept these four propositions, for they object to the theory that all literature lends itself to composition. Consciously or unconsciously, they resent the possibility of staling literature by having pupils use its subject matter for their grubby little themes. They feel that a pupil's enjoyment of literature, that his real pleasure in reading, should not be imperiled by the drudgery accompanying theme writing. This attitude has been delightfully expressed by the late Professor S. S. Seward of Stanford University, who, in describing the teacher's use of literature as a basis for composition, compared it to the use a teacher in shop might make of a picture of the Colosseum should he hold it up before his class with the injunction "Look; then go build a woodshed like it." Teachers who agree with Professor Seward would tend to draw theme subjects from activities, surroundings, the pupil's thoughts, observations, or imaginings, not from his reading.

Lastly, there are those teachers, greater in number probably than any group so far represented, who steer a middle course. They would not have pupils write letters from King Arthur to Guinevere or from Gareth to Sir Kay, for they wish to keep a

Colosseum uncontaminated by woodshed possibilities. Similarly, they would not ask a class to retell Silas Marner's search for his gold, or Sydney Carton's exit from the world, for they would realize that it had been done rather creditably already. For somewhat the same reason they would never ask a class to outline a chapter of fiction, once a favorite kind of busywork, or to describe a character (such as Hepzibah or Dr. Manette) who has been amply and more skillfully described by the author.[1] Would they, I wonder, in deference to the College Board examinations, ask pupils to write out in their own words the gist of Shelley's "To a Skylark," or Keats's "Ode to a Nightingale," or Mr. Frost's "Mending Wall"? Since discretion rather than valor has, in scholastic circles, become an admired virtue, they probably would—but secretly, shamefully, and with twinges of conscience. In spite of these reservations, however, they would still find in literature a basis for a half, or a third, or a fourth of the theme work given. A half, probably, if College Board examinations loomed close; a fourth, perhaps, if they felt free to do as they desired, uninfluenced by any consideration except the development, interest, and pleasure of the pupils before them.

It is much simpler, however, to point out the ways in which teachers would not use literature than to generalize on the subject of how they would. For its use must, of necessity, depend upon class interest in the thing read, class ability, and individual ability. Above all, it depends upon the teacher's skill in awakening interest and in developing a desire to write. It depends upon her own ability in writing, her sensitiveness to words, and her enthusiasm for the work. Some teachers write and submit for class criticism their own version of the class assignment. This united effort and shared criticism (for the teacher's output will

[1] Incredible as it sounds, I have heard of classes that outlined the entire novel of *Ivanhoe,* and other classes that outlined in detail Palmer's complete translation of the *Odyssey.*

frequently be inferior to the high points in students' themes) banish the old teacher-pupil attitude, and make for a spirit of honest, co-operative labor.[1]

II. WHEN AND HOW MIGHT YOU COMBINE THE TWO?

But after these generalities, you ask for concrete suggestions. Where would a teacher use literature if she believed it should form a basis for some part of the composition work, and how should she use it?

I shall skim through an imaginary course of study, a course that is more or less duplicated in some two-thirds of the high schools throughout the United States, and indicate some of the types of literature that I believe lend themselves to composition work—provided, remember, that the lessons are skillfully and enthusiastically presented; then I shall sketch in detail certain specific assignments that have produced good work.

A. Classical Material

Let us begin with classic myths. There, so many people are transformed into some unusual form—stars, trees, fountains, rivers, insects, animals, flowers—that the formula is ready-made. A transformation myth is easy to imagine; the cause for the transformation calls for originality; the language demanded is exceedingly simple; and the climax, the transformation itself, ends the theme naturally and speedily. To avoid plagiarism, the pupils should be given one or more objects and asked to decide in each case upon the original form and the cause for the change. For example, any one of the following topics would provide material for various explanations, so that each pupil would be working upon an original theme even though each member of the class chose the same topic.

---

[1] An interesting and stimulating record of informal instruction will be found in Mr. Sidney Cox's *Avowals and Ventures: The Teaching of English*. It must not, however, be taken too literally by the secondary-school teacher, confronted, as she is, by disciplinary problems nonexistent in college teaching.

1. Why the fog hangs over San Francisco Bay
2. Why one buffalo is white in the Montana herd
3. Why pine trees grow needles, not leaves
4. Why the water snake coils and strikes
5. Why Cascade Falls talks to itself
6. Why the blue jay has a crest

If the teacher writes a sample theme first, with her own explanation, the class has a model, probably is more interested, and very possibly is more stirred to invention. But with certain classes this use of a model would kill interest; hence the teacher must steer her course carefully according to her class, aware of the devil of overguidance on one side and the deep sea of ignorance on the other.

The *Odyssey* offers many possibilities in the realm of imagination. There is a new monster to be introduced and described in fitting language (language that approximates the pupil's idea of Mr. Palmer's idea of Homer's idea of the way the Greeks of a fabulous age spoke and thought). If you have never tried to awaken a freshman class to creative effort with the strong wine of Homer, beware! In a good class with a teacher who herself loves "the surge and thunder of the *Odyssey*," strange and interesting dramas, descriptions, adventures, will develop. Tales will be told, tales less artistic but as gruesome as that of the bubbling eye of the Cyclops or of the maids hanged in a row whose ending Homer laconically records in the comment, "Their feet twitched a little, but not long." Tales will be told of hardship, influenced, it is true, by the movies but close rivals to Odysseus' exploits between Scylla and Charybdis. Tales of disguise will be written, disguise revealed at last by everything except a scar on the foot; and tales of faithful dogs will abound, of dogs who recognize their long-lost masters but who never, except at the hands of some lachrymose little girl, are allowed to die miserably.

Some of these stories can be enjoyably done by good or average classes, the limitation often being one of time rather than one of interest. But any class will delight in the dramatic presentation of the Circe story, the conversation having been carefully constructed, written, distributed, conned, and rehearsed before the final Homeric program.

B. Ballads

Old ballads, like classic myths, invite imitation. And the genuine pleasure of the practical-minded boy who makes a successful rhyme reminds one of the pleasure small children take in certain couplets, couplets often lacking desirable international outlook. It is an odd and significant fact, this pride in the creation of certain pleasing sounds. You as teacher may be convinced that Bob or John not only has no music in his soul, but has no interest in putting words together. Then you lure him, helping him probably more than he is aware, into some rhymed combination approximating verse. If the future does not appear too difficult and too fraught with danger to his grade, he will go further. *You have awakened in him a little flicker of artistic pride in writing.*

Many teachers err, I believe, in leaving freshmen without suggested subject matter for their original ballads. The form alone is quite enough to cope with, but form plus the making of a terse, clear narrative (such narrative as they cannot write in prose) is no easy combination. There are, however, the ready-made short stories, the classic myth read earlier, the Howard Pyle adventure of Robin Hood, an incident from *Ivanhoe* or any other romantic novel with which they are familiar—any of these will provide ballad material of suitable kind. With these stories provided, the pupil has a chance to produce something of which he may be proud. At least these ready-made tales from real literature insure better work than do original stories, or the Frankie and Johnnie episodes, all too familiar in the Northwest, or the romantic incidents gleaned from the movies.

C. Novels

When novels such as *Ivanhoe, Silas Marner, A Tale of Two Cities* are read, a more distinct pattern may be obtained. Pupils are no longer asked, I hope, to be Gurth or Silas or Nancy, but they are led to scan certain scenes critically in order to find out how the author has done them. Then they are asked to draw upon their own information, use as much of the author's obvious technique as they can, and turn out something of real interest to the class. Does this work sound too ambitious? Is it playing the "sedulous ape" too obviously? Before we decide, let us see just how it might be done.

In *Ivanhoe*, you will remember, there is a telling scene in which Rebecca, looking from the window of Front de Bœuf's castle, reports to the wounded Ivanhoe the progress of the battle below. It is a good, fairly quick description interspersed with questions. The characters and words of the two are clearly shown in what is said and in the gestures occasionally introduced. Much is, of necessity, eliminated because of the narrow boundaries of the castle window; much must be left to conjecture. You, as teacher, might suggest that those interested take one of the following topics or make up a similar one.

1. A football player is hurt and placed upon the ground while the game goes on. A grade-school boy near him describes to him the last three minutes of play.

2. A private-school girl with a broken leg lies in her room overlooking the school grounds while her brother describes what he can see of the May fête below in which she was to have played the part of queen.

3. A college track meet is in progress. An office boy and the janitor's son obtain a pair of field glasses and, perched in an office window, see about five minutes of the meet before they are sent about their duties. Of course only one can see at a time.

4. Marian, who is taller than her friend, describes to her the last few minutes of a basketball game.

It is true that the slightly archaic language of the conversation in *Ivanhoe* makes it a less good model than some later novels, but the class is quick to recognize that Scott, addicted to description though he is, yet tells an admirable story.

In *Silas Marner* you can also find models, though chiefly of characterization. Examples are found in the picture of the Christmas party with its rapid drawing of the individual guests; the whimsical discussion at the inn with its portrayal of the characters of Mr. Macey, Tookey, the contentious farrier, and the husky-voiced butcher; the contrast between Nancy and her sister; the punishment of little Eppie; and even the tiny detail so beautifully done in the phrase "such a linen weaver" in the second paragraph of the book. This phrase gathers up all the mystery, distrust, isolation of those "pallid, undersized men—who look like the remnants of a disinherited race" and transfers it undiminished to the weaver Silas. Because the story, with its detailed setting and explicitly stated motives, calls for little imaginative creation on the part of the reader, many teachers place this novel early in the high-school course. There are other teachers, however, who place it later because older pupils, they feel, profit more by discussion of all the network of motive and of social problems excited by a reading of this novel. They wish with younger pupils to emphasize plot; with older pupils they prefer to stress motive and characterization.

A Tale of Two Cities, probably one of the most popular books taught in high school if the story is not ruined by an over-conscientious teacher, provides admirable patterns for high-school writing. As I have said earlier, training in the choice of verbs not only improves the pupils' themes, but is a sensible device for interesting a class in the artistry of writing. Suppose, for example, *A Tale of Two Cities* is being read and the class has taken gleeful pleasure in young Jerry's flight. You remember how he was pursued by the ubiquitous coffin that hid in doorways too, rubbing its horrible shoulders against doors, and drawing them up to its ears, as if it were laughing. It got into shadows on the road, and lay cunningly on its back to trip him up. All this time it was incessantly hopping on behind and gaining on him, so that when the boy got to his own door he had reason for being half dead. And even then it would not leave him, but followed him upstairs with a bump on every stair, scrambled into bed with him, and bumped down, dead and heavy, on his breast when he went to sleep.

What would you do with it? There is the description; the class has enjoyed it; you also teach composition. Suppose you ask them if as children they have ever been frightened. Then you tell them, perhaps, as vividly as you can, some brief absurd incident of your own. Shortly each of them will, presumably, have an experience, real or imaginary, to offer. Then follows discussion of how Jerry suffers. "Purely imaginary suffering, of course," you may say. But the average class will be quick to assure you that one suffers just as much, even though it is imaginary and unnecessary, if the sufferer thinks the adventure real. Then will come absurd childish fears of ghosts, of the dark, of haunted houses, of cubbyholes on the stairs to bed. Unwholesome? Not at all, if the subject is rightly handled, but an admirable place to pooh-pooh certain fears, encourage purposeful telling, pit pupil against pupil in an attempt to give tersely and vigorously the most sinister significances to some trivial incident. What have always been favorite themes with children? Battle, murder, and sudden death, and all those woes, romanticized and unreal, from which we as adults devoutly ask deliverance.

Another pattern from the same book—for the book abounds in them—that strengthens the sophomore writing, occurs in that famous scene of the breaking of the wine cask:

All the people within reach had suspended their business, or their idleness, to run to the spot and drink the wine. The rough, irregular stones of the street, pointing every way, and designed, one might have thought, expressly to lame all living creatures that approached them, had dammed it into little pools; these were surrounded, each by its own jostling group or crowd, according to its size. Some men kneeled down, made scoops of their two hands joined, and sipped, or tried to help women, who bent over their shoulders, to sip, before the wine had all run out between their fingers. Others, men and women, dipped in the puddles with little mugs of mutilated earthenware, or even with handkerchiefs from women's heads, which were squeezed dry into infants' mouths; others made small mud embankments, to stem the wine as it ran; others, directed by lookers-on up at high windows, darted here and there, to cut off little streams of wine that started away in new directions; others devoted themselves to the sodden and lee-dyed pieces of the cask, licking and even champing the moister wine-rotted fragments with eager relish.

Below is a theme frankly modeled upon those obvious tricks of the trade that a sophomore finds, with teacher guidance, when he reads the foregoing scene. The class, a city group, has been asked to reconstruct in their own minds what might happen in a certain crowded city street if a fruit peddler's cart broke down and fruit rolled in all directions. To give all a fair start, and to eliminate the long introduction common in high-school themes, the first sentence was, I believe, agreed upon in the classroom. Here is an effort sent me by the teacher, Miss Hazel Poole, of Newark, New Jersey.

FORBIDDEN FRUIT

One minute it was a peaceful apple cart, the next a heap of wreckage. The stone which the vender had placed in front of the cart had slipped, and the cart had rolled down the hill, landed against a brick wall, and turned over.

Apples flew everywhere. As fast as the apples scattered, people gathered. Down upon their knees, crawling on their stomachs, clamoring, yelling, biting, kicking, and swearing, they went after the rosy fruit. Just like the fruit, these people had come down that hill and landed here, human wreckage.

Children were knocked down and hands trampled upon by the fighting crowd. In one place a little child, gathering a few pieces of fruit in his arms, tried to sneak into a hidden corner to eat them. A big brute of a man reached out with a grimy hand and knocked the little boy to the ground, taking the fruit for himself. No one saw or cared that the child was unconscious from the blow. His own parents were too occupied fighting for themselves.

A little farther on, an old crone, her scraggly gray hair falling about her unwashed face, crammed her mouth full of one apple while she snatched at more.

Two women scratched and tore at each other, their clothes half torn off their bodies, their hair falling about their waists, all over some pieces of fruit.

Apples covered with mud went into greedy mouths. Apples that had rolled through the filthy streets were grabbed up and eaten. Still, when no more apples remained, the fighting continued. Those who had not got many blamed it on their neighbors, and a fight ensued. Others who remembered a kick or a punch received in the scramble decided to make up for it now that there were no more of the rosy prizes to take up their attention. A few lucky ones who were able to conceal some greatly battered pieces in the folds of their clothing, sneaked off to eat them unmolested.

If you have had no experience with sophomore themes, you will not at once recognize the virtues illustrated in the composition just quoted. Glance at it again. Note its admirable terseness. Note the variety in the sentence beginnings. Observe—of course you cannot avoid doing so, for the theme is badly overloaded— the verbs, vigorous, live, smashing. No matter if they are too numerous and a little childish. Wait until you have toiled through themes—colorless, aimless, dead themes. Then you will see that Dickens in the hands of a skillful teacher has galvanized this style. Is it perfunctory writing? I believe one senses here the pleasure of the writer. How he enjoyed the "big brute," the "unconscious" child, the glorious tumult (as noisy as the graveyard fight in *Tom Jones*) indicated by "clamoring, yelling, biting, kicking, and swearing." Remember, it is not sweetness and light but vigor, action, vitality, that attracts the average schoolboy. If you are too refined for him, he will bring his body to class, but his spirit will remain in the real land of football, science, shop, or perhaps the battles and adventures of history.

D. *Informal Essays*

The Sir Roger de Coverley Papers offer an inviting model to many teachers, a model that affords opportunity for training in the delicate, whimsical use of words. Here pupils find humor gained from implication rather than from obvious statement. And it is an interesting thing, by the way, to see how juniors or seniors in high school, accustomed to the "club of statement," awaken but slowly to Addison's "needle of insinuation." Much reading in class, much half-whimsical comment by the teacher, are perhaps necessary with literal young Americans. But when once they see that deliberate understatement, grave-faced exaggeration, precise and delicately adjusted wordings, form part of Addison's technique for amusing and gently ridiculing his age, they are usually eager to play observer to their own school or community. The value of this work, I believe, lies principally in the fact that it forces the writer to choose and to maintain a certain point of view and certain mood, to select words and trivial foibles that will accord with this mood, and to refine his own (often crude) sense of humor. And may I add that any writing which calls for originality, close observation, exactness, and which, at the same time, may be entered into with all the enthusiasm of a game is a godsend to both class and teacher?

Modern essays, too, offer an opportunity for half-humorous writing. Many essays should be read aloud by the teacher just for the chuckle that they produce, and much individual reading should have been carried on before the pupil is advised to try his own hand at this form. An inconsequential diary kept for a week or a month or during the period of time allotted to essay reading is no mean source for the germ of a good essay. It must, of course, be made clear that factual records are of no aid but that a record of those fugitive thoughts, those little wonderings, "the rubs, the tricks, the vanities on which life turns," is the stuff of which good essays are made. That lucky woman who "could wonder herself crazy over the human eyebrow" had the makings of a familiar essayist. Some such essays as Robert Benchley's "A Little Debit in Your Tonneau," or Ralph Bergengren's "Furnace and I," or Heywood Broun's "On Holding a Baby," or that stand-by of all teachers, Lamb's "Roast Pig," [1] will furnish an amusing beginning, for a class must always be amused and lifted over the first prejudice against any form of writing in which story interest is lacking.

E. Exposition and Formal Essays

But what of the more serious essays, orations, expositions? If your juniors and seniors are concerned with problems of student government, election of officers, school politics, why not make your classroom a political forum? Student-body presidents, athletic commissioners, members of the board of control—many, to be sure, never to hold loftier offices than those of class secretary and sergeant at arms—may try their powers. To be effective, these compositions must of course be oral, but your class will soon learn that a successful speaker seldom attempts a maiden speech without a copy of his extemporaneous remarks in his pocket. Then, too, pleas for some long-cherished project such as a little theater, a new assembly hall, a new athletic field, a system of entertainments provided by students for the blind institute or the orphan asylum—any or all of them can follow class study of a well-made speech in which some project has been logically and warmly advanced.[2]

[1] All but the last-named essay can be found in Mr. Pence's *Essays by Present-Day Writers.*

[2] Under Miss Marian Brown's guidance an interesting organization called the Rainbow Club was carried on for years in University High School connected with the University of California. Its object was "to bring rainbows into the lives of others." But, incidentally, it greatly aided the work in oral and written English. Its various projects, all projects that any teacher of English could utilize, included: weekly programs for the Blind Institute, for

Then there is the other type of informational essay represented by Huxley's "On a Piece of Chalk," found in his *Lay Sermons,* or by Mr. Palmer's *Self-Cultivation in English,* or by Mr. Ross's *Latter Day Sinners and Saints.* In these, but particularly in the first two, the pupil sees, perhaps for the first time, the beauty of organization, and the artistry of articulation. In the first and last he recognizes the desirability of much illustration so that each proposition, at first unfamiliar to the reader, is made completely familiar to him by the use of homely comparisons. Of course in all composition work, but particularly in work of this kind, the interest and knowledge of the class, the location of the school, the occupation of the parents, will determine what essays are read. Naturally these factors will also determine what original material the pupils can use. Chemistry, botany, general science, home economics, may serve. Work in the mines, in car barns, in a garage or factory, in the five-and-ten-cent store, may provide new material for some which will be unknown to the rest of the class. Mr. Palmer may prove a comfort to a few of the girls, for often their activities are confined to music lessons, school, and housework. But if they read, they can tell of literary explorations, of milestones in their reading, and of literary friendships that may provide them with good, thoughtful material.

the Orphans' Home; committee plans and reports for philanthropic work such as raising money for a dental chair, cleaning and papering a room at the local clinic; the making of booklets and scrapbooks; the writing of original stories for hospital children.

In a small Montana town off the railroad one of my students, Miss Ruth Creveling, found a means of motivating her high-school writing by having pupils make storybooks for the children of the lower grades, who had almost no library facilities and practically no supplementary readers. The community had no newspaper; hence the high school attempted to supply that lack by a mimeographed sheet reporting community happenings, and running ingenious advertisements of the local business houses. The editorials provided essay work. I cite these two extremes, a city and a remote village, to indicate that a resourceful teacher studies her community and adapts her work to it so that her composition writing may, when possible, have a definite motive and an assured audience.

F. Poems

Of the connection between the reading of poetry and the writ-ing of verse, one need say nothing, since Mr. Mearns has pro-vided us with that stimulating record, *Creative Youth*. But it is not Mr. Mearns's wizardry alone that calls forth such unusual contributions from high-school pupils. There is the *Scholastic Magazine,* with its yearly volume of student verse (*Saplings*), to reassure high-school teachers that others have done almost as much in gaining poetic expression from their pupils as Mr. Mearns himself.

On an assignment given by Miss Hazel Poole after a class had completed reading "The Coming of Arthur" and had been par-ticularly impressed by the beauty and solemnity of Tennyson's lines, she reports as follows: "After we had read about the coro-nation of Arthur, the class was asked to write, either in prose or in blank verse, a description of some ceremony with which they were familiar, emphasizing *beauty* and *solemnity* of the scene." Note that only the emotional pattern of the Arthurian passage is demanded, not the material unfamiliar to twentieth-century boys and girls. I shall quote from one paper called "First Commu-nion." It is not good blank verse, but the appeal to the senses, the use of color, the atmosphere of solemnity—all obvious in the model—have been adapted to the description of a ceremony familiar to the writer, familiar but perhaps never before so keenly realized.

FIRST COMMUNION

It is a bright, glad day in May. The scent
Of apple blossoms fills the air. Clear light
Streams in the little church through bright stained glass,
And shines on the mellow cream of painted walls
And casts on well-worn benches multicolored
Patches. The high white altar, decked with flowers
Pure and white, with gleam of gold and flash

Of glittering, polished candlesticks, is seen
Against a shining golden background, while
The light of tiny vigil lamps, bright blue
And red and yellow, is reflected on
The lovely marble statues of great saints.
Slowly, majestically, the white-clothed priest
Now moves; and chimes ring out so low and sweet
They seem like whispers of the angels; then
Great peals of music swell and rise, then fade,
And solemnly through the hushed and quiet church
They echo. Down the spacious central aisle
With careful steps they come, the white-clothed girls
With flowing veils, the little boys who march
With folded hands and lowered heads. As they near
The altar rail to receive the Sacred Host
The candles seem to leap up high, like souls
That try to rise to Him who reigns above.

G. Shakespeare's Plays

Perhaps further illustration of what I have termed the pattern assignment is not necessary. In an earlier chapter under a discussion of the unit method of composition I have already made suggestions as to original composition work in connection with the reading of short stories. Of plays I have not yet spoken, but in the past I have urged many teachers to avoid that repetitious introduction to Shakespeare's plays found in many schools. Whether the class be freshman, sophomore, junior, or senior, there are teachers who, convinced apparently that nothing is ever acquired permanently, begin every Shakespearean drama with a sketch of the author's life, follow it with a glimpse of the sixteenth-century theater, and then reverently approach the play. This lack of variety and of growth in the presentation of the plays is, to put it mildly, stupid. And I have suggested that some shift in emphasis similar to the one outlined below might be used throughout the four years:

1. **Freshman year.** Shakespeare's home in Stratford, his boyhood, sports of the period, country customs.

2. **Sophomore year.** The playhouses of the period, methods of presenting and of staging plays.

3. **Junior year.** Shakespeare and his contemporaries, London life, times, customs, obvious sources of his plays, the Mermaid Tavern, his probable friends.

4. **Senior year.** Shakespeare the philosopher. His portrayal of various types. The "modern dress" productions and the possible influence upon his plays. Famous interpretations by famous actors.

If some such shifting in emphasis is introduced, the teacher will almost automatically find herself asking her freshmen to imagine themselves living in the sixteenth century. She will ask for stories of sixteenth-century sports and home life compared with country life and sports of today. Her sophomores will write letters telling of their trips by boat across the Thames to attend a performance of *The Merchant of Venice,* of how their ruffs were wetted by spray from the oar, and of how the dandies on the stage interrupted the performance, until even the groundlings grew disgusted and threw fruit and nuts in their direction. The juniors will perhaps be reading Alfred Noyes's *Tales of the Mermaid Tavern,* will be dipping into his *Drake* and into Mr. Strachey's *Elizabeth and Essex.* They will be writing of old London, will, perhaps, speculate over poor Robert Greene and young Marlowe, and wonder if Bacon wrote Shakespeare's plays. And the seniors? Either *Macbeth* or *Hamlet* opens up speculation and heated discussion. To clarify class thinking and to give all an opportunity to express opinions, the wise teacher will in part have these opinions expressed in writing after the subject has been well started in class.

Here, you will note, for almost the first time I have suggested taking the material from a former age, not merely borrowing technique. True. But there is a robust and realizable quality about the life of the sixteenth century that the high-school pupil can catch, just as he can catch the spirit of the *Odyssey* or relive the gay adventures of Robin Hood.

H. Outside-Reading Reports

Before we discuss composition in its relation to outside or home reading, it might be well to consider: (1) what the term "outside reading" means, and how it is conducted in many schools; (2) how important it is compared with other phases of work in English; and (3) what type of problem in connection with literature confronts the teacher of composition.

Aside from the study of class texts such, for example, as *The Merchant of Venice, Ivanhoe,* or a volume of essays, pupils are, as a rule, asked to select and read each term a certain number of books. These books are not necessarily connected in either type or subject matter with the work carried on in class, but in many schools are chosen as the fancy of the pupil dictates. In other schools less freedom is given, and the pupils are asked to read from the list each term at least one book of each of three types, the listed books being divided into biography, novel, poetry, drama, essay. Another variation, once widely popular and still found in certain schools, is the practice of using a list in which all books are classified as "fiction" or "nonfiction," and of asking the pupils to choose an equal number from either list, or to choose one nonfiction book for every two books of fiction. Unfortunately the connotation which springs up about the term "nonfiction" renders this classification less desirable, I believe, than that in which books are listed by type. Under this latter method the pupil is in a way prepared beforehand for the kind of book he is to read. If he is not forewarned, he may approach all books with the same expectation of romance and sentiment with which he would meet a Zane Grey or a Gene Stratton Porter.[1]

To avoid such possibilities of disappointment for their pupils,

[1] See Appendix G for reading lists.

many teachers hold book-discussion days. Then the teacher and pupils talk over the books listed. Pupils volunteer information concerning the books they have read; the teacher sketches lightly the stories or ideas of those books which may have particular appeal. Or she reads extracts from some half-dozen to give the class an idea of the contents. At the end of the hour she volunteers to lend these books.[1] Such a day, informal and spontaneous as it seems, requires careful organization and skillful handling in order to make the reading a pleasurable, even an exciting, experience.

In still other schools no reading list is used, but pupils are given credit for reading any book that bears the stamp of either the school or the public library. The objection here is, it seems to me, much the same as the objection made to exposing an untrained pupil to the dictionary. In both cases the wealth of material is perplexing. In the library the pupil is prone to seize upon the first attractive title. He may, of course, be fortunate. But I recall one little girl who struggled in silence with Ibsen's *The Doll's House,* and another who liked *Pollyanna* and thought that she would therefore enjoy Mrs. Wharton's *House of Mirth.* The pathos of the often-heard comment "I don't like it, but now I've read so many pages I can't afford to stop," tells much of the attitude of these unguided pupils toward the dull task of reading. On the other hand, many pupils like to read. One principal

---

[1] In connection with the city or county library, teachers often make themselves personally responsible for some ten or twenty books at a time, take them to their classrooms, sketch their contents, and lend them direct to the pupils. Of course some may be lost, but if the teacher appoints a responsible pupil-librarian, is herself reasonably systematic, and sees that pupils pay for books lost, most librarians will be more than willing to enter into such an agreement. You should remember that the item in the monthly report about which most librarians are deeply concerned is the number of books taken off the shelves. By this plan you help them to swell the number. But you also give a tremendous impetus to pupil reading, for, as a rule, students prefer to read even a difficult book thus personally recommended and placed in their hands than to read a much easier one which they must find for themselves. Until library reading is an established habit, it is wise to do all in your power to make book reading an enjoyable exercise.

finally located a boy who had cut three classes, and been excused from the fourth because of headache, in the basement with a book. The boy explained that he had found a story about a man named Jean Valjean who got into the sewers of Paris and added, "Golly, you see for yourself I couldn't leave him there!" Many of your pupils will like to read. Many more will like to be considered readers. Some will frankly avoid reading. Why not assume that most of them will find *some* books delightful, and then do all in your power to make that assumption true?

A system better than that of complete freedom, but one where no book list is supplied, is this: A teacher asks her pupils to jot down the titles of books which they have enjoyed; she jots down a number of such book titles herself. Then together, teacher and pupils attempt to make a suitable list for their school. The teacher skims many books brought by pupils; the pupils read many books approved by the teacher. The making of the list is a year's undertaking.

How important does this work in outside reading seem to you? Is the amount of good voluntary reading over and above the required minimum a test of the success of your literature teaching? Why do you teach literature? Is it not to enable pupils to read intelligently, profitably, pleasurably? In other words, is not this so-called outside reading the best preparation for life outside of the schoolroom? Personally, I count it as the most important part of English work. But even teachers who agree with that statement, you will find, are loath to give up time from class reading and mechanics to develop this phase of work.

Do you know how outside reading correlated with composition is conducted in many reputable schools? The teacher announces to a class of varying reading ability and varying mental ages that in three weeks' time a book report will be called for. She doubtless reminds the class at least twice. The day of trial at last arrives. It is a sort of literary Judgment Day when the just and the

unjust are tried. The teacher writes on the board some enlighten
ing queries suitable to any type of book that her forty pupils
may have stumbled upon either with or without a guiding list.
They, presumably, include such favorites as these:

1. Describe the most exciting scene in your book.
2. Tell the *last* important incident in your book.
3. Describe the hero (or heroine) and tell one characteristic incident about him (or her).
4. Tell clearly in good essay form why you did or did not like
the book read.
5. If your book is not a novel, sum up for us the main idea that
the author gave and illustrate this idea so that we see his method
of developing it.

(Do you wonder that, educated under this system, many college
freshmen confess to having never read a book while in high
school, but to having secured the necessary information by word
of mouth?) These questions the pupils answer in writing. The
papers are collected, corrected, returned, and placed in the pupils'
notebooks. Credit is given each pupil for one book read; and a
new literary Judgment Day is announced. Thus enjoyment of
reading is cultivated. Thus penetration and sensitivity are developed.

What is the matter with this plan? Suppose that Tom Bush
reads *Les Misérables*. It is long, and he spoils the end by gulping
it down the night before the test in order to find out if the hero
lives or dies. Mary Brannon reads *Mrs. Wiggs of the Cabbage
Patch* and, because she can both spell and punctuate, gets a better grade on her outside reading than Tom. The book is so short
that she can read it the night before and can readily remember
the easy names of the characters. Helen is reading *David Copperfield* with real enjoyment. She has a sensible mother who makes
her go to bed at ten. Helen reports that she has not been able to
finish her book—and is given a failure for the day.

What effect does this set day of judgment have upon outside

reading? It makes reading a task. It overshadows the book. Again and again you will hear pupils say, "I don't like to read a book if I have to make a report on it"; "That's a good book; it's easy to remember"; or "Read this book; it's short."

But there are many other ways of securing evidence that a book has been read aside from those just described. Are you familiar with the booklet, often beautifully lettered, illustrated, and tied with ribbon, in which pupils discuss some phase of the book read? At times this booklet is an interesting, artistic effort that enhances the pupil's insight into and enjoyment of reading. Sometimes it is mere busywork that is allowed to exist in the name of outside-reading reports. How can you tell its worth? Ask yourself: "Is it an end in itself or does it increase the pupil's pleasure in reading—in intelligent, enthusiastic reading?"

So far I have made no constructive suggestions. In composition work, what use shall you make of the books read outside of class? I shall suggest several devices below, but the best method, I believe, of reporting upon books read calls for no composition. When you can, make the book report merely a private discussion with the pupil during which he fills out his reading card with you, talks over with you the type of books that he likes, discusses the last book read in the light of other reading, and gives you an opportunity to advise him intelligently as to his next choice.

SUGGESTIONS FOR OUTSIDE-READING REPORTS

1. The dust-cover announcement. Ask your class to write on a 3″ x 5″ card their final draft of a bookseller's statement. This announcement is supposed to appear on the dust jacket of the book. It should both attract readers by its terseness and interest, and provide them with an honest estimate of the book.[1]

2. Thought questions copied by the pupil a week before his report is due from the teacher's file of questions on books for outside reading. At home with the aid of his book he is to write out

---

[1] This idea was given me by a teacher who had used it successfully in her high-school classes. Since then, other teachers have reported its use and its encouraging effect upon formerly unenthusiastic readers.

adequate answers to these two or three questions, questions that call for reasoning *about* the book, not mere knowledge *of* it.[1]

3. A comparison of two books in which the pupils select parallel points and contrast them. (To be done at home after the topics have been approved by the teacher.)

4. Booklets made at home and decorated as the pupil sees fit. Such a booklet might contain:

a. A diary written by the heroine of *Standish of Standish*.

b. A log written by the hero of *Captains Courageous*, telling of a brief part of the trip.

c. A comparison of the pupil's home town with that pictured by William Allen White. (One might hesitate to compare it with *Main Street*.)

5. An oral discussion with the teacher, but also a 3″ x 5″ card upon which each pupil files, with his name and the name of the author and the title, two sentences of advice or criticism for other pupils who might wish suggestion concerning what book to read. These cards are placed on file in the library. (If you can get a football hero to endorse a book strongly, the book's popularity is assured.)

6. A class period, probably a laboratory period for the class, or a study period for the pupil, when a student takes an examination upon his book. This examination might be one question, a test of his insight into the book read but also a test of his powers of organization.

And yet, in spite of these various possibilities for securing compositions, why not minimize outside-reading reports? Might they not be a mere statement kept by both teacher and pupil on a permanent reading card—a record that remains on file for the length of the pupil's school life? On "book-chat" day when, with the reading cards before her, the teacher throws out questions concerning books pupils might choose to read, she could soon ascertain whether or not the books listed had been read intelligently. Some teachers would gladly renounce any formal report.

[1] The idea of systematizing this method of report by keeping an ever growing file of questions, several sets for the books that are read often, was given me by Miss Hazel Poole of Newark, New Jersey, whose article in the *Newark School Bulletin*, Vol. IX, No. 6 (February, 1930) presents the plan in detail.

Others would point out that unless a pupil thinks over his book, gets perspective upon it, compares it, perhaps, with other books, he has not extracted its full essence. In other words, the book, they would say, is hardly his until he has speculated about it.

What do you think? Your opinion, of course, will depend in part upon your own enjoyment of books. It will depend in part upon your own conception of what a book has to offer an immature reader. It will depend in part upon your whole conception of the purpose of outside reading. This section will, however, have served its purpose if it leads you:

1. To eliminate a "Judgment Day" when all reports are due.

2. To guard against decreasing the enjoyment of reading—intelligent, thoughtful reading—by the bugbear of reports.

3. To avoid mere busywork about books that distracts pupils from the book itself.

4. To emphasize the importance of the pupil's creative reaction to the book and, conversely, to minimize the importance of convincing the teacher that the details of the book have been honestly mastered.

5. To stress the all-importance of a proper introduction of books and pupils, sufficient guidance, and much classroom discussion. In other words, to stress the adventure of meeting books so that outside reading may be as delightful to your pupils as browsing in a library can be to one who enjoys books.

6. To make clear that composition and literature should often be combined, but *never* to the disadvantage of the literature read.

III. WHAT SHALL YOU DO AND HOW SHALL YOU DO IT?

In spite of the discussion just ended, I am convinced that it is wiser to draw much of the material for themes from the pupil's own experience, actual or imaginative, rather than to force him back into a century not his own. Any teacher must, of course, watch her class and discover for herself what awakens their interest, what strengthens their powers of thinking, and what deadens and conventionalizes their work. Remember that primarily your own honest liking for and honest enthusiasm about literature and literary figures predetermines to a very large degree the interest and the enjoyment of your class. Also they have a right, no matter how poor their mechanics, to discover the pleasure that springs from creation. But here a new caution is necessary. Even if they create only a poor thing, remember it is their own; and, as you know, parents are prone to love the defective child. Therefore after you (1) have aroused enthusiasm, (2) have, through prevision, guarded your pupils from too great disaster, (3) have provided a pattern for them that they can enjoy and comprehend, and (4) have received their little woodsheds from them, your business is to treat those original productions tenderly. Admire where admiration is possible, even if only a word or a sentence is good. Leave unsaid much that might be termed adverse. Move on to other patterns from which they can profit more. Not to utilize to some degree the literature read, limits, I believe, the pupil's appreciation of literature quite as truly as it limits his ability to develop quickly some traces of good style in his own writing. But there is a grave danger in utilizing literary material for *all* writing. After all, composition training should be training in the use of English as a flexible medium for expressing the writer's own thought. It should be a tool. Be careful that you make it a tool and not merely a doubtful ornament paraded under compulsion.

SUGGESTED EXERCISES

Read a number of the references listed at the end of this chapter before attempting these exercises. All of the following suggestions presuppose a recent review of the book or form mentioned. Do not attempt them with but a hazy idea of the model given. These exercises allow you to discover your own sensitivity to the technique of writing.

1. Write a brief transformation myth that you could read to a freshman class as a means of stimulating interest in that form of writing.

2. Write in ballad form one of the well-known classic myths, or your own transformation myth, or a single adventure from Scott or from Homer.

3. Take some Bible narrative (the story of Esther, of Job, of Saul, of Samson, or of young Benjamin) and write one detail of the story, stressing the character of the main actor. Keep the simplicity and dignity of the original.

4. In the chapter entitled "Echoing Footsteps" in *A Tale of Two Cities* reread that paragraph beginning "Headlong, mad, dangerous footsteps . . ." Note by what means the crowding and the vast horde of people are made real to us. Then take a familiar sight such as a football crowd leaving the stadium or swarming to a bonfire rally. Give that sense of pressure and numbers which you find in the passage cited.

5. Reread in *A Tale of Two Cities*, Book I, Chapter V, the sixth paragraph beginning, "And now that the cloud settled on Saint Antoine . . . ," noting how the sense of hunger is driven home through repetition. Take some one impression familiar to you, such as rain, wind, heat, cold, and in a brief sketch that you could present to your class give that impression, filling it with concrete detail and using much repetition, as in the model.

6. In *The House of Seven Gables* or *North to the Orient* or *Silas Lapham* select one pattern that you believe high-school pupils might use profitably. Write out your assignment for the class, based upon the passage selected, and compose a brief original paper which would meet the requirements that you make.

7. After you have read the first six or eight essays from the *Spectator*, write a brief original essay in the mood and tone of those read. Take one of the following topics or choose one of your own: The Author, Three Members of My Club, My Hobby, Athletics in Our Institutions of Higher Learning, The Art of Rushing.

8. Read Huxley's "On a Piece of Chalk." In one paragraph discuss Huxley's method of persuading his audience into belief. Take any scientific fact with which you are familiar and explain it as he does, simply, interestingly, and with much concrete detail. Plan this explanation to interest a child of ten.

9. Read several modern informal essays. Look about you. Choose a subject, no matter how insignificant in itself if you can make it

significant of some human frailty, peculiarity, or interesting trait. Work it out, not too seriously, in an essay of reasonable length.

10. Choose from a volume of modern poems three that you feel high-school pupils should like. Perhaps Mrs. Wilkinson's *New Voices* may aid you. Suggest an assignment for each of these in which the pupil is to seize upon some trait of the poem and embody it either in prose or in verse. You might wish to have him catch the movement suggested by a boat, a cradle, a trotting horse: or you might wish to have him sense keenly the play of light or the interweaving of color. Take one of the assignments made and write a verse that would serve as a model.

NOTE: A whole chapter has been spent upon the subject of composition motivated by literature, but do not gain the impression that pupils *must* have models. "Motivating Composition in Relation to Pupils' Reading" happens to be the title of this chapter, but doubtless the best writing is done without a realized model. Literature here is used much as if it were a springboard. You have to start your pupils; here is one way. Do not overuse it, or you will divorce your composition work from life.

SUGGESTED READINGS

A. References for Your Own Guidance

The English Language Arts, Vol. I, N.C.T.E. Curriculum Series, Dora V. Smith, Director

Read Part I, Chapter 3, "Goals and Experiences in the Language Arts Program." What part may literature play in pupils' development?

1. Quiller-Couch, Sir Arthur: *On the Art of Writing*, Putnam, 1916, pp. 1-51

Read these two humane, delightful chapters and then determine not to blind your pupils "with a swarm of little school books" that are "wrong from beginning to end," nor to obstruct education by "obtruding lesser things . . . until what is really important . . . is seen in distorted glimpses." Why not own this book?

2. Piercy, J. K., ed.: *Modern Writers at Work*, Macmillan, 1930, pp. vii-xii

Note the letter sent blithely forth to the great—and if you skim through the volume, note the amazingly satisfactory response. This preface breathes faith in teaching and enjoyment in the work. Read it.

3. Lubbock, Percy: *The Craft of Fiction*, Scribner, 1921

4. Wharton, Edith: *The Writing of Fiction*, Scribner, 1925

5. Mirrielees, Edith: *Story Writing,* The Writer, Inc., Boston, 1947
These three books (entries 3-5) will aid you in your analysis of fiction.
There are, of course, many others equally helpful.

6. Appy, Nellie: *Pupils Are People,* Appleton-Century, 1941
A book to read, reread, and own. Recognition of individual differences
in students, in their reading, in their writing provides opportunity for all
to work happily and creatively.

7. Mearns, Hugh: *Creative Power,* Doubleday, Doran, 1929

8. Two books planned for college but helpful background for teachers
are:

a. Frank, Neal: *Studies in Poetry,* Doubleday, 1949

b. Cooper, Charles W.: *Preface to Poetry,* Harcourt, Brace, 1946

9. Ciardi, John: *Mid-Century American Poets,* Twayne Publishers,
New York 4, 1950
If 1950 poetry puzzles a teacher, this book will prove interesting and
informative.

10. Lieberman, Elias, ed. *Poems for Enjoyment,* Harper, 1931
Excellent but simple poetry with other suggested readings, aids to interpretation, and "Creative Self-Expression" illustrated with students'
poems.

11. Auslander, Joseph, and Hill, F. E., eds.: *The Winged Horse,*
Doubleday, Doran, 1927

12. Thrall, William Flint, and Hibbard, Addison: *A Handbook to
Literature,* Doubleday, Doran, 1936
A useful book of general information on terms used in literature, with
brief illustrations. A type of dictionary.

13. Wilkinson, Marguerite: *New Voices,* Macmillan, 1926
This book has been popular with high-school juniors and seniors because "it makes sense." In teaching, the author's discussion of "The
Pattern of a Poem" and "Organic Rhythm" encourages students to attempt verse writing.

B. References Concerned with Teaching Composition
from Literary Models

1. Axley, Lowry: " 'Originative' Writing," *English Leaflet,* Vol. 29, No.
257 (April, 1930)
Do you believe that models act as "springboards for pupils that wish
to create," or as curbs to originality? What characteristics mark the
papers quoted?

2. Hitchcock, Alfred: *Bread Loaf Talks on Teaching Composition,* Holt, 1927, pp. 44-59
Read this chapter carefully. It contains much truth.

3. Werry, R. R.: "Benefits of Teaching Creative Writing to Non-Creative Students," *School and Society,* Vol. 68 (Nov. 20, 1948), pp. 355-57

4. Chapman, Lucy H., and Cauley, Thomas: *Language Skills* (Grade Ten), Harcourt, Brace, 1947
"Things to Write About," pp. 136-64, discusses the use of models before writing biographies, radio scripts, stories. The models given are "springboards" for tenth graders.

5. Hartley, L. C.: "Approach to Teaching Creative Writing," *High School Journal,* Vol. 32 (January, 1949), pp. 19-24

6. Lodge, E.: "Sound Films Motivate English Composition," *Clearing House,* Vol. 23 (1949), pp. 274-75

C. References from the *English Journal*

1. Graham, Helen: "A Plan for Teaching the Biography," Vol. 30 (1941), pp. 238-41
Various biographies of Americans were read by individual students and discussed in class. Then the class composed a radio script, based upon their reading, called "Cavalcade of America."

2. Oetjen, M. E.: "Stepchild of the English Course: Book Reports," Vol. 38 (1949), pp. 41-43

3. Frank, Robert: "An Experiment in Senior English," Vol. 38 (1949), pp. 10-22
Do not miss this admirable work with a hostile class. Students can and will write when thoroughly interested.

4. Webster, Edward Harlan: "Imaginative Writing: A Unit of Work," Vol. 16 (1927), pp. 613-23
This article is an excellent example of intelligent building toward a definite goal. What are the writer's five major objectives? What characteristics do you note in the final product?

5. Wilds, Mildred Helen: "Enlarging Experiences Through Essays," Vol. 23 (1934), pp. 554-57
Essays as a basis for stimulating talk and writing.

6. Williams, Paul A.: "Creative Reading," Vol. 36 (1947), pp. 454-59
Writing based upon reading, but in a new, amusing way so that literature applies to their own ideas.

PART TWO

Literature Reading and Study

CHAPTER XI

Attitudes toward Literature

I. LITERATURE TEACHING

A. What Are Some of the Barriers, Raised by Teachers Themselves, That Block Successful Teaching of Literature?

Y OU REMEMBER your own high-school experience with books. Was it a happy one? It is to be hoped so, for teachers are prone to reproduce in their own teaching the type of instruction they received; hence high-school work tends to remain stationary unless young teachers, aware of the danger, make a conscious effort to question their own practices. If your own high-school teachers thought of literature in terms of life experiences to be made an integral part of their pupils' lives, and if they were genuinely interested in teaching their pupils both to read for exact information and to read for enjoyment, then you have an excellent basis upon which to build. But if they were not teachers of this type, or if, as in many small schools today, they were excellent teachers of science or mathematics who, forced to teach English because of schedule difficulties, conceived it their duty merely to present a series of books to be read, then your high-school experience may seriously handicap your teaching. Analyze your own school days in the light of this and subsequent chapters; then discard or retain what seems wise to you. To start your own thinking, it might be well to consider what ideas some teachers of literature have had that are detrimental to their teaching. Following are a few obvious examples.

Many teachers, luckily a steadily decreasing number, think it their duty to teach one book, and one book, and one book. In other words, they do not think of any one piece of literature as

a part of a larger unit in which a problem is broached, investigated, and explored by different pupils. They do not think of
using literature either as a means of further developing the problems discussed in other departments in high school or as a means
of linking books, poems, articles, pictures, music, and historical
and sociological problems. Nor does it occur to them that literature might have more meaning if the reading were centered about
one topic, and each book treated as a part of a general theme. If
they thought out the situation, which they do not, they would
say that just as the teacher of physical education completes
swimming and goes on to basketball with no entangling alliances,
so they step neatly from *Silas Marner* to *Julius Caesar* and from
Julius Caesar to the *Odyssey,* and from the *Odyssey* to "The Ancient Mariner," clipping and typing all the threads of one piece
of literature before advancing on the next.

Of course this statement is exaggerated, but, unfortunately,
not so greatly exaggerated as you might suppose. Use your common sense. Don't let a course of study that says, "Four books
chosen from the following list are to be taught in the freshman
year," lead you to believe that those four books are isolated units
representing your literature course. Your responsibility is to
teach your pupils to read as intelligent adults read, sensing the
social and economic problems involved, dipping here and there
into magazines, newspapers, histories, poems, and biographies.
You wish your pupils to be alert. You wish them to correlate
what they read in class with what they see in their family life
and in their community life. The isolation policy, easy as it is
for the teacher, is deadly for the pupils. One book with its human
problem should be considered merely an introductory step into
the world of ideas, of books, of articles all about us. Both you
and your pupils must realize *why* you are reading literature in
and out of the classroom, and *how* this literature throws light
upon the physical and social problems that have confronted mankind, or are now confronting them. If you make of yourself a

connecting link between all kinds of collateral material, if you keep yourself an enthusiastic recipient and showman of the miscellaneous illustrative material that, if encouraged, pupils will bring from home, you can soon make literature an integral part of the students' lives. Your classroom should not contain a kind of rarefied atmosphere into which, white-gloved, you lead your flock. The English class should be an essential, normal part of their everyday lives in which they are led to understand the society about them. And to understand that society, they must know not only facts concerning it, but the problems, ideals, and emotions of past and present social groups. Unless literature is made a part of the pupils' discovery of the world about them—past and present—it would be more useful for them to be studying history or science. Do you agree? Perhaps at the present moment you do not. But wait. Try teaching isolated books with emphasis upon the literary excellence of each masterpiece. The futility of making a potential street cleaner, and a cook, and a garage mechanic, or even a potential minister, actor, or college professor (multiplied by ten or by fifty) burn with desire to question you further on the subject of Homeric poetry one month, Shakespearean comedy the next, and old ballads the third, will so depress you that you will prefer Woolworth's as a source of livelihood. And who knows? Perhaps should you follow this preference, you might do less harm to the next generation.

But do not be led into the error of believing that merely some *new method* of teaching can make literature study profitable to your classes. Probably certain teachers have in the past taught as excellently as any of our present teachers. The secret of success still lies, as it has always lain, in the teacher's conception of literature as a part of the long record of man's hopes, and fears, and struggles, of his successes or of his failures in overcoming physical difficulties and in building up a social framework in which he can live. As Mr. Canby has remarked in another sense, "A small wire cannot carry a heavy current." But unless the teacher herself has a vision of literature in its relation to history and economics, she cannot, of course, impart this vision to others.

Many teachers suffer from what Robert Frost has termed "the overconscientiousness of the second-rate teacher." They are so fearful lest details are not mastered that both they and their classes lose sight not only of the basic problems but of the novel, drama, or poem as a whole. They also fear lest the full study period which should be devoted to literature be given instead to algebra or chemistry—both more accurate, both lending themselves to more exact grading, and hence more important, they fear, in the eyes of their pupils. Conscientiously regarding "The Ancient Mariner" or *Ivanhoe*, they devise busywork which can be exactly graded. And they may be wise or they may be worse than foolish, according to the value of the work that they invent. Do not misunderstand. If pupils are to enjoy literature or to profit by its study, they should and must work. But the work itself must be worth the doing. In some parts of the country the change in the college-entrance examinations may perhaps already have affected the meticulous type of teacher. The emphasis in the newer type, the comprehensive examinations, is laid upon a grasp of the important aspects of the book or poem. But as yet, College Board examinations have but little effect upon the high schools of the West and Middle West. Wherever you teach, be "conscientious" certainly, but not "second-rate." And even when you are confronted by rows of squirming boys and girls, remember that no piece of literature is the sum of all its parts. It is something greater; hence you must see that no book or poem or drama is mangled into a series of isolated exercises to serve as busywork for mischievous sophomores.

Many teachers, and often teachers of real ability, take their literature classes too solemnly. They are fearful of levity. They forget that in literature as in life humor and pathos, tragedy and comedy are mingled. They forget too a more essential thing. Literature is a laboratory in which pupils may see life analyzed. There they see causes, motives, results; they see characters twisted by circumstance, and characters twisting circumstances to their own ends. To the degree that your pupils are capable of imaginatively re-creating the situations and emotions portrayed, they themselves become artists. And unless you develop their ability to respond quickly and correctly to the various emotional stimuli presented, literature will mean comparatively little to them. A roar of laughter, a chuckle, a smile, an amused shrug, or a perfectly audible and respected snuffling over sad portions of a book or play should be expected. Why not? People laugh and cry at a movie. Is literature so different? Make your classroom a simple, human, natural place, one where, if possible, it is the blasé pose of the mascara-eyed sophomore which becomes slightly absurd, rather than the frank emotional response of the less-sophisticated little girl or boy. Naturalness on your own part, a quick laugh or changes of tone from serious to light, will do much to create a genuine and dispel a "schoolroom" atmosphere. And the country over, the rapid transformation of the conventional schoolroom into a study room with movable chairs and tables, into an informal library, theater, or workshop, has gone far toward eliminating the artificial formality that once dominated the classroom.

Many teachers, particularly those whose education ended from fifteen to thirty years ago, resent the growing practicality of the age. The idea of classrooms called "workshops" and assignments termed "contracts" is to them thoroughly repellent. To them the pupil still remains the passive learner; the teacher still stands as authoritarian, dispensing information and, unquestioned, inspiring love and reverence for the literature of the past. They are unwilling and perhaps unable to accommodate themselves to the active, eager boys and girls of today whose knowledge of the world of movies, transportation, commerce, gangsters, sports, and mechanics far surpasses their own. They know the classic writers.

Chaucer and Milton, Shakespeare and Shelley, have given them inspiration, beauty, peace. It is their desire to make their class-rooms quiet retreats where the words of master writers of the past are read and meditated upon until they become a part of the in-tellectual sinew of their pupils. And when the modern high-school boy or girl refuses these riches and prefers public speaking or journalism or handicrafts, the teachers turn back to their ivory towers in disappointment with the age. What can you learn from them? One thing perhaps. All the literature of the past which is vital to high-school boys and girls *is* vital because it throws light upon human relationships and human struggles. These teachers know the older literatures, but if their reading had been vital it would not have divorced them from life. It would have enriched life for them and for their pupils. You can-not teach modern boys and girls from an ivory tower, but neither can you lead them to the best in literature unless you have lived with it yourself and made it an integral part of your own experi-ence. Perhaps you have never had time to live with books. If that is so, busy as you are, take one or two great poems, fine essays, great plays, and read and reread until you begin to realize them fully. You may have within you the finest possibilities for litera-ture teaching: love of literature, understanding of its funda-mental problems, and practical appreciation of the difficulties awaiting high-school pupils. Experiment. Don't be content to be artisans if, as some of you undoubtedly can, you might be artists.

But you have one advantage over this older type of teacher. It is to be hoped that you do not think of literature as a purely cul-tural subject. You are state-trained teachers in a democracy to whom is intrusted the training of the future citizens. And your business is so to train them that they can live intelligently in the co-operative, democratic society we hope to see emerging out of the welter of the present day. It is a practical problem that con-fronts you. Your boys and girls must read directions, write busi-ness letters, prepare to take their places in science, in business, in the economic development of our country. Many will never open a book after they leave you, but will confine themselves to the daily paper and to magazines. In such cases, have you failed? Not if they read the paper intelligently; not if they can follow written directions, or if they can forget factory life or illness or poverty in some tale of adventure. Not if they leave school with a social rather than an antisocial attitude toward society. In a public high school you have all levels of intelligence and all types of home life represented. Do not make the mistake of thinking that the pupil who will not voluntarily read the best literature has failed to profit by his schooling. The classics are not for him a daily diet, but you may have opened to him the possibilities of the better magazines, the popularized scientific books, and the fictionized biographies; and even though you have not made him a student, you have not failed if you have given him some recognition of his responsibility to society.

Some older teachers bewail the expenditure of time and instruction upon commercial-minded pupils, and judge that expenditure wasted because pupils out of school do not pick up Shakespeare, read Addison, turn to Milton or Scott or Shelley. Do not let this fallacy discourage you. You yourselves know Homer, Chaucer, Milton, Wordsworth, Shelley, and Browning. Is it your habit to read at length from these older writers? And yet you would be loath to say that they had contributed nothing to your own development and your own judgment of later poets. The majority of your pupils will not go on to college. You are providing them with the last instruction in literature that they will have. What must you do? Give them *important* literature from the past, of course, literature that is for some reason significant to them, but mingle with the classics as many modern plays, novels, essays, poems, biographies, magazine stories and articles as you can find time and material to use. You are preparing them to be reading adults, not students of literature. Face the issue squarely. If they leave you with no knowledge of literature later than Matthew Arnold—well, there is always for them the movie, the card game, the radio, gossip, or still less innocent recreation.

Many teachers assume that if individual words are correctly pronounced, those words, often rich in content for the adult, are likewise rich in content for the pupil. But the story told by the late S. A. Leonard showing the possibilities of a barroom-dance-hall interpretation of Scott's line "The stag at eve had drunk his fill," and the example of the boy who wrote "The benediction of Arnold was a serious thing for our country," both illustrate the numerous misconceptions that, unrecognized by the teacher, linger in the mind of the average or below-average high-school pupil.

Teachers frequently take it for granted that high-school pupils know how to glean ideas from printed material; hence they put printed matter before a pupil but give no instruction as to how meaning is to be extracted from the rivers of black print that flow over the white page. They are not *teaching*; they are merely allowing pupils to *learn* and that only if those pupils are already sufficiently well taught to teach themselves. There is, of course, an excuse for this attitude on the part of the teacher. From 5 to 50 per cent of the class probably read well. But before you present material to a class, might it not be wise to discover who can and who cannot gain accurate information from a passage?[1] Rest assured that in every normal group you will find many who read almost as well as you, but also you will find many who have about fifth-grade ability. Your first task therefore is to discover the reading power of each member of your class; then you have laid a foundation on which you may build intelligently.

Oftentimes teachers, like the proverbial Martha, are too occupied with many things to discover whether or not their pupils are visualizing the scenes and characters about which they read. Per-

[1] Are you familiar from your education classes with the Morrison plan of pretesting?

haps it would be wise to discover your own power of visualization. If that familiar primrose by the river's brink remains
merely the two words, adjective and noun, "yellow primrose" to
you, you are not ready to teach others to read, for you yourself
have not yet succeeded in reading successfully. Don't, however,
be discouraged. Probably you will find that you do visualize. Because you see the primrose or the castle or the cowboy instantly,
you are hardly aware of the process which has gone on in your
own mind. Hence you do not realize why the scene or character
has for you genuine beauty or awe or repulsion, while it remains flat, stale, and unprofitable for your pupil. Experiment;
close your eyes while someone says certain nouns to you. Discover for yourself your own mental equipment. Next try lines of
sensuous poetry. Sharpen your own power of visualization. When
you recognize what words mean to you in color, sound, form,
space, connotation, then you are ready to attempt to teach your
pupils what visualization is.

B. What Are Some of the Difficulties That the High-School Pupil Faces in His Study of Literature?

Does the discussion thus far lead you to believe there should
be no *work* for the pupils in their study of literature? Does your
own experience in college English confirm that impression? What
work awaits the entering high-school pupil when you lay before
him *Silas Marner* or the *Odyssey* or *Selected Short Stories* or a
modern play? [1] Up to the time of their entrance into high school,
your pupils have probably read children's books, movie magazines, or airplane or motorboat tales. Do you realize how unprepared the majority of them are to cope with the material of the
average high-school curriculum? In a later chapter you will find
discussion of courses made as you might wish to make them.
This, however, is a practical world based upon precedent, courses
of study, supervisors, and an enormous regard for "discipline."

[1] La Brant, Lou: *The Teaching of Literature in Secondary Schools.*

Since you will be young teachers who must fit into a ready-made system, and since your success depends largely upon your letters of recommendation from your first school, I am here discussing courses of study as you will find them. Remember, though, that even without wrecking the curriculum of your school you can do much to render a bad course of study less objectionable. In the schools that you mean to enter what work awaits the *average* or *below-average* high-school pupil?

1. He must cope with literature that is longer, more complex, more mature, more remote from his own experience than any he has read before.

2. He must quickly enlarge his vocabulary, a vocabulary which often is smaller and more distorted than you suspect.

3. He must learn to analyze simple prose for the meaning, gathering the bare thought, undistracted by encumbering detail.[1]

4. He must, having conquered word meanings and the sense of the passage, learn to visualize, so that the words and sentences he reads are rich in sense impressions.

5. He must learn not only to gain the full meaning from *one* passage or *one* book but to compare or contrast that idea and recognize, perhaps, in what way it throws light on problems of today.

6. He must learn to respond emotionally to those rivers of black print which flow before him. It is to be hoped he may sensitize himself and to a certain extent refine his sense of humor. He may even learn to distinguish between pathos and the bathos of the cheaply sentimental, to demand reality rather than fairy-tale success stories, and to appreciate the workings of cause and effect rather than the blithe evasion of natural but unpleasant consequences. And, too, while he is spending his time on these five necessary steps in his advance upon your literature course, the library awaits him with its row upon row of books, its dictionary, magazine rack, shelf of new plays, and daily papers.

7. If he attends a conventional type of high school where department lines still exist, he must struggle to see the relationship be-

---

[1] Do you recall your own difficulties in note-taking when you were a freshman in college? As teachers you will come to know the pupil's habit of remembering nonessential but striking illustrations and forgetting the principle illustrated.

tween what he learns in history, in science, in English, and what he knows is to be his life in the machine shop or office or store. Probably the student's inner dissatisfaction arising from the apparent uselessness of the information offered him is one of the chief causes for lack of interest, with its resultant disciplinary problems and failures. How responsible it is for the more serious matters of maladjustment and emotional difficulties is as yet unknown.

But to return to our original question, is there to be no *work* for the pupil in his study of literature? You will find that this ironical fact confronts you: He must work and work hard in order to enjoy his reading, but if his contacts with literature are not enjoyable, if they do not teach him to read for the pleasure of reading, then his work is largely—though not entirely—wasted. *How are you, the teacher of literature, to solve the problem in your own schoolroom?*

C. How Shall You Improve Your Pupils' Reading Ability?

How Do You Read? As has been stated in previous chapters, your business is to *teach* your pupils to read, not merely to place books before them. But teaching pupils to read who think that they have read for some eight or eleven years is perhaps more difficult than you now realize. Probably the first and most useful step in your thinking about the subject should be an analysis of your own reading activities. What are they? At breakfast you scan the headlines and the first editorial in the morning paper.[1] You look up the exact address of the barber or the dressmaker; then you study history for an hour. At noon between bits of conversation you skim the last chapter of a thrilling detective tale to discover who killed whom and why. In the library on your way to class you glimpse the copied line in your neighbor's eighteenth-century notebook, "Dies of a rose in aromatic pain," and as you say it over to yourself on the way to class you wonder, perhaps, that Pope could have written a line so full of sensuous beauty.

[1] Do you know the comments upon American reading habits made by Ernest Dimnet in his *Art of Thinking?*

Later you go to the encyclopedia to find whether prison reform laws were passed in England before or after Fielding published *Amelia*. But first you see in the *New Yorker* a cartoon with a Biblical injunction below it that makes you chuckle. And that night at home you read a letter that you were asked to send on at once, in which you are advised in detail how to apply for a certain teaching position, whom to see, what to say to each person, and where to find the principal or clerk of the board.

During this rather busy day you have indulged in eight reading activities; and yet if you were, at any point, asked what you were doing, you would have responded that you were "reading" or that you were "looking something up." But what have you done?

1. Skimmed the paper in lazy fashion to gain an *approximate* idea of how France feels toward England, what sport writers think of the latest baseball pitcher, whether the Ellis Island scandal or the San Francisco crime wave has any new and sensational angles.

2. Looked in the telephone book for *one isolated* bit of information to be remembered exactly.

3. Read a chapter of history slowly, *attempting to outline paragraph by paragraph* and to hold in mind the main statements, the sequence, and the relation of facts.

4. Skimmed a detective tale to experience the feeling of suspense and to unravel a complicated mystery.

5. Read one line of verse, visualizing a rose and faintly recalling its "aromatic" odor.

6. Read hastily, glimpsing whole paragraphs, until you found in what year prison reform was first enacted in England.

7. Glimpsed a drawing, read the line below, and connected it with the original dignified use of the same words. Chuckled over it, and mentally exaggerated the cartoon until it fitted an acquaintance of yours.

8. Read exact instructions in a letter, and made careful mental note of each one.

Had the day been longer, you might have done a number of other types of reading, but these eight examples will illustrate the fact that you "read" each time, but in each situation different abilities were called into play.

How Can You Teach Pupils to Read? If you look at a roomful of college freshmen confronted with a long list of reference reading, you soon discover that some of them have never learned the art of selection. They must read each paragraph and each word; no hasty glimpse will suffice to prove to them that a particular paragraph does not apply to their topic. Often these same freshmen if given *one paragraph* for intensive study will be unable to answer correctly any specific questions concerning its contents. They know the general trend of thought, but not the exact facts. Or they may have a fairly definite impression but a wrong one, as illustrated by the student who called a certain urbane philosopher "rude" because he had said to his companion, "That was a pertinent remark you just made." (Unfortunately even a B.A. degree does not confer upon its recipient all the "rights, privileges, and obligations" of our English vocabulary.) And as to quick association of ideas—"seeing the point" as we term it—well, perhaps some of us are born obtuse and no amount of schoolroom training will do much for us.

But, you say, true as it is that many pupils can and many cannot read, what are we to do about it? If the grade-school teachers have not taught them, why should we think that we can? Probably they are not capable of doing high-school work anyway.

Maybe they are not capable of the type of high-school English work that your course of study prescribes. If they are not, stretch the course of study here and there, and find what they are capable of and what they need. But of this be sure; all of them need to learn:

1. How to read directions or instructions.
2. How to glean a specific fact from a mass of print.
3. How to get a correct general impression from a single paragraph or from a book.

4. How to read fiction at some level, even though they can never cope with adult fiction, and to read it with enjoyment.

5. How, even though the selections are most elementary, to enjoy verse.

You might teach admirably if you could keep those five requirements before you and not become too deeply enmeshed in the various snares called "Following the Course of Study," "Teaching the History of English or American Literature," "Spending One Semester upon Grammar," "Requiring Written Book Reports for Outside Reading." And there are more; probably the most embracing and engulfing of all snares has the trivial-sounding title "Outside Activities." But these "activities" can so sap your energies that in self-defense you become a mere automaton by day in order that you may coach plays, supervise clubs, chaperon dances, hear debaters, and proofread the school paper by night. Be warned. Do not, in your eagerness to be useful, accept more activities than you can manage adequately. Do you recall the sign "School. Go Slow"?

D. What Kinds of Literature Will You Be Asked to Teach?

When you view the texts in use today, you may feel that only a Francis Bacon, who took all learning for his province, could cope with the material. And when you face your classes, "sitting so proper in their seats," you may wonder how (1) the literature and (2) Gladys Mae Smythe are to be fused. But many of the teachers under whose excellent guidance you yourself conquered Hector, Madame Defarge, Lincoln Steffens, or "Lycidas," good teachers though they were, were not supermen nor superwomen. So take courage. They knew boys and girls; they knew and enjoyed literature. They realized that their business was to cultivate in those boys and girls a *desire to read, enjoyment of reading, increased power in appreciation of literature,* and a *deeper understanding of life itself*—its opportunities and *responsibilities in a democracy.* Or, to put the matter negatively, they realized that teaching literature was not primarily presenting material to be read, nor testing for facts obtained from that reading. (That statement will bear much thinking about on your part.)

In order to give you at once a swift survey of a more or less typical literary menu presented to junior-senior high-school pupils, I have listed under each literary form a number of titles. These titles give you a cross section of selections used in high schools in the North, South, East, West, and Middle West. Probably no one school uses all of them, but they give a fair example of the material used "to provide points of departure" for more extended reading. This scanty list may, perhaps, give you some sense of what is expected of you, and also some hint as to the adequacy of your own preparation.

E. What Are the Forms of Literature That Confront You?

NARRATIVE POETRY

The Epic

A long heroic narrative poem. It presents characters in high positions in a series of adventures. These form an organic whole through their relation to the central figure, one of heroic proportions. It gives also much as to the customs and development of a nation or race. *Examples:*

Folk Epics

The Iliad and *The Odyssey*—Greek
Beowulf—Saxon
The Kalevala—Finnish
The Song of Roland—French
The Nibelungenlied—German

Art Epics: Classic

The Aeneid—Virgil (selected books)

Paradise Lost—Milton (first three books)

Art Epics: Modern

Drake—Alfred Noyes
John Brown's Body—Stephen Vincent Benét
The Song of Hugh Glass—John Neihardt

The Florida *State Course of Study* stresses the epic in the junior high school. Among the titles listed to be considered by the teacher are:

Adventures of Odysseus and the Tale of Troy, retold by Padriac Colum

Boys' Cuchulain: Hero Legends of Ireland, compiled by Eleanor Hull

Story of the Iliad, retold by Alfred John Church

Story of the Aeneid, retold by Alfred John Church

The Song of Roland, translated by James Baldwin (also on the Minnesota list)

The Story of Siegfried, James Baldwin (also suggested in the Minnesota course of study)

Texas lists both *The Iliad* and *The Odyssey* as translated by Alexander Pope.

Minnesota stresses the tales from *The Kalevala, The Eddas, Beowulf,* as well as the modern epics *The Song of Hugh Glass* and *John Brown's Body.*[1]

References on the Epic

Guerber, H. A.: *The Book of the Epic*
A valuable book for school libraries. "The object . . . consists in outlining clearly and briefly . . . the principal examples" of those epics of all countries "which have supplied endless material to painters, sculptors, and musicians ever since art began." (p. 16)

Dixon, W. M.: *English Epic and Heroic Poetry*

Ker, W. P.: *Epic and Romance*

The Metrical Romance

A romantic tale in verse. The term is specifically applied to the medieval romances (*Sir Gawain and the Green Knight,* etc.) but applies to Scott's romances in verse and all truly romantic verse stories. *Examples:*

Medieval Romances	"Matter of France"
"Matter of Rome the Great"	*The Song of Roland, Huon of*
Ancient history: *The Troy-Book*	*Bordeau,* Stories of Charlemagne

---

[1] Perhaps one should add here that almost all courses include some work on the Greek myths. Some include the myths of many lands, including the Indian legends of our own country.

"Matter of England"
King Horn, Havelok the Dane, Guy of Warwick
"Matter of Britain"
Arthurian literature such as *Sir Gawain and the Green Knight*

Modern Metrical Romances

Spenser: *Faerie Queene* (Renaissance)
Scott: *Lady of the Lake, Marmion, Lay of the Last Minstrel*
Tennyson: *Idylls of the King*
Robinson: *Tristram*

The Arthur material as represented in *Idylls of the King* and Scott's metrical romances are widely used, but you as teacher should know the older material.

References for the Metrical Romance

Weston, Jessie: *Chief Middle English Poets*
Ker, W. P.: *Epic and Romance*
MacCallum, M. W.: Tennyson's *Idylls of the King and Arthurian Story*
Chambers, E. K.: *Arthur of Britain*

The Metrical Tale

A story in verse. *Examples:*

Chaucer: *Canterbury Tales* (any story)
Longfellow: *Tales of a Wayside Inn* (any story)
Noyes: *Tales of the Mermaid Tavern*
Burns: "Tam O'Shanter"

Longfellow: "Evangeline"
Holmes: "How the Old Horse Won the Bet" and "Grandmother's Story of Bunker-Hill Battle"
Masefield: "Dauber" and "Reynard the Fox"

All but the last title appears in most courses of study.

The Ballad

The old ballad was a poem meant for singing made by people quite free from literary influence, and handed down by oral tradition. Usually a single heroic episode of dramatic nature; physical courage and love, happening to common rather than royal people; supernatural events—all mark this form. Little characterization, abrupt transitions, action, dialogue, tragic situations stated but not enlarged, impersonal treatment, a summary statement in the last stanza, are usual traits. The usual stanza form is of four lines, the first and third of eight syllables each, the second and fourth of six each. The rhyme scheme is usually abcb, the meter iambic. Typical stanza:

> "Haf owre, haf owre to Aberdour,
>   It's fiftie fadom deip,
> And thair lies guid Sir Patrick Spence,
>   Wi the Scots lords at his feit."

Examples:

Old Ballads	*Modern Ballads*
"Sir Patrick Spence"	Coleridge: "The Rime of the Ancient Mariner"
"Hind Horn"	
"The Wife of Usher's Well"	Macaulay: "Horatius at the Bridge"
"A Gest of Robyn Hode"	
"The Hunting of the Cheviot"	Browning: "Hervé Riel"
"Kinmont Willie"	Arnold: "The Forsaken Merman"
"Lord Randal"	
"Edom o' Gordon"	Longfellow: "The Skeleton in Armor"
"Bonnie George Campbell"	
"The Three Ravens"	Kipling: "Fuzzy-Wuzzy"
"The Twa Sisters"	Lowell: "The Courtin' "
"Robin Hood" (many of them)	Service: "The Cremation of Sam McGee"
"Fair Margaret and Sweet William"	

(Here belong such cowboy and frontier ballads as "Roll on, Little Dogies, Roll On" and "Casey Jones.") Practically all this material, plus much more, is taught in every high school.

References on the Ballad
(Collections)

Gummere, Francis B.: *Old English Ballads*
Child, Francis James: *The English and Scottish Popular Ballads*
Quiller-Couch, Sir Arthur: *The Oxford Book of Ballads*

(Discussion)

Louise Pound: *Poetic Origins and the Ballad*
This book upsets the old concepts as to the origins of the ballad.

Francis B. Gummere: *The Popular Ballad*
John A. and Alan Lomax: *Cowboy Songs and Other Frontier Ballads*

THE LYRIC

A brief subjective poem, creating for the reader a single unified impression marked by imagination, melody, and emotion. Through the ages there have been many concepts of the lyric. Today we name "lyric" such forms as songs, sonnets, odes, elegies, light verse, artificial French forms (rondeau, rondel, ballade). The expression of personal emotion imaginatively phrased seems to be the one important quality common to all forms.

References on the Lyric

Rhys, Ernest: *Lyric Poetry*
Reed, E. B.: *English Lyric Poetry from Its Origin to the Present Time*
Palgrave, Francis, ed.: *The Golden Treasury*

The Ode

Any strain of enthusiastic and exalted lyrical verse that is directed to a fixed purpose and deals progressively with one fixed theme. It is elaborate, imaginative, dignified, and intellectual in tone. It is the most intricate in form of all the lyrics. *Examples:*

Dryden: "Alexander's Feast"
Wordsworth: "Ode on the Intimations of Immortality"
Shelley: "Ode to the West Wind"

Markham: "Lincoln, the Man of the People"
Moody: "To a Soldier Fallen in the Philippines"

The five odes listed above are usually included in the English course.

References on the Ode

Gosse, Edmund: article in the *Encyclopaedia Britannica*
Shafer, Robert: *The English Ode to 1660*
Alden, Raymond: *English Verse*

The Elegy

A lyric poem expressing either personal or public loss. At times merely a contemplation of death. This form was popular with classical writers. Two of the most widely known poems of this type are Gray's "Elegy Written in a Country Churchyard" and Milton's "Lycidas." *Examples:*

Shelley: "Adonais" (on the death of Keats)

Arnold: "Thyrsis" (on the death of Clough)

Tennyson: "In Memoriam" (on the death of Arthur Hallam)

MacKaye: "To the Fire Bringer" (on the death of William Vaughn Moody)

Gray's "Elegy" is universally used. In some schools, "Lycidas" and "In Memoriam" (the latter in a cut version) are listed.

References on the Elegy

Gayley and Kurtz: *Methods and Materials of Literary Criticism*
Bailey, J. C.: *English Elegies* (See the Introduction.)

The Sonnet

A lyric form of fourteen lines. The two widely recognized types are the Italian (Petrarchan) and the English (Shakespearean). The Italian form is divided into two parts, the octave (rhyming abba, abba) and the sestet (rhyming cde, cde). The octave asks the question, or expresses the desire or passion or resentment. The sestet solves this problem—answers the complaint or philosophically eases the unhappy mood. Since Shakespeare's day the English form, slightly varied, has been most widely used by English writers. .*Examples:*

Milton: "Sonnet on His Blindness"

Wordsworth: "Composed upon Westminster Bridge, 1802"

Keats: "On First Looking into Chapman's Homer"

Hagedorn: "Doors"

A few of Shakespeare's sonnets and the first three listed above appear in practically all courses, as do many others if time and pupil interest make them desirable.

References on the Sonnet

Tomlinson, C.: *The Sonnet, Its Origin, Structure, and Place in Poetry*
Alden, Raymond: *English Verse*

The Simple Lyric

A. The Song

A lyric adapted to musical expression. Usually it is short, simple in wording, a spontaneous and lilting expression of emotion. All types and topics exist: love, war, yearning, patriotism, drinking, dance— all have inspired songs. *Examples:*

Shakespeare: "Who is Sylvia?"

Ben Jonson: "Drink to Me Only with Thine Eyes"

Burns: "Scots Wha Hae"

Stephen C. Foster: "My Old Kentucky Home"

Francis Scott Key: "The Star-spangled Banner"

Kipling: "Recessional"

Robert Frost: "The Road Not Taken"

Charles Wesley: "Hark! the Herald Angels Sing"

Robert Nathan: "I Ride the Great Black Horses of My Heart"

B. Simple Lyrics Not Sung

Examples:

Old English: "Deor's Lament"

Chaucer: "The Complaint to His Empty Purse"

Housman: "When I Was One-and-Twenty"

Yeats: "The Lake Isle of Innisfree"

Frost: "House Fear"

Wallace Stevens: "Peter Quince at the Clavier"

Milton: "L'Allegro"

Whitman: "Song of Myself"

Aiken: "Morning Song from 'Senlin'"

You will note the wide variety of types grouped as "simple lyrics." Most of these listed, plus many more, occur in all courses of study for high school.

References on the Lyric

Rhys, Ernest: *Lyric Poetry*

Reed, E. B.: *English Lyric Poetry from Its Origin to the Present Time*

Palgrave, Francis, ed.: *The Golden Treasury*

Untermeyer, Louis, ed.: *Modern American Poetry* and *Modern British Poetry* (combined edition)

Consult for modern lyrics.

DRAMATIC POETRY

Poetry that utilizes such dramatic qualities as monologue, dialogue, vigorous diction, strong emotion. Usually a situation or crisis is presented in which conflict, emotion, often tragedy are mingled. *Examples:*

A. Drama in Verse

Greek tragedies
Shakespeare: *The Tempest*
Browning: "Pippa Passes"

Anderson: *Winterset* and *Elizabeth the Queen*

Reference on Drama in Verse

Matthews, Brander: *A Study of the Drama,* Chap. 12

B. Dramatic Monologues

A monologue in which a soul reveals the conflict within. Browning is given the credit for first using the form, which has since become popular. *Examples:*

Browning: "Andrea del Sarto" and "My Last Duchess"   Kipling: "M'Andrew's Hymn"

Robert Frost, Amy Lowell, E. A. Robinson, Carl Sandburg, and many other moderns have used this form or a variant of it.

C. The Masque

A survival of the ancient pageant. The best-known example is Milton's *Comus.* In medieval times *The Dance of the Seven Deadly Sins* was a masque. In most courses, Browning's dramatic monologues, Shakespeare's poetic dramas, and "free reading" of Maxwell Anderson's plays are listed. *Comus* is read by many college preparatory classes, but is not widely read by other groups.

References on the Masque

Sullivan, Mary: *Court Masques of James I*
Green, A. W.: *The Inns of Court and Early English Drama*

PROSE

The Essay

An attempt to set forth some of the author's thoughts and feelings concerning life in any of its various phases. These may be trivial or serious; they may be rambling or concise; they may be whimsical or deeply philosophical. Most people divide them into what they term "formal essays" and "informal essays." The division is not exact, but the formal essay *informs;* the informal essay, highly personal, wanders at will. *Examples:*

Informal Essays

Montaigne's and Bacon's essays	Bernard De Voto: "Easy Chair"
Lamb: "Poor Relations"	(*Harper's Magazine*)
Hazlitt: "On Going a Journey"	Stephen Leacock: "On the
Crother: "Dame School of Ex-	Weather"
perience"	Robert Benchley: "What Col-
E. B. White: "One Man's Meat"	lege Did to Me"
(*Harper's Magazine*)	

These informal essays are often termed "familiar essays."

Formal Essays

Carlyle: "Burns"	Emerson: "The American
Macaulay: "Essay on Johnson"	Scholar"
Burke: "Conciliation"	

In the typical high-school course Macaulay's unfair picture of Dr. Johnson, and Emerson's essays, are widely taught, as are numberless familiar essays.

References on the Essay

Alden, R. M.: *Essays, English and American*
Bryant, W. F., and Crane, R. S.: *The English Familiar Essay*
Walker, Hugh: *English Essays and Essayists*

Prose Fiction

Here the myth, the allegory, and prose romance would be classed, but aside from the first they play but small part in the high-school course. The allegory would be represented by Bunyan's *The Pilgrim's Progress*—little read, unfortunately. The romance would be represented by *The Travels of Sir John Mandeville,* More's *Utopia,* and the famous *Mort d'Arthur* by Sir Thomas Malory. Only the last is used occasionally for reference.

The Novel; the Novelette; the Short Story

These three forms are too familiar to need discussion.

References for the Novel

Baker, E. A.: *The History of the English Novel,* 10 vols.
This is an admirable survey from the earliest beginnings.
Lovett, R. M., and Hughes, H. S.: *A History of the Novel in England*
Lubbock, Percy: *The Craft of Fiction*
This is a stimulating book.
Wharton, Edith: *The Writing of Fiction*

References for the Short Story

Pattee, Fred: *The Development of the American Short Story*
Frederick, John T.: *A Handbook of Short Story Writing*
Mirrielees, Edith R.: *The Story Writer*
Bement, Douglas: *Weaving the Short Story*

You would, of course, consult the *O. Henry Prize Stories* and the O'Brien *Best Short Stories of* (the year).

Prose Drama
References

Thorndyke, Ashley: *Tragedy*
Nicoll, Allardyce: *British Drama* and *A History of Late Eighteenth Century Drama*
Clark, Barrett: *A Study of Modern Drama*
Mantle, Burns: *The Best Plays of* (the year)

Biography
References

Nicolson, Harold: *The Development of English Biography*
Balch, Minton, ed.: *Modern Short Biographies and Autobiographies* (Introduction)
Maurois, André: *Aspects of Biography*

Travel Books

Books of General Information [1]

II. HOW SHOULD YOU PLAN YOUR WORK IN LITERATURE?

Though each of you must solve that question for yourself, according to the particular conditions under which you teach, yet there are some general principles that are applicable to practically all conditions.

In the majority of progressive classrooms today, daily class recitation in literature with assigned reading for the whole group has been abandoned. The English room is a workshop, a studio, a theater, or a library—not a classroom as the term was understood thirty years ago. During the English period, after the teacher has once launched a carefully planned unit of work in travel, adventure, heroism, man's conflict with himself or with nature—whatever the unit may be—the pupils pursue their personal investigation.[2] The teacher is a guide, a prod, and an adviser. When necessary the pupils come to her for help. She in her turn must feel free at any time to interrupt a group of pupils, or the whole class, for discussion or added information. Such a plan of work, *after it is once successfully launched*, tends to carry itself more or less satisfactorily; but at no time can the teacher retire from the scene, trusting that a class can or will manage itself. Little by little, as it proves worthy, responsibility can be

---

[1] Do you know Arthur G. Kennedy's *A Concise Bibliography for Students of English, Systematically Arranged?* It is published by the Stanford University Press, Stanford University, Calif., 1940. See if your college library has the book. You would find it wise to own it. A second book that you should own is *A Handbook to Literature* by William Flint Thrall and Addison Hibbard, Doubleday, Doran, 1936. The material, arranged in alphabetical order (from "Abstract Terms" to "Wit and Humor") defines, illustrates, and provides references for practically all terms dealing with literature or used in literary criticism. If you have not done so, examine carefully McCall, W. A., Cook, Luella B., and Norvell, G. W.: *Experiments in Reading*, Books 1, 2, 3, 1934; and McCall, W. A., and Norvell, G. W.: *Improve Your Reading*, 1942—both Harcourt, Brace. These booklets, planned for the junior high school, will give you definite information as to how reading may be taught.

[2] See the Introduction: "Some Experiments in Present-Day Teaching."

placed in the group, but the election of class officers and the fond hope that the class will run itself has wrecked many a potentially excellent unit. Before such a unit is begun, the teacher must:

1. Know thoroughly the objectives she desires to achieve.

2. Know and have organized exactly the minimum work to be required of even the dullest pupil, and the possible work for those of greater ability.

3. Know exactly the tests and exercises that she will use to spur the lazy and to stimulate the bright.

4. Know definitely what library material and other illustrative material may be either displayed to, or "discovered" by, the pupils.

5. Know in a general fashion what activities (pantomime, dramatization, original dialogues, informal debates, library talks, etc.) may be adapted or created that will further some phase of English study; and learn, according to the pupils' interests, what allied arts (music, painting, soap-carving, drawing, etc.) may be wisely encouraged to further the student's appreciation and enjoyment of reading.

In other words, no teacher can arrive the day before instruction begins, a stranger to the school and the school resources, plunge into the unknown course of study, and hope to do intelligent teaching. The work must be organized around definite centers of interest, and the material must be carefully planned and skillfully graded so that unit one leads to unit two and is more simple than unit four.[1]

But, you may question, how is it possible to plan before you see your pupils? Luckily, different as each one is, you can usually find in pupil activity a common denominator of interest. Remember this: Unless you are unusually stimulating, beautiful, magnetic, and charming, most pupils, unresponsive as they may seem, would rather talk than listen to you; rather adventure for themselves than be led by you; rather elaborate a hint from you until

[1] Have you read Lou La Brant's *The Teaching of Literature in Secondary Schools?* It would repay you to do so.

it appears their own idea than undertake a project which you have explained to them in detail. At the same time you can rely upon awakening their interest in almost any fundamental human problem not too subtle or too far removed from their experience. A difference in centuries or in civilizations will not prove a barrier (that is, of course, if the vocabulary used is one with which they can cope) [1] so long as they can interpret the emotional situation and so long as the *reason* for reading is apparent and, to their minds, adequate.[2]

To the sophomore mind and to your own, the meaning of that term "adequate" may not be identical, but of this be sure: Every unit you plan must be clean-cut, definite, must include different kinds of work as well as different kinds of reading, and must come to some kind of climax so that there is a sense of completion and personal accomplishment. To get real work from your pupils you must also have (1) frequent factual tests to insure careful reading; (2) thought-provocative questions to increase the pupils' skill in interpretation; (3) collateral reading of such nature as to develop both the pupils' power of viewing books as units and of seeing the relationships of one book to another; and (4) guided, intelligent library work so that your brighter pupils have adequate occupation and so that the use both of reference books and of magazines and fiction may, one hopes, become habitual.

The only warning that you may need is this: Do not attempt too much at first. Pupils have to understand clearly *what* they are to do and *why* they are to do it. They have to be led to undertake—or at times driven to undertake—the work planned. You will at first be surprised at how slowly a class moves. But remember that discussion, if it is serious, is in itself educational. A day for organizing your group into a series of committees to look into school-library conditions (which you know), and town-

---

[1] Sweeney, Barry, and Schoelkopf: *Western Youth Meets Eastern Culture.*
[2] See the Introduction: "Some Experiments in Present-Day Teaching."

library conditions (which you also know), to consult with the social-science teacher (whom you have seen) is probably time well spent. You could cover the ground more quickly by telling your group many of the things which they will find out for themselves, but you would not develop their qualities of initiative, resourcefulness, and co-operation, nor would you give them drill in simple parliamentary procedure and extemporaneous speaking. Just as soon as you have the individual working seriously to pass his own tests, and groups of pupils working seriously together to produce a play or a booklet or a report or an assembly program, you have welded your class together successfully. What you have to do next is to see that their effort is not misspent, nor their span of interest too brief. The bright pupil whose interest flames one day and is extinct the next becomes a serious problem. Sometimes special responsibility to the group may hold him; sometimes individual work more exacting but also more spectacular may tickle his vanity. The pupils are in your hands, and you must study them to see how you can best get each one to develop his own native ability. Easy? Not at all. But both challenging and interesting.

SUGGESTED EXERCISES

1. After you have read two of the references in Suggested Readings listed under "A. References Concerning Your Own Equipment," think over your own training, personality, appearance, dress, manners. Then think back to your own liked and disliked high-school and grade-school teachers. Class discussion of the readings assigned might prove stimulating. More than you realize, perhaps, each individual can change manners, habits, appearance, and even outlook upon life, if he turns his intelligence upon himself.

2. After you have read two or more references from the *English Journal* under each of the six headings listed, come to class prepared for a discussion of fundamental changes apparent in the modern junior-senior high school. Be ready (a) to hand in a brief outline of the important changes; (b) to discuss in class those

changes, illustrating from the reading done; and (c) to draw some tentative conclusions as to which changes seem most beneficial.

3. In a brief article (300 to 500 words) that later may be used for general class discussion, summarize your present opinions upon *one* of the following topics:

a. The loss of the textbook in literature—its advantages and disadvantages

b. The advantages and disadvantages of an activity program in which the pupils are the moving spirits

c. The advantages of a "unit" assignment in literature. Define the term before you discuss it.

d. The advantages and disadvantages of the "contract" in literature teaching

e. The use of literature for inculcating ideals of personal and national conduct

SUGGESTED READINGS

A. References Concerning Your Own Equipment

The English Language Arts, Vol. I, N.C.T.E. Curriculum Series, Dora V. Smith, Director

Read Part III, Chapter 16, "The Program in Literature," and Chapter 15, "Mass Modes of Communication." Do you agree?

1. Thomas, Charles Swain: *The Teaching of English in Secondary Schools,* Houghton Mifflin, 1927, pp. 510-15

A veteran teacher presents questions so that each beginner in the field of English teaching may survey his own weak and strong points.

2. Sharp, Russell A.: *Teaching English in High School,* Houghton Mifflin, 1924, Chap. I, "The Teacher in the Making"

3. Carpenter, G. R., Baker, F. T., and Scott, F. N.: *The Teaching of English in the Elementary and Secondary School,* Longmans, Green, 1913, Chap. V, "The Training of the Teacher"

Note the dates of these three books. Do you agree with their views?

4. *An Experience Curriculum in English: A Report of a Commission of the National Council of Teachers of English,* W. W. Hatfield, Chairman, Appleton-Century, 1935

Appendix C, "Teachers' Education in English." What ought you to do before you begin teaching? What future college work should await you?

Chapter III, "Selecting and Providing Literature Experiences." Here you will find the conclusions of our leading educators. *Study carefully.* Chapter V, "Literature Experiences: Grades 7-12." List for future reference the various primary objectives stated.

5. Broening, Angela M., chairman: *Conducting Experiences in English,* Appleton-Century, 1939

A report of a committee of the National Council of Teachers of English. Based on the contribution of 274 co-operating teachers of English.

6. Herzberg, Max J.: "The Teacher of English in the Modern World," *English Journal,* Vol. 40 (1951), pp. 86-90

A fund of common sense given imaginatively.

7. Ruud, Evelyn: "Reading List—Design for Living," *English Journal,* Vol. 28 (1939), pp. 45-50

An attempt to break away from the conventional course and give the children of migratory workers something appealing and "real."

8. Hatfield, W. W.: "Put First Things First," *English Journal,* Vol. 37 (1948), pp. 486-87

Read this provocative article. The writer is the editor of the *English Journal* and wise in his judgment of teaching.

9. Perrin, P. G.: "A Realistic Philosophy for Teachers of English," *English Journal,* Vol. 37 (1948), pp. 64-72

Considers briefly four philosophic attitudes.

10. Treanor, J. H.: "Moral Overtones of English Literature," *Education,* Vol. 69 (1949), pp. 315-16

11. Carter, M.: "Case for World Literature," *School Review,* Vol. 56 (1948), pp. 415-20

12. Quin, Marion: "Why Not Study All America?" *Progressive Education,* Vol. 19 (1942), pp. 379-83

A discussion of Latin-American friendship. Excellent bibliography.[1]

13. American Council on Education, Hilda Taba, director: *Reading Ladders for Human Relations,* rev. ed., Washington, D. C., 1949

Gaining sensitivity toward and understanding of people.

14. Zorn, J. W.: "Vitalizing the High School English Curriculum, with

[1] Do you belong to the Book-of-the-Month Club or to the Literary Guild? Do you take the *Saturday Review of Literature* or the *Herald Tribune Book Review?* How do you keep up with your pupils?

Special Reference to Nonacademic Students," *Education*, Vol. 69 (1948), pp. 250-53

Do you approve?

From the English Journal

1. Pollock, T. C.: "English for Maturity," Vol. 38 (1949), pp. 66-72

2. Phelps, F. B.: "Literature a Guide to Social Living," Vol. 39 (1950), pp. 340-41

Do you agree with this attitude?

3. Deighton, Lee C.: "Shall Reading Be Free?" Vol. 25 (1936), pp. 399-402

Does this article agree or disagree with your text? Note that it is not written by a teacher, but by a man whose business leads him to many schools.

4. Herzberg, Max J.: "Later May Be Too Late," Vol. 32 (1943), pp. 8-12

Here the role of the teacher in wartime is discussed in stimulating fashion. Read.

5. Rothenbush, Verona F.: "Developing Active, Thinking Citizens," Read.

Vol. 32 (1943), pp. 188-95

6. Rose, Elizabeth Lamar, and Davis, Mary Houston: "An English Unit on Aviation," Vol. 32 (1943), pp. 126-32

Includes a bibliography. Useful, particularly for boys.

7. Carlsen, George Robert: "Understanding the American Heritage," Vol. 36 (1947), pp. 116-20

Teaching American literature well.

8. Miller, Helen Rand: "The American Education for Life," Vol. 37 (1948), pp. 193-95

A terse, interesting summary of purposes.

9. La Brant, Lou: "Diversifying the Matter," Vol. 40 (1951), pp. 134-39

Ways of broadening the students' outlook, and the teacher's?

10. Pooley, Robert C.: "English in the Coming High School," Vol. 37 (1948), pp. 284-91

An excellent survey of a possible future. ". . . The function of the English teacher is the introduction to the love of literature. Notice I said 'to the love of literature' not 'to the knowledge of literature.' "

CHAPTER XII

Teaching the Art of Reading

READING of some type and at some level is one of the most universal and important businesses and pastimes of the American people. The cook reads the instructions left by her employer, the recipe for some complicated dish, the newspaper for war happenings and movie news, the pulps for escape and romance. The millworker or the miner reads his labor paper, reads the local paper, comparing its presentation of the news with that of his own labor press, considers the union communications at the Trades and Labor Council, skims pulps, *Liberty*, or the *Saturday Evening Post* for relaxation. The farmer reads the catalogue for seeds, machinery, household goods; the United States *Farmer's Bulletins*, the *Farm Journal*, the weekly paper of his Farm Bureau, Grange, or Farmers' Union. And for most of these people the information, the stimulus, the widened horizon of the city or county public library exists (in adequate or inadequate form) *only* if teachers the country over impart the Art of Reading to their pupils. I stress this need for reading, for, discouraged, teachers forget at times that not only the college-preparatory group and the prospective white-collar class but also the great, solid working class in city, town, and country are readers—good or poor.

Our business above all else is to teach these hordes of youngsters to read, and to read intelligently. To be sure, the radio has somewhat lessened man's dependence upon the printed page. It has not, however, lessened but perhaps increased his need for an adequate vocabulary. It has not lessened but increased his information and his curiosity about the world in which he lives—a world that for all of us has now become tragically alive and real.

A sophomore remarked after the Japanese attack on Pearl Harbor, "World events are becoming terribly personal." There it is: the awakening of countless people to world citizenship, to a need for greater understanding—gained largely from books and papers. And with tragic events there comes, too, the need for escape, and for imaginative experiences—at some level. For the poorer readers books provide escape; for the better readers they both educate and sensitize, adding to life savor, depth, and greater comprehension.

Are you convinced? Desirable as it is for pupils to appreciate the best that has been thought and said, to use speech and writing unsullied by error or rhetorical awkwardness, *ability to read intelligently and with fair speed tops all other factors in an English course.* The son of the street-cleaner or of the best scholar in your community must carry on his own education throughout a long or a short life. How? Largely through reading.

So much for generalization. In your classrooms, what are you going to do? Show your pupils that just as the football player on the field is helpless if unaware of the significance of the signal 7-2-5-9, so a reader is helpless if he cannot understand the words on a page. Vocabulary—that is a basic factor. But just as no painter, actor, cook, or inventor has won success and yet hated his medium, so it is with your potential readers. All your work to build readers must be *motivated* by you, must be *challenging* and *interesting* to your pupils. Variety in presenting the *same* type of reading situations or drill; patience, humor, understanding, persistence, and logical organization of that material—these must mark your work. Reading, however, unlike community singing, is not a mass but an individual activity; hence you must grasp the individual difficulties and attempt to cope with them both in class and in brief private conferences.

I. WHAT IS THE TEACHER'S FIRST DUTY?

Convinced of the need for training, aware of the vocabulary difficulties (see Chapter V), what should be your first responsibility? Naturally you do not expect the athlete in the back row and the semi-invalid in row one to compete on the race track with equal success. Why, then, do many teachers expect an I.Q. of 85 to march, lock-step, through literature with an I.Q. of 140? Perhaps they don't, but how without first securing intelligence ratings of her pupils can a teacher be certain that she is not wasting time on the 85 I.Q. pupil who is reading at a rate normal *for him,* or neglecting the retarded reader with an I.Q. of 100 or better? The first can, doubtless, improve a little, but he is not retarded. The second presents a problem demanding investigation.

Obviously it is your duty as a teacher to discover how well or how poorly your pupils read. Undoubtedly the quickest and least painful way of securing this information is to give them a diagnostic reading test. Both they and you, however, should recognize the fact that such a test is neither a teaching device nor an examination. And, too, even though you are fairly expert in test-giving and test-grading, both they and you should be aware that the test is in no sense to be considered a final judgment rendered upon the intelligence or the ability of the pupil. A solitary test is merely a straw in the wind, nothing more. But straws are useful.

Many high-school teachers, if they were honest with themselves, would have to admit that a large percentage of their pupils (1) recognize the meaning of a sentence or paragraph no more rapidly, (2) read with no more comprehension, (3) interpret an author's meaning no more skillfully, and (4) appreciate and evaluate literature with no more maturity at the end of a year than they did at the beginning. Does such a condition suggest success, or failure? Teachers are—and perhaps must be—optimists, but it is unfortunate when they remain optimists only because they have never tested the results of their teaching. So much for generalizations. What are you to *do*?

1. Discover the I.Q. of each member in your class.
2. Test each pupil's reading.
3. Analyze those tests.
4. Provide adequate training according to the need of each pupil.

Testing is not of necessity a timetaking procedure. For example, the *Monroe Standardized Silent Reading Test, Revised,* can be given in about five minutes. Since it is aranged in three forms suitable for grades three to five, six to eight, and nine to twelve, you could use it in either junior or senior high school. And since two forms of the text exist for each level, you can test your own teaching ability by repeating the test in a different form in the middle or at the end of the year. It is not at all a bad plan to give the first one in September, give the second in January, and in June repeat the test given in September. When school opens you give a diagnostic test; until January you and the pupils work for improvement; in January you discover what progress seems to have been made; until June you redouble your efforts; in June you and your pupils discover the results of the year's work. How does this method compare with that used in some classrooms where teachers place book after book before their pupils, hoping that they will improve? What is the result? Those who can read with enjoyment, read. But they read no better. The slow readers plod along at their usual pace—or daydream, for there is no incentive to hasten or to concentrate. And the nonreaders? When reading tests are used, attention is centered upon learning how to extract the substance of a reading assignment quickly, accurately, and imaginatively. And, too, the responsibility for making progress seems to be shared with the pupil; it no longer rests upon the teacher alone.[1]

[1] For tests consult Appendix C, pages 576-79.

II. WHY DO SOME PUPILS READ POORLY?

Consider again the case of the pupil with an I.Q. of 100 or better who in spite of that rating is a poor reader. There are several possible explanations. Perhaps his is a language difficulty; he may come from a home where he hears and speaks only a foreign language. Discover tactfully what his home environment is. Your pleasure at finding his knowledge of Italian or German or Polish, and your deferential attitude toward him in vocabulary discussions, can offset any embarrassment he may feel as to his "alien" origin. His difficulty may be a mechanical one. Perhaps he uses his lips as if reading aloud. Watch your pupils to see which of them form each word with their lips. Probably all of us use lip movement at times if the material is excessively difficult, and now it is admitted that some slight vocalization is carried on by even the most sophisticated reader. That fact, told to your lip-reading pupils, will soothe their self-respect, but its being a fact does not reduce the damage done by overuse of the lips in reading. If a pupil uses lip movement continuously, you can be sure that he is retarding his speed of reading and is still placing a preponderance of emphasis upon word recognition. It has been found that by calling the pupil's attention to his habit and getting him to attempt to inhibit this lip movement and all movements of articulation, insofar as that is possible, his rate of reading can be increased. Much practice in rapid silent reading is of course essential.

Unfortunately, teachers as well as the fathers and mothers of slow readers have in the past tended to build up a legend about slowness. You know the hoary maxim "Slow but sure." Later you will meet the slow pupil who tells you, either defensively or apologetically, "I don't read fast, but I *remember* what I get," the implication being all too plain concerning the pupils who finished reading ahead of him. Scientific investigation does not, so far, support the axiom. It seems to prove that there is a close correlation between the rate of reading and the degree of comprehension. Good readers are usually fast readers; poor readers are usually slow ones.[1]

But the most usual difficulty, and one that you should investigate early, is faulty eye use. In your first school you may not have access to any of the mechanical devices used for eye-testing and eye movement. You can, however, gain a rough estimate of the pupil's eye movements by sitting beside him and watching, as he reads, his eyes reflected in a mirror placed before him. By close watching you can judge the approximate number of fixations (pauses while the eye impression is conveyed to the brain), the number of regressions (returns to look again at a word or phrase), and then swings back to the left margin at the conclusion of each line. What then? Count the words read; then divide by the number of fixations. Just as some speakers hesitatingly scoop out one word at a time while others pour out a lavish number, so some pupils read a word at a time, some a phrase at a time, and some apparently sweep a whole sentence into their minds at a glance. *Make it your business* to learn how eyes work when reading and what mechanical devices exist to test eye conditions and to measure eye span (the number of words covered between each fixation). There are several devices: the Ophthalm-O-Graph, Metron-O-Scope, Ophthalm-O-Scope, Catchistoscope, Stereo-Orthopter and Telebinocular. All of these machines are manufactured by the American Optical Company, Southbridge, Massachusetts.

A study that you should investigate has been made by Stella S. Center and Gladys L. Persons called *Teaching High School*

[1] Many a teacher, worried by discipline, occupied by too many tasks to be performed at once, does her pupils grave injustice by inadvertently encouraging slow reading and putting her stamp of approval upon it. Why does she? Because she has not planned for and obtained sufficient material; because she wants (and wisely) to carry on conferences while members of the class are reading; or because—you can imagine for yourself situations where peace at any price, even the slowing down of your pupils' reading rate, may seem desirable.

Students to Read, a publication of the National Council of Teachers of English, Monograph 6, Appleton-Century, 1937. It contains a detailed study of the use of these mechanical testing devices, with case histories recorded. But you can do much for your pupils' improvement in reading without such elaborate equipment. Do you remember the flash cards of your first-grade days? The Metron-O-Scope works on much the same principle, but like the roll on an automatic piano, one whole line, not just a word or phrase, is unrolled, appears, disappears, and is followed by the next and then the next. It can be rolled slowly or quickly. One ingenious teacher constructed a rough imitation with an old window shade which she lined, lettered, fastened to the chalk tray and, by means of a cord through a staple at the top of the blackboard, was able to draw up, thus exposing between two parallel sheets of wrapping paper across the shade one line of print at a time. I am by no means sure that the benefit received and the labor expended by the teacher and the class were commensurate. But I am sure that the interest aroused, and the general recognition that eye training was important, secured an unusually desirable class attitude in which to carry on remedial reading.

III. WHAT BOOKS SHALL POOR READERS READ?

What kind of material should you use? It must be interesting. It must be reasonably simple in vocabulary and in idea. Simplified texts, appropriate for junior-high-school texts, might be used successfully for poor senior-high-school readers. But for most non-readers the incentive to read on and on depends upon the amount of suspense and excitement or upon the topic in which they have special interest. The books listed below interest most poor readers who wish to improve their comprehension and speed. Give many brief drills, encourage pupils to use drill pads, but rely chiefly upon much easy free reading. Knowing each pupil, you could attempt to fit the book to his hobbies or to his background.

TEXTBOOKS AND WORKBOOKS FOR TEACHING READING SKILLS

Roberts, Holland, and others: *Let's Read* series, Henry Holt

Book I. *Reading for Experience*, seventh grade, 1941

Book II. *Growing Up in Reading*, eighth grade, 1939 (Exceptionally good)

Book III. *Reading for Life*, ninth grade, 1937

Book IV. *Reading for Work and College*, tenth through twelfth, 1940

Hovious, Carol: *Following Printed Trails;* and *Flying the Print Ways*, D. C. Heath, 1937

Hovious, Carol, and Shearer, Elga: *Wings for Reading*, D. C. Heath, 1942

McCall, William A., and Norvell, George W.: *Improve Your Reading*, Harcourt, Brace, 1948

For the teacher:

Strang, Ruth, Checkovitz, Alice, Gilbert, Christine, and Scoggin, Margaret: *Gateways to Readable Books: An Annotated Graded List of Books in Many Fields for Adolescents Who Find Reading Difficult*, H. W. Wilson Co., 1952

For the busy teacher or for the librarian this book is almost indispensable.

These textbooks are intended for classroom use. But remember, youngsters reach excellence, as do skaters, violinists, or acrobats, only by long-continued practice. Pupils gain facility in reading only by much free reading where they put into practice those principles learned in the classroom. Here the problem that confronts you is to make your follow-up work an individual problem. You must provide each pupil with as much material, simple in form, interesting in substance, as he can absorb. At once you will recognize the difficulty of finding time for individual instruction. Visualize the conditions. You may have as many as a hundred and fifty pupils divided into four or even five or six classes. Probably you will not have more than two or three separate class preparations, but in a small school you might. You may have one or two study-hall hours where you vacillate between being policeman, walking encyclopedia, dictionary, and school nurse. If clubs, debates, and dramatics abound, you will also have some outside responsibilities. How can you do individual work?

Fortunately for you there are some admirable and inexpensive books which contain enough vitality and variety to interest retarded readers.[1] But the simple articles in the *Reader's Digest*, accounts in sports magazines, short stories in which the plot interest sweeps the reader on in spite of some unknown words— any of these may serve your purpose until suitable books can be secured.

In all probability you cannot afford a battery of tests. Often you will find no tests for exactly what you need. But with training you and your better pupils can make objective tests that will at least prove how carefully or how intelligently reading has been done. Naturally, a test has little value if it is so easy that all members of a class can gain a perfect score. If true-false questions are used, the statements must of necessity be absolutely true or absolutely false, and must be so worded as to afford no clue to the correct answer. In true-false tests, completion tests, matching tests, or multiple-choice tests the chief thing to keep in mind is this: Unless the question is itself of some importance, ability to answer it proves nothing.

You wish, of course, to discover whether or not your pupils have done the assigned reading, but you also wish to know if they have grasped the underlying idea of the poem or story. These brief tests, however, serve another purpose. In every class there are pupils who are well read but inarticulate, and others who are instantly vocal. Unless you guard against it, your discussion periods may be monopolized by the few, and you may conclude that the silent ones are ignorant. Or your talkative pupils may so monopolize your attention that you are deceived into thinking that all in the class have read intelligently. In ten minutes an objective test can reveal who has and who has not understood the reading assignment. Bluffers are detected; the shy are given credit for their real work; and if the test is well made,

[1] A few books for retarded readers are listed at the end of the chapter.

all the members of the class recognize that they have been rewarded according to their actual knowledge.[1]

IV. HOW CAN YOU MAKE READING AN INDIVIDUAL PROBLEM?

Tests, however, are mere sounding-rods to discover the depths or shallows in each pupil's ability. Your *teaching* is another matter. Just what confronts you? You wish to cultivate three types of reading: rapid reading to locate specific information; careful reading for purposes of study; and recreational reading, in high school often termed "outside reading."

You have perhaps thirty pupils in your class; for texts you have some five or six individual books or one of the widely used anthologies similar to *Hidden Treasures in Literature, Adventures in Literature, Explorations in Literature,* or *Literature and Life.* You have also a library, probably limited but not completely hopeless, as a source for information or for recreational reading.

First, it would be wise to consider the pupils. Not only do they differ in age, family training, background, interests, and disposition but, remember, they differ also in intelligence. If you expect all thirty to *read* the same material, *progress* at the same rate, *find enjoyment* in the same situations, *participate* enthusiastically in the same activity—well, you will be expecting only what many teachers have expected in the past. But you will be about as reasonable as the person who expects uniform rate of progress from an airplane, a racing automobile, a truck, a freight train, a horse and buggy, a bicycle, and a kiddy car. In fact you would be less reasonable, because human emotions and desires are even less predictable than mechanical aberrations. In other words, you must, busy as you are, treat each pupil as an individual. You will find that soon, as in Swedenborg's Heaven, each will rise or

[1] Consult Appendix C. There you will find what an experienced teacher considers desirable in objective tests for literature.

sink to his own level so that you will have three or five or seven little groups in each of which the members are more or less equally equipped. But even then do not make the mistake of thinking that you need not treat each person in each group as in need of individual consideration.

As a teacher, you are genuinely interested in increasing the reading rate of your pupils. As a college student, you can see daily the advantages of rapid reading. But speed minus accurate comprehension is both a menace and an annoyance; hence you should provide numerous comprehension tests aside from the regular work in literature, which is of course, after a fashion, a continuous test of the pupil's comprehension. For such work brief paragraphs followed by specific questions, longer passages followed by true-and-false statements or completion exercises, simple précis work—all place the emphasis not only upon rapid reading but upon accurate comprehension of the material read. In a less-direct but probably in an even more effective way than by the use of reading tests you can increase your poor reader's ability to grasp the meaning of a passage. Vocabulary work, if it is intelligently conducted, careful study of topic sentences for key words, and selection and organization of the central thought in isolated and then in related paragraphs will prove effective ways of increasing his reading ability—granted, of course, that the pupil has normal intelligence.[1]

Throughout this chapter tests have been frequently mentioned.

V. WHAT IS THE PURPOSE OF ALL THIS WORK?

I have known student-teachers whose interest in the process of this training led them to lose sight of its purpose. The reason that pupils are urged to increase their ability to read is, of course, that they may read with both pleasure and profit. Not all pupils can learn to read philosophical or scientific essays, or learn to project themselves imaginatively into foreign settings or emo-

[1] See Chapter V.

tional situations. But all can learn to read with some pleasure if you give each the opportunity to read at his own level. Interest is the great lever; discussion, guidance, enthusiasm, and patient searching for suitable material, material that (as Miss Teitge in "Follow the Romany Patteran," referred to in Chapter XVI, has shown) leads on from story to story, from book to book, from article to article. Never make reading an isolated activity. One book leads to another; a book leads to class discussion and comparison; an "interest trail" leads to talk and friendships and the trading of bits of information.[1] Make reading vital, reading on *whatever plane is suited to the pupil's background and brain power*.

SUGGESTED EXERCISES

Before you attempt these exercises read a number of the references listed at the end of this chapter. Remember that since you attended high school the method of testing a pupil's reading has changed materially. Investigate literature tests; inform yourself concerning the various ways in which pupil reading may be studied and improved. If you do not, you will probably continue in the old laborious, timetaking method, and your pupils will leave you as they came to you—good, mediocre, or poor readers.

1. Divide your class into four groups, each group to acquaint itself thoroughly with one of the tests suggested earlier, and to try out the test on some member or members of the class. If possible the tests should be *put on call at the library loan desk,* examined, and then discussed by members of the class.

2. Divide your class into four groups to investigate these tests in literature. Class reports and class discussions should follow.

a. *Abbott-Trabue Exercises in the Appreciation of Poetry* by Allan Abbott and M. R. Trabue, Teachers College, New York City, *Forms X and Y*. Sample, 5 cents each. An abridged account of the test you will find in the *Teachers College Record*, March, 1921. You will find that this test awakens interest in the reading of verse, and tests interestingly the ear and the taste of your pupils.

b. *Prose Appreciation Test* by Herbert A. Carroll, Educational

---

[1] See Appendix G, "Additional Reading Lists."

tests for (1) 7-9; (2) 9-12, 3334 Walnut St., Philadelphia, Pa.

c. 1. *Cooperative Literature Comprehension Test,* 9-12; 2. *Cooperative Literature Acquaintance Test,* 10-12. Addresses: p. 576

d. *Logasa-Wright's Six Tests for Appreciation of Literature,* 9-12, college. Public School Publishing Co., Bloomington, Ill.

e. *National Literature Test,* 6-8. Gregory, C. A., 347 Calhoun. St., Cincinnati 19, Ohio

f. 1. *Barrett-Ryan Literature Test,* 9-12, college; 2. *Davis-Roahen-Schrammel American Literature Test,* Kansas State Teachers College, Bureau of Measurements, Emporia, Kansas [For 1 and 2]

g. 1. *Stanford American Literature Test,* 9-12; 2. *Stanford English Literature Test,* 9-12, Stanford University Press, Stanford, Calif.

Reading and Library Information

a. *Peabody Library Information Test,* 7-9 (See f2 above)

b. Bennett: *Use of Library,* 9-12, college (See f2 above)

c. Ulman-Clark: *Test on Classical References and Allusions,* 7-12, Bureau of Research, State University of Iowa, Iowa City

d. *Jones' Book-a-Day Test,* 7-9, Box 41, Hill City, South Dakota
A check on outside reading, factual not interpretive.

e. *I. Roody's Completion Test,* N.C.T.E., 211 West 68th St., Chicago 21, Ill.

Fictitious problems listed; solutions probable or fantastic to be chosen.

SUGGESTED READINGS

References for Your Own Guidance

1. National Council of Teachers of English: *Reading in an Age of Mass Communication,* William S. Gray, ed., Appleton-Century-Crofts, 1949

If possible, read this book entire; its 108 pages have much to offer you. The chapters are:

I. "The Changing Role of Reading," by Ralph C. Preston

II. "The Enriching Values of Reading," by Louise M. Rosenblatt

III. "Personal Factors Influencing Reading," by Lou La Brant

IV. "Basic Competencies in Efficient Reading," by William S. Gray

V. "Reading and the Art of Interpretation," by Russell B. Thomas

VI. "Distribution of Responsibility for the Reading Program," by Robert C. Pooley

2. *Keeping Reading Programs Abreast of the Times* (Conference on Reading Held at the University of Chicago, 1950) compiled and edited by William S. Gray, *Supplementary Educational Monographs*, No. 72, The University of Chicago Press, 1950

Consult those chapters dealing with junior-senior high-school reading considered in various lights. Of value to you is the list of "New and Timely Books" (pp. 238-42) for upper grades and high school.

3. Rosenblatt, Louise M.: *Literature as Exploration* (A Publication of the Progressive Education Association), Appleton-Century, 1938

This is a book to own and to absorb during your first years of teaching. "Through books, the reader may explore his own nature, become aware of potentialities for thought and feeling within himself, acquire clearer perspective, develop aims and a sense of direction. . . . literature deals with human personalities and human problems."

4. Blayne, Thornton C.: "Validity of Self-Evaluation Charts in Developmental Reading Programs," *Elementary English*, Vol. 26 (1949), pp. 280-81; 292

5. Broening, Angela M.: "Trends in Secondary-School English: Developing Attitudes Favorable to Good Reading," *National Education Association Journal*, Vol. 38 (1949), pp. 666-67

6. Green, Rosemary M.: "The Role of Semantics in a Secondary School Reading Program," *Education*, Vol. 69 (1949), pp. 590-94

Study of semantics profits a serious reader in three ways. "He will understand better what he hears and reads. He will talk and write more effectively. He will think more accurately." (Her quotation is from Walpole's *Semantics*.)

7. McCullough, Constance M., Strang, Ruth M., and Traxler, Arthur E.: *Problems in the Improvement of Reading*, McGraw-Hill, 1946

See Chapter II.

From the *English Journal*

1. Carlsen, George Robert: "Literature and Emotional Maturity," Vol. 38 (1949), pp. 130-38

Read; then reread.

2. Farnsworth, Burton K.: "The Reading Approach to English," Vol. 32 (1943), pp. 435-37

Excellent advice for the harassed teacher.

3. Herzberg, Max J.: "The Teaching of English in the Modern World," Vol. 40 (1951), pp. 86-90

4. Pooley, Robert C.: "Using Periodicals in the English Classroom," Vol. 40 (1951), pp. 266-70

5. Ranous, Charles A.: "A Sample Lesson in Reading," Vol. 34 (1945), pp. 428-34

A discussion of two types of reading: emotional truth and objective and verifiable truth. A distinction between them in the minds of practical students will increase their understanding of literature.

Nonacademic Readers

6. Horst, J. M.: "English in Human Relationships," Vol. 37 (1948), pp. 524-29

7. Robinson, Esther Agnew: "Reclaiming the Slow-Learning Boys and Girls," Vol. 36 (1947), p. 134

Reading for the socially starved.

8. Sprague, Lois: "Non-Fiction Books for Retarded Readers in the Upper Grades," Vol. 28 (1951), pp. 19-34

A book list given.

9. Grey, Lennox: "Radio—A Means, Not an End," Vol. 40 (1951), pp. 144-49

Radio and other mass media are discussed in the first class meetings with a group of nonreaders. A good idea before reading begins.

10. Lutz, Una Dell: "Books for Severely Retarded Junior High School Readers," Vol. 39 (1950), pp. 439-47

A list of 14 sources from which book lists for retarded readers—both junior and senior high school—can be obtained. Be wise and list these sources. Also 150 book titles suitable for junior high school are given.

11. Rickert, Mary O.: "Motivation for Slow Learners," Vol. 38 (1949), pp. 43-44

The plan seems practical, different, successful.

12. Blayne, Thornton C.: "Telescopic Briefs in Building Reading Comprehension," Vol. 34 (1945), pp. 154-56

Advises teaching slow readers from up-to-date magazines.

13. Kinney, Lucien, and Dresden, Katharine, eds.: *Better Learning Through Current Materials*, Stanford University Press, 1949, Chapter III, pp. 39-50

Newspapers used in a ninth-grade remedial reading class, pp. 216.

14. Pilant, Elizabeth: "American Folklore for Remedial Reading," Vol. 40 (1951), pp. 207-08

". . . First requirement for remedial reading material is that it have high interest level and low difficulty rating." Folk tales answer this requirement.

15. Anker, Lieber: "America in the Classroom," Vol. 39 (1950), pp. 447-50

Seventeen books listed (nonfiction) used by a nonacademic ninth grade.

16. Lobdell, Lawrence O.: "A Classic as Reading Material for Retarded Readers," Vol. 39 (1950), pp. 491-96

A simplified version of *A Tale of Two Cities* encouraged confidence. They were reading "regular" pupils' literature.

17. Frogner, Ellen: "Inexpensive Books for the Junior High School," Vol. 39 (1950), pp. 385-87

". . . Books for individual recreational reading" priced from $1.25 to 25 cents. Get acquainted with The Teen Age Book Club (TAB), 7 East 12th Street, New York 3, New York, and the *Scholastic* Book Service at the same address.

18. Gulick, James: "A Method for Organizing Classroom Book Reading," Vol. 39 (1950), pp. 387-90

Note the common sense shown in the type of reports made.

A FEW BOOKS FOR RETARDED READERS[1]

Author	Title	No. of schools reported books enjoyed
Alcott, Louisa M.	Little Women	26
Blackmore, Richard D. (adapted by Jordan, Berglund, Washburne)	Lorna Doone	18
Hough, Emerson	The Covered Wagon	18
James, Will	Smoky	21
Kipling, Rudyard	Captains Courageous	17
London, Jack	Call of the Wild	28
————	White Fang	16
Miller, H. A., and Leary, Bernice, eds.	New Horizons	32

[1] A list compiled by Glenn Meyers Blair, *English Journal,* Vol. 30 (1941), pp. 42-47. Reprinted by permission of the editor. From a long list I have taken only those titles reported by seventeen schools or more as enjoyed by their retarded pupils.

Author	Title	No. of schools reported books enjoyed
Moderow, G., and Sandrus, M. Y., eds.	Six Great Stories	24
Persing, Chester L., and Leary, B., eds.	Adventure Bound	43
—————— eds.	Champions	27
Persky, Louis J.	Adventure in Sport	21
Spyri, Johanna	Heidi	18
Stevenson, Robert Louis	Treasure Island	21
Tarkington, Booth	Seventeen	20
Terhune, Albert Payson	Lad, a Dog	17
Twain, Mark	The Adventures of Tom Sawyer	25
——————	The Adventures of Huckleberry Finn	19
Webster, Jean	Daddy Long Legs	22
Williams, Blanche C.	New Narratives	23

BOOKS SPECIALLY PREPARED FOR PUPILS WITH LOW READING ABILITY

1. Today, simplified classics or abridged classics can be obtained from numerous book companies. For example, Scott, Foresman has published for grades 7-12 but with a fourth or fifth grade vocabulary, the following books: *David Copperfield, Huckleberry Finn, Last of the Mohicans, Lorna Doone, Moby Dick, Silas Marner, Tom Sawyer, Treasure Island, When Washington Danced,* and two books of famous short stories.

2. Strang, Ruth, Burns, Barbara S., and Puls, Helene S.: *Here and There, and Home; Seven Days at Sea,* Teachers College, New York City, 1938. Also simplified.

3. Written to bridge the gap between fiction and informative reading for retarded readers in high school.

"Discovery Series," Harcourt, Brace

New Horizons by Augustus Miller and Bernice Leary

Tenth-grade interest and seventh-grade difficulty

Champions by Chester L. Persing and Bernice E. Leary

Eleventh-grade interest and junior-high-school difficulty

4. *A Tale of Two Cities, Great Expectations,* and *Silas Marner,* abridged, illustrated, and with introduction and notes, Harcourt, Brace, 1950

CHAPTER XIII

The Teaching of Poetry

Do you enjoy poetry, good poetry? If you do not, before you begin teaching, a whole summer's private reading course should await you, a reading and rereading of certain poems and poetic plays until you yourself are ready to adventure pleasurably and with self-confidence into the realms of verse. If you attempt to teach before you are yourself both at home in verse and delighted by it, you are confronted by one of two dangers. You may tramp heavy-shod over lyric and epic and dramatic monologue, extracting "meanings" as if you were prying cockles from their shells. Or, less evil but still wasteful, you may evade all teaching of verse by supplying your classes with numerous anthologies and by urging them to read for themselves, hoping that they may find what has somehow escaped you. A few pupils may make such discovery, but the majority doubtless will be convinced that poetry, with its singsong lines and odd indirection of speech, is not for them. And what have you done? Closed a possible avenue of enjoyment, cut off some twenty or one hundred and twenty human beings from one of the ancient delights—a delight neglected and debased today, yet still for many a vital source of release and comfort.

Many people take literature so much for granted that until they are confronted with the responsibility of leading others into it, they are unaware both of their own quality of appreciation and of the possibilities that literature teaching offers. They are also oftentimes unaware of the difficulties that verse presents to the boy or girl who has not grown up with it as a normal part of his home life. It would be interesting to try a poetry test with the same persons at four, at eight, at twelve, at sixteen, at twenty.

Unless those persons had had excellent schooling, I venture that this would be found true: At four and still at eight they delighted in rhyme and in rhythm. They liked jingles. They responded to nonsense, to whimsy, to pictures and fanciful ideas. They enjoyed stories in verse. They learned easily not only the counting-out rigmaroles, but such friendly verses as those found in *When We Were Very Young*. Then what happened? By sixteen they were "off" poetry, as many a high-school boy has explained impatiently. And at twenty? Some had found their way back, but for the majority an occasional prosy bit of newspaper verse sufficed. It is pathetic and embarrassing to find many a man or woman, otherwise adult and refined, cherishing a platitudinous bit of doggerel which discovers to the reader with rhymed emphasis that home is a good place to be, that Mother is a boy's best friend, or that time cures all ills.

In our twelve years of grade-school and high-school literature teaching, what has happened to kill the child's native delight in verse? Is it possible that "The Children's Hour," "Thanatopsis," "Evangeline," mulled over and "studied," have wearied them? Or that the sledge hammer of rhythm of

> Life is real! life is earnest!
> And the grave is not its goal

has deafened their ears to a more subtle refrain? Might it be true that in both grade and high school, poetry even more than prose has been seized by the would-be moralist as a means of providing instruction? In some classrooms even "The Ancient Mariner" has been mangled to show that boys should not shoot birds.

But there is another reason. In the present age, when moving pictures flash information to our minds or radio pours news into our ears without demanding effort on our part, when picture magazines give us foreign news with a minimum of reading, when even our best magazines carefully break up articles into Parts I,

II, III so that we can grasp their organization with little effort, poetry still makes demands upon the reader. True, one can grasp light or narrative verse at one reading, but just as a symphony demands effort and careful attention, so great poetry rewards us only when we grasp both its obvious and its implied meanings, feel its music of word and line, appreciate its pictures, re-create in our own minds the mood and thought of the poet. Don't expect too much at first. Make clear to your class that a poem is like a potential friend. The boy or girl whom you know through and through in half an hour is hardly the one whom you wish for a lifelong friend. Build slowly. Mingle humor and pathos. Mingle narrative, dramatic monologue, and lyric. *Build slowly, but build.*

I. THE DIFFERENCES BETWEEN PROSE AND POETRY

A. First: The Difference in the Writer's Purpose

You will, of course, lead young pupils (young in their ability to appreciate poetry) into narrative verse for the pleasure that they get from a good story well told. There the purpose of poetry and the purpose of prose narrative are not far apart. But what of the lyric? It is essential that a practical-minded class understand (1) what a poet is about, and (2) *how* his whole purpose differs from that of the prose writer, *before* it reads much poetry aside from narrative verse. With such understanding, pupils avoid the bewilderment, resentment, and dislike of poetry found in many classes. Some teachers begin with an informal discussion of what *prose writers* are attempting to do.

Obviously, prose writers try to tell a story, long or short, as clearly and as impressively as they can; or to present an idea as clearly and as convincingly as they are able; or to amuse us with whimsical thoughts which may, as in some familiar essays, lead us to some serious or semiserious ideas; or to explain a process, an institution, or a situation with clarity and accuracy. Also you and the class will, doubtless, agree that the prose writer attempts, no matter what form he uses, to express his ideas with (1) clarity of thought, (2) logical organization or pattern, (3) imaginative appeal, (4) emotional appeal, and (5) carefully chosen wordings. He may also, depending upon his purpose, use (6) comparison or contrast, (7) symbols rather than factual statements, (8) references from literature, history, contemporary events, (9) implication (as in satire) rather than direct statement.

In the summary, you and the class might agree that his purpose is primarily to *appeal to our minds,* but at the same time in certain forms of prose he desires to *excite our imaginations and our emotions,* and to *please our aesthetic sense* by his pattern and expression.

What is the purpose of such a discussion, a discussion with ample illustration of each type volunteered by your pupils? Many pupils, approaching lyric poetry as they approach prose, find poetry unreasonable, obscure, silly. You have heard pupils protest, "If he wanted to say it, why didn't he say it so people could understand?"[1]

First of all, then, your business is to make sure your pupils realize:

1. that lyric poetry is a reasonable, individual form of art.

2. that the lyric poet is neither striving for the same ends nor desirous of exactly the same reactions from his readers as is the writer of prose. If you glance back at the list of qualities found in prose, you will of course recognize that all of them (plus a more or less regular rhythm) are characteristic of poetry. If that is so, why list them? Because you must make your class realize (particularly if it is somewhat hostile to poetry) that a poet is

---

[1] Unfortunately this rebellious attitude, an attitude of unwillingness to attempt to understand or to grant a poet the right to use his medium as he chooses, is not confined to the young. Many Americans roar at all foreign peoples as if they were deaf; many Americans belittle as absurd or "funny" all music or painting that they cannot understand. And modern poetry they treat with impatience, condescension, or contempt. Don't join the ranks of the ignorant.

not completely different from the "doctor, lawyer, merchant, chief" whom you and they know. Of course you admit that if he is a great poet, he is more philosophical, more sensitive, more imaginative, more keenly aware of beauty, more able to see resemblances, and more at home in the use of figurative language. He has also 'a more musical ear for words and for rhythms, and takes more pleasure in words and phrases. Some teachers, in order to drive home the resemblance between the poet and the members of the class, produce pupils' themes. From them they glean such figurative language as they can find. One pupil may speak of "the pools of gold," meaning the fallen leaves about the poplar trees; another, speaking of a wreck, may mention "the cold breath of fear." In one theme a pupil remarked, "My life is like a jigsaw puzzle, but I can't put the parts together to make sense." Later he also tried to reproduce sound (with no knowledge of the word "onomatopoeia") in the sentence: "All we heard was the PLUNK . . . plunk, plunk, plunk . . . PLUNK . . . plunk, plunk, plunk, of the dying motor."

All of us, you would insist, are for brief moments poets. The poet has, you would add, in abundance what we perhaps have in mere drops or teaspoonfuls. Why labor the point? You are—without apology—pleading the cause of poetry, good poetry, before a practical, hardheaded audience. You hope to deepen and sensitize their emotions, to develop their imaginations, to spiritualize and to a degree ennoble their bread-and-butter attitude toward life, thus opening to them lasting pleasures. (Man, to be man, must walk upright, not on all fours.)

How shall you begin? Probably, first you lure your pupils into enjoyment *after* they have read narrative poems with pleasure— by reading brief lyrics to them which express emotions and experiences familiar to them. Then, second, you must make clear the purpose of lyric poetry, and the difference between that purpose and the purpose of prose.

BRIEF LYRICS FOR CLASS READING AND DISCUSSION

You will notice that the *only* likeness between the poems represented here is their brevity. Do not tire your pupils. Always offer a mixed menu of simple and more difficult poems so that even the slowest or least imaginative pupil has an opportunity to understand and comment.

American Poets [1]

Edna St. Vincent Millay: "Wild Swans," "The Pear Tree," "Departure"

E. E. Cummings: "Chanson Innocent"

Langston Hughes: "Homesick Blues," "Brass Spittoons"

Countee Cullen: "Three Epitaphs"

Edward Rowland Sill: "Opportunity"

Sidney Lanier: "A Ballad of the Trees and the Master"

Lizette Woodworth Reese: "Women"

Bliss Carman: "A Vagabond Song"

George Santayana: "O World, Thou Choosest Not the Better Part"

Richard Hovey: "At the Crossroads," "Love in the Wind"

Edwin Arlington Robinson: "An Old Story," "Richard Cory," "John Gorham," "New England"

Edgar Lee Masters: "Anne Rutledge," "Lucinda Matlock" (from *The Spoon River Anthology*)

Stephen Crane: "The Blades of Grass"

T. A. Daly: "The Song of the Thrush," "Mia Carlotta," "Between Two Loves"

Robert Frost: "The Runaway," "Tree at My Window"

Carl Sandburg: "Chicago," "Fog," "Grass," "Cool Tombs," "Jazz Fantasia," "Losers"

Adelaide Crapsey: "Cinquains"

English Poets [2]

William Davies: "Leisure"

A. E. Housman: "When I Was One and Twenty," "With Rue My Heart Is Laden"

---

[1] The poems marked American are to be found in the Louis Untermeyer anthology *Modern American Poetry*.

[2] The poems listed as English are to be found in the Louis Untermeyer anthology *Modern British Poetry*.

Robert Graves: "It's a Queer Time"
Wilfred Owen: "Greater Love"
John Masefield: "Laugh and Be Merry," "The Tewkesbury Road,"
"Sea Fever"
Rupert Brooke: "The Soldier"

Before considering lyrics—I repeat this statement—you have
led your pupils into reading narrative poems for the interest and
excitement of the story; you have casually enjoyed with them
the rhythm, the pictures, the wordings. Now you are bridging
from that simpler form of narrative verse to lyrics.[1]

In discussing the difference between prose and poetry, you and
your class might reach some such decision as this:

The purpose of poetry is not to *state* the meaning, but to *suggest*
it; not to *tell*, but to *picture;* not to *inform*, but to *lure the reader
to create for himself;* not to *speak,* but to *sing;* not *only to sing,* but
to *awaken song* in the reader.

[1] No other step in the teaching of poetry is more perilous. If you continue
discussion of simple poems too long, you disgust your better students. If you
suggest too difficult verse, you discourage all the class. This transition calls for
understanding, tact, good judgment.

POPULAR NARRATIVE POEMS

Coleridge: "The Ancient Mariner"
Arnold: "Sohrab and Rustum"
Tennyson: "The Revenge"
Browning: "The Pied Piper of Hame-
lin"
Vachel Lindsay: "The Congo," "Gen-
eral William Booth Enters Heaven,"
"A Negro Sermon: Simon Legree,"
"Abraham Lincoln Walks at Mid-
night"
Robert Frost: "Death of the Hired
Man"
Rudyard Kipling: "The Ballad of
East and West"
Amy Lowell: "Evelyn Ray"
John Davidson: "A Ballad of Hell"

SIMPLER VERSE

Bret Harte: "Plain Language from
Truthful James," "Jim"
John Hay: "Jim Bludso"
Oliver Wendell Holmes: "Grandmoth-
er's Story of Bunker-Hill Battle,"
"The Deacon's Masterpiece," "Bal-
lad of the Oysterman," "How the
Old Horse Won the Bet"
Edgar Allan Poe: "The Raven"
The narrative poems in Peters' *Hun-
dred Narrative Poems* or in *Poetry
of the People*

A more practical class might prefer some such classification as this:

Prose	Poetry
Primarily tells; hence it requires greater space.	Primarily pictures; hence it tells much in small space.
Speaks primarily to our heads. Although it also to a *lesser degree* may contain the various appeals of poetry.	Speaks to our heads (through the idea); our hearts (through emotions); our ears (through music); our eyes (through pictures); our bodies (through rhythm).
	More than prose, it can make a total appeal.

Or again, you and your group might prefer to wander into poetry, reading much, before any discussion of the differences between prose and poetry is broached. You must decide and judge your results by the intelligent enjoyment that your group finds in reading excellent poetry. Note that word "excellent." Begin where your pupils can enjoy, but do not continue on the Riley or Eugene Field or Robert Service level longer than is necessary.

See that your pupils both understand and admit as reasonable the difference in purpose which exists in the mind of the writer (1) when he composes a prose story or essay, and (2) when he composes a poem. (Is it necessary to remind you that no one ever learned to swim by avoidance of water or to read by avoidance of books? Surround your pupils with easily accessible verse. A card catalogue is at first a serious barrier.)

How, you may ask, are you to make these various differences between prose and poetry interesting and appealing to the rather stolid members of your group? For you do want your pupils, after their first unconscious response to poetry, to attempt to sensitize themselves to changes in rhythm, pattern, rhyme, general mood evoked by sound and word music. (Note that these qualities make strong physical appeal.) At the same time pupils should strive to grasp, with your aid, *meaning, plan, reference, symbol,* and *implication.* The physical response and the intellectual recognition of the idea must go hand in hand. I have known earnest student-teachers who disgusted their practical, scientific-minded students by lush quotations divorced from meaning, mere bits of figurative and onomatopoetic writing, and thus alienated pupils who might have enjoyed the poets if thought and rhythm and word music had been introduced as one indivisible unit called poetry. Be warned. Start with simple verse in which the idea is evident.

B. Second: The Difference in Form: Rhythm, Rhyme, and Metrical Pattern

The most obvious difference between prose and poetry is the difference in rhythm. It would be wise to discuss rhythm with your class, asking for as many examples as possible: the rhythm recognized in breathing, walking, swimming, marching, dancing, or in a running engine, ocean waves, work songs, heartbeats. Not until the essence of rhythm (the regular recurrence of stress —unstress, stress—unstress, stress—unstress) is perfectly clear even to the most stolid of your pupils is it well to talk of the uses of rhythm in poetry. And even then you must at first use only the most obviously rhythmical measures.

Many pupils are unaware of stress or accent. Try them out. Suggest first the accent in words, their names, perhaps; then take longer words like *Mediterranean* or *institutionalize, complication, companionable.* If a pupil is unable to determine where stress occurs in a word, naturally he is unable to discover it in a line. Build from the foundation. In much the same way you must build from the foundation in teaching rhythm. Many pupils have little sense of rhythm. Others feel it, perhaps, more keenly than you; they respond to every change. They are like musical instruments upon which every poem plays its appropriate accompaniment. But be forewarned. It is of course impossible for a pupil to appreciate and enjoy the rhythm of a poem if he cannot feel the music and actually experience the rhythm. I. A. Richards expresses the idea as follows:

Words in sequence have a form to the mind's ear and the mind's tongue and larnyx, even when silently read. The gulf is wide between a reader who naturally and immediately perceives this form and movement (by a conjunction of sensory, intellectual and emotional sagacity) and another reader who either ignores it or has to build it up laboriously with finger-counting, table-tapping and the rest; and this difference has most far-reaching effects.[1]

Most pupils will recognize the fact (when you suggest it) that their minds are half-occupied by what they read and, at the same time, half-occupied by tomorrow's track meet or today's assembly or yesterday's dance or quarrel or illness. All reading has to fight against this normal preoccupation. But rhythm soothes this busybody, practical element in the mind, putting it to sleep as it were, so that the reader or listener receives the mood or picture or idea of the poem more vividly, more instantly, than he would were the idea given in prose. In other words, rhythm puts the reader or listener in tune with the poem. Here is an example I have often used in my classroom. It is the familiar

> Tramp, tramp, tramp, the boys are marching!
> Cheer up, comrades, they will come.

The class at once recognizes the marching rhythm, the determined, noisy optimism inherent in the rhythm itself. But to make obvious that it is the *rhythm*, not the *idea*, which they feel, I try other words. For example:

> Trip, trip, trip, the fairies enter.

[1] Richards, I. A.: *Practical Criticism*, Harcourt, Brace and Company, p. 14. Printed with permission of the publishers.

At once the elephantine proportions of these fairies raise a smile.
Or try a lullaby such as

> Sleep, sleep, sleep, the babe is resting.

And again the class recognizes that here too the rhythm, itself
a definite entity aiding or marring the idea, would awaken any
normal child.

By some such device, what have you accomplished? You have,
superficially and in part, answered that annoyed but honest high-
school boy who inquires, "Why don't the poets say what they
want to say in prose so you can get it?" But you can go farther,
at first dealing with only the most obvious rhythms. Take, for
example, a real lullaby from *The Jungle Book*. Here, the baby
seal is rocked to sleep in the ocean. Note how the rhythm of the
waves is carried to you in the rhythm of the verse.

> Where billow meets billow, there soft be thy pillow;
> Ah, weary wee flipperling, curl at thy ease!
> The storms shall not wake thee, nor shark overtake thee,
> Asleep in the arms of the slow-swinging seas.[1]

By tactful questions you could lead the class to discover for
themselves that rhyme here aids in marking the rhythm,[2] thus
increasing the musical quality for the reader. Pupils will recognize
that the soft two-syllable rhymes—*billow*—*pillow; wake thee*—
take thee—suggest the flowing rise and fall of ocean waves. Most
pupils easily recognize such rhymes as *ease* and *seas*. They are
more accustomed to end than to internal rhymes, but do not be
misled by your more vocal pupils. In any class you may find
pupils willingly rhyming *come* with *comb, statement* with *comment, progress* with *horses.*

---

[1] This and the next verses are from *The First Jungle Book* by Rudyard Kipling, copyright 1893, 1921, reprinted with permission from Mrs. Kipling and
Doubleday, Doran and Company, Inc., as are the other Kipling verses.

[2] See "rime" in Thrall and Hibbard's *A Handbook to Literature*, Doubleday,
Doran, 1936; and Brooks and Warren's *Understanding Poetry*, Holt, 1938.

After Kipling's lullaby, try the contrast of his "Road Song of the Banderlog" in the same volume. There you get the quick breathless leaps, four at a time, through the leafy boughs of trees, as the monkeys make their heedless way through the jungle.

> Here/ we go/ in a flung/ festoon
> Half/ way up/ to the jeal/ ous moon!
> Don't/ you envy/ our pranc/ ing band?
> Don't/ you wish/ you had ex/ tra hands?
> How/ would you like/ if your tail/ were so—
> Curved/ in the shape/ of a Cup/ id's bow?

Here again, you would point out, rhyme marks the metrical pattern, timing the leaps and pauses in the monkey's progress.

In fact, Kipling's volume of verse will supply you with admirable, obvious examples. Any group of youngsters will respond to his

> You couldn't pack a Broadway half a mile—
> You mustn't leave a fiddle in the damp—[1]

> Loud sang the souls of the jolly, jolly mariners;
> "Plague upon the hurricane that made us furl and flee—[2] "

But there is neither East nor West, Border, nor Breed, nor Birth
When two strong men stand face to face, though they come from the ends of the earth.[3]

The old ballads offer easy comprehension and a simple rhythm.

> High upon highlands and low upon Tay,
> Bonnie George Campbell rode out on a day;
> Saddled and bridled and gallant rode he,
> A plume in his helmet, a sword at his knee.[4]

[1] "The Song of the Banjo."
[2] "The Last Chantey."
[3] "The Ballad of East and West."
[4] "Bonnie George Campbell." In these first steps, avoid oversolemnity. You like light verse; surely from time to time you have chuckled over a limerick, a parody, or some neat, sarcastic turn of words. Share that enjoyment with your class. Consider the poems of Dorothy Parker, the lighter verses of Edna St. Vincent Millay, Oliver Herford, T. A. Daly, Gilbert and Sullivan's songs in

Not all rhythm, of course, will prove so obviously suitable or
so easy of comparison as are the rhythms in these poems. A class,
however, will at once recognize the lightness, the superficiality,
in such tripping lines as

> There's nothing very beautiful and nothing very gay
> About the rush of faces in the town by day,
> But a light tan cow in a pale green mead,
> That is very beautiful, beautiful indeed . . .[1]

They will recognize the change in speed and tone wrought by
vowel sounds in the last line of this poem:

> And better is a temple made of bark and thong
> Than a tall stone temple that may stand too long.

They will feel the striking contrast to this light, running melody
in the sonorous line:

> Glory of warrior, glory of orator, glory of song . . .

the fragile delicacy found in Robinson's "John Gorham":

> You are what it is that over rose-blown gardens
> Makes a pretty flutter for a season in the sun;
> You are what it is that with a mouse, Jane Wayland,
> Catches him and lets him go and eats him up for fun[2] . . .

the neat precision in Pope's couplet:

> Know then thyself, presume not God to scan;
> The proper study of Mankind is Man.

At first strong contrasts are necessary. The noise, excitement,
and high tide of feeling in the march of the Crusaders is obvious in

the various operas (*Pinafore, The Mikado,* etc.), Arthur Guiterman, Edward
Lear, E. A. Robinson's "Miniver Cheevy," or the light French forms as represented by Austin Dobson.

[1] Orrick Johns' "Little Things" from *Asphalt and Other Poems.* Reprinted by
permission of and arrangement with Alfred A. Knopf, Inc.

[2] From Edwin Arlington Robinson, "John Gorham," by permission of The
Macmillan Company, Publishers.

> Strong gongs groaning as the guns boom far,
> Don John of Austria is going to the war [1] . . .

which contrast with Browning's

> Where the quiet-colored end of evening smiles,
>   Miles and miles
> On the solitary pastures where our sheep
>   Half-asleep . . .

or his "Boot and Saddle":

> Boot, saddle, to horse and away!
> Rescue my castle before the hot day
> Brightens to blue from its silvery gray.

Here again the pupils feel the influence of the double rhyme, *smiles—Miles* and *miles*, increasing the dreamy atmosphere of the poem and contrasting sharply with the speed in "Boot and Saddle," emphasized by the three successive end rhymes in three successive lines: *away, day, gray.*

Pupils might be interested to know that a poet may vary his rhythm and rhyme in the different parts of a poem to gain different effects. I use Stephen Vincent Benét's *John Brown's Body* to illustrate this fact. He writes of the simple Northern soldier, Ellyat, in the unrhymed lines:

> . . . Ellyat huddled under the tall tree
> Remembering what he could. He had run for years,
> He had slept for years—and yet it was still not dawn.

This is nicely contrasted with the gallant bravado of the Southern gentleman, a bravado made the more apparent by the use of the three-syllable rhyme:

> He turned to Shepley with his punctilious
> Air of the devil turn supercilious.

[1] Chesterton, G. K., "Lepanto."

For advanced college students, of course, the various rhythms might become the basis of intensive study, but for your beginners in verse it is enough if they feel the rhythm, grasp its use, and try sympathetically to understand the poem.

Is this work technical? Not unless you make it so. Note that feet and names of meters do not enter. Later, if the pupils wish to write verse and to scrutinize their lines for rhythm, names are as necessary perhaps as they are for an intelligent discussion of carburetors, spark plugs, or differentials.

Robert Frost, impatient with the dry dust of some teaching, has said whimsically, "There is only *one* foot in English verse: the iambic—and its variations."

How sensitively aware to changing rhythms are you? It might be wise to consider the poems listed in this chapter, examining them for the rhythm and deciding how you would make rhythm a live and delightful topic in your classroom. How much emphasis you will put upon poetic form will depend somewhat upon your pupils and their interests.[1]

C. Third: Differences in Music—of Word and Line

Are you sensitively aware of assonance and of tone color? Perhaps you can make your pupils more aware of vowel music

[1] Consider the various rhythms in these poems.

AMERICAN POETS

(Selected from Louis Untermeyer, ed., *Modern American Poetry*)

William Rose Benét: "The Horse Thief"

Vachel Lindsay: "The Congo," "The Chinese Nightingale," "A Negro Sermon: Simon Legree"

Robert Frost: "Once by the Pacific," "Two Tramps in Mud Time"

E. A. Robinson: "Luke Havergal," "Richard Cory," "Miniver Cheevy"

Countee Cullen: "Heritage"

ENGLISH POETS

(The first three are found in Louis Untermeyer, ed., *Modern British Poetry*)

Alfred Noyes: "The Barrel-Organ"

James Elroy Flecker: "The War Song of the Saracens"

Robert Graves: "Neglectful Edward"

John Masefield: "The West Wind"

Edith Sitwell: "Aubade"

Algernon Charles Swinburne: "The Garden of Proserpine"

in verse if you liken the poet to an organist who at will sounds the high or low notes of his organ. His melody consists in blending these tones. So the poet plays back and forth on the sharp *i*'s and *e*'s, the gray *a*'s as in *care*, the mellow *a*'s as in *calm*, or the deep *o*'s and *u*'s.

Of course the historic example is Poe's "The Bells." Pupils who know nothing else about poetry can point with pride to "The icy air of night" and contrast it with "Hear the mellow wedding bells," but less spectacular examples of vowel music may elude them. And yet they derive pleasure from discovering that it is the regularity of vowel music which arrests their attention in Tennyson's lines—

> On one side lay the Ocean, and on one
> Lay a great water, and the moon was full—

just as it is the *i* sounds at the beginning and end of each line, contrasting with the quick dip into the mellow *u* and *o* in the center that, in part, render Blake's lines unforgettable—

> Tiger, tiger, burning bright
> In the forests of the night.

And this same vowel play, your pupils will find, makes it imperative to read verse aloud if it is to be fully realized and enjoyed. Much more obvious than vowel music is alliteration; much more subtle is tone color such as one finds in Robert Frost's

> The woods are lovely, dark and deep.

In the same poem we see the use and beauty of repetition, frequent in verse even to the point, as in the old ballads, of becoming a refrain.

> The woods are lovely, dark and deep,
> But I have promises to keep,
> And miles to go before I sleep,
> And miles to go before I sleep.[1]

[1] Reprinted by permission of and arrangement with Henry Holt and Company from Robert Frost's *Collected Poems*.

Remember, that although this is familiar to you, it is not familiar to your high-school pupils. Certainly it is not desirable to make it immediately familiar to them. Build slowly, a little at a time.[1]

D. Fourth: The Difference in the Importance of Word Pictures

In narrative and descriptive prose there is, of course, an abundance of sense impression and often much use of imaginative comparison. Figures of speech—arresting, amusing, provocative—strew the pages of novel or an article. But, true as this fact is, prose is more directly aimed at our common-sense, everyday selves, poetry at our emotional and aesthetic selves. Both appeal to the intellect, but in different ways. Because the beautiful, the aesthetic, has been associated with poetry, you should recognize early that in the minds of many high-school boys poetry is considered effeminate. Hence at first, if your pupils frankly dislike verse you would do well to choose as an entering wedge virile poems, poems of action, of power, of high endeavor. Do you yourself know Neihardt's *Song of Hugh Glass;* Stephen Vincent Benét's *John Brown's Body;* Frank Ernest Hill's *Westward Star;* Alfred Noyes's *Drake* and *Tales of the Mermaid Tavern;* D. G. Rossetti's *The King's Tragedy?*

Aside from rhythm and metrical pattern, perhaps the most important difference between verse and prose is that the poet, in contrast to the prose author, seldom says directly what he means. He awakens, suggests, stimulates the reader's imagination so that the reader will re-create for himself the poet's experience. Make your students aware of the difference. All of them will at once recognize a matter-of-fact quality in the statement "A match was

---

[1] Consider the following poems for the word music:

G. K. Chesterton: "Lepanto"
William Butler Yeats: "The Lake Isle of Innisfree," "Fairy Song" (from *The Land of Heart's Desire*)

Walter de la Mare: "Nod," "Silver," "The Listeners"
Conrad Aiken: "Morning Song from 'Senlin'"

lighted." In the following line they will then see how Browning transforms a prosaic occurrence into poetic form by suggesting the picture, instead of stating the fact:

The blue spurt of a lighted match.

In the same way Walter de la Mare might have remarked that the world was flooded by moonlight, a sensible matter-of-fact comment, but the moonlit world becomes visual to the reader not through prosaic statement but through the series of pictures which the poet conjures up.

Couched in his kennel, like a log,
With paws of silver sleeps the dog.

. . . . .

A harvest mouse goes scampering by
With silver claws and a silver eye.

. . . . .

And moveless fish in the water gleam
By silver reeds in a silver stream.[1]

A poem popular with high-school pupils, and one rich in pictures, is Alfred Noyes's "The Highwayman." Perhaps with older pupils a close second and third are Vachel Lindsay's "The Congo" and Carl Sandburg's "Chicago." All three are rich in picturization, but "The Congo" and "Chicago" show unmistakable modernity. In them is that juxtaposition of fact and imaginative interpretation, ugliness and beauty, lusty strength and vigor of feeling, that makes strong appeal to modern youth. Our pupils live in the twentieth century. Give them much of the idealism and beauty of the past, but keep them aware by means of modern poetry that poets still live, portray, and interpret the life about them.

---

[1] Louis Untermeyer, ed.: *Modern British Poetry,* 4th rev. ed. Reprinted from Walter de la Mare's *Peacock Pie* by permission of and arrangement with Henry Holt and Company.

E. Fifth: The Difference in the Amount of Figurative Language

With your aid, a class soon discovers that many pictures, many comparisons, in poetry are merely implied, demanding of the reader that he sense the resemblance, that he too, like the poet, create from the poet's suggestion a picture or a comparison of his own. This demand on the reader is not, of course, made by the Homeric simile. There the comparison given is rich in detail. Note how little effort is required of the reader by this passage from Arnold's "Sohrab and Rustum":

> As some rich woman, on a winter's morn,
> Eyes through her silken curtains the poor drudge
> Who with numb blacken'd fingers makes her fire—
> At cock-crow, on a starlit winter's morn,
> When the frost flowers the whiten'd window panes—
> And wonders how she lives, and what the thoughts
> Of that poor drudge may be; so Rustum eyed
> The unknown adventurous youth, who from afar
> Came seeking Rustum.

But the majority of poets, you might point out, are less explicit:

> The fog comes
> on little cat feet.

And Carl Sandburg leaves the reader to sense the quietness of both cat and fog.

> Like a small gray
> Coffee-pot,
> Sits the squirrel.
>
> *
>
> Clean as a lady,
> Cool as glass,
> Fresh without fragrance
> The tulip was.[1]

[1] Untermeyer: *Modern British Poetry*, 5th rev. ed. From *Kensington Gardens* by Humbert Wolfe, reprinted by permission from Doubleday, Doran and Company, Inc.

Here in both his poems Humbert Wolfe presents the comparison, but the furry-tailed handle of the coffeepot or the cool elegance of the tulip must be conjured up by the reader himself. Simple as is the picture, you will at first be surprised at how slowly pupils sense what is not told in detail.

Often, however, poets demand more of their reader. Perhaps you recall the lines in "L'Allegro":

> Straight mine eye hath caught new pleasures
>
> .   .   .   .   .
>
> Towers and battlements it sees
> Bosomed high in tufted trees.

And you may remember the quick pleasure it gave you when you realized that "bosomed" suddenly transformed those towers and battlements into regal ladies gazing out above the trees. Personification is, of course, much used in verse, and easily recognized, but many readers miss its more subtle implications. Insofar as they do, they miss one of the pleasures of poetry: exploring in their own minds the many bypaths suggested by the poet.

You and I know that pedagogues, not poets, have catalogued and labeled the various kinds of comparison or imaginative expression, herding them together under the general term "figures of speech." Did you too in your high-school days hunt this fragile quarry, pinning down a living metaphor or a quivering simile in your notebook, satisfied that next day "Teacher" would be convinced that you had "done" your reading? It was busywork, but probably it was worse, for you mutilated the poem. When I began teaching, not knowing how to keep my pupils occupied, I indulged in this questionable sport with vigor and enthusiasm. No simile [1]

---

[1] *Figures of Speech:*

Simile—a direct comparison

Metaphor—an implied comparison

Allegory—an implied comparison extended into a descriptive story

Personification—speaking of some animal or thing as if it were alive

Apostrophe—direct address to a person, or thing, that is absent as if it were present

escaped my eager hunters; every example of metonymy and synecdoche was traced to its lair and dissected before the awed eyes of the class. Poetry study was enjoyed, but the pleasure resembled that gained from a good detective tale. The poet had committed a certain number of figures of speech; we classroom sleuths were on his trail. Sooner or later detection was inevitable. We had zest for the hunt, but we had no appreciation for the poetry. It was some years before common sense came to my rescue, aided by Max Eastman's injunction " 'Figures of Speech' —'metonymy,' 'synecdoche,' and other long-tailed monsters—are what bar the entrance of a simple human into the realm of poetry." [1] If you wish to avoid those errors that, too often, pedagogical human flesh is heir to, you too would do well to consult his *Enjoyment of Poetry,* a book to read, mark, learn, and inwardly digest.

But don't avoid the pleasure and profit arising from vigorous comparisons, comparisons that set the mind racing. You recall the Wife of Bath's love of fine clothes, strolls in the fields, and gay company? It lives again in her lines:

> Thou seydest this, that I was lyk a cat;
> For whoso wold senge a cattes skyn,
> Thanne wolle the cat wel dwellen in his in;
> And if the cattes skyn be slyk and gay,
> She wol nat dwelle in house half a day,
> But forth she wole, er any day be dawed,
> To shewe hir skyn, and goon a-caterwawed.

Anthesis—contrast for effect
Hyperbole—exaggeration for effect
Epigram—a short, witty saying often embodying a truth
Irony—using words to convey a meaning opposite from their apparent meaning
Metonymy—substituting one word for another closely associated with it

There are, of course, other figures, but certainly you would not insist upon your pupils knowing many of them. To confine yourself to the term "figurative language," and to stress the imaginative quality in poetry, leading pupils to see its value, is certainly wiser than to lead pupils into a scientific classification of the various types.

[1] Eastman, Max: *Enjoyment of Poetry,* p. 78.

Katherine Mansfield's quick comparisons I have used, without the key word. "The bathers' hats on the beach were like great ———." Pupils suggest flowers, cabbages, mushrooms, then, finally, shells. Soon they are off into the fascinating realm of figurative language.

F. Sixth: The Difference in the Use of References, Implications, and Symbols

You might point out to your pupils that in reading poetry much of the charm lies both in the suggested pictures—pictures which each reader re-creates in his own brain—and in the subtle references which, suddenly, give new meaning to the lines. About the words he reads flock meanings and memories that enrich the bare statements and fill them with significance. If, for example, a reader knew nothing of Christ's words to Peter, "Verily I say unto thee, That this night, before the cock crow, thou shalt deny me thrice," what could he make of the last lines of Hardy's poem "In the Servants' Quarters"? A man has denied all knowledge of his companion, the criminal who is being questioned in the hall above; then:

> —His face convulses as the morning cock that moment crows,
>   And he droops, and turns, and goes.[1]

Or without knowledge of the Bible story, the reader loses much of the beauty in Keats's lines:

> Perhaps the self-same song that found a path
> Through the sad heart of Ruth, when, sick for home,
> She stood in tears amid the alien corn.

It is also true that the pupil innocent of all information of Greek mythology, to whom the term "lotus" suggests only the drugstore "Lotus Lavender," must make strange reading of Tennyson's

[1] Untermeyer: *Modern British Poetry*.

"The Lotos-Eaters." Matthew Arnold's "Philomel," with its reference to "thy dumb Sister's shame" must seem ultramodern, but a bit scandalous. Shakespeare's choice of Philomel to "Sing our sweetest lullaby" gives no picture to the uninformed. And in Milton's companion poems "L'Allegro" and "Il Penseroso," filled with classical reference (Cerberus, Venus, "Ivy-crowned Bacchus," Vesta, Saturn, "Ida's inmost caves," Cynthia checking her "Dragon Yoke," Hermes) the pupil is either confused and bored or stimulated, his reaction depending upon whether these terms, or many of them, are a pleasant recall of junior-high-school myths or he finds them merely a series of unknown terms added to the poem to "show off" the poet's classical knowledge.[1] It is not only in the older poets that classical reference plays an important part. Your twentieth-century poets, used as they are to airplane and television, yet turn to Ulysses, Icarus, Venus, Narcissus, Medea and Jason. Convince your pupils of that fact.

References and implications, puzzling as they are to the uninitiated, provide the understanding reader of poetry with one of his major pleasures. Give your pupils the pleasure of this sudden shock of recognition. How? By intelligent prevision.[2]

Any normal pupil can get at once the simple comparison:

I have seen old ships like swans asleep . . .

[1] By intelligent foresight the junior-high-school teacher can provide a thoroughly interesting unit on myths. (There is the amusing activity of collecting modern advertisements to illustrate the businessman's use of these myths.) But also she can provide the pupils with a background for the enjoyment of music, art, poetry—in fact, for all reading.

[2] An excellent example of prevision: Time was spent in a class of mixed ancestry upon the American immigrants' contributions to American culture. Later Schauffler's poem "Scum o' the Earth" was read in class. The shock of pleased surprise on the pupils' faces as they understood (actually alone and unaided) the poet's references to and names of artists and musicians and other famous men, was both touching and embarrassing—touching, for the frank, unconcealed pride exhibited in "gettin' the meanin'" without Teacher's help; embarrassing, for its emphasis upon the stupidity of much of our teaching in which adequate prevision is nonexistent.

> The years ride but out from the world
> like courtiers gone to a throne
> That is too far for treaty . . .

calls for far more imaginative grasp. And the following lines
need, for full comprehension, some knowledge of life:

> Familiar as an old mistake
> And futile as regret.

> Tell them ye grieve, for your hearts know today;
> Tell them ye smile, for your eyes know tomorrow.

Any normal pupil can, with proper prevision and some aid
from the teacher, grasp references of a simple type. Most pupils
would, however, be puzzled by Francis Thompson's lines:

> The angels keep their ancient places;
> Turn but a stone, and start a wing!

Far more difficult for the high-school mind (and for the adult
also) is the poets' use of symbol and images.[1]

I see no advantage in distinguishing between *image* and *symbol*
when discussing figurative language with your pupils. Your concern is to make your pupils realize that a second meaning lies
beneath the obvious one which the words convey. For example,
Robert Frost in "Mending Wall" pictures the actual stone wall
so common in New England. But to the foreign child whose
family cannot enter the United States because of filled quotas
and to the political-minded senior advocating "Union Now" the
wall will symbolize different things.

Make clear to your pupils that here, as in many poems, the
interpretation of the image varies with the reader, the creative
reader. However, in Robert Frost's poem "Fire and Ice," the

---

[1] This topic is excellently treated in *Understanding Poetry* by Cleanth
Brooks, Jr., and Robert Penn Warren.

reader has no choice but to accept his symbols: *fire* as *desire* in man; *ice* as man's *hate*.[1]

Another of Frost's poems—I stress them because they have much to offer you and your pupils—"The Road Not Taken," will charm any understanding pupil used to the woods in winter, but the image of the path "no foot had trodden black" leads the reader on to recognize the path as life. Simple? Not for the pupil unaware of symbols and images, but most satisfying to him when he realizes that he *can* understand. Give him often this opportunity to understand, until you build up his self-confidence. From our own reading you and I know that certain things in nature are used over and over again with certain significances. In Tennyson's "Idylls of the King" we recognize the shrouded mystery of man's life before birth and after death in his line

> From the great deep to the great deep he goes.

And Tennyson uses the same image in "Crossing the Bar," while to Arnold in "Dover Beach" the ocean recalls "the sea of faith," now at ebb tide. To Beowulf this "whale's path" was a symbol of the unknown and the fearful, but your pupils, remember, are unaware of these concepts.

In beginning this discussion of symbols I should remind the class, were I you, of our constant use of symbols in newspaper and speech. Trade "follows the flag"; we salute "the Stars and Stripes"; we wonder if "the Rising Sun" or "the Hammer and Sickle" or "the Swastika" will dominate in such and such a country. From some such discussion you can go on and on until your pupils recognize that all of us use figurative language daily. Then and then only are the less imaginative pupils convinced that it is a way in which a poet may "say what he means." You must remember that you are the advocate of poetry, good poetry, but do

---

[1] Frost's amusing satire "Departmental, or the End of My Ant Jerry," provides food for classroom thought and classroom chuckles over rhyme and wording.

not *impose* your ideas; merely make possible for your pupils the understanding and the liking of poetry. If they still do not enjoy it after you have done your best, but grant that other people do—just as some people are nonmusical and some people are color-blind—you have, even so, accomplished something.[1]

Compression, vital to poetic wording, gives keen satisfaction to the adult reader. But to the pupil, that very lack of deliberate expression and that omission of the prose steps (which if over-long we condemn as "pedestrian prose") are again a barrier for them. Thomas Hardy in the poem "In the Time of the Breaking of Nations" gives the whole rhythm of life—birth, work, love, war, passing of dynasties—in the scope of three quatrains. Shakespeare in "Sonnet 29" gives in fourteen lines a penetrating analysis of self-discontent and hopelessness; then the swift up-surge of spirits, the sudden joyous arrogance of happiness—compressing into sonnet form the gist of a novel or drama.

SONNET 29

When in disgrace with fortune and men's eyes
I all alone beweep my outcast state,
And trouble deaf heaven with my bootless cries,
And look upon myself and curse my fate,
Wishing me like to one more rich in hope,
Featur'd like him, like him with friends possess'd,
Desiring this man's art, and that man's scope,
With what I most enjoy contented least;
Yet in these thoughts myself almost despising,

---

[1] Symbols: From "The War Song of the Saracens" by James Elroy Flecker:

"And the Spear was a Desert Physician
    Who could cure not a few of Ambition
And drave not a few to perdition
    With medicine bitter and strong."

From "To the Virgins, to Make Much of Time" by Robert Herrick:

"Gather ye rosebuds while ye may,
    Old Time is still a-flying;
And this same flower that smiles to-day
    To-morrow will be dying."

Haply I think on thee—and then my state,
Like to the lark at break of day arising
From sullen earth, sings hymns at heaven's gate;
    For thy sweet love remembered such wealth brings
    That then I scorn to change my state with kings.

You will have no difficulty in finding numerous examples of compression in the poems which you and the class consider. Remember, just as some people are at a loss to recognize a word from which letters have been deleted (recall the eighteenth-century method of writing, Al-x-nd-r P-p-, or J-hn Sw-ft), so many pupils find compression peculiarly difficult. They have ears and hear not the word or phrase charged with meaning; they have eyes and see not the image which illuminates the passage. Reading aloud, if well done, is often the best method of making clear the meaning, making it clear without that type of discussion which wearies the spirit. They need to have your aid, particularly with cryptic expression or compressed meanings. Often pupils "read all the words" but the whole idea, what is said, what is implied or omitted, escapes them until they hear the poem well read. Stephen Crane's poems, deceptively simple in wording, illustrate the point.

THE WAYFARER

The wayfarer,
Perceiving the pathway to truth,
Was struck by astonishment.
It was thickly grown with weeds.
"Ha," he said,
"I see that no one has passed here
In a long time."
Later he saw that each weed
Was a singular knife.
"Well," he mumbled at last,
"Doubtless there are other roads." [1]

[1] Printed with permission of Alfred A. Knopf, Inc., from Stephen Crane: *Complete Works.*

You must make your pupils realize, in all this consideration of poetry, that the poet (even though he sets to work the moving-picture machine in our heads and awakens whole trains of associations or recollections or emotions) is addressing himself to our brains. He has in every poem that is a poem *an idea* which he is putting before us. Both pupils and poetry suffer at the hands of a teacher who, grasping the idea herself or indifferent to the idea, takes it for granted that the silent pupils share her enthusiasm and understanding—or indifference. Do you need to be convinced that misunderstandings arise?

An intelligent teacher of English confessed to me that in her high-school years she had read but had failed to understand Browning's "My Last Duchess." As nearly as she could remember, this was her impression of the poem:

"There was an Italian Duke, an educated, proper kind of man, who had married beneath him. He wanted his beautiful wife to behave herself. Finally he reprimanded her. Resentful, she grew sullen and unsmiling. Without explanation to the reader, Browning said that the Duke sought a second wife." It was years, the teacher added, before she could think of this poem without remembering her embarrassment in high school. Her remark to me was "I made an ignorant comment about that wretched poem which caused general laughter."

Have you had such an experience? Sometimes misunderstandings arise from the failure to grasp one word or phrase. Note that "my *last* Duchess" and "all smiles stopped together" needed explanation, an explanation that would have saved one pupil unhappiness and a sense of inferiority. But there are other causes for misunderstandings. Often lack of understanding arises because the pupil has no comprehension as to *why* the poem was written. Or misunderstanding may arise because of the pupil's ignorance of the background and beliefs of the period. The embarrassed but determined college student who asked in a Chaucer class, "Was Criseyde a 'good woman'?" exposed her own ignorance of the whole code of chivalric love, but she exposed even more disastrously the instructor's failure to provide adequate background for an intelligent understanding of the poem.

The teaching of poetry is, more than any other form of literature, fraught both with possible danger and with delight. Between the devil of overconscientiousness and the deep sea of ignorance you will have to pick your way carefully. Beware of teaching either too little or too much. Unless your pupils are aware of comparisons and implications, poetry will mean little to them; but unless you lean lightly on any *one* poem, you may ruin for them not only the one poem, but the whole field of poetry, a field that might readily have been for them a lasting source of pleasure. Some teachers believe, apparently, that it is wise to dissect one poem with care and thoroughness, spoiling it, to be sure, but "teaching" it thoroughly, on the theory that then pupils can apply to the enjoyable reading of other verse what they have learned from the sacrificed poem. But your own common sense will convince you that, in the high-school phrase, "picking to pieces" one piece of literature will not be conducive to greater enjoyment of another. And if you are unconvinced that high-school pupils *can* enjoy the reading of poetry, go to Hughes Mearns's *Creative Youth*. There you can glimpse an artist's teaching.

II. CLASS PRESENTATION OF POETRY

So far, all this discussion of poetry has been general. Suppose that you have thirty-five not-too-attentive high-school pupils before you. Your business is to interest them in verse. Your business is to make this group into discriminating readers who can draw pleasure and inspiration—whatever that means—from their reading of poetry. First of all, what difficulties must you foresee and guard against?

It would be wise to turn to I. A. Richards' *Practical Criticism*, pp. 12 to 18, and there discover what types of difficulties and misunderstandings you should foresee. Aware of these, you will be much more explicit, much more comprehending, in your attempt to combine pupils and poetry.

Summarizing these difficulties which confront the pupils and from which you must protect them, I list Mr. Richards's points briefly:

The pupils have difficulties in:

1. Making out the plain sense of the poem—(grasping the meaning)

2. Grasping the sensuous approach (form, rhythm, music)

3. Visualizing the images presented

4. Receiving the correct idea of the poem because of erratic associations arising from personal experiences or emotions (mnemonic irrelevances)

5. Avoiding an automatic response when the poem expresses some idea or emotion about which the reader has ready-made views or responses

6. Giving neither too much (sentimentality) or too little (inhibition) emotional response to a poem

7. Rejecting a poem for the beliefs expressed which are not held by the reader (doctrinal adhesions)

8. Appreciating a poem when it is not written in the form of other poems that the reader has enjoyed or not appreciating it when written in a form previously disliked

It would be wise to consider these eight difficulties. If you do so, you will bridge from your pupils' moods and experiences to the world of the poet much more carefully than if you are ignorant of them.

Suppose that, as was suggested earlier in this chapter, you have talked with your group concerning rhythm and concerning the different musical effects that poets obtain. Now you wish to interest them in some specific poems that will serve as a starting point for their individual reading. It might be wise to recall your own experience with certain poems to see what reactions were aroused and in what order your own liking grew. You will find that even now as an adult you seldom get the full meaning of a great poem at the first reading, just as you seldom sound the depths of a new acquaintance immediately upon introduction. He may have a vast and beautiful soul, but at first you are only aware that his eyebrows are bushy and his smile is pleasant. We like or dislike people at first for trivial things; this fact, too, is true of your meeting with poems. I recall my first introduction to Francis Thompson's *The Hound of Heaven*. I heard it quoted. Immediately I was charmed, not with its symbolism, not with the spiritual beauty of the poet's experience, but with the lilt of those first lines, and the ingeniously lovely use of the word *labyrinthine*. Trivial? Yes, but it was a mere superficial acquaintance. Later I learned of the medieval concept of Christ as a hound pursuing the soul of man. I recalled the lean black-and-white hounds in pictures of St. Dominic, and still later heard the legend of St. Dominic's mother, who the night before her son was born dreamed she had brought forth not a child but a black-and-white dog that, seizing a flaming brand in its mouth, ran through the land, setting the world on fire. All that came later; at first the delight lay in the sound, in the use of two words, and in the picture and echo conjured up in my own mind by *labyrinthine* and *running laughter*. Do you know the poem?

Read these lines several times—

> I fled Him, down the nights and down the days;
>   I fled Him, down the arches of the years;
> I fled Him, down the labyrinthine ways
>   Of my own mind; and in a mist of tears
> I hid from Him, and under running laughter.[1]

What is the purpose of this autobiographical account concerning a poem? Informally, without apparently telling you, I am

[1] Untermeyer: *Modern British Poetry,* 5th rev. ed. Reprinted from *The Hound of Heaven* by Francis Thompson. Copyright 1922 by Dodd, Mead and Company, Inc. Used by permission of the publisher.

letting you know what to expect of *The Hound of Heaven*. I am trying to prevent your turning to it, in case you do not know it, expecting that it is a ballad of adventure or a light song. Also without, I hope, being too stilted, I am trying to share with you my own pleasure. Just some such simple preparation on your part before your class begins a book or poem or play would insure a more sympathetic and understanding approach. This particular poem will tax your comprehension; it, of course, is not for the immature, but the method for high-school freshmen or for seniors is the same. Do you resent so much information before you meet the poem itself? Remember that you are far more at home with literature than are the high-school boys and girls in your classes.

There is another reason for this bridge to a poem. No high-school pupil likes to appear stupid. Many a teacher reads a poem without previous comment. Her purpose is to have the class see and feel as the poet saw and felt. If you recall I. A. Richards's analysis, you realize that one or more of eight different difficulties may arise to distort that poem in the minds of the pupils. The teacher has thrown them this bit of verse. Then she asks how they like it, or what it means to them, or what they see. Suppose that you in a group of your peers have answered honestly and found that you have made an absurd misjudgment. You have tried and failed. Also you have been made a little ridiculous. Have you a friendly feeling toward verse? Many a high-school pupil has been turned from imaginative poetry because of such an experience. In your teaching, remember that painfully few of us adults trained in literature are ready to give a judgment after one reading. When we read a new book, we are, I fear, prone to see what others think, what reviewers say; and we wait to see what changes take place in our own minds after we have had time to consider the book in perspective.

A poem is not a criminal; a class is not a jury. Judgment, final and irrevocable, need not be pronounced at once. Eventually you do want your pupils to know the better from the poorer poems, but be content to build slowly.[1]

In order to illustrate these statements with a poem that is popular among high-school pupils, one might choose Walter de la Mare's "The Listeners." Were you introducing it to a class, what would you do? Something like this, would you not? First, you would practice reading it until you read it well. And for a class you must increase your emotional pressure a little, for there are thirty or forty different individualities to whom you hope to appeal. You must appreciate, too, the necessity of reading slowly, not only so that every *word* is given due value, but also so that the pictures presented and the comparisons made may have time to form themselves in the minds of your hearers. Then you must decide how much or how little to say in order that the class may be attuned to the poem. It is wise—for listening is not always easy—to give pupils some special picture or pattern or phrase to listen for as you read. When it comes to their ears, it comes with the pleasure of the expected.[2]

Before you began to read, probably you would say something like this: 'The Listeners,' by Walter de la Mare, is an odd poem. It doesn't tell you very much as to what has gone before, or why the man in the poem returns. You have as good a right as I to imagine what you like, but I always think of a village deserted after the war, half in ruins probably, and overgrown by grass and ferns. It is moonlight and the Traveler, for some promise made in the past, comes back. As I read, note how the sound of knocking is echoed in the poem itself." (Perhaps as you read you will tap lightly on the desk for the second, eighth, twenty-seventh, and twenty-eighth lines to emphasize the echoed knocking.) You

[1] Look up Hughes Mearns's amusing verse quoted from a high-school pupil, "B.C. (*Before Cliché*), A.D. (After Discovering—'Em)"—*Creative Youth,* Doubleday, Doran, 1925, p. 22.

[2] You will recognize this same sensation at a musicale when, after many unfamiliar numbers, a violinist plays a familiar air and the audience rustles its pleasure.

might add that a contest goes on in the poem between sound and silence and that it is interesting to see which in the end wins.

Many teachers are afraid to *teach* because they are obsessed with the idea that work must not be made too easy for the pupil. But if your purpose is to show a class *how* to enjoy a poem with the expectation that their reading of poetry is not to be confined to this one poem but is to spread over many, then why should you not share enjoyment with them and aid them as much as will prove stimulating to their imaginations and emotions?

The high-school students' prejudice against poetry can be attributed, I believe, to two causes:

1. The teacher's failure to plan a series of unified, interesting units adapted to each individual class's interest and maturity

2. The teacher's failure to provide careful, thorough preparation of each individual class and for each individual unit, so that the pupils know exactly what to expect from the unit. This work should be introduced so that they:

a. Interpret correctly and with enjoyment the "core" (read by all the class) poem in introducing the unit

b. Build from that poem to many others which *without too much effort,* delay, or disappointment they "discover" [1]

c. Receive gratifying encouragement and approval for class contributions

d. Participate actively upon *whatever level of poetry* and with whatever type of activity is possible and appropriate for each pupil (The class I.Q.'s, perhaps, range from 70 to 150. Environments range, perhaps, from gutter to university library. Be certain that you let each shine where and how he can.)

After so dogmatic a statement, it might be wise to illustrate by a series of possible units what teachers can and do plan and carry out. By the term "core" poem, I mean the poem or poems read by all the class which serve as a point of departure, each

---

[1] In mining countries the term "salt a mine" is not unknown. An expert goes forth and "plants" gold, for example, so that the person whom he plans to dupe "discovers" it. Don't dupe your pupils, but "plant" material for them conscientiously.

member of the class working independently to enrich the group unit by contributing his discoveries. In Appendix H you will find several illustrations of poetry units, units adapted to various ages and types of interest. In these various units you will find much material, material that lives, excites, educates, and produces intelligent thinkers and readers of poetry, or material that produces a bored class, sullen or impudent, who refuse to do more than a bare minimum of work in order to escape from you and further boredom. A teacher of English published the frank comments of her pupils, who after a study of lyrics were asked to write honestly on what they thought of the work just completed.[1] Ponder these three statements:

1. "The teacher's presentation made me tired. When left alone to read it, I found much to think about and thoroughly enjoyed it."

2. "It is my contention that the teacher was not very enthusiastic about it and handed it out as if it were a matter of routine."

3. "The teacher tried to impress us too much with her views and meanings. She was too free with her own opinions and not very liberal with the opinions of her class."

Not every adult can appreciate opera, painting, architecture, or even the beauties of nature. Two intelligent but bored travelers returning from one of the grandest mountain prospects in our land remarked: "No use going to the top. Nothing to see but clouds and a bunch of peaks." Poetry—that is, all but light verse or narrative poetry—for some in your class may remain nothing but clouds punctured here and there by an occasional peak of thought. Be prepared for that rather disappointing prospect.

Perhaps, however, you can decrease the number of uninterested readers by motivating the study of poetry through the *idea*—as suggested by the various skeleton units given in Appendix H. You cannot expect a class of practical, busy boys and girls to remain long entranced by the purely aesthetic qualities of poetry.

[1] Rule, Marjorie G.: "Less Lyric Poetry," *English Journal* (High School Edition), Vol. 26 (1937), pp. 389-93. There were also favorable comments.

Supply a strong motive for reading. Cultivate appreciation of rhythm, music, picture, figurative language, but make that appreciation a by-product. You and the class attempt to read poetry for what it says to awaken your minds and emotions, to give you a new or a heightened sense of and understanding of life.

How are you going to get from your pupils a responsive attitude in class when poetry is considered, and a respectful recognition of poetry's right to exist?

Before attempting to answer that question by a few specific examples, I shall list four attributes of procedures on your part that seem essential to successful teaching. In *almost* any group of normal pupils you can secure a responsive attitude from the class toward poetry if you, the teacher, are:

1. Clear, tactful, and patient in building slowly from the simple to the more complex; from narrative poetry to the more easily grasped picture, situation, mood, of the shorter lyrics

2. Constantly alive to the necessity of cultivating in your class a sensible, matter-of-fact recognition that in poetry appreciation, as in learning to play the trombone, some pupils are, naturally, quicker than others, but that slowness in learning to appreciate is no disgrace—if some progress is made

3. Careful to distribute opportunities for active class participation and to encourage reading *on a level* and *on topics suitable* for each individual, and to provide strong motivation for that reading (which must, I again insist, be made easily accessible)

4. Genuinely appreciative of student ideas and student effort as shown by your cordial reception of suggestions, tentative ideas expressed about the poems, or those verses "brought in to read." Some will be banal. All you can do is to lead the pupils gently to something a little better, but no poem should be condemned if a pupil thinks it good until the pupils themselves find fault with it.

The interesting method tried by I. A. Richards of having each student read the same poem daily for several days and then note his changing opinion of it suggests a good way of "trying out" a poem. Many times the easier, cheaper poem attracts at first;

then its charm wanes with each reading. Why not try that method yourself?

A discussion of general attitudes and procedures, although useful, may prove inadequate as a guide without more concrete discussion of specific poems. What shall you do aside from reading a lyric aloud as well as you can and attempting to share with your class your own enjoyment of it?

A. Class Preparation and Presentation of Masefield's "Sea Fever"

Suppose you have a class of landlocked pupils who know neither ocean nor lake. Pictures of ships they know, but their own modes of travel consist of trains, automobiles, perhaps airplanes or even horses. The prairie and mountains are familiar to them. You wish to introduce them to Masefield's "Sea Fever," a favorite, as you observe, from eighth grade on. What would you do?

First, in preparation you would acquaint yourself with Masefield's life. You would also read and reread the poem until you were certain of the total meaning (the meaning of the poem as a whole and the exact meaning and picture of each word and phrase). Then you would read it softly aloud, feeling the desire expressed, seeing the pictures suggested. As you read, you would try to convey that desire and those pictures (the total and the specific meanings) by your voice—its change of pitch, intonation, illumination of certain words. You would, in other words, make Masefield's experience your own. You would prepare to tell it, simply but graphically, in his words to your class.

Second, when your class is assembled you might speak of the out-of-doors, of "wanderlust," of "the call of the open road." You would be certain to draw your class into the discussion. Trains they know, doubtless. You might refer to Miss Millay's "Travel":

> Yet there isn't a train I wouldn't take
> No matter where it's going.

or the lines of Fanny Stearns Davis's "My Self and I":

> O gypsy hearts are many enough
> But gypsy feet are few.

Such restlessness is not confined to Miss Millay, nor to adults only. Or hunting season, fishing season, may have arrived with its lure for every able-bodied boy. The material with which you begin building your bridge from the pupils to the poem, and the illustrations which you use, must depend upon your group.

Third, you would speak of Masefield's restless adventures and of his days on the sea as a boy and young man. (Have you read Miss Armstrong's *Trelawney,* or Conrad's "Youth"?) You would speak of the lure sea life seems, throughout the ages, to have exercised in spite—or because—of its loneliness, dangers, and remoteness from land. The class might compare this life with the lure of lonely expeditions to the pole; expeditions alone into the mountains; the solitude on the prairie at night. You would guide them to the physical thrill of driving in an open car at high speed, or feeling the rush of wind in an open plane. Perhaps some have tried skiing or skating and can speak of the rush of wind, the icy air as it whips past them as they coast down the steep, snow-covered hill. For some, and do not discount this source, motion pictures have provided experiences that life has not as yet offered them.

Fourth, you would read the poem, first suggesting that the way Masefield feels about the sea may recall to each of them some out-of-doors experience (in automobile, train, plane, on horseback, on skates), or may recall some moving-picture hero whose adventures are a bit similar to those of the poet's.

Fifth, after you have read the poem aloud to the class once, you will return to these phrases which need repetition:

the wheel's kick	running tide
a star to guide her by	wind like a whetted knife
flung spray and blown spume	sea gulls' crying
wind's song	long trick's over

(Did you realize how much "illumination" was needed for these pupils far from the sea?) Any of your pupils who drive a car can explain "the wheel's kick," and it would be wise to leave as much explanation to them as you can. To you the feel of a driving rain would be a poor substitute for "flung spray"; perhaps the unexpected sprinkling from a garden hose will serve better? "Spume," perhaps someone will explain, looks like the foam on milk, or like the whitish scum on the top of an irrigation ditch. Does it seem absurd, this translation of the unknown into the known? Any devotee of speed will understand and again feel "wind like a whetted knife," as will also those pupils accustomed to blizzard weather. The picture and the sound of "the sea gulls' crying" and the picture in "the gull's way and the whale's way" probably need mention only.

Then you will read the poem aloud again, so that all may see the pictures. The class is then probably ready to speak of the implication in the last line:

A quiet sleep and a sweet dream when the long trick's over.

It gives some pupil the satisfaction of discovering a meaning behind the words.

Sixth, many teachers, excellent teachers, go no farther. They have "illuminated" a lyric by their introduction, by class discussion, reading, discussion of phrases and pictures, and second reading. Perhaps they are right. But it seems a pity not to lead the class to "discover" (always make such a "discovery" easy) Masefield's "Tewkesbury Road." Here are echoes of their own experiences, easier to grasp because more familiar. Either in fact or through moving pictures most of the pupils will know this gypsying along the highway

Through the gray light drift of the dust in the keen cool rush of the air.

And they, too, have felt

. . . the beat of the rain, and the homey smell of the earth—

even if their excursions are limited to a city park.

They can, even before reading more of Masefield's verse, begin to have some opinions as to the kind of man he is. You will find the pupils producing evidence to show that John Masefield must have a keen eye, much energy, a happy temperament, and pleasure in living. When or if they discover his "Laugh and Be Merry," they feel pleasantly reassured as to their ability to understand poetry, for they can substantiate their opinion by his lines:

The splendid joy of the stars; the joy of the earth . . .

and the final line

Laugh till the game is played; and be you merry, my friends.

Through this search to know the man, you have also guided your pupils into reading poetry filled with figurative language. They must interpret "till the game is played"—a repetition of "till the long trick's over"; and some of them have progressed far, perhaps, when they grasp the line

Guesting awhile in the rooms of a beautiful inn

as meaning man's life on earth.

Seventh, from this point you can build as you like: (1) poems of nature; (2) poems of joy in action; (3) poems of joy in work; (4) poems of the sea; (5) poems of the open road; (6) poems of the common, everyday peoples of the world.

Your pupils might each select one of these paths, band into groups (Do you recall Edith Wharton's comment on women's clubs who sought culture in groups, "afraid to face it alone"?) and go scouting for poems. You would have made that scouting easy, for your library would be provided with a shelf of anthologies and poets' works. After the various pupils had reported to the group, the class as a whole would, perhaps, pass upon these selections. Later the poems, if brief, might be copied for a school-library anthology for either their own library or one in some less-favored school. Or the poems might be listed as a guide for next year's class, or selected poems might form the basis for a program, each group represented by its best reader.

B. Class Preparation and Presentation of Browning's "My Last Duchess"

First, in your own preparation you would acquaint or re-acquaint yourself with the main facts and many interesting details concerning the life of Robert Browning, particularly of his life in Italy. (You and the class are fortunate if you have visited Florence and have firsthand information.) Then you would formulate a little information about the Renaissance spirit, enough to make the Duke's character understandable.

You would make sure that you:

1. Know something of the Renaissance life: its culture, and its cruelty.

2. Know something of Florence, its position as an art center, the art galleries within easy walk of Browning's home, and Browning's deep love for the Italy of the past. (Recall his lines from "De Gustibus":

"Open my heart and you will see
Graved inside of it, 'Italy.' ")

3. Know something of Ferrara, where the poem is placed, and of its famous marble.

4. Have pictures to illustrate graphically the rich interiors—tapestries, wall decorations, carved chairs—of the Renaissance castles, and pictures to illustrate the magnificent clothing of the period. We are prone to forget that children reared in the ugliness of the prairie town or the commercial city, or in the loneliness of a tiny village, find it hard to conceive of leisure, luxury, beauty, or of a mode of living and a set of values utterly alien to their own.

5. Make a study of the poem for every turn of phrase, reading it

aloud in preparation for the class reading, thinking yourself into the cultivated, aristocratic mind of the Duke, visualizing the position of the speaker, of the silent envoy, of the picture of the Duchess, of the stairs which they are to descend, of the bronze sea horse.

Second, for your class presentation you would build your "bridge" according to your class's intelligence, background in history and art, experiences in dramatic monologue and in drama reading. It is probable that your class will consist of a stolid group of average children, plus a sprinkling of imaginative pupils.

1. Probably you would open by a discussion of the dramatic monologue. You would suggest the difference between it and the now familiar soliloquy found in Shakespeare's plays. You would draw from the class statements as to the demands made on the reader by such a form. (The imagined setting, appearance and actions of the speaker, position and probable actions of the listener, interpretation of the speaker from his words only and from his unconscious assumptions.) [1]

2. You would speak briefly of the poem to be read and of the setting, the beauty, culture, artistic heights, reached in the Renaissance. You would explain the term "Fra" (Brother). Why? To keep your movie-trained pupils from suspecting a secret romance.

3. You would then read the poem simply and with the minimum of action—a slight gesture for the withdrawing of the curtain, the position of the picture implied by your raised eyes, the envoy given a position in the same manner, a slight, casual gesture perhaps indicating the bronze sea horse. In other words you certainly would not *act* out a monologue; but just as certainly you would imply or sug-

---

[1] Here once more is an opportunity to discuss briefly that term "assumptions"—the accepted bases from which the Duke reasons—one of the most interesting revelations because of the speaker's unconsciousness of their being questionable. To illustrate the term, you might ask the difference in the way the term "slave" would be said by Julius Caesar and by Abraham Lincoln. The difference in the way "Christian" might be said by an aristocrat of Rome in the year 90 A.D. and in the year 1900. Miss no opportunity to break down the ignorant concept that the pupils' own "home-town" standards are, have always been, and will always be "right" for all inhabitants of the globe. You are both teaching a poem of a different age and broadening your pupils' general education.

gest faintly the probable action of the Duke in order to get before
your class at one reading the way in which you wish them to live
through the monologues to be read later. Your reading would of
course be casual, conversational, as if you were yourself carrying on
the monologue.[1]

4. Then discuss the pupils' questions, questions which in the time
left cannot be—fortunately—fully answered; hence a rereading by
the pupils becomes necessary. Probably they would ask some such
series as: "Why did Browning write it; what was he doing?" "What
happened to the wife?" "Did he kill her?" "Why did he drag in
that sea horse?"

5. The next day, after the pupils have studied the poem thoughtfully, the class discussion should reveal not only the Duke's character and that of the Duchess but also the Renaissance spirit.

Third, after this discussion of the poem, you would probably
lead your class to a rather wide selection of poems in this most
popular form. I prefer to have some few questions, general questions, to guide the reading rather than the more specific questions
for each poem. You would probably read with them a part or
all of "Andrea del Sarto," having copies of some of the artist's
Madonnas and that single picture of his beautiful Lucrezia, the
model for all his Madonnas. "Andrea del Sarto" is not a simple
poem, not so easily understood as "My Last Duchess," but if well
taught these are for many high-school seniors two of the best-
liked and longest-remembered poems in their high-school course.
Why? Because human relations are discussed. Your pupils, both
the good and the poor, are hungry for experience, for authentic
information about life, love, marriage, work, friendships, death.
The better motion pictures provide a source of much vicarious
experience, but in literature, as the pupils may eventually realize,
the individual character and the interrelation of characters are
often analyzed more subtly and interpreted by a skillful writer
with more wisdom and philosophy than is possible in a film. Re-

---

[1] Few errors in judgment meet with greater dislike or contempt on the part
of practical high-school pupils than does the teacher's error in overdramatizing
any class presentation. Interest your group; never embarrass them.

member, particularly with juniors and seniors, that this avid curiosity about life exists—carefully hidden from you until you introduce for impersonal discussion some problems in life relationships—these natural hungers, ambitions, repulsions, mixtures of good and evil. By the heightened interest in the class, by a new tension which you can feel, you realize that you have hit upon a topic of vital importance in the lives of your group.

Fourth, you might provide your class with some such mimeographed list of poems as the one given below, poems made clear and inviting. You would be careful to mark the most difficult— a warning to the easily discouraged reader, a challenge to your better students. You would see that simple and difficult alike were discussed, either in groups, or in conference, or in class. Some of your readers, although in the senior class, read at freshman level; some read as well as or better than you. (You recall the old saying "Milk for babes and meat for strong men"?) Provide for both types and encourage both.

POETRY

Revelation of Character and of Human Relationships as Shown in Monologue, Dialogue, or the Dramatic Lyric

(Poems marked * are difficult reading.) [1]

Note: Ask yourself after each of these poems that you read:

1. Why was the poem written?
2. What is the character revealed by the speaker? How is it revealed: in words? in assumptions? in omissions? in implications?
3. Does it reveal an age also—as in "My Last Duchess"?
4. What life problem is discussed?
5. Which problems are applicable to the present world?

---

[1] The starred poems might not be appropriate for certain schools and for certain communities. Unless, for example, you can make your pupils conscious of the historical reasons for the worldly lives of many Renaissance priests—priests made priests for political reason by some worldly-minded ruler, or forced by poverty into holy orders—it would be wise to omit "The Bishop Orders His Tomb." Aid from the art department or from some pupil interested in art would add interest to the discussion of "Fra Lippo Lippi."

Author	Title	Comment
Robert Browning	"My Last Duchess"	A Renaissance husband discusses his late wife as he displays her picture while arranging for his next marriage.

Robert Browning ... "Andrea del Sarto" .. The "faultless painter,"
held by a beautiful but
Ah, but a man's reach should exceed his brainless woman, dreams
grasp, of rivaling Raphael—
Or what's a heaven for? were he free. A delicate
analysis of conflicting
passion and ambition.

* Robert Browning .. "The Bishop Orders
His Tomb" ...... Of this poem Ruskin says:
"I know no other piece of
One block, pure green as a pistachio-nut, modern English prose or
There's plenty jasper somewhere in the poetry in which there is
world— so much told . . . of the
And have I not Saint Praxed's ear to pray Renaissance spirit . . .
Horses for ye, and brown Greek manu- its worldliness, inconsist-
scripts . . . ency, pride, hypocrisy, ig-
norance of self, love of
art, of luxury and good
Latin."

* Robert Browning .. "Fra Lippo Lippi" .. The Renaissance worldly
painter, modern in his art,
(Said sarcastically) whom chance and poverty
placed in a monastery.
A fine way to paint soul, by painting body (See the bulletin board
So ill, the eye can't stop there, must go for a picture of Fra Lip-
further pi's worldly face in his
And can't fare worse. own painting surrounded
by angels before the Ma-
donna.)

* Robert Browning .. "Saul" .... A difficult poem, but rewarding. David, the He-
brew harpist, tells of his
playing before Saul, the

Author	Title	Comment

How good is man's life, the mere living!
How fit to employ
All the heart and the soul and the senses forever in joy.

King, in an attempt to lure him from melancholia by awakening, step by step, his desire to live and act. Tracing the appeals made from physical, to mental, to spiritual desires shows you David's skill and knowledge.

Robert Browning . . . "Count Gismond" . .

. . . The lie was dead,
And damned, and truth stood up instead.

A story told by the woman (whom slander had wronged) of the steadfast goodness of her protector, Count Gismond.

* Robert Browning . . "Mr. Sludge, 'the Medium'" . . . . . .

We find great things are made of little things,
And little things go lessening till at last Comes God behind them.

Mr. Sludge reveals his own mind, the mind of a charlatan, but he makes a good case for his deception when denounced for his trickery.

* Robert Browning . . "Soliloquy of the Spanish Cloister" . .

If hate killed man, Brother Lawrence,
God's blood, would not mine kill you!

A charlatan, clothed as a pious monk, reveals his petty meannesses while the reader sees beneath his spiteful picture of the brother whom he hates the speaker's real character.

Edwin Arlington
Robinson . . . . "John Gorham" . . . .

And I dare say all this moonlight lying round us might as well
Fall for nothing on the shards of broken urns that are forgotten
As on two that have no longer much of anything to tell.

The last meeting of lovers where the man, wearied by the flirtations of his companion, speaks his mind.

Author	*Title*	*Comment*
Edwin Arlington Robinson	"How Annandale Went Out"	Before a jury, a doctor explains why he ended his friend's suffering (showing his hypodermic needle). It is a brief example of Robinson's cryptic style.

A wreck, with hell between him and the
end,
Remained of Annandale; and I was there.

* Edwin Arlington
Robinson ...... "Ben Jonson Entertains a Man from
Stratford" .... A discussion of Shakespeare, the house-building
citizen and genius, by
Ben, the poet. A long
but beautiful analysis of
Shakespeare's mind and
moods.

It's all a world where bugs and emperors
Go singularly back to the same dust
    Each in his time.

Robert Frost ...... "Two Witches: The
Witch of Coos".... A ghost story in which
the murdered man's bones
wander restlessly from
cellar to attic. Told by
an old countrywoman.

Summoning spirits isn't
    "Button, button,
Whose got the button," I would have
    them know.

Robert Frost ...... "The Death of the
Hired Man" ..... Here five characters
emerge from the discus-
sion of wife and hus-
band: the secure wife and
husband, the hired man,
the young college boy
who liked Latin, and the
hired man's brother. Note
the nature touches which
tell much of both the
woman and of Robert
Frost.

Home is a place where, when you have
    to go there
They have to take you in.

Author	*Title*	*Comment*
Robert Frost	"The Code"	An amusing revelation of the touchy pride and sturdy self-respect of a New England farm hand.

The hand that knows his business won't be told
To do work better or faster—these two things.

| Robert Frost | "The Fear" | A woman's fear (the reason for that fear implies a past life of which we are told little) that she is being spied on by some man sent to watch her. Her mind and the calm mind of the stranger are briefly revealed. |

. . . Every child should have the memory
Of at least one long-after-bedtime walk.

| Robert Frost | "Snow" | An account of the itinerant preacher's brief stop in a snowstorm, and the fear, annoyance, and relief it provoked. An excellent revelation of two types of people. (This poem has also been used, slightly altered by cuttings, as a one-act play.) |

You can't get too much winter in the winter.

Notice how completely all of these poems of Robert Frost's echo the rhythm of speech.

| Matthew Arnold | "The Deserted Merman" | This old legend tells of the mortal who married a merman and lived under the sea until the Easter church bells called her back to the earth. |

Where great whales go sailing by,
Sail and sail, with unshut eye
Round the world for ever and aye.

Author	*Title*	*Comment*
Lady Anne Lindsay Barnard	"Auld Robin Gray"	A poor Scottish girl in love with a sailor tells her tragedy, for she was persuaded to desert her lover and marry in order to support her old parents.

They gi'ed him my hand, tho' my heart was in the sea;
Sae auld Robin Gray he was guidman to me.

Austin Dobson	" 'Good-night, Babette' "	A tired old man remembers, forgets, and drops off to sleep. Given in light, delicate verse.

Thomas Augustine Daly	"Mia Carlotta" and "Between Two Loves"	These are Italian dialect poems, brief bits revealing the tenderness, amusement, and pride of the Italian immigrant.

Giuseppe, de barber, he maka da eye
An' lika da steam engine puffa an' sigh
For catcha Carlotta w'en she ees go by.

You will note that in this list are many poems seldom found in the average high-school text. No pupil ever developed the habit of wide, discriminating reading by single poems scattered through a text. Pupils must *read* in order to develop skill in reading. Open to them the world of literature, old and new. If they read only the old, they have rare material, but they are prone to forget that literature is today a living force.

You may be successful in making your pupils recognize your interest in their opinions of long-accepted poems, but unless they are unusually naïve they are aware of the fact that Milton, Keats, Wordsworth, and Shelley are discussed at length in every history of English literature and discussed not by high-school students but by adequate critics. The great advantage of using modern literature and of combining it with older writings lies in the greater freedom felt by students, particularly by better students. Then, too, the world changed in 1914. It is changing rapidly in 1943. Your pupils like to feel that they are, in part at least, reading those poets who are attempting to interpret the present world. And your pleasure and their profit will arise in part out of your so combining old and recent literature that your pupils realize at last the *sameness* of man and of human emotion from age to age.[1] The teaching of poetry to young Americans is challenging, calls for "all that a man has of fortitude and delicacy," but is richly rewarding.

One resource—aside from radio readings of poetry and poetic drama—which adds much to the successful teaching of poetry appreciation is the series of victrola records prepared from readings by living poets. When a class actually hears Robert Frost himself read his own poetry or hears Archibald MacLeish give part of one of his poetic plays, the pupil knows that poetry *is* a living thing, a thing of interest to thousands of adults. If it is possible, know and use these recordings. Then there are the records prepared by the National Council of Teachers of English, produced by the Columbia Recording Corporation.[2] Even if you cannot afford to get them for your first school, it would be wise to file away a record of them.[3]

SUGGESTED EXERCISES

Before you attempt any of these exercises it would be wise to read as many as you can of the listed references. Be certain that you read these two: Brooks and Warren: *Understanding Poetry* and Reed Smith: *The Teaching of Literature*. Both books discuss poetry teaching and will supply you with numerous illustrations. Reed Smith

[1] Examples of older and modern poetry: Wordsworth: "Daffodils" and Lizette Woodworth Reese: "Daffodila"; Keats: "Ode to a Nightingale" and Harold Munro: "The Nightingale Near the House"; Walt Whitman's and Vachel Lindsay's poems on Lincoln.

[2] Album No. I is entitled *The Appreciation of Poetry*. Here are six ten-inch records, twenty-nine poems, read by Norman Corwin, radio author and producer. A teachers' manual is included in the price of the album. More of these albums will be announced in the *English Journal*.

[3] More detailed information is given in Chapter XIV on radio, phonograph records, recording, and films.

gives an outline or a précis for many of the old favorites to be found in every high-school course. Both books ought to be familiar to you. From Mrs. Wilkinson's *New Voices* you will find many possible reading assignments for your high-school pupils; the book is eminently readable.

1. From your reading of poetry bring to class ten illustrations of well-used: (a) symbols, (b) onomatopoeia, (c) assonance, (d) alliteration, (e) comparison—simile or metaphor, (f) phrases that in themselves you would term particularly poetic.[1]

2. Test your own ability to interpret poetry. Select one of the following.[2] Exactly how would you interpret to a questioning high-school senior? (a) Hagedorn, Hermann: "Doors"; (b) Millay, Edna St. Vincent: "Euclid Alone Has Looked on Beauty Bare"; (c) Dickinson, Emily: "I Like to See It Lap the Miles"; (d) Brooke, Rupert: "The Hill."

3. Select one of the following poems; prepare to present it in class. Be able to read it in part or entire so that it is not only clearly understandable to your audience but also an enjoyable experience for them. Your ten-minute class presentation should include: (a) a "bridge" from the class to the poem; (b) a reading of significant parts; (c) a brief discussion; (d) an appropriate assignment for the next day.

It is wise to remember that your "bridge" should never distract but should concentrate interest and attention upon the poem; hence a discussion of the author may or may not be appropriate. Do not waste time nor exceed the allotted ten minutes:

a. Shelley, Percy Bysshe: "The Cloud"

b. Untermeyer, Louis: "Caliban in the Coal Mines"

c. Lowell, Amy: "Patterns"[3]

d. Hodgson, Ralph: "The Bull" or "Eve"

e. Hardy, Thomas: "In Time of the Breaking of Nations"

f. Auslander, Joseph: "Ulysses in Autumn"

[1] Have you ever taken the test prepared by Allan Abbott and M. R. Trabue called *Exercises in Judging Poetry,* Teachers College, New York City? There are two forms, *X* and *Y.* You would find the test an admirable way of arousing interest in your high-school classes and of showing pupils their ability in reading verse. It can be given orally if you have not money enough for individual copies.

[2] See Untermeyer: *Modern American Poetry* and *Modern British Poetry.*

[3] See *New Voices* for suggestions.

g. Sassoon, Siegfried: "The Dugout" and "Every One Sang" (written in 1918)

h. Brooke, Rupert: "The Great Lover"

i. Owen, Wilfred: "Dulce et Decorum Est"

j. Lindsay, Vachel: "The Chinese Nightingale"

k. Aiken, Conrad: "Morning Song from 'Senlin'"

l. Tennyson, Alfred: "Ulysses"

m. Robinson, E. A.: "Ben Jonson Entertains a Man from Stratford"

n. Frost, Robert: "Death of the Hired Man"

4. Select a poem suitable for study in junior or senior high school. It might have for its main interest the woods, home, exercise, animal life, social conditions, heroism, adventure—anything that you yourself enjoy and can present interestingly. About this poem group as much related prose and verse as you can. Add pictures and music if possible. Build up enough material to make a thoroughly profitable week or two-week exploration for a high-school class. If the different members of your college class work on this project and then pool their findings, you could begin your teaching with a wealth of interesting suitable material.

5. After you have consulted "Mounting Pegasus" by Mildred Wright (*English Journal*, Vol. 25 (1936), pp. 376-81), divide your college class according to the topics listed, have each group investigate the poems named, and then have each member submit a bit of original verse. How accurate is your ear? How aware are you of the demands poetry teaching will make on your own creative ability?

6. If you have the opportunity, read the chapter on poetry in *Junior Book One* of the Canby, Carter, Miller series called *High School English*, Macmillan, 1936. Then compare it with the poetry section in Book One of the Cook, Norvell, McCall series called *Hidden Treasures in Literature*, Harcourt, Brace, 1935. Both books are intended for the seventh grade. When you have examined the two, plan a three-day program in which you introduce the study of poetry to a seventh-grade group. (If you feel uncertain as to the maturity of seventh-grade pupils, attempt to meet some children. No teacher would object to your visiting her classes, particularly if you explained your reason for coming.)

7. Below are listed those poems usually found in any high-school course. You would find it most advantageous to divide your class, each member taking one of these poems. For each poem a member

of your class would: (a) write a brief "bridge" to the poem; (b) write a brief précis or outline; (c) list obscure words, lines, or references with suggested explanation or comparison well within the high-school pupil's experience; (d) list illustrative material (giving its sources so that you, too, can find it readily for: (1) the author, (2) the poem, (3) pictures and music if appropriate, (4) other poems or prose writings to be used in connection with the "core" poem.

This material should be mimeographed and should become the property of each member of the class. Do you realize how invaluable such a collection could become?

a. Lowell: "The Vision of Sir Launfal"
b. Tennyson: "Ulysses"
c. Milton: "Il Penseroso"
d. Milton: "L'Allegro"
e. Bryant: "Thanatopsis"
f. Tennyson: "Gareth and Lynette"
g. Tennyson: "The Passing of Arthur"
h. Tennyson: "Launcelot and Elaine"
i. Shelley: "The Cloud"
j. Shelley: "To a Skylark"; "To the West Wind"
k. Wordsworth: "Tintern Abbey"
l. Coleridge: "The Rime of the Ancient Mariner"
m. Keats: "The Eve of St. Agnes"
n. Arnold: "Sohrab and Rustum"
o. Burns: "Tam O'Shanter"
p. Gray: "Elegy Written in a Country Churchyard"
q. Markham: "Lincoln, The Man of the People"
r. Markham: "The Man with the Hoe"
s. Wordsworth: "Earth Hath Not Anything to Show More Fair"; "The World is Too Much with Us"; "The Solitary Reaper"
t. Holmes: "Old Ironsides"; "Grandmother's Story of Bunker-Hill Battle"
u. Whittier: "Snow-Bound"
v. Longfellow: "The Courtship of Miles Standish"

8. Devise a unit on modern inventions as a topic for poetry. You might begin with Emily Dickinson's "I Like to See It Lap the Miles," Percy MacKaye's "The Automobile," Robert Frost's "The Egg and the Machine," and some of the numerous airplane poems, including those of Frank Ernest Hill's in his volume *Stone Dust,* Longmans, Green, 1928. The last section of *The Winged Horse* (Hill and Joseph Auslander) might also aid you.

SUGGESTED READINGS
References for Your Own Guidance

The English Language Arts, Vol. I, N.C.T.E. Curriculum Series, Dora V. Smith, Director

Reconsider your reading of Part I, Chapter 1, "The Purpose of Teaching the Language Arts," and Chapter 2, "The Language Arts and the Growth of Young People." What type of development in pupils does well-taught poetry foster?

1. Richards, I. A.: *Practical Criticism*, Harcourt, Brace, 1927

Read at least the introduction without fail, and Part IV, the Summary.

2. Eastman, Max: *Enjoyment of Poetry*, Scribner, 1921

You will find all of this book worth your careful consideration.

3. Wilkinson, Marguerite: *New Voices*, Macmillan, 1921

Consider the first four divisions of the book: "The Pattern of a Poem," "Organic Rhythm," "Images and Symbols," and "The Diction of Contemporary Poetry." A good library reference for students.

4. Auslander, Joseph, and Hill, Frank Ernest: *The Winged Horse*, Doubleday, Doran, 1927

This is a simple, readable account of poetry and poets by two men who are themselves poets. Library reference.

5. Harrison, Joseph B.: "Poetry and the Lay Reader," *Pacific Spectator*, Vol. 5 (1951), pp. 16-27

Modern verse seen through the eyes of a layman. Tone humorous but intent serious.

6. Viereck, Peter: "Parnassus Divided," *Atlantic Monthly*, Vol. 184 (1949), pp. 67-70

7. Boas, Ralph, and Smith, Edwin: *Enjoyment of Literature*, Harcourt, Brace, 1934, pp. 1-176

Make thoughtful enjoyment of poetry your objective.

8. Ciardi, John, ed.: *Mid-Century American Poets*, Twayne Publishers, New York, 1950

An enlightening discussion of the work of thirteen poets not recognized before 1910, in which each explains his own ideas about poetry as illustrated by his poems in this anthology. The editor discusses in his "Foreword," "What does it take to read a poem?" and "What is modern poetry?"

9. Brooks, Cleanth, Jr., and Warren, Robert Penn: *Understanding Poetry*, Holt, 1931

Here two modern writers discuss poetry in the terms of the "under-standing" necessary in order to grasp and enjoy it. *Read.*

10. Buchanan, Walter: "The Nature of Rhythmic Talent," *Pacific Spectator*, Vol. 5 (1951), pp. 16-27.

A highly readable analysis of the development of a sense of rhythm.

11. *Saturday Review of Literature*, Vol. 26 (March 27, 1943)

The whole issue is devoted to the memory of Stephen Vincent Benét.

12. Ciardi, John: "What Does It Take to Enjoy a Poem?" *Saturday Review of Literature*, Vol. 32 (Dec. 10, 1949), pp. 7-8.

From the *English Journal*

A General Discussion of Poetry

1. Engle, Paul: "Poetry in a Machine Age," Vol. 26 (1937), pp. 429-39

If you are more familiar with Wordsworth than with T. S. Eliot or Stephen Vincent Benét, read this article.

2. Manicoff, Rose: "The Effects of Extensive Teacher Reading of Poetry," Vol. 28 (1939), pp. 50-56

3. Breymer, Marjorie: "The Sound of the Seas," Vol. 40 (1951), pp. 192-97

A report on the results of teaching a high-school class to read poetry.

4. Endres, Mardie Weatherby: "Poetry in the Junior High School," Vol. 39 (1950), pp. 505-08.

Deals both with poetry presented to class and verse written by students. Suggests kinds of poems with which to begin in a class where many are prejudiced against poetry.

5. Rule, Marjorie G.: "Less Lyric Poetry," Vol. 26 (1937), pp. 389-93

Here you find the basis for much of the practical-minded pupils' dislike of English. Do you see a different possible conclusion? Consider Hugh Mearns's *Creative Youth.* (This article was quoted in part in the text.)

6. Warren, James E., Jr.: "Two Creative Approaches to Lyric Poetry," Vol. 37 (1948), pp. 415-21

7. Jacobs, Leland B.: "Millay's Poetry for the Junior High School," Vol. 26 (1937), pp. 745-48

The poems here listed will convince you that some nineteen or more are not only suitable but most pleasurable for a junior-high-school group.

8. Szekler, Juliet M.: "Timeliness in Literature," Vol. 23 (1934), pp. 849-50

Urges study of such writers as Milton and Blake, Milton and Swift. The class points out inevitable comparisons with economic conditions of today.

9. Wheeler, Paul Mowbray: "Comparing Poems on Like Topics," Vol. 40 (1951), pp. 154-61

The article with its illustrations plus its list of twenty-five desirable comparisons should prove useful.

10. Oxley, Chester Jay (Mrs.): "Lyrics to the Teen-Agers," Vol. 36 (1947), pp. 197-99

"Lyrics" not "poetry" have popular appeal.

11. Wright, Mildred: "Creative Writing of Freshmen," Vol. 19 (1930), pp. 297-301

Poetry reading and the writing of verse.

12. Stewart, Annarrah Lee: "Freedom with Direction," Vol. 19 (1930), pp. 357-63

An experiment in verse writing.

13. Partridge, Ruth: "Students Discover Universal Themes in Poetry," Vol. 36 (1947), pp. 99-200

Looking at yesterday and today.

14. Fenn, Henry Courtenay: "The Tavern Idea in English," Vol. 21 (1932), pp. 378-84

Mermaid Inn Club instead of English class—began with Chaucer at the Tabard Inn and surveyed English literature from inns and coffeehouses.

15. Carpenter, Robert H.: "A Unit in Poetry," Vol. 21 (1932), pp. 744-48

American literature (eleventh grade) began with Lindsay and rhythm; Robinson and rhyme schemes next; then poems about war.

16. McGraw, H. Ward: "Teaching for Appreciation: A Suggested Procedure for the Eleventh and Twelfth Years," Vol. 19 (1930), pp. 44-48

Poems two writers read; for example, Guest and Nichols. Difference between good and poor poetry discovered.

17. Ciardi, John: "Poets and Prizes," Vol. 39 (1950), pp. 545-52

Lists of Pulitzer Prize winners, and discussion of the basic difference between the older and the more recent poets.

18. Le May, Elizabeth: "Teaching the Romantic Poets by Way of the Contemporary," Vol. 23 (1934), pp. 558-67

Rupert Brooke, Edna St. Vincent Millay, Bliss Carman, etc., read in conjunction with romantic poets and compared with them. Try 1950 poets also.

19. Pettigrew, Ruth: "Ballads—Old and New," Vol. 27 (1938), pp. 746-50

20. Malm, Marguerite: "No Post-Mortems," Vol. 26 (1937), pp. 654-56

Note here the pleasant method of "bridging" to a poem. Read, and list the seven steps suggested.

21. Parks, Carrie Belle: "Poems for Any Fine Day," Vol. 18 (1929), pp. 653-58

A list of poems for the "would-be truants" in class, with a description of methods of presenting the poems.

22. Campbell, Marian Wendeln: "Teaching *The Lady of the Lake* Creatively," Vol. 20 (1931), pp. 139-44

The teacher makes this poem a delight or anathema to the pupils. Beware!

23. Enos, Bertram: "Odysseus' Latest Adventure," Vol. 19 (1930), pp. 141-47

Mimeographed copy in manuscript form used as introduction to the epic. Handwork and reading of associated poems (list).

24. McCracken, Fern: "For the Sake of Poetry," Vol. 30 (1941), pp. 224-30

Be sure to read this article. It is a wise and amusing approach to real poetic appreciation.

25. Deutsch, Babette: "Poetry for the People," Vol. 26 (1937), pp. 265-74

Here you will find an understanding discussion of Carl Sandburg's "The People, Yes," a poem that appeals to modern youth.

26. Smith, Mary Elinore: "City Poems for Ninth and Tenth Grades," Vol. 21 (1932), pp. 716-25

27. Bashefkin, Sara S.: "Teaching Poetry by Contagion," Vol. 24 (1935), pp. 21-27

Approach to poetry for "young hoodlums."

Poetry Reading Combined with Other Activities

1. "Criticizing Our Pupils' Poems," Vol. 22 (1933), pp. 392-98

2. Messenger, Ruth: "The Art to Praise," Vol. 22 (1933), pp. 662-66

3. Shaw, Charles E.: "Usable Musical Settings," Vol. 20 (1931), pp. 508-09

4. Anderson, Harold A.: "Literary Recitals in the Secondary School," Vol. 23 (1934), pp. 119-26

CHAPTER XIV

The Teaching of Drama

WHEN you advance upon a play, whether it is with your freshmen or with your seniors, one obvious word of warning will be appropriate. *Remember that a play is a play.* It is not a reading exercise; it is not a study of characterization; it is not a geometric puzzle to be worked out upon the Freytag design showing preliminary exposition, inciting forces, rising action, climax, falling action, and denouement. It is a *play* demanding actors, the human voice, and audience. And, too, it is a form of literature far more difficult for high-school pupils to grasp than is any other form that you attempt with them. But although it is the most difficult, you will find that it can be one of the most satisfying and educational.

I. RECOGNIZING THE PUPILS' DIFFICULTIES IN DRAMA READING

Why is it difficult? Wipe from your mind all memory of expectant audiences, an orchestra, the curtain's rise, the lighted stage, and actors to whose voices you respond emotionally much as a piano responds under the fingers of a skilled player. Then look at the list of characters printed in formidable array before the beginning of the drama. You see that someone is the son of someone else; you dutifully read through the ten or twenty names. But you cannot remember all of them. Then, unless the play is by Shaw or Barrie, you are confronted by "Act I" and the illuminating comment "A baronial hall" or "A library." After that brief statement come bewildering *L's* and *R's* and numerous exits. Then comes a name, and a speech, another name and another speech, and so on for pages, interrupted occasionally by

436

"Exit" or "Enter" or a direction in brackets such as *excitedly,
jokingly, proudly,* or *his voice sounding above the hubbub.*

Do you see the difficulty? If you read plays well, *you* imaginatively supply all the glamour of the theater. You build from the
sketched *L's* and *R's* a library that forms an appropriate background for the actors who possess it; you also supply face and
form and personality to the names and words as you read. Mrs.
Maurrant and Mrs. Jones in *Street Scene* are not only easily dis-
tinguishable to you, but are distinct human beings, made, probably, if you have not the moving-picture version to aid you, in
the likeness of certain people whom you know. To you their
speeches are not "speeches," but human conversation; and if
you are a good reader of drama, the printed words are impreg-
nated with their tones of voice. Mrs. Maurrant's wistful "It seems
as if a person should get more out of life than just looking after
somebody" is for you sharply contrasted with Mrs. Jones's nasal
comment, "Well, I hope to tell you, after all I've done for mine,
I expect 'em to look after me in my old age." But in even so
simple a play as *Street Scene,* with its pageant-like quality and
its characters easily differentiated by their nationality, dialect,
and comparatively fixed positions in the house windows, you will
find students confused and troubled. If you wish to realize their
difficulties, turn back to one of Shakespeare's chronicle plays
with which you are unfamiliar. See how the Earl of Northum-
berland and Lord Willoughby and the Earl of Salisbury produce
at times even in your mature mind a vexing incertitude. And as
for that astute politician "Henry, surnamed Bolingbroke, Duke
of Hereford, son of John of Gaunt; afterwards King Henry IV,"
do you remember how hard you found it in high school to recognize the gentleman under his various names?

II. RE-CREATING STAGE SETTINGS

Drama is a difficult form. How are you to simplify it for your
beginning pupils? How are you to help them make from the

printed page a play containing living human beings? You may
be called upon to teach *The Merchant of Venice, Julius Caesar,
Coriolanus.* How shall you do it? Since your pupils, bred up on
movies, are familiar with all the sensuous beauty that a lavish
director can introduce, I should not at first ask a beginning class
to think of a Shakespearean play as produced on a sixteenth-
century stage. Present it to them and ask them to present it to
themselves in modern, beautiful setting. Later the Shakespearean
stage in all its austerity can be considered, but not now, not
while you are attempting—what? To evoke from mere printed
words people with voices, facial expressions, figures, clothes, personalities; to evoke scenes, emotions, and ideas from words used
in figurative sense and in blank verse at that. Build up a setting
that will assist your pupils, spoiled as they are for austerity by
the wonders of the cinema. Recall the most beautiful setting that
you have ever seen for the play and re-create it for your class.
Show them what can lie back of "Venice. A street" or "Belmont.
Portia's house." Perhaps you have seen some well-known actors
in *The Merchant of Venice.* There the casket scene and the court
scene would charm even the critical eye of a high-school sophomore. Or if you have not seen *The Merchant of Venice* well
staged, go to the *Variorum* edition, edited by Dr. Furness, which
you can find in any college library, and build up a background
for your class. Clothe these actors in the velvets and plumes of
sixteenth-century grandeur; contrast Gratiano's yellow trunks
and hose with Bassanio's royal purple, and set them both off in
contrast to Shylock's brown gaberdine—not forgetting the small
red cross on his shoulder. Think of your stage sets, too. One
producer opened the play with a small bridge vaulting a Venetian
canal, below which floated a gondola, a red light glowing in its
prow. Shylock's house, its second story frowning above the re-
cessed first, stood on one side. Throngs of merrymakers with
and without masks, an occasional page, a girl with castanets,
singing for the coins flung her, crossed and recrossed the bridge

or the street before it. Finally Antonio and his two flippant, indistinguishable companions pre-empted the stage—and the play began. Why all this elaborate detail when Shakespeare's words, which have lived through the ages, can still dominate men's minds without these nonhistorical trappings? Don't be pedants. Suppose you do put an electric light in the prow of the gondola. You conceal the wire. Suppose Shakespeare did not have stage settings and vaulting bridges reminiscent of Japanese gardens. Remember that presumably Shakespeare knew far less of Venice than the high-school pupils of today, bred up as they are on Pathé newsreels.

III. CONVERTING THE PRINTED PAGE INTO SPEECH

You are working for an imaginative experience for your pupils. You are working to make Shylock a real tragic character, whose voice slides from servility to command, from anger or triumph to bewilderment. Shylock sums up his life on the Rialto in competition with the "Christian" Antonio; in words all too applicable to twentieth-century problems he challenges the "Christian" creed of man's brotherhood, and if you can but make him real, your high-school boys will thrill to these speeches and enjoy and profit by giving them. Then, too, the whole trial scene, broken in the middle perhaps to let a new cast try its skill, offers an admirable opportunity for making the play live. And Shakespeare's humor in the form of Launcelot Gobbo—dull as it seems to us after many, many repetitions—becomes humor when acted before the class by pupils who have rehearsed it with their manager and who yearn to excel, hoping perhaps to appear on an assembly program, or a program before another section of the same grade. Timetaking? Yes. But it is worth the time if your class lives the play. Other pupils who are not to act can read while the actors are learning their parts for a *B* contract, or for extra credit, or for glory. But it is important that all, not merely the bright few, take some part in bringing the play to life, and it should be fully alive. You should not be afraid of Shakespeare's horseplay. Make your classes aware of the levels of humor, and show them how essential low comedy was to please the groundlings; then let Sir Toby hide behind the desk while Malvolio struts, or let Launcelot kneel before his blind father presenting his hair, not his beard, his fingers, not his lean ribs, for Old Gobbo's trembling touch. These are timeworn jests, but they are not timeworn to your pupils. And, by the way, as you look over your class, do you think that most of your pupils would have been in the pit or galleries had they been in attendance for the first production of "the Venesyon comody" in 1594?

IV. TEACHING CERTAIN STAGE CONVENTIONS

When your students hold a Shakespeare text, for example, *The Merchant of Venice,* in their hands for the first time, what aside from its many characters and its terse statement of place may be confusing to them?

For one thing, they may not realize until you point it out to them that this play, like many others, does not begin at the beginning of the story but near the climax. Hence they are forced to build up for themselves all that has gone before. They must take for granted Antonio's maritime interests, his frequent clashes in the past with the Jewish moneylender, and the existence of that deep friendship, fully developed before the play opens, between the staid merchant and the romantic Bassanio. At first they need much help, the most obvious being the proper pronunciation of the names that look formidable until they are put on the board and discussed by the class. To young America, Bassanio is a difficult character to understand, and the whole attitude toward money, interest, debt, deserves discussion. Perhaps the old saying "Friends tie their purses with a spider's thread" may be useful in explaining a point of view concerning money radically different from their own and may make them

more tolerant of the romantic situation, for many find it hard
to conceive of friendship not wrecked by unpaid debts.

Necessary as it is to tell your class much when they approach
their first, or second, or third play, all that you *tell* them has
little teaching value. It is purely a prologue to the far more
important matter of having them deduce from the lines themselves what lies behind. At first much help is necessary, but by
hints and questions you can bring pupils to build imaginary pictures implied but not stated by the writer. You must show them
that just as a playwright telescopes the action, omitting much
preliminary material in order that the climax may be soon
reached, so too he cuts all preliminary conversation and brings
his characters on in the midst of discussion. You and I accept
this stage convention, but a character seems strangely abrupt and
unreal to the beginner unless he realizes that much conversation
has preceded the remarks heard by the audience. For example,
Shylock and Bassanio appear, and the first words of the scene are:

Shylock. Three thousand ducats; well?
Bassanio. Ay, sir, for three months.

Antonio opens the play with the announcement to two casual
friends:

In sooth, I know not why I am so sad.

And Shylock and Launcelot Gobbo omit all mention of Old
Gobbo's intended departure and begin:

Shylock. Well, thou shalt see, thy eyes shall be thy judge,
The difference of old Shylock and Bassanio.

In the matter of implied action too, even action seemingly so
obvious that we forget to enlighten the pupil concerning it, a
class frequently proves unimaginative. In novels the readers are
told when the hero rises, sighs, points, or shrugs his shoulders.
From a play in book form they expect the same explicit information. Unless stage directions are given, it rarely occurs to them

to interpolate action as they please. Without help they do not imagine the shifting of stage pictures as actors cross and recross, the possibility of a soliloquy when there is no statement of the fact that the other actors are talking softly together, the absurd nonsense when Launcelot discourses with the fiend and his con-science, and the pushing and pulling of Old Gobbo in the scene with Bassanio. And as for Launcelot's palm-reading at the end of the scene, often they can make nothing of the nonsense be-cause the term *palm* is not specifically mentioned.

Then there are more important actions implied, essential to the meaning or to the full dramatic effect. In *Julius Caesar,* perhaps even more popular than *The Merchant of Venice* for beginning classes, there is Antony's dramatic exposure of Caesar's mutilated body. You and I know that he flings back the dead Caesar's robe, but no mention is made of that action. Do you recall the lines?

> Kind souls, what! weep you when you but behold
> Our Caesar's vesture wounded? Look you here,
> Here is himself, marr'd, as you see, with traitors.

When pupils know that the sixteenth-century theater had no programs and realize that the actors must themselves keep the audience aware of what character is about to enter, they will be interested to note the skill with which these announcements are made. Lucius reports:

> Sir, 'tis your brother Cassius at the door.

Bassanio meets his friend and explains to Shylock:

> This is Signor Antonio.

And an even more difficult entrance is made clear by Coriolanus when his mother, wife, and little son approach:

> My wife comes foremost; then the honour'd mould
> Wherein this trunk was fram'd, and in her hand
> The grandchild to her blood.

But often Shakespeare goes farther than a mere announcement, as in the entrance of Caesar where his very expression and the manner of his followers are given in the lines by Brutus:

> But, look you, Cassius,
> The angry spot doth glow on Caesar's brow,
> And all the rest look like a chidden train:
> Calpurnia's cheek is pale, and Cicero
> Looks with such ferret and such fiery eyes
> As we have seen him in the Capitol
> Being cross'd in conference with some senators.

So also in the lines where Coriolanus, returned triumphant, greets his wife, he conveys both her action and her quiet dignity and gentle nature:

> My gracious silence, hail!
> Wouldst thou have laugh'd had I come coffin'd home,
> That weep'st to see me triumph? Ah! my dear,
> Such eyes the widows in Corioli wear,
> And mothers that lack sons.

Just as pupils must be led to realize that actions of individuals and of stage groups are implied in the lines, so too they must realize that the scenery and stage effects are also implied, since Shakespeare wrote for a comparatively bare stage. As soon as pupils recognize—and you will soon make them—that without twentieth-century stage properties the audience was forced to imagine its own scene from the lines it heard, then each pupil should be led to assume that same responsibility when he reads a play. You will be surprised to find how much a little drill in visualizing scenes from the lines given will stimulate the imaginative and open the eyes of the practical. For example, call your pupils' attention to the picture (the backdrop for the stage) contained in these lines:

> The gray eyed morn smiles on the frowning night,
> Chequering the eastern clouds with streaks of light.

Lady, by yonder blessed moon I swear
That tips with silver all the fruit-tree tops.

✓

Look how the floor of heaven
Is thick inlaid with pattens of bright gold

✓

How sweet the moonlight sleeps upon this bank

✓

Night's candles are burnt out, and jocund Day
Stands tiptoe on the misty mountain tops

✓

and yon grey lines
That fret the clouds are messengers of day

Simple as this work seems to you, you will find that many pupils read "words, words, words" with never a picture clearly conjured up in their brains. By all means acquaint yourself with the *Mercury Shakespeare Texts,* those charming editions with tiny sketches of the characters and stage directions running along the margin of the page. No class which has used those texts and also listened to the accompanying records for *The Merchant of Venice* and *Twelfth-Night,* could fail to appreciate Shakespeare.[1]

V. RE-CREATING CHARACTERS

What is the next step in teaching drama? You have begun admirably when you bring your freshmen or your eighth-graders to understand what past occurrences, present actions, and stage pictures should be implied from the lines read. But since plays concern characters and character conflicts, your teaching, though successfully done, is by no means completed until these mere names in lists come to life and become people. Many teachers discuss the characters, asking the pupils to describe their own

[1] The McGraw-Hill Book Company distributes both the Mercury texts and the Mercury recordings.

pictures of them—their voices, carriage, manners. The character's past life is surmised and his future forecast. Such questions are wise or futile according to the wisdom of the teacher and the amount of proof pupils are led to find in the play itself. Mere imaginative flights discourage or disgust the literal-minded and lay no foundation for future reading. As with stage picture and action, the lines portraying character must be read imaginatively. This re-creation of character as attempted at the ninth-grade level is well illustrated by the following quotation for the Kansas state course of study.[1]

LITERARY AIM I: DEFINITION AND REFINEMENT OF PERSONAL VALUES
SELECTION: "THE PATCHWORK QUILT," BY RACHEL LYMAN FIELD

I. Analysis of "personal values" as a literary aim:

The term "personal values" is such a general one that any definition becomes largely subjective. Without being dogmatic, however, we may consider such values as individual standards of worth or excellence, criteria by which the person measures and chooses for himself that which is worth while in life. It is not so much the problem or duty of literary study to teach the pupil *what* to choose as it is the aim of such study to teach him *how* to choose for himself those values which will enrich his life long after he has left the English classroom. Infinite are the possibilities of training the pupil's emotions and guiding the formation of his attitudes by means of the many personalities which appear in most literary selections. This refinement of a pupil's responses to the human qualities of the persons around him is in itself a worth-while aim. Perhaps literature may lead the pupil to a sympathy for old and young alike, to an understanding of their hopes and fears, their love and hate, their kindness and selfishness. Not an impossible dream is the development of the pupil's ability to understand his fellow men, but at the same time to think for himself and to refine his own system of values. In such a way does literature contribute to individual enrichment, as it leads ever forward into the endless realm of appreciation.

[1] *Manual of Guides,* Part II, *English,* State of Kansas, Department of Education, issued by Geo. L. McClenny, State Superintendent of Public Instruction.

II. Realization of aim through reading and study of "The Patchwork Quilt," by Rachel Lyman Field.[1] (Selection for freshmen.)

   A. Subject matter.

      1. Qualities of the play:

         a. Realism in characters and setting.

         b. Fancy in dream characters of the past.

      2. Characters:

         a. Old Mrs. Willis—a frail old lady who is unhappy and out of place in the luxury of her daughter's home, a grandmother who begs for her old patchwork quilt which brings back to her the memories of an earlier day.

         b. Anne Wendall, her daughter—a nervous, twentieth-century woman who obviously tries to be patient with her mother, but whose condescending attitude shows that she looks upon old Mrs. Willis as a child.

         c. Joe Wendall, Anne's husband—a practical business man, interested chiefly in getting the deed to the farm owned by Mrs. Willis.

         d. Betty, the granddaughter of old Mrs. Willis—a merry little girl about six years old, who understands her grandmother and is fascinated by her stories of the past.

         e. Molly—old Mrs. Willis as she appeared on her wedding day and in her early married life. (In the fantasy.)

         f. William—Molly's husband. (In the fantasy.)

         g. Emily—the daughter of Molly and William. (In the fantasy.)

      3. Scene—an upstairs bedroom and sitting room, stiff and luxurious rather than homelike.

      4. Plot:

         Characters overshadow plot in this one-act play. The plot is a simple one centering around a deed to a farm which belongs to Mrs. Willis. This deed is closely connected with the patchwork quilt which Mrs. Willis cherishes because of the memories which each patch brings back to her. Mrs. Willis appears dazed and bewildered amidst her strange surroundings when deprived of her quilt. But as soon as the little granddaughter brings the quilt from the cook's bed, old Mrs.

[1] H. Ward McGraw, *Prose and Poetry for Enjoyment,* The State of Kansas, 1939, pp. 734-750.

Willis recalls the past vividly, even the "secret" of the central white piece of the quilt, the piece which contains something that "crackles." Anne and Joe want that deed and try to coax Mrs. Willis to reveal its hiding place, but first they command the patchwork quilt to be removed, in spite of the old lady's protests. Immediately Mrs. Willis's sentences become incoherent. She goes to the bed and fingers the gray silk covering and says, "It's all gray now."

B. Techniques.
  1. Activity of first day:
    a. Discussion of how plays differ from stories (pp. 673 and 674 of McGraw text).
    b. Discussion of how to read plays (pp. 673 and 674 of McGraw text).
    c. Introduction of play by teacher.
      (1) Reading and explanation of scene.
      (2) Reading of first speeches to give an idea of characters.
    d. Assignment of parts to members of class for reading in class on the following day.
    e. Assignment for entire class—to read play for understanding of plot and characters before next class period.
  2. Activity of second day:
    a. Reading of play by pupils chosen on preceding day.
    b. Reading of stage directions by teacher with necessary explanation.
  3. Activity of third day:
    a. Discussion of characters as a means of revealing personal values.
      (1) Importance of memories to old age—consequently need for pleasant memories.
      (2) The searching for the familiar.
      (3) Value of the familiar as compared with the luxurious.
      (4) The selfishness of youth intent on its own benefits.
      (5) The stinging condescension toward an old person.
      (6) The pathos of a wandering mind.
      (7) The sympathy and understanding of a little child.
      (8) The joy of a return to the familiar.
      (9) Realization that old persons were once young and active.

> (10) The charm of the romance of an earlier day.
> (11) The desire to give a most cherished possession as a token of love—the deed.
> (12) The loneliness of age when dreams have fled.
> (13) Disregard for the wishes of age.
> (14) Weariness of age in the midst of rushing persons who do not understand.

b. Discussion of why Mrs. Willis thought so much of Betty.

c. Discussion of how the title fits the play.

III. Outcomes and results for high school students.

A. Greater sympathy for older persons among family and friends.

B. Contempt for human selfishness.

C. Realization that luxury does not necessarily bring happiness.

D. Greater interest in memories and stories from an earlier day.

E. A standard of values based upon human interest rather than upon dollars and cents.

F. Greater appreciation of the one-act play as a type of literature.

G. Introduction to the art of reading plays.

Much this same method would be used in any play and at any level. (But the more obvious attempts at moral training would, of course, be more and more tactfully concealed as readers become more sophisticated.) Since all high schools teach Shakespearean dramas, I shall use Shakespeare's plays for further illustration.

For example, consider Portia's courteous response to the tawny Prince of Morocco. It will take a minute's thought before the pupils see behind the lady's gracious mask, but a question from the teacher will recall to the pupils' minds the wearily ironic woman beset by unwelcome suitors. Then they grasp the meaning of Portia's:

> Yourself, renowned prince, then stood as fair
> As any comer I have look'd on yet
> For my affection.

Or they will realize that Brutus' whole scholarly, philosophic life and his tenderness appear in the apparently unimportant lines:

> Look, Lucius, here's the book I sought for so;
> I put it in the pocket of my gown.
>
> .   .   .   .   .   .
>
> If thou dost nod, thou break'st thy instrument;
> I'll take it from thee; and, good boy, good-night.
> Let me see, let me see; is not the leaf turn'd down
> Where I left reading?

VI. DETERMINING YOUR POLICY

A question that may puzzle you is this: How much time should you expend upon Shakespearean language, upon classical allusions, upon the sometimes involved phraseology of certain passages? What does your common sense tell you? You desire to give your pupils an imaginative experience; you desire to cultivate their ability to read comprehendingly; you desire above all else to teach this play so interestingly that your pupils will want to read more Shakespeare plays, to act certain isolated scenes from them, and to go on to the reading of other dramas. Suppose your pupils find that this first play of Shakespeare's is hedged about with sources, classical allusions, words to trace, and numerous notes to study? Will they have either courage or desire to advance upon another play, alone and unaided? It is easy to overteach the first play. Leave much for the second or the fifth or the eighth. Be content to build slowly. But build you should. Personally I feel that Portia might to advantage have chatted less cryptically than in the lines:

> such a hare is madness the youth, to skip o'er the
> meshes of good counsel the cripple.

I believe that the teacher should explain the general idea. And surely there is no reason to look up the classical references in the lines:

If Hercules and Lichas play at dice
Which is the better man, the greater throw
May turn by fortune from the weaker hand:
So is Alcides beaten by the page.

Hercules the class knows; Lichas is unknown. But one question as to the meaning of the lines will, without the aid of Gayley's *Classic Myths,* show Lichas a weakling compared to his opponent.

I am not counseling you to keep your class as ignorant as possible—far from it!—but I do urge you to keep a play a play. As you progress, more study will be given passages and whole plays. But, simple as this beginning work appears, it takes imagination, genuine skill, and much enthusiasm to present a play so that it is an imaginative adventure. After pupils learn how to read a play, they can then learn how to consider character, plot, setting, and can attempt to develop some criteria for judging the excellence of the plays read or seen. Remember that your plan of teaching should be progressive. When you consider plays with your juniors and seniors, the study and outside reading should concern itself more with the development of character, the social and philosophic problems presented, the interpretation of lines, and the deft unfolding of plot than does your work with younger pupils. But here, too, a play must remain a play. In this chapter I have emphasized the beginning steps, for too often they are taken for granted. When they are, drama is likely to remain a closed book to many high-school students. At the end of this chapter you will find reading references that deal excellently with this problem of developing the reading powers of your pupils *after* they have learned how to grasp a play. Consult one or more of these reading references, for this chapter gives you merely the preliminary steps in high-school drama study.

So far, I have discussed only Shakespearean drama as taught in the early years of high school, for some two or more of Shakespeare's plays are either suggested or required in practically every American classroom. But study of the drama, even in the early years, should not begin and end with the sixteenth century. Drinkwater's *Abraham Lincoln,* Peabody's *The Piper,* Barrie's *Peter Pan* and *The Admirable Crichton,* Maeterlinck's *The Blue Bird,* Rostand's *Chantecler,* Noyes's *Sherwood,* and many other full-length plays as well as many one-acts offer contemporary drama that is neither too difficult nor too sordid for the eighth grade or for the early years of the high school. Thanks to Burns Mantle's best plays of the year and to numerous inexpensive editions of modern plays, it is usually possible for your more mature students to read the plays which are being discussed in the current magazines and papers. School study then ceases to be a thing apart, for English classes become reading clubs of contemporary drama, a part of the adult reading world. In those schools where the last two years in English work are divided into separate, specialized courses, drama study is always a popular course. Why? Because in that course pupils feel themselves in contact with real life.

VII. PREPARING YOURSELF FOR DRAMA TEACHING

It would be wise for you—unless drama has been one of your major interests in college—to prepare yourself carefully for this rather specialized type of instruction. You are familiar, of course, with Shakespeare's plays and possess, doubtless, both annotated texts and bibliographies, but are you well versed in Shaw, Barrie, Galsworthy, O'Neill, Peabody, Synge? Do you know Elmer Rice, Marc Connelly, George Kaufman, Maxwell Anderson, Sidney Howard, to name only a few of the many English and American dramatists to whom your pupils could turn with pleasure? One play should lead to another play just as one novel should lead to another, and often a play will be better realized and better appreciated through comparison than it could possibly be if read alone. Bookmakers, recognizing this fact, have published a school edition containing both *Macbeth* and *The Emperor Jones.* Why? To show the same theme, overweening ambition, in two different

centuries and in two different levels of society. And do you realize
how alive for a class *The Emperor Jones* becomes after seeing
Paul Robeson in the cinema version?

The theatrical world has always held a fascination for youth.
You would do well to utilize this natural interest. At some time
most of your freshman girls have, in imagination, seen themselves as movie stars; and even many of your high-school boys,
loath as they would be to admit it, feel a measure of identification with some intrepid, handsome hero. Why not familiarize
yourself and your older students with those actors and actresses
who have played or are playing famous roles: Laurence Olivier
as Caesar and Henry V, Vivien Leigh as Cleopatra, Uta Hagen as
Joan of Arc, Helen Hayes as Queen Victoria, and José Ferrer
as Cyrano de Bergerac—these names and many more afford an
interesting and illuminating bit of research for your upperclass-
men. From this research they will find lying behind the printed
words in their text possibilities of interpretation that had never
occurred to them. A play, even a Shakespeare play, is not a thing
of the past: and if you focus attention upon the stage interpretation of certain lines, you do two things: (1) you vitalize the
printed page; and (2) you connect the life of the pupil outside the
classroom—his life made of work, daydreams, and moving pictures
—with his school experience.

VIII. UTILIZING THE MOTION PICTURE AND THE RADIO IN CLASSROOM DISCUSSIONS

Here another question arises. How seriously do you take moving pictures, and how much do you really know about them?
How well informed are you concerning radio drama? Do you
know William Lewin's work? Do you read the *Audio-Visual
Guide?* Do you listen to many programs?

Very possibly your pupils will be better informed than you.
But unless you have followed the subject rather carefully, you
would do well before beginning your teaching to consider both

radio and motion pictures and how you can gain them as allies in your approach to literature teaching. Luckily you need not wander here unguided, for in recent years, and particularly since the studies made by Mr. Henry Forman and others, motion pictures have come to be recognized as either an educational menace or an aid so important that they must be reckoned with.[1] In 1934, Mr. William Lewin, chairman of the Committee in Photoplay Appreciation, a committee appointed by the National Council of Teachers of English, brought out a monograph in which were given the results of a study made with sixty-eight different towns or cities. With each group a definite program of education was carried on. Films were viewed, discussed, studied, and the improvement in the judgments of each group recorded. The fact that often teachers were as much in need of film instruction as were their pupils added a certain difficulty but also a certain zest to the experiment. The committee reports:

Valuable as will be the use of the photoplay to the experienced teacher of literature, its value to the less experienced teacher will be even greater. From the standpoint of the average young teacher in the earlier grades of the high school, the chief problem is that of pupil behavior. . . . The cinema becomes a scientific visual aid to the teacher of literary appreciation. With assistance of the photoplay, the work of the teacher of literature becomes more interesting to the pupil, and the necessity of compelling attention through discipline practically disappears.[2]

As is obvious, however, the value of the study of both films and radio depends upon the quality of the programs. Use moving pictures and use radio, by all means, but use them wisely. They offer admirable material for oral work, for written or oral comparison with plays read, for discussion of such topics as dramatic incidents, well-timed entrances, character contrasts, artistic inter-

[1] Forman, Henry James: *Our Movie-made Children,* Macmillan, 1933.
[2] Lewin, William: *Photoplay Appreciation in American Schools,* Appleton-Century, 1934, pp. 98-99.

pretation, and appropriate setting. But they also offer a side field for discussion of ethical, psychological, and sociological problems. True, many films are cheap, are vulgar, and give a distorted view of life. But if films are viewed by the majority of your pupils, might it not be wise to draw on this well of experience, and to attempt to lead pupils to discriminate in favor of those where artistic presentation is combined with sense, morality, and idealism? Both moving pictures and radio may aid you in motivating your drama units. They may also cheapen your work and waste precious time. Consider them well, for they are a strong force in the modern world, one which you cannot ignore. Written drama may or may not continue as an important factor in the lives of your boys and girls, but apparently the cinema and the radio, doubtless changed and improved, will continue to provide the people's favorite amusement. Many admirable plays have been produced. Much that is cheap, vulgar, and dangerously anti-social still remains. Is it too optimistic to suggest that you and thousands of other teachers like you may perhaps by your teaching have some influence on the cinema and radio programs of the future?

The effect of radio dramatizations as a spur to reading is effectively shown in the article by Joseph Mersand "Radio Makes Readers," *English Journal*, Vol. 27 (1938), pp. 469-75. Consider it; then see what—with careful teacher guidance—*you* can accomplish with *your* own pupils.

Fortunately it is a simple matter to inform yourself on radio, recording, and films in case you are not well acquainted with these three fairly new educational devices for increasing the students' appreciation and interest in drama. Below is a list of nine reliable sources of information. A letter from you to any one or letters to all of them will bring you pamphlets and newsletters full of information. Collect at least some of these pamphlets so that you are prepared to be intelligent on the subject before you begin teaching.

Sources for Timely Information

In this text, audio-visual aids are mentioned frequently. But only in Appendix J will you find listed names and addresses of those organizations from which you can obtain free or inexpensive material. A second source of timely information comes from the following magazine departments.

1. *Elementary English:* "Look and Listen"
2. *Nation's Schools:* "What's New for Schools"
3. *N.E.A. Journal,* "Audio-Visual Aids"
4. *Scholastic* (Teachers' Edition): "It's a Daisy," "Tools for Teachers," and "Visually Yours"
5. *School Review:* "Educational News and Comment"
6. *Audio-Visual Guide,* repeatedly mentioned in Appendix J

Good Listening, an eight-column folded sheet, published October through May, by the Wisconsin Association for Better Radio and Television, has a different purpose. It attempts to educate listeners so that they will demand better programs. Each issue lists continuing programs ranked as good. The networks represented are: A.B.C., C.B.S., N.B.C., and Mutual. Might such a fold-sheet page, up-to-date and easy to read, increase your students' interest in better class programs? Why not risk five cents and order one copy, or, if extravagant, risk even twenty cents for ten copies which you could share with your students? [1]

One aspect of radio and television, the drama, provides an excellent introduction to the reading of plays, as Milton A. Kaplan's article points out.[2] And if you or the school owns a recorder, you have an excellent means of arousing interest in radio drama. Remember, however, that discussion, both before and after listening

---

[1] Subscription price: 2 cents a copy for ten or more; 1½ cents for 100 or more; 5 cents singly. Order, if possible, before the 15th of the previous month, from Mrs. J. R. McCarthy, Raulf Hotel, Portage, Wis. General Memberships Co., Better Radio Listening—$1.00 and includes a year's subscription to *Good Listening.* Sustaining membership, $5.00.

[2] "Radio Plays as an Introduction to Drama," *English Journal,* Vol. 39 (1950), p. 23. See also Appendix H, "Drama."

is essential. And for speech improvement and increased student effort, a tape-recorder serves admirably.[1]

But for fear that you might think after this outpouring of information about mechanical devices that drama teaching consists primarily of radio programs, films, and recordings, may I remind you that all three are merely highly useful ways of increasing what must first of all be obtained: thoughtful, intelligent reading, with enjoyment, of many dramas. No devices are particularly valuable except in the hands of a competent teacher.

SUGGESTED EXERCISES

Before attempting these exercises read the chapter on drama in *Enjoyment of Literature* (Boas and Smith), and as many of the other references listed as possible.

1. Select and reread a not too familiar play by Shakespeare; then prepare a ten-minute oral presentation before the class, such a one as you might use with your high-school class to awaken interest in the play and to insure an intelligent approach to it.

2. Select an isolated scene from one of Shakespeare's comedies not usually taught in high school; cut for reading. Work out a brief introduction to it, with sufficient explanation so that the scene can be enjoyed by a class unfamiliar with the play. If possible, present both your introduction and the scene, entire or in parts, before the prospective teachers in your group.

3. Go through some half-dozen Shakespearean plays and select as many outstanding characters. Your plan should be to interest your high-school class in reading by presenting a portrait gallery of characters which they can enjoy. It might be practical and timesaving to appoint different members in your college class each of whom is to (a) select one character, (b) prepare an appropriate analysis or introduction and (c) arrange a cutting of one speech or a series of speeches which will illustrate the personality of the character. Use for each play act, scene, and line numbers, so that each cutting, if put on file, may be consulted by other members of the class.

4. Make an annotated reading list giving author, title, publisher, price, and comment for a senior class studying *one* of the following topics: (a) Modern American drama; (b) Modern British drama;

[1] See Appendix J, III, No. 1 and No. 2. Tape Recording.

(c) Modern one-act plays; (d) Poetic drama; (e) Outstanding plays not British or American.

(If different members of your group combined upon this assignment, you could compile a list of suitable material that might prove both stimulating and timesaving for you in case you wished to carry on individual project work with outstanding pupils.)

SUGGESTED READINGS

A. References for Your Own Guidance

1. Baker, George P.: *Dramatic Technique*, Houghton Mifflin, 1919

2. Chambers, E. K.: *The Medieval Stage*, Oxford University Press, 1903
An authoritative source for information concerning minstrelsy, folk drama, religious drama.

3. Chandler, Frank W.: *Aspects of Modern Drama*, Macmillan, 1922
Here you will find an extensive review of the drama of late nineteenth and early twentieth centuries. A useful book.

4. Nicoll, Allardyce: *An Introduction to Dramatic Theory*, G. G. Harrap, London, 1923
A stimulating presentation of the nature of both tragedy and comedy.

5. Dickinson, T. H.: *Chief Contemporary Dramatists*, series 1, 2, 3, Houghton Mifflin, 1915, 1921, 1930

6. Mantle, Burns: *American Playwrights of Today: The Best Plays of* (every year), Dodd, Mead [1]

7. Samples, David M.: "Production Problems in Play-directing," *English Journal*, Vol. 38 (1949), pp. 86-91

8. Cook, Dorothy, and Holden, Katharine M.: *Educational Film Guide*, annual edition, H. W. Wilson Company, New York

9. Kenny, Rita J., and Schofield, Edward T. (revised by Catherine Bordman): "Audio-Visual Aids for the English Teacher," *Audio-Visual Guide*, February, 1951 (1630 Springfield Ave., Maplewood, New Jersey)
This list of motion pictures, filmstrips, recordings, and directory of sources can be obtained, a reprint, for 25 cents. All phases of English. A valuable possession for any school.

10. Harshfield, H. W., and Schmidt, P.: *Playing Out Our Problems in Socio-Drama*, Ohio State University, Columbus, Ohio, 1948

11. Boas, Ralph Philip: *The Study and Appreciation of Literature*, Harcourt, Brace, 1931, "Dramatic Literature," pp. 148-216

---

[1] In Appendix H you will find books dealing with high-school dramatics.

A thoughtful discussion, most concise, of drama, plus judgments made and illustrated from plays of specific characteristics at different periods.

12. Chute, Marchette: *An Introduction to Shakespeare,* E. P. Dutton, 1947

Read before teaching a class in Shakespeare. In this book Shakespeare lives, writes, acts. Miss Chute writes from scholarship, but has created a disarmingly simple, fascinating picture of the man, the theater, the times.

B. References Concerned with the Teaching of Drama

1. Boas, Ralph P., and Smith, Edwin: *Enjoyment of Literature,* Harcourt, Brace, 1934, pp. 281-395

A careful study of the various problems discussed under the general term "drama"; both stimulating and profitable.

2. Thomas, Charles Swain: *The Teaching of English in Secondary Schools,* rev. ed., Houghton Mifflin, 1927, Chapter X.

Deals with the teaching of plays and suggests various ways of arousing interest.

3. *Theater Arts,* February, 1941, celebrated its 25th anniversary with articles by O'Neill, Lunt, Fontanne, Sherwood, Rice, Saroyan, and Wilder. This copy should be of interest to your classes.

4. Nickerson, P. S.: "A Study of the Value of Recordings in the Teaching of Shakespeare," *Radio and English Teaching,* Max J. Herzberg, editor.

"Good recordings added effectiveness to the teaching of drama." But unless these records are played *after* the students understand how they fit into the play and what situation exists, even the best Shakespearean actors sound ridiculous to the student in any tense, emotional scene. Build bridges to it first.

From the English Journal

First Steps in Drama Teaching

1. Brickell, Henry M.: "What Can You Do with Sociograms?" Vol. 39 (1950), pp. 256-61

Banish self-consciousness. Not Teddy but the "Rev. M. J. Sutton" is talking before the class. Why should Teddy be embarrassed?

2. Hastings, Margaret Florence: "Let's Act It Out," Vol. 20 (1931), pp. 670-72

Describes acting out stories (Old Testament, etc.).

3. Ellis, Marion L.: "Dramatization—under Difficulties," Vol. 21 (1932), pp. 44-50

4. Stieglitz, Sarah Thorwald: "Review by the Court," Vol. 39 (1950), pp. 452-54

A high-school class stages a "trial" to decide whether Silas Marner may keep Eppie. The writer emphasizes that she chooses this form of interesting the class in the book because of the number of students who are related to lawyers.

5. Phelps, Frances Brownell: "Mrs. Wiggs in the High-School Patch," Vol. 39 (1950), pp. 161-63

A senior-high-school class does its own dramatization of "Mrs. Wiggs," using the writing as basis for three weeks' work in composition and then presenting the play to a town audience.

6. Rider, Virginia: "Modern Drama Educates for Tolerance," Vol. 36 (1947), pp. 16-22

A unit for the twelfth grade.

7. Johns, Kingston, and Smith, Donald E.: "A Drama Course: Planned, Used, Evaluated," Vol. 39 (1950), pp. 571-74

A twelfth-grade course of study in contemporary drama for average and higher than average students.

8. Benner, Helen F.: "Eighth Graders Learn from Plays," Vol. 37 (1948), pp. 40-42

An entertaining account of plays developed and given through student initiative, with a minimum of teacher assistance. The writer recommends the monthly magazine *Plays,* 8 Arlington Street, Boston.

Shakespeare in High-school Classes [1]

1. Palmer, Dora E.: "The Play's the Thing," Vol. 38 (1949), pp. 568-71

Julius Caesar, Henry IV, and *Romeo and Juliet* became, with the teacher's aid through stimulating questions, a popular and successful unit.

2. Tolman, Helen Louise: "Julius Caesar Up to Date," Vol. 29 (1940), pp. 830-32

The similarity between Caesar and the German and Italian dictators.

3. Welles, Orson, and Hill, Roger: "On the Teaching of Shakespeare and Other Great Literature," Vol. 27 (1938), pp. 464-68

A plea for Shakespeare study that is enjoyed. Uses records.

4. Ginsberg, Walter: "How Helpful Are Shakespeare Recordings?" Vol. 29 (1940), pp. 289-300

[1] Barker, Fred: *Forty-Minute Plays from Shakespeare,* Macmillan, 1927.

A discussion of the records made from Orson Welles's version of *The Merchant of Venice* and *Twelfth Night,* to be used in connection with the Orson Welles and Roger Hill, Mercury Shakespeare texts.

5. Taggert, Louise, and Haefner, George E.: "Two Methods of Teaching *Macbeth*," Vol. 23 (1934), pp. 543-53

6. Simons, Henry W.: "Why Shakespeare?" Vol. 23 (1934), pp. 363-68
A list of "bad" practices in the study of Shakespeare's plays.

7. Royster, Salibelle: "Shakespeare for the Superior," Vol. 36 (1947), pp. 34-37
Students volunteered to form a Shakespeare class (not on the schedule). "Not all were top students, but all were Shakespeare fans." Throughout the term note how the students thought that they chose the plays. Note all depended upon their participation.

8. Hartinger, Elizabeth A.: "As We Like It," Vol. 20 (1931), pp. 764-66
Class acted out parts of *As You Like It,* then worked out programs for class presentation: songs, puppet shows, miniature stages, etc.

9. Goldberg, Sam: "Romeo and Juliet and 'Vocational' Boys," Vol. 39 (1950), pp. 159-60
An encouraging example of student activity and enjoyment coupled with learning.

10. Mersand, Joseph: "Building Audiences for the American Theater," Vol. 27 (1938), pp. 246-52
This article classifies many plays as to the particular appeal they can make and the important use they can have in helping pupils to grasp personal, social, and political problems.

Motion Pictures, Radio, and the Class in Drama Study

1. Lewin, William: "The Business of Running a High-School Movie Club," Vol. 23 (1934), p. 37

2. Lewin, William: "Two Units in Photoplay Appreciation," Vol. 22 (1933), pp. 817-23

3. Hamilton, Delight C.: "An Experiment with *Treasure Island*," Vol. 20 (1931), pp. 415-16

4. Rosenkranz, Samuel: "English at the Cinema," Vol. 20 (1931), pp. 823-28

See Appendix H, pp. 601-02.

CHAPTER XV

The Teaching of Fiction

I. WHAT ARE SOME GENERAL PRINCIPLES APPLICABLE TO ALL LITERATURE CLASSES?

As HAS already been said, when you are confronted by a class in high school, you have represented in the pupils before you probably from ten to twenty different reading abilities. You may have the same number of different backgrounds represented. The daughter of the professor of Italian sits next to the son of the Italian garbage collector. Across the aisle is the German gardener's son; behind him is the stodgy little American whose mother takes in washing, and in front of him is the daughter of the local banker, in whose residence *Fortune* is the only magazine displayed. Social position, you will find, is no index of the pupils' literary backgrounds. In reading taste this group varies from Hardy to *Breezy Stories,* from Shelley to Edgar Guest, although they are all labeled "10A English" and for forty-five minutes confront you daily. One thing is obvious: you cannot treat them all alike without boring the best, teaching the mediocre, and discouraging the poorest. You cannot, therefore, plunge into fiction without first discovering not only how well or how poorly your pupils cope with the mechanics of reading but also upon what level of literature they feel at home. I have watched teachers attempting to "teach" *Treasure Island* to pupils who could and did read *Les Misérables* or *The Three Musketeers* by themselves, and to whom any extended class discussion of Stevenson was worse than weariness of spirit. And, too, I have seen *The Lady of the Lake* required of every pupil in class when it was patently evident that the little Chinese in one corner and the slightly subnormal girl in the front seat never could grasp the language nor work out from inverted sentence to inverted sentence the meaning of the lines. Such stupidities in teaching English are not uncommon. In fact they are as common as the differences in ability and background that I have just sketched. And why? Unfortunately the differences in pupils' minds, unlike the differences in their bodies, are well concealed. Such regimentation would become at once absurdly apparent if a teacher tried to fit each body in the class with a size sixteen uniform.

Again remember Swedenborg's Heaven where every soul sinks or rises to its own level. Test. Break your class up into groups. Make of your classroom a workshop with occasional class meetings. On days when you meet to help the mediocre, excuse the brighter pupils. Let these brighter ones prepare reports, rehearse a play, plan a cinema production, read a book for comparison, or do one of a dozen things that will throw light on the general topic under discussion and increase the pupil's power of using the library, organizing material, and co-operating with other pupils in a common enterprise. Or allow them time for reading done for its own sake. *Often teachers underestimate the intrinsic interest* of books. Afraid to trust to the charm of a given novel, they encourage readings for some future activity, such as a dramatization of the material. This may be an excellent idea when its purpose is to interest the pupil in reading, but many students can and do enjoy wide reading without the bait of a future activity. When such is the case, the activity becomes perfunctory and therefore a serious waste of time.[1]

But in spite of what has just been said, some reading in common is essential. You must realize this fact, even though through your education courses, you have, doubtless, become familiar with many plans for individual work. The Morrison plan, the Dalton plan, the long-unit assignment, and the contract method are probably familiar to you. Perhaps you know Dr. Burke's individual method, adopted, with certain changes, at Winnetka,

[1] Hitchcock, Alfred: *Bread Loaf Talks on Teaching Literature*, p. 84.

and now spoken of as the Winnetka technique. The fundamental likeness in all these plans, and in the programs of the progressive schools or experimental schools, is that each pupil, insofar as it is possible, studies at his own rate, takes his own objective tests when he is ready, and makes his own individual contribution to the class.[1] The excellences of these methods are many. One danger, though, they have in common. Unless the teacher guards against that danger, pupils are likely to feel themselves *isolated*, drawing from their work only the values to be found in, say, a correspondence course. Pupils, remember, are social human beings, and for many of the antisocial ones learning to work with others and learning to talk about ideas with others are all-important. For this reason it is almost imperative that some small body of literature should be read by all members of the class in order to provide a common fund of interest.[2]

Suppose that you have a class reading *Ivanhoe,* and among those students a Japanese or a German or a French pupil whose brain is good, but whose language ability is limited. Involved sentences, numerous characters, and the terms and customs of chivalry are all stumbling blocks for his foreign brain. Yet one of the most essential things is for you to make him a part of your class group, to offer him opportunity of contributing, and to allow him to excel.[3] Your course of study calls for *Ivanhoe.* What can you do? There are always the simple stories of chivalry such as Howard Pyle's or Eva Tappan's, which it would be well to give him first. There ought to be some student who could "keep him straight" on the story, so that he has a reasonably clear idea of what goes on in class. There are to be found accounts in simple prose of heroic adventures in Japan, in Germany, in France,

[1] Curtis, Frances D.: Unit Assignments, *Junior-Senior High-School Clearing House,* Vol. 9 (1935), No. 9, pp. 539-542.

[2] Thomas, Charles Swain: *Teaching English in Secondary Schools,* p. 183.

[3] Too often teachers excuse blunders in their own teaching by laying all blame on the course of study. Any course of study, no matter how rigid, can be manipulated if a teacher has sufficient courage and ingenuity.

which, if you find them for him, he might master readily. And then there is always the possibility of his contributing a cover for the class notebook, a drawing of a knight or an illustration of medieval armor. Why have him bother his foreign brain with *Ivanhoe?* Because he needs to be a member of a class; hence it might possibly be well to juggle one pedagogical principle with another and exact from him the minimum of actual reading of a historical novel with the maximum of class participation. **But** also a teacher has to remember that no novel and no considerable number of a class should be sacrificed for any one individual. Do not bore a bright class by allowing a backward or foreign pupil numerous opportunities of appearing before his fellows. It is commonly recognized, however, that the teacher by her own attitude can usually evoke a like attitude in her pupils. Instead of boring your group, it is possible to have your whole class pride itself upon the advancement of some shy or foreign class member.

II. WHAT DANGERS AWAIT YOU IN "TEACHING" FICTION?

If you have grown up in a home where books formed an integral part of each day's living, and where as a matter of course the children read and lived in books, you may wonder just what you can "teach" about a novel that was obviously planned for recreational reading. In your various classes you are confronted with *Captains Courageous, Treasure Island, Silas Marner, The House of Seven Gables, A Tale of Two Cities, The Scarlet Letter,* or *Tess of the D'Urbervilles.* Each was written to be read. Each was meant to be enjoyed. Not one, even *A Tale of Two Cities,* which in the hands of certain teachers becomes a course in French history, was meant to convey exact information or to provide an adequate excuse for training in the use of the library. What are you to "teach"? Furthermore, "character building," "the inculcation of right standards of living," "better citizenship" were hardly the ultimate aims of Stevenson or Dickens or Kipling. (By omitting Eliot and Hawthorne I avoid possible controversy.) And for young readers, readers who should be engaged with *Treasure Island* or *Silas Marner* or *David Copperfield*, a study of technique such as "the interaction of setting, plot, and character," or a study of "static and kinetic characters" is too advanced.[1] You should not attempt to develop a critical attitude in your pupils until after you have developed the power to read. You will agree to that statement at once—in theory. In practice, however, many young teachers, fresh from college, aware that they must "teach" something, and in possession of notebooks well stocked with critical terms, offer simple high-school freshmen slightly simplified college courses. And the result? Books that might have been enjoyed are closed avenues of pleasure, so that if pupils read at all, juvenile fiction, Western thrillers, or the saccharine *True Story* remain their recreational reading.

And last in this discouraging catalogue of lost opportunities for "teaching" fiction comes the most common and perhaps the most pernicious item. Kipling, Dickens, Hawthorne, Eliot—almost all novelists except Joyce and Virginia Woolf—divided their novels into chapters. Each chapter contains of necessity much description, numerous minor incidents, several characters. If one is seeking to "teach" something, and if one is just a little desperate as to how thirty pupils are to be kept fully occupied, one may even descend to daily quizzes on the chapter assigned, to dictionary drills on unknown words, to retelling the entire chapter, bit by bit, "in your own words." (The inference here, I suppose, is that the author has done an inferior job which a freshman can improve.) I have witnessed, too, in certain classrooms interruptions of the course of a story by diagraming exercises, so that a whole paragraph of *A Tale of Two Cities*, for example, was worked through for subject, predicate, and modifiers while Dr. Manette's fate was, supposedly, under languid discussion. This last practice

[1] For your own pleasure and for intelligent discussion of fiction with your upperclass students you will find Boas and Smith's *Enjoyment of Literature* a helpful and stimulating book to consult.

seems to me a little more vicious even than that of asking a class to outline a chapter; but since both are bad, perhaps comparison of evils is profitless.

What has been said so far? When you "teach" a novel:

1. Do not spoil the novel by overloading it with history and literary research. What will add to, what will detract from, genuine enjoyment and realization of the story is for you to decide.

2. Do not make your class overconscious of the "moral." If the book is a true picture of life, of course it shows truthfully causes, actions, and results of those actions. I know nothing more profoundly moral—in the lofty sense of the word—than watching a human soul work out its own destiny. But beware of twisting and prostituting a work of art so that it conveys some lesson that you —not the author—desire to teach. You are interested in character building; you wish to promote good citizenship. You believe in ethical discussion in class, and in inculcating sound morality. Of course you do. But you are harming, not helping, your pupils if you spoil their interest and understanding of books by overloading literature with moralistic teachings *not implicit in the book itself.*

3. Do not stress novel technique until your pupils have for a time experienced identification with the characters and complete absorption in the story. Little by little you wish to make them conscious of *how* a book is written and of *what* is good and what is inferior fiction. But just when your pupils will be able to enjoy and profit more by seeing how books are written and which characters live and which are papier-mâché is, again, a question that you must decide. Your purpose is to open up wholesome, profitable fiction as a constant pleasure, an imaginative experience, an interpretation of society's manifold moral, social, and economic problems. You must question yourself as to the training that each book is to provide. To repeat the same type of experience may be profitable for a time, but the wise teacher repeats these life situations knowingly.

4. Do not dissect a novel chapter by chapter, the class advancing upon it in lock step, reading no more than is assigned, working through that assignment, transforming an imaginative creation into a drill book for words and sentences. Here again your tact and judgment are needed. The words must be understood; the pupils' vocabularies

must increase; the sentences and paragraphs must be comprehended. And certainly if pupils always read that which is easily grasped, their type of reading would remain permanently juvenile. How much "teaching" a novel will endure and yet remain an imaginative experience you must *decide with each book*. But in your own mind and in your own practice you must always distinguish between *informational* and *imaginative* reading. For these two types, the teaching technique is radically different.

III. AT VARIOUS LEVELS OF NOVEL READING WHAT SHOULD YOU TEACH?

What you teach depends upon three things: (1) the reading ability of your pupils; (2) the books you have at hand; and (3) the amount of time you mean to devote to a specific text. More than you now realize, it will be worth while for you to consider this last factor, the time element. Just as many a short story can be improved or ruined by tampering with its time scheme, so can the presentation of a book. No one but you, the teacher in charge, can arbitrarily decide how many days it will take a class or an individual in your class to extract from a book the maximum amount of imaginative experience with the minimum waste of time. I stress this point as a caution, because many state courses of study set an arbitrary limit.[1] Treat such courses of

---

[1] One state course of study lists in part for the ninth year:

Novel (ten days; choose one)
Boyd: *Drums*
Dickens: *Nicholas Nickleby*
Eliot: *Silas Marner*
Kipling: *Captains Courageous*
Stevenson: *Treasure Island*

Drama (ten days; choose one)
Barrie: *Quality Street*
    Peter Pan
Drinkwater: *Abraham Lincoln*
MacKay: *Jeanne d'Arc*
Maeterlinck: *The Blue Bird*
Shakespeare: *Julius Caesar*

Epic Material (nine days)
Homer: *Odyssey* (Palmer's translation)
    Iliad (Bryant's translation),
    especially Books 1, 6, 22, and 24

Old Testament Narratives. Book of Esther; others.

Remember when you are teaching that not a grain but a whole salt shaker should be taken with any course of study.

study respectfully, of course, but remember that a teacher must use her own judgment. To leave a book before it has been imaginatively realized, or to linger over it after a class has absorbed all that it should *at its level* is both wasteful of effort and injurious to class interest.

What do you wish to "teach" concerning novel reading? Although novels, of course, differ materially, yet in one regard all are alike. They are created to give the reader an imaginative experience. We read a book on fly-fishing to gain from it specific information; we read Walter Lippmann or Frank Simonds for certain ideas that in turn open interesting bypaths of thought in our own minds. But we read a novel in order to share vicariously the life, scenes, emotions, and ideas of others. The first two types of reading are termed informational; the latter, a literary experience.[1]

In your entering class what will you probably find? As has already been said, most of your pupils will have read juveniles, easy episodic tales with a maximum amount of adventure, minus plot in the strict sense, and a minimum amount of detailed setting or subtle character analysis. The characters for the most part announce themselves or are pronounced by the author as good or bad. Though almost invariably their social position rises, what at the beginning of the book they are fundamentally, they remain to the end. There are no puzzling changes in character; hence there are no disconcerting alterations necessitated in the reader's judgment of those characters. The background against which they appear is either negligible or is given in a specific, straightforward manner. Practically nothing is implied; practically everything is told. And for a child there is here a satisfying certainty—for no adults can be more conservative than children —which makes reading a safe and pleasant recreation. The out-

---

[1] These terms have been so used by Fries, Hanford, and Steeves. See reading suggestions at the end of the chapter.

come of the story may remain unsuspected, but there are no hidden meanings or troublesome symbols to irk the reader.

If you question just what literature might be termed "safe and pleasant recreation," demanding little from the immature or retarded reader, consult the article by Glenn Meyers Blair, "The One Hundred Books Most Enjoyed by Retarded Readers in Senior High School"—(*English Journal,* Vol. 30, 1941, pp. 42-47).

A. Teach the Characteristics of an Adult Novel

Given, then, a group who enjoy simple reading, what is the next step in aiding them to an imaginative realization of adult fiction? As I see it, you have four general services that you can render them. *First,* you have to explain the nature of a novel. Rather slowly and explicitly you tell your group when they approach their first adult novel that they are advancing upon a slow-moving story. Something does not happen on every page. They must develop patience, for they cannot discover the outcome at once, and they must develop the ability to hold in mind many characters and remember many incidents which eventually will prove important.[1] Later, after they have read part way into the book, you will show them how one incident leads to a second and a second to a third. Then, too, you wish to keep them alive to surmises and hints dropped by the author both as to plot and as to proper interpretation of character. Still later, by questions and suggestions you will lead them to realize the relation of cause and effect. In other words, you are teaching your pupils to understand plot—something quite different from the chronological happenings or series of adventures their juvenile books have provided them.

Thanks to the moving picture, both relation of incident to incident and complication of action are fairly well understood,

---

[1] See La Brant, Lou: *The Teaching of Literature in Secondary Schools.* Because Miss La Brant has discussed so well the difficulties pupils meet in fiction reading, it is hard to avoid a mere paraphrase of what she has already said. Consult the reference to her book at the end of this chapter.

but *to see* and *to read* require, apparently, two quite different processes. Why? Because the cinema makes all things visual, but the novel provides description that remains mere words unless by an imaginative process these words are transformed into pictures.

B. Aid Your Pupils to Visualize

Here lies your *second* task. Many teachers, unconscious of a pupil's difficulties in visualizing, overlook the necessary training. As Miss La Brant has pointed out in her discussion of *Silas Marner*, the teacher needs to discuss the pictures that she sees in a sentence; the pupils need to contribute what they see. A laboratory experiment is really being conducted here. In what? In discovering and increasing (1) the pupil's power of visualizing; (2) his power of evoking from the pictured word clear-cut, concrete images rather than mere vague impressions; (3) his power of supplementing details to complete a picture that is merely suggested.

Is training in visualization possible? Of course. Recall your psychology laboratory experiments and, within reason, utilize some of that training in your teaching procedure. Have some drill in the fifteen minutes at the end or the beginning of the hour. Present carefully selected sentences to your class and ask them (1) to read or listen; (2) to close their eyes and discover what they see; (3) to list what they actually see. At this point you should help your pupils to distinguish between what they *see* and what an instant later they add to the original image.[1] What are you doing? Stimulating the imaginative pupils, jogging the brains of the more stolid, and opening the minds of all to the amazing idea that for the accomplished reader words are really pictures. Then, too, you are impressing even the dullest pupils with the realization that reading is an art which can be cultivated and improved. This last realization can be both an encour-

---

[1] Observe that you have here the basis for good extemporaneous oral work.

agement and a stimulus, encouraging to the slow, stimulating to the clever.

Try your own skill. Here is a sentence from Somerset Maugham's *On a Chinese Screen:* "You see a string of coolies come along, one after the other, each with a pole on his shoulders from the ends of which hang two great bales, and they make an agreeable pattern. It is amusing to watch their hurrying reflections in the padi water. You watch their faces as they pass you."[1] Close your eyes and consider the sentences. What do you, the prospective teacher, see? Are there many coolies or few? How do they in your mind make "an agreeable pattern"? Do they go fast or slow? Are they tottering along, or marching, or shuffling? Are they walking together or in single file? Do you see the road wide or narrow or like a footpath on a dyke? How do you picture the "padi water"? Does your "agreeable pattern" include their reflections? And what pictures pass through your mind when you read the words "You watch their faces"? In other words, how well do you visualize? Take the deserted ruins of a former civilization sketched in the words "A great dead, red city lying out on honey-colored sands." Or take "There is nothing stiller in the world than the skeleton of a house in the dawn after a fire." Yes, you can teach pupils to visualize. Many, of course, do it without instruction, and some will put you to shame, for they will live in a scene more imaginatively and completely than you, conscious as you will be, like the eldest of the Ruggles children, of the "mannerses" of your group.

It is hardly necessary to remind you that in all fiction, particularly in fiction at junior-high-school level, the main interest lies in the story. Your pupils are concerned with what comes next. You are too, but you are aiding the pupils to read so that "what comes next" is supplemented by enjoyment in pictures,

[1] From Maugham, Somerset: *On a Chinese Screen,* by permission of and arrangement with Doubleday, Doran and Company, Inc.

both those written in full and those more subtly suggeste
tures which each reader must build for himself.

C. *Assist Your Pupils to Comprehend Character Portrayal*

Your *third* responsibility in teaching novel reading is to give
direct aid to your pupils in understanding the more complicated
characters found in adult fiction. Pupils need to learn to suspend
judgment. The unprepossessing character may be either honest
or dishonest or both, as circumstance molds him; or the attractive heroine may be vain, ungenerous, and lovable. In fact, little
by little, pupils must be led to see that in good adult fiction the
characters are as inconsistent and as complicated as are real
people. Hence if disappointment is to be avoided and at least
some of your group are to be lured away from juvenile fiction
rather than driven back to it, you must be alert to show them
why characters act often as disappointingly as they do. Constantly you need to emphasize the idea that in good adult fiction, even though persons and events are fictitious, the author is
honestly attempting to portray men and women whose characters
are changed and shaped by happiness or disaster. If teachers in
the past had consistently shown the business of the author to be
the drawing of psychologically true characters, no matter how
fantastic the occurrences that befell them, and if they had constantly taught that in worth-while literature the actions grow out
of the character and the character in its turn is molded by the
action and the environment, what changes should we not see now
in the reading habits of thousands of literate adults! The many
pulp magazines, with their sugarplum tales, unreal characters,
and actions divorced from inevitable results, if they did not cease
altogether, would at least be reduced in number. Reduced also
would be the number of those readers who reject all "unpleasant"
literature, and who denounce the writers employed in presenting
and interpreting the sordid and the unhappy social and economic
conditions of today.

Just as paintings or statues present a lifelike representation of some object or person, so a novel or short story may be also an artistic production presenting some life study. You and I know that fact. But you will find that many of your pupils and even many of your pupils' parents place all fiction in the class of Coca-Colas or ice creams, a means of passing the time pleasantly. They do not grant to fiction the same honor accorded to the plastic arts, nor admit that the fiction writer should be allowed even the modified freedom of the sculptor to portray life as he sees it. Try to lead your pupils—not all at once but slowly—to realize that they must suspend judgment and first strive to understand all the factors molding a character before they judge that person.

Among the books listed at the end of the chapter, you will find much material for just this type of slow consideration. *Why* did Arrowsmith turn back to science? *Why* did Beret and *why* did Silas Lapham develop as they did? If biography, drama, short story, and novel are mingled—not a logical arrangement, but most desirable for intelligent teaching—you will more closely approximate the conditions of adult reading. You will also observe that a few of these books might be questioned, not by your pupils but by their parents. It is my contention that such questioning will not arise *if* you lead your pupils along, step by step, from juvenile reading to semijuvenile, and then to the simpler adult books.

It requires much more adult thought and feeling to appreciate *The Late George Apley* than *My Ántonia*, or to read *Babbitt* with comprehension of the pathos hidden beneath the humor and grasp of Lewis's indictment of American life, than to read *Gone with the Wind*. Do not discourage your poor readers by plunging them into material too difficult for them. But, just as surely, do not encourage pupils to read long at the same level unless that level is the highest. With some groups and in some communities you might never deal with the neurotics in *Mourning Becomes Electra;* you might never introduce Santayana, even to the best senior in your class, delighted as you may have been with *The Last Puritan*. The book demands maturity; you can be certain that the pupils are only as mature in their reading as their emotional development allows. Your main purpose is to develop *as far as you can,* but not to discourage voluntary reading.

When you have guided your pupils into adult books, when you have awakened their curiosity as to *why* characters develop as they do, or *why* they should have developed differently (Avoid ·hat deadening certainty, "The book is always right"), you have done literature a genuine service. Many adults never reach that stage. For them, as has been said, Chaucer's lovely Criseyde remains "a bad woman," *Anna Christie* a book to be banished from the library; and they wonder, rather pathetically but with "unco" self-approval, why authors do not write about pleasant people. Undoubtedly some of your pupils will join their ranks, yet surely by the end of four years you can lead the majority to realize that a great novel or play or poem is not merely a literary sweetmeat but is an honest attempt to picture or to interpret life either directly or by parable, and that the author must draw his characters as those characters are. Anna Christie is "bad"; Dunstan Cass is "bad"; yet you can show your pupils that it is more important to seek to realize what forces made them what they are than merely to pass judgment upon them. Discussion of environment and heredity may lead them to understand Dunstan and Godfrey and to realize this important fact: *The business of a novel, if it pretends to realism, is to portray faithfully some aspect of life as it has been or as it is lived.*

Although you yourself recognize that many vivid characters are also characters scarcely tinged by reality, it would not be wise to point out that fact to your amateur reader. To him Barkis, Mrs. Micawber, Jerry Cruncher, are delightfully real because they are delightfully obvious. Let him enjoy them. Perhaps later you will show him how some other characters like those of Dickens but drawn by a less skillful hand are mere caricatures of real people. Until he has lived with fiction for a time, do not crowd critical observation upon him. At first—though your teaching should not end there—work for enjoyment of story, character, setting. If at first you teach in a tiny school where no course of study exists and where you are the entire "Department of English," it will be your duty to assign to different years the books, concealed in some dusty closet, provided by the school board. Remember that novels of adventure, of action, belong in the earlier years, and that the psychological novel is by far the most difficult for young pupils to appreciate. It would be wise for you to dip back into your earlier reading, and if possible to talk with some librarian as to the books pupils read. Do you know Zane Grey? Your pupils do, and enjoy him. Do you know Dumas and Victor Hugo, and such tales as *The Red Badge of Courage, The Long Roll, The Crisis, Reds of the Midi, Kidnapped,* and *The White Company?* And do you also know that delightful series of boys' books by Howard Pease, books full of sea life, tropical islands, and breathless adventure, but written with all the skill of an experienced writer for adults? It would be wise to read, mark, learn, and inwardly digest the article by Carrie Belle Parks listed at the end of this chapter. It has imagination, vitality, and common sense, qualities that, if you read the *English Journal,* you will come to associate with her contributions. After reading it, you will realize that one of the great barriers in teaching the novel in high school is the teacher's ignorance of those tales of danger and daring which do and should meet junior-high-school demands for a "good, interesting book." You doubtless prefer a more adult fare, but unless you know the type of fiction your younger pupils read for pleasure, how can you lead them from that level to a more adult type? At first the conventional hero, the heavy villain, the caricature of a heroine, may satisfy your group. Little by little *after* they have read with enjoyment (within limits, what they read is of minor importance) you can bring them to adult fare, to such a text for example as *Silas Marner*, which after all has a real mystery, a crime, and rather easily understood motivation of character. By their senior year most of them should be reading thoroughly adult fiction: Hardy and Conrad perhaps, but surely Willa Cather, Somerset Maugham, Hugh Walpole, H. G. Wells, Arnold Bennett, and the "Book of the Month." In fact some of them will read what you read; but some will spend the rest of their lives on the level of youthful adventure or fairy-tale romance.

You may question just how and where this information concerning the proper book for the proper age can be obtained. It would be wise to know suitable books and to possess a few well-selected lists. One of the first things your principal in high school may ask of you is to give him a list of suitable fiction for the library. If, by chance, you begin teaching in a one-teacher-in-English school, this task of selection of books falls to you. In Appendix G you will find a set of references to excellent reading lists, annotated lists from which you can order with some assurance even those books which you have not read. Yet firsthand acquaintances is most desirable, even if it consists of only twenty minutes spent in a rapid survey of a modern book. Read Miss Isabelle M. Hall's article listed at the end of this chapter. Pupils, you will find, do not like to live *exclusively* in the "horse-and-buggy days" of literature. Think over that remark.

Why not prepare a list of suitable novels similar to the one by Dr. John McClelland, Associate Professor of English, Stanford University, a page of which is given below?

A READING LIST OF MODERN FICTION

This list is designed, not as a guide to the best fiction, but as a guide to some better fiction. . . . In preparing this list I have had in mind the student who has a desire to read, but who is somewhat at sea when it comes to selecting a book. With a view of assisting him, I have tried to supply a sentence or two of commentary on each book's nature and content; and, in most cases, some hint as to the mind and personality of its author. . . .

Bennett, Arnold. (Englishman: 1867-1931)

The Old Wives' Tale. (Manufacturing town in the pottery district of England: Paris during the siege of 1870) A celebrated modern realistic novel; too long, in my opinion, but presenting a convincing picture of the lives of two English women of the middle class. Crowded with minute details, but interesting. (400 or more pages)

Crane, Stephen. (American: 1871-1900)

The Red Badge of Courage. (American Civil War) A remarkably artistic performance. One of the most modern of modern novels; yet it appeared a generation ago. The psychology of a raw recruit, a farmer boy, during his first experience under fire. You have probably never read a war story quite like this. (300 pages)

I selected here two books with which, I am sure, you are familiar. But suppose you were not familiar with them; suppose you were "at sea" as to what to read. Would you not find the comment, the date, the number of pages, reassuring, particularly if you must obtain your book by way of the card catalogue?

Why do not the members of your class combine to make carefully annotated bibliographies, each selecting either a grade level or a topic? Unlike many college classes, a class in the teaching of English is of value only if it functions later in the high-school classroom. Recognize that fact, and provide yourself with material as well as with ideas immediately useful to you in your first year of teaching.

An enlightening discussion of why people read fiction is to be found in Bernard De Voto's "Snow White and the Seven Dreads," a discussion particularly applicable to the high-school reader who is seeking to know about life and living.[1] One sentence from this article has seemed to me particularly important to remember: "Delivered over to emotions that crucify and exalt him, the individual is helpless; all emotion happens to him for the first time and his need is to know what it is." Fiction tells

---

[1] De Voto, Bernard: *Minority Report*, Little, Brown, 1938, or "The Easy Chair," *Harper's Magazine*, November, 1938.

him what that emotion is and how others have met and coped with it. Fortunately most high-school boys and girls have the ability to assume during school hours a nonchalant exterior—but do not be misled. In these strenuous days of world unrest, many of them come from households facing poverty, failure, death. These "boys and girls" may be the wage-earners for the family. Love, marriage, the struggles of life on an insufficient wage, may be theirs in another three or six months. Remember, these students are faced by life; the boys are faced by a year or more in an army camp. There is not time to have them learn of standards and morals and responsibilities in some adult tomorrow. In the literature classroom is the place where life should be faced, problems discussed, standards of conduct and standards of taste considered. Often it is the teacher, not the class, who seems bent upon juvenile discussions. Feel out your class interests; then make the classwork as adult as your group can absorb with enjoyment and profit. A class need not be a solemn place; but the problems faced in much fiction are in themselves serious. What are some of the problems, you may ask?

Everybody, at some time in his teaching, meets *Silas Marner*. What problems arise that are profitable for discussion—not from the standpoint of novel technique, but from the standpoint of the pupils' future attitudes of mind and preparation for living?

1. The influence of home life on growing boys and girls
2. The need of man to be a part of his community
3. The needless suffering caused by secret marriage
4. The unhappiness arising from marriage if the husband and wife come from widely different social backgrounds
5. The inevitable bitterness arising from concealment and deceit

Does that list sound as if you were to ruin a story by over-moralizing? Just start a class (without self-consciousness on your part) on a serious problem that affects life and society. They, not you, will carry it on. Times have changed; the taboos of yesterday are the "social problems" of today. Motion pictures, magazine stories, newspapers, the talk of the neighborhood, inform your pupils about all the happenings of society; your business is to help them interpret and philosophize on those happenings and the emotions and results ensuing. If literature interprets life, as we agree that it does, you, the teacher of literature, must see that that particular interpretation is not only understood by your pupils, but is also translated into *general* terms.

If you glance over the books listed at the end of the chapter, you will realize that every one, even those on the list for retarded readers, offers *some* education as to the way people ought or ought not (for their own and for others' good) meet the joys and sorrows of life. Here pupils see the difference between large-souled and petty-souled individuals, between those concerned with the verities of life and those who float, unaware that life expects something from them if they are to gain something from life. Here are concepts of courage, persistence, generosity of spirit, democratic living, enjoyment of the simple things, humor, whimsey, courageous bravado, humility. Much can be learned vicariously of parent-child relationships and husband-wife relationships, desirable and undesirable; of love resulting in happiness or in disaster. Here, too, pupils may get their first awareness of the existence of an all-absorbing intellectual life, or the beauty of spiritual living, since, in a materialistic age and in a strictly materialistic home, such concepts may never have crossed their horizon. In the more adult novel, as suggested in the lists given on page 499, social problems (as those problems affect the individual and society as a whole) open the reader's eyes to an interpretation of happenings and social misadjustments of which as a child he was possibly unaware. Through fiction he can grasp, since it is ordered and interpreted, what might remain a puzzle until, by trial and error, he too has misinterpreted and been penalized for that stupidity. Luckily you, the teacher of English, are responsible for only a small part of the pupil's education, but you must do what you can to fit him (1) as a citizen of a democracy and (2) as an individual with a life before him. *Most of all* your special responsibility is to provide him with one joy that cannot fail him—the joy of reading.

D. Develop an Open-minded Approach toward Literature

A *fourth* responsibility that faces you when you teach fiction in high school is that of attempting to develop open-mindedness not only in the pupils' judgments of characters but in their approach to books themselves. Nothing is accomplished by forcing on pupils material that they read groaningly. But it is often true, particularly in nineteenth-century fiction, that the first thirty pages of a book may seem uninviting, and yet, after that difficult beginning, the book itself proves more fascinating than did the easy material to which pupils are accustomed. Explain that fact to them. Attempt to win from your class a tolerant attitude until a book has been given time to prove itself. Some teachers explain who the characters are and what the beginning chapters include, and then launch the pupil into the full stream of the story. This personal work takes time and knowledge, but, particularly with certain types of nonreaders, it is an effective method. Often it is possible to delegate some share of this conference work to a willing pupil who will not only take pride in launching a fellow member, but, to uphold his own reputation, will also be stirred to improve the quality of his reading. Such work also affords an opportunity for pupils to utilize in well-motivated oral work—conversational in tone but well ordered—material that they have read.

Perhaps the most valuable aspect of this work, however, has not been mentioned. If you can make reading a community affair, where practically all are interested in their own and their neighbors' reading, you are approximating the situation existing in that adult reading world of which you hope your pupils will some day be members. Encourage two pupils to read the same book, so that they can discuss the story. Throw out a conjecture of your own concerning a character or situation. Forget—publicly of course—how a book ends or why two characters are led into conflict, or what causes some character's degeneration. Then it becomes the pleasure and the duty of those who have read the book to inform you. Elsewhere I have discussed the use to be made of a teacher's ignorance. Often, of course, since you cannot know all books, this ignorance need not be assumed. But you will soon find that from one pupil you can pick up enough about a book so that you can give useful hints to the second or the twenty-second student who reads the same story. Do you observe what a far cry it is from this type of work to the old-style, Judgment Day book report, written apparently for the sole purpose of convincing a suspicious teacher that the book had been gone through? Compulsion, grades, perfunctory reports, all combined to make "outside reading" a burdensome task even for those who enjoyed fiction. Yet—so great is the power of literature—there were many pupils brought up under this system who read widely and well.

In the matter of wide reading, there exist many schools where no compulsion is used to secure either quality or quantity, but where teachers are accustomed to give strong approval to good material. Courteously they tolerate or even approve juvenile fiction, making plain, however, that each person must read at his own level. Their conviction is this: No pupil wishes to be thought immature by his fellows; therefore he will strive to improve the quality of his reading, not to fulfill an assignment, not to secure the teacher's approbation, but to win the respect of his fellow readers. Such a practice presupposes three things:

1. The presence in the class of at least a few well-read pupils who will set a fair pace in wide and discriminating reading
2. An understanding, friendly atmosphere in the class itself, one in which it is possible for the teacher and pupils to adventure into the field of literature with a minimum of teacher-pupil discord

3. A teacher whose tact and understanding make it possible for her to encourage reading upon various levels without belittling the achievement of the permanently immature [1]

Many teachers, feeling some compulsion necessary to goad their pupils into wide reading, use a point system. Each book to be read has first been evaluated by the teacher—or a point-system book list is used—and allotted from one to five or more points according to its value and difficulty. If, for example, *Mrs. Wiggs of the Cabbage Patch* were scored one point, probably *The White Company* would be given two, and *David Copperfield* four or five. Each pupil must secure a certain number of credits for wide reading. This system, it is thought by many, gives a fairer reward for reading done than is possible when any book, within limits, is counted as one book read. And many pupils are permanently immature. We all know people who "dislike any book about the sea," or "like to read about America but can't stand foreign settings." What do they really tell of themselves? That they have never learned to read imaginatively. As Mr. Canby has phrased it: "Take the story out of their street and they will not follow it. Their minds will not travel, and therefore they do not properly read." [2]

Just how you can break down these barriers remains a question, but much can be done by seeing that these inhibited pupils do read, and read the type of novel they enjoy. Then perhaps they can be led to like not a foreign setting, but at first a Canadian forest or a bit of New Mexico. Naturally you cannot begin a campaign against your pupils' prejudices, but you can bring into class material that is vivid, dramatic, appealing, and attempt to charm them into desiring more adventurous imaginative experiences. You can—if you can—read a piece of fiction aloud so well that all enjoy it. To awaken interest, you can dip into various types of books and into books of various settings. Then you can

[1] See Chapter X, "Motivation of Composition in Relation to Pupils' Reading."
[2] Canby, Henry Seidel: "On Reading Fiercely," from *Definitions, Second Series.*

"lend" the book to those who wish to go farther. Often the most effective spur is provided by the comments of other students; hence the wisdom of book-chat days. If the books read by the various pupils in the class or by the various groups of pupils center about some common problem (a man's sense of patriotism, a woman's relation to herself and to her family, the influence that one individual can have upon a community, the right of a country to dominate men's lives, the effect of war upon a community) or if it is closely fused with the social problems arising in history or social studies—these book-chat days are given a significance far greater than if they were mere scattered conversations on books of widely differing content. Analysis, deduction, judgment, are called into play. Books are considered as finished units, and plots become exciting vehicles for conveying a life situation. In such discussion suddenly a sixteenth-century setting, a Utopian dream concerning the year 4000 A.D., a modern realistic story, may take on new meaning for a class, who see that novels, no matter what the age, actually do portray the same human problems and human reactions to those problems.

E. Develop Adult-minded Readers

Does all this sound too adult for high-school pupils? Try it. I know college classes where such discussion would be "too adult," and I have known at least one literary club where such discussion would be impossible. Why? I should like to think that it was because many adults were unintelligently taught in their grade and secondary schools; because they had "studied" a text in detail but had never "read" a book as an adult should read it, fully conscious of the fundamental idea illustrated. Little by little while your classes read as widely as time, inclination, and your library will permit, you can build up with your pupils some concepts as to (1) types of novels, (2) theme as distinct from plot, (3) static characters as distinct from those who change and develop, (4) the interaction of plot, character, and setting, (5)

and the varying emphasis placed upon these three elements. Your seniors should also know some of the developments in the present-day novel.

IV. WHAT IS YOUR RESPONSIBILITY IN GUIDING PUPILS' READING?

It is evidently true that while some teachers of fiction try to invent material to "teach" in connection with fiction study, the great majority of these industrious instructors do not teach their pupils *how* to read a novel intelligently. Why? Sometimes, doubtless, because they have pupils who cannot think logically. But largely, I am afraid, because they themselves have neither discovered their pupils' level of reading nor analyzed fiction to find what information about novels renders fiction reading an intelligent, pleasurable, broadening experience. In other words, just as a fountain, even a mere bird bath, has behind it the whole city water system, so a teacher must have behind her a wealth of accumulated knowledge—much more than she intends to pour forth for her pupils. To be a stimulating teacher she must be well read and widely read. And though her reading must not be confined entirely to past writings, she must know the past if she hopes to have a sound basis for judging present-day work. Some of your upperclass boys, themselves workers, may find interest in the social aspect of life in present-day America as presented in Albert Halper's *The Foundry,* Robert Cantwell's *The Land of Plenty,* or the pictures of social unrest so excellently drawn by Dos Passos. Or they may, if brought up on farms or ranches, find interest in that calm-flowing picture of life shown in Elizabeth Madox Roberts's *The Time of Man;* or in Willa Cather's *My Ántonia.* Some teachers might point out that these books are not in their course of study or on their "outside" reading list. True. But any book that has social significance and is within the high-school student's intellectual and emotional grasp may serve to open up the world about him.

One question will always arise: What is and what is not suitable for high-school reading? You may question, for example, having your pupils read present-day naturalistic fiction. You may question William Faulkner, Vardis Fisher, or Erskine Caldwell as suitable material for youth. I should most certainly. To these particular moderns I should be reluctant to lead my students, but of this I am convinced: If of their own accord they read these books, it is far wiser for them to discuss what they have read with you than for them to pass the books secretly from hand to hand, brooding over them without intelligent adult guidance. Here they find mental horror, sex, and brutality blended with skill and sometimes with artistry. Obviously these are not the writers best suited to high-school youth, but I am confident that if you teach your pupils to regard literature as a record of man's hopes, fears, ideals, phobias, rebellions against life, and escapes from living, even the naturalistic fiction of today can be fairly judged by them. *What you want to give your pupils is a sane and honest view of life—pleasant and unpleasant—through the literature of the ages.* But it is wise, nonetheless, to guide pupils away from the psychopathic and steer them in the direction of what we term normal relations and normal reactions toward love, birth, death, and the various episodes that lie between.

How much or how little you can do in individual conferences will depend upon your tact and judgment, upon your ability to set each member of a class to carrying on his own work, and upon the amount of your own teaching. But of this be sure: You can accomplish more in arousing interest in reading by giving a word of encouragement to one, lending a book that you like to another, comparing notes on some episode with a third, than you can ever accomplish by regimented work with a class group. To what end, then, does this discussion of books and pupils lead? Obviously there are three things which you, a prospective teacher of literature, must attempt:

1. To increase your knowledge of books, recognizing in each the imaginative experience that it affords

2. To increase your sensitivity to the moods and reactions of others, so that intuitively you realize the perplexities and needs of your pupils

3. To increase, through practice, your skill not only in stimulating a pupil's desire to read a particular book but also in awakening in him an intellectual curiosity which he must satisfy

It is a big order. But until you have read widely, how can you know what types of reading will fit the various types of pupils? How can you bolster up the courage of one pupil whose father is out of work, whose mother is ill, and who, discouraged and perhaps undernourished, needs to believe that life can be worth living just to find the courage to go on trying to get an education? And how can you suggest a book that will distract the ugly adolescent little girl in need of an ideal to dignify living for her, or the little boy who knows that in him lies hidden another Lindbergh but who quietly refuses to exert himself in school? They are all different. Fiction, at high-school level, you will find, will serve to encourage, to ennoble, to energize, even more than it will serve to build literary appreciation or offer material for artistic creative work; and if it does accomplish these former ends, you will find that you are teaching not English or American literature but boys and girls who are entering upon the task of living. Already they are distracted by far too many interests. They are all avid—blasé as they appear—to know more about life and about themselves in relation to other people. Recognize their differences and their common interests. Then make wide reading an exploration into the very problems that await them: how people in the past and in the present have met or are meeting hardship, ease, peace, war, love, marriage, parenthood, civil and political problems, social maladjustment, justice and injustice. Show them through literature how men and women have been in the past and are today—in spite of suffering and injustices—building lives profitable to themselves and to their community because they have the fortitude and the persistence to labor for a social state in which freedom and justice for all, not for a favored few, shall exist. It is only by a long view of the world's history that one can gain some perspective upon the changing social and economic conditions of the present day. Strive for such a philosophical perspective in order that you may lead your pupils intelligently. Fiction is not a thing apart, a plaything for "leisure reading"—delightful and desirable as that view of it may be. It is an artistic presentation of life, from which adolescent youth may learn much concerning the emotions, ideals, successes, and defeats of persons like themselves, confronted by the same problems which confront them and meeting those problems in craven or in courageous fashion.

V. THE SHORT STORY

Novels are not the only fictional form known to your pupils. Most of them will be familiar either with such tales as "Rip Van Winkle" or with the short story itself in some form. What they have read and how they read is your first interest. Of one thing you can be certain: The short story, upon some level, is the only fiction many of your pupils read and will continue to read long after they have forgotten English 10A or 12B. Hence the short story provides an excellent bridge to other literature. It is briefer than the novel; it is simpler than the drama; it is more easily grasped than poetry. Moreover, it is a form with which almost every seventh-grade pupil has had some experience.

In college you have, doubtless, learned much as to point of view, time scheme, character contrast, setting, shift in moods, uses of dialogue, repetition, thesis implications. But a story is primarily a *story*, a narrative told to entertain. Until your pupils can read a story intelligently, can grasp its purpose and some of the shades of meaning and implications, they have little business with the technique of telling. Concern yourself first with your pupils' grasp and enjoyment of the plot, of the characters, of the bits of description which provide background or delay action. Give in class just enough discussion of technique to enhance that comprehension and enjoyment. Do not spoil for your immature pupils all stories above "pulp" level by attempting a college course in story technique.

VI. WHAT SHOULD HIGH SCHOOL PUPILS LEARN ABOUT THE SHORT STORY?

First you must decide what collections of short stories are suitable for high school. To aid in that decision, I suggest that you secure *Basic Book Collection for High School*,[1] ALA, 1950 and the Oregon State Library supplements to it, 1950 and 1952. Here is a well-selected and annotated list of novels, but of particular value to you are the carefully selected short-story anthologies, each with a detailed table of contents. Other lists exist, but few are so helpful and up-to-date as this one, plus its supplements. After consulting such a bibliography, you cannot plead ignorance of what pupils might, can, or do read; you might rightly ask, however: Just what does a teacher *do* with a story after asking the pupils to read it thoughtfully? Much that has already been said about novel reading is of course equally applicable to this briefer form of fiction. But a short story is not an exceedingly short novel. Just as the writer of poetry has a purpose different from the writer of prose, so the short-story writer has a different problem from that confronting the novelist, and has somewhat different designs upon his reader.

As pupils outgrow the tales of childhood and advance to plot stories, I like to provoke discussion which reveals the short story as a wedge or section cut out of the characters' lives and presented to the reader as a unit. The wedge, of course, implies that life for these characters has gone on before the story opened. Probably it infers that life goes on for them after the reader has

[1] ALA, Chicago, Ill. Supplements from Oregon State Library, Salem, Ore.

closed the book. Pupils then attempt to see how much about this former life is told or implied. (Such inferences on their part are later used in recognizing the conventions of the drama.) Naturally the questions arise: "Why did the writer select this particular wedge?" "What does it contain that makes it, above all the years or days in the characters' lives, important?" (You might, of course, pour out upon your freshmen's heads Poe's definition of the short story; but how unwise you would be! Let your pupils discover for themselves.)

Freshmen reading Homer's admirable short story of Odysseus and the Cyclops have puzzled excitedly over the question "What is the very first detail that you, as editor, could not cut without spoiling the plot?" Finally a pupil may remember that convenient bag of wine—ten times stronger than other wine—which makes possible the escape of Odysseus. From that or some similar incident grows discussion of the writer's selection of events, and his preparation for later events. Pupils are quick to show that this preparatory material must be casually introduced, so that the reader remains unaware of its significance until he looks back over the story.[1] We also discuss what a good time Homer (in the ninth grade we think of him as *one* man) must have had writing that story, how he worked for suspense; how he enjoyed the Cyclops' putting his hand right on the ram under which Odysseus was hidden; and how, what with all the noise of sheep and their baaing, of course the Cyclops couldn't hear Odysseus' heels dragging on the ground. We consider how casually Homer mentioned the sticks for the fire, those sticks which came in handy later, and how he disposed of all the neighbors so that none would come near the cave when they heard cries issuing from it. We consider Odysseus, too, his coolheadedness, his com-

---

[1] In my classes I speak of "signposts" (a term borrowed from E. R. Mirrielees, Stanford University) and draw little posts on the board, indicating that one side is blank; on the other the number of miles is given to the city of X. We, the readers, see the blank side, but when we arrive at our destination (the end of the story), looking back, we see the information conveyed by each post.

mon sense, his cunning. We agree that "it was just like him" to stop long enough in his escape by boat to hurl taunts at the Cyclops. We have earlier spoken of Homer's evident enjoyment of suspense, but we mention it again as it is shown by the Cyclops' parting rock, flung at the fleeing Odysseus, that rock which washed the little boat back and back toward the Cyclops' island.

Why, you might ask, at this point import Homer and the *Odyssey* into the discussion of the short story? It is a great adventure story, a story pupils enjoy, and when a class is living through an adventure, it enjoys a sympathetic discussion of those perils. You recall that "As the twig is bent, the tree inclines." From some such informal discussion the pupils learn how to visualize the scenes, but also how to look with critical eyes at the way stories are told. Who knows? Later they may develop taste and critical judgment.

High-school youth likes humor and adventure. Begin with a class reading of some humorous stories which will put your freshmen in a pleasantly anticipatory mood. Be sure that, as with other units, you take time to launch the story *pleasantly*. A happy class period when the pupils chuckle with genuine amusement *with* not *at* you, the teacher, forms an unforgettable bond uniting you, the class, literature. Naturally, every class varies, but in spite of that fact I shall suggest three levels of short-story consideration: the first for the ninth grade; the second for the tenth grade, and the third for the eleventh and twelfth. But please remember that the freshman work may be appropriate for some of your seniors, or the senior work be appropriate for your sophomores.

SHORT STORIES FOR THE NINTH GRADE

Story. "Miss Letitia's Profession" by Lupton A. Wilkinson

Miss Letitia, a fragile, dainty New England spinster, whose inefficient brother is the ill-paid editor of *Hot Clues*, a cheap confession magazine, has, through her desire to aid that brother, trained herself to write crime confessions, becomes proficient, becomes well-to-do, and is secretly fascinated by the thieves' slang and argot, which she studies diligently. Alone, she confronts a thief in her dining room; from her ladylike lips falls a string of epithets that routs the thief. A little tired, she returns to her needlepoint for the church social.

Reason for Selection. The story is humorous; the character is convincingly drawn; each event is carefully prepared for. The argot itself, the incongruity of those words from those lips, would delight the class. It is a steppingstone, and an amusing one, from pure adventure to adventure plus character. It would lead well (as suggested in *Twenty-two Short Stories of America*) to a consideration of O. Henry's "After Twenty Years" (a much poorer story). At this level I should also introduce the heroic story "Turkey Red" by Frances Gilchrist Wood, a frontier tale blending near-tragedy, idealism, and a happy ending. The story of the dull Pennsylvania Dutch girl by Elsie Singmaster, "Mr. Brownlee's Roses"—a girl who is competent in trying circumstances—again blends humor with pathos.[1]

SHORT STORIES FOR THE TENTH GRADE

Stories. "The Monkey's Paw" by W. W. Jacobs
"Miss Hinch" by Henry Sydnor Harrison
"The Hands of the Enemy" by Charles Caldwell Dobie

"The Monkey's Paw" you'll find in many anthologies. "Miss Hinch" and "The Hands of the Enemy" are in the Gerould and Bayly anthology *Contemporary Types of the Short Story*, Harper.

Contents. All are adventure stories. "Miss Hinch" gives the prolonged chase of detective and criminal, the reader being uncertain which is which; "The Monkey's Paw" is a gruesome tale of a magic paw by means of which the possessor may have three wishes granted, but always with tragic consequences. "The Hands of the Enemy" gives the adventurous night of a professor interested in psychology

---

[1] "Turkey Red" in H. C. Schweikert's *Short Stories*. "Miss Letitia's Profession," "After Twenty Years," and "Mr. Brownlee's Roses" in E. R. Mirrielees' *Twenty-two Short Stories of America*.

For tenth-grade nonreaders try the *American Boy Anthology*, Crowell Co., New York. It contains the popular story "Captain of the *Araby*" by Howard Pease, noted writer for boys.

and sociology. The skillful character-drawing and repetition of situation makes it memorable.

Reason for Selection. Through their series of events all three are interesting to the reader, although the last two call for careful reading and each calls for some understanding of character. The point of view from which the story is told becomes important. The first is told by the Godlike author; the second, "Miss Hinch," is told objectively; the last is told by the professor, but the reader is kept aware of the differences possible were the story told from another point of view. With these tales of adventure plus character I should combine such stories as Fanny Hurst's "Ice Water, Pl————" and O. Henry's "The Third Ingredient." Here character and home environment are important.[1]

SHORT STORIES FOR THE ELEVENTH AND TWELFTH GRADES

Stories. "A Source of Irritation" by Stacy Aumonier
"I'm a Fool" by Sherwood Anderson
"Haircut" by Ring Lardner
"Night Club" by Katharine Brush
"The Killers" by Ernest Hemingway

Contents. All reveal character; three reveal social conditions. "A Source of Irritation" is amusing in its presentation of a stolid, unimaginative farm worker suddenly caught in romantic adventure. "I'm a Fool" is a boy's analysis of his own desire to "show off" and the resultant unhappiness. The reality of the mood and the speech makes this an unforgettable story. "Haircut" and "Night Club" both give the dull, unimaginative, and hence insensitive person's view of uncomprehended tragedy. "The Killers," told almost completely through conversation, is a gangster story with an unforgettable ending.

Reason for Selection. These five stories are thought-provoking. The first, "A Source of Irritation," is humorous. It lays a good foundation for the third, where it becomes obvious that stupidity and cruelty are often akin. "I'm a Fool" puts before the pupils clearly both the hopelessness of the drifter and the folly of pretense. (It often provokes a frank and helpful discussion of the difficulties of youth.) "The Killers," often understandable at first to high-school age, calls for reading between the lines, and recognition of the use

[1] Both stories are in H. C. Schweikert's *Short Stories.*

of conversation to cover the nervousness of the two gangsters. All but the first story call for much interpretation, much reading between the lines. "Haircut" is an indictment of the small town; "Night Club," of the unsatisfying, unthinking life of the city.

You will note that I have selected modern short stories for this discussion. Do you recall the pupil's comment on "horse-and-buggy days" in literature? First interest your pupils; interest them in plot, character-drawing, theses, pictures of society and of man's relation to himself, to his fellow men and to his country, and to his Maker. The short story, though short, is not trivial; it is not, if you choose above the cheap level, a mere ice-cream soda with which to pass the time. Interest your pupils with both new and old material; then give them as much thoughtful reading of excellent stories, both old and new, as time and their ability permit. If you choose stories wisely, you are providing a laboratory course in analysis of character, environment, problems in living handled by an artist. The great advantage here, as in drama and novel study, is that pupils can receive a preview of life, but an orderly preview in which cause and effect are logically related.

By the time your pupils graduate, most of them should know that cheap fiction is cheap largely because the author has not concerned himself with a nice adjustment between *motive, action, result*. He fails to build convincingly; hence we are not persuaded that the motives ascribed are sufficient to produce the resulting action. Then, too, he disregards those inevitable consequences which would of necessity follow the act. In class I have often used an old play, *The Man Who Came Back,* to illustrate this point. In one scene the man is the lowest of the low in a Shanghai opium den; the next, clad in white, and married to a sweet young thing, he is the happy and apparently healthy proprietor of a sugar plantation. Such a play or story, purporting to be realistic, in which the inevitable results are sheared off as they are in numberless pulp magazines, from my point of view is immoral, and certainly poor training for the young. It is hardly necessary to add that it is poor art.

For your convenience I am appending at the end of this chapter material to be found in anthologies of modern stories, some of them planned not for children but for adults. Use these latter books with your advanced students, those students who need more grown-up fare than do the rest of the class.

SUGGESTED EXERCISES[1]

Before you attempt these exercises, read a number of the references listed at the end of this chapter. It might be wise to file papers in order to have them for future use in your own classrooms. Perhaps an exchange with other class members might prove profitable.

1. Select some rather simple well-known book suitable for high-school use; then, *after* you have read Miss Parks's article "Literary Escalators: Literature for Everybody," construct a literary escalator of your own, leading to this book. A suitable novel for your goal might be such a book as *The Black Arrow, The Three Musketeers, The Red Badge of Courage, Kidnapped,* or a more mature book such as *The Rise of Silas Lapham, Song of the Lark, Vanity Fair, Typhoon, The Scarlet Letter, Barren Ground.*

2. Take this problem: You have a retarded group of tenth-grade pupils. Decide how you will teach some modern novel. Prepare for the class an outline for the work, plus lists of books to be used as an extended "free-reading" list.

3. Select five stories for each selection given below. Take stories not discussed in your text; prepare to teach them as (a) a unit in home relations; (b) a unit in courage; (c) a unit in character study.

4. Decide with five modern novels—consider *The Yearling* for one—what type of unit would be most interesting in building these five into a required list, surrounded, of course, by many for free reading.

5. Select one volume from the following list of anthologies. Go over it carefully as if you were selecting a possible text for high school. Consult the criteria for judging textbooks, given in Appendix L. Decide what reasons dictated both the material selected and

---

[1] For further reading lists see Appendix G.

the order of its arrangement. Before you begin work on the anthologies listed below, turn to page 658 in the text. Read carefully "Criteria for Selecting a Graded Series of Anthologies of Literature." How should you begin this research? Read the introduction and table of contents; then read or glance through several units, noting the different types of literature and the various aids given for each different type. Consider the pupils' probable interest awakened by this material, and the possible educational value gained from it. If possible it would be wise to devote some class time to discussion of these anthologies. Remember that it is usually the teacher who selects from an approved list the texts for class use, a serious responsibility. From anthologies you can learn (1) how reading units may be organized, (2) what books for free reading are considered appropriate at each grade level, and (3) what kind of guidance is given to aid the reader.

The following anthology series will offer you contrasts in purpose, material, guidance, and that subtle quality termed inspiration. If your own schooling lies some distance behind you, the modernity of more recent anthologies may surprise you. The junior-senior high-school student today, surrounded by radio and other audio-visual programs, needs to understand the present of which he hears so constantly. But he also needs to understand the past through the best literature that *at his level of development* has vital human interest for him. Literature, well selected, becomes vital, as anthology makers know, if tactfully presented. There must be sufficient (1) background material, (2) aids in reading and vocabulary, and (3) lists of appropriate free reading. But all this equipment, unless so presented as to arouse a feeling of vitality and genuine pleasure in literature, depresses rather than stimulates the student. Remember also that different types of literature demand different types of reading. Examine the anthologies. Have their makers lived up to this responsibility? There is need too for education of the emotions at each stage of development. Judged by present national and international conditions, what intellectual and emotional qualities must future citizens develop if they are to serve as good citizens and as happy individuals?

Anthologies—Junior High School

1. Invitation to Reading Series and Adventures Series, Harcourt, Brace, provide two different levels of instruction. In the first series,

designed for the "book-shy adolescent," the literature is fitted to his interests, reading ability, and intellectual capacities.

Adventures Series, *Challenge to Grow, Challenge to Explore,* and *Challenge to Understand,* presents in each book through modern and traditional literature twelve to fifteen challenges to the reader. The purpose is to develop personal, intellectual, and emotional growth.

2. Cultural Growth Through Reading—Literature-Speech Series, Laidlaw, offers a sharp contrast to the books listed above. Here strong emphasis is placed upon the development of speech skills such as enunciation, pronunciation, voice quality; and upon widely different speech situations in connection with the literature or the general idea of each unit. The books, divided into two parts, are designed to provide material for each term.[1]

Anthologies—Senior High School

1. Adventure Series, Mercury Edition, Harcourt, Brace, 1952. The format of these texts with their eight-page colored picture-and-text section at the beginning of each volume provides a vivid, artistic, and most inviting introduction to literature. The understanding and enjoyment of literature throughout the books is heightened by means of highly artistic colored pictures, photographs, and sketches. For many students this combining of literature with other arts should open to them a new realm of enjoyment. Each book provides much material not in earlier editions and often preceded by preparatory suggestions, followed by suggestions for study. Footnotes, a glossary, charts and maps, and lists for free reading, annotated in the first two books, provide material that increases the enjoyment of reading.

The series:

I. *Adventures in Reading*

II. *Adventures in Appreciation*

III. *Adventures in American Literature:* Part I, "Modern American Literature"; Part II, "The Growth of American Literature"

IV. *Adventures in English Literature:* Part I, "The Anglo-Saxon Period" through "The Victorian Age"; Part II, "The Modern Age"

[1] Investigate other anthologies. Few differ from others as radically as do the series listed above.

2. The World in Literature Series, Ginn, 1946. This series offers an interesting comparison, particularly the first two volumes, with the series just described. Quite aside from the usual purposes of improvement in reading skills, growth of vocabulary, enjoyment, and thoughtful appreciation of literature which are basic factors in practically all anthologies, as they are in this one, in the first two books a new factor enters. It is the determined purpose that pupils in the United States shall broaden their horizons by reading selections of high literary quality, in translation, from countries not their own as well as material from England and the United States. Books I and II, for the first two books are interchangeable, are:

The series:

I. *Within the Americas.* The units are: U.S.A., North of 49, The Animal World, South of the Rio Grande, Treasure Island, and The Americas (selections from the Western Continent)

II. *Beyond the Seas* provides freshmen or sophomores with sympathetic understanding of peoples east and west of the United States and of their types of living

III. *Writers in America*

IV. *Writers in England*

The last two volumes follow the conventional pattern. All the volumes are illustrated, and in the first two the illustrations, in color and black and white, do much to increase interest and understanding of the foreign countries.

3. America Reads Series, Scott, Foresman, 1951. Only two volumes are in print (March, 1951), but these two, I. *Good Times in Literature* and II. *Exploring Life Through Literature,* have one quality that differentiates them from the two series discussed. Note the discussion, "The Author's Craft," following most of the selections. Here freshmen and sophomores are made aware, through statement and questions, of the writer's skill and by what means he holds the readers' interest. Accompanying the first volume is a work book called *Think-It-Through Book.* Look at it if you can. In tone is it similar to the various texts listed?

SUGGESTED READINGS

A. References for Your Own Guidance

The English Language Arts, Vol. I, N.C.T.E. Curriculum Series, Dora V. Smith, Director

Summarize what you have read in Part I, Chapters 1 and 2, and Part III, Chapter 16. Then apply that reading to the study of fiction. How may fiction hasten growth and development?

1. Poley, Irving: "English as a Help in Developing Mature Personalities," *Bulletin of the National Association of Secondary-School Principals,* Vol. 30 (February, 1946), pp. 163-69

2. Loban, Walter: "Evaluating Growth in the Study of Literature," *English Journal,* Vol. 36 (June, 1948), pp. 277-83

Words from an outstanding teacher of literature.

3. Rosenblatt, Louise M.: *Literature as Exploration,* Appleton-Century, 1938

4. Taba, Hilda: *Literature for Human Understanding,* American Council on Education, Washington, D. C., 1949

5. Carlsen, George Robert: "Creating a World Outlook Through Literature," *English Journal,* Vol. 30 (1944), pp. 526-37

6. Boas, Ralph Philip: *The Study and Appreciation of Literature,* Harcourt, Brace, 1931

See also *Enjoyment of Literature* by Boas and Smith, Harcourt, Brace, 1934. An even better book, one desirable to have on your desk.

B. References Concerned with Teaching

From the English Journal

1. Gulick, James: "A Method for Organizing Classroom Book Reading," Vol. 39 (1950), pp. 387-90

2. Wilds, Mary Edmund: "Experimenting with an Outside Reading Program," Vol. 38 (1949), pp. 29-33

3. Magalander, Marvin: "Pitfalls in Modern Reading," Vol. 38 (1949), pp. 6-10

4. Miller, Georgia E.: "Adapting Reading Materials to Varying Ability Levels," Vol. 27 (1938), pp. 751-59

5. Gillum, Margaret: "Interpreting Family Relations Through Literature," Vol. 26 (1937), pp. 539-47

6. McLaughlin, Ora C.: "Reading Lesson," Vol. 29 (1940), pp. 810-18

7. Chambers, Helen L.: "The 'Extensive' Method in Junior High School Literature," Vol. 29 (1940), pp. 32-36

8. La Brant, Lou: "A Little List," Vol. 38 (1949), pp. 37-40

C. Novels to Encourage Thoughtful Reading [1]

Our American Scene

Rise of Industry and Social Consciousness

Howells: *The Rise of Silas Lapham*   Norris: *The Octopus*
Addams: *Twenty Years at Hull House*   Tarkington: *Alice Adams* and *The*
Gilfillan: *I Went to Pitt College*   *Turmoil*
Glasgow: *Vein of Iron*   Wharton: *The House of Mirth*

Civil War and the South

Crane: *The Red Badge of Courage*   Dowdey: *Bugles Blow No More*
Benét: *John Brown's Body*   Glasgow: *The Battle-Ground*
Churchill: *The Crisis*   Young: *So Red the Rose*

Middle Western—Twentieth Century

Lewis: *Arrowsmith*   Lewis: *Babbitt*
Anderson: *Winesburg, Ohio*   Masters: *Spoon River Anthology*
Cather: *Song of the Lark*   O'Neill: *Ah! Wilderness*
De Kruif: *Microbe Hunters*   Ostenso: *Wild Geese*

New England and Down East

Wharton: *Ethan Frome*   Wilder: *Our Town*
Chase: *Mary Peters*   Wilkins, Mary E.: Short stories

Pioneers and Early Settlers

Rölvaag: *Giants in the Earth*   Cather: *Death Comes for the Arch-*
Aldrich: *A Lantern in Her Hand*   *bishop, My Ántonia,* and *O Pio-*
Sandoz: *Old Jules*   *neers!*

Why not build further so that the students glimpse conditions in the United States since 1918?

D. The Short Story

From the *English Journal*

1. Neville, Mark: "Summer Reading for Junior and Senior High School Pupils," Vol. 38 (1949), pp. 341-48

See also Vol. 37 (1948), pp. 297-306.

[1] Selected from Lucyle Hook's admirable list portraying "Our American Scene," *English Journal,* Vol. 28 (1939), pp. 17-18. Printed by permission of the editor.

2. Kelley, Ruth: "Extensive Reading of the Short Story," Vol. 21 (1932), pp. 651-54

3. Brown, Carroll E.: "Why Do Boys Like to Read Frank Merriwell?" Vol. 19 (1930), pp. 483-84

4. Vickery, Thyra: "Narration Recollected in Tranquillity," Vol. 30 (1941), pp. 299-306

5. Mirrielees, Edith R.: "Short Stories, 1950," Vol. 40 (1951), pp. 247-54

From Other Sources

1. Smith, Dora V.: "Make Friends with Books," *Elementary English,* Vol. 28 (1951), pp. 70-75

2. Carr, Constance: "Substitutes for the Comic Books I," *Elementary English,* Vol. 28 (1951), pp. 194-200; 214

3. ————: "Substitute for Comic Books II," *Elementary English,* Vol. 28 (1951), pp. 276-85

4. Witty, Paul A.: "Children's Interest in Reading the Comics," *Journal of Experimental Education,* Vol. 10 (December, 1941), pp. 100-04

5. Pancost, M. H.: "Need English Be Boring to Boys?" *Education,* Vol. 71 (1950), pp. 17-18

6. Webb, Marian A.: "Regionalism in Young People's Books," *Elementary English,* Vol. 28 (1951), pp. 76-81

7. Smith, W. F.: "Literature: Students Tell Why They Elect It," *Clearing House,* Vol. 24 (1949), pp. 244-45

Aids

1. Order from The National Council of Teachers of English, 211 West 68th Street, Chicago 21, Illinois.

Books for You, a Reading List for Teen-Agers, 1500 titles listed and annotated (for grades 9-12). Selected by the N.C.T.E. Committee, Mark Neville, Chairman. Single copies, 40 cents; ten or more, 30 cents.

E. Recent Collections of Short Stories

1. Jaffe, Adrian H., and Scott, Virgil: *Studies in the Short Story,* William Sloane Associates, 1949

2. Wood, William Ransom: *Short Short Stories,* Harcourt, Brace, 1951

3. Heydrick, Benjamin A., and Thompson, Blanche Jennings: *Americans All,* rev. ed., Harcourt, Brace, 1949

4. Certer, Henry: *Short Stories for Our Times,* Houghton Mifflin, 1951

CHAPTER XVI

Nonfiction and the School Library

I. METHODS OF ENCOURAGING NONFICTION READING

Do you remember your own reaction at twelve, or fourteen, or sixteen, to the term "nonfiction"? If you do, perhaps you will better understand those pupils for whom the term is synonymous with dullness. And often their estimate is for them correct. Fiction they know in either book or film form, and they enjoy identifying themselves with the heroes and heroines of many thrilling adventures. They like the sense of suspense, the rapidity of action, and the appeal to their imaginations and emotions. One day a teacher confronts them, unskillfully perhaps, with factual material, or—worse—with an abstract idea embellished by many puzzling illustrations and references. What is the result? A fixed dislike of all nonfiction, and a conviction that it must of necessity be dull. This idea has been fostered in certain schools by the often unwise insistence upon a three-to-one proportion, one nonfiction book to three fiction, in each student's so-called voluntary reading. From this ruling, pupils draw the deduction that to buy the pleasures of fiction, one must endure nonfiction. Naturally such a student attitude hampers intelligent reading.

A. Why Is Nonfiction Unpopular in High School?

Students, however, as has already been suggested, are not entirely to blame for this widespread prejudice; teachers are in part responsible. If you could spend one day with a skilled librarian in a public library frequented by pupils of junior-high-school age, you would soon find the chief source of pupil prejudice. Teachers as a class, particularly senior-high-school teachers, do not know the nonfiction books that appeal to boys and girls of twelve to fifteen. Regardless of this ignorance, they attempt to hurry their pupils into nonfiction, nonfiction of an adult type. Before you lead your pupils to reading of this kind, you should, of course, acquaint yourself with books that they can enjoy. Are you familiar with Paine's *Girl in White Armor* (Joan of Arc), Lindbergh's *We*, Rickenbacker's *Fighting the Flying Circus*, or Miss Ferris's many delightful books for girls? Have you read, at least in part, Cornelia Meigs's *Invincible Louisa* (Louisa M. Alcott), Nordhoff and Hall's *Falcons of France*, Thomas's *Boy's Life of Colonel Lawrence?* These books and books like them are steppingstones from juvenile fiction to adult article, biography, and essay. When pupils are led through them, enjoying the fine courage and sense of accomplishment found in them, they are not only willing but eager to adventure further. By twelve or fourteen, many pupils, particularly boys, desire something "true." For them an easy transition from tales of childhood is the "true" adventure: Adams's *Stonewall* (Jackson), Ross's *South of Zero* (some early expeditions to the pole), or Davidson's tale of Australia called *Red Heifer*. But even such alluring books as these need proper introduction. A mimeographed list of titles in the hands of nonreaders is a poor guide to the riches of the school or town library. At this point one intelligent librarian is probably of more value than are a dozen willing but uninformed teachers of English, for the librarian, if she is intelligent, has knowledge of books, sympathy, and intuitive appreciation of the pupils' needs. She knows at once a book for the pupil wanting "something that really happened," "a book about airplanes," "something about Indians," or "something about boats and machines." The same intuition guides her in finding a wholesome book for the overdeveloped girl who seeks romance in *True Story* or *She Done Him Wrong*. And she is wise enough to know from her long handling of books and readers that the girl who finds genuine interest in Cades's *Good Looks for Girls* will seek the library again and later will find there books of less specialized interest.

But not all the work can be left to the librarian. Just as a carpenter owns his tools, so you, a teacher of English, must be well supplied with tools for your trade; hence you should know many, and possess some, reading lists. You will find in Appendix G a list carefully selected from lists that have been compiled by librarians and teachers well versed in the reading interests of high-school pupils.

B. How Can You Popularize Nonfiction?

Different teachers, of course, attempt in different ways to lead their pupils to nonfiction reading. When school boards are sufficiently generous, some teachers maintain a magazine table in their classrooms. There junior-high-school pupils find such attractive reading as the stories and articles in *American Girl, Story Parade, National Geographic, Popular Mechanics* and *Popular Science*. In the senior-high-school group, magazines such as *Harper's, National Geographic, Travel*, the *Nation, American Magazine*, the *Atlantic*, and *Life* are popular. If, even by rotating these magazines, different classrooms cannot secure them, then a library magazine table is established. In either case the teacher makes it her business to see that the fare provided is appetizing. For her younger pupils she reads bits from the magazines, finds a picture of a ski-jumper, a streamline train, or an account of an outboard-motor boat race. These very simple articles, because of their brevity, provide an excellent means of interesting pupils in nonfiction. A *Collier's* article, for example, on the American boy who, alone and without money, sauntered into the English field and won the world's championship in rifle-shooting may have three values. It may (1) furnish a connection with a modern magazine found in many homes; (2) lure the nonreader into the reading of simple prose; and (3) perhaps provide some pupils with an oral report in which a boy's skill, energy, and persistence are stressed. Is this literature? No, certainly not, but you are building wisely nonetheless, so long as, dissatisfied with that level, you are consciously building to a higher one, and at the same time are securing interest and enjoyment at each step.

C. What Use Shall You Make of Magazines and Newspapers?

Perhaps never before in the history of the American high school has it been easier to interest pupils in the modern newspaper and magazine article. Today, economic activities directly affect large numbers of high-school pupils. Today science offers spectacular changes that are absorbingly interesting to the scientific-minded, and industry opens new possibilities for training. On the part of high-school pupils there is a serious, practical attitude of mind unknown before. These various conditions, plus the increased simplification of magazine material, have made nonfiction in magazines far more popular among pupils than it was, say, ten or fifteen years ago. The magazines of today, beginning with the simple ones—the *American Boy*, the *American Girl*, *Scientific American*, *Scholastic* (an admirable magazine planned exclusively for high-school English classes)—and leading up to our best weekly and monthly magazines, offer a broad field that you must not fail to utilize. For you, busy as you will be, the *Reader's Digest* may serve perhaps to save your time and put you quickly in touch with a wide range of topics. The annotated list of articles given in each issue of the *English Journal* may also prove useful to you, since in the welter of magazines that appears today pupils need suggestions as to specific articles. You must guide them, of course, but also you must encourage each one to explore for himself and to read widely, more widely than you yourself have time to read.

Some teachers question the wisdom of introducing high-school pupils to this contemporary literature. They feel that in the little time allotted to literature reading in high school, it is wrong to divert any of it to this modern, frankly ephemeral material. Much is to be said for their contention. In drama, fiction, and poetry, all based as they are upon human relationships and human emotions, pupils can usually gain more from certain great masters of the past than from modern writers. To live wisely in the present they need a knowledge of how past peoples have met situations fundamentally similar to their own, and where these people have succeeded and where failed. If through certain carefully selected classics you as teacher have the wisdom to show your pupils how the same ethical or social problem that confronts men today appeared in Greece, in Rome, in eighteenth-century England, and in Puritan America, these older authors can provide a more vital educational experience than can lesser writers of the present. Don't neglect the better modern writers, though.

But the case with nonfiction is entirely different. The nonfiction which your pupils now read, and which they will read as adults, deals largely with economics, sociology, psychology, science, and exploration. In these fields they must primarily read the writers of their own century. And for the great majority this reading will consist of nonfiction magazine articles rather than of nonfiction books. Train them so that they know the better-type magazine and newspaper, and attempt to save them from accepting as true the sensational, the vicious, the antisocial, merely because it appears in print. There is important work awaiting you here. You might be surprised to find the number of families represented in your school who believe the printed page implicitly because they have never been led to question it. You will have done much for your pupils, the future citizens of the United States, if you liberate them from the tyranny of print.

What can you do with the contemporary newspaper and magazine? Of the two, the problem of the newspaper will prove the simpler. In all probability newspaper reading will be closely associated with the work in social studies. Such a paper as the *American Observer*,[1] carefully prepared for students, can be used

---

[1] The *American Observer*, Civic Educational Service, 1733 K St., Washington, D. C. Planned for class use.

for accurate information concerning domestic and foreign questions. But the local daily paper, the papers read in your vicinity, and, if possible, such papers as the *New York Times* and the *Christian Science Monitor,* should be consulted, discussed, and questioned. Breed incredulity, a wholesome quality. Before they accept or reject an idea, accustom your pupils to discover *who* expresses it, and what grounds he has for his belief. Are you familiar with Ernest Dimnet's *The Art of Thinking?* His discussion of the American method of newspaper reading might serve as an excellent stimulant to your own thinking on the subject.

D. What Problems Confront You When You "Teach" Magazines?

What can you do with contemporary magazines? Perhaps a visit to a newsstand will prove profitable. Look over the display and note for how many the one claim to popularity is the exploitation of sex—sex vulgar, blatant, alluring or disgusting, according to the taste and sophistication of the reader. What use can you make of that material? At first with some emphasis you would say "None." But I am not so sure. If your pupils do not read on this level, certainly you would not drag them down to it. But what if they do, or if some of them do? And no matter what their reading level, if they are normal boys and girls, they are interested, as they should be, in the relations of men and women. There is much question as to whether discussion of sex should be given place in high school. Probably teachers are agreed that science classes offer the most logical setting for scientific discussion, but for a certain type in your high school, boys or girls who are fed on cheap films and cheap fiction and on those smoking-car tales, hoary with age even in Boccaccio's day, merely scientific explanation of physical facts is not sufficient to lead them to a wholesome, normal attitude toward the relation of men and women and toward love, marriage, and the begetting of children.

Again it is your own attitude that will in some measure determine their own. Probably it is less what you say than what you imply that is important. If you give no undue importance to the subject and yet make occasion to treat it simply and honestly as one of the normal functions of the body accompanying the union of those who find physical, intellectual, and spiritual satisfaction together, you can to a certain degree make the neurotic tales and articles of our cheapest magazines appear puerile and silly. But it would be wise for you to investigate your own mind. The nineteenth-century concept of romantic love, a concept carried over into some of our frankly romantic magazines of today, and long regarded as "wholesome for the young," is probably unwholesome for many because of its unreality. Either it entrances the romantic readers and makes them dissatisfied with the workaday aspects of marriage (note our divorce-court records), or it disgusts the cynical. Define your own attitude, for two things are true: 1. Normal high-school pupils are deeply concerned and deeply curious about sex relations. 2. By silence on your part you can allow them to continue curious, secretive, perhaps prurient-minded; or by your attitude, implications, and an occasional remark you can help to diminish a neurotic attitude connected with sex relations and perhaps place the whole subject on a wholesome basis. Look over a magazine stand; then you will realize how essential it is to predetermine your attitude toward sex in classroom discussion before you introduce the contemporary magazine.

Many teachers try at the beginning of the year by means of an informal questionnaire to discover what magazines are read by their pupils. Such a practice is wise, for then the teacher does not find herself in the absurd position of attempting to attract pupils by the *Saturday Evening Post* or *Collier's* or *Story Parade* who at home are familiar with *Harper's Magazine*, the *National Geographic*, the *New Yorker*, or the *Atlantic*. And yet it is not absurd to use those lighter, nonliterary publications for nonreaders or for pupils devoted to the pulp magazines. Some teachers encourage unselected lists of all outside reading done during a week, asking only that each pupil record *all* that he reads, together with a word or a phrase as to its worth as he sees it. Sometimes those lists will prove to be blanks; sometimes, if they are honestly made, they may cause you consternation. But such a list should be regarded as a confidence. Whatever such lists contain, you must avoid complete condemnation of a magazine which a pupil enjoys. Instead, substitute something better. For the girl who seeks romance in those cheap publications designed for the lowest mental denominator, you can surely find some love story, sentimental doubtless, yet interesting, wholesomely conceived, and told with sufficient simplicity so that a low intelligence can grasp it. It is natural that your overdeveloped girl of twelve or fourteen, a girl who perhaps at night frequents public dance halls, should crave what for her spells romance, just as it is natural for boys of her age to yearn toward wild tales of slugging and murder. When you understand and admit these natural, human instincts, you are ready to meet your pupils intelligently, and to try, with humor and sympathy, to win them from the neurotic or the antisocial to something better both in attitude and in form.

E. What Types of Books May Arouse Interest?

If you glance at the list of high-school boys' preferences, for lists of their preferences have been made, you will note that humor, sport, and science are the most popular. Do you know much about the last two fields of interest? Certainly no English course, you will agree, at least no English course to which you were exposed, dealt at length with these topics. You were busy with Shakespeare, Milton, Homer, Dickens. But today your business is to do many things. One is to teach some of the great literature of the world, literature that has an intrinsic interest for the boys and girls at whatever level they have reached. Many older teachers bewail the fact that too little literature and too much general reading is now encouraged. What do you think? Is it not possible that through the interests which pupils already have you can lead them to more adult, more intellectual interests? Whatever you think, it would be wise to acquaint yourself with some of the material in science which boys and some girls have found interesting.

Your business is to make readers, not to teach some specific book or books. But be comforted, for it is not a long journey from magazine accounts of people and things to book accounts, if those books are books prepared with boys and girls in mind. Hermann Hagedorn's beautiful contribution to biography, *The Book of Courage,* such a Junior Guild book as Jeanette Eaton's *Young Lafayette,* or bits of Halliburton's wanderings or Beebe's deep-sea adventures, if read aloud, discussed, lent to students, may do much to lure boys and girls into the habit of reading.

But mere reading aloud by the teacher, even excellent reading, needs a running gloss of pertinent comment, discussion, class contribution, and mention of other books available in the school or town library. Often teachers arrange with the school, town, or county librarian to borrow twenty or thirty books at a time and, with the assistance of a pupil-librarian, lend them to members of the class. Naturally certain difficulties arise. Occasionally books are lost; occasionally pupils are loath to pay for books that they damage. But when boys and girls are just beginning to read nonfiction, no other way lures them so successfully into intelligent wide reading. Much good reading aloud by the teacher from well-selected passages that "show what the book's about" is here wise, and much private comment and courteous, helpful encouragement for pupils for whom reading is difficult. It is essential, too, that the teacher should always be willing after fair trial to have pupils drop one book in favor of another which may prove more interesting. Eventually, of course, it is wise to have some plan, some continuity, back of each pupil's reading.

Perhaps a girl interested in Miss Ferris's *Girls Who Did* or *When I Was a Girl* will be led to read Helen Keller's life, and from that will go on to a consideration of numerous lives and a study of what qualities make outstanding women. Or a boy may center his reading in the old West, building from Lamb's *Sign of the Buffalo Skull* to Barrows' *Ubet* and then to Parkman's *The Oregon Trail*—a book with real appeal if presented in a good edition. A third might turn to Lincoln or Lawrence or Joan of Arc or Martin Johnson, lion-hunter, but go on to a consideration of greatness and the factors that contribute to it. Of course the secret lies in the teacher's enthusiasm, in her tact, and, most of all, in her knowledge, for the first qualities, desirable as they are, can further reading but little without the last.[1]

Perhaps either biography (excellent modern biography) or travel books most successfully bridge the gap between fiction and nonfiction. As an example of such bridge, consider this travel unit. It is devised to lure freshman-sophomore nonreaders into living adventurously through travel books.

TRAVEL UNIT: "THE ROYAL ROAD TO ROMANCE": RICHARD HALLIBURTON

This book (by Robert Henderson) would have endless appeal to the freshmen and sophomores because of the adventure and excitement, the unusual elements, and the variety which it contains. Real interest can be developed. The pupils are almost unconscious that they are "studying."

1. Teacher's preparation

a. Pictures of the Matterhorn, the Alhambra, the Eiffel Tower, Monte Carlo, the Pyramids, the Taj Mahal, and Fujiyama. (A great deal of material could be found in the *National Geographic*.)

b. Kipling's tales of India and the Near East, a rich source of supplementary material.

---

[1] One teacher had a series of folders into which she dropped pictures, anecdotes, or any illuminating material concerning writers whom she would touch upon in class. The value of such collection both for bulletin board and for a quick refreshing of her own memory is obvious.

c. Washington Irving's *The Alhambra,* and other stories of Spain. Spanish songs such as "Borrachita me voy," and "Estrellita."

d. A bulletin board used as a map, on which Halliburton's journey would be traced, with cartoons or pictures illustrating important happenings.

e. Articles concerning the fate of Richard Halliburton—*Time* magazine, Vol. 33, June 13, 1939, pp. 59-60; *Publisher's Weekly,* Vol. 136, August 12, 1939, pp. 455—would open much speculation as to what really happened to him.

f. Other books by Halliburton should be read and reviewed by members of the class: *The Glorious Adventure, New Worlds to Conquer, The Flying Carpet* (airplane).

g. Other books for outside reading:

Bullen, *The Cruise of the Cachalot after Sperm Whales*

Dana, *Two Years Before the Mast*

Chase, *Mary Peters*

Franck, *Vagabond Journey around the World*

Stockton, *Buccaneers and Pirates of Our Coast*

Synge, *Book of Discovery*

Gatty and Post, *Around the World in Eight Days*

Lindbergh, *We*

Anne Lindbergh, *Listen! the Wind*

—— *North to the Orient*

Byrd, *Skyward*

Hedin, *My Life as an Explorer*

Buck, *The Good Earth* (if the pupil is sufficiently mature)

h. Great scenes of the book *Royal Road to Romance*

1. "Beginning the Road," pp. 1-33
2. "Southern Europe," pp. 34-98
3. "Eastward Bound," pp. 99-225
4. "The Near East," pp. 226-326
5. "The Far East," pp. 327-91

Miss Azile Wofford has compiled a bibliography entitled "A List of Biographies of Authors of Books Read by Young People." [1] Here the pupils again meet in adult literature those authors whom they enjoyed as children. But biography must not, of course, be limited by childhood reading. Byrd's *Skyward,* Janet Scudder's *Modeling My Life,* Sugimoto's *A Daughter of*

[1] *English Journal,* Vol. 30 (1941), pp. 377-82.

the Samurai, Jane Addams's *Twenty Years at Hull House,* M. I. Pupin's *From Immigrant to Inventor*—all these offer inviting prospects *if* the material is motivated and *if* both time to read and time to talk of what has been read is offered the class.

F. How Can You Bridge the Gap from Junior to Adult Nonfiction?

After pupils of junior-high-school age have read simple magazine articles, easy travels, and lives of great men and women retold for the young, what comes next? Too often in the leap from junior to senior high school it is the full-grown literary essay, packed with bookish reference from the well-stocked mind of a scholar, and whimsical or playful with an adult humor which to the practical boy or girl of fourteen seems either puzzling or silly. Many a teacher has given thanks for that one masterpiece known to every American child and remembered gratefully by every teacher. I refer to Lamb's "Roast Pig." Glance back to your own high-school days. Was it not an oasis? But since there is but one "Roast Pig," what shall you do? Instead of the familiar essay, probably adult biography is the most simple approach: Garland's *A Son of the Middle Border,* De Kruif's many brief biographies in which zeal and heroism are related with vigor and clothed with romance. For many, Parker's *An American Idyll,* Jensen's *An American Saga,* Graham's *Tramping with a Poet through the Rockies* or Jane Addams's *Twenty Years at Hull House* will have charm. Many a high-school pupil will admit that his or her interest in biography and adult reading began with Marietta Hyde's *Modern Biography,* an unusually stimulating text. For other pupils the open sesame to adult reading may be the historical novel, blending fact and romantic fiction, or cruel fact as in Hubler's *Lou Gehrig: the Iron Horse of Baseball,* or George Stewart's *Storm* or *Fire,* picturing the power, beauty, and horror in natural forces.

Today the public libraries, provided, as many are, with a

personal-guidance department, offer excellent suggestions to the teacher of English. Miss Teitge in her article on the gypsy patteran remarks:

If we aim to give reading guidance to boys and girls, if we hope to strengthen their old interests and to create new ones, if we wish them to acquire a reading habit that will carry over into their future, then let us induce them to follow from one book to another the patteran laid by their individual interests, a game that is more fun and also more profitable than is the reading of books chosen wholly at random.[1]

To illustrate her theory, Miss Teitge traced the reading of several boys and girls whom she started on Donald Culross Peattie's *Singing in the Wilderness: A Salute to John James Audubon,* Putnam, 1935. In his book, Mr. Peattie hints that Audubon might be the lost Dauphin. One boy, interested in this suggestion, followed this "trail of interest":

FIRST TRAIL

1. Minnigerode, Meade: *Cockades: A Romance,* Putnam, 1927, and *The Son of Marie Antoinette: The Mystery of the Temple Tower,* Farrar and Rinehart, 1934

Then, interested in disappearing folk, he read Orczy, Emmuuska: *The Scarlet Pimpernel,* Putnam, 1905.

SECOND TRAIL

This was followed by a girl.
Singing in the Wilderness and *Audubon* (see above), which led to
Rawlings, Marjorie Kinnan: *The Yearling,* Scribner, 1938.
Cranes watched by Jody led to
Matschat, Cecile Hulse: *Suwannee River: Strange Green Land,* (Rivers of America Series), Farrar and Rinehart, 1938.
She became interested in habits of animals and odd people remote from cities. This interest led to

---

[1] Virginia Teitge (Chicago Public Library): "Follow the Romany Patteran," *English Journal,* Vol. 29 (1940), pp. 206-207. Printed with permission of the editor. The gypsy patteran is a handful of leaves on the ground.

Sheppard, Muriel Earley: *Cabins in the Laurel,* University of North Carolina Press, 1935. Then came

Campbell, Olive Dame, and Sharp, Cecil J.: *English Folk Songs from the Southern Appalachians,* Putnam.

This book led on to mountain people:

Chapman, Maristan: *The Happy Mountain,* Viking, 1928.

Audubon's interest in science led to

Robinson, Mable L.: *Runner of the Mountain Tops: The Life of Louis Agassiz,* Random House, 1939, and

Fenton, Carroll Lane: *Life Long Ago: The Story of Fossils,* John Day in association with Reynal and Hitchcock, 1937.

THIRD TRAIL

A second girl followed brave women in hardship.

Audubon (interest centered in his wife) led to

Roberts, Elizabeth Madox: *The Great Meadow,* Viking, 1930;

Lane, Rose Wilder: *Let the Hurricane Roar,* Longmans, Green, 1935; and

Binns, Archie: *The Land Is Bright,* Scribner, 1939 (a story of the Oregon Trail).

Such lists indicate one way in which reading, intelligent reading, may be encouraged and guided, but the guide must himself be a well-informed reader.

G. What Concessions Must You Make and What Demands?

Time and credit must be allowed for this adult reading; not only should you expose your pupils to good books, but you must accommodate your demands to their reading program. At present in many schools a situation exists which is wholly illogical. Both principal and teachers do lip service to the need for and benefits received from wide reading, but they fill the pupil's time with specific textbook assignments, and place the weight of their approval upon textbook knowledge. Wide reading, except for an occasional independent soul, ceases to exist, and is replaced by an occasional book report, squeezed in between the textbook assignments. It is even true in some communities that no "outside" or "recreational" reading may be carried on during school hours, the theory being that reading, a form of play, is unsuited to the serious study-hall atmosphere. Such an attitude toward wide reading may arise in part from the principal's realization that many upperclass students, like many of their parents, can never read on an adult level. But to surrender in practice what they subscribe to in theory is an undesirable way of meeting the situation. And a situation does exist in our modern schools that demands from the teacher time, patience, knowledge of books, and understanding of her pupils. In our educational melting pot it grows more and more difficult and yet more and more essential as the school population becomes increasingly cosmopolitan for the teacher to differentiate and discriminate in her class suggestions or demands. Remind yourself often of the old saying "Milk for babes and meat for strong men." For one senior you would suggest a book as simple as Stewart Edward White's *Daniel Boone, Wilderness Scout,* and for his good friend, Colonel Lawrence's *Revolt in the Desert* or even perhaps Robert Graves's sophisticated autobiography *Good-bye to All That.*

In the past it is true that we have at times presented dull pupils with too adult fare, but it is also true that we have often erred in the other direction. Allowing the best intellects in your class to lounge over books below their reading level, books that provide no intellectual stimulus, is probably an even graver error than to rebuff the nonreader by too difficult a reading program. This former group, often your intellectual equals, needs special consideration. Since you will find in any high-school class that you may have to adjust yourself to reading ability and emotional response varying from fifth-grade level to complete maturity, be careful that the lower level does not completely engross your attention. Recognize and in some way distinguish from their fellows those who are your intellectual equals. Aside from the regular conference period, seize a few hurried moments in the hall, or after school, or during laboratory period, to exchange

ideas about these mature books that they and you have discovered. If you do, it will be to your mutual advantage. Both of
you will draw from these moments a much-needed stimulus, surrounded as you will be by immature minds. Also the discipline
and atmosphere in your classes will improve. A teacher's failure
to recognize outstanding ability and adult interests is not only
wasteful, it is also stupid, for it invites these brilliant students
to misbehave like children.

H. How Can You Awaken Interest in the Essay?

If you have consulted past courses of study in English, you
will recognize that in the modern high school much of the formal
exposition earlier taught has disappeared to reappear as outside
reading for science or social studies. This material is not, however, entirely lost to the English class of today, for often, even
in highly departmentalized high schools, popularized books of
science or economics read for other departments form a basis for
oral and written work in the English classroom. But in those
schools where other departments do not utilize expository material, the elastic term "English" is still expanded to include not
only such veteran articles as Huxley's "On a Piece of Chalk," but
also some one of the numerous recent anthologies of popularized
scientific material selected for high-school use. Though formal
exposition in itself is largely lacking, except when used in connection with composition work, one type of literary exposition is
still popular and useful both for itself and as a transition to the
adult light essay. It is the simple factual essay founded upon
personal experience. One book providing such material is Essie
Chamberlain's *Essays Old and New,* which offers thoughtful
essays and literary exposition that even your most practical
pupils will admit are in sensible prose. In it they will find neither
those flights of humor nor those obscure literary references which
for many pupils mar the adult light essays.

But surely by the time your pupils have become juniors, if not before, they are ready to meet whimsical writing, particularly if the introduction is an oral one, the teacher reading aloud from numerous authors. Usually, in this kind of reading the near-contemporaries of your pupils are easier for them to enjoy than are any of the older essayists, even Charles Lamb. Heywood Broun, Don Marquis, Donn Byrne, Robert Benchley, A. A. Milne, G. K. Chesterton, Samuel Crothers, Agnes Repplier—any of these offer possibilities for successful introduction to a new and delightful literary experience. Where student prejudice against nonfiction is openly expressed, some teachers even withhold the term "essay" for a time and begin by reading aloud whimsical essay after whimsical essay, apparently for the mere fun of the doing. High-school humor is a peculiar article. Also high-school pupils are prone to think of class periods as dull—whether they are dull or not. It is a convention, and a convention that it is well to shatter. To enjoy a bit of skillfully worded humor many levels above the slapstick variety is in itself worth while. And the next step is to have the class browse through books on the essay shelf, discovering their own favorites, which they will bring to class, or confide to you or their notebook, or imitate perhaps, or record in a permanent file that may be of use to future readers. If it is not made a burden, there can be much lively vocabulary work, much noting of skillful exaggeration or understatement, much observing of ideas suggested and then left tantalizingly unsaid so that the creative reader can himself explore and build a second essay merely hinted at in the one read.

As the reading continues, a class, even a good class, will sometimes become forgetful and confused as to just *why* people write familiar essays, and an unimaginative one will state that wonder openly. Then comes the time for again pointing out the serious thread woven into the lighter material and for rediscovering how that one thread of truth gives substance to the whole. From these light essays some pupils can be led to enjoy the possibilities of exploring their own minds. What do *they* feel concerning lawn mowers, furnaces, ears, holding babies, wearing hats, going a journey, or consulting wrist watches in the wilderness? With a volume of familiar essays at hand it is possible to show them that writers—real writers who are paid for what they write—have let personal likes and dislikes, whims, and daydreams spin themselves into loosely connected records that charm because of the unexpected sidelights they throw upon some object or idea and, of course, because of the personality that lies behind them. If you desire to give your class a quick series of mental shocks, try reading the first sentence of each of several light essays. Here are a few:

When Adam delved and Eve span, the fiction that man is incapable of housework was first established.

I do not recall that anyone has written the praises of a lawn mower.

"When I have one foot in the grave," said Tolstoy to Maxim Gorky, "I will tell the truth about women."

There persists much of the harem in every well-regulated home.

There has been some discussion of late as to the etiquette of the revolving door. When a man accompanied by a woman is about to be revolved in it, which should go first?

Lying in bed would be an altogether perfect and supreme experience if only one had a colored pencil long enough to draw on the ceiling.[1]

As a class listens, some of its members begin to see possibilities in their own experience: the cellar door, the attic, the hot-water boiler that from time to time explodes, the lilac tree that wears

[1] From Pence, Raymond W.: *Essays by Present-Day Writers*.

its glory of bloom for so short a season. Dozens of things, they discover, are entertaining or tiresome, insignificant or significant, according to the way human intelligence invests them with meaning. And what greater boon can you give your prospective garageman, stenographer, housewife, or businessman than the power of discovering pleasure in his own mind and interest in following its workings? [1]

After a class has been lured into wide exploration of the familiar essay, and has an appreciation of the purpose behind this kind of writing, it is a relatively simple matter to lead the group to more philosophical reading. For many an adolescent boy or girl Stevenson's *Virginibus Puerisque* has provided a rich personal experience. Dr. Jordan's "Life's Enthusiasms" or "Without Mark or Brand," obviously moralistic as they may seem to older readers, may suggest a courageous philosophy needed by many of your class. And since

> Gypsie hearts are many enough
> But gypsie feet are few,

those would-be wanderers who inhabit your classroom may find pleasure in such an essay as Hazlitt's "On Going a Journey." If they have found pleasure there, it is an unskillful or overbusy teacher who does not see that Hazlitt's essay becomes a pathway leading to W. H. Hudson, Thoreau, Dallas Lore Sharp, John Burroughs, John Muir, or William Beebe.

I. How Important Is Your Presentation of the Essayist's Life?

With all these authors the pupils' own enjoyment of the out-of-doors provides him with a friendly introduction to their writing. No such common interest is immediately discoverable with

---

[1] As you see, a study of the light essay almost demands an accompanying composition project. Addison and Steele provide models for contemporary observation of fashions and foibles; Lamb suggests delightful comparisons and whimsical exaggeration. See Chapter X.

such men as Montaigne, Bacon, Sir Thomas Browne, Carlyle, or Cardinal Newman. Not only is there no one general topic that they share in common with high-school pupils, but there are, of course, the barriers of time and changed vocabulary. These are barriers difficult enough to pass, but there exists, I believe, an even greater one. Too often the teacher, whether with a respectful bowing acquaintance or with an intimate knowledge of these writers, is not sufficiently specific and helpful in her suggestions or assignments. The pupils flounder about in this older material uncertain as to what they should expect or should find. For in reading an essay, a form as intimately personal as a lyric, it matters a great deal who the writer is, how he has lived, what his profession was, and with what authority he speaks. Montaigne and Newman are both churchmen, but how different is the way in which an informed reader approaches them. Addison and Swift both wrote in the eighteenth century, but, again, unless the pupil sees the decorous Sir Joseph and the malign Dean, who yet is capable of the "little language" to Stella, the mere words that he reads lose significance. A personal essay demands that you, the teacher, build a personality behind it. Lamb's tenderness, his dreary occupation and family sorrow, add depth and meaning to the humor and wistfulness of his work. Washington Irving's temperament and his position in American letters, Goldsmith's Irish humor, sadly misunderstood by the John Bulls surrounding him, Macaulay's amazing childhood memory and the easy living which divested him of certain types of sympathy—all are essential to a pleasurable and intelligent understanding of their essays. I am not advising that biographical study precede all reading; but the informed teacher can in five minutes build picturesquely a concept of a writer's personality and position that will give zest to essay reading. Not gossip about a literary figure but a discriminating estimate of the man's mind and personality is the type of information the pupil needs.

J. What Training in Citizenship Should You Attempt?

So far, I have said little of one of the objectives that throughout junior and senior high school should play an important part in your selection and presentation of material. Literary appreciation will in certain districts be restricted to a fairly small number of your pupils. But all of them—dull and brilliant alike—are sooner or later to become voting citizens. Throughout your work in nonfiction you can guide them away from the unwholesome and toward honest work in which the recognized responsibilities, virtues, and accomplishments of altruistic men and women are interestingly recorded. High-school boys and girls, in spite of the cynical pose many assume, are most of them quick to respond to heroic action. Service to mankind, particularly if that service can be presented picturesquely and without a too moralistic note, accomplishment and success not confined alone to the accumulation of wealth, generous giving and spectacular daring such as one finds in Dr. Grenfell's labors, or in the quiet sacrifice of men for the scientific investigation of yellow fever on the Isthmus of Panama—all have appeal. And the frankly moralistic talks made by the students themselves in earnest discussion of a man's responsibility to himself or his family or city or nation convince one of the fact that modern youth, like youth of all time, wants reality and an honest facing of the social and economic problems which will confront them. Odd as it may seem, it is often the teacher rather than the pupils who veers away from the actual, and who seems to deprecate discussion of moral or economic problems. Sometimes, doubtless, such hesitation arises from knowledge of her own inadequacy in the field of world problems or philosophy. Sometimes it arises from fear of exciting adverse criticism or of beginning a discussion the end of which she cannot foresee. Occasionally it may arise from a wrong concept of her function as teacher, pouring information into her pupils' minds appearing more important than allowing those minds to develop the power of thought and clothe that thought in words. But if these discussions are not mere duplications of the discussion carried on in other classes, and if they are discussions, not wild assertions and idle contradictions, they should be encouraged.

Today, when democracy is battling for its existence, high-school pupils should be aware of what democracy is and of what problems confront it. Probably the foreign correspondents' articles or diaries offer the easiest and most interesting reading to high-school pupils. They hear Vincent Sheean on the radio; it is an easy transition to his *Personal History* with its problems as to college life and the life of a young American. From that they can easily go on to his *Not Peace but a Sword*. Then there is Duranty. Edgar Snow, too, with his long years in the Orient, offers them a realistic picture in *Red Star over China* and other books that will, perhaps, open a new continent to them. Van Paasen in *The Days of Our Years*, for the junior or the senior, offers adult fare. Gerald W. Johnson in *Waste Land* or Stuart Chase in *Rich Land, Poor Land* confronts pupils with the problem of soil erosion, a problem that to many of them is no academic question. Mr. Shirer's *Berlin Diary* may seem too horrible in many of its aspects for high-school reading, but I sometimes question if it is not unwise for America to insist upon treating youths and girls of seventeen or eighteen as if they were children.

Much of this new material for discussion of citizenship and the problems of our civilization will grow out of the fiction and drama read and will be merely supplemented by nonfiction reading. Such a combination of many forms of writing bound together by one theme gives, I am convinced, a normal out-of-school reading experience. Also it has greater appeal than a unit composed of one type only, since pupils' interest in types varies. But there is a second point in its favor. The pupil addicted to fiction but strongly repelled by nonfiction is here given an opportunity to see why nonfiction is perhaps necessary to show skeptical readers the authenticity of the facts given in novel or drama. Pupils cannot be forced, but they must be weaned away from their preconceived ideas as to what is and what is not desirable reading. The following list, given in part only, illustrates one successful example of blending types and a provocative series of themes.[1]

I. THE LITERATURE OF SOCIAL PROTEST—THE POET AS PROPHET IN THE BIBLICAL SENSE

Charles Dickens, *David Copperfield, Oliver Twist, Nicholas Nickleby, A Tale of Two Cities;* Selections from the Old Testament; Irwin Shaw, *Bury the Dead* (expurgated); Stephen Crane, *The Red Badge of Courage;* Frank Norris, *The Pit;* Jack London, selected short stories; Grace Lumpkin, *Make My Bread;* Josephine Johnson, *Now in November;* Susan Glaspell, *A Jury of Her Peers* and other short stories; Untermeyer, Kreymborg, Whitman, Wordsworth, Hunt, Masefield, Sassoon, poems, a sufficient number of which are found in any of the standard collections; Erich Maria Remarque, *All Quiet on the Western Front;* John Galsworthy, *Justice* and *Loyalties;* James M. Barrie, *The Admirable Crichton,* and *The Twelve-Pound Look;* James Stephens, *Mary, Mary* and *The Crock of Gold.*

II. THE LITERATURE OF SOCIAL PROBLEMS

Ibsen, *The Doll's House* and *The Enemy of the People;* William Shakespeare, *Macbeth, Julius Caesar;* John Galsworthy, *Strife;* Tompkin, *To Earn My Daily Bread;* Kingsley, *Dead End* (expurgated); Anton Chekhov, *The Cherry Orchard;* Karel Capek, *R. U. R.;* George Bernard Shaw, *The Apple Cart, Saint Joan, Man and Superman;* Sinclair Lewis, *Babbitt;* Stuart P. Chase, *Men and Machines;* Thorstein Veblen, *The Instinct of Workmanship;* Edward Levinson, *I Break Strikes;* Leo Huberman, *The Labor Spy Racket* (from the La Follette Committee reports); Justice Brandeis, *Other People's Money;* Sinclair Lewis, *It Can't Happen Here;* Walter Lippmann, *A Preface to Morals;* George Soule, *A Planned Society; The Autobiography of Lincoln Steffens;* Lewis Mumford, *Technics and Civilization* (selections); Joseph Wood Krutch, *The*

[1] *A Program for English Study* by Joseph W. Gallant, Benjamin Franklin High School, New York City. Printed with permission of the editor from the *English Journal,* Vol. 30 (1941), pp. 399-401.

Modern Temper; Samuel Butler, *Erewhon;* James Harvey Robinson, *The Mind in the Making;* Charles and Mary Beard, *The Rise of American Civilization;* Kallett and Schlink, *100,000,000 Guinea Pigs;* Paul de Kruif, *Seven Iron Men* and *Why Keep Them Alive?;* Childs, *Sweden: The Middle Way;* Herold Rugg, *Changing Civilization in the Modern World;* Robert and Helen Lynd, *Middletown.*

K. What Responsibility Have You for Providing Ethical and Aesthetic Material?

Another question, too, should concern you. There is in American schools, in contrast, for example, with the French, a serious lack of what might be called philosophical reading and discussion. Ethical problems—the struggle of man with his own spirit, with his relationship to the universe and to other men—receive scant attention in our educational system. But if those problems are made sufficiently clear-cut (and nonfiction offers opportunity for this type of discussion), you will find that the average high-school class is both puzzled and fascinated by a kind of thinking often new to them, deprived as many of them are of the church and Sunday-school training of an older generation.

Fiction and drama will, of course, provide endless possibilities for discussion of social and personal topics involving ethical problems. The relation of friend to friend, of man to woman, of wife to husband, of child to parent, of man to society, of man to his country, and of man to God—these lie at the root of all fiction. But it is in essays that these relationships, stripped of confusing particular incident or detail, appear, clear and generalized. Emerson may become for some of your pupils a lifelong comfort. For example, his "Friendship," and "Compensation" offer such thought-provoking lines as: "I do not wish to treat friendship daintily but with the roughest courage," and "In the nature of the soul is the compensation for inequalities of position."

Pupils need not accept Emerson's point of view, but the possibility of discussing an abstract question may never have occurred to some of them. People divide themselves, do they not, into those who are totally concerned with *things* and *personalities* and those to whom an *idea* is important? Certainly much of your teaching should undertake to develop the second type, and in the teaching of nonfiction you have an opportunity. Many high-school students have found comfort and inspiration in David Starr Jordan's "Life's Enthusiasms," and "The Strength of Being Clean," both simply moralistic but breathing strength, hope, confidence—qualities much needed in this unsettled age. Then there are Sir James Barrie's "Courage," Cardinal Newman's magnificent "Educated Man," and "Gentlemen," James Truslow Adams's "The American Dream," Stevenson's slighter essays in *Virginibus Puerisque* (for many pupils the first serious consid-eration of the relations and thoughts of youth put in discussible form), and Crothers's various essays in *The Dame School of Ex-perience*. Montaigne's "Of Conscience" with the well-known line "Punishment is born at the same time with sin" is for modern youth a puzzling document. But perhaps it is in such a biography as Hans Zinsser's fine and courageous *As I Remember Him* that the problems of living are presented even more convincingly than in the abstract essay. Pupils—and adults—think in terms of persons and of concrete situations; you, as teacher, will try to lead your pupils to generalize from the concrete.

But *essays are not all serious nor are important problems lim-ited to the serious aspects of living*. It is most important to re-member this fact. For years I have had an affection for that woman described by Stevenson who could laugh herself sick over the quirk of an eyebrow. (Memory may have altered Stevenson's meticulous wording.) Each of your pupils is going to be closely acquainted with himself for, perhaps, seventy years. During that somewhat long span of life, is he to be factual-minded? Is he to speak without quirk of humor or amused exaggeration? Is he to find himself without internal resources sufficiently amusing and profitable, so that a period of two hours of solitude appalls him, and a movie or a game of cards is essential? ("Cards are to a woman what business is to a man," I was informed recently.) Perhaps through all reading, but particularly through discriminating work with vocabulary and through carefully selected light essays, you can awaken in many of your pupils appreciation and enjoyment of the whimsical, at first as echoed in their own minds, then as created. Christopher Morley, Chesterton, Crothers, James Thurber, Agnes Repplier, Katharine Fullerton Gerould (in her lighter moments), E. B. White, Saroyan, Leacock, Benchley, Ring Lardner, Clarence Day, Charles Lamb—these and many others can delight a student or can fill him with infinite disgust at the frivolity of a writer who "ought to say something worth while." Break up your class into groups. Let each group read at its own level. The ultrafactual can be brought to recognize that an author has a right to do what he wishes, and they may even by tactful leading (I advise Charles Dudley Warner) come to enjoy the simpler and more obviously humorous essays.

May I mention one other responsibility? ("All that a man can do is his best" has often consoled me; if I seem to be piling too many responsibilities upon the teacher of English, just recall that comforting statement.) Many pupils are deprived of beauty, deprived of the "wonder and the wild delight" that poetry may bring them or of that "faerieland" entered through the covers of a book. Remember, in spite of the wave of practicality which is sweeping over the United States, that the hyacinths of beauty and of imagination are yours to provide, and that the bread of all the factual courses and factual transactions in and out of school hours is already within the reach of the student. In the past, many teachers have turned entirely to hyacinths, thus forfeiting the respect of their factual pupils, or entirely to bread, thus depriving their pupils of the beauty and imaginative experience rightfully theirs. It would be wise to remember that a steadily diminishing ratio of bread for your better students and as large a ratio of hyacinths as your poorer students can receive with understanding should be the ideal that you hold before yourself.[1]

II. YOUR RELATION TO THE SCHOOL LIBRARY

Much so far has been said of the aid to be received from the co-operative librarian in the school library, with its magazines, posters, alluring displays of biography and drama. But in the high school where you, an inexperienced teacher, do your first teaching, it is entirely possible there may be no librarian; even a library in the real sense of the word may be nonexistent. If that is the case, you can be reasonably sure of one thing. Just as the supervision of dramatics, declamation, debate, and the school paper tends to gravitate to the teacher of English, so does the supervision of whatever books the school may possess. And, on the whole, in spite of the added responsibility, it is probably a good thing to have under your care the place that bears much the same relation to English teaching that the laboratory does to the teaching of chemistry. In the library are the tools necessary to your successful teaching. It is wise, therefore, to assume library responsibility cheerfully, for if a library, so-called, is locked except for a few minutes after school or is converted into a study hall where any movement or consulting of the shelves is frowned upon, your English classes are sadly handicapped.

A. How Might You Organize Your School Library?

If you know little of library methods, what are you to do? I suppose the first thing is to use your common sense and secure the most advantageous room possible, in case, as is true in some tiny schools, the books have heretofore been locked in a hall closet. Naturally, your common sense will tell you that it is un-

---

[1] If of thy mortal goods thou art bereft,
And from thy slender store two loaves alone to thee are left,
Sell one, and with the dole
Buy hyacinths to feed thy soul.—Muslih-ud-Din Saadi

wise to do all of the work yourself. Lay your plans as specifically as you can; then, when you can, consult and enlist other teachers so that the library becomes a school, not a department, project. But by all means enlist the aid of pupils. Perhaps you have forgotten how at twelve, at fourteen or fifteen, you yearned to be in some fashion distinguished from your fellows. Look for those pupils who are both eager and conscientious. Consult your principal; after all, it is his school; let him see that you recognize that fact. Remember, however, when you select your pupil assistants that most high-school pupils are little snobs. Even more than in college, perhaps, students in high school fear strange paths that may prove unfashionable. If it lies in your power, consult several of the prominent students. Interest them and get from them their stamp of approval. Then, after approval has been secured, in all probability some obscure, conscientious pupils will carry the load of work. Parents can be utilized here to the advantage of the school, the new English teacher, and the parents themselves. You want curtains, a flower box, a homemade bulletin board [1] and shelves that possibly can be manufactured by school boys and faculty from donated lumber. (The American Library in Paris still proudly displays its shelves made during the war from the packing boxes in which books for American soldiers were transported.) And even if it were easier to don a smock and dust and clean and paint in solitude, why would it still be wise to enlist these various agencies? Probably the answer is obvious.

Doubtless you have little choice as to where your library is to be located, but long experience shows it to be most used when near or opening into the study hall. If a glass partition is possible, the dragon guarding the study hall can extend her vigilant eye to include the library. Where no room is available, then the only possibility is to get shelves in your classroom and conduct

[1] See Appendix F.

a library as best you can. Such a course has its difficult moments, but having books in your room and always at hand has also its great advantages.

If some sort of library exists, what aids can you find in case you are untrained in library methods? First, what do you need to know? You must know how to (1) select and order, (2) classify, (3) accession, (4) prepare books for use, (5) shelve, (6) check out and in, and (7) most important of all, control your library with the minimum expenditure of energy and nervous force. Does this program sound appalling? I have known some young teachers without library training who did excellent work equipped only with common sense, enthusiasm, good temper, and one or more of the numerous aids provided for the inexperienced.[1] The task may seem less overwhelming when you remember that if your library is not yet catalogued, you presumably have comparatively few books. Then, too, you must lighten the load by using pupils. Use pupils not only as aids in establishing a library but as student-librarians and give them credit—an outside activity credit —for work well performed. It is wise to use them not only as a means of arousing and maintaining interest in the library, but also as a means of saving your own energy.[2]

Perhaps it is unnecessary to give detailed suggestions concerning the use of students, the buying of books, or the acquisition of well-made reading lists; but if a teacher-librarian position confronts you, it would be intelligent to work through the teacher-librarian activities suggested at the end of the chapter. Naturally, genuine library training would be desirable, but since teachers must of necessity do many things for which they have never been prepared, the hints given there may prove useful.

[1] Consult "Suggested Exercises" at the end of the chapter.
[2] In the Woodrow Wilson Junior High School, Oakland, California, numbering some nine hundred pupils, a substitute librarian was called in because of the librarian's illness. At the end of the first day the principal discovered the substitute in a corner of the library where the efficient pupil-librarians had set her repairing books while without confusion or delay they conducted the real business of the library.

B. *What Might Your Library Mean to Your Community?*

You and I recognize that a library should be made attractive by gay book jackets, occasional posters, flowers, and pictures; and we are inclined to take such accessories for granted. But if the pupils in your small school are accustomed at home and at school to the ugly and purely practical, you will find yourself astonished at the pride and pleasure you can engender in a library which still seems to you barren and unattractive. A few prints, a bulletin board, gaily colored oilcloth if tables are too splintery for comfortable contact, a vase donated perhaps by the English teacher and filled by the flower committee when flowers are available, can alter the whole atmosphere of a room that in itself is cheerless and ugly. Such a room demands thought, care, organization, and—most of all—energy and enthusiasm on the part of the teacher. Why, you might ask, when you are employed to teach English, should you waste your time, energy, and, I suspect, some of your books, magazines, and a little of your money on this school project? You are employed to teach English, but aside from music and art English is compelled to stand for almost all the cultural influences with which your pupils come in contact. First, of course, consider your own health and strength; then, in so far as your energy permits, create an atmosphere congenial to wide, intelligent reading.

In rural districts where no library exists, some teachers have sought to interest the community in transforming the school library into a county library, thus opening it to adults after school hours or for one evening a week. As is obvious, the purpose is to make the school a community center and not only to educate the pupils in school but also to supply a reading room and books and magazines for unemployed graduates and for parents. There are real difficulties, many of them, the chief being the added hours of work and the added responsibility. In certain communities, however, responsible married women in the

P.T.A. have co-operated generously and have effectively relieved the teacher of much if not all of the additional load.[1]

SUGGESTED EXERCISES

Read several of the listed references at the end of this chapter before you attempt these exercises. In the following exercises you should evince your ability to talk of literature not only clearly and interestingly, but in a provocative and stimulating manner that will lead pupils to read eagerly. If possible, use original methods for awakening interest and for utilizing the material read in some form of class or individual activity. This material, if time allows, should be given before your college group.

1. Huxley: "On a Piece of Chalk," found in *Lay Sermons*.
a. Prepare a three-minute introduction to awaken your high-school pupils' interest.

b. Give some general directions to them so that they will read intelligently.

c. Select two examples from the essay to illustrate for them its two outstanding qualities.

d. State to your college group the uses you plan to make of this essay: (1) for oral exposition; (2) for written exposition; (3) for an introduction to later literary-scientific essays (be specific here); (4) for awakening interest in evolution, biology, or other scientific work. (The purpose here is to have a live, interesting unit on "Science in Literature," of which "On a Piece of Chalk" is to form a part. Are you familiar with De Kruif's many brief biographies?) [2]

2. Addison: *The Spectator Papers*. Select six essays that might serve as a series of portraits of Sir Roger and his contemporaries. Consult Boas and Hahn's *Social Backgrounds of English Literature* or Ashton's *Social Life in the Reign of Queen Anne* for the life of the times. Then:

a. In three minutes present a picture of the times (with specific references) that would encourage your pupils to read farther.

[1] *The Wilson Bulletin for Librarians*, H. W. Wilson Co., 950-972 University Avenue, New York City ($2.00 a year), will provide you with much material on modern writers and many suggestions for making a library attractive.

[2] Fred B. Millett's *Contemporary American Authors; A Critical Survey and 219 Bio-Bibliographies* (Harcourt, Brace, 1940, text ed. $3.75) is almost a necessity if you wish information and references concerning early twentieth-century writers.

b. Introduce one of the characters so that the class realizes Addison's purpose, method, and charm.

c. Give a minimum reading assignment from Addison and Steele and suggest some *three* or *four* lines of investigation that would call for wide reading in both the eighteenth-century and the contemporary essay.

3. Macaulay: "Essay on Johnson." **a.** In a three-minute talk awaken interest by introducing Dr. Johnson to your high-school pupils.

b. Indicate briefly those qualities in Dr. Johnson which the brilliant Macaulay could and could not deal with sympathetically.

c. Select one or two sentences from the essay that seem to you typical of Macaulay's style; read these to the college group if time allows, and point out those qualities that you think would have some significance for high-school seniors—who are little interested in style in itself.

4. Pence, R. W.: *Essays by Present-Day Writers,* or any other collection of modern light essays. **a.** Select three similar or contrasting modern essays.

b. Work out a stimulating approach to them.

c. Present to the college group if possible. Your object should be to awaken interest in either the topic or the writer so that your pupils will wish to read farther. Have at hand a bibliography of some dozen suitable essays that you have investigated.

5. Plan to have your senior class read a whimsical group of essays. (Choose where you like, but include Charles Lamb and Samuel Mc-Chord Crothers.) Introduce the group of essays to your college class as you would launch it before your seniors. Have clearly outlined your (a) objectives, and (b) some five possible lines of interest that different individuals could investigate.

6. Prepare a stimulating three-minute introduction to Hans Zinsser's *As I Remember Him,* or some other biography of value. Your purpose is to awaken interest in it.

7. Consult the current issues of *Harper's, Atlantic, Free World, National Geographic, Travel, Scholastic, United Nations World,* and *Saturday Evening Post.* Select from each some nonfiction material that has worth for high-school juniors. Be ready to report on author, article, magazine, volume, pages, and the specific use (oral, written) that could be made of each.

8. Select on three levels of difficulty several light essays. Plan for each the approach that you would use with factual-minded pupils. (If several of your group worked on this project, and the material were mimeographed, you might find it most useful later in your schoolroom.)

SUGGESTED READINGS

NONFICTION

A. References for Your Own Guidance

The English Language Arts, Vol. I, N.C.T.E. Curriculum Series, Dora V. Smith, Director
Read Part III, Chapter 10, "The Language Arts and the Library." What must be your own relation to the school library?

1. Boas, Ralph P., and Smith, Edwin E.: *Enjoyment of Literature,* Harcourt, Brace, 1934, pp. 523-36

2. Zimmerman, Helen: "Making Magazine Study a Vital Part of the Curriculum," *Minnesota Journal of Education,* Vol. 15 (1934), pp. 142-43

3. Dale, Edgar: *How to Read a Newspaper,* Scott, Foresman, 1941

4. Smith, Reed: *The Teaching of Literature,* American Book Company, 1935
See "Selected Reading Lists in Biography," pp. 368-73. Check this list with your library books.

5. Nicolson, Harold: *The Development of English Biography,* Harcourt, Brace, 1928

6. Balch, Marston, ed.: *Modern Short Biographies and Autobiographies,* Harcourt, Brace, 1940
The introduction discusses and contrasts old and new biography. By all means read; then show your upperclasses how the techniques of drama and short story function in modern biography.

B. Reading Biography and Other Nonfiction

From *Elementary English*

1. Heriot, Grace Miller: "Children and Biography," Vol. 25 (1948), pp. 98-102
The 50 biographies and 14 autobiographies listed here are most of them suitable for grades 7, 8, 9, or for nonreaders in higher grades.

2. Brecht, Ethel L.: "Adventures in Free Reading," Vol. 24 (1947), pp. 13-17

3. Sprague, Lois: "Non-Fiction Books for Retarded Readers in the Upper Grades," Vol. 28 (1950), pp. 28-34

From the English Journal

1. Roberts, H. D.: "Late Biography for the Literature Class," Vol. 20 (1931), pp. 408-13

2. McHarry, Liesette J.: "A Plan of Correlation," Vol. 21 (1932), pp. 302-09

3. Graham, Helen L.: "A Plan for Teaching the Biography," Vol. 30 (1941), pp. 238-41

4. Lemon, Babette: "Biography and Autobiography in the Ninth Grade," Vol. 32 (1943), pp. 81-84

5. Pooley, Robert C.: "Using Periodicals in the English Classroom," Vol. 40 (1951), pp. 266-70

Reading Papers and Magazines
From the English Journal

1. Carney, Elizabeth: "An Effective Newspaper and Magazine Unit," Vol. 25 (November, 1936), pp. 752-56

2. Simmons, Josephine: "A Semester of Current Literature," Vol. 30 (1941), pp. 47-53

3. Varner, Marian S.: "Students Discover Newspapers," Vol. 39 (1950), pp. 391-92

4. Woodford, Mary E.: "A Reading Course for Juniors," Vol. 30 (1941), pp. 24-31

5. Andrews, Katherine: "A 3B Class Studies the Newspaper," Vol. 35 (1946), pp. 497-99

6. Dowling, Kathleen: "Reading to Grow," Vol. 40 (1951), pp. 392-93

7. Doonan, Caroline M.: "Magazines for Developing Literary Taste," Vol. 37 (1948), p. 245

8. Glenn, Clara: "A Class Study of Trash Magazines," Vol. 32 (1943), pp. 27-29

From Elementary English

1. Price, Denova M., and Mulryan: "Let Newspapers Improve Your Reading," Vol. 27 (1950), pp. 515-20

2 Lester, R., and Wheeler, Viola D: "Newspapers in the Classroom," Vol. 22 (1945), pp. 324-29

Bibliography for: I, "Using Comics," and II, "Using Newspapers."

3. Berwald, R.: "Learning to Use the Newspaper," Vol. 17 (1940), pp. 257-61

C. The School Library

Books Helpful to the Teacher-Librarian

Small or large, all school libraries should have:

1. Monroe, Isabel S., and Jervis, Ruth: *Standard Catalog for High School Librarians,* A Selected Catalog of 3,800 books, H. W. Wilson Company, 958-72 University Avenue, New York

2. Fargo, Lucile F.: *The Library in the School,* rev. ed., American Library Association, Chicago, 1947

Aids

1. *The Wilson Bulletin for Librarians.* See note, page 531

2. Pamphlets

a. *How to Use the Readers' Guide to Periodical Literature and Other Indexes,* H. W. Wilson Company

These and the following list may be obtained free upon request, enough for each class member. Excellent for class exercises.

b. *How to Use Webster's New International Dictionary, Workbooks for Use with Webster's New International Dictionary, An Outline for Dictionary Study, Quirks and Quizzes: Six Tests on Your Vocabulary,* and *Vocabulary Quiz,* G. & C. Merriam Company, Springfield 2, Massachusetts.

3. Encyclopedia Britannica, 20 North Wacker Drive, Chicago, and F. E. Compton and Company, 1000 North Dearborn Street, Chicago, will on request send free pamphlets.

4. Woodring, M. N., Jewett, I. A., and Benson, R. T.: *Enriched Teaching of English in the Junior and Senior High Schools,* rev. ed., Teachers College, Bureau of Publications, Columbia University, New York, 1934

These 354 closely packed pages are "A Source Book for Teachers of English, School Librarians, and Directors of Extra-curricular Activities, listing chiefly free and low-cost illustrative and supplemental materials."

5. Cross, E. A., and Carney, Elizabeth: *Teaching English in High Schools,* rev. ed., Macmillan, 1950, Chapter 17, "The Library and School Anthologies."

Book Sources: Inexpensive

1. Scholastic Book Service, 7 East 12th St., New York. (Obtain 25-35 cent reprint editions. Over 250 titles.)

2. Noble and Noble, 67 Irving Place, New York. (Two comparative classics in one book.)

3. Scott, Foresman, 114 East 23rd St., New York. (Simplified classics.)

4. The Globe Book Company, 175 Fifth Avenue, New York. (Simplified classics.)

5. Harcourt, Brace, 383 Madison Avenue, New York. (Classics abridged *not* rewritten. Shortened 40 to 50 per cent.)

6. Teen Age Book Club (TAB), 7 East 12th St., New York. (Write for material explaining this organization and its books.

7. Pocket Book, Jrs., 30 Rockefeller Center, New York. (For junior high school.)

Selecting Books and Magazines

1. Lathrop, Edith A.: *Aids in Book Selection for the Secondary School Libraries*, Superintendent of Documents, Washington, D. C.

2. Martin, Laura Katherine: *Magazines for School Libraries*, H. W. Wilson Co., New York

3. *Books for You*, edited by Mark Neville, National Council of Education, 1951

4. Watch for lists of books in *Elementary English, English Journal*, and reviews in the *Saturday Review of Literature, New York Times Book Review Digest*, and *New York Herald Tribune Book Review*

Write for information from the companies listed under "Book Sources" above.

5. Two magazines concerned with audio-visual information are:

Audio-Visual Guide—Aids to Education (an official organ of the N.E.A. Department of Secondary Teachers), 172 Renner Avenue, Newark 8, New Jersey, $3.00 a year. "Audio-Visual Aids for the Teacher of English," February issue, 1951, is available in reprint for 25 cents. Order from 1630 Springfield Ave., Maplewood, New Jersey

Library Atmosphere

See Appendix F, "Pictures and Bulletin Boards," pages 589-92. Plants, curtains, pictures, book jackets, pupils' artistic donations—all these make the library unlike a classroom.

CHAPTER XVII

Problems Confronting the Prospective
Teacher of English

WHEN you enter teaching, you suddenly discover that you are no longer a private individual. No longer can you talk, dress, jest, with the comfortable certainty of being understood, as you can in your college community, securely indifferent to the opinions of the world. At first you will probably obtain a position in a small town where you will be "the new teacher," a possible social asset, a possible "joiner" of clubs, of church organizations, of reform movements. With fifty, or a hundred and fifty, pupils whom you meet daily, your chance word in the classroom, the clothes that you wear, the "Good morning" that you do or do not say, will all become fit material for speculation and comment. But do not let this statement of the case overwhelm you; it really is not so bad as it at first sounds. I mention it, however, because so many inexperienced teachers blunder into difficulties or find themselves lonely merely because they have never thought of themselves as grown-up members of a community, or realized that they have become professional women with professional relationships to maintain. There are intelligent people, really intelligent people, who spend less thought upon how to order their lives and how to maintain pleasant relationships with those about them than they spend in planning the furnishings of their houses or in ordering their meals. And yet both furnishings and meals are but ashes in the mouth if one is unhappy in one's professional and social contacts.[1]

---

[1] In a textbook is it too elementary to suggest that a teacher is supposed to (1) .return first calls and make calls after accepting an invitation to dinner; (2) repay some social debts by an occasional invitation to tea, dinner, luncheon; and (3) live as graciously as is financially expedient?

In the schoolroom and in the community a teacher, though young, must assume adult responsibilities.

Would it not be sensible, therefore, before you go adventuring, to consider the various factors in your new environment, and to decide what attitude toward each you think it desirable for you to maintain? Then, aware of what possible problems may confront you, and supplied with some standards (generally termed "professional ethics"), you can go forth, "fearless and unperplexed," to conduct life as you *choose*, not as you *chance* to do it.

I. YOUR RELATION TO THE COMMUNITY

The community in which you find yourself, if small, may be split into various factions. Often these factions are divided on church lines, on club or anticlub lines, on divisions between school-board members. Each side may attempt to enlist the new teacher of English, since she is supposed to speak, to act, to know parliamentary law, and to have an unfailing supply of activity suggestions.

Your duty is, naturally, to maintain a thoroughly friendly, thoroughly impartial, thoroughly uninformed attitude toward the various cliques and clubs. It is, of course, wise to allow yourself to be told as little gossip as possible, and to enter no organizations when you first arrive. New, unfamiliar work and the need for knowing your school and community libraries ought for the first few weeks to serve as adequate excuses. As a teacher of English, however, you should be ready to give occasional talks for the various organizations. It would be sensible to go armed with one or two subjects: an author, a place of historic interest which you have seen, a literary form, a biography, or a modern play. You should remember, though, that your community may be much more conservative than your college friends. You personally may enjoy Hart Crane, T. S. Eliot, or Robinson Jeffers, but a reading of *The Bridge* or *The Wasteland* would probably leave your audience puzzled and bored. Then, too, when you are asked by some enthusiastic maker of programs to speak for an hour, you will often find yourself at the end of a long, breathless afternoon faced by a polite but frankly restless audience. It is wise, therefore, to have your topic so organized that it can be compressed into twenty minutes. Pictures add much to such a talk; hence it would be foresighted of you to provide illustrations for a few possible lectures as well as for your schoolwork.[1]

The Parent-Teacher Association (P.T.A.) is an organization which may be either a most desirable adjunct to a school or a grave liability. Without wise leadership it may degenerate into a center of gossip and discontent. Under wise leadership it can be a source of strength to the school, and a mutually profitable meeting place for parents and teachers. From time to time you as teacher of English may be called upon for a program. In that case it is wise to remember that parents enjoy an inferior program provided by their children more than a superior one provided by adults. Such a possible entertainment might be singing of the glee club, if that is under your direction, reading of compositions, acting of some classroom scene, displaying notebooks and illustrated compositions, or serving tea with the members of your class.

In your classroom, too, it is wise occasionally to have, as a climax to some unit of work, a program to which parents are invited. Although such an afternoon takes added energy, you will find that those efforts to know the community which are also outlets for your classes in English serve as motivation in classwork, and are therefore more worth while than are many other types of community contact.

The person in your community who can be your greatest aid and ally is the public librarian. If she is not, the fault probably lies with you. It is well to visit the public library early, to know its resources, to make friends with the librarian and attendants. Perhaps if you take the initiative and ask the librarian to luncheon, tea, or dinner, and in the advantageous position of hostess tactfully ask for suggestions as to possible co-operation

[1] See Appendix F for suggestions concerning "Pictures and Bulletin Boards."

between the library and the classes in English, you may gain her friendship and her support immediately. You and she, remember, are the two persons in the community most intelligently interested, presumably, in getting young people to read wisely. But you must be careful. Remember that a sudden call for all of the material about Scott, Louis XI, or dry farming is annoying. The library may be supplied with display material for all of these topics, but there is no time to assemble it. On Saturdays and after school are the library rush hours. Be considerate; do not try to discuss work then. Also show consideration by supplying the librarian *at least ten days in advance* with a list of those topics and those books which you mean to ask your students to investigate. May I suggest that you approach the librarian humbly? She may perhaps have been cogitating upon the problems of outside reading when you were in the second grade.

II. YOUR RELATION TO YOUR SUPERIOR OFFICERS

Who are your superior officers? The members of the board of education, the superintendent, the principal of your school, and— if there is one—your head of department. Though you should be thoroughly friendly, sensible, frank, with any and all of these persons, a safe rule to follow is this: Never consult with a higher official upon any school problem until *after* you have laid the matter before your immediate superior. As teacher of English the problems of dramatics, journalism, and graduate addresses may involve you in more complicated situations than you at first realize. But remember this fact: When you enter a school system, you enter an army. It is as discourteous for you to run to the school board or to the superintendent with some problem as it would be for a private in the army to accost the colonel with suggestions concerning adequate mess equipment. Your ideas may be admirable; tell them to the head of your department or to your principal. Practically never should you, a teacher, of your own volition carry any matter to a member of the school board. For you, the final authority is the superintendent. Be sufficiently professional in attitude to realize that you weaken the whole organization if you weaken the authority of your principal or superintendent. To discuss the policies of either man adversely with members of the community or with pupils is not only a breach of professional etiquette, but is a serious menace to the school. If you cannot approve, you can be silent, or you can resign. It is true, however, that if you wait, the situation may clear itself or you may discover that the principal is, in reality, coping with problems of which you realized nothing. Your position must not make you cowardly—yet for the first year Kipling's advice to the man-cub is not to be despised.[1]

On the other hand, when you are teaching English there are many possibilities of augmenting your principal's power and popularity with the students. For one thing, a principal wishes to know what is going on in your classroom. Often he suffers more than you when he comes to visit your classes. He must come, however, for he has, as a rule, to send in a rating about you to his superintendent. If you are tactful, you will make these visits easy and pleasant by inviting him and your department head to see a dramatization, to judge a contest, or to hear an open-forum discussion. One principal remarked to me: "I never dare go past Miss X's English room when I am busy. If a youngster sees me pass, without a 'by your leave' to the teacher, he slips out to invite me in to see what they are doing. And they are always doing something interesting, too." This condition is pleasant and mutually helpful.

When you have invited the principal or head of department to hear a class program, it is courteous to call upon the one who comes or to have your pupil chairman call upon him for some comment. They are, you remember, your immediate superiors; the principal is for the pupils the chief representative of the

[1] "But the Jungle is large and the Cub he is small. Let him think and be still." Maxims of Baloo, *The Jungle Book*, p. 46.

school. He may make some courteous comment about the work that will give a sense of its importance to the class and will spur them on to greater effort, or he may have a criticism or a suggestion that will be of genuine value. Occasionally an undeserved or unkind criticism from a thoughtless principal binds a class and teacher more closely together, for youth is prone to side with youth; and, to your amusement, you may find your class defending you even when you are unconscious that defense is necessary. Best of all, perhaps, these invitations to visit indicate that you are striving for that ideal relationship in which teachers and principal are working together toward the common aim: live, purposeful teaching.

On what qualities must your principal judge you?

1. Discipline and the appearance of your room. All other virtues, you will find to your disappointment, sink into utter insignificance if you cannot control your group.

2. Prompt and efficient handling of the machinery involved in reporting absences, securing excuses, handing in reports, etc.

3. Apparent interest and satisfaction of your pupils in their English work.

4. Pleasant relationships with other teachers and willingness to co-operate. There will be extra duties: a study hall when someone is ill, an assembly room to put to rights for some emergency, a club that needs a sponsor, or a P.T.A. meeting to be engineered.

5. Your method of presenting work and of conducting classes, as well as your ability to have ideas, to suggest them tactfully, and to take no credit when your original idea emerges as a part of your principal's policy. Does that last statement sound as if he were ungenerous? No executive has time to originate detailed changes such as co-operation in the teaching of mechanics of writing, a "hospital" class, a class in journalism, an alternative third-year course in literature or in public speaking, a club for girls, a discussion group for teachers. If the plan is successful, the credit is in reality his, for you as teacher could not, unaided, carry out any of these schemes; hence you should be content to suggest them, discuss them with him, work for them, and give him credit and enthusiastic support. If you are honestly interested in the idea and not concerned with

the hope of self-advertisement, you will not mind the loss of credit. Few things, remember, undermine your teaching so quickly as does the feeling of not being appreciated; be sure that you avoid that form of self-pity. If your full energy goes into making each class period both profitable and enjoyable, you will not only find teaching high-school pupils an absorbing adventure, but you will also find little time to worry about your superiors.

There are, however, certain problems, legitimately yours, which extend beyond your own classroom, for English in high school must always remain in part a "service" department. It must provide tools for other studies; hence certain problems are so vital that they become the concern of the whole school. Some of these problems presenting schedule difficulties (a "hospital" class for those deficient in mechanics, a class for repeaters, ability grouping in English classes) or demanding co-operative effort (teaching mechanics of writing) are considered in the reading references at the end of the chapter. Even as a prospective teacher of English you should know something about these questions; these references will provide you with further information when you need it.

III. YOUR ATTITUDE TOWARD OTHER TEACHERS AND TEACHER ORGANIZATIONS

In regard to other teachers and teacher organizations, a few moments' thought will show you what is and what is not a professional attitude. A criticism of another teacher made to a principal, pupil, or citizen is of course not only in very bad taste but also distinctly unprofessional. To criticize a former teacher by stating or implying that she seems to have taught your group little is, to put it mildly, rude and unnecessary. You are a part of a larger organization; do not weaken that organization by undermining any of its members. Since in composition you cultivate a close personal relationship with pupils, they may try to share their grievances with you. Mr. X has been unfair in chemistry. Miss Z is dull in history and has favorites. Mr. Y used bad English, loses his temper, and does not know his subject. Perhaps, unfortunately, the pupils are correct, but on your own part a serene indifference, a humorous comment as to the pupil's own mood, a flat statement "Don't talk to me about the faculty," will, in many cases, suffice. In rare instances, of course, when a pupil has really been hurt, a more sympathetic attitude and the suggestion that the pupil go to the teacher in question may be your wisest and kindest course.

Other teachers are quick to realize whether you are friendly, sensible, and willing to carry your full share of outside work, or whether you are ready to take affront, eager to escape responsibility, or—just as bad—to seize upon every opportunity for self-advertising. Certain outside activities (dramatics, commencement addresses, journalism, annuals) gravitate to the department of English, but it is an unwise department that seeks to absorb into itself *all* outside activities, even though the department receives publicity through this concentration. You are a part of a school as well as a teacher in a department. It is most unwise to augment the reputation of the department at the expense of the pleasant, friendly relationships which should exist in the school. Often, for example, debate clubs and open-forum discussion clubs are guided much more successfully by teachers of the social sciences than by a teacher of English. The art department and the classes in sewing—if they will co-operate—should be given full responsibility and full credit for stage settings and stage costumes. But quite aside from the question of pleasant school relations there is another and even more serious question. You can carry only a certain number of activities. *Beware of attempting so much that your real occupation, classroom teaching, suffers.*

There are three teacher organizations of which you should be aware: the National Education Association (N.E.A.), the State Teachers Association with its yearly institute, and the National Council of Teachers of English, with its various local organizations and two official organs: the *English Journal* and the *Elementary English Review.* Dues for the N.E.A. help to finance research studies concerning the educational situation in the United States. The state association attempts to solve state problems such as the maintenance of fair salaries, or seeks to popularize such innovations as sabbatical leave, equal salary for equal training, or bonuses for summer travel or study. The third organization, the English Council, is the only well-known association devoted exclusively to a study of the problems arising in the teaching of English. Certainly its organ, the *English Journal,* should be a part of your professional equipment. Later, perhaps, it may become the recorder of some of your more successful classroom experiments.

IV. YOUR RELATION WITH YOUR PUPILS

With pupils your relationships resolve themselves into out-of-school and in-school contacts. In some ways the two are dissimilar, but the teacher of English who becomes "just another high-school student" outside of school and who accepts invitations and attentions from high-school boys, soon loses control and respect within the classroom. A safe rule to follow is this: Accept no invitation from a boy in high school unless you are invited in the capacity of chaperon. Even at school dances, as you will realize when you stop to consider it, it is well to avoid dancing with high-school boys if your dancing means that high-school girls are left without partners. You can refuse to dance or, better far, if the boys are in the minority, you can dance with high-school girls, thus setting the example so that girls can dance together. You may like to dance, but it is better to curb your desire than to set some high-school girl envying you, wondering if you are partial to your partner, presently, therefore, questioning your fair grading, and regarding you rather as a social rival than as a teacher.

On the other hand, you can be admirable friends with high-school boys and girls, warm personal friends, and yet maintain a clear-cut teacher-pupil relation. They want an older person, not of their own family, with whom they can talk as one adult to another. Your business is to know them, if possible, both inside and outside the schoolroom, to be a friendly, stimulating, sympathetic friend who, for many of them, opens up a wider field of interest than they would find for themselves. But no matter how sympathetic or how stimulating a teacher may be, she should at the same time both encourage and practice decent reticence. It is easy to dabble with a younger person's emotions and feel godlike in molding character. A teacher of English can do much good; she can also do much harm. The best teachers that I have known have been men and women with strong, keen minds who were cool, detached, friendly, always sympathetic but bracingly, not relaxingly, so. They discouraged self-pity and overmuch introspection, but were not afraid of a frank meeting of minds and an honest discussion of serious topics. Their personal honesty, kindliness, sympathetic insight, and sound, humorous common sense were qualities that demanded both respect and liking.[1]

Aside from classroom contacts, you, as teacher of English, will meet your pupils in connection with various activities. Although your judgment and good taste should be your principal guides, you should know what others have done and what principles have guided them. Enthusiasm is, of course, essential, but mere enthusiasm unguided by principle breeds difficulties, particularly if unguided enthusiasm flowers into anything so permanent as print. In Appendix H you will find "References on Extracurricular Activities." It would be wise now or later to know these refer-

[1] A stimulating book by Mr. Sidney Cox, *Avowals and Ventures: The Teaching of English,* is well worth reading and contains much truth, but young teachers in high school should beware of rushing unadvisedly into the "friendships" mentioned which pupils may misunderstand, and should avoid a sentimental questing for self-revelation that may easily degenerate into a display of teacher egotism or adolescent morbidity.

ences. After the list is a space for additions. If when you find an article that seems to you helpful, you record it here, you can soon build up for yourself a brief, useful bibliography.

Within the classroom the practice of some purely mechanical devices may save you from embarrassment and from the possibility of certain disciplinary difficulties. Although it is true that in many schools no problem of discipline arises, you should be very careful until you know your group thoroughly to give them no opportunity to take greater liberties than you desire. *It is always easier to relax your discipline than to strengthen it.* The two main factors that make, at first, for disorder are anonymity and lack of occupation. To avoid the first, get from your pupils as soon as they enter your room slips recording their names and the seats they occupy. All students, even the deaf and the shortsighted, choose to sit in the back seats; hence before passing these slips you will, doubtless, ask those in the back of the room to move forward, and others to shift into the scattered empty seats left in the various rows or at tables. You may not realize at first that, particularly in composition work, a concentrated group talks more easily and more readily than one scattered about a large room, but after a few recitations, you will find that both for you and for the class a solid grouping is pleasanter. These slips can be passed to one pupil in each row or at each table, quickly distributed, and filled according to some such board model as this (students have a genius for misunderstanding spoken directions):

Please write:

1. Your name (last name first)
2. The row occupied (Row A, B, C, etc. Row A is nearest the front of the room)
3. The seat occupied (Seat 1, 2, 3, etc. Seat 1 is nearest the window in each row)

You will find that this work must not be hurried, for from these slips your seating chart will be made. Since after the second day you will waste no time in roll call, this chart becomes your means of recording absences. (A mistake on your part means difficulty in the office and an inquiry concerning your error.) As soon as these slips are collected by rows or tables and passed to you, you can, by glancing at them, call a pupil by name, an excellent way of creating a sense of responsibility. By the next meeting you should have temporary charts for each class so that you apparently know by name every pupil in the room—an effective way of maintaining order. Later, changes in seating may be necessary, but a temporary chart in pencil can be easily changed to a permanent record.[1]

A second device for securing good discipline and a businesslike attitude toward the work is to begin teaching as soon as you receive the name slips upon the first day, to make a definite assignment requiring some forty minutes of preparation for the day following, and to require assignment books, both for yourself and for your pupils. Such a book is important to you because often a pupil is absent several days and desires the missed assignments, or he is to be absent and wishes to obtain the work in advance. Usually he will come to you when you are busy. If you have your book, dated, paragraphed, usable, you can give it to him without hesitation. He respects your good workmanship, for pupils are quick to recognize efficiency and well-planned procedure. This book will also enable you to give fairer examinations and more intelligently distributed drills, tests, reviews. In fact your assignment book shows you to be a methodical or a methodless teacher. If on Saturdays you will plan the work for six days in advance (one week and the following Monday) you will find life simpler, pleasanter, and more efficiently conducted. Unless there is a definite reason to the contrary, the assignment for advanced work should be given at the first of each period, as you will realize if some day the bell rings and you are left—pathetic, futile, undig-

[1] See Appendix A, II, for "Your Teaching Equipment."

nified—shouting instructions at the backs of your departing pupils.

A third device for maintaining discipline and for getting your class into working mood is to have a daily plan showing what is to be done during the class period. Sometimes, of course, you will depart from it. Bypaths will appear that you judge profitable; pupils will misunderstand what seemed to you obvious; a topic will suddenly unroll in a fashion that you had not foreseen. But your plan is there to save you from waste of time, from embarrassment, from floundering when you discover—a condition often found in English work—that some pupil is intentionally attempting to sidetrack the class discussion because he has not prepared the assigned lesson. In cases of drill work (dictation, spelling, grammar, etc.) it is well to have your plan timed so that you do not allow yourself to spend too much of the period upon one phase, or fail to call for the work assigned for that day. No class can long respect a teacher who consistently runs behind schedule, and yet in English it is particularly easy to do so. If you make an assignment, see that the work is required upon the date set. If papers are to be handed in, collect them as soon as the class enters, so that the attention can be centered upon classwork, not divided between it and last-minute revisions. Also a definite plan for collection and for distribution of papers by rows and tables, and a specified pupil to arrange them, saves time, is businesslike, and avoids a disorder that might be difficult to curb.

Many young teachers have no idea as to how much or how little the students in the back of the room are missing. To avoid the usual low-voiced confidences from the front seats, walk about; conduct your classes from all parts of the room, for composition is, in the words of Dr. Leonard, "a social problem." If in addition to this peripatetic habit you establish audibility as one of the necessary factors of a satisfactory pupil recitation, your classwork will increase in value and interest. After a class

discussion, analyze it. You may be surprised to find that comparatively few have done all the talking. You can avoid such
monopoly by distributing questions, by frequent brief tests and
test discussions, by trusting only in part to volunteered information. But you must be fair and not force your pupils into bluffing
or into downright dishonesty. Preparation demanded daily but
called for only occasionally, erratic assignments of outside reading or notebooks made once and not referred to until the date
required, ill-considered assignments—all these breed evasions of
the truth. And such announcements as "Credit will be given to
those who state that they have finished their assigned reading,"
or questions in examinations such as "Have you or have you not
read the references listed?" encourage dishonesty. In such cases,
the teacher, I believe, is more culpable than the pupils, but it is
the pupils who suffer.

You may say that all of these admonitions are needless if the
teacher possesses one certain quality. I agree. Class behavior and
class and individual breaches of discipline must be met and
handled by common sense. (Is it our egotism that leads us to
term this rarest of all human attributes "common"?) Perhaps the
best possible advice is this: First, have your work so well in hand
that you can devote your full attention to the class; second, never
let a disturbance get well started. Check it before it is more than
begun. Composition work requires freedom; it is spoiled by disorder. Never tolerate for one minute whispering, inattention, note
passing. Find yourself unable to talk if any other person in the
room is talking (I refer to discussion, not to laboratory periods).
If you think of yourself as a combination of hostess and chairman, and of your class as your fellow workers and guests, you
can, as a rule, by means of your own perfect politeness make the
atmosphere very much what you wish it. Much, too, can be accomplished by the teacher's obvious belief that all are interested
and working for a common objective. If a pupil whispers he must,

therefore, have some idea which seems to him so important that he is impatient to contribute it. Of course there are cases where this polite subterfuge will not work. This subterfuge is the velvet glove, but a class, much as it appreciates this glove, also appreciates an iron hand. When it is necessary, strike and strike hard. Never pretend to overlook a serious breach in discipline. If you do, pupils will try you farther. (Have you read the chapter entitled "Miss Jones" in Hugh Walpole's novel *Jeremy?* Do.) Usually, however, a reasonable, sensible discussion with the class, with a request for co-operation, is effective, for high-school pupils, you will find, are as a rule both sensible and responsive to the idea of fair play.

If a real disciplinary problem arises, deal with it summarily. Never handicap a class or yourself with a disturbing element in the room. At first, however, you may not realize that few things are more disruptive to a school system than the thoughtless practice of sending pupils from your room without specifying their destination and the time that they are to arrive. They may as a rule be sent to a study hall, to the library, to the principal's office. But to send a pupil out into space soon brings the principal and perhaps other teachers inquiring into your methods of discipline. Of course it is unwise to "scold" a pupil before his classmates. First of all, it is unfair because you, as teacher, have the advantage. Have an offender report to you in private. You will find as a rule that, unsupported by a class, he is rather defenseless. Remember that complete courtesy and a reasonable "Just what is the matter? Why don't we get on better in class?" is probably your best approach. Often there are two sides; at least it is well to take for granted that there may be. If a pupil is difficult, it is sometimes wise to ask him to write out his side of the affair (this procedure gives him time to think, and you, a teacher of English, should encourage motivated writing), and in twenty minutes, when you are ready for him, he may be able to meet you more reasonably. After a serious talk, a friendly "Good night" and the next day a complete ignoring of past difficulties will often win a pupil's liking and respect. (Some teachers would profit by a study of the Black Panther's disciplinary methods applied to the man-cub, Mowgli, as pictured by Mr. Kipling.)

Should you analyze a great number of cases of pupil-teacher disagreements, you would find that most of them were summed up by the pupils in one of two ways, either "She doesn't like me" or "The class isn't interesting; there's nothing to do but listen and answer questions." And those two statements should be your guides. You must convince your pupils that you like them, that you enjoy the class, that you find pleasure in the give-and-take of classroom discussion. Four words arranged in de-scending scale denote the highest praise that pupils can give a teacher: "She is *fair, hard, interesting, friendly.*" With pupils to "have favorites," to be "easy," to be "dull," to be "unsympa-thetic," are the four opposites. These unfavorable terms, however, are often bestowed because a teacher is unprepared and does not know how to organize her work rather than because of her natu-ral disposition. In many schools, remember, discipline and good manners are synonymous. Hence there is no need to worry about the possibilities until they emerge, but to be prepared for them is wise and comforting.

What can you do to affect your class pleasantly?

1. You can always enter a classroom as if teaching that particular class gave you real pleasure. This kind of entrance has an admir-able effect upon both you and the pupils.

2. Your attitude can be optimistic, your manners simple, friendly, natural.

3. Your voice can be clear, easily heard, pleasant in tone. A badly pitched voice wears out the nerves of a class and the throat of the speaker; hence it is wise to consider your voice carefully, and perhaps have some instruction in placement and reading if you have not already done so.

4. You can dress so that your general appearance is pleasing and your costume reasonably varied.[1] There was a time when powder and rouge were taboo; remember that even now a lavish use of rouge and lipstick is undesirable.

5. You can so plan your work that the work is varied, that pupils take an active part in definite projects, and, if possible, have an expectant attitude toward future assignments.[2]

6. You can make your classroom attractive. English is an art, and deserves an artistic setting. But even if you cannot make your room artistic, you can

a. See that the lighting is not injurious, by having properly adjusted shades and perhaps by securing curtains and drapes.

b. See that fresh air is plentiful and drafts avoided.

c. See that your pupils are so seated that they sit, see, and hear as conveniently and comfortably as possible.

After these three primary considerations have been taken care of, you should consider

d. Bulletin boards.

e. Pictures.

[1] Just remember that many a high-school notebook cover records the number of ties, the different dresses, the color of hose worn by Teacher. Less pleasant to contemplate, but as inexorable, is the high-school record of failure in dress. One notebook bore the anticipatory entry: "Number more spots this term: . . ."

[2] MEET THE FAMOUS DOCTOR. DR. JOHNSON WILL BE WITH US TOMORROW were the signs that greeted students the day before they were to begin Macaulay's "Essay on Johnson." The class was frankly curious, but no explanation was offered. Before the next meeting the teacher secured blank booklets, cut them in half, and provided each prospective Boswell with a blank diary of convenient size in which he recorded daily his experience with the mighty Doctor.

Many teachers allow their classrooms to be metamorphosed into a Greek museum, a little theater, a library, a Scottish castle, a newspaper office, or a post office according to the junior-high-school project then on foot. The pupils (carefully guided but apparently free) are eager to contribute because the work has for them a sense of reality.

Some teachers pass out mimeographed sheets indicating the kind of subject, the specific purpose, the treatment, and the method of the theme due a week later. Thus they make the work specific, insure understanding of and some thought about the subject each must choose for himself, and give the paper to be written importance.

These three examples are merely concrete illustrations of the type of junior- and senior-high-school work that is carried on all over the United States.

Don't fail to recognize the fact that presenting material in various surprising ways arouses interest.

f. A table for magazines, books, and displays.

g. A bookcase and books.

h. A filing cabinet for pictures and a filing place for pupils' notebooks and themes.

Of course if you are among the wanderers who teach from room to room, only the first four will be possible, but if you have a permanent room, a desirable thing to strive for, you can do more. Above all, your classroom should be a workshop filled with the tools that you need. You will find that a class can usually be awakened to pride in their room if the room is really theirs and their ideas are considered. And, absurd as it may sound, many a dull pupil finds English more interesting after painting a bookcase or devising ways of securing a bulletin board.[1]

V. YOUR ATTITUDE TOWARD YOURSELF AS A PRIVATE INDIVIDUAL

As a private individual you need occasionally to take stock and to discover what your duty is to yourself. Robert Frost, the noted poet, who gives lectures and serves as a consultant in numerous colleges, suggested to a class in the Bread Loaf School of English that teachers of English should rank the three elements in teaching in the following order of importance: themselves, their books, their pupils. Many a teacher whom I meet has, I judge, reversed the order to read: pupils, books, self. I doubt the wisdom of that reversal. I doubt it in spite of speeches heard and articles read on the duty of service to others, the beauties of self-sacrifice, the moral responsibilities of the teacher for her group. Your duty as a teacher is, I am convinced, first, to make yourself a thoroughly interesting personality capable of both making independent judgments and receiving others' points of view. Your health, your live interests, your reading, your amusements, you should regard as important factors for enriching your life and

[1] In Appendix F you will find a discussion of bulletin boards, pictures, and other illustrative material.

making you a more worth-while character. One serious danger in teaching is the danger of cutting yourself off from adult thought, of becoming permanently juvenile in interest, and therefore intellectually flabby and incapable of sustained abstract thinking. All of us know teachers—worthy, self-sacrificing teachers—whose conversation is punctuated with "One of the children in my room said . . ."

Long ago Benjamin Franklin, in the maxim "An empty bag cannot stand upright," uttered a warning particularly applicable to the great army of teachers in America. In the schoolroom there must be so much intimate human contact, so much pouring out of interest, sympathy, enthusiasm, that a teacher, more than other persons, must look to her physical, spiritual, and intellectual refreshment. It is particularly true that you, a young teacher, may overestimate your own importance to the school, and remain unaware that you owe a duty to yourself. It might be more wholesome for you to remember that the system is vastly larger than you are. To this system you owe the best that you can give, but the best can only come from a rich, bountiful, interesting personality. I am not urging selfishness. Teachers are as a group energetic, idealistic, hard-working. Many of them, however, have from a mistaken sense of duty stunted themselves while young so that they cannot develop as fully and as richly as they might have done. The pity of it is that they not only mar their own lives and fail to realize their own best possibilities, but also bring to growing boys and girls, pulsing with life, humorless teachers of lowered vitality, frayed nerves, and narrow, conventional interests.

What can you do? Travel, study, play, rest. Summer school once in two or three years may be wise; a camping trip every other year may be wiser. One night each week set aside for reading adult literature, a workday on Saturday, but Sunday freed from all school thoughts, a summer working in a National Park or a seaside resort, a summer in England actually viewing the scenes about which you may talk daily during the school year, a dramatic club of adults in which you read and act plays, an automobile, golf, swimming—all or any of these may suggest possible excursions into realms beyond the classroom that would enable you to bring a richer personality, a broader experience, to the boys and girls in your charge. You will find that teaching is a profession in which you sow and reap in exact proportion. Since, as you know, personality is the basis upon which all teaching rests, you, as an intelligent teacher, should turn your intellect upon yourself, examine your attributes—mental, emotional, physical—think out your relationships with others, order your time to the best advantage, and then plunge into your year's work determined to make it for yourself and for your pupils a profitable and enjoyable adventure where you shall "Hold the hye wey, and lat thy gost thee lede."

SUGGESTED EXERCISES

At the end of this chapter a number of references are listed. Read as many as you can before you attempt these exercises.

A. Community Contacts

1. A talk for the literary section of the women's club. Collect a bibliography (author, title, publisher, pages consulted, and a sentence statement as to the type of material) for a half-hour's talk on any modern literary figure not a dramatist. If possible have illustrative material.

2. A talk for the dramatic section of the women's club. The members desire a modern play read aloud with a five-minute introduction concerning the author and the outstanding points of interest in the play. Write out the talk; indicate the cuttings to be made in the play. (Never read *more* than an hour.) Are you familiar with *The Best Plays of* (the year), edited by Burns Mantle? These plays, cut for reading, have been published each year since 1919.

3. Plan a twenty-minute talk before the Parent-Teacher Asso-

ciation on some phase of high-school reading or writing. How can the home aid the school? Remember that a talk, no matter how "noble," is poor if uninteresting. Outline the talk and add any references that may have aided you. A good story adds much to a talk at four-thirty in the afternoon.

A laboratory meeting of the class during which two or three talks from each group are given and discussed with reference to the types of audiences and of audience appeals used might be genuinely valuable.

B. The Library

1. Send two representatives from your class to visit the county and the city librarian in your college community. Have these representatives discover and report to class:

a. What special privileges or aids are given to teachers in regard to:

(1) Ordering books for the school libraries.

(2) Advising teachers as to the expenditure of school moneys.

(3) Lending books to schools within the county.

(4) Circulating old magazines to city and county schoolrooms.

(5) Lending pictures or free material.

(6) Preparing library displays for high-school classes.

b. What plan, if any, exists for recognition of and guidance of grade-school or high-school reading? (Often a whole system of medals and rewards is carried on without any co-operation from classroom teachers.)

Since librarians are busy people, a preliminary letter suggesting a time for this visitation, stating its purpose, and asking if the time set is convenient, would be a wise precaution and would doubtless insure a cordial welcome.

2. Have two representatives from your class investigate and collect for your class group some five high-school reading lists with cost, publisher, and a descriptive statement as to makers and kind of list. To a young teacher, for example, an annotated reading list is much more useful than is a mere series of titles.

See Woodring, M. N., and Benson, R. T.: *Enriched Teaching of English in the High School* (revised). It would be wise for all the class members to expend 40 cents on *Books for You* (see "Reading Lists and Aids to Reading" in Appendix G).

C. Schoolroom Conditions

1. Have two of your members without consulting each other make a seating chart for your college class. Have these charts discussed to decide which is the better and why.

2. Have three members of your class consider the college classroom as if it were their high-school room for English classes and have them suggest for class consideration practical, economical, and effective improvements in its appearance; ascertain where and for how much the materials could be obtained; and make a joint written report that can be filed for the benefit of other members of the class.

It would be well to consult the college art department and picture catalogues to ascertain the cost and kinds of bulletin boards, and to give addresses for all recommended material.

3. Do you know?

a. *Booklover's Map of the British Isles?*

A map showing the locale of the stories of English literature from ancient to modern times.

b. *Booklover's Map of the United States?*

c. *Picture Posters*, in color, of England and Scotland's castles, countryside, villages, famous buildings. See Appendix F for details. Enliven literature with maps, foreign posters, and pictures.

D. Contemporary American Magazines

Using Periodicals, Ruth Mary Weeks, Editor. National Council Office, 211 West 68th Street, Chicago 21, 1951, $.60.

An invaluable book for the teacher who would know magazines. Informative, stimulating, useful.

SUGGESTED READINGS

I. THE ENGLISH TEACHER'S PERSONALITY, TRAINING, AND POSITION IN THE COMMUNITY

A. References for Your Own Guidance

1. Brown, Rollo: *How the French Boy Learns to Write*, Harvard University press, 1915, pp. 174-207 and 229-37

Here are two portraits: the teacher (as he is) in France, and the teacher (as he should be) in America. Consider the two positions suggested—in classroom and in society.

The American Teacher

2. Hartley, Helene: "Preparation and Selection of Teachers of English," *Bulletin of the National Association of Secondary-School Principals,* Vol. 30 (February, 1946)

3. Thomas, Charles Swain: *The Teaching of English in Secondary Schools* (Revised), Houghton Mifflin, 1927, pp. 510-15
Here in questionnaire form is a suggested scheme for self-measurement.

4. Witty, Paul A.: "The Teacher Who Has Helped Me Most," *Elementary English,* Vol. 24 (1947), pp. 345-54
Traits found desirable in teachers as given in 14,000 letters collected from grades 2-12

5. Lane, Bess B.: "The Teacher Looks at Herself," *Progressive Education,* Vol. 8 (March, 1930), pp. 211-13
Here is a self-rating scale that includes: personal characteristics; emotional and mental characteristics, conditions of classroom; ability in teaching skills. Be sure to ponder the list.

6. Hart, Joseph K.: "Personality Problems of Teachers," *Progressive Education,* Vol. 8 (1931), pp. 219-22
In the schoolroom is there "a subtle intellectual violence" worse than the brutality of olden times? (All of this March number should interest you.)

7. Summarized from *Scholastic Magazine:* "What is Your Ideal Teacher?" *English Journal,* Vol. 36 (1947), p. 209
The nine leading characteristics selected from 1700 replies. Are they well chosen?

8. Poley, Irvin C.: "A Third Aim," *English Journal,* Vol. 32 (1943), pp. 374-79
Do not fail to read this article.

9. Hatfield, W. Wilbur: "Let's Take the Offensive," *English Journal,* Vol. 37 (1948), pp. 367-69
Urging school activities that will inform parents and the community of the purposes and accomplishments of the school.

10. Horn, Gunnar: "The English Teacher and Public Relations," *English Journal,* Vol. 39 (1950), pp. 243-49
Good advice if you have time.

11. De Lima, Agnes: "Democracy in the Classroom," *Progressive Education,* Vol. 8 (1931), pp. 196-98

A picture is given here of Bess Crumby, a democratic teacher. Consider it.

From the *English Journal*

1. Rounds, Robert W.: "Respect for Personality," Vol. 36 (1947), pp. 126-29

2. Mersand, Joseph: "Homogeneous Grouping," Vol. 39 (1950), p. 394
Why not, tactfully, use grouping in the classroom?

3. Cook, Alice Rice: "The Exhibition Table," Vol. 17 (1928), pp. 672-73

4. Painter, Margaret: "Oral Emphasis in the English Class," Vol. 36 (1947), pp. 348-52

5. Dias, Earl J.: "Three Levels of Listening," Vol. 36 (1947), pp. 252-54

6. Forsdale, Louis: "Films on American Writers," Vol. 39 (1950), p. 334

7. Shoemaker, C. C.: "Management of Group Discussion," Vol. 36 (1947), pp. 508-13
Since discussion (not lectures) is basic in every classroom, faculty meeting, and PTA program, consider this problem—in which tact should play a predominant role.

8. Bernstein, Julius C.: "Recording and Playback Machines: Their Function in the English Classroom," Vol. 38 (1949), pp. 330-41
You may have none, but what an absorbing topic for investigation, discussion, and even a demonstration.

OTHER PROBLEMS

9. Preston, Ralph: "How English Teachers Can Help Retarded Readers," Vol. 36 (1947), pp. 137-40

10. Foust, Clement E.: "Practical Co-operation," Vol. 17 (1928), pp. 162-64
Round table. What are the six practical suggestions?

11. Glendenning, Marion: "An Improved Reading Program in Rochester Junior High School," Vol. 36 (1947), pp. 513-18

12. Meade, Richard A.: "Organization of Literature for Juniors and Seniors," Vol. 36 (1947), pp. 366-70
Major methods of organization in fifteen states provides an interesting cross-section. Note which type arouses most interest.

13. Miles, W.: "Outside Reading Inside the Program," Vol. 36 (1947), pp. 380-81

National Book Week celebrated. Why not have an exhibit—made by pupils?

14. Carter, Joseph C.: "Features Make the School Paper," Vol. 36 (1947), pp. 353-56

15. Boyle, Regis Louise: "Devising a Journalism Curriculum," Vol. 36 (1947), pp. 188-91

If possible make journalism (the school paper) classwork, not outside activity.

16. Joyce, John F.: "S. A. O. Toward the Renaissance of the Theater in the Secondary School," Vol. 36 (1947), pp. 481-86

From Various Sources

1. Eckelmann, Dorothy, "If Johnnie Stutters," *Elementary English,* Vol. 22 (1945), pp. 207-13, 233

The advice here is equally useful in senior high school.

2. De Boer, John J.: "Cultivating Powers of Discrimination in Reading," *School Review,* Vol. 57 (1949), pp. 28-36

3. Harshfield, H. W., and Schmidt, P.: *Playing Out Our Problems in Socio-Drama,* Ohio State University, Columbus, Ohio, 1948

Co-operation in the Teaching of Mechanics

4. Thomas, Charles Swain: *The Teaching of English in the Secondary School,* Houghton Mifflin, 1927, pp. 164-78

For future use with principals and teachers opposed to co-operation, remember the "spoon dam" comparison given here.

5. Templeton, Payne: "Putting the English Department in Its Place," *High School Teacher,* Vol. 5 (1929), pp. 214-15

CURRICULUM

6. Bennett, R.: "Integrated Programs in Secondary Education," *High School Journal,* Vol. 31 (1948), pp. 22-26

7. Broening, Angela M.: "Integrating English and Social Studies," *Baltimore Bulletin of Education,* Vol. 25 (1947), 112-14

8. Weeks, Ruth Mary: *A Correlated Curriculum,* Appleton-Century, 1936

A "pioneer" book in this field by the chairman of a N.C.T.E. Committee on Correlation.

9. Lagerberg, M. N., and Foley, H. K.: "World History and English," *Social Studies,* Vol. 38 (1947), pp. 295-98

From the *English Journal*

1. Pooley, Robert C.: "Basic Principles in English Curriculum Making," Vol. 30 (1941), pp. 709-12

2. Neville, Mark: "English as a Positive Factor in Correlation," Vol. 27 (1938), pp. 44-49

3. Smith, Dora V.: "A Curriculum in the Language Arts for Life Today," Vol. 40 (1951), pp. 79-85

There is much wisdom here.

Appendices

APPENDIX A

Laborsaving Devices

I. YOUR FILING SYSTEM

IF YOU move from school to school, as you probably will for a time after you begin teaching, the size and weight of your possessions become matters of concern; hence it is wise to think out a practical method for filing your materials, to decide upon *one* system, and then to adhere to that system religiously. Your files are your equipment. It is about as reasonable for you, a teacher, to "clear your desk" at the end of each term or year as it is for a doctor to throw away his patients' records at the end of every twenty or forty weeks. Develop a system. Below are some suggestions; doubtless you can improve upon them.

A. Index Filing Cards

1. **Index filing cards** are made in the following sizes: 3″ x 5″, 4″ x 6″, 5″ x 8″, 6″ x 9″; and in five grades of cardboard. The B grade, 180, may be obtained in white, buff, blue, and salmon, but the less expensive cards are made only in white.

2. **Uses of index filing cards** are many; a few of them are as follows:

a. The 3″ x 5″ size is convenient for: Listing reading references on topics connected with work studied. (The Conrad or Walpole reference, mentioned, would be given here with volume, page, and cuttings indicated.)

Listing book questions for outside-reading reports, questions that may be given to pupils to copy and then be returned to you.

Listing suggestions for your various units of composition, each unit having its separate title card, and *each card bearing the unit heading*. (At times you file in a hurry.)

b. **Cards 5″ x 8″ in size** are desirable for recording vocabulary or dictation exercises, drills in spelling, grammar, punctuation. Colored cards in this size bearing thought-provoking quotations culled from your reading—quotations that lend themselves to speculative thought within the range of high-school boys and girls—do much to awaken interest and to correlate your schoolroom with the world of thought outside. Why colored? Because the gay card indicates that the reading is purely voluntary; the card is a bit of extracurricular activity on your part that has no relation to announcements that should be read.

B. Aids to Filing

Filed material, to be of use, must be easily discoverable. Some teachers buy the more expensive cards, using a different color for each of the four types of work: class literature, outside reading, theme units, mechanics; but this method has grave disadvantages.

1. **"Blank Card Size Guides in Color,"** advertised under that title, made to fit the various sizes of filing cards and obtainable in gray, buff, blue, and salmon, are necessities if your files are to be entirely convenient.

2. **Fiber-board card trays** with covers are probably the most convenient containers, for wooden boxes are both heavy and expensive.

3. **Loose-leaf notebooks,** arranged according to topic, each topic indicated by a marginal sticker, are used by many teachers in preference to cards. They are more easily handled, and can be lent to pupils with less danger of loss or confusion of material.

4. **Manila envelopes** clearly labeled are usually considered the most convenient retainers for bulletin-board clippings, pictures, and other bulky material. If you find admirable illustrative material it should serve year after year, but unless you have a convenient filing system, you are too busy to discover it when you need it. You probably will not have a suitable filing case in your

schoolroom, but the manila envelopes, each properly labeled, can be filed upright in a gaily painted apple box in your schoolroom. Your pupils can be encouraged to enrich your equipment, to have bulletin-board committees and filing committees. You are forcing order and system upon yourself; you are acquiring material for future classes; but you are also teaching order and system to your pupils and arousing interest and pride in *their* bulletin board. Furthermore you are acquiring tools for future teaching.

5. **Your desk** is your private file. Usually it contains four large drawers, one deep one capable of division. Since few mishaps are more annoying than the losing of a pupil's composition (if the teacher loses it, it miraculously increases in value—until found), the dedication of each drawer to a specific class and the faithful adherence to that dedication will save you worry and distracted hunting for themes, themes occasionally *not* handed in because the pupil reckons upon his teacher's lack of system.

Dozens of times daily you will use the drawers of your desk. Many teachers fit the top one with a series of low pasteboard boxes—one each for pencils, clips, rubbers, string; one for classbook with charts, absence book, assignment book; one for theme paper; and one for cut slips, those useful and necessary slips used for getting written information quickly from the class. Does all this orderliness sound too methodical? Remember that every class period should be either an orderly and systematic laboratory period or an artistically conceived and executed voyage of discovery. Do not invite disorder and waste state money by delay in discovering your materials.

II. YOUR TEACHING EQUIPMENT

A. Seating Chart and Dated Book for Absences

The making of a seating chart has been discussed in the text, but there are fine points in the manufacture of a chart that you may not at first recognize. What are they?

1. It is convenient to have the chart small enough to fasten in your grade book, particularly if you must travel from room to room.

2. The chart should show the full name of the pupil, for both you and your substitute, if you are ill, must use it in reporting absences to the office.

3. It should show the pupils' seats in correct relation to your own desk as you stand facing the class.

A CONVENIENT SMALL CHART

	1	2	3	4	5	6	7
D		X	X	X	X		
C	X	X	X	X	X	X	X
B	X	X	X	X	X	X	X
A	Mary C. Smith	John L. Jones			Martin C. Jones	Maude White	

```
Teacher's
Desk
```

4. If there is a broken seat in your room, or if a pupil drops your class, your chart should show this vacancy by an empty rectangle.

5. Even though *you* can get along with a poor chart, make one comprehensible to a substitute, for it and your assignment book should be available for her. Her intelligent use of both will do much to prevent disorder.

Many teachers, in order to speed up roll-taking, carry with them a long narrow tablet similar to a spelling blank, dated for each school day. At the beginning of each class period, the names of those absent are written in this blank book under the appropriate date and class. At the end of the day when reports must be made to the office, the entire list can be transferred to the office blank and into the teacher's grade book. (This method is by many considered more efficient and less wasteful of class time than the marking of each class in the grade book, upon the correct line, and the copying from each class list at the end of the day.) Often pupils can be detailed to make this final transfer from dated book to blank and book, *but no teacher should trust the original discovery of absentees and roll taking to a pupil.* As far as your superiors are concerned, you had better break five commandments than make repeated errors in reporting absences.

B. *The Assignment Book*

Pupils are usually required to have, keep, use, and occasionally display assignment books. These ought to be pocket-size, since they should be used both at home and at school, and since no boy can reasonably be expected to carry a large notebook with him to football or after-school work. In many schools the form used is as follows:

| Mon. Jan. 16 | 1. Choose some game, not too difficult. Think it through. Write out directions; then read to someone to see if he can follow each step.
2. Look at sentence construction.
3. Examine use of connectives.
4. When directions are as brief as you can *courteously* make them, copy.
5. Hand in to be read in group. |
| Tue. Jan. 17 | Laboratory. Outside reading. Committee meeting at noon in basement —if raining. |

The back of this assignment book is useful for personal charts, personal spelling lists, titles of books that the pupils may want to read or consult, and any jottings that are relative to the English course. But since you are hoping to instill some conception of system and order, these books ought to be well and neatly kept.

C. Class Procedure Plan

You will keep, of course, an assignment book similar to those kept by your pupils. But life will be more comfortable, your sleep will be sounder, and your classes will be more interesting, more personal, and more efficiently conducted if you cultivate the habit of making a brief *class procedure plan* for the morrow's work before you go to bed. This need be no elaborate, student-teacher avowal of "Principles; Aims—Major and Minor" such as you may have to make for your practice teaching. But it should show you what you think should take place during class time. Here are three sample plans:

12A
1. Roll.
2. Announce Friday's special program.
3. Remind Martin and Helen to see committees are at work.
4. Read *Nigger of the Narcissus* XIII. "Fiction—if at all" to XV. "Sometimes . . ." (Takes 15 min.)
Stress: "impression conveyed through senses."
See Rothwell has chance to talk on music.
Ask Anne about shipwreck in *Lord Jim*.
Stress: "feeling of unavoidable solidarity."
John and Helen—give chance for their pet theory.
5. Show connection with our theme work.

9A
1. Roll.
2. Find out why Mary was absent. (Miss Prince saw her in library.)
3. Return Harry's folder. Arrange for individual test.
4. Give surprise dictation. (Folder A. "A Moment's Pause.")
Stand near George. See if he hears easily.
Keep Martin quiet. Have him help George correct.
5. Return Wednesday's themes.
Read from Helen's, George's, Tom's.

Show how Walpole also wrote of a dog in *Jeremy*—p. 46. Begin "The dog went . . ." to p. 52, "farcical tail." Praise sentences marked in John's and Martha's themes.

STOP AT 9:50.

6. Give drill on verbs. Folder A. "He and I have seen . . ."

7. Make class leave quietly. Speak of people below.

10A

Laboratory.

1. Give 3-minute dictation of directions for correction of folders.

2. Personal progress charts: Look at Maud's, John's, Helen's, Edith's.

3. Commend Matthew. Speak to class about it.

4. Try to get in two outside-reading reports.

STOP AT 10:55.

5. Announce that "Tigers" must have competition questions in on Wednesday. "Lions" must submit replies Friday.

6. Give chairmen time to speak to committees.

7. Read principal's request for quiet in halls.

You will, Martha, be busy about many things, but why not intrust them to paper, and then forget them until class time arrives?

Listening, Audio-Visual Aids, and Other Language Uses

THROUGHOUT this text you have been referred over and over again to *The English Language Arts*, Volume I, N.C.T.E. Curriculum Series.[1] In 1945 the Commission on the English Curriculum was appointed, under the skillful leadership of Dr. Dora V. Smith, University of Minnesota. The Commission began at once its nation-wide study of the language arts curriculum, basing its work upon the growth, interests, and needs of young people from preschool through college. For each phase—reading, literature, writing, speaking, and listening—and at each level of instruction, a chairman from the Commission was appointed. Working with the chairman were five or six classroom teachers from different sections of the country. But the published volume has involved the participation of more than 176 persons representing more than thirty states and 350 school systems. This six-year study, illustrating the types of experiences needed at each level for healthful growth, provides you with (1) authoritative reasons and standards for modern teaching; and (2) many suggestions, methods, units, and illustrations. Best of all, it will give you a feeling of assurance —a feeling much needed in the first years of teaching.

A knowledge that your work is guided by outstanding teachers of *The English Language Arts*, teachers of experience, should lead you to experiment with suggested programs, units, or methods for teaching skills that they have found useful.

In 1953 two more volumes of the series will be published: Vol-

---

[1] *The English Language Arts*, by the Commission on the English Curriculum, Appleton-Century-Crofts, April, 1952. $3.75.

ume II. *Language Arts in the Elementary School* and Volume III. *The Language Arts in the Secondary School.* The other volumes now in preparation are: Volume IV. *The College Teaching of English* and V. *The Preparation of Teachers of the English Language Arts.*

From Elementary English

1. Bontrager, O. R.: "Some Possible Origins of the Prevalence of Verbalism," Vol. 28 (1951), pp. 94-104, 107

2. Knopf, Helen Bachman: "The Development of Thinking and of Concepts," Vol. 28 (1951), pp. 290-97

3. Strickland, Ruth G.: "How the Curriculum May Contribute to Understanding," Vol. 28 (1951), pp. 226-36
Excellent teaching rests upon these generalizations and suggestions, as applicable for senior high school as for fifth grade.

4. Gray, William S.: "Reading and Understanding," Vol. 28 (1951), pp. 148-59

5. Wilt, Miriam K.: "What Is the Listening Ratio in Your Classroom?" Vol. 27 (1949), pp. 241-49

References from Many Sources

1. Starr, Cecile, Editor: "Ideas on Film," *Saturday Review of Literature,* Vol. 27 (January 27, 1951), pp. 32 a-d
A list of 215 film libraries in 37 states that may be consulted concerning 16 mm. films for rental or sale.

2. Taba, Hilda (and others): *Reading Ladders for Human Relations.* Washington, D. C.: American Council on Education, 1949

3. For timely information and bibliographies on all audio-visual aids to education consult:

a. *Audio-Visual Guide,* William Lewin, Editor, 172 Renner Avenue, Newark 8, New Jersey. Price $3.00 a year. A course in radio is offered free with a two-year, and one in television with a three-year, subscription. The February, 1951, issue contains an eleven-page bibliography of excellent audio-visual aids for the English teacher. Reprints for 25 cents from 1630 Springfield Avenue, Maplewood, New Jersey.

b. *Educational Screen,* Paul C. Reed, Editor, 64 East Lake Street, Chicago 1. Price $3.00 a year. Much information here on 16 mm. films.

c. Less "timely" but useful is Corey, Stephen M., "Audio-Visual Materials of Instruction," *Forty-eighth Yearbook* of the National Society for the Study of Education, Part I, Nelson B. Henry, Editor, University of Chicago Press, 1949.

4. *Experiencing the Language Arts,* Bulletin No. 34, 311 pages, the result of a Bulletin Production Workshop conducted at the Florida State University, 1948, Angela M. Broening, Consultant.

"The Bulletin may be purchased by writing to the State Department of Education, Capitol Building, Tallahassee, Florida." Price one dollar.

LISTENING

1. Solheim, A. K.: "School and Good Radio Listening Habits," *Journal of the Association for Education by Radio,* Vol. 5 (January, 1947), pp. 67-68

2. Rankin, P. T.: "Listening Ability," *Chicago Schools Journal,* Vol. 12 (1930), pp. 177-79, 417-20

3. Burkhard, R.: "Radio Listening Habits of Junior High School Pupils," *Bulletin of the National Association of Secondary-School Principals,* Vol. 25 (1941), pp. 45-48

4. Sullivan, G. W.: "Listening Behavior in the Secondary Schools," *American Teacher,* Vol. 31 (1946), pp. 12-13

5. Armentrout, W. D.: "Discriminate Listening Basic," *Journal of the Association for Education by Radio,* Vol. 5 (1946), p. 87

6. In the magazine *Audio-Visual Guide,* November and December issues for 1950, the first eight units of a course in "Radio Appreciation," were published. There is also a course in "Television Appreciation" which may be obtained free with a three-year subscription to the magazine. Both courses are written by Alice P. Sterner, Chairman, Department of English, Barringer High School, Newark, New Jersey.

From the English Journal

1. Arnat, C. O., and Husband, John: "Listen!" Vol. 29 (1940), pp. 371-78

2. Tyler, I. Keith: "The Listening Habits of Oakland (California) Pupils," Vol. 25 (1936), 206-15

3. Freeman, Bernice: "Listening Experiences in the Language Arts," Vol. 38 (1949), pp. 572-76

4. Glicksberg, Charles I.: "Practical Logic in the Classroom," Vol. 35 (1946), pp. 14-21

"One never knows when the lightning of discussion will strike in the classroom." If often, it indicates interest. The article stresses how to make discussion profitable.

5. Minton, Arthur: "Hard-Easy Words," Vol. 35 (1946), pp. 500-02
Not spelling but simple words often misunderstood.

6. La Brant, Lou: "Analysis of Clichés and Abstractions," Vol. 38 (1949), pp. 275-78
Read this practical illustration of how to meet in classroom teaching the students' use of abstractions.

7. Neumayer, E. J.: "Teaching Certain Understandings about Language," Vol. 39 (1950), pp. 509-15
Be sure to read this article.

8. Hayakawa, S. I.: "Recognizing Stereotypes as Substitutes for Thought," Vol. 38 (1949), pp. 155-56

9. Adams, Harlen M.: "Learning to be Discriminating Listeners," Vol. 36 (1947), pp. 11-15
Many references are given and judgments expressed. An excellent article.

APPENDIX C

Tests for Mechanics, Reading, Vocabulary, and Literature

I. TEST FOR MECHANICS

1. *Barrett-Ryan-Schrammel English Test* for grades 7-12 and college. Forms: 3. Cost: $1.70. Specimen Sets: 35 cents (Bureau, Educational Measurements, Kansas State College, Emporia)

2. *Cooperative English Test. Test A Mechanics of Expression Test* for grades 7-12 and college. Time: 40 min. Cost: $3.20 for 25 tests.[1] Specimen Sets: 50 cents (1952)

3. Cross, E. A.: *Cross English Test* for grades 9-12. Forms: 2. Cost: $1.75. Specimen Set: 35 cents (World Book Co., Yonkers, New York)

4. Smith, Dora V., and McCullough, C.: *Essentials of English Tests* for grades 7-12 and college entrance. Forms: 3. Time: 45 min. Cost: $1.60 (1950). Specimen Set: 50 cents (Educational Test Bureau, Minneapolis, Minnesota)

5. Tressler, J. C.: *Revised Tressler English Minimum Essentials Test* for grades 8-12. Forms: 3. Cost: 90 cents (1950). Specimen Set: 20 cents (Public School Publishing Company, Bloomington, Illinois)

II. READING AND VOCABULARY TESTS

1. *California Reading Tests* for grades 7-9 and 10-13. Time: one period. Forms: 4 and 3. Cost: (subject to change) $1.50.

---

[1] All costs given are for packages of 25 tests plus equipment.

Order Cooperative Tests for the East: 20 Nassau Street, Princeton, New Jersey; for the West, 4641 Hollywood Boulevard, Los Angeles, California. If saving is desired, order the *Single Booklet Edition* for $3.90 (1952) which contains this test, Effectiveness of Expression, and Reading Comprehension.

Specimen Set, any level, 35 cents (California Test Bureau, 5916 Hollywood Blvd., Los Angeles 28, Calif.)[1]

2. *Cooperative Vocabulary Test* for grades 7-9 and college. Scores depend upon range of words, not speed of recognition. Time: 30 min. but all scales need not be attempted. Cost: $3.45. Specimen Set: 50 cents. (See note for *Cooperative Tests*.)

3. Haggerty, M. E.: *Haggerty Reading Examination*, Sigma 3. Grades: 6-12. Forms: 2. Time: not given. Cost: $1.40. Specimen Set: 35 cents (C. A. Gregory Company, 345 Calhoun Street, Cincinnati, Ohio)

4. *Iowa Silent Reading Test* for grades 4-8 and 9-12. Forms: 2 each. Time: 45 min. Cost: $1.80; advanced, $2.40. Specimen Set: each 45 cents (World Book Company, Yonkers, New York)

III. LITERATURE TESTS

1. Abbott, Alan, and Trabue, M. R.: *Exercises in the Appreciation of Poetry*. Forms: X and Y. Cost: (1950) 20 cents (Bureau of Publications, Teachers College, Columbia University, New York, N. Y.) Excellent. Analyzes for pupils why one likes or dislikes poetry.

2. Burch, Mary C.: *Stanford Test of Comprehension of Literature*. Grades: 7-12. Forms: 2. Tests (1) Narration and Description, (2) Character Portrayal and Emotional Appeal, and Exposition. (Stanford University Press, Stanford, Calif.)

3. *Cooperative Literary Comprehension and Appreciation Test* for grades 10-12. Forms: R and T. Time: 40 min. Cost: $3.20 (1952)

4. *Cooperative Test: Interpretation of Literary Materials*. Grade 12—and adults. Tests sensitivity to situation, character, literary devices, author's meaning, and point of view. (See note page 576 for address of *Cooperative Tests*.)

[1] Other addresses: 110 South Dickinson St., Madison 3, Wisconsin; 206 Bridge St., New Cumberland, Pa.

IV. ADDRESSES

A card to each of the following addresses will bring you a descriptive catalogue of tests.

1. Bureau of Publications, Teachers College, Columbia University, New York

2. Public School Publishing Company, Bloomington, Ill.

3. World Book Company, Yonkers-on-Hudson, N. Y.

4. C. A. Gregory Company, 345 Calhoun Street, Cincinnati, Ohio

5. Educational Test Bureau, Minneapolis, Minn.

A list of tests is given in Chapters IV and XII.

V. OBJECTIVE TEST QUESTIONS ON LITERATURE

The following statements as to the purposes served by objective literature tests and the type of questions that should be asked, written in 1941 by Luella B. Cook [1], deserve close study. They provide you with a means by which to measure the value of your own tests. Note that *thinking*, not memory, is demanded.

Four purposes these tests are meant to serve:

1. To give you a definite opportunity to exercise original thought and critical judgment, under circumstances conveniently organized to measure reading progress.

2. To provide a kind of formal assignment with which to conclude each section of the text.

3. To provide convenient material for a laboratory period in the study of literature.

4. To teach specific elements of appreciation.

In these carefully prepared objective tests, the pupils are tested for:

1. Essential points in a series of short stories.

[1] Quoted from *Objective Tests to Accompany Adventures in Appreciation*, 2nd ed., Harcourt, Brace, 1941. Reprinted by permission of the publishers.

2. Identification of characters from brief descriptions, actions, or remarks.

3. Recognition of the motive behind specific actions.

4. Recognition of the underlying idea of story, novel, or poem.

5. Ability to draw correct inferences from the remarks made by characters.

6. Identification of the authors as judged from the tone, style, or topic of brief essay quotations.

7. Ability to distinguish accurately between whimsical and serious comment.

8. Ability to absorb the dominant idea of an essay.

9. Recollection of incidents in prose or verse.

10. Recognition of the allegorical significance of a poem.

11. Appreciation of the differences in vocabulary and idiom used in different centuries.

(I have given this list because you have here an excellent example of objective tests which are not superficial but which cut to the essentials in content, judgment, and discrimination.)

(

APPENDIX D

Correcting and Grading Papers

1. Symbols used in correction. In any handbook you can find a conventional list of symbols used for correcting themes, but it would be wise to discover what symbols have been used formerly in the school where you are teaching. It is both confusing and uneconomical to make your pupils accommodate themselves to a new set.

2. Symbols abandoned for numbers. Instead of adopting symbols unfamiliar to you or asking pupils to adopt symbols unfamiliar to them, a good compromise device exists. With class aid list the minimum essentials for each grade, each item bearing a number, and perhaps the amount of credit deduction to be made when the principle each represents is violated. (Errors would, of course, be differently weighted in freshman and senior themes.) This list should be permanently posted on the consultation board. To indicate an error in a theme you would place the appropriate number in the margin opposite the line in which the error occurred.

3. Existence but not type of error indicated. When you correct a theme it might be well for the first few weeks to place the specific number in the margin so that the pupil can see what error he should look for in the indicated line. But as pupils progress in comprehension of the minimum essentials, and as their errors continue more and more to be errors arising from haste or from carelessness rather than from ignorance, a different method should be employed. When correcting themes a teacher should beware of eliminating the pupil's personal responsibility for his paper; making the corrections on his own theme should be an important part of a pupil's learning process. The complete ab-

surdity of circling each specific error, of inserting the correct form, of doing all of the work for the pupil, cannot be asserted strongly enough. The pupil learns by doing, not by being done for. Ideally it would probably be better to make no line check in the margin but at the end of the theme to list thus the number of errors made:

Comma fault 1
Punctuation 8
Spelling 3

But though this method may be good theoretically, practically it penalizes you, the teacher, too heavily. It forces you to reread the whole theme, not merely the checked line, when the pupil cannot find his listed errors; hence the check in the margin is a desirable compromise.

4. The rubber-stamp method. Some teachers have a rubber stamp which they use on all freshman-sophomore themes. It would resemble this model although it might differ in detail.

Fragment	Punctuation ....
Two sentences	Spelling ....
Grammar	....

The theme is stamped either at the top or the bottom of the written page. As the teacher reads, she checks errors in the margin (if the theme is of any length) and also keeps tally on the appropriate line within the stamp. The blank line in the stamp allows her to vary her emphasis. It may be placed upon the varied beginnings of sentences; it may be placed upon repetition of *and* and *said*. It may be used to check some individual error of the writer's. When the theme is corrected, no adverse comment concerning the use of mechanics is necessary, for the number of tally marks tells the story. The pupil sees his record; he sees, perhaps, that he does not know complete sentences; he finds that he must go over his theme, one by one find and correct his errors, and check off on this tally each error as he finds it. The final record if, for example, he cannot find one error marked, will look like this:

Fragment	*ʎ*	Punctuation	*ʎʎʎʎ*
Two sentences	*ʎʎʎ*	Spelling	*ʎʎ*
Grammar	*ʎ* 1?	"And" misuse	*ʎʎʎʎ*

Obviously there was a grammar error that he did not understand. By elimination of the checks in the margin (which he should cross off), he *could* find it, but that Sherlock Holmes method may not occur to him until you point it out.

5. **Common sense necessary in application of any principle.** The suggestions listed above are merely suggestions. To play a technical "button, button, who has the button?" with a class ignorant of foundation principles would be wasteful, stupid, cruel. You as master mechanic should *teach* your apprentices, but if you do all the work while your apprentices look on, you teach little but lazy incompetence. You must determine—perhaps by diagnostic tests—whether the principles are understood; then you must proceed intelligently.

6. **One practice in determining grades.** Since there should be some connection between the number of words written and the number of errors made, the pupil states the approximate number of words in each theme. The teacher corrects, checks only the errors on the minimum-essentials list for the grade, and lists the number of errors plus their penalty in deducted credit. The number of errors is divided by the number of words in the theme. The answer to this division is subtracted from one hundred; the remainder gives the pupil's grade on form. Of course errors are weighted. Two sentences might count five times as much as a misspelled word, or one misspelling of a particular word might count four times as much as some other misspelling. Then too, in a junior or senior theme an error would count more than if it

occurred in a freshman theme. The process is really simple. Suppose, for example, that a theme contains four hundred words and ten errors. Multiply the errors by ten, divide by four hundred and subtract the answer, which is twenty-five from one hundred. The seventy-five obtained is the theme grade on form. A second grade is given on content, but if a pupil continues to fall below 70 (a passing grade) in form, he is required to attend an "opportunity" class in the afternoon and to remain there until his work is permanently improved.

Although this seems a fair and logical method, it is not one that I would use. This mechanical device subordinates the more important element, the ideas expressed.

APPENDIX E

Methods in Composition Work [1]

IN GENERAL, the criticism of students' compositions may be accomplished in three ways—by the teacher, by the pupil himself, and by the pupil's fellow class members. Each of these will be dealt with in turn.

I. TEACHER CORRECTION AND CRITICISM

The following are the principal methods and devices discovered from the sources consulted in this phase of the investigation:

1. Pass through the room and note errors as the children write, calling each individual pupil's attention to his own. Thus incorrect usages are discovered before they become fixed.

2. Go from desk to desk noting the most common errors and then get the attention of the whole class for a moment while the teacher warns them all against these common dangers.

3. Delay discussion of papers for at least a day in order to give time for the teacher to read and pick out the more typical errors that are made by a large number of the students.

4. Make a blackboard list of all the errors that were in a given set of papers. Then have the guilty parties go to the blackboard, check their own errors, and tell what should be used instead.

5. Tabulate the most common types of errors in a set of papers and give the whole class oral concert drill on the correct forms until they are reduced to habit.

6. Keep a separate card or page in a notebook for each student and make an entry on it for each paper, indicating the one outstanding item that needs most improvement. Make this record cumulative throughout the entire course.

[1] Quoted by permission from an article by S. C. Crawford and Marie C. Phelan; quoted here by permission from the *English Journal*, Vol. 19, No. 8 (October 1930), pp. 616-620.

7. Hold conferences with the individual pupils about their written work, calling one after another to the desk for this purpose while the rest of the students are engaged in writing.

8. Mark a set of papers for only one error or type of usage at a time and, to avoid dividing the child's attention, do not point out other errors. For example, one set of papers may be marked for commas, another set for agreement of subject and verb, and so on.

9. Use a prepared list of errors, such as that obtained from the Charters-Miller study, as the basis of the work, taking up one error at a time and putting it upon the blacklist with such emphasis that all students will notice it whenever anyone commits it.

10. Select a few of the papers that are best in regard to the particular principle, rule, or quality of merit most emphasized on a given day and show or read them to the class. Thus one day's selection may be based on neatness, another day's on punctuation, and so on.

11. Put the papers that are best in the items stressed for a particular day on the bulletin board, where they can be inspected by others and where enough people will see them to make it a real honor to win a place in the exhibit.

12. Do something to be sure the child actually devotes attention and thought to the errors which he has committed and to their correct form after the papers have been checked and returned to their owners.

13. Mark each child's paper for all errors and have him copy it correctly and return the revised form to the teacher with the original.

14. Put in the margin as many check marks as there are errors in a given line, leaving the child to find the mistakes himself.

15. Draw a red line under what is wrong and return to the child, who must find out what the error is and correct it himself.

16. Commend the students who have fewest errors or highest quality of composition work in order to take advantage of the positive motive for improvement.

17. Before giving adverse criticism, find something worthy of praise in the paper in order that the sting of criticism may be removed.

18. When returning corrected papers, put the correct form on

the blackboard and use it as a model in discussing the specific errors in the individual papers.

19. Find out the reason for a child's error instead of assuming that it was merely due to chance. If the same cause is allowed to continue to operate, the same blunder is likely to appear again.

20. Create a state of mind which will make the child more critical of his own work as regards the types of errors which have been corrected.

21. Treat repetitions of errors previously corrected as matters of utmost seriousness and insist that the same error be not repeated over and over.

II. PUPIL SELF-CORRECTION AND CRITICISM

The following are some devices which have been reported by teachers and which involve having the student correct his own written work.

1. Require each student to keep a section in his notebook entitled "Points I Must Remember," and have him add items as the need for them is revealed by the papers.

2. Give all pupils a rather detailed list of items on which they are to check their work. For example, "Does each sentence begin with a capital?" "Is each proper name capitalized?" and so on.

3. Mimeograph or put on the blackboard a list of the desired standards, specifications, or rules recently taught, and have each pupil check his paper against this list before handing it in.

4. Mimeograph or put on the blackboard a list of the common errors and have the pupil check his paper against this list before handing it in.

5. Have all pupils correct their papers at the same time, all hunting for a single type of error at a time while the teacher goes through the list of errors previously prepared.

6. Create the impression in the class that a pupil is not qualified to correct another person's papers until he can correct his own.

7. Dictate a given unit of material and have a perfect copy of it put on the blackboard as a model by which to make corrections in individual papers. Collect papers after pupils have corrected them and penalize for any errors which the pupil has failed to detect or mark in his own paper.

8. Require each pupil to state in writing at the end of his paper that he has reread it before handing it in.

9. Have a pupil write a letter to the teacher every six weeks, listing his own most serious errors, telling what progress he is making in correcting them, and telling what he hopes to accomplish during the next six weeks.

10. Have each student keep all his papers in a large envelope and at intervals go back and criticize earlier papers after new usages or principles have been studied.

III. MUTUAL CORRECTION AND CRITICISM BY PUPILS

The list below gives devices and procedures which involve the principle of having one student correct or criticize the work of another.

1. Cultivate a social spirit or atmosphere in the room which will make individual pupils willing to take criticism kindly from their fellow students.

2. Have students write their exercises on the blackboard where all can see them when they are being discussed and criticized.

3. Read the five best papers to the class and have the group vote on which is best, a vote not being allowed to count unless it is accompanied by a reason.

4. Read a few of the papers which have most mistakes, without mentioning names, and let the class suggest the corrections that are needed.

5. Have a pupil go to the front, read his paper, and ask for corrections, criticisms, or suggestions from his fellow students.

6. Require a student who criticizes another person's paper to be able to tell why it is wrong and to give the correct form himself.

7. Encourage favorable criticism but insist that if praise is given it must be based on some actual merit or good quality that can be definitely described in objective terms.

8. Let each child read his paper while the others listen and indicate the grade on an unsigned slip of paper. Later have a committee assemble the grades from all students and make a report.

9. Have pupils exchange papers, check errors lightly, and return to their original owners for correction.

10. Have several pupils read each paper, so that errors which one overlooks will be discovered by another.

11. Permit considerable freedom for pupils to ask questions while they are correcting others' papers, so that they may clarify their own ideas of what is correct usage and good form.

12. Pair students so that each pair contains a good student and a poor one and then have the good one explain to the poor one how to improve his work.

13. Appoint a committee to read the entire set of papers, each member of the committee reading each paper, all members of the committee being required to agree on the final rating given to each paper.

14. Divide the class into four groups, one to meet in each corner of the room, and let each group correct papers in committee fashion.

15. Correct papers after pupils have corrected them and charge the pupil critics with any errors which they missed or any correct forms which they marked as being wrong.

16. Permit and encourage pupils to question the decisions of those who have marked their papers, thus providing a thoughtful and critical study of the papers after they are returned to their owners.

17. Have a definite understanding that the teacher is at liberty to revise any mark given by a student if it is found to be wrong.

The reader should bear in mind that the above devices deal largely with the mechanics of written composition and that it would be possible to assemble a supplementary list of methods and procedures designed to teach the oral phase of expression.

APPENDIX F

Pictures and Bulletin Boards

BELOW are a few suggestions for improving the appearance of your classroom. You will need a bulletin board, neatly lettered announcements, pictures. If your school lacks money, you should investigate the various sources of free material: travel bureaus; steamship companies; publishers' pamphlets, announcements, biographical material; the various sources listed in *Enriched Teaching of English in the High School* by Woodring and Benson.

1. **Making a bulletin board** is not difficult. For groundwork you might use beaverboard or celotex and for frame, molding strips, both of which are obtainable from any lumber company; for covering, use burlap, which is made in green, blue, brown, or maroon.

2. **Lettering signs for your board** is more difficult perhaps. You should know how to print or to do manuscript writing. If you do not, the following information may be useful to you:

Wise, Marjory: *On the Technique of Manuscript Writing*, Scribner, 80 cents

Drafting Alphabets (Dewey 740: Lefax 00, 11–572 and 5–242), Lefax Company, Philadelphia, Pa. These two sheets (cost about 30 cents) give ten different types of alphabets.

Drawlet Pens for Printing can be ordered from Esterbrook Pen Co., Camden, N. J. The Speed-Ball pen (A No. 1 and C No. 1) can be obtained from any art-supply house.

3. **Frequent changing of pictures on your bulletin board** makes a fair-sized collection a necessity. Below are listed various sources from which you can get inexpensive prints.

I. PICTURE COLLECTIONS

1. Art Institute of Chicago, Michigan Ave. and Adams St., Chicago.

Photographs of every object in the museum, 8" x 10", black and white; sepia. Photogravures, 6" x 8". Portraits of American and foreign artists, 11" x 14" and 5" x 7". A sketch of the life of the artist accompanies each picture. Postcards, statuettes, books, for sale. Write for price list.

2. The Boston Public Library, Boston, Mass. Abbey pictures of the Sir Galahad story, in color, postcard size, formerly $1.50 a set. Desirable for any class studying Arthurian legends.

3. Brown's Famous Pictures, Geo. B. Brown and Co., 38 Lovett Street, Beverly, Mass. Write for catalogue. Not free.

Many subjects, reproductions of famous masterpieces. In sepia and colors. Miniature pictures: 3" x 3¼"; extra size: 9" x 12"; 5½" x 8", pictures in packets.

4. Copley Prints, Curtis and Cameron, 12 Harcourt Street, Boston, Mass. Illustrated catalogue.

Many of the subjects come both in sepia monotone and in color. 4" x 5". Many pictures of literary subjects. Grail pictures of Edwin A. Abbey, taken from the frieze decoration in the Boston Public Library. These are the best pictures available for use in the teaching of *The Idylls of the King*. Also sold (No. 2) by the Library.

5. Perry Pictures Co., Malden, Mass. A 56-page catalogue (illustrated and with sample pictures), 25 cents.

Perry pictures are half-tone reproductions from photographs or steel engravings. Many prints are in soft brown or sepia tone on rough paper. These good, inexpensive prints, 3" x 3½", 2 cents for 50 or more, are sometimes used for illustrating pupils' notebooks; particularly used to familiarize pupils with the Greek gods, goddesses, and people often mentioned in literary allusions. (Niobe, Psyche, etc.) Larger pictures, 5½" x 8" and 10" x 12" are also available.

6. Frebault, Marcella, *The Picture Collection*, H. W. Wilson Co., 950 University Ave., 1943, $1.25 (1950 cat.).

A list of sources of pictures, with information on processing, filing, and giving effective service.

7. Teachers Aids Service to the Library, Lili Heimer, Director. A free list of available booklets, ranging in price from 25 cents to $1.00. Booklets on various subjects, each booklet giving annotated listings of pictures, exhibits, recordings, films, charts, publications, etc., with prices indicated.

8. Metropolitan Museum of Art, Fifth Ave. at 82nd St., New York. (Reproductions)

A rare collection, much of it in both postcard size and large prints. A catalogue is a good investment.

9. Denoyer-Geppert Co., Scientific School Map Makers, 5235-5259 Ravenswood Ave., Chicago 40, Ill.

a. Desk Outline Maps: for less than fifty per map, the prices (1951) 8½″ x 11″—2 cents; 11″ x 16″—3 cents; 16″ x 22″—5 cents.

b. (M13a) England and Wales, 27″ x 39″ (scale 10 miles to the inch). A colored wall map showing locations of famous cathedrals, castles, battlefields, etc. Border, colored escutcheons.[1]

c. Pictorial Maps of U. S. in Color: America in Folklore, illustrating popular characters in folklore and legend. 33″ x 23″ (-1 P)—$2.50; C.B.F.—$8.00.

d. Booklover's Maps, 30″ x 24″ (-1 P)—$1.50; (-14)—$4.25.

e. A pictorial map in six colors (P 9 UN World) of the United Nations. The Charter appears on the map. (-1 P)—$2.50; (-10)—$5.75; more elaborate—$10.50-$18.50.

10. Travel Information Sources

a. British Railways, 9 Rockefeller Plaza, New York.

Available are Picture Posters for sale of castles, countryside, villages, famous buildings in both England and Scotland. Beautiful, in color.

b. French Government Travel Bureau, 610 Fifth Ave., New York.

c. Study Abroad, Inc., 250 West 57th St., New York.

A card to each address should prove useful.

11. F. E. Compton and Co., 1000 North Dearborn St., Chicago, Ill.

Compton's Picture Units: Later Middle Ages (Begins with Cru-

---

[1] Types: (-1 P) Paper sheet—$2.00; (-10) Plain wood, rods top and bottom, $4.00; (-14) on spring roller and board, dust proof—$6.50; (C.B.F.) Panel, lacquered frame—$16.75.

sades); Modern Period, Life in Feudal Europe, $1.75 (in 1951). Teacher's booklet, but only a limited number.

12. A. J. Nystrom and Co., 3333 Elston Ave., Chicago, Ill.

Goode Literature Map of British Isles, 44" x 60" (muslin). Marks all locations concerned with authors' lives or their works. $9.50 (in 1951).

Bibliographies, Readings, Reading Lists

I. BOOK LISTS

1. *Books for You,* a List of Leisure Reading for Student Use in Senior High School, Mark Neville, Chairman, N.C.T.E., 40 cents.[1]

2. *Gold Star of American Fiction, Rev., 1823-1949,*[2] 60 cents

3. *Basic Book Collections for High School,*[2] 1950, $2.75
1700 titles classified and evaluated.

4. *Basic Book Collections for Junior High Schools,*[2] 1950, $1.75

5. *Basic Book Collections for Elementary Grades,*[2] 1951, $2.00

6. *By Way of Introduction,*[2] 1947. Single copies $1.25; 10-100 copies, 65 cents each
A recreational reading list for high school of 1000 books grouped under 20 headings.

7. *Vocations in Fiction,*[2] 2nd ed., $1.25
Indexes 463 titles under 102 subjects.[2]

8. *A 1952 Supplement,* Oregon State Library, Salem, Oregon, 1952. Probable price 35 cents

9. *Reading Ladders for Human Relations,* American Council on Education, 744 Jackson Place, Washington, D. C.

10. *Recommended Reading,* Sisters of Charity, Mount St. Vincent-on-the-Hudson, New York City

11. *Using Periodicals,* Ruth Mary Weeks, ed., N.C.T.E., 1950, 60 cents

---

[1] A junior-high-school list will be published before June, 1952.
[2] Published by the American Library Association (ALA), 50 East Huron St., Chicago, Ill. (Order direct.)

Desirable for selection of periodicals and for suggestions on teaching.

12. *Magazines for High School: An Evaluation of a Hundred Titles*, Laura Katherine Martin, ed., H. W. Wilson Co., 1946

13. *Periodicals for Small and Medium-sized Libraries*, ALA, 1948

14. *Standard Catalog for High School*, 5th ed., H. W. Wilson Co. Supplement in paper can be ordered later.

II. READING MATERIAL FOR HOBBIES

A. Books for Boys

1. Scacheri, Mario, and Scacheri, Mabel: *The Fun of Photography* (illus.), Harcourt, Brace
A complete handbook for the amateur.

2. Teale, Edwin Way: *The Boy's Book of Photography*, Dutton
Hints on how to get better pictures and have more fun with a camera.

3. Micoleau, Tyler: *Power Skiing Illustrated*, Barnes, A. S.
Describes and pictures skiing technique, beginning with first principles, but only skiing enthusiasts would profit from this book.

4. Mason, Bernard S.: *Woodcraft*, Barnes, A. S.
Written for those who enjoy hiking, campfire cooking, woodcraft.

5. Wood, William R., and others: *Just for Sport*, Lippincott
A collection of short stories and articles about sports and those who participate.

These titles are in *Books for You*, pp. 59-61. Students who own this approved list can make intelligent choices in the public library.

B. For Girls

1. Ferguson, Ruby: *A Horse of Her Own*, Dodd
How Jill gets a horse and acquires fine horsemanship.

2. Boylston, Helen: *Sue Barton, Student Nurse*, Scholastic,[1] 25 cents
A lovable redhead begins in a big hospital.

3. Head, Gay: *Boy Dates Girl*, Scholastic,[1] 25 cents
Answers the questions teen-agers ask most often.

4. Tunis, John R.: *Champion's Choice*, Harcourt, Brace
A story of a girl's struggle to reach championship in tennis.

III. A FEW BOOKS TO LURE THE NONREADER

1. Cades, Hazel R.: *Good Looks for Girls*, Harcourt, Brace
Practical suggestions on care of skin, hair, clothes, etc.

2. Hope, Anthony: *Prisoner of Zenda*, Scholastic, 25 cents
A romantic thriller.

3. Meigs, Cornelia: *The Story of Invincible Louisa*, Little, Brown
Biography of Louisa M. Alcott.

4. Halliburton, Richard: *The Royal Road to Romance*, Garden City, N. Y.

Exciting Adventure, Grades 8-12

1. Pease, Howard: *The Tattooed Man*, Doubleday
The Jinx Ship, Doubleday
Shanghai Passage, Doubleday
Bound for Singapore, Doubleday
All four are stories of Tod Moran's adventures at sea.

2. White, Stewart Edward: *Daniel: Wilderness Scout*, Doubleday

Easy Reading, Grades 7-9

3. Tunis, John R.: *Son of the Valley*, Morrow

4. Means, Florence Crannell: *Assorted Sisters*, Houghton Mifflin
Story of girls in a settlement house in Denver.

---

[1] Scholastic, 351 Fourth Ave., New York 10, N. Y. Books in 25 and 35 cent editions which have been approved by ALA, N.C.T.E., and others.

5. Stevens, James: *Paul Bunyan,* McClurg

6. Wister, Owen: *The Virginian,* Grosset and Dunlap

7. The Discovery Series, Harcourt, Brace

a. *Adventure Bound*—ninth-grade interest level; sixth to eighth grade in reading difficulty

b. *New Horizons*—for high-school sophomores; fifth to seventh grade in reading difficulty

c. *The Open Road*—ninth- or tenth-grade interest level; seventh grade in reading difficulty

d. *Champions*—biographies for high-school juniors; ninth grade level or below in reading difficulty

e. *Conquests of Science*—a science reader for high-school juniors and seniors; low reading difficulty

For other titles, see Chapter XII.

IV. DEVICES FOR A GOOD READING PROGRAM

(Reported by Agnes Roycroft, Ardmore High School, Ardmore, Pa., and printed by permission from *Conducting Experiences in English,* Monograph 8, a report of a committee of the National Council of Teachers, Angela M. Broening, Chairman, Appleton-Century.)

1. Naturally, first discuss how to choose books: the relative value of selecting by color; conversation; title; standing of author; opinion of family, friend, teacher, librarian; book review; advertising; appearance on radio, stage, or in movie. Set up flexible standards for first class, second class, third class, and the rod riders. Stress the superficiality of the Halliburtons, the Guests, and the Van Dines. I have found this to be a safe and inoffensive policy: "Read what you want, but in class discuss the best only. Otherwise the weeds will crowd out the flowers. There are attractive weeds, to be sure, and there are misleading weeds. If you can't decide what you are cultivating, bring your problem to class."

2. Encourage "must" lists or "What I should read before I receive my diploma?" lists.

3. Make the most of Book Week, since it comes in the fall: favorite author contests, posters, book exhibits and reviews, dramatizations.

4. Subscribe through any bookstore to the *New York Times* and *New York Herald Tribune* literary magazines (a quarter each, yearly, to cover postage) or have two students bring their weekly issues in on Monday morning. Keep the previous year's supply until September for class textbook use. Before they are finally thrown away, have all prominent authors' pictures clipped. When you have at least one good-sized picture of most great writers, make a Book Week project of the mounting of them on colored paper with suitable printing about dates, types, and major works. These may then be used collectively as a pictorial survey of literature, or individually as the need arises.

5. Be on the mailing list for the monthly booklist of any bookstore. Post on the bulletin board along with such book-club notes as will be brought from home.

6. Use a blackboard border of book covers brought from home. Prune the collection to the best only, and it will be a popular consulting list as well as a quick reminder of titles or authors.

7. Have an author bulletin board: "Authors in the News." When ten students bring in the same set of pictures of the Pulitzer Prize winners, post the first and suggest that the others add to their clipping notebooks. This encourages proper reading of the newspaper and magazine.

8. Have one class responsible for annotating for the benefit of all a "Radio Program for the Week," another "Drama," and third "Movies," always with the emphasis on dramatization of good literature and deliberate, not accidental, attendance. Occasionally give movie assignments, George Arliss in *Disraeli,* for instance.

9. Have students collect literary allusions and quotations. In two recent cases, the accused has been called by the judge a modern Jean Valjean. Some penny scales have the inscription "O, that this too, too solid flesh would melt!" Eventually there is material for a Professor Quiz program.

10. Constantly make strong recommendations of good authors and specific titles so that the pupil will have them in mind when he goes to the library without a list.

11. Encourage the bringing of books to class. Be enthusiastic about the good ones; have them exchanged. Read a sample here and

there; the violin lesson from the Day essays, the "Barkis is willin'" passage from Dickens, "Grass" from Sandburg's poems. Soon there will be too many stopping at the desk before class to tell you how much they like their latest book. Turn these into extemporaneous before-the-class recommendations. Timid pupils sometimes overcome their shyness this way.

12. Allow books to be discussed in small groups with one class report from each group.

13. Sponsor the club feeling with books. Suggest that John let Henry know when the book goes back to the library. "Who knows where Jane can get a copy of ———?" Borrow a book from a student occasionally. If the right spirit is created, no pupil will claim to have read or finished a book when he has not.

14. Air the "I don't likes." Encourage frankness but frankness backed by specific detail. This year one girl freely professed a dislike to *The House of the Seven Gables,* but her discussion persuaded four members of her class to start reading it at once.

15. Suggest the rereading of some books for better understanding, the noticing of details, comparison of reaction between junior-high reading and senior. Illustrate by a class exercise in rereading a play, perhaps.

16. Encourage some intensive unit reading: several books by one author, several books on one subject, books by and about an author.

In the Hammond, Indiana, High School, a similar problem was met in a similar fashion, Emma Jane Bender reports. Her ninth-grade group was largely composed of boys, and so an animal-story unit was presented. Assigned work-corrective drills and class discussion of articles on animals occupied four days of every week; the fifth was devoted to free reading of materials, within the pupils' ability, available on the shelves. After the animal unit, more attention was given to developing specific reading skills, but some part of each day was free for individual reading. The results were satisfactory.

The free-reading program of the Sudlow Intermediate School, Davenport, Iowa, reported by Helen Ackermann, is particularly rich in devices for getting poor readers to try to read.

V. NATIONAL COUNCIL OF TEACHERS OF ENGLISH PUBLICATIONS

The *English Journal* and *Elementary English* are published monthly during the school year by the Council, and should be on the desk of every English teacher. In addition to the magazines, all Council books are sold to members at a reduced price. A few books and pamphlets [1] are listed below:

English in Common Learnings, Lou La Brant, ed.

> The values to be secured through English and conditions necessary for attaining them in any curriculum. 50 cents

Teaching English Usage, Robert C. Pooley

> A survey of present-day language. The book is practical, enlightening. Use it in teaching. $2.00 (members—$1.15)

Pupils Are People, Nellie Appy

> A vivid and practical discussion of excellent teaching that can stimulate a class and meet the needs of the individuals. $2.50 (members—$1.45)

Books for You, Mark Neville, ed. A Reading List for Teen-Agers

> A bibliography with topical arrangement, Grades 9-12, published in 1951. One copy, 40 cents; ten or more, 30 cents

Using Periodicals, Ruth Mary Weeks, ed.

> Use of periodicals to teach students to select, evaluate, gather and organize material, and to read "modern" poetry and fiction. 60 cents

Reading in an Age of Mass Communication, William S. Gray, ed.

> A committee report on high school and college reading today. $1.50 (members—90 cents)

Substitutes for the Comic Books, Constance Carr

---

[1] You can order magazines, pamphlets, and books from the National Council of Teachers of English, 211 West 68 Street, Chicago. Ask for free pamphlet "Tools for Teaching English."

Extracurricular Activities

I. JOURNALISM

Two books are essential in every teacher's library: *How to Read a Newspaper*, Edgar Dale (Scott, Foresman) and *Using Periodicals*, Ruth Mary Weeks, *et al.* N.C.T.E., a 1950 pamphlet. The first is a mine of information; the second, information, methods, objectives, and educational opportunities.

Other useful aids are:

1. Arnold, Elliott: *Nose for News*, Way of Life Series, Row, Peterson, 1941

2. Hyde, Grant M.: *Journalistic Writing*, Appleton-Century-Crofts, 1948

Excellent, simply done high-school text.

3. Mott, George Fox, and others: *New Survey of Journalism*, Barns and Noble, New York, 1950

4. Otto, W. N., and Finney, N. S.: *Headlines and By-lines*, Harcourt, Brace, 1946

Separate sections on "Reading the Newspaper," "Writing the Newspaper," "Producing the Newspaper."

5. Staudenmayer, M. S.: *Reading and Writing the News*, Harcourt, Brace, 1947

A workbook-textbook teaching students to read and evaluate modern newspapers and covering the problem of publishing a school paper.

6. Reddick, D. C.: *Journalism and the School Paper*, Heath 1948

7. Whipple, Leonidas: *How to Understand Current Events*, Harper, 1941

From the English Journal

1. Green, Elizabeth: "Utilizing School Publicity,"[1] Vol. 30 (1941), pp. 548-50

2. Horn, Gunnar: "A School News Bureau,"[1] Vol. 33 (1944), pp. 156-59

3. McNamee, Mary L.: "Surveying News-paper Policies," Vol. 28 (1939), pp. 57-59

4. McAndless, M. Thelma: "Guiding the Citizenship Program through School Publications," Vol. 33 (1946), pp. 241-47

5. Alverson, Maxine: "A Class Who's Who," Vol. 30 (1941), p. 591

This takes the place of an expensive yearbook, but leaves a permanent record in the library.

P. L. S. Journalism Test, 10-12 and college. Kansas State Teachers College, Emporia, Kansas.

II. DRAMA AND DRAMATICS IN HIGH SCHOOL

A. Awakening Interest in Drama

1. Turner, Alice V., and Bodin, W.: *A Course in Motion Pictures,* Educational and Recreational Guides, Inc., Newark, N. J.

2. Lass, Abraham Harold, and others: *Plays from Radio,* Houghton Mifflin

Planned for high school. Included are: discussion questions, casting, and sound effect suggestions, a production manual, and radio glossary.

3. Galbraith, Esther E., ed.: *Plays Without Footlights,* Harcourt, Brace

Ten short plays selected for high school. Discussion questions, notes on production, authors, and the plays.

---

[1] Both 1 and 2 illustrate close co-operation between school and the town paper.

4. Shay, Frank, and Loving, Pierre, eds.: *Fifty Contemporary One-Act Plays*, World Publishing Co.

5. Griffith, Francis, and Mersand, Joseph, eds.: *Modern One-Act Plays*, Harcourt, Brace

Sixteen one-act plays, most new to textbooks, with hints about play-reading, play-going, and acting.

B. Practical Advice: Library Reference Books

1. Chalmers, Helena: *The Art of Make-up for the Stage*, Appleton-Century-Crofts

The illustrations aid in showing one how effects are gained.

2. Heffner, Hubert C., Selden, Samuel, and Sellman, Hunton D.: *Modern Theatre Practice*, Appleton-Century-Crofts

Although planned for college courses in play production, it is a valuable reference for high-school teachers in dramatics. Directing, scenery, and lighting are excellently presented.

3. Selden, Samuel, and Sellman, Hunton D.: *Stage Scenery and Lighting: A Handbook for Non-Professionals*, Appleton-Century-Crofts

Practical directions for those unskilled in producing plays.

4. Grimball, Elizabeth B., and Rhea, W.: *Costuming a Play* (illus.), Appleton-Century-Crofts

5. Dazian's Inc., establishments in New York and Los Angeles; [1] offices in Boston, Chicago, and Dallas, Texas. A theatrical fabric organization. Schools or professional productions: a free booklet, "What Fabrics Can Do for Your Show."

III. DEBATE

1. Menchhofer, J. D., and Sponberg, H. E.: *Rules for Parliamentary Procedure*, 2nd rev., Michigan State College Press, 1951, $1.00

---

[1] New York, 142 West 44th St.; Los Angeles, 731 South Hope St.

2. *University Debaters' Annual,* Appleton-Century-Crofts, 1949-50, $2.50

3. McBurney, J. H., and others: *Argumentation and Debate,* Macmillan, 1951, $3.50

See "Suggested Readings," page 266. Free copy of *Teaching Controversial Issues,* Junior Town Meeting League, 400 South Front St., Columbus 15, Ohio. Begin request: "Please ask publisher of *Our Times* to send me . . ."

IV. LIBRARY EXPLORATION IN POETRY (See Chapter XIII)

Poetry Units

These units were made by teachers for teachers so that the material on any one theme might be collected to be "discovered" later by the high-school pupils. Since these units were made by various students in my class in the Teaching of English or were compiled by the entire class, only occasionally can I give credit to an individual student.

A. WANDERLUST

by Catherine Morris

This work is seasonal, used to advantage in the spring, when the students themselves feel the wanderlust.

"Sea Fever" (core poem)

1. "A Vagabond Song," Bliss Carman
2. "Road Hymn for the Start," Moody
3. "Wander Thirst," Gerald Gould
4. "A Mile with Me," Henry van dyke
5. "A Song of the Road," Stevenson
6. "The Sea Gypsy," Richard Hovey
7. "The West Wind," "Tewkesbury Road," "Sea Fever," John Masefield
8. "The Old Grey Squirrel," Alfred Noyes (A man who couldn't travel)
9. "The Traveller," Cicely Fox Smith (A man who did travel)
10. "The Hills," Burton Braley
11. "The Feet of the Young Men," Kipling
12. "The Barrel-Organ," Alfred Noyes

Most of these poems are found in *Poems of Today*, Alice Cooper, ed., Ginn.

B. THE SEA

The unit given below, again using Masefield's "Sea Fever" as core poem, turns to a study of the sea, ships, and "men who go down to the sea in ships," you will note, not wanderlust. Though much of the material is not difficult, I think that you will realize that it was planned for seniors.

"Sea Fever," and "A Song for all Seas and All Ships" (core poems)

1. "The Sea Gypsy," Robert Graves
2. "I Wonder What It Feels Like to Be Drowned," Robert Graves
3. "The Sea Is Wild," Richard Hovey
4. "The Sea Serpent Chantey," John Hall Wheelock
5. "In Cabin'd Ships at Sea," Vachel Lindsay
6. "Song for All Seas and All Ships," "The Ship Starting," "On the Beach at Night," "As I Ebb'd with the Ocean of Life," "Aboard at a Ship's Helm," "After the Sea-Ship," Walt Whitman
7. "Break, Break, Break," Alfred, Lord Tennyson
8. "Dusk at Sea," Thomas S. Jones, Jr.
9. "An Old Inn by the Sea," Odell Shepard
10. "The Schooner," T. E. Brown
11. "Ships," Margaret Widdemer
12. "Sea Fever," "Cargoes," "Captain Stratton's Fancy," John Masefield
13. "By the Pacific," Joaquin Miller
14. "The Master Mariner," George Sterling
15. "Once by the Pacific," "Sand Dunes," Robert Frost
16. "Sea-Scapes," James Branch Cabell
17. "Sea Surface Full of Clouds," Wallace Stevens
18. "Swimmers," Louis Untermeyer
19. "Old Ships," David Morton
20. "Water," Hilda Conkling
21. "The Main Deep," James Stephens
22. "The Old Ships," James Elroy Flecker

C. BIBLIOGRAPHY FOR THE STUDY OF "THE SANTA FE TRAIL"

by Shirley Knight

The following list illustrates well the many different avenues of thought the members of the class may follow, each selecting his own route and still remaining a part of the class through the use of a "core" poem.

Rhythm

1. "The Bells," Edgar Allan Poe
2. "The Congo," Vachel Lindsay
3. "Hiawatha," H. W. Longfellow
4. "The Rime of the Ancient Mariner," S. W. Coleridge
5. "Lepanto," G. K. Chesterton
6. "How They Brought the Good News," Robert Browning
7. "Tarantella," Hilaire Belloc

Bird Poems

1. "To a Waterfowl," William Cullen Bryant
2. "To the Wood Robin," John Bannister Tabb
3. "The Sandpiper," Celia Leighton Thaxter
4. "The Mockingbird," Paul Hamilton Hayne
5. "Woodnotes," Ralph Waldo Emerson
6. "The Little Beach Bird," Richard Henry Dana
7. "The Wild Duck," John Masefield
8. "The Eagle," Alfred, Lord Tennyson
9. "Ode to a Nightingale," John Keats
10. "To a Skylark," Percy Bysshe Shelley
11. "To a Skylark," William Wordsworth
12. "The Black Vulture," George Sterling

Poems of Industry

1. "Chicago," "Smoke and Steel," Carl Sandburg
2. "Song of the Shirt," Thomas Hood
3. "A Rhyme about an Electrical Advertising Sign," Vachel Lindsay
4. "The Song of Iron," Lola Ridge

Travel Poems

1. "Cargoes," "Roadways," "Sea Fever," John Masefield
2. "Where Lies the Land?" Arthur Hugh Clough
3. "Columbus," Joaquin Miller
4. "Know Ye the Land?", Lord Byron
5. "The Master Mariner," George Sterling
6. "Song of the Open Road," Walt Whitman
7. *Songs from Vagabondia*, Richard Hovey

Nature Poems

1. "Lines Written in Early Spring," William Wordsworth
2. "Hymn before Sunrise," Samuel Taylor Coleridge
3. "The Cloud," "The World's Wanderers," "To Night," Percy Bysshe Shelley
4. "The Cloud Confines," Dante Gabriel Rossetti
5. "The Hounds of Spring," Algernon Swinburne
6. "The West Wind," John Masefield
7. "Loveliest of Trees," A. E. Housman
8. "Day That I Have Loved," Rupert Brooke
9. "God's World," Edna St. Vincent Millay
10. "Stopping by Woods on a Snowy Evening," "Birches," "Reluctance," Robert Frost
11. "Lilacs," Amy Lowell
12. "Laughing Corn," Carl Sandburg
13. "The Groves Were God's First Temples," William Cullen Bryant

D

The following list (a skeleton list) is given to illustrate a unit in which three possible topics are suggested, but pupils are supposed to weed out the poems which do not help them to prove the American attitude—or the poet's attitude on one of the following topics: *Democracy, Problems of Society, Poetry in the Common Place.* Wide reading is encouraged, and pupils "trade" poems, talk of their "finds," and are led to pursue *one* interest undiverted by others. Naturally, this unit belongs in the senior high school.

1. "I am the People, the Mob," "Cool Tombs," "Grass," *The People, Yes*, Carl Sandburg
2. "Years of the Modern," Walt Whitman
3. "Cry of the People," John G. Neihardt

4. "Caliban in the Coal Mines," Louis Untermeyer
5. "The Man with the Hoe," Edwin Markham
6. "The Leaden-Eyed," Vachel Lindsay
7. "Scum o' the Earth," Robert Haven Schauffler
8. "The New World," Witter Bynner
9. "Saturday Night," James Oppenheim
10. "The Common Street," Helen Gray Cone
11. "Broadway," Hermann Hagedorn
12. "Roses in the Subway," Dana Burnet
13. "Nights Mardi Gras," Edward J. Wheeler
14. "The Flower Factory," "The Fugitives," Florence Wilkinson
15. "The Time Clock," Charles Hanson Towne
16. "Factories," Margaret Widdemer
17. "Cherry Way," R. C. Mitchell
18. "Factory Girl," Maxwell Bodenheim
19. "Old Men and Old Women Going Home on the Street Car," Merrill Moore
20. "Portrait of an Old Woman," Arthur D. Ficke
21. "Michael," William Wordsworth
22. "The Farm Died," Malcolm Cowley
23. "The Shadow Child," Harriet Monroe
24. "The Golf Links Lie So Near the Mill," Sarah Cleghorn
25. "Atlantic City Waiter," Countee Cullen
26. "An Old Woman of the Roads," Padraic Colum
27. "I Am the Mountainy Singer," Joseph Campbell
28. "Old Susan," Walter de la Mare
29. "The Dead Lover," "To an Athlete Dying Young," A. E. Housman

E. SUPPLEMENTARY READING LIST FOR "SONG OF HUGH GLASS"

by Vivian Bower

This last unit given below represents a type of which I highly approve, for it combines prose and poetry. The factual-minded student finds this type of unit satisfactory. The core poem here, *The Song of Hugh Glass*, is one of those indispensable books for luring pupils into enjoyment of poetry. Here they read with genuine pleasure, for heroism, rapid mingling of fear, hope, despair, and final triumph (plus a prairie background and lurking Indians).

Neihardt, John: *Collected Poems*
"Indian Tales and Others"
"The Stranger at the Gate"
"Two Mothers"
"Song of Three Friends"
"Song of the Indian Wars"
House, Julius T.: *John G. Neihardt—Man and Poet*
Linderman, Frank: *American Indian Old-Man Stories*
Indian Why Stories
Old Man Coyote
On a Passing Frontier
Red Mother
Harte, Bret
"The Luck of Roaring Camp"
"Outcasts of Poker Flat"
"Tennessee's Partner"
Clemens, Samuel L. (Mark Twain): *Life on the Mississippi* (cuttings)
White, Stewart Edward: *The Blazed Trail*
James, Will: *Smoky* and *Sand*
Parkman, Francis: *The Oregon Trail*
Sandburg, Carl, ed.: *The American Songbag*

Coleman, Rufus, ed.: *Western Prose and Poetry*
Lomax, J. A.: *American Ballads and Folksongs*
Cowboy Songs and Frontier Ballads
Songs of Cattle Trail and Cow Camps
Barrow, John R.: *Ubet*
Boyd, Thomas: *Shadow of the Long Knives*
Aldrich, Bess S.: *A Lantern in Her Hand*
Laut, A. C.: "A Story of the Trapper"
Kellogg, Louise Phelps: *Early Narratives of the Northwest* (early Fathers)
Hughes, Helen: *Trails Thru the West Woods*
Abbott, N. C.: *Montana in the Making* (chapter on Jesuit missionaries)
Judson, Catherine: *Land of the Shining Mountains* (chapter on early missionaries)

V. ENJOYING PHOTOPLAYS

Reported by the Technical and Commercial High School in Newark, N. J., through Alexandra B. Lewis. Printed by permission from *Conducting Experiences in English*, National Council of Teachers of English, Angela M. Broening, chairman, Appleton-Century.

I. *Objective*

To learn to select movies intelligently so as to make them pay in enjoyment and education

II. *Activities*

A. In order to help you with later assignments, prepare a bibliography on varied phases of modern movies for the section of your notebook devoted to the cinema. Include books, pamphlets, and articles.

B. Draw from the library one (or more) title that seems significant to you. Bring these books to class. Write titles on the board. Members may add to their bibliographies. The chances are good that there will be books on scenario writing, costuming, make-up, acting, directing, development of the cinema, etc.

C. Report on the history of the movie industry. What part did Porter, Ince, Griffith, and Sennett play in the evolution of this art?

D. With the advent of Fairbanks, what type of film became popular?

E. If possible, get information on *The Cabinet of Dr. Caligari; The White Hell of Pitz Palu.* These are early foreign films. What influence did they exert on American films?

F. Think back over the films you have seen. Make a classification of types.

G. What do these names stand for? René Clair, Alexander Korda, Alfred Hitchcock, Pudevkin

H. What was the outstanding picture of each of the following? Vidor, Van Dyke, Capra, Cukor. Add other directors and titles to this list.

I. What are the requirements of a good scenario?

J. Point out the differences between a stage play and a screen play.

K. State the factors that give the screen drama its appeal to the masses.

L. Do not be too technical, but come to class prepared to tell about one or more of the following:

How film is made	What is meant by "16 frames a second"?
Kinds of films—positive, negative, reversal	How slow motion is attained
Kinds of films—widths	Explain "iris-out" and "flashback"
Movies are the result of an optical illusion	

Lens stops   Trick photography
Fade in and fade out   How to take interiors with a
Lap dissolve—and   movie camera
    wipe   Sound track
Double exposure   Editing—cutting

M. Gilbert Seldes says, in *Saturday Review of Literature*, "Movies will never arrive at their highest level until they begin to create their own material as well as they have created their own methods." Comment on this.

N. Explain block-booking. Is it necessary? Why? What evils does it foment? Could producers afford to turn out pictures always on highest levels?

O. Do "stars" make the pictures, or vice versa?

P. What are the elements of a good review?

Q. Bring reviews to class clipped from magazines or from your local paper. (What is a blurb?)

R. State the aesthetic principles of a good photoplay.

S. Ruth Bryan Owen once made this statement: "We must keep our trashy movies at home. They give foreigners a distorted impression of American life." Explain.

T. Did the coming of sound add to or detract from the photoplay as an art?

U. Place a composite of the group's reactions on the blackboard. Have the group judge on these principles a picture the majority has seen. Use excellent (4), good (3) fair (2), poor (1), as indices. If the group has decided there should be six basic principles adhered to in the production of every picture, a top-notch picture that is excellent on every point would have a score of 24. Include such items as story and plot, acting, direction, photography, dialogue, sound, good taste; social, educational, inspirational values; settings, costumes, casting, diction, tempo, or timing, etc.

Blank page for additional references

Blank page for additional references

References for Vocabulary Use

LEVELS OF WRITING[1]

RELIANCE upon the affectiveness of facts—that is, reliance upon the reader's ability to arrive at the judgment we want him to arrive at—varies considerably, of course, according to the subject we are dealing with and the audience. When we say, for example, "His temperature was 105 degrees," practically any reader can be relied upon to feel, "What a bad fever!" but when we say, "Mr. Jones's favorite poets were Edgar Guest and Shakespeare," there are among the possibilities such judgments as these: "How funny! Imagine not being able to distinguish between Guest's tripe and Shakespeare's poetry!" and "Mr. Jones must be a nice fellow. They're my favorites too." Now, if the remark is intended to be a sarcastic comment on Mr. Jones's undiscriminating taste, the sarcasm will altogether escape those who would give the latter response. This is what is meant by a remark being "over people's heads."

In this light, it is interesting to compare magazines and stories at different levels: the "pulp" and "confession" magazines, the "slicks" (*Good Housekeeping, McCall's, Esquire, Saturday Evening Post*, and so on), and the "quality" magazines (*Harper's, The New Yorker, The Nation*, for example). In all but the "quality" magazines, the writers rarely rely on the reader's ability to arrive at his own conclusions. In order to save any possible strain on the reader's intelligence, the writers *make the judgments for us*. In this respect there is little for us to choose between "pulps" and "slicks": they may give us statements in

---

[1] Hayakawa, S. I.: *Language in Action*, pp. 154-56. Printed with the permission of the author.

the form of reports, but they almost invariably accompany them with judgments, to make sure that the reader gets the point.

In the "quality" group, however, the tendency is to rely a great deal on the reader: to give no judgments at all when the facts "speak for themselves," or to give enough facts with every judgment so that the reader is free to make a different judgment if he so wishes. Passages of this kind, for example, are not uncommon in "pulps" and "slicks":

Elaine was—well, let's put it frankly—a trifle vulgar. She was pretty, of course, although in an obvious sort of way.

In the "quality" group, the treatment leaves a good deal more up to the reader:

Elaine dropped her cigarette into the remains of her coffee. As she stood up, she gave a couple of tugs at her skirt, and patted the ends of her curls.

WORDS AS THE SYMPTOMS OF DISTURBANCE[1]

Human beings, however, probably because they consider it beneath their dignity to express their anger in purely animalistic noises, do not ordinarily growl like dogs, but substitute series of words, such as "You dirty double-crosser!" "You filthy scum!" Similarly, instead of purring or wagging the tail, the human being again substitutes speeches such as "She's the sweetest girl in all the world!" "Oh, dear, what a cute baby!"

Speeches such as these are, therefore, complicated human equivalents of snarling and purring and are not symbolic in the same sense that the statement, "Chicago is in the state of Illinois," is symbolic. That is to say, "She's the sweetest girl in all the world" is not a statement about the girl, but a revelation of the speaker's feelings—a revelation such as is made among lower animals by wagging the tail or purring. Similarly, the ordi-

[1] *Ibid.*, p. 59. Printed with the permission of the author.

nary oratorical and editorial denunciation of "Reds," "Wall Street," "corporate interests," "radicals," "economic royalists," and "fifth columnists," are often only protracted snarls, growls, and yelps, with, however, the surface appearance of logical and grammatical articulation. These series of "snarl-words" and "purr-words," as it will be convenient to call them, are not reports describing conditions in the extensional world, but *symptoms of disturbance,* unpleasant or pleasant, in the speaker.

EXAMPLES OF BASIC ENGLISH[1]

The following extracts are written in Basic English.[2]

"ON SCALES," FROM J. B. S. HALDANE's "Possible Worlds." "The unending quiet of those unending spaces," said Pascal, looking at the stars and between them, "puts me in fear," and this fear, which has little enough reason in it, has been sounding on in men's minds for hundreds of years.

It is common to say that one is unable to get any idea of the distance even of the nearest fixed stars, and to make no attempt to get an idea of the number of *atoms* in one's thumbnail. This tendency makes it quite unnecessarily hard for the man in the street to get clear in his mind about the chief discoveries of present-day science; a great part of which are quite straightforward, but for the fact that the numbers they are based on are of some size. Pascal's feeling, in fact, has nothing to do with science, or with religion. "I will be over the top of him in a short time," said Sir Thomas More, when he took his last look at the sun before his head was cut off; and in the view of the present-day expert in *astronomy* the sun is a somewhat small but more or less representative star.

There is no reason for the belief that outer space is unlimited.

---

[1] Ogden, C. K.: *The System of Basic English,* Harcourt, Brace and Company, 1934, p. 233. Reprinted by permission of the author.

[2] The words in italics are not part of the 850-word vocabulary but are supplementary words permitted in using Basic English for special subject fields.

Very probably all space is of fixed size, and certainly the distances to all the stars we see are not outside the range of man's mind. To be unlimited is a property of mind and not of material things. We have the power of reasoning about what is unlimited but not of seeing it. As for the quiet of outer space, one would be unable to go on living in it, and so would be unable to say if it was quiet or not. But if one was shut up in a steel box in it, like the men in Jules Verne's book who went to the moon, there would probably come to one's ears quite frequently, at any rate when near a star, the sound of a very small bit of dust moving at a very great rate and coming up against the box.

ADAM AND EVE[1]

Genesis, II. 1. In this way were the *heavens* and the earth made, and everything which is in them.

2. And on the seventh day God came to the end of the work which he had made; and he took rest on the seventh day from all his work which he had made.

3. And God gave his *blessing* to the seventh day, and made it *holy*; because in it he had taken rest from all his work.

4. These are the *generations* of the heavens and the earth when they were made.

5. In the day when the Lord God made the earth and the *heavens* no plant of the field was in the earth, and no grass of the field had come up; because the Lord God had not sent rain upon the earth, and there was not a man to do work on it.

6. But there went up a *mist* from the earth, and all the face of the land was watered.

7. And the Lord God made man of the dust of the earth, and put into him the breath of life; and man was made a living *soul*.

8. And the Lord God made a garden in the east in Eden; and there he put the man whom he had made.

9. And out of the earth the Lord God made every tree come

---

[1] *Ibid.*, pp. 266-67. Reprinted by permission of the author.

up which was a pleasure to the eye and good for food; and the
tree of life in the middle of the garden and the tree of knowledge
of good and *evil.*

THE ABC OF WAR PAYMENTS[1]
(From *International Talks*, Wickham Steed)

THE LAUSANNE MEETING
Its Purpose and Outlook

It would be a good thing if persons talking and writing about
"reparations" or "war debts" were made to say what it is all
about to boys and girls at school. Then they would have to get
their ideas clear and be simple. If they had a true knowledge of
what they were talking about, it seems to me that they would
say something like this:

Not so very long back there was a Great War. It was started
because every nation in Europe was in fear of all the rest. They
were fully armed and all had the same fear—that others might
have designs to get control of them. At last two of the nations,
Austria and Germany, made up their minds to give the others
such a hard and sudden blow that they would go down before it.
They did a great amount of damage. But the others gave back
harder blows and made Germany and Austria put their names to
a paper saying that these two countries were responsible for
"starting it," and give an undertaking to make payment for the
damage done. This undertaking to make payment for damage
was named "reparations."

AN EXAMPLE OF BANTU SPEECH[2]

(The Bantu is a member of one of the great Negroid tribes
occupying equatorial and southern Africa. The Bantu language

---

[1] *Ibid.*, p. 247. Reprinted by permission of the author.
[2] From Jespersen, Otto: *Language,* p. 353. Printed by permission of Henry
Holt and Company and George Allen and Unwin, Ltd., 46 Museum Street,
London, W.C. 1.

constitutes the most important linguistic family in Africa south of the Sahara.)

In the Bantu language the word for 'man' is *umuntu*. Just as in "Pig Latin" of childish speech, each word in a sentence having any reference to man (*umuntu*) must begin with some letter to remind the listener of the word *umuntu*. This will be, according to fixed rules, either *mu* or *u*, or *w* or *m*. In the following sentence, the meaning of which is 'our handsome man appears, we love him,' these reminders (as I shall term them) are printed in italics:

*umu*ntu	*w*etu	*omu*chle *u*yabonakala,	si*m*tanda (I)
man	ours	handsome appears,	we love

If, instead of the singular, we take the corresponding plural *abantu*, 'men, people' (whence the generic name of Bantu), the sentence looks quite different:

*aba*ntu	*b*etu	*aba*chle	*ba*yabonakala,	si*ba*tanda

BEACH-LA-MAR

Beach-la-Mar, or Beche-le-mar, or Sandalwood English, is a speech used for trade in the Western Pacific. The tongue grew, it is believed, from the habit of "blackbirding" (seizing slaves). Since these slaves spoke different dialects but had, doubtless, picked up a few words of English, a corrupt form of English approximating the sound of English words became their second tongue. Below are sample words:

Nusipepa—(a letter or any written document)
Mary—any woman
Pisupe—(from pea soup) all canned goods
Bullamacow—cattle. Jespersen states that because a bull and a cow were left on the island, the islanders thought the two words were one.
Bulopenn—ornament—from blue paint

The round-about expressions for terms that to us are simple is illustrated by:

A piano—of course shipped in a box, "big fellow bokus (box) you fight him he cry."

A concertina is "little fellow bokus you shove him he cry, you pull him he cry."

The term 'inside' indicates a person's mental state.

jump inside—be startled
inside tell himself—consider
feel inside—to know
feel another kind side—to change one's mind
Woman he got faminil (faminly) *inside*—she is with child or pregnant
He took daylight a long time—to be awake
To bring a corkscrew: *Bring fellow belong make open bottle*

The number 101 is "ten fellow ten one fellow."

We say "The butcher is here"; their expression is: "Man belong bullamacow him stop."

There is a pleasantly human quality in the term for a young banana plant, "piccaninny blong banana."

Familiar to us is their term, "He savvy too much" (knows too much).

Pidgin-English, used in China, Japan, and parts of California is described in Otto Jespersen's *Language,* p. 221, and other corruptions of English are treated by Professor Jespersen, pp. 221-33. In certain communities your pupils would be particularly interested in Jespersen's treatment of one Indian language, the Chinook.

Audio-Visual and Oral Activities

I. REFERENCES FOR EDUCATION IN RADIO AND TELEVISION

1. *C.B.S. Listeners' Guide* to Public Affairs

Programs on C.B.S. Radio and Television. The Columbia Broadcasting System, 485 Madison Ave., New York 22, N. Y. Free. A useful year's guide for broadening students' interest and raising their level of listening.

2. N.B.C. mimeographed articles (free) upon topics concerning radio, bibliographies such as Radio Drama Collections. National Broadcasting System, Department of Education, RCA Building, Radio City, New York 20, N. Y.

3. The Office of Education: *School Life*

Lists of all material prepared for sale or distribution free on request. Superintendent of Documents, Federal Security Agency, Government Printing Office, Washington 25, D. C., $1.00 a year.

4. *Can Radio Listening Be Taught?* (Pamphlet)

Wisconsin Association for Better Radio and Television, 2545 Van Hise St., Madison, Wisconsin. 25 cents. These units, chiefly for English, aim to teach the art of radio listening (elementary and high-school level). Are practical.

5. *Using Current Materials*

Junior Town Meeting League, 1400 South Front St., Columbus 15, Ohio.

6. Two *magazines published for school use* are:

a. *Audio-Visual Guide,* 1630 Springfield Ave., Maplewood, N. J. Discusses records, television, tape recording, films; analyzes current motion pictures. Offers courses in television and radio, $3.00.

b. *Listenables and Lookables,* Leon C. Hood, ed. A four-page pamphlet, 27 issues a year, $2.50.

English Journal Articles

7. Kaplan, Milton A.: "Radio Plays as an Introduction to Drama," Vol. 39 (1950), p. 23

8. Cullimore, Catherine M.: "A Radio Workshop Club," Vol. 37 (1948), pp. 318-20

9. Boutwell, W. D.: "Radio—'Industry' or 'Art'?" Vol. 38 (1949), pp. 525-26

10. Larrabee, Carlton H.: "Radio, a Public Servant," Vol. 38 (1949), pp. 92-94

See also Appendix B.

II. REFERENCES FOR EDUCATION IN MOTION PICTURES AND FILMS

B. Bibliographies, Magazines, and Pamphlets [1]

1. Lewin, William, *Photoplay Appreciation in American High Schools*, an annotated list of 158 books and pamphlets. *Audio-Visual Guide*, 1630 Springfield Ave., Maplewood, N. J., 25 cents.

2. Lewin, William, *A Kit of Tools for Teaching Photoplay Appreciation and Discrimination*, Audio-Visual Guide, 1950, 15 cents.

3. *The National Board of Review of Motion Pictures, Inc.*, 31 Union Square, New York, $3.00 a year. Reports on films, books, reviews.

B. Films and Filmstrips

1. *Educational Film Guide*, H. W. Wilson Co., 950 University Ave., New York, 1951. Price on request. An index to 8,251 motion pictures (16 mm.). F. A. Kram, comp.

2. A Directory of 2,000—16 mm. Film Libraries. (State-by-state and city-by-city list.) Superintendent of Documents, U. S. Government Printing Office, Washington 25, D. C., 30 cents.

[1] Consult the *Readers' Guide*. It now carries a bibliography of magazine articles on moving pictures. The 1951 list covered 21 pages.

3. Life Filmstrips in color (35 mm. Films), 9 Rockefeller Plaza, New York, $4.50 each.

4. "Audio-Visual Aids for the English Teacher," a reprint from *Audio-Visual Guide*, 1630 Springfield Ave., Maplewood, N. J., 25 cents. A valuable bibliography for every English teacher.

5. Decker, Richard G.: "Making an Inexpensive Sound Film," Monograph No. 2 (mimeographed), New York State English Council, Colgate University, Hamilton, New York, 25 cents.

A play-by-play account of making a short movie.

6. Teach-O-Discs, Teach-O-Filmstrips, Audio-Visual Division, Popular Science Publishing Co., 353 Fourth Avenue, New York.

A catalogue of recordings of English and American classics. Free.

7. *Tools for Teaching English*, National Council of Teachers of English, Chicago, Ill.

A list of N.C.T.E. recordings by American poets, Robert Frost's new records (1951) included.

8. Work-films and motion pictures for teacher-student aid.

a. *Improve Your Spelling*. In color, rental: $4.50; in black and white, rental: $2.50. Coronet Films, Inc., Chicago, Ill.

Described in *English Journal*, Vol. 41 (February, 1952), p. 112.

b. Andrews, Joe W.: "Audio-Visual Reading Guidance," *English Journal*, Vol. 46 (1951), pp. 33-36. Method and use of films: *To Read a Book, Find the Information,* and *Know Your Library,* Coronet Films, Inc.

c. *Producing a Play*, International Film Bureau, 6 N. Michigan Ave., Chicago 2, Ill. *English Journal*, Vol. 41 (1952), p. 112, gives details.

d. Hanford, Ellen: "Radio Club Activities," *English Journal*, Vol. 29 (1940), pp. 148-151

An adventure in finding and adapting stories and plays for radio or the school's public address system. The article lists also the types of training needed and enjoyed by students and teacher.

Papers for or by High-School Pupils

IN SOME schools before an assignment is discussed, the teacher writes a paper which will illustrate just those qualities that she desires the class to consider. Do you like the idea? The following three papers plus the class assignment were written by student teachers.

I. TWO PATTERN ASSIGNMENTS AND ILLUSTRATIVE PAPERS

1. **Assignment for high-school juniors** made by Maxwell Gates: Based on your reading of the story of Joseph and Benjamin, select one detail of the story which appeals to you particularly and write it, placing yourself in the situation of one of the characters. Try to make that character alive and his environment real. Suggestions: Joseph sold by his brothers; Benjamin traveling through the famine area to Egypt; the cup discovered in Benjamin's corn sack; Benjamin's reaction to the discovery of Joseph's identity. Remember that through sense appeal you can gain an impression of reality.

Model

BENJAMIN TRAVELING THROUGH THE FAMINE AREA

The dust of the road burned in Benjamin's nostrils and muddied his lips. The heat of the sun trudged through his head and stirred up clouds of pain as inescapable as the clouds of dust stirred up by the donkeys' trudging.

Benjamin looked at the black fields; he saw the carcasses of cattle in the fields like censers burning foul incense; and he knew that all the way into Egypt he and his brothers would taste the sun-dried dust; they would see the sun-scorched fields and the sun-split earth;

and the vile vapors from the sun-cooked flesh would crawl after them until they had come to Pharaoh's commissioner.

Yes, the power of the sun was great, and it was to be feared as all power was to be feared, as Jehovah or the great man in Pharaoh's court. For all things which had strength and all men who had power used it to destroy the weak. He had learned that from the sheep-hungry howling of wolves and from the famine and from the bloody altars of the Almighty God, Jehovah. And now it was the seer of Egypt who was mighty. And all of them, Benjamin, Reuben, and their father, Jacob, were as defenseless against him as corn sprouts against the sun or huddled sheep against the wolf.

"Must I, then, lose two sons? Must these gray hairs be brought down in sorrow to the grave?"

Those words of his father, which Benjamin had heard him speaking to Reuben in the Big Tent, had followed him over all the hills of Canaan. They were as ever present as the dust kicked up by the donkeys' hooves, as the sun-heat kicking in his head.

He ran past the donkeys to where Reuben led the caravan. He pulled at Reuben's robe which had been so fine when their journey began. Reuben looked down at him, and Benjamin saw that his red beard was gray with dust as his father's was gray with age, that his eyes were like a wolf's eyes and his nose like the beak of a hawk. And Benjamin was ashamed to let the tears come out of his eyes, to tell Reuben he was afraid, that he was tired and his head full of pain.

"Reuben," he said, "I am going to be a wolf, too. Not a sheep, like Joseph, to be slain; but a wolf, Reuben, like you."

He wondered why Reuben put his hand to his eyes and walked away from him.

2. **Assignment for high-school freshmen** made by Maxine Esgar: Write a very simple story that you might tell to your small brother of five or six. Remember that children like detail.

HOW WE CAME TO HAVE A CONSCIENCE

Many many years ago a little boy was walking through the woods when suddenly he came to a small cottage. It was a funny little cottage—not at all like any he had ever seen in the city. It was built of large pebbles, each one a different color. The roof was made of grass and sloped up to meet a queer white chimney. There were two shiny windows, and a small red door which was very crooked.

The little boy looked wide-eyed for a few moments and thought to himself, "I wonder who lives here." The glimmering light from the windows fell across his path and seemed to coax him to come nearer. He approached slowly, looking backward over his shoulder with each step.

"It wouldn't hurt to just peek in," he thought, but when he came closer he discovered that he could not see because the light was so bright.

"Maybe if I knocked on the door someone would come," and with this he took hold of the heavy iron knocker and knocked somewhat timidly. "Doesn't seem to be anyone home." He knocked again, and still no answer.

"I don't think anybody would mind if I just stepped in and looked around," and trying the doorknob, he found that the door opened invitingly.

The room was dark, and he closed his eyes for a moment in order to accustom himself to the darkness. When he opened them he saw that it was bare, except for a little bed, the covers of which were quite mussed up. Near the bed a square table, covered with all sorts of good things to eat, was set for one person. Beside the table stood a chair, with funny spindly legs.

"Whoever lives here must be very small," he thought. "This chair is just big enough for me, and I know this fork is the same size that I have on my own table at home, and—oh, my favorite pie, lemon custard! Maybe I could just take one teeny bite." He sat down, took the fork in his hand, and cut off a little corner of the pie. Just as he was about to raise it to his mouth he heard a heavy footstep beside him. The fork clanged against the plate, and he looked up into a pair of piercing black eyes.

"What are you doing in my house and eating my dinner?" a sharp voice demanded.

The little boy opened his mouth to answer, but he was so terrified that no words would come. He just looked at the sharp-voiced person. Gradually his terror was replaced by awe. This fellow was no bigger than himself, and what a queer creature he was! On top of his fat red face stood a purple cap, the end of which wound downward to a pair of green pointed shoes. His cloak was yellow, and beneath it showed a pair of red stockings. A smile danced across the little boy's face, and he said almost laughingly:

"I knocked on the door, but no one answered, so I just stepped in to see who lived here. I wasn't really going to eat your dinner. I just wanted to taste the pie."

The sharp voice replied.

"But it is my house and it is my dinner."

"Yes," answered the little boy, "but," he paused—"Who are you, anyway?"

"My name is 'Conscience,' " was the answer, "and to punish you I am going to remain near to you the rest of your life. And every time you are tempted to do something wrong, you will hear my voice."

The little fellow was true to his word. And from that time on, whenever the little boy was about to do something that he should not do, he heard a voice saying to him, "My name is Conscience."

Last, is an attempt by the teacher to make Browning's "My Last Duchess" live and take form before the eyes of the senior class. Perhaps the pupils themselves might enjoy such an attempt, although it is not the type of assignment that should be required.

"MY LAST DUCHESS"

by Helen Lane

His hand, with its fat, sausage-like fingers heavily weighted with rings, held the goblet of wine high.

"This wine, my dear, was purchased by my great-grandfather, the fifth Duke of Ferrara, over one hundred years ago."

At the opposite end of the long table, she languidly twirled the delicate silver stem between thumb and forefinger, staring the while into the mahogany-red depths of the liquid. With a sigh she litfed it to her lips, then politely smiled her approval. It was useless to comment, she thought. Last night it had been the cheese, the night before it had been the tapestry from Persia, the night before that the terra-cotta figurine which some illustrious ancestor had brought from Sparta. And besides, it seemed a futile effort to raise one's voice so that it would carry the length of the long table only to utter the usual "It is excellent." So she relaxed against the hard carved chair with its intricate inlay of mosaic and watched the dying rays of the sun sift through the stained-glass windows, shooting glints of blue and gold and crimson into the crystal candelabra.

One of the servants, stiff and erect in his gold braid, padded to the head of the table. She heard the wine gurgling into the goblet. She continued to stare at the twinkling crystals. They began to glitter less and less until they looked like tiny blocks of ice with gray shadows.

"My dear Duchess!"

She peered over the bowl of pomegranates and oranges into the soft, puffy face of the Duke.

"My dear, you must maintain a more dignified bearing while eating."

Quickly she drew her hands from the marble chair arms, folded them on her brocaded lap, and sat with prim docility.

Again she heard the servant pad to the head of the table, again the gurgling of wine. She sighed.

Suddenly, the sweet, clear notes of a reed pipe came to her ears. Her clasped fingers flew apart, from her lips came a gasp of delight. Again the shrill, piping notes, recalling rolling meadows, crystal springs! Her embroidered slippers tapped softly in time to the lilting melody.

Once again a servant padded to the head of the table. The scraping of a chair. Then the portly figure of the Duke waddled past the row of servants and stopped before her. He bowed slightly.

"If you'll excuse me, dear Duchess, Goldoni has an excellent bronze Neptune which he wishes me to see immediately."

Lightly he kissed her hand.

"I trust you haven't forgotten that Fra Pandolf will be here at eight o'clock tomorrow morning to continue work on your portrait. Retire at an early hour so that you may look fresh and rested."

She smiled in compliance.

As she listened to his footsteps echo down the long room, she realized that it was becoming difficult to smile. For a time everything had pleased her. She had felt delight in the mere joy of living: common courtesies from the servants, or a slight compliment from old Fra Pandolf as he worked on her picture these past several weeks. But, a few days ago, she had overheard the Duke discussing her with a friend:

"Yes, she is indeed a lovely creature. Eyes like the deer in my park. Fra Pandolf claims the cast of her skin is remarkable. She does not, however, as yet fully realize the significance of my name and my position."

She knew then that he looked upon her not as a person with a mind and a heart, but merely as an ornament like the bronze Neptune or the terra-cotta figurine. That same evening just at sunset she had heard the reed pipe.

The door closed.

She swept from her chair to the balcony and gazed down into the garden, soft and blurred in the dusk. The clear pipings ceased. She skimmed down the winding stairway, her skirts billowing out behind her. On the bottom step she stopped, breathless.

From around the fountain he came, leading the white donkey, a smile on his lips, a bough of cherries in his outstretched hand.

II. STUDENT THEMES

In the papers to follow you will find work of different types, kinds, and qualities. The chart is merely to suggest to you the six items which any competent teacher will consider. Naturally, the *type* of theme, the *objectives* in the composition unit, and the *maturity* of the pupil determine the emphasis and type of criticism. Most pupils thrive upon favorable comment.

A. Themes with Comments

The following papers were written chiefly by high-school students. Read the selections carefully. Do not correct, but write an analysis of each under the headings given below.

ANALYSIS OF THEMES

Selection No.

1. Value of idea	4. Vocabulary and skill in sentences
2. Organization and development	5. Mechanics
3. Naturalness, simplicity, and vigor (the opposite of an attempted "literary" style)	6. Total impression (Grade—if one is required)

In a busy schoolroom, teachers cannot write out full comments on every theme, as is expected of them, but all comments should convince the writer that his paper has been read sympathetically, with interest in *what* is said as well as in *how* those ideas are expressed.

Below are three freshman themes with the teacher's comments. Remember that there is no *one* right way to correct or comment; no two teachers would write identical comments; hence feel free to disagree, but have definite reasons for your difference of opinion.

I. PARTING OF WAYS
by Olive Ross, Freshman

It was a cold, tingling winter day long ago. The steady untiring, crunching sound of footsteps on the white, crusted snow could be heard. The footsteps belonged to three men who were plodding laboriously along pulling a sled behind them.

They looked twice their size for they had on big, heavy coats. Twisted around their necks were several scarfs, and on their heads were enormous, fur-lined, wind-proof hoods.

On the sled were huge bundles of freshly killed meat, for the friends had been very lucky on this hunt. But they wanted just one more deer before they started home.

Suddenly they came to a stand-still for in the distance they saw something move. Each declared he had seen it in a different place. Hastily deciding that each man should follow his own idea, they parted. The sleds, being heavily loaded, sank into the snow leaving tracks and ruts as they moved.

As the winter gradually turned into spring the sun shone brighter and warmer and started sparkling little streamlets of water trickling here and there. Many of them chose to run in the tracks made by the sled and as they ran along they cut deep gorges.

Finally, after running a very long distance, they came together at the spot where the men had parted, making a still larger stream.

As the years went by they kept cutting deeper and deeper, growing wider and swifter until today we call the larger river the Missouri and the three smaller ones the Madison, Jefferson, and Gallatin after the men who parted at the Three-Forks of the Missouri to go their various ways.

Comment: *This is good original work.* I've often wondered about the "Three Forks." You might combine the first three paragraphs and combine the fifth and sixth. Why? You use a good, simple style here except in paragraph 1, sentence 2. Read it aloud several times. What's the matter? Why not begin "On the crusted snow" and then combine sentences 2 and 3? Avoid dead passives like "could be heard." Why? Later you have some excellent wording: "plodded laboriously," "trickled." The second sentences in paragraph 4 and paragraph 6 show real promise. You build well to the end, but the last sentence in paragraph 4 confuses me: "as they moved" is not clear. Keep up this good work; think over this paper; then see me.

2. DAYS OF GLADNESS

One minute it was a peaceful school ground, the next a yard of merry children. Little children, fat chubby ones, laughing and clapping their rosy hands in merry glee, joyful over their sudden release at recess time. Little girls in clean pinafores and little girls with uncombed hair, dirty faces, and faded dresses; all ran out together. Little boys, casting shy looks at pretty little girls, lingered a little behind, with a rosy apple or cooky thrust behind them in cherubic hands; some skipping, some running, some lagging behind, laughing and jumping up and down in glee.

They came out as snow does when it falls. Some snow comes in a hurried, flurried way; some comes dancing along with a bit of wind, while some falls slowly and gently to the warm earth. The snow is intent on reaching the earth; the children on reaching the ocean wave.

They climbed on with happy laughter, some standing, some sitting; yet all grabbed something to hold to. Then each, with a rolling motion, started to pump. Little boys panted and pumped the harder. Little girls stopped a moment to catch their breath. Every face was beaming with a wholesome joy. A gust of wind came by and billowed out their gingham skirts, making them resemble miniature ladies who might have lived in Washington's day.

The clang-clang of a big bell warned them that recess was over. Each scrambled off the ocean wave in a second's time. Once more they were on their merry way to the school building.

An old man, aged and sad, passed by. He shaded his eyes with his old shrunken hands and whispered in a cracked voice:

"Oh, to be a child again,
To feast on happy glee.
Oh, to be a child again,
Once more to forget
Years of toil and sadness.
Oh, that I were young enough
To live in simple gladness."

Here is an example of one of the peculiarly difficult problems which confronts you in high school. This theme was written after a study of *The Tale of Two Cities* advised in the text. But for this girl it was not a happy assignment. Your business would be to woo her away from sentimentality and artificiality without hurting her feelings. She has no idea that she is not sincere. Probably she and her family agree that she has a flair for writing.

Comment: You have chosen a difficult subject; it is much easier to write about one person or two persons whom you can describe in realistic fashion than it is to give an impression of a group. You can see this fact yourself. Look how real you make the little girls with "uncombed hair, dirty faces, and faded dresses." If you were describing just one child, you could show how her hair, brown, unwashed, hung in her eyes, and how her face looked with a smudge on her chin and one cheek. Do you get the idea? Then you could make your reader say, "Why, I can just see that myself." It is a vague term like "beaming with a wholesome joy" that rather spoils your picture, because we can't see it clearly. I suppose, don't you, that good writing is as much as possible like our talk—when we talk well. That's why paragraph 2 is so good. Read it aloud. You'll see just how simply and how well you have shown us three kinds of snowfall. In paragraph 2 you get much action; your *ing* words are excellently live. I think you have real promise, but do work *hard* to make your writing sound like good talk. That touch about the gingham is excellent, too. It is always better to *show* than to *tell*. That's why I wish you'd work to picture, and would avoid words like "merry way" and "merry glee." You write well enough so that you can make us *see* and do not have to *tell* us what you are trying to show. Go on. I'll be interested to find out how well you can picture exactly. It's fun to write, isn't it?

You will note that "cherubic" goes untouched; that the old man, who is also "aged" is ignored. The problem is: With some praise, with a little disapproval, with some good advice, and with a shared experience—she and I are writers—can I correct her unspeakably bad writing? What is your solution for such a case?

3. SISTERS

Being sisters is fun. I have a sister and she is so like me
√ the teachers get us mixed up, she is just my size and color.
√ √ We wear clothes alike to, and its alright with mother if we
√ √ trade cloths. Mother likes us to look alike, she says sisters
√ should, for when we are grown we'll feel closer togeather
√ because we are so alike now. And we are not alike inside
√ √ one bit, we are as diferent as black and white, we don't even
like the same things. Being right musical, if you know what
I mean, makes one much more sensitive, and I feel things
more than my sister. Being right down fussy, if you know
√ √ what that means, is another way of saying it my sister says,
she's sharp with her tongue. We both have lessons on the
√ piano, she pounds. I play rather good, but I don't brag
or leave my music laying about for folks to see like she
√ √ does, she pretends to have a music soul. Anyway its fun
to be sisters and fool the teachers even if we do fight
some days.

Comment: There are several excellent touches here; I believe that you should grow to write well. Do you know why? In spite of all the errors in spelling and sentence construction, you have admirable energy and life in this paper. Another good thing about it is that excellent first and excellent last sentence. You have a good sense of form, of rounding out what you say so that it seems complete.

Well, what about the faults? We'll work on just *two* to begin with: spelling and running sentences together. Every complete statement that would make sense by itself and is not connected by an *and* or some such word ought to end with a period. You know subjects and predicates? Look for them, underline them; then see where you have headlong collision of sentences. Note: "*She is* like me, *she is* my size." Here are *two* sentences. Put a period between them. In the margin I have checked where errors occur. Find them. Read your theme out loud softly and *listen*—carefully. Do it several times; then see where you need to improve your sentences. But first of all, do give each sentence its own period. Don't lose the life and sense of fun here. After you have found all the errors that you can, bring the theme to me. You almost convinced me that it must be fun to be twins.

Until this writer can make sentences and spell a few of the common words, I feel that "laying" and "good" can wait. Do you? It is a temptation to correct everything, and to comment on the writer's assurance of her own superiority, but don't. In conference, "music" and the other errors might be discussed, but *one* thing at a time is wiser.

B. *Themes from Montana*

The following five papers were taken from the Gallatin County High School publication *Scribblings,* with the permission of the instructor in charge, Miss Esther Niebel, Bozeman, Montana.

I. WHY RED BUFFALO BERRIES TURN WHITE IN WINTER

by Helen Jean Finch, Freshman

Long ago in one of the greatest Indian tribes of the West there was a young warrior. As the young Indian grew older he became one of the outstanding braves of the tribe, because of his excellent qualities in hunting and fighting. Soon he was greatly honored in his own tribe and admired and feared by the other tribes of the West. However, in spite of all his pretended valor the young Indian was a coward. As this was known to no one in the world but himself, he decided to continue showing his false bravery. But this false front was not to last long.

A few years later the cowardly warrior was killed, and after his death he was transformed into a buffalo berry. When this berry is first seen it appears a brilliant red, which undoubtedly stands for courage. But when this berry is heated by fire, as was the warrior in the heat of battle, it turns a cowardly white, thus showing the true character of this supposedly brave warrior.

2. WORKING IN THE LETTUCE

by Allen Embery, Sophomore

There I stood helpless, lettuce up to my waist and more lettuce coming all the time. I would soon be buried in lettuce. What was I to do? What could I do? Nothing but wake up and begin wondering what time it was. I hadn't been awake long when I heard someone whoop. This meant that I was to go to the cabin for my breakfast before going to work in the lettuce field. I scurried out of bed and put on my clothes.

I wasn't long in dressing because it was cold, good and cold, as it is every morning up the Gallatin when you get up long before the sun.

I went to the cabin to get my breakfast. I hadn't been there more than ten minutes when dawn began to break. This meant we must go to the lettuce field and begin picking the fresh heads. When you are picking lettuce you must begin as early as possible, for when the sun shines on the lettuce the heads become soft and cannot be packed.

We left for the field in an old car in which Sam and I hauled the lettuce from the patch to the cabin where it was trimmed and packed for shipment.

The crew consisted of two pickers, who cut the solid heads and two girls, who put the heads in crates. Then Sam and I hauled the crates to the cabin in the trailer, where we dumped the lettuce onto a platform. That morning the lettuce was trimmed and packed in the crates neatly and carefully to keep the heads from bruising and wilting. Each crate held from forty-five to fifty heads of neatly trimmed lettuce. When it reached the town where it was to be sold an inspector examined the crates and marked on them the grade of lettuce in each crate as number one, two, or three. If it was number one this meant that the lettuce in this crate was in good condition, if it was marked number two it was in fair condition, and number three meant poor condition.

3. ON THE WEATHER

by Margaret Linfield, Sophomore

Mr. Hotercol was mad! Furious! What the blazes did people think he was anyway?

They must think he was a magician or something, but then he wasn't! He couldn't perform miracles.

He'd given them a perfect Thanksgiving both of them. The football fans had wanted good weather and he had given it to them super-collosal. The hunters too, he hadn't made them walk around in snow and slush had he? But still they weren't satisfied.

Why did he have to be blamed because it hadn't snowed yesterday. He was only the weather forecaster not a creator.

Yes, that's the way it always was. If the sun shone all day, people wished for rain. They complained that their crops were drying. If it rained they said all it did was rain. What was the matter with that darn weatherman anyway?

Well, he'd show 'em. He'd leave, go away, far away, where no one ever cared about the weather. The same weather all the year round, wasn't that perfect? Florida perhaps, yes, that was it, Florida. He'd pack right away.

The phone was ringing, answer it? No, let it ring, let them get along without him for once. He'd show them. Let it snow, let it rain, let it shine, he should care.

Oh, hello. No Miss, sorry, no snow tomorrow.

Well after all, it was his work, he'd chosen it and he was paid for it.

4. THE RETURN
by Rhoda Anne Hoverson, Junior

Arabelle Ella Lorans ruefully studied her frowning image in the oval mirror propped against the foot of the bed. Face; long, narrow, and framed with a stubborn mop of stiff blonde hair; she turned the pages of a thick red book frantically and read. Presently she looked up and grasped a comb. Consulting the book at frequent intervals, she combed her mottled locks this way and that and finally after sticking some pins here and there she gazed at the reflection in utter amazement. She'd hit it at last! Joyously she shoved all her equipment on the floor and slept the sleep she deserved.

Four stuffy days in the public library and as many sleepless nights she had already spent studying. In two more she would be ready; she would know exactly how she would look, act, and what kind of personality she would have. Poor old "Pilgrim's Progress" had suffered many a hard blow while she practiced determinedly walking up and down stairs with it on her rigid head. One by one she had painfully picked out those eyebrows that should not be there. Then to top it all she had had to break Oscar one day. He had sat on her desk since she could remember and he had the sweetest smile for a pig, but she found that all those nickels and dimes that she had so generously put into him just wouldn't shake out. So she resolutely took a hammer and put an end to the miser who yielded in death three dollars and ten cents. This she immediately invested in cosmetics which, according to Hollywood stars, best set off her type of beauty; and dumped the faithful Oscar in the trash can.

All her life she had lived in the slim, smooth shadow of her more sophisticated sister. In everyone of those years there had been one dull summer and as dull a winter but this summer was bound to be different. With sister Ann away on her cruise and a closet-full of clothes thoughtlessly left behind at her departure, it had all the ear-marks of the perfect summer. To the ambitious Arabelle the seashore seemed to offer the opportunity of a lifetime. Even though her hair was too dry and her face too brown and her nails too short a week could do wonders.

When Arabelle, accompanied by her mother, put in an appearance at the beach a week later, she was a changed girl. From the tip of her colorfully sandalled feet to the top of her smartly hatted head she was the latest word in chic apparel. Her mother was changed too; at first she had been so terrified she had nearly fainted but after a few days of it she only looked dazed and slightly worried once in awhile.

So after a spectacular arrival they settled in an ivy draped cottage in the cove. One introduction followed hot on the heels of the one before and soon Arabelle had all the eligible young men clamoring for her evenings. By day she languished on the sands in her becoming bathing suit; she never went near the water because it's hard on hair, and her's was smooth and shiney and not-to-be messed. Or perhaps she might picnic on some far beach if it pleased her. By night she danced or sailed when the moon laid it's luminous path across the surging beach or if it were later, sleepily watched the milkman come in the front gate behind her. And no matter how late it was she must coax her hair around some curlers and cream her tired face before she could get a wink of sleep.

As the weeks wore on, certain changes took place. Everywhere Arabelle went female eyes followed her with daggered looks and older women whispered "hussy." Arabelle found it harder to be gay and even harder to get out of bed.

Then one day she could stand it no longer. She forgot her curlers, her creams, her fingernails. She jumped into the surf without a cap and when she had swum far enough, she ran along the hot beach like some wild thing and climbed the rocks. That evening she came home with a bad case of sunburn, two skinned knees, and ten broken fingernails. To put it mildly, she was a mess.

When Arabelle arrived home she gathered all her books and threw all of them, together with glamour, into the furnace. Then she gathered Oscar and painstakingly glued him together till he was a little crooked but otherwise as good as new. Then she tied her hair back from her face with a gaudy red ribbon and went to play tennis in the afternoon sun.

5. RICHARD CARVEL

by Mildred Grande, Junior

How would you like to find yourself a prisoner aboard a slaver? How would you like to know that you are to be sold to a wealthy planter on a far off island, where you will work out your keep in slavery? This is what nearly happened to Richard Carvel, the beloved grandson of Lionel Carvel, a wealthy Maryland landowner.

He was rescued by the famous seaman, John Paul Jones, who took him to his home in Scotland. Later Richard persuaded Jones to accompany him to London, where Richard tried to secure money from his grandfather's account. Unfortunately because he was unable to identify himself to the satisfaction of Mr. Carvel's London agent, he failed to get any money and was therefore placed in prison because of his debts.

But wait, I shall tell you no more as I think you will enjoy reading the book. It is full of fast-moving adventure. There are good word pictures of life in London in the eighteenth century. You will meet with the young blades of society such as Horace Walpole, David Garrick and Edmond Burke. The story gives you a colorful picture of these great men. The book enables one to become better acquainted with the noted coffee-houses, the gathering places of the time. For those desiring romance, there is a good love story and the social set of today can learn about the society of London and of the colonies of that day. The reader who must have fighting, will have a plenty, when he reads the experiences of Richard and John Paul Jones in the American Revolution. I advise anyone who likes adventure stories to take a chance on "Richard Carvel."

C. Themes from New Jersey

The following two themes from Miss Hazel Poole, Newark, New Jersey, are the product of class laboratory periods.

1. A CITY STREET

by a Freshman

The stranger, waiting at the corner, knew at last what people meant by the voice of the city. The rumble of trucks and buses was very confusing to him. It was made even more confusing by the fact that he was lost. How he wished he were back in Hungary! His brother John had failed to meet him at the dock, but he had secured from a policeman directions for reaching his house. He had been so awed by the tall buildings that he had wandered and now did not have the slightest idea where to go. Taxis screeched to a stop. A fire-engine clattered down the street. The policeman's shrill whistle pierced his ears. People rushed by, all intent on something and none paying any attention to the people surrounding them. He walked across the street. The trolley clanged its bell for him to get out of the way. An ambulance rushed down the street like mad, with its siren shrieking. All these things made him more lonely than ever. Didn't these noises ever stop? Was everybody always in such a hurry? He looked into the store window at the toy train running around on its track. How much like the people and traffic it was— rushing ahead, never stopping! It even had a little whistle that made a noise. He wandered aimlessly on, finally stopping to look at a sign post. P-I-N-E. That looked familiar. Hurriedly he pulled out the paper with his brother's address on. Three hundred sixty-five Pine Street. Why, this must be the street John lived on. Now to find number three hundred sixty-five. He stopped at the first house and rang the bell. "Can you tell me," he said, "where— John!"

"Peter! Where have you been?"

The two went inside. Peter is now very happy. Every time he walks near the downtown district he thinks of the day he stood on the corner, lost and lonely.

2. VERA VAMP

(An echo from study of *The Spectator*)

From the general appearance and attitude of this pert maiden, you can be sure of the fact that she takes more than an ordinary interest in boys. As Vera goes walking down the corridors at school, the boys stop to whistle to the time of her steps. The red lips and finger-nails make it next to the impossible to overlook Vera, as from a distance, she looks like a Christmas tree all bedecked with the latest. If a good-looking boy happens to pass her way she immediately has a cinder in her eye, or else one of her books slips accidentally to the floor. We find it hard at times to get her to keep the minutes of our club correct, as she can't keep her eyes off Percy Stacomb. If you wonder why she gets such good marks, a little investigation will disclose that she has all men teachers. Who goes to the football games with an escort fit for the president? Even a person with a sub-normal mind could find the answer. One of the reasons for the increase in male membership to our club is Vera, and if you ask the boys she is the main reason. Percy Stacomb hasn't a chance with Vera, as she is constantly rushed by other fellows, keeping Percy in the background. Whenever there is some homework which Vera doesn't feel capable of doing one thousand boys immediately offer to do it. If she drops her handkerchief, one thousand males rush for it. Do football players talk of the next play when in a huddle? No! They say, "Give me the ball! Vera's in the stands watching me. I have to do something good." Every day she is seen with a new boy-friend. I assure you that the others have found how soon their money disappears after their having been associated with her for a short time, and you'd be surprised in how short a time money disappears when Vera is in the vicinity. It's really quite amusing to look in on a dance if Vera is present. The girls are found huddled together at one end of the room, while at the other end is a conglomeration of male dancers clustered about a lone female, seemingly quite at home. Of course, Vera is the girl in question. To sum up her general character, when it comes to boys Vera is a very good authority.

D. More Themes from Montana

The following four papers, sent from various high schools, were published with permission of the editor of *Sluice Box, High-School Number,* printed at Montana State University, Missoula, Montana.

I. MOTHER'S DAY
by Gladys Landon, Bearcreek High School

Warden Smart eased his bulky frame into the big swivel chair and puffed on a fifty-cent cigar. He looked long and intently at the calendar, then turned to Miss Smith, his gum-chewing secretary.

"Tomorrow is Mother's Day," said he. "Phone and order a dozen carnations and a box of candy. Send them to my mother. Here's the address." He threw a slip of paper on the cluttered desk. "Now take a letter."

Down in Cell 15, two convicts were talking. Young, eager Johnny Andrews contrasted sharply with the prison-stamped Irish Pat.

"Calendar says Mother's Day tomorrow," said Pat, pointing with a blunt, dirty forefinger.

"Yes, I know. I used to buy my mother a bunch of violets, and once I told her she'd get carnations some day. Just as well she doesn't know I'm cooped up here. It'd kill her. Swell of the warden not to write and tell her."

"Well, kid, me ole lady kicked the bucket; I never knew about Mother's Day anyhow. Yer lucky you only got to stay t'ree monts. I'm here fer fifteen years."

That afternoon Miss Smith ordered a dozen expensive red carnations and a box of chocolates. After looking around the table she found a slip of paper bearing the address.

"Didn't know the old lady got married again. Oh, well, Andrews is a better name than Smart. And her living in that place! With the money the boss's got she ought to be on Fifth Avenue," she mused as she got the package ready for mailing.

The next morning the postman stopped at the little brown house on the corner in far-away New York. Every day he was greeted by little Mrs. Andrews, who asked him every morning if he had a letter for her from Johnny.

"Well, Mrs. Andrews, I have a nice package for you and you better open it up right away because I think it's flowers," said the postman.

"I knew Johnny wouldn't forget. He must be doing well to send me carnations and candy." Her eyes filled with happy tears.

2. MY PET PEEVE

by Harold Swan, Missoula County

It is a fact well known to all that women have single-track minds. Deluge them with a barrage of information concerning the clutch, brake, gearshift, lights, and steering apparatus, and they become so completely confused that your life is placed in much danger.

Women instinctively find the ignition and the gas, and can be taught, over a period of years, how to shift gears. It also takes them but a short time to discover how to operate the horn. It has been ascertained through complete and thorough research that it is impossible to teach them when *not* to blow it, so you needn't try.

If you wish to show a woman how to operate the brake, clutch, and steering wheel, a good place to make your effort is on the plains of Iowa, Nebraska, or Kansas. If your resources are sufficient you may instruct her on the Sahara Desert. Utah's famed salt flats are also an excellent location.

The first step before attempting to teach one of the creatures to drive is to invest in $10,000 worth of life insurance and go to one of the aforementioned spots. Place her in the front seat, sit back, close your eyes and attempt to relax. When the automobile overturns or when the gasoline tank is empty, you'll stop, probably not before. Constant drill and practice bring results, and if you demonstrate often and let her try often, you will find that within two months it is possible to go easily twenty-five miles without a wreck.

When you start her on city driving, take out $25,000 more in life insurance. Turn the automobile over to her, put on a football helmet, place plenty of padding around you, and clamber into the back seat. When your charge takes the car through an opening, presumably three inches wide at 40 m.p.h. beware of swallowing your gum or chewing-tobacco. If you have one fender left, and if you have stopped for one out of ten red lights after an hour of practice, you may consider yourself an expert instructor.

The next day you will receive a surprise! If you have sharp ears and an earnest desire to evesdrop you will hear your pupil state, in effect, "Yes, my dear, I've been learning to drive; and just yesterday I took the car right through town—and without a scratch."

3. ON SKIING

by Isabel Brenner, Missoula County

You will undoubtedly expect this dissertation to be on the behalf of the thrills and humorous spill of skiing. In short, you will expect me to ramble on like the many ski enthusiasts whose perverted fiendish glee contends that smashing head first through an icy drift is uproariously funny, or that the sensation identical to having the bottom of one's stomach ripped out is a thrill. You are due for a shock and the privilege of meeting someone who hasn't been swept away by a fad.

Let's say that you, after having been told that, though you had never skied before, you'd "learn in no time," have consented to be dragged out of a warm bed at seven o'clock some delightfully frigid morning. These friends, who have it in for you, are all gay and talkative and full of skiing stories. People like that are usually conceited in the morning and stupid in the afternoon anyway.

The first four hours of small hills aren't so bad. The terror begins when some particularly malicious person suggests climbing a little higher. You protest, but are quickly squelched by cries of "Look at Beatrice. She's never skied before either." Not to be outdone by Beatrice, you start. It seems that everyone brought climbers, but no one told you about them, so you take off your skis and, putting them over your shoulder where they hurt the least, try walking up the hill. At each step your foot sinks some two feet so that you flounder and are often thrown down. The rest, who are several hundred feet ahead, point back and shout loudly to each other. "Ha, ha," they say, "just look at poor old George down there!"

About half way up you notice that the rest are just reaching the summit, with Beatrice leading them all. But you—you fool—are still game. You thrust bravely ahead, but at the echoing yell "Track," you know enough to try to get out of the way. This you barely do, and are left with the breathless feeling that your life has been miraculously spared.

As you reach the top you find that you're alone, everyone else having gone down and decided that, since it is four o'clock and a chilly wind has come up, it would be better to go on the cars. The wind *is* chilly—"bitter" you say—enough so to freeze your clothes, leaving you encased in ice. You get the panicky feeling that if you don't go down immediately, they will leave you to die a horrible frozen death. You look down the hill and realize that it is utterly preposterous even to think of running it. This leaves you one course: strap your skis together and, sitting on them, get to the bottom as quickly as possible and run for the cars, avoiding everyone you can. On the way home think up as many excuses as possible to avoid further experiences such as this, and ignore, or answer by throwing the dried crusts of your sandwiches, such questions as, "Did you learn much about skiing, George? I don't see how you could have if you *sat* on them!" (This last with deep scorn.)

Now your object and only thought is to get home to bed and stay there until supper time Tuesday.

4. CAN WAR BE JUSTIFIED IN THE MODERN WORLD?

by Robert Howard, Missoula County

The justification of war is the most difficult task which man has ever undertaken. The fact that the task has never been done successfully is sufficient clue to its difficulty. Of course most wars have been justified at the time they were being fought, at least in the minds of the masses. But few indeed are the cases where modern historians have found satisfaction in the ostensible reasons for conflict.

As a general rule there are three main classes under which these reasons fall. Briefly, they are self-defense, acquisition of territory and prestige, and the necessity of spreading a religious or moral teaching.

Let us take up self-defense first. There have been a few cases (very few indeed), in ancient and medieval history especially, where the self-defense motif for war was justifiable. And most of these, when scrutinized carefully, fail to hold water. In the first place, nations, at least modern nations, do not go to war simply to get territory. Land is not an end in itself. It's what the land can give the nation that counts. It may be raw materials or natural resources, it may be factories and industrial plants, but it is never land for the sake of land. Quarrels over the Sahara desert have not been very numerous in history.

Bearing these things in mind let us look a little more closely at the self-defense "excuse." If the nation whose territorial integrity was violated had been willing to scale down her trade barriers and restrictions so that her aggressive neighbor could have access to the things she needed for her very life, a war in self-defense would have been unnecessary. So we see that the nation who cries self-defense is, more often than not, just as responsible for the war as the invading power.

With that myth exploded, we can turn to the next reason which need not detain us long because of its infrequent use today. The age has past when a lord could calmly declare that he was going to invade the neighboring domain on a maurading expedition and get enthusiasm from the populace. Today we must camoflouge the desire for land with an appeal to racial and political prejudice, but the task is becoming increasingly harder.

All of which brings us to the third reason for war, the necessity for spreading a religious belief or moral doctrine. The tragedy of this reason is that it has been proved false again and again through the course of history. No convert was every really made to a religion or no one ever accepted a principle under the threat of force. Outwardly perhaps, but in their heart of hearts—no. These zealots failed to see that in their enthusiasm they were disregarding the most precious thing in the world—human life. No matter what the cause may be, no matter what its inspiration, if it is formed to take human life it is unworthy of the name it bears. That is why no war, whether religious or political, can ever be justified before the eyes of thinking man. That is why the modern world must reject war and seek a new path towards peace and light, a path that means the regeneration of man and his destiny.

III. POEMS

BEAUTIFUL THINGS I LOVE

Barren sand dunes along lake shores,
Low-lapping waves washing white sand;
White caps, and sail boats,
And struggling tugs;
All these things I love, and hundreds more.

Miles of straight highway across
the great plains;
Contented cattle on the open
range;
Stern-wheeled river boats covered with lights
A wheeling bold eagle almost
out of sight,
The lone beacon's beam on low
clouds at night.

High timbered hills; green val-
leys below,
Tall pine and fir trees and short
sturdy oaks,
Great bridges, tall buildings;
dwarfed humans below,
Mid-winter, an elk herd battling
deep snow;
Plain nature pictures are the
best I know.

A faithful dog straining to talk,
Sunrise and sunset from a high
mountain peak,
A tiny pink baby just learning
to walk;
New hats and gloves fresh from
the store,
A well-arranged room with fresh-
polished floor.

Beautiful clothes on a beautiful
girl,
Curled hair well kept with bows
and pins;
Clear eyes expressing their "will-
not" or "will;"

Fresh golden bread and a siz-
zling steak;
All these I love and hundreds
more.
　　　—Lester Van Dusen,
　　　　Missoula

CLOUD ROPE

Cowboys of Empyrean
Are riding their horses high;
They're swinging their red ban-
danas
Into the western sky.

The range on the horizon
With prairie sage grows blue;
The pioneer clouds are moving
Slowly in ghost review.

Indian chiefs are dancing,
Tossing their blankets away;
Feathers of war-paint are falling
Over the edge of the day.

Sands of the trail are sifting
On the spectre caravan,
Hiding the sad melancholy
Wrapt in the soul of man.

Cowboys of Empyrean
Are swinging their cloud ropes
high,
Pulling the horns of their steer-
stars
Into the western sky.
　　　—Virginia Anderson, Fergus

THE WEAVER [1]

Lock and lintel, shutter and
broom—
Silken threads that fly the loom;
Grey-wing, witch ring, dusty
thatch;
Tears of a princess rust the
latch,
And her hands turn wan to the
warp and woof
As a pale moth fluttering under
the roof.
Now is the grass at the threshold
still,
And silence listening at the sill;
Shadow of ivy on the floor,
Grey moss feeling the oaken
door.
The moon has frozen to elfin
laughter
Carven monsters that flank the
rafter,
And of her witchery let fall
A shadow pattern on the wall—
Shine and shimmer, fold and fold
The drifting pattern of cobweb
gold
Drawn from the shuttle, as scat-
tered, found,
It lisps and whispers from loom
to ground;
And gold to gold and silken fair

Floats to the loom the weaver's
hair.
Yet far in the forest and faint
with dew
A leprechaun taps at the elf-
queen's shoe;
And over the forest, across the
spell,
Thistle, oak bough, cliff and fell,
The far-off sound of a hunter's
horn
On the trail of a flying unicorn.
—Jean Allred, Ogden
High School, Utah

DESIRE

Give me waving grass and lofty
trees—
And plains that stretch to Western seas;
Where white gulls fly,
Where under snowy sails, brave
men have lived and died.

Show me a sandy beach, where
lofty palm trees wave;
Where tiny boats go plowing
through the surf;
And coral pink shells lie beside
the sea
While jungle creatures peer
through grass and turf.
—Mariam Newhall,
Fort Benton

[1] Quoted from "Weavers."

DAWN

Dawning
Will rise as wraithes
From eastern earthen pots—

The gray hills. Twining incense
heralding
The day.

—Randall Ruechelle,
Kalispell

IV. COLLEGE ENTRANCE THEMES

The two following papers were written in a college entrance examination by recent high-school graduates.

I. MANY PEOPLE FEEL CERTAIN THAT DEPRESSION WILL COME WITH PEACE

I have often heard the saying, "What will become of us after this war" mentioned by quite a few people. Many people say that if and when there is a depression again, it will be worse than the last one. In my opinion I think one should not think of something like that, because after all where will it get them—nowhere. This country is at the present time, spending and using up alot of money for defense, which is an entirely good thing. When and if peace comes among the nation, many seem to think it will put many boys and men out of work and therefore lead into another depression. But why worry about that now; let good come for and worse come for worse. Anyway if a depression is going to come out of peace, it isn't going to stop and ask the people. People have their points about depression, too I guess, because it is an awful thing and I know there is not one of us who would like to live through one: especially if one has heard about some of the tales about the last depression. It was said that many were starving and didn't have any money with which to buy food and many froze to death.

Let's hope that this country uses its head sensibly and none of us have to live through one. But I think when peace comes this country will be able to stand upon its own feet satisfactory and everything will go on just about the same as today, oh, of course it might not be just like it is now, at least everyone I imagine is hoping it won't. But again why look forward to it, take it if it comes and then after that one just about has to like it.

2. MANY PEOPLE FEEL CERTAIN THAT DEPRESSION WILL COME WITH PEACE

Many people feel certain that at the end of this war our country will again find itself in a state of depression.

The argument is based upon the fact that during the last war prices were high and times were good but there followed the depression of the twenties and thirties.

For this reason Leon Henderson and his assistants have been appointed by the president as price administrators.

This problem is a very difficult one because in the first place many people do not understand the need for this office and to them controlled prices mean dictatorship.

Just why is there a need for controlled prices? This is the reason. At the present time we are on a ratio of 7-1. By this we mean that seven hours of our working day are spent making commodities and one hour making defense materials. By the end of this year we hope to have our factories on a 5-3 basis. And we may have to go farther than that. England is even now on a 3-5 basis—that is 3 hours of a working day on commodities to 5 hours on defense materials. But what does this mean? What is the connection between hours spent making materials and price control? The obvious answer is this:

Our factories are going to be so busy with defense that they cannot make all the commodities which have become necessities to the American people.

Furthermore, materials used for these commodities are also essential materials for defense, for example the steel used in ice boxes, automobiles and hundreds of household appliances; the zinc used in galvanizing the farmers fence; and the gasoline we need in our cars.

Other materials essential to manufacturing will be difficult if not impossible to obtain. We are already feeling the silk embargo, and many similar items will soon be at the same premium. Our ships are needed for defense. They cannot haul our luxuries.

Therefore, we establish the fact that because of a shortage of labor and materials there will naturally be a shortage of commodities.

This will automatically mean price rises. But to this people are prone to answer "So what? Rising prices—rising wages; rising wages—prosperity."

But people with this idea have failed to realize that there are two distinct types of price rises. The first is a gradual raising of wages, then prices, then standard of living; a slow and tedius process by which we have been gradually climbing out of depression during the past few years. The second is inflation.

Economists have diagnosed inflation as the gun which causes most of our depression ills. But unfortunately they have found no cure.

Just what is inflation? It is the quick rising of prices because of shortage of products; the wild bidding of one buyer against another because each wants those products. It is soaring wages and unreasonable extravagant spending.

Inflation is like a balloon. For a few minutes it is a full and beautiful thing, but then comes the pin prick of after war, with soldiers returning; with no shortage of labor or materials and like the balloon the bubble of inflation breaks, leaving nothing.

Thus our Price Administrator, Leon Henderson, Mr. Henderson and his staff cannot of course prevent shortage. Neither can they single handed prevent inflation. They must have the full cooperation of the American people.

It is necessary that Americans understand their problem and each one do his part.

"But what can I do?" is the usual question.

You can do this, or rather to make it negative not do these type of things:

Don't go to the market and buy 1000 pounds of sugar because you hear its going up. By doing this you are bidding the sugar up and helping to cause inflation.

Don't trade in your automobile every year just for a new one. Leave the automobiles for people who don't now have them and need them in their business.

If everyone helps many people will be wrong in feeling certain depression will come with peace.

APPENDIX L

Criteria for Textbook Selection [1]

INDIVIDUAL teachers and book-selection committees have found the criteria which follow helpful in selecting language-composition books, anthologies of literature, and practice material.

CHECK-LIST OF QUESTIONS FOR CONSIDERATION IN THE SELECTION OF A TEXTBOOK IN COMPOSITION

Directions: 1. Place a "3" on the line in front of each item to which you can answer an unqualified "yes" for the textbook under consideration.

2. Place an "n" before each question to which you must answer an unqualified "no."

3. If your answer is qualified but nearer "no" than "yes," put a "1" in front of the item.

4. If your answer is qualified but nearer "yes" than "no," put a "2" in front of the question.

5. Total your points within each of the sections indicated by the roman numerals. These figures may then be compared with the ratings of other textbooks for the same section. It is the consensus among members of the committee that no textbooks should be considered for adoption which average less than 2 on the points starred.

—— I. *The Viewpoint of the Textbook*

    —— * A. Does the author recognize that composition is a social activity?

    —— * B. Does he recognize the uses of composition in everyday life?

—— II. *The Author's Style*

    —— A. Is the style stimulating, suggestive, vigorous?

[1] Prepared by a committee of the National Council of Teachers of English, Dora V. Smith, chairman. Reprinted by permission from *Conducting Experiences in English,* English Monograph No. 8, D. Appleton-Century Company, 1939.

—— B. Is there sufficient concrete detail to develop general concepts?

—— * C. Is the exposition clear, accurate, and simple enough to be readily understood?

—— * D. Is it suited to the age of child for whom it is intended?

—— E. Does it address itself to the pupil?

—— III. *Proportion and Organization*

    —— A. Does the author give adequate attention to

        —— 1. The motivation of expression?

        —— 2. The stimulation of interests and ideas?

        —— 3. The selection and organization of ideas?

        —— 4. The development of power of expression?

        —— 5. The habituation of correctness in speech and writing?

    —— * B. Does the author give to oral composition the proportion of time dictated by its prominence in the activities of everyday life?

    —— * C. Does he give to letter-writing the emphasis demanded by its practical importance in everyday life?

    —— D. Does the author stress the subordinate and contributory function of correctness in speech and writing in relation to the larger purpose of expression?

    —— E. Does the author organize his material into sectional divisions large enough to stimulate interest, to give perspective, and to promote well-rounded growth?

    —— * F. Does the author organize his materials in such a way as to

        —— 1. Care for pupils of varying abilities and interests within the same class?

—— 2. Make both pupil and teacher conscious of the ends toward which they are working and the degree of progress attained?

—— 3. Provide for flexibility in adapting the assignment to the individual classroom situation?

—— IV. *Motivation*

—— * A. Does the author create in the pupil the desire to express himself?

—— * B. Does he identify the composition work of the classroom with the expressional activities of life both within and without the school?

—— C. Does he keep before the pupil the purpose of each activity in which he is asked to engage?

—— D. Does the author stimulate observation and interest in a wide variety of subjects?

—— E. Does he arouse the initiative and originality of the student?

—— * F. Does he stress the importance of thinking?

—— * G. Does he use the social purposes of composition to encourage not merely correct but clear, vigorous, and interesting expression?

—— H. Does he identify his composition activities with actual experience instead of merely setting up series of topics for "theme writing"?

—— I. Does he promote additional activities among superior pupils?

—— * J. Does he promote progress by offering numerous means of self-criticism:

—— 1. By providing standards for the evaluation of one's own writing?

—— 2. By offering bases of comparison with the work of others?

—— 3. By furnishing means of comparison with earlier achievement?

—— K. Does he throw the responsibility for progress upon the pupil himself?

—— V. *Activities Proposed*

    —— A. General characteristics:

        —— * 1. Are the activities suggested by the author suitable and interesting to the grades for which they are recommended?

        —— 2. Are they representative of a wide range of experience and thought?

        —— 3. Are there projects suggested which allow for class, group, and individual activity?

        —— 4. Are these projects timely, interest-arousing, and thought-provoking?

        —— * 5. Is sufficient direction given for the execution of these projects?

        —— 6. Are the tasks specific, not general?

        —— 7. Are the illustrations pertinent to the pupils' experience?

        —— * 8. Does the book contain sufficient practice material for applying principles developed?

        —— 9. Are the practice materials so graded in difficulty as to be easily adaptable to the needs of groups and individuals of varying ability?

        —— 10. Does the book offer a wide range of choice in suggestions for assignments?

        —— 11. Does the author stimulate creative writing among pupils capable of more literary achievements?

        —— 12. Is there plentiful correlation of activities with those of other subjects of study?

—— * B. Does the text furnish adequate experience in the following language activities of everyday life?

—— Announcements

—— Book reviewing

—— Conversation

—— Creative writing

—— Current event discussion

—— Debating

—— Dictionary, use of

—— Explaining or giving instructions

—— Gathering and reporting information

—— Informal discussion

—— Interviewing

—— Letter-writing

—— Magazine materials, use of

—— Note-taking

—— Public discussion according to parliamentary form

—— Reporting speeches or committee findings

—— Speech-making

—— Story-telling

—— C. Does the author offer sufficient aids and devices for

—— * 1. Development of vocabulary and use of the dictionary

—— 2. Development of feeling for phrasing

—— * 3. Development of effectiveness in sentence structure

—— 4. Selecting and organizing material before writing

—— 5. Outlining

—— * 6. Development of well-rounded paragraphs

—— 7. Making of skilful transitions

—— 8. Effectiveness of beginning and ending

—— VI. *The Mechanics of Expression*

    —— A. Grammar:

        —— * 1. Is the grammatical material motivated by constant relation to actual language situations?

        —— 2. Does the author provide for measurement and stimulation of progress both for the individual and for the class?

        —— * 3. Does he provide for individual diagnosis and remedial work?

        —— * 4. Is there large stress upon sentence sense and sentence structure with repeated review of the topic?

        —— * 5. Is the content chosen on the basis of function in accord with the findings of scientific investigations:

            —— a) With relatively large stress on points of difficulty such as verb and pronoun?

            —— b) With recognition of points of debatable usage?

            —— c) With emphasis upon function not classification (i.e. Are classifications of adverbs into adverbs of degree, cause, manner, etc., omitted, and the use of the adverb versus the adjective stressed? Is power to express thought relationships with exactness made more important than ability to label sentences as compound or complex?)

—— * 6. Is there ample provision for repeated drill upon a few specific points instead of inadequate drill upon many non-essentials?

—— 7. Is the program cumulative with adequate provision throughout for review?

—— B. Capitalization and punctuation:

—— * 1. Are the requirements limited to matters of usage in our own day as revealed by the report of the Minimum Essentials Committee of the National Council of Teachers of English?

—— * 2. Are distinctions between required and optional usage clearly made?

—— * 3. Are ample drill materials provided?

—— 4. Is the program cumulative with adequate provision for review?

—— 5. Does the author provide for measurement and stimulation of progress both for the individual and for the class?

—— * 6. Does he provide for individual diagnosis and remedial work?

—— 7. Is there constant provision for use of the skills mastered, in actual writing situations?

—— VII. *Physical Format*

—— A. Mechanical make-up:

—— 1. Is the textbook a good standard size, easily handled by the pupil?

(i.e. roughly 5½ inches x 7¾ inches)

—— 2. Is it easily opened and durable in binding?

—— 3. Has the paper a non-gloss surface?

—— 4. Is it heavy enough to insure that print on the obverse side shall not show through?

—— 5. Are the margins wide enough to insure an uncrowded page?

—— 6. Is the page well-spaced so as to emphasize outstanding points?

—— 7. Are the lines not more than 90 mm. long?

—— 8. Is the type dark, plain, and distinct —not less than 10 point?

—— B. Attractiveness and effectiveness of form:

—— 1. Is the book attractive in appearance?

—— 2. Has it appropriate and effective illustrations?

—— 3. Has it graphic devices for aid in outlining, letter form, work derivations, etc.?

—— 4. Are the chapter and section captions clear, brief, well-spaced, interesting?

—— 5. Has the book a usable index?

—— 6. Has it a usable table of contents?

—— 7. Has it a clear and impelling preface, giving the purpose of the author and suggestions for use?

—— C. Does the copyright date (issued or revised) suggest that the book is recent enough to reflect modern tendencies in teaching?

CRITERIA FOR SELECTING A GRADED SERIES OF
ANTHOLOGIES OF LITERATURE

—— 1. Are all aspects of a literary experience provided for?

—— 2. Are several repetitions of the same literary experience given in new situations and with fresh literature so that the student may practice with satisfaction the reading method appropriate to that experience?

—— 3. Is the pupil helped to mature through stories of realistic folk literature into stories of modern science? From imaginative hero stories to realistic biography? From light verse to great poetry? From short stories to long fiction? From one act to five act plays?

—— 4. Is provision made for pupils to understand at first simple social situations and gradually more complex ones?

—— 5. Has provision been made in every book in the series for three levels of literary material: (1) that which the teacher presents, (2) that in the reading of which she guides the pupil, and (3) that which the pupils can read for themselves without the teacher's direction?

—— 6. To what extent will using the series aid him in finding books of value to him personally?

—— 7. Will using this series encourage him to apply his reading and library skills in providing himself with good books?

—— 8. Will he acquire an intimate knowledge of some artist's works and an extensive knowledge of many others?

—— 9. Is provision made that the child will feel the desire to guide his own reading?

—— 10. Is the literature program as set up helpful to the child in finding the creative experience that will guide his avocation or vocation?

—— 11. Does it provide practice in the desirable library skills developed in each grade?

—— 12. To what extent will the series help the pupil to use his leisure time for reading?

—— 13. Will use of the series make the pupil care enough for books to own some for himself? To use carefully the books he borrows?

—— 14. Will the literature program as set up make him more sensitive to real experiences?

—— 15. Will the literature program as set up influence him to choose wisely among the mass of modern literature that clamor for his attention?

—— 16. Does the series provide content and activities suitable for slow, average, and bright pupils? If not, does it provide adequately for the type of pupil for whom it purports to be written?

CRITERIA FOR SELECTING PRACTICE MATERIAL IN READING, USAGE, SPEECH IMPROVEMENT

—— 1. Will the use of this material tend to center the pupil's attention upon a desirable aspect of the subject?

—— 2. Are directions to pupils clearly and definitely stated? Are sample exercises given to demonstrate the directions?

—— 3. Does the material focus the pupil's attention on a sufficiently small unit at a time?

—— 4. Does the material utilize all relevant motives for learning the associations being fixed?

—— 5. Does the material give diffuse practice in skills previously learned while it gives intensive drill on a new item?

—— 6. Is the material so arranged as to be self-administering and self-corrective by the individual pupil?

—— 7. Are the associations being drilled upon important enough to warrant their being made automatic?

—— 8. Are check tests included so as to help the pupil see how near he is to the goals set up in the unit of learning and to help him diagnose where he needs to straighten out his facts and improve his skills?

—— 9. Is the material selected or written so as to furnish a challenge to the type or types of learner (slow, average, bright) for whom it was prepared?

—— 10. Does the material suggest applications of the skills, in school and out-of-school situations?

APPENDIX M

Publishers' Addresses

Abingdon-Cokesbury Press, 150 Fifth Ave., New York 11
Allyn & Bacon, 50 Beacon St., Boston, Mass.
American Book Co., 55 Fifth Ave., New York 3
Appleton-Century-Crofts, Inc., 35 West 32 St., New York 1
Baker & Taylor Co., 1429 North Broad St., Hillside, N. J.
Barnes, A. S., & Co., 232 Madison Ave., New York 16
Barrows, M., & Co., 114 East 32 St., New York 16
Beckley-Cardy Co., 1632 Indiana Ave., Chicago 16
Benson, W. S., Co., 109 East 5 St., Austin, Tex.
Benziger Bros., 12 West 3 St., New York 12
Blakiston Co., 1012 Walnut St., Philadelphia 5
Bobbs-Merrill Co., 724 North Meridian St., Indianapolis 7
Boni, 3 Grove Court, New York 14
Bowker, R. R., Co., 62 West 45 St., New York 36
Bruce Publishing Co., 400 North Broadway, Milwaukee 1
Century. *See* Appleton-Century-Crofts
Columbia University Press, 2960 Broadway, New York 27
Coward-McCann, 210 Madison Ave., New York 16
Crofts. *See* Appleton-Century-Crofts
Crowell, Thomas Y., 432 Fourth Ave., New York 16
Dodd, Mead & Co., 432 Fourth Ave., New York 16
Doubleday & Co., Garden City, New York
Dryden Press, Inc., 31 West 54 St., New York 19
Dutton, E. P., & Co., 300 Fourth Ave., New York 10
Follett Publishing Co., 1257 South Wabash Ave., Chicago 5
Franklin Publishing & Supply Co., 1931 Cherry St., Philadelphia 3
Freeman, W. H., & Co., 549 Market St., San Francisco 5
French, Samuel, Inc., 25 West 45 St., New York 36
Funk & Wagnalls Co., 15 East 24 St., New York 10

Ginn & Co., Statler Bldg., Boston 17

Globe School Book Co. *See* World Book Co.

Gregg Publishing Co. *See* McGraw-Hill Book Co.

Hammond, C. S., & Co., 515 Valley St., Maplewood, N. J.

Harcourt, Brace & Co., 383 Madison Ave., New York 17

Harper & Bros., 49 East 33 St., New York 16

Harvard University Press, 44 Francis Ave., Cambridge 38, Mass.

Heath, D. C., & Co., 285 Columbus Ave., Boston 16

Herder, B., Book Co., 15-17 South Broadway, St. Louis 2

Hinds, Hayden & Eldredge, Inc., 105 Fifth Ave., New York 3

Holt, Henry, & Co., 383 Madison Ave., New York 17

Houghton Mifflin Co., 2 Park St., Boston 7

International Textbook Co., 1001 Wyoming Ave., Scranton, Pa.

Iroquois Publishing Co., 106 East Fayette St., Syracuse, N. Y.

Irwin, Richard D., Inc., 1818 Ridge Road, Homewood, Ill.

Johnson Publishing Co. *See* Beckley-Cardy Co.

Jones, Marshall, Co., Francestown, N. H.

Knopf, Alfred A., Inc., 501 Madison Ave., New York 22

Laidlaw Bros., 328 South Jefferson St., Chicago 6

Laird & Lee. *See* Laidlaw Bros.

Lippincott, J. B., & Co., 227 South 6 St., Philadelphia 5

Little, Brown & Co., 34 Beacon St., Boston 6

Liveright Publishing Corp., Inc., 386 Fourth Ave., New York 16

Longmans, Green & Co., 55 Fifth Ave., New York 3

Lothrop, Lee & Shepard Co., 419 Fourth Ave., New York 16

Lyons & Carnahan, 2500 Prairie Ave., Chicago 16

McGraw-Hill Book Company, 330 West 42 St., New York 36

Macmillan Co., 60 Fifth Ave., New York 11

Merriam, G. & C., Co., 432 Federal St., Springfield 2, Mass.

Merrill, Charles E., Co., 400 South Front St., Columbus 15, Ohio

Metropolitan Museum of Fine Arts, Fifth Ave. at 82 St., New York 28

National Tuberculosis Association, 1790 Broadway, New York 19

Nelson, Thomas, & Sons, 19 East 47 St., New York 17

Noble & Noble, 67 Irving Place, New York 3

Norton, W. W., & Co., Inc., 101 Fifth Ave., New York 3

Odyssey Press, Inc., 101 Fifth Ave., New York 3

Orchard Hill Press. *See* Bobbs-Merrill Co.

Oxford University Press, 114 Fifth Ave., New York 11

Pitman Publishing Corp., 2 West 45 St., New York 36

Putnam's, G. P., Sons, 210 Madison Ave., New York 16

Rand, McNally & Co., 536 South Clark St., Chicago 5

Regents Publishing Co., Inc., 45 East 17 St., New York 3

Reilly, Peter, Co., 133 North 13 St., Philadelphia 7

Rinehart and Co., 232 Madison Ave., New York 16

Ronald Press Co., 15 East 26 St., New York 10

Row, Peterson & Co., 1911 Ridge Ave., Evanston, Ill.

Sadlier, William H., Inc., 11 Park Place, New York 7

Sanborn, Benjamin H., & Co., 221 East 20 St., Chicago 16

Saunders, W. B., Co., 218 West Washington Square, Philadelphia 5

Schwartz, Kirwin & Fauss. *See* William H. Sadlier

Scott, Foresman & Co., 433 East Erie St., Chicago 11

Scribner's, Charles, Sons, 597 Fifth Ave., New York 17

Sears Publishing Co. *See* Dodd, Mead & Co.

Silver Burdett Co., 45 East 17 St., New York 3

Sloane, William, Associates, 119 West 57 St., New York 19

Smith, Turner E., & Co., 441 West Peachtree St. N. E., Atlanta 3, Ga.

Southern Publishing Co. *See* University Publishing Co.

South-Western Publishing Co., 310 Huguenot St., New Rochelle, N. Y.

Standard Publishing Co., 20 East Central Parkway, Cincinnati 10, Ohio

Stechert-Hafner, Inc., 31 East 10 St., New York 3

Translation Publishing Co., Inc., 67 Irving Place, New York 3

University of Chicago Press, 5750 Ellis Ave., Chicago 37

University Publishing Co., 1126 Q St., Lincoln 1, Neb.

Van Nostrand, D., Co., 250 Fourth Ave., New York 10

Wahr Publishing Co., 103-105 North Main St., Ann Arbor, Mich.

Webb Publishing Co., 55 East 10 St., St. Paul 2, Minn.

Wheeler Publishing Co., 2831 South Parkway, Chicago 16

Wilcox & Follett Co. *See* Follett.

Wiley, John, & Sons, Inc., 440 Fourth Ave., New York 16

Williams & Wilkins, Mt. Royal Ave., Baltimore 2, Md.

Winston, John C., Co., 1010 Arch St., Philadelphia 7

World Book Co., 313 Park Hill Ave., Yonkers, N. Y.

INDEX

This index contains: 1, Names of: (a) all persons other than authors who are named in the text; (b) all authors except those of student themes, and all editors, named in the text, in "Suggested References," and in all reading lists. 2. Titles of: (a) anonymous books, and a few others referred to by title alone; (b) units; (c) *not* those of themes, poems, stories, etc. References are often slight; (a) and (b) indicate bibliographical reference to book or article. See the second index for authors named in "Suggested Exercises," "Suggested References," and bibliographical lists in the text.

665

Speech, the teacher's, 152, 240-42, 244, 249 n. *See also* English, subhead.
Speech work, 152, 239-64
  corrective, 262
  correlated with other subjects, 253-57
  criteria for selecting material on, 659
  importance of, 242-44
  mechanical aids for, 259-60
  class vs. individual, 261-64
  See also Oral work.
Spelling, 115-24, 143, 146
  changing fashions in, 118-21
  dramatizing, 120
  oral, 121
  rules, indecision regarding, 122-23
  rules for teaching, 116-18, 120, 124
  speech work correlated with, 257
  "sugar-coating," 119
  tests, 117, 124, 146; list of, with publishers, 150
  trouble spots, 120-21, 125-26
  variations in, 257
  words often misspelled, 45, 48, 116-18, 120-21, 126
Spenser, Edmund, 347
Spyri, Johanna, 378
Stage
  conventions, 440-44
  settings, 437-39
State Teachers Association, 544-45
Steamships (in italics), 131
Steed, Wickham, in Basic English, 617
Steele, Richard, 519 n. *See also Spectator, The.*
Steele, Wilbur Daniel, 288
Steeves, Harrison R., and others, 468 n.
Steffens, Lincoln, 344, 523
Steinbeck, John, 200
Stephens, James, 523, 604
Sterling, George, 604, 605, 606
Stevens, James, 596
Stevens, Wallace, 351, 604
Stevenson, Robert Louis, 287, 378, 461, 464-65, 467 n., 475, 494, 519, 525, 603; quoted, 111
Stewart, William K. *See* Inglis, Rewey B.
Stick drawings, 102, 139
Stockton, Frank R., 511
Stormzand, Martin J., 122
"Story," calling a composition, 255
Story Parade, 507
Strachey, Lytton, 316

Strang, Ruth, and others, 378
Stratton, Clarence, 378
Subjects (sentences), 78-90
  shifts in, 102-03
"Substantive" an advisable term, 85 n.
Suffixes, 153, 172, 176, 182, 257
Sugimoto, Etsu I., 511-12
Sullivan, Sir Arthur S. *See* Gilbert.
Superficiality, danger of, 19-20, 193
Superintendent of schools, 540-41
Swedenborg, Emanuel, ref. to, 371, 462
Sweeney, Francis G., and others, 357 n.
Swift, Jonathan, 405, 520
Swinburne, Algernon Charles, 393 n., 606
Syllabus in English (New York State), 213
Symbols
  in correcting composition, 580
  poetical use of, 387, 400-07, 429
  prose use of, 382
  words as, 62-63, 64, 65-66
Synecdoche, 399
Synge, M. B., 511
Synge, John Millington, 451
Synonyms, 159, 174-75

Tabb, John Bannister, 605
Tanner, Edwin P. *See* Mace.
Tappan, Eva M., 10, 463
Tarkington, Booth, 291 n., 378, 498
Teachers, English
  appearance of, 553
  characteristics and qualities of, 13, 28, 115, 235, 310-11, 334, 363, 411
  considered "easy," 51, 552
  creative, 4
  education of, broad, 20-21
  equipment used by, 567-71
  lack of vision of, 21
  need to save energy, 40
  mistakes of, 78-79, 92, 97, 100, 108, 232, 241, 269-72, 331-39, 367 n., 412, 421 n., 463 n., 465, 515, 520-22, 543, 550
  outside (extracurricular) activities, 344, 369-70, 527, 544, 546-47; references on, 600-03
  overconscientious, 334, 407, 411
  point of view of, 7
  problems of, 537-56
  small-town restrictions for, 537-38
  testing their own knowledge, 72-73
  unfitted for teaching, 21

BIBLIOGRAPHICAL INDEX

Including all bibliographical references in "Suggested Exercises," in "Suggested Readings," and in bibliographical lists in the text.

Books and Articles

Organizations and Publications

Note: For publishers' lists, see main index.